The Cultural Context of Childhood

The Cultural Context of Childhood

Ronald W. Henderson
University of Arizona

John R. Bergan
University of Arizona

Charles E. Merrill Publishing Company
A Bell & Howell Company
Columbus, Ohio

Published by
Charles E. Merrill Publishing Company
A Bell & Howell Company
Columbus, Ohio 43216

This book was set in Caledonia and Spartan Black.
The Production Editor was Lynn Walcoff.
The cover was designed by Will Chenoweth.

Library of Congress Catalog Card Number: 76-7251

ISBN: 0-675-08599-3

CREDITS:

Reprinted materials: Specific acknowledgments of permissions to use materials appear on p. vi, which is to be considered an extension of this copyright page. Standard credit and source information appears in the *References*.

PHOTOS:

Four-color photo essays—Fetuses on p. 1 of essay © Donald Yeager, 1976; Mother breastfeeding infant on p. 2 of essay © Carroll H. Weiss, RBP, 1973.

B/W photos—Photos on pp. 79, 129, 200 by Bernstein Photo. Photo on p. 108, 114 by Editorial Photocolor Archives/Blair Seitz; p. 139 by EPA/Arthur Sirdofsky; p. 139 by EPA/James Carroll, p. 271 by EPA.

1 2 3 4 5 6—80 79 78 77 76

Printed in the United States of America

To our wives and children:

Kathy, David, and John;
Lea, Holly, Paige, and Tom

Acknowledgments

The following are arranged in alphabetical order by author (or title if more appropriate).

Bronfenbrenner, U. Material from *Two Worlds of Childhood: U.S. and U.S.S.R.*, by Urie Bronfenbrenner, © 1970 by Russell Sage Foundation, New York.

Chomsky, N. Material from *Language and Mind*, Englarged Edition, by Noam Chomsky, © 1968, 1972, by Harcourt Brace Jovanovich, Inc., and reprinted with their permission.

deMause, L. Material from "Our Forebears Made Childhood a Nightmare," by Lloyd deMause. Copyright © 1975 Ziff-Davis Publishing Company. Reprinted by permission of PSYCHOLOGY TODAY MAGAZINE.

"Gee, Officer Krupke." Lyrics reprinted from *West Side Story*. Copyright © 1957, 1959 by Leonard Bernstein and Stephen Sondheim. Used by permission.

Jencks, C. Material from *Inequality: A Reassessment of the Effect of Family and Schooling in America*, by Christopher Jencks, et. al, © 1972 by Basic Books, Inc., Publishers, New York.

Lorenz, K. Material from *King Solomon's Ring* by Konrad Z. Lorenz, copyright © 1952 by Thomas Y. Crowell Co., Inc. Reprinted with permission of the publisher.

Piaget, J. Material from *The Child's Conception of the World* by Jean Piaget. New Jersey: Humanities Press, Inc., 1963. By permission.

Rest, J. Material from "Developmental Psychology as a Guide to Value Education: A Review of 'Kohlbergian' Programs," *Review of Educational Research*, Vol. 44, No. 2, 1974, pp. 243 and 245. Copyright 1974, American Educational Research Association, Washington, D.C.

Skinner, B. F. *Beyond Freedom and Dignity*. New York: Alfred A. Knopf, Inc. © 1971 Alfred A. Knopf, Inc. By permission.

Skinner, B. F. Material reprinted by permission from the *New York University Education Quarterly* IV, 2 (Winter, 1973): 2-6, © New York University.

Williams, R. Material from "Stimulus-Response: Scientific Racism and IQ," by Robert L. Williams. Copyright © 1974 Ziff-Davis Publishing Company. Reprinted by permission of PSYCHOLOGY TODAY MAGAZINE.

Contents

Preface

This book provides an introduction to child development for prospective parents, teachers, and others who will be involved in guiding the growth of children. Traditionally, books on child development have taken the stance that their task is to impart to the reader objective, scientific facts about growth and development. Our view is that the scientist does not stand apart from his culture as he plys his trade. The facts he chooses to investigate are dictated not only by the structure of his discipline, but also by politics, economics, and social need. Introductory treatments of development often shield the reader from these issues on the premise that the objective facts of the discipline must be mastered before the reader will be prepared to deal with the controversial issues or matters of application. In our view developmental principles and processes tend to lack vitality and meaning when presented in isolation from the social issues and events in which they are grounded. For this reason we have chosen to present developmental concepts in the context of contemporary cultural issues and events.

The growing fund of knowledge in developmental science provides an increasingly valuable resource for guiding the socialization of the young, and for identifying environmental characteristics which may have restricting effects on development. In recognition of this fact, we not only present basic information on developmental characteristics and processes, but also attempt to deal with the implications and applications of such information in socialization.

We have avoided the tradition of organizing the book according to ages and stages because we feel that this kind of structure makes it difficult to reveal the nature of those developmental processes which have longitudinal applicability in socialization. Relevant information on ages and stages is integrated into the substantive discussions of developmental processes and the social settings in which they take place.

The book is composed of five parts. In the first part we present basic sociocultural and developmental concepts as they relate to child growth and socialization. Chapter 1 discusses cultural concepts and themes relevant to human development in contemporary society, while the second chapter provides an overview of the science of development and its implications for socialization.

Biological and physical processes are discussed in Part II. Chapter 3 summarizes hereditary and prenatal influences on development, and chapter 4 discusses physical growth and motor-skill development.

Part III deals with cognitive development. In chapter 5 we consider the measurement of intellectual development. Chapter 6 presents material on the process of intellectual development organized in terms of the major theoretical perspectives in the field. Chapter 7, which deals with language development, concludes Part III.

Part IV covers personal and social development, beginning with an overview of theoretical perspectives in chapter 8. Chapters 9 and 10 discuss social, emotional, and motivational development. Our approach here has been to focus on behaviors and capabilities that enable individuals to deal competently with their interpersonal and physical environments. The facts of development are embedded in a presentation of the psychological conditions and processes that contribute to social and personal competence.

The final section of the book examines the implications of previously introduced concepts for socialization. Chapter 11 focuses on socialization processes, and chapter 12 deals with socialization institutions such as family, extrafamilial child care institutions, schools, and mass media.

The book contains a number of features intended to facilitate student efforts to learn the material presented. An overview of chapter content at the beginning of each chapter affords an advance organization of the material to be discussed. Key words and phrases presented in the margins signal the presence of significant concepts. Suggested readings provide resources to augment content presented in the text. Finally, instructional objectives covering a range of cognitive skills are provided to assist students not only to gain knowledge of the material presented, but also to apply the principles discussed in the guidance of development. Throughout our discussion we have departed from the traditional use of the masculine pronoun in our examples. Instead, we have alternated the use of masculine and feminine pronouns in an attempt to assure equal representation of the sexes.

We wish to express our appreciation to Ruth Kingsley, Richard Koussa, Tom Kratochwill, Arthur Pearl, Margaret Ronstadt, and Rosemary Swanson who read all or portions of the manuscript and made constructive suggestions. We also wish to thank Professors Lorraine Dennis, Patricia Leonhard, Stewart Cohen, Toni Lenahan, and William Cerbin for their thoughtful and constructive reviews of various drafts of the manuscript. We would also like to thank Jean Godier, Jenny Needham, Linda Chatterton, and Nedra Dow, for translating illegible prose into accurate typescript.

Special thanks are expressed to Gene Brody, who piloted the manuscript for us to test its effectiveness as an instructional tool in several sections of introductory child-development classes. We are also grateful to his students who provided us with feedback and constructive suggestions on the manuscript and the test items included in the professional supplement.

We are especially grateful to our wives, Lea and Kathy, for their painstaking editing of the manuscript and constructive suggestions, and especially for the weekends and evenings they have given up during the preparation of this book.

Part One

Development, Culture, and Science

1

Human Development in a Technological Society

Instructional Objectives	Recognize or recall
	Compare and contrast
	Describe or demonstrate
	Evaluate

influences of beliefs about the nature of children on child-rearing practices.

the definitions of culture, society, enculturation, socialization, goals, values, themes, acculturation, and assimilation.

child-rearing themes and practices in colonial America.

the influence of theories of childhood on educational practice.

Locke's ideas on the disciplining of children.

themes of the westward expansion period.

changes in family life associated with the beginnings of the industrial revolution.

early effects of the industrial revolution on the treatment of children.

influences of themes in an industrial society on child rearing.

relationships among industrialization, family structure, and developmental environments of children.

early and contemporary developmental environments of children.

implications of cultural pluralism for child rearing.

major tenants, strengths, and limitations of humanism and empiricism.

CHAPTER CONTENT

Basic concepts

    Culture

    Society

    Cultural goals, values, and themes

    Cultural change

    Cultural pluralism

Selected cultural themes

    Early cultural beliefs

    Themes in a pioneer society

    Themes associated with industrialization

    The culture of change

    Humanism: The individual and society

Beliefs about the nature of children and the appropriate procedures for raising them differ greatly from one culture to another at any given period of time. Even within a given culture beliefs change markedly over time. Recognition of this fact is particularly important to the study of child development, because what people believe about children influences the ways children are treated. Furthermore, such beliefs also affect the science of child development by giving direction to scientific inquiry. Consider the following quotation which represents a view that was once widely held by English-speaking people.

> *Native depravity* is certainly the source of all moral evil in the conduct of mankind: and as we bring with us into the world a nature replete with evil propensities, and as these propensities begin to manifest themselves as soon as the mind is capable of expression or action, so the first emotions of a mind, in such a state, will be emotions of evil, and the first efforts of powers so depraved will be evil; and hence it will be easy to trace the follies of youth, as well as the crimes of maturity, to the impurities of the heart, which is declared by the highest authority to be "Deceitful above all things, and desperately wicked." (Martin, cited in Kessen, 1965, pp. 37-38)

What kind of creature is the child? The theory of the child cited above was incorporated into a manual of advice for Sunday school managers and teachers published by Thomas Martin, a Wesleyan Methodist minister, in 1818. His theory, no doubt, represents the beliefs of very few people today. It is unlikely that many people today would see wickedness and evil in a babbling, smiling infant, but such a conception of childhood was very much a part of nineteenth-century English and American life (Kessen, 1965).

Changes in theory of the child   Through time and space the weight of opinion on the question "What kind of creature is the child?" has shifted. As we shall see from time to time in the chapters that follow, changes in beliefs concerning the nature of children and opinions about how they should be raised sometimes reflect broader changes in the prevailing social philosophy of the nation. The prevailing "spirit of the age" is referred to as the *Zeitgeist*. Changes in the prevailing conditions of life, as those associated with the transition from an agrarian to an industrial economy, may also bring about changes in attitudes because of the shifts in relationships between children and their caretakers which they may occasion.

Other changes in beliefs about the nature of children and about how they should be treated may result from the public dissemination of ideas from theory and research in child development. In future chapters we shall see that these ideas are not always in harmony with one another. Some theories stress maturational changes that are by definition largely biologically determined as the most important factors in development. Other theories emphasize the role of experience, while still others are concerned primarily with the interactions between experiential and biological factors.

Differences in theoretical emphasis

The diverse points of view that have been derived from the study of development may compete for the attention of parents and other "care-givers," such as teachers, but all recognize that the development of children results from the influences of *both* biological and environmental factors, even though the competing theories differ in the degree to which they emphasize one set of influences over another. In future chapters we shall emphasize the fact that biological and environmental influences find expression largely through their interactions rather than as a result of unitary influences of either.

As you read about the facts, processes, and theories of child development which are presented in this book, we hope also to draw your attention to the fact that people's beliefs about the nature of children, and their notions about the qualities that they should develop in order to function effectively as adults in the society, influence the ways in which people typically interact with their children and the experiences they typically provide for them. The requirements of life in a particular society and the kinds of skills and abilities valued by that society also influence the kinds of problems presented to be solved by developing children. All these factors constitute a most important set of influences on the child's development. They compose the child's social environment, and from one cultural group to another there are vast differences in the nature of the social influences which shape the behavior and development of children.

Social environment

It is not only the child who is influenced by the cultural milieu in which he is raised. The scientist who is occupied with the study of development and the conditions which affect it is also responsive to his social environment. Granted, the status of the body of knowledge of the child development field influences the kinds of questions that are chosen for study. But just as surely, the *Zeitgeist* of the scientist's society influences the kinds of questions he or she chooses to investigate, and even the ways in which objective data are interpreted.

In brief, cultural and social phenomena influence both the development of children and the research activities of developmental scientists. In this chapter we will introduce some of the concepts which will be used in later discussions of these influences to provide illustrative examples of sociocultural influences that have helped to shape the development of children and a developmental science.

BASIC CONCEPTS

Culture

Like many concepts used in the social sciences, the term *culture* has both a popular and a scientific meaning. In the popular sense we tend to think of a

...ne who has cultivated tastes. The meaning is quite similar
...m in agriculture, when a "cultured" crop is one that has been
...icial conditions. A person who has cultivated a taste for the
...mphony may be thought of by some people as "having culture."
...all what social scientists mean when they use the term culture.
...culture was first used by nineteenth-century anthropologists to refer
...iman custom (Keesing, 1958). Sir Edward Tylor, a noted armchair
...ogist of that era, defined culture as ". . . that complex whole which
...knowledge, belief, art, morals, law, custom, and any other capabilities
...ibits acquired by man as a member of society" (1958, p. 1). The habits,
...icts, and capabilities that constitute culture do not come from an individual's
...i creative activities. Rather, they are his legacy from the past and they are
conveyed to him through formal and/or informal education (Lowie, 1937).

The use of the term culture spread from anthropology to the other social
sciences, and it has been defined in somewhat different ways by various writers.
One pair of anthropologists (Kroeber & Kluckhohn, 1952) writing on the concept
of culture found over 160 different definitions of culture in the literature. What
most of the definitions seem to specify in common is that culture is composed of
patterns of behavior which are characteristic of a particular group of people.

Cultural patterning To say that behavior is patterned means that behavior occurs with some predictable regularity. As Tylor's original definition implied, culture is learned. It is
transmitted primarily through symbolic communication (Kroeber & Kluckhohn,
1952), which includes oral and written language, as well as gestures which have
standard meaning and through overt modeling or demonstration.

Inclusiveness of Behaviors, arts, customary products, and other manifestations of culture are
the concept shared among the members of some specifiable group of people. In a sense then
it is possible to speak of the culture of the United States, because in spite of the
diversity of groups and individuals in America, there are some patterns of
behavior that are widely shared among its citizens. At another level one can
refer to the culture of a particular ethnic group within the larger culture. The
culture of Mexican-Americans in the Southwest differs from both their Anglo
and their native-American neighbors, and the culture of Papago native-Americans
is distinctly different from that of Navaho or Apache native-Americans.

From the definition and discussion offered above it should be clear that
customary social behavior is a most significant aspect of culture. It is the aspect
of culture we most frequently emphasize in this book.

The term culture is often used to designate the existing body of customary
behavior, attitudes, values, and products of a given group of people. But culture
does not simply *consist of* those things—it also *induces* these behaviors in new
members of the culture. The process by which the skills and behaviors characteristic of a culture are transmitted to an individual is often referred to as

Enculturation and *enculturation* (Keesing, 1958; LeVine, 1973). A similar term, *socialization*, de-
socialization notes the process by which the child's roles in a social system are transmitted to
him (Keesing, 1958; LeVine, 1973). In practice the two terms are often used
interchangeably. This more general application of the term *socialization* is the
usage we have followed in this book because we assume that the same psychological processes are involved in the transmission and acquisition of social roles
as with other customary behaviors.

Society

Society is another of those terms which have popular and scientific meanings
that are quite discrepant from each other. The social scientist's use of the term

has little to do with the people whose names appear in the society pages of a daily newspaper. Those people are part of a society, but they might be offended to know what a small part they are. Some anthropologists, especially British ones, use *society* to designate that class of human activity which we have designated by the term culture in the previous discussion (e.g., Evans-Pritchard, 1951; Radcliffe-Browne, 1957, 1948). Among American social scientists, society is more frequently used to refer to the aggregation of individuals who live together in an organized population. The focus is on the people. The term culture puts the focus *Society defined* on the customary behaviors that are shared among that group of people (Linton, 1936, 1945). Through their institutions, such as family, religion, government, and so on, the behavior of individuals toward one another is organized. These well-established patterns of conduct are based upon the *culture* of the population that comprises a given *society*. These patterns of conduct form the *social organization* of the society. The concept of social organization will be developed in more detail in chapter 11.

Cultural Goals, Values, and Themes

Within each society there are culturally defined goals that are considered as *Goals* legitimate aims for its members. These goals are the things which group members consider to be worth striving for (Merton, 1949). They are usually ordered according to some hierarchy of values. Values involve preferences among alter- *Values* natives, and the value preferences of a group tend to be emotionally charged (Keesing, 1958). Along with the goals there are culturally defined regulations and controls which dictate the acceptable modes for obtaining the goals. These controls are the regulatory norms of the society (Merton, 1949).

A number of societal goals may be subsumed under an overriding postulate which may direct or stimulate action. Such postulates constitute cultural themes *Themes* (Opler, 1945), which may be explicitly stated or merely implied. As we shall see in the illustrative material at the end of this chapter, some of the major themes which have given direction to activity in American society have been called into question in recent years.

Cultural Change

Some cultures are more stable than others, but in general cultures do change over time. Of the many concepts which deal with different types of change, the processes which are most central to the topics of this book are the processes of *acculturation* and *assimilation*.

Acculturation refers to those changes which take place when individuals from *Acculturation* societies having different cultures are in direct and usually prolonged firsthand contact, and when that contact results in changes in the cultural patterns of one or both groups (Redfield, Linton, & Herskovitz, 1936). Each culture maintains much of its own character, but change is reflected in the cumulative transfer and reformulation of cultural elements.

In the process of assimilation the members of one group become completely *Assimilation* integrated and absorbed into a more dominant group. Members of an ethnic group that had been assimilated into a dominant culture could not be distinguished from other members of that culture.

Cultural Pluralism

Assimilation was the aim of the "melting pot" theme in American society. More recently minority groups and their advocates have begun to assert that minority ethnic groups have a right, if not a positive responsibility, to maintain valued elements of their ethnic cultures (Kopan, 1974). It has been argued that the coexistence of multiple cultural traditions within a single society provides a variety of alternatives which should enrich American life. The implications of this proposition for child rearing and education will be touched upon repeatedly in ensuing discussions.

SELECTED CULTURAL THEMES

Earlier we indicated that people's conceptions of the nature of the child and their ideas about the qualities that should be instilled in developing children influence socialization practices. Profound changes in our ideas about the nature of children and in the ways we treat them have occurred since the quote by Martin given at the beginning of this chapter was written. A few examples of cultural influences will illustrate the changing social and cultural context of childhood. Many of these changes have been associated with industrialization and the shift from an agrarian to a technological society.

Early Cultural Beliefs

In the United States early ideas about children and child training were influenced by religious doctrine. A broad segment of the colonial population was influenced by the Calvinist belief that regarded children as being innately wicked. Parents

Native depravity

were advised to deal with this evil nature by breaking the child's "will." "Will" was defined as defiance of the parents' wishes, and children of any age were expected to comply quickly and completely to every command. Crying babies were to be left alone, because it was thought that crying would strengthen the child's lungs and because if the baby were given prompt attention, it would make constant demands and become the ruler of the house. If a child were repeatedly allowed to cry until it stopped its will could be broken (Sunley, 1955). Parents and teachers were admonished to develop in their children the

Desired qualities

qualities which were considered desirable in adults. These qualities included obedience, honesty, industry, and piety (Cotton Mather, cited in Rippa, 1969). Children were considered to be merely imperfect versions of adults (Kessen, 1965).

At the same time other ideas had an influence, albeit a more limited one than religious doctrine, on conceptions of childhood. The eighteenth-century social philosopher Rousseau, for example, believed that civilized environment had a corrupting influence on children. He believed that their basic nature was good and that the effects of a civilized environment were bad. Accordingly, he stressed the importance of bringing out manly virtues against the weakening effects of civilization. The male child could become vigorous through such acts as taking cold baths, which presumably would give him Indian-like qualities of strength.

Interestingly enough, although Calvinist and Rousseauistic conceptions of the nature of the child were the exact opposite of one another, their recommended child training practices, such as forcing the child to do difficult things, were remarkably similar (Sunley, 1955). However, Rousseau's influence in colonial America was quite limited, and children were more generally regarded as evil than as pure.

Influences on education

Judging from historical documents (e.g., Rush, cited in Rippa, 1969), by the early 1700s a major purpose of proposals for a uniform education system in America was to produce a more homogeneous population who could therefore be easily governed. In the schools, physical punishment was a major means of

Disciplinary measures

controlling and disciplining children. But here too, other voices suggested alternative procedures. Even Cotton Mather (1710), an influential Calvinist minister, suggested that teachers make more sparing use of punishment and more liberal use of rewards. Earlier yet, the English empirical philosopher John Locke offered the following observation:

> I grant, that Good and Evil, *Reward* and *Punishment* are the only motives to a rational Creature; these are the Spur and Reins, whereby all mankind is set on work, and guided, and they are to be made use of to children too. For I advise their Parents and Governor's always to carry this in their Minds, that Children are to be treated as rational Creatures (p. 61). First, children (earlier perhaps than we think) are very sensible of *Praise* and Commendation. They find a Pleasure in being esteemed, and valued, especially by their Parents and those whom they depend on. If therefore the Father *caress and commend them, when they do well, show a cold and neglectful countenance to them upon doing ill;* And this is accompanied by a like Carriage of the Mother, and all others that are about them, it will in a little Time make them sensible of the Difference; and this if constantly observed, I doubt not but will of it self work more than Treats or Blows, which lose their Force when once grown common, and are of no use when Shame does not attend them. . . . (cited in Kessen, 1965, p. 62)

Locke's influence was very limited during this early period, but later his influence was strongly felt in psychology. Locke's thinking anticipated important psychological ideas about children and their upbringing by over 200 years.

Themes in a Pioneer Society

Some of the themes which were prominent during the period of westward expansion in America are of particular interest because the values and actions of the pioneer movement provide a popular stereotype for the idealized qualities of the American character. Somewhat romantically we tend to regard our pioneer forebears as practical, self-reliant, independent, adventurous, and individualistic. The horizons of vast unsettled spaces provided an open invitation to pioneers who have been characterized as optimistic and idealistic.

Valued qualities

Future orientation. The optimistic and adventurous spirit of pioneer Americans was directed toward the future. It was widely assumed that hard work would lead to a better future. This premise, sometimes referred to as effort-optimism, suggested that the world is like a machine which can be repaired, improved, and mastered for human purposes. Through work people might even achieve the goal of their own perfectability (DuBois, 1955). Writers who tried to characterize American society and culture in the early 1900s often emphasized an orientation to the future. This orientation was often accompanied by a general disregard for the past, and an anti- or non-intellectual attitude. One writer expressed these themes in the following words:

Effort-optimism

> What has existed in the past, especially in the remote past, seems to him (the American) not only authoritative, but irrelevant, inferior, and outworn. He finds it rather a sorry waste of time to think about the past at all. But his enthusiasm for the future is profound; he can conceive of no more decisive way of recommending an opinion or practice than to say that it is what everybody is coming to adopt. This expectation of what he approves, or approval of what he expects, makes up his optimism. It is the necessary faith of the pioneer. (Santayana, cited in Rippa, 1969, p. 398)

Practicality. Idealism in America has had definite limits. The future-oriented idealism of the pioneer Americans has generally been concerned with only a

Immediate and long-range futures

very immediate future. Their interest in the future has been directed toward very pragmatic ends. Those goals and consequences most immediately in view seem to have been most influential on action. Long before the contemporary concern about ecology, the American humorist Will Rogers commented on the fact that the pioneer, romantically remembered for his close association with nature, was likely to cut down a tree but not to plant one. The themes that are effective in realizing societal goals may appear to be advantageous at one time yet turn out to be dysfunctional at another.

Children in the pioneer society. The pioneer existence was full of hardships, but it had its rewards as well. Many of the rewards were in the future, and were available only to those with the courage, energy, and ingenuity to pursue them. Children reared under such conditions very likely developed a practical approach to coping with the immediate future. The outlook was optimistic for those willing to put forth the effort.

Consistent with the Protestant ethic, the pioneers' idealistic objectives could not be achieved without self-denial, as well as effort. Immediate gratification could be had only at the expense of greater and longer range goals. Children had an important role to play in the efforts of the family to obtain a better future. From a very early age they could contribute valuable work to the collective efforts of the family.

Themes Associated with Industrialization

The Industrial Revolution

A little over two and a half centuries ago, a series of events took place which profoundly influenced the place of the child in society. The flying shuttle, a device which increased the speed and efficiency of weaving, was invented in England in 1733. The spinning jenny, capable of spinning numerous threads at the same time, was invented in 1770. The following year saw the invention of the water frame, which utilized the power of a water wheel in running looms, jennies, and other equipment. The next few years witnessed the emergence of other developments in the mechanization of textile industries, which, in a sense, culminated in James Watts' development of the steam engine in 1785. This invention proved to be a very versatile source of power for running factory equipment.

These developments, which provide some visible indications of the beginnings of the Industrial Revolution, started a far-reaching series of events that influenced views of childhood and the treatment of children.

Just prior to these events, handcrafted goods, primarily textiles, were produced for sale through a domestic system. Businessmen supplied raw materials to women and girls on farms who produced cloth. The domestic system offered advantages to both the businessmen, who made a good profit through such arrangements with a number of women, and the wives and daughters who could supplement the meager income from the family farm. Moreover, mothers could work in the relative comfort of their homes and be present to care for their children. With the coming of the Industrial Revolution, this situation changed markedly. The status of the family as a basic economic unit was altered.

It is true that the open frontiers of the United States provided an alternative; families could continue to function together as an important cooperative economic unit in the agrarian West. But at the same time, the Industrial Revolution brought basic changes in urban areas of America and western Europe. This development interrupted a nascent reform movement to regard children as worthy human beings. Rather abruptly, not only women, but children as well,

were required to fill the need for cheap labor to operate the new factories and
the mines, which produced coal to power the factories. As Kessen (1965) puts it,

> Just as the reforms of the mid-eighteenth century were giving some hope that the
> lot of the child might improve, the factory system began its comprehensive growth
> in Western Europe. With the demand for cheap labor that resulted, the child was
> again in jeopardy. Under an ugly alliance of parents, officers charged with
> responsibility for the parish poor, and factory managers, children were sold into
> effective slavery. They not infrequently worked, ate, and slept at their machines,
> with neither education or continuing adult care. (pp. 31-32)

From a contemporary perspective, it is almost impossible to envision the
conditions under which children were required to labor. Some feeling for the
lot of children who served the purposes of the emerging mechanistic society may
be gained from a speech in which the Earl of Shaftsbury argued for child labor
regulations. Here is an example of information he presented regarding the use
of children in the mining industry.

Child labor

> In Derbyshire many (children) begin at 5, many between 5 and 6 years, many
> at 7. In the West Riding of Yorkshire it is not uncommon for infants even of 5
> years old to be sent to the pit. About Halifax and the neighborhood children are
> sometimes brought to the pits at the age of 6 years, and are taken out of their
> beds at 4 o'clock. (cited in Kessen, 1965, p. 46)

Concerning the working conditions, the Earl reported:

> In the West Riding of Yorkshire it appears that there are very few collieries with
> thin seams where the main roadways exceed a yard in height, and in some they
> do not exceed 26 or 28 inches; Nay, in some the height is as little as 22 inches; so
> that in such places the youngest child cannot work without the most constrained
> posture. The ventilation, besides, in general is very bad, and the drainage worse.
> In Oldham the mountain-seams are wrought in a very rude manner. There is very
> insufficient drainage. The ways are so low that only little boys can work in them,
> which they do naked, and often in mud and water, dragging sledgetubs by the
> girdle and chains. (cited in Kessen, 1965, p. 48)

And regarding the nature of the tasks performed, and the pain endured, he
reported:

> The child, it appears, has a girdle bound round its waist, to which is attached a
> chain, which passes under the legs, and is attached to the cart. The child is
> obliged to pass on all fours, and the chain passes under what, therefore, in that
> posture, might be called the hind legs; and thus they have to pass through
> avenues not so good as a common sewer, quite as wet, and often times more
> contracted. This kind of labour they have to continue during several hours, in a
> temperature described as perfectly intolerable. By the testimony of the people
> themselves, it appears that the labour is exceedingly severe; that the girdle blisters
> their sides and causes great pain . . . Robert North says, "I went into the pit at 7
> years of age. When I drew by the girdle and chain, the skin was broken and the
> blood ran down . . . If we said anything, they would beat us." (cited in Kessen,
> 1965, p. 49)

Efficiency.   Our society places a high value on efficiency, the aim being to produce as many goods as possible with the smallest possible expenditure of time
and resources. Efficiency, in fact, is often translated into monetary terms, an
attitude of great longevity as illustrated in the advice of one of our major folk
heroes. Benjamin Franklin admonished his readers to:

Remember that Time is Money. He that can earn Ten Shillings a Day by his labour, and goes abroad, or sits idle one half of that Day, tho' he spends but Sixpence during his Diversion or Idleness, ought not to reckon That the only Expense; he has really spent or rather thrown away Five Shillings besides. (cited in Rippa, 1969, p. 103)

Productivity and efficiency. The emphasis on efficiency has permeated almost every aspect of contemporary society. Perhaps it is seen most dramatically in the systems approach now widely advocated in industry, government, and even education. Efficiency represents the triumph of effort-optimism over a mechanistic universe. The more successful one is in exploiting nature, the greater the productivity. Products are the tangible signs of success in getting the greatest productivity and return with the least cost from the mechanistically conceived universe (Dubois, 1955).

Practicality. A longstanding emphasis on practicality over abstract intellectual interest is evident in psychology and education, as well as business and industry. William James (cited in Rippa, 1969), an early leader in American psychology, admonished teachers about the inadequacy of abstract verbal instruction. "Verbal reactions," he cautioned, "useful as they are, are insufficient. The pupil's words may be right, but the conceptions corresponding to them are often direfully wrong" (p. 335). James advocated practical work in the shop or laboratory as a means of teaching students to know the difference between accuracy and vagueness.

Efficiency in the molding of children

A growing belief in humans' ability to control the environment for their own ends came to include published advice to parents on how to mold the kind of child they wanted. The theme of efficiency is reflected in the following observations:

> Parents apparently forced infants and younger children to perform beyond their physical or mental level. Babies were sometimes required to sit upright before being able to do so. Some babies were not permitted to go through the crawling stage (perhaps to prevent dirtiness), and walkers and leading strings were used to get the baby to walk as soon as possible. Mental precociousness was much admired, children being taught lessons far beyond their years, so that they could be shown off before company. (Sunley, 1955, p. 156)

The work ethic. To exploit the "mechanistic" universe required effort, just as effort was required of pioneers who set out to mold the frontier environment to their own ends. Horatio Alger, whose novels were widely read in the early years of this century, popularized the image of the boy of humble origin who, through hard work, acquired the most cherished rewards of the society.

Importance of the early years

A parent who wished to mold a child according to the desired specifications of piety, obedience, honesty, and industry had to invest a considerable effort in the child-rearing enterprise. The first few years of life were considered the most important time for lasting influence to be exercised, and as industrialization developed and children were apt to move to the cities when they grew up, proper early training was stressed as a means of preparing the individual to cope with the temptations of city life (Sunley, 1955). Both love and strict physical discipline were advocated as means of producing the kind of child desired. In the long run, however, a shift in roles associated with industrialization may have had a more profound effect on disciplinary and child management practices than advice of authorities. With husbands and fathers away from home during the day and often during the evenings as well, to attend to the affairs of business, the mother took over increased responsibilities for discipline, and her

Shifts in disciplinary roles

methods are reported to have been milder than those of male disciplinarians. Similarly, female teachers became the rule as free public education spread.

The Culture of Change

The values and institutions which developed with industrialization have brought us to the brink of a period that has been variously identified by the terms "the second industrial revolution," "the super industrial revolution," "the second phase industrial state," and kindred designations. It has become a popular academic pastime to predict what lies ahead for humankind. One quality which all predictions have in common is that the rate of change in social institutions and in the private lives of individuals will increase at a breathtaking pace. Since the rate of cultural transition will provide little opportunity to carefully design and test new societal values and institutions, and since trial and error is of particularly dubious value under unstable conditions, the next generation of citizens will face major problems dealing with the changes that will confront them. In the estimation of Carl Rogers (1972), the greatest problem which will face man in the years to come

Rate of change

. . . is not the hydrogen bomb, fearful as that may be. It is not the population explosion, though the consequences of that are awful to contemplate. It is instead a problem which is rarely mentioned or discussed. It is the question of how much change the human being can accept, absorb, and assimilate, and the rate at which he can take it up. (p. 411)

The single most prominent outcome of the changes which have taken place has perhaps been the relegation of the family to a less prominent role as a socializing agent than it held in previous years. Bronfenbrenner (1970) reaches such a conclusion in his comparison of child rearing in the Soviet Union and in America, and he stresses that this is not a change which we planned for or wanted. "Rather it is itself the by-product of a variety of social changes, all operating to decrease the prominence and power of the family in the lives of children" (p. 99).

Among the important factors that have served to decrease the influence of the family on the development of their children are changes which may be categorized as "the shrinking world of caring," "the temporary family," and the "transient family."

The shrinking family. It is commonplace to talk about our shrinking world. The technological advances which the mechanistic society has brought about in travel and communications have indeed made it a small world in many ways. Through television, children have knowledge about places and events which escaped their parents until adulthood. The increased mobility of upper-middle-class professional families has also increased the firsthand knowledge of their children. But the world is also shrinking in other ways that may serve to *restrict* the range of experience available to children.

The composition and nature of the family and neighborhood have changed markedly, in part because families now tend to have fewer children, but also because the number of relatives who live near enough to influence the child has diminished. In the past, families tended to be larger than they are today. The family of the past was more like the extended family, which some minorities, such as the Mexican-Americans, are struggling today to preserve. Bronfenbrenner (1970) recalls that in the past,

Family composition

. . . everyone minded your business. They wanted to know where you had been, where you were going, and why . . . And it wasn't just your relatives . . . People on the street would tell you to button your jacket, and ask why you were not in church last Sunday. Sometimes you liked it and sometimes you didn't—but at least people *cared*. (p. 96)

The American family is growing smaller.

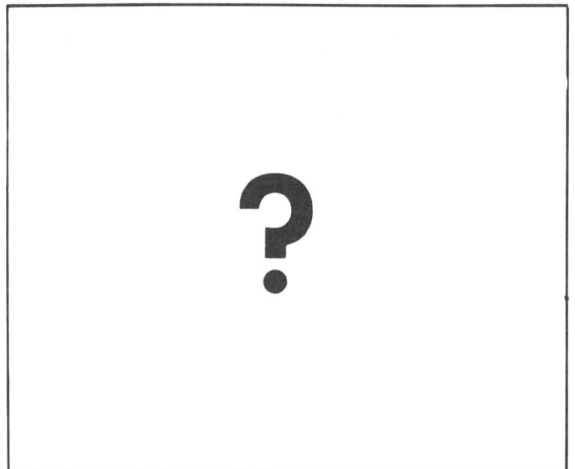

Characteristics of
suburban life

Nothing of the sort is true for most children in America today. One of the side effects of industrialization, and the accompanying urbanization, is that the nuclear family—the family unit composed of a man and woman and their biological offspring—has almost universally replaced the traditional extended family.

In spite of the large number of people who are in close physical proximity to the urban or the suburban child, she may experience caring relationships with relatively few people. The sphere of associations of her small nuclear family,

. . . has withered to a small circle of friends, most of them accessible only by car or telephone. Paradoxically, the more people there are around, the fewer the opportunities for meaningful human contact. Whereas, before, the world in which the child lived consisted of a *diversity of people* in a *diversity of settings*, now for millions of American children the neighborhood is nothing but row upon row of buildings where "other people" live. One house, or apartment, is much like another—and so are the people. (Bronfenbrenner, 1970, emphasis added, p. 97)

So whereas today's children give an appearance of sophistication which may be a constant source of amazement to their parents, their sophistication may be superficial in many respects. They may know a lot about places and things because of experience obtained vicariously through the technological miracles of rapid travel and instant communication. But the same children may have a very limited range of direct experience with members of families which are much different from their own in income, occupational status, or educational background. In a nation that avows to value diversity, the benefits of technology may be a mixed blessing.

In some low density suburban neighborhoods people are seldom seen outside their homes.

The transient family. Besides the change from the extended to the nuclear family form, our mechanistic society has set in motion other transitions in family roles. Toffler (1970) summarizes these shifts in the following statement:

> Industrialism demanded masses of workers ready and able to move off the land in pursuit of jobs, and move again whenever necessary. Thus the extended family gradually shed its excess weight and the so-called "nuclear family" emerged—a stripped-down portable family unit consisting only of parents, and a small set of children. This new style family, far more mobile than the traditional family, became the standard model in all industrial countries. (p. 242)

This account suggests that the requirement for mobility which came with industrialization may in part account for the reduction in size of the American family. Beyond the changes in children's home environments resulting from reduced family size, the high rate of mobility has introduced additional changes into the developmental milieu of the child. With increased transiency among American families, one can only guess at this point what difficulties children may encounter in repeatedly making and breaking relationships. Toffler (1970)

Disrupted friendships

has summarized the results of a study by Harry R. Moore of the University of Denver, indicating that no differences were found in the test scores of highly transient and nontransient students. But when the researchers looked beyond the test scores they found

> there was a definite tendency for the more nomadic children to avoid participation in the voluntary side of school life—clubs, sports, student government and other extra-curricular activities. It is as though they wished, where possible, to avoid new human ties that might only have to be broken again before long—as if they wished, in short, to slow down the flow-through of people in their lives. (p. 122)

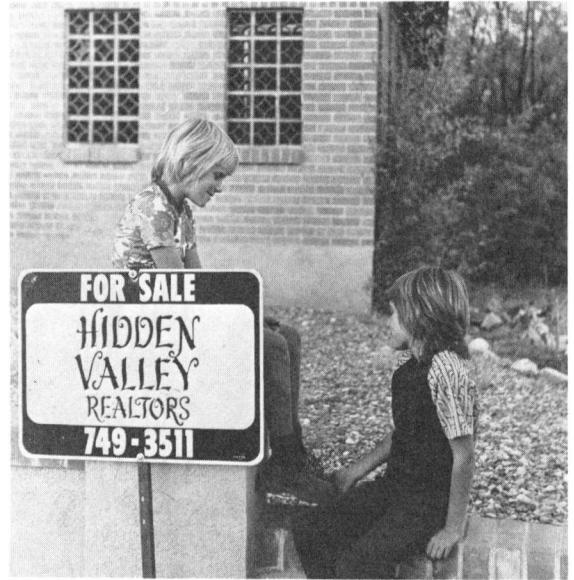

High mobility among families results in disrupted friendships.

The use of the term *nomadic* in the quotation above may be misleading. In most truly nomadic human groups, a relatively stable aggregate of people migrate together, so that they are among familiar people, and established role relationships are not markedly disrupted. This is not true, for example, for the family of the corporation executive in an industrialized nation. As people are transferred, promoted, and maneuvered for better positions, relationships are continually disrupted, and little is known about the long-range effects of continually uprooting children during their formative years. At this point we can only say that there is, in this nation, a growing concern among educators and child care professionals about the need some psychologists feel developing children have for a certain amount of continuity in their relationships and experiences. If the only source of continuity is provided by interpersonal relationships within the nuclear family (which itself is unstable), is this sufficient? If not, what adequate sources of continuity can be planned for environments in which these children live?

The temporary family.   For many families conflicts between careers and parenthood are already sufficiently serious to demand that alternative institutions be developed to care for children whose parents are unable to devote sufficient time to them. The United States has been particularly slow in recognizing the strains which competing needs place on families, and we have been even more hesitant in developing new social institutions to cope with the problem. Millions of American women, including mothers, wish to work as a means of personal ful-

Restrictions on alternatives to home care

fillment. Other millions of American mothers must work—as a matter of survival rather than choice. But there has been a notable lack of enthusiasm in this country for the provision of day care opportunities.

Beyond the problems posed by the shrinking of the circle of people who have an intimate caring relationship with the child, and beyond the strains introduced by the increased geographical mobility of families and employment of mothers, there is yet another fundamental change in the nature of families that must be coped with. This problem is simply that the developmental environments of children are subject to threat because of the increasingly temporary nature of the family.

In at least some sectors of the population, these transitions in the family have been gathering momentum for some time. In 1930, John B. Watson, a pioneer American behaviorist, gave his view on this trend. He reported:

> American family life in large cities is admittedly on the wane. This is shown in many different ways: by the greater number of divorces, fewer marriages, increased age of the men at marriage, fewer children among the well-to-do, the great increase in the number of men who have playmates and the number of women who are interested in men other than their husbands. Just as surely but along different lines is the same trend shown in the ever-increasing number of boys' and girls' camps which take the children away from the home for the whole of the summer and the number of children who go to boarding-school while their parents go to Europe. The latest invention is the outdoor winter camp to take the children from Friday afternoon to Sunday night. Parents are becoming even more willing to shunt the care of the children into well-trained hands. The kindergartens, even in the great universities, now take youngsters at 18 months, and in at least two institutions, infants are taken at or near birth for observation and psychological care.
>
> All this is sensible. I believe the children are enormously better off. Nevertheless it is an open admission that the home is inadequate, unqualified and unwilling to care for children. (p. 55)

There are clear signs that the family may become even more temporary than it is now, as the forces of the mechanistic society work to reduce the bonds that have held families together in the past.

While families are becoming smaller, more transient, and less stable, other stressful conditions resulting from urbanization impinge on family life. The crowded conditions of city life constitute one source of stress.

Violation of personal space. Just as people learn the language of their culture without being consciously aware of the abstract rules that govern their linguistic behavior, so also do they acquire rules that govern the interpersonal spatial relationships which are normative in the culture. Edward T. Hall (1966), an anthropologist, has studied the territorial limits which people in a given culture establish as proper for various kinds of interpersonal transactions. The individual is likely to experience emotional discomfort and stress whenever the territorial limits for a given type of interpersonal exchange is violated.

Increasingly, the crowding which accompanies urbanization makes it difficult for individuals to maintain dimensions of personal space that keep stimulation at a level with which they feel comfortable. Experimentation with several species of animals has shown that the stress resulting from overcrowding produces disturbances in behavior and endocrine functioning (see Dubos, 1968; Calhoun, 1962). The effects on humans are less clear, but Rene Dubos (1968), a microbiologist, experimental pathologist, and humanitarian, has concluded from his observations that

Urbanization and crowding

The things children learn are influenced by their environment.

Crowding, regimented life, environmental pollution, and disturbances of fundamental biological rhythms are aspects of life which are common to all highly
technicized and urbanized societies, rich or poor. These influences elicit from the
human organism responses from which are emerging the physical, mental, and
social disorders commonly called diseases of civilization. (p. 56)

*Crowding and
anonymity*

Paradoxically, the more people there are crowded into our environments, the
more difficult it may be to form close interpersonal relationships. Under conditions of urban crowding, an individual can be anonymous in the midst of a
crowd. Individuals and groups may be subject to stress because urban environments and geographical and social mobility make it difficult to develop durable
and dependable relationships with others. Anthropologists have indicated that
one of the functions of group membership is to help individuals maintain their
equilibria under the impact of the ordinary shocks of life. When group life is
shattered, men and women are lonely and unhappy (Dubos, 1968).

Certainly there have been attempts to design environments in ways to help to
provide privacy and preserve intimate interpersonal relationships, but these
ventures have not been notably successful. Dubos (1968) has remarked:

Some urban planners advocate social and architectural arrangements which provide
each individual person with three or four intimate contacts at every stage of his
existence. But the great mobility of our populations, the high levels of crowding,
and the increased complexity of social life make such intimate associations almost
impossible for the larger percentage of the public. From all points of view,
population pressure probably constitutes the most important single handicap to
creating urban environments with proper biological qualities. (pp. 166-67)

*Adaptation to
change*

One of the most remarkable things about human beings is their ability to
adapt to changing circumstances. Undoubtedly there are certain social advantages

in this, but adaptation may also present problems. Physiological research has shown that increased secretion of various hormones accompanies crowding, and excessive hormonal activity may have harmful effects on the human physiology (Dubos, 1968).

The damaging effects of crowding may not be immediately apparent. In fact, children socialized under conditions of high crowding may feel very uncomfortable in the *absence* of social stimulation such that they cannot feel happy or safe outside a crowd of their own kind. Just as with overeating or many other sorts of habits and addictions,

> such habituations provide temporary relief or even satisfaction, but they are of course dangerous. This is probably true of habituation to overcrowding. Architects have shown that more ingenious design of human settlements can compensate to some extent for insufficient space, but there are limits to what can be achieved by architectural ingenuity. Beyond these limits, overcrowding is likely to cause psychological damage. (Dubos, 1961, p. 154)

Even though the long-range effects of crowding on human populations are not clear, there is sufficient cause for concern over the possible consequences of this trend. It is a problem that warrants attention from those who wish to design environments which will facilitate the optimal development of children and youth. Much of the rebellion against the traditional values and institutions of the mechanistic society have centered upon the depersonalization and the stress from overstimulation common to technological societies. From the counter-culture to encounter groups to mysticism and religious cults, we see groping attempts to discover ways of coping with these factors.

Pluralism. Many observers of the contemporary social scene have remarked that societal values are undergoing transition. Among the reasons for these changes one hears that ". . . many values alter as a consequence of perceiving that past values are leading us into untenable solutions" (Purple & Belanger, 1972, p. 21). As we have noted before, those values associated with technocratic economic goals and the depersonalized aspects of the "computerized bureaucracy" are favorite targets for attack (Purple & Belanger, 1972).

Stating that our traditional value system is undergoing change does not really explain very much. To see that a significant number of Americans still ascribe to the traditional values one has only to consider recent political rhetoric calling for a return to the tested virtues of the work ethic and respect for authority. As we suggested earlier in this chapter, what we see today is more likely a movement toward a pluralistic society, in which different groups hold different values, rather than a uniform transition in the values of the society in general. Such pluralism may be yet another unanticipated consequence of events set in motion by industrialization. Toffler (1970) has noted that as technology advances, overchoice is created ". . . with respect to available goals, cultural products, services, subcults, and life styles" (p. 432).

Overchoice

Among the most powerful of the mechanisms by which people are exposed to optional values and life-styles is television. The potential influence of this medium is evident when one considers that, according to a study done several years ago (Witty, Kinsella, & Conner, 1963), second graders spend an average of 17 hours per week watching television. By the sixth grade they are putting in about 38 hours per week watching the tube. So, by the time the average child is 16 years old, he has spent the equivalent of 15-20 solid months, 24 hours per day watching television.

Television and optional values

The popular media, now so persuasive, are much more likely to introduce people to the emerging alternative values and life-styles than are the traditional institutions. Silberman (1970) comments on this influence:

> In particular, the mass media teach people how to consume and play in this increasing consumer- and pleasure-oriented society, in sharp contrast to the schools, which still emphasize the nineteenth-century virtues of work and thrift. Unlike the schools, too, the media are able to respond to changes in taste or in life style, for example, inducing young people into the new youth culture and the legitimizing parts of it for the adult population. (p. 34)

Value conflict   While the media are ahead of the schools in depicting the plurality of values and life-styles followed by various segments of the population, Silberman (1970) assesses the view of the contemporary society that is presented on television as a partial and distorted representation. Rarely does it realistically depict, for example, the conflict experienced by people caught between the values and expectations of the ethnic subculture of their home and the dominant values of middle-class America. Such conflicts appear to be more common than ever before. In the past the ideal of the American melting pot was widely accepted as a goal by the majority and minority groups alike. This has been a theme of long standing, as we saw earlier in Rush's argument for an educational system to produce a more homogeneous populace.

The melting pot ideal has now fallen into widespread disrepute, as minority groups increasingly come to value and promote cherished aspects of their own languages and cultures. There is now a strong movement to value diversity and to promote cultural pluralism. This trend has definite implications for the rearing and education of children. We see a concern on the part of parents to have their children learn and preserve the values and skills associated with the subculture, in addition to learning the competencies required in the dominant culture. A few years ago it was common for educators to talk about poor and minority group children as *culturally deprived*. Accordingly, *compensatory* education programs were developed to "fill in the deficiencies" left by their native subcultures. These terms are now out of fashion, for cultural and psychological reasons to be discussed in subsequent chapters.

Humanism: The Individual and Society

In this chapter we have provided examples of some of the themes that have influenced the ways in which children are regarded and trained in our rapidly changing culture. The themes and values mentioned here are only illustrative and for every statement made about model group values and activities it is possible to think of numerous exceptions, even for those times in the past when our society was more homogeneous in some ways than it is today. Descriptions of themes refer to average distributions, and many individuals and groups fall outside of or at the fringes of distributions. For example, while suburban children in general may have proportionally less opportunity to engage in shared activities with their parents or other adults than might have been the case in a bygone age, there are nevertheless many suburban parents who violate the mode by devoting a great deal of time to their children. And the descriptions rendered by social historians may not at all capture the themes and values of the various ethnic and racial minorities who have contributed to the making of America. Effort-optimism, for example, hardly describes the expectations of Americans of traditional Mexican ancestry (Paz, 1961). But even though there are many exceptions to the trends described in this chapter, some broad pervasive themes of change are nevertheless discernible, and these trends raise a number of issues relating to child rearing, health, and education.

One trend is seen in the fact that many Americans have recently become awakened to the fact that the stereotyped ideals of American character, reflected in song, legend, and school book, ignored the individual and group uniqueness of vast segments of the American population—primarily those who were poor and of minority group racial or ethnic identity. From colonial times onward, the dominant values favored a relatively restricted sector of the population, and the idealized melting pot was our trademark. It was difficult for a person to maintain the individual characteristics associated with an ethnic subculture and still obtain the benefits of production which came from the exploitation of natural resources. Today, people in many sectors of the society are coming to feel that cultural diversity adds to the richness of experience and cultural heritage of the nation. It is widely felt that the cultural contributions of differing groups should be preserved as a national resource, and that individuals should have freedom of choice in the cultural norms by which they choose to live. Sex roles in the past were also passively accepted on the basis of cultural prescriptions for appropriate masculine or feminine behavior. Today more and more people feel that roles should be a matter of individual choice.

There is also a growing feeling that the effects of industrialization have served to mechanize not only people's conception of the universe, but their conception of themselves as well. Science and technology have held a prominent and prestigious position in American society, and the precise and efficient methods of the physical sciences have been emulated by the human sciences. Prestige in the scientific community has been closely correlated with the degree to which methods and procedures approached the control and exactness of physics and chemistry. Therefore, in psychology, the "pure" branches, such as experimental psychology, have been held in highest esteem, while descriptive and applied branches, such as developmental and educational psychology, have been accorded low status. The reward systems associated with status surely have had an important influence on the kinds of questions asked and the nature of the research pursued. Many psychologists are now rebelling against such a system, objecting to the depersonalized picture of human beings presented by the experimentalist point of view. The humanistic cause is supported by a great number of psychologists and educators. This is part of a widespread search for alternatives to the values and institutions of a mechanistic society.

Humanistic themes. Humanism is not a unified position. A very diverse spectrum of views, operating principles, and theories are evident among psychologists and educators who view themselves as humanists. Nevertheless, there are some widely shared characteristics (Rich, 1971). Among these themes is an emphasis on people's active role in making decisions and directing their own behavior (Rich, 1971; Child, 1973). "Man is a conscious agent. . . . He experiences, he decides, he acts" (Child, 1973, p. 15).

A sub-theme related to humans' character as self-directed beings is the notion that humans have an inner need to fully develop their potential. Our contemporary institutions and favored methods of child rearing and education are frequently regarded as environmental barriers to the realization of human potential for vast numbers of individuals.

The humanist's emphasis on growth toward one's potential and the process of continuous movement from "being" to "becoming," sets the human species qualitatively apart from animals that occupy a "lower" position on the phylogenetic scale. It is a view which also takes strong exception to the notion that humans are completely, or even primarily, controlled by external forces—as just one more element in a mechanistically designed universe.

Another common characteristic among humanists of varied persuasions is the belief that the individual operates as an integrated whole (Rich, 1971; Child, 1973). It is often argued that psychological theories which deal primarily with discrete, observable behaviors regard humans erroneously, as little more than a collection of parts, always reacting to environmental stimuli without initiating or creating. Some writers (Rich, 1971) characterize such approaches as structural, and argue that only a process approach, such as humanism is supposed to offer, can adequately capture the complexity, self-directedness, and individuality of human beings.

Structural and process approaches

Limitations of humanism. The humanistic conception of the nature of humanity is probably congruent with the "intuitive" notion of the human character accepted by most people. Irwin Child (1973) of Yale University has argued that this agreement between the humanist's model and the impression that most people hold about what it is like to be human is a most important factor supporting the value of the humanistic model. Most of us like to think that we exercise free will, that our individual uniqueness should be accorded dignity and respect, and that we are more than just interchangeable cogs in an automated world.

However attractive these ideas may appear, contemporary humanism has some serious limitations. Child (1973) has identified a number of characteristics which he judges to be deficits in the humanistic position. First, the concepts associated with humanism are often vague and ambiguous. At anything more than an impressionistic level, it is far from certain that concepts such as "authentic person," "self-actualization," "process approach," "inner-experience," or even "human potentiality" convey the same meaning to different people. Because of the vagueness of humanists' concepts, empirically oriented psychologists, who strive to define their concepts in terms of observable operations or behaviors, often regard humanists as "fuzzy thinkers."

Conceptual vagueness

Romanticism

A second limitation of much humanistic writing is its sentimental (Child, 1973) or romantic character. It may be well to regard humans as controllers of their own destiny, but to do so in the face of everyday evidence that many people are buffeted about by their environment is to take a romantic, or at least overly optimistic view of things. Many people lack the skills and resources to exercise any degree of independence from the sometimes capricious external influences of environmental forces.

Communication and verifiability

Effective communication, to say nothing of scientific inquiry, requires that statements be verifiable. The value of insight, no matter how creative or brilliant it seems, is limited if it remains essentially a private experience. The vital quality of verifiability is lacking in much humanistic writing (Child, 1973). This is a very serious limitation indeed.

Empirical psychology—limitations. Although there have been spokespersons for the humanistic point of view since the beginnings of American psychology, until recently the dominant spokespersons for the humanistic model were Europeans. In America the empiricist tradition has been dominant. Experimental psychology has received some reflected glory and status from the hard sciences which contributed directly to the growth of technology in the mechanistic society. The research tradition in American psychology has had the advantage of being objective and precise. A frequently heard criticism, however, is that topics of inquiry

Neglect of significant problems

in the research tradition are restricted to those which can be studied most directly with the objective techniques already available. As a result, important problems which do not lend themselves to study with existing methods and technology are neglected (Child, 1973).

Another criticism of empirical psychology is that in its eagerness to emulate the physical sciences, it too soon became preoccupied with the experimental study of cause and effect relationships, at the expense of important descriptive work. The psychology of child development is an exception to this pattern. In some ways research in this area appears to have become fixated at the descriptive level.

*Neglect of
description of
naturalistic
behavior*

Perhaps as an artifact of the historical development of psychology in America, the domain of human behavior which seemed to lend itself best to empirical investigation was that of intellectual performance. At an early point in the development of verifiable observations of human behavior, techniques were developed which permitted the measurement of certain aspects of intellectual performance—first through the development of intelligence tests, and then by applying the same procedures to the assessment of academic achievement. These tests provided an acceptable means for obtaining information that was not only verifiable, but which could also be communicated clearly. Even the amount of error reflected in the observations could be specified. In recent years researchers have become aware of the limitations of these measures, but they are still used very routinely for many purposes, and it seems clear that in the past, the *availability* of such measures influenced the nature of the questions that have been studied by American psychologists.

Humanists, reacting to the narrowness of research concerns, have urged a broader consideration of human capabilities. This seems to be a worthy aim. They have also urged the adoption of broader aims for American education than those reflected in the activities of most schools. Traditionally, from the elementary grades to graduate school, the bulk of resources and effort has been directed toward the teaching of academic skills and knowledge. Other important aspects of life, particularly the affective life, have not received systematic attention. Contemporary humanists were certainly not the first to recognize this unbalanced state of affairs and to advocate a more awakened conception of man. Pestalozzi, a Swiss educational theorist whose life bridged the seventeenth and eighteenth centuries, expressed many of his ideas about education through a character whom he called Gertrude. Advising a young man who was organizing a school, Gertrude said one day,

*Neglect of
significant aspects
of behavior*

> You should do for your children what their parents fail to do for them. The reading, writing and arithmetic are not, after all, what they most need; it is all well and good for them to learn something, but the really important thing is for them to be something,—*for them to become what they are meant to be* . . . . (Emphasis added, cited in Rippa, 1969, p. 88)

The challenge held out by the humanist is for us to discover ways to facilitate the development of all facets of human life. Empirical psychology has fallen far short of meeting the challenge. Psychologists have learned a great deal about how to facilitate the acquisition of knowledge and information. Beyond simple descriptions, less is known about how people learn to make judicious use of their knowledge and skills, how to foster the development of a satisfying affective life, or how to deal competently with other people.

The shortcomings of science, as applied to human behavior, are evident also in relation to the humanistic theme of inner-directedness. Sophisticated principles and procedures have been developed to manage the behavior of children in our charge. But procedures to teach self-management skills have only recently begun to be explored. At a time when children and adults alike are faced with more and more choices to make, there is still a tendency to manipulate the individual, and to place the responsibility of choice in hands other than one's own. Conversely, humanists often assume that if a rich variety of options is available to individuals, they will make growth-facilitating choices on the basis of some kind of inner wisdom. Both views seem naïve. Individuals do differ from one another in their ability to set goals for themselves, to choose alternative modes of action in pursuit of those goals, and to evaluate their own progress. Presumably these skills can be taught, and the individual who learns to use such strategies would have greater freedom of choice than one lacking such an ability. Some progress is now being made along these lines, but empirical psychology has gotten a late start in the search for means of providing individuals with the tools required to have a role in designing their own freedom.

Science and humanism. The principal strength of humanism is its potential for identifying worthwhile goals for human endeavor. The ability of humanism alone to achieve these aims is limited because the goals are not clearly conceptualized in terms that provide for lucid communication. Nor does humanism have a means of verifying whether given actions do indeed lead to the cherished goals. In short, humanism offers goals which have widespread appeal, but it has not provided replicable methods for attaining them. On the other hand, scientific psychology has sound methods, but lacks a guiding philosophy to discern the difference between more and less significant applications of its techniques. As a result, research has often been concentrated on topics lacking broad human significance, but amenable to study with existing measures and techniques.

The psychology of child development is undergoing a transition. The nature of the transition will be described in the next chapter, but we can say here that the time seems to be ripe to bring the scientific method to bear on humanistic objectives. We count ourselves as humanists, on the basis of our goals and values, and empiricists, on the basis of our methods. In this context, humanism means to us a balanced concern for the optimal development of all of a human being's facets—those pertaining to physical, intellectual, social, and emotional life. It means providing developing children with skills with which to take an increasing responsibility for managing their own lives—skills in evaluating alternatives, setting goals, and choosing courses of action articulated to those ends. That is the essence of personal autonomy.

SUGGESTED READINGS

Bronfenbrenner, U. The changing American child—A speculative analysis. *Merrill-Palmer Quarterly,* 1961, 7 (2), 73-84.

Bronfenbrenner, U. *Two worlds of childhood: U.S. and U.S.S.R.* New York: Russell Sage Foundation, 1970.

Dubos, R. *So human an animal.* New York: Charles Scribner's Sons, 1968.

Kessen, W. *The child.* New York: John Wiley & Sons, 1965.

Mead, M., & Wolfenstein, M. *Childhood in contemporary cultures.* Chicago: Phoenix Books, 1955.

2

The Science of
Human Development

Objective	Recognize or recall	Compare and contrast	Describe or demonstrate	Evaluate
the definition of developmental psychology.	●			
the meanings of and the influences on genotype, phenotype, ontogenetic traits, and phylogenetic traits.	●	●		
the early biological model of development including relevant research and cultural origins of the model.	●		●	
Hall's influence on socialization practice.	●		●	
the behaviorist model including views regarding genetic and environmental influences on behavior.	●		●	
applications and cultural origins of behaviorism.	●		●	
criticisms and rebuttals of the behavioral commitment to the technology of behavior.	●	●		
the interactive model.	●		●	
the interactive stance as it has been articulated in the study of intellectual and social development.	●	●		
the biological model of development from the standpoint of the behavioral viewpoint.				●
the behavioral model of development from the standpoint of the interactive viewpoint.				●
the interactive model of development from the standpoint of the behavioral viewpoint.				●
descriptive and experimental methodology.	●	●	●	
the cross-sectional and longitudinal methods of research.	●	●		
what makes an experimental or descriptive study a developmental study.	●			
the definitions of the terms *independent* and *dependent* variable.	●			
the definition of the term *developmental process*.	●			
views on and interpretations of situational and temporal stability in growth.	●	●	●	
the meaning and societal use of the term *developmental norm*.	●			
the characteristics of individual differences in growth.	●			
the implications of findings concerning individual differences for socialization practice.	●		●	
the different bases for the construction of developmental stages.	●	●	●	
major goals of socialization in contemporary culture.	●			

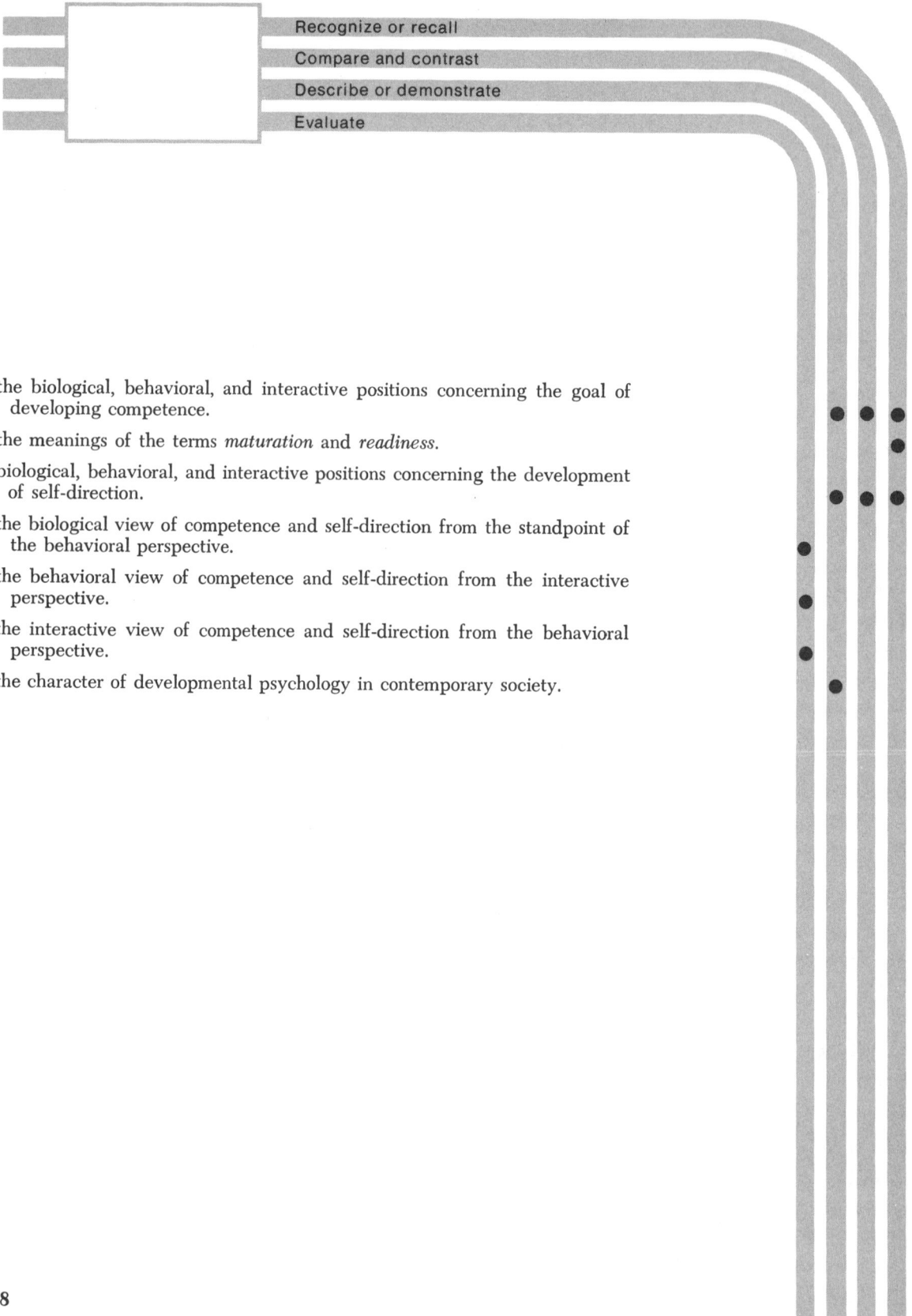

the biological, behavioral, and interactive positions concerning the goal of developing competence.

the meanings of the terms *maturation* and *readiness*.

biological, behavioral, and interactive positions concerning the development of self-direction.

the biological view of competence and self-direction from the standpoint of the behavioral perspective.

the behavioral view of competence and self-direction from the interactive perspective.

the interactive view of competence and self-direction from the behavioral perspective.

the character of developmental psychology in contemporary society.

CHAPTER CONTENT

Developmental psychology defined

Conditions of development: nature versus nurture

Basic concepts in the nature-nurture controversy

Developmental theories and the nature-nurture issue

Developmental research and the nature-nurture issue

Developmental processes

Stability in developmental processes

Commonality versus uniqueness in growth

Developmental stages

Developmental psychology and socialization

Developing competence

Developing self-direction

Developmental psychology: a changing science in a changing society

In chapter 1, we put forth the view that child development and socialization can best be understood in terms of the cultural context in which they take place. Throughout the remainder of the book we shall examine childhood and its relationship to culture using theory and research findings from the science of developmental psychology. The present chapter provides an overview of developmental science which sets forth the basic concepts and theories to be used in explicating developmental processes and socialization practices in succeeding chapters in the text.

DEVELOPMENTAL PSYCHOLOGY DEFINED

Developmental psychology is that branch of psychological science committed to the study of changes in behavioral capabilities and processes occurring as a function of time. Developmental psychology is based on the assumption that developmental changes take place in an orderly fashion. The principal tasks of the developmentalist are to discover the processes through which change is effected and to determine the conditions which bring about change. As will soon become apparent, the history of developmental psychology has been marked by continuous controversy and debate with respect to both of these tasks.

CONDITIONS OF DEVELOPMENT: NATURE VERSUS NURTURE

The central issue of contention in the field of developmental psychology has been that of determining the conditions which shape development. In the history of developmental science, this issue has been referred to as the nature-nurture controversy. Early developmentalists took the position that developmental change was produced in the main by genetic influences. Later theorists challenged this position by asserting that environmental factors played the central role in determining behavioral change. After an initial period of protracted and heated debate, concern shifted from the polemical argument of whether nature or nurture controls development to the more subtle issue of the relative contributions of nature and nurture to development. Today, a major concern in the field is that of revealing how the influences of nature and nurture combine to produce changes in behavioral capability and functioning. Within the various sub-specialties in developmental psychology, the shift from the early extreme positions in the field to an interactive stance is still very much in progress. Polemical views remain and continue to attract wide attention and to affect socialization practices in the nation. Yet there are movements within all sub-specialties toward an interactive stance emphasizing combined genetic and environmental influences on growth.[1]

As we examine the nature-nurture controversy, keep in mind that the debate is not simply a dispassionate scientific argument. It is a controversy which has evolved in the context of social and political forces affecting the economic well-being of every individual in society. Western culture has always distributed goods and services to people in unequal ways. Throughout the course of history justifications for economic inequalities have been linked closely to presumed genetic and environmental influences on behavior. As a result, prevailing views regarding the contributions of nature and nurture to development have had important economic implications for large segments of the population. For example, social policies regarding the origins of poverty and the development of programs for minimizing economic privation have been markedly affected by assumptions concerning hereditary and environmental influences on development. The massive educational programs initiated in the 1960s to wipe out intellectual deficits of poor children are a case in point. These programs were based in part on the assumption that environmental factors played a major role in determining intellectual growth. They derived support for this assumption in large measure from the work of psychological theorists who presented evidence suggesting that environmental variables had a significant influence on intellectual development in the early years of life.

Basic Concepts in the Nature-Nurture Controversy

The nature-nurture debate has evolved from the consideration of two types of information. The first has to do with the fact that overt characteristics of behavior can be determined by predispositions transmitted from generation to generation through genes or by environmental factors. The second involves the fact that some predispositions are shared by virtually all members of a species, while other predispositions vary greatly among various members of a species.

Genotype, phenotype, and development. The fundamental assumption underlying the nature-nurture controversy is that the overt characteristics or behaviors of an individual can be influenced either by genetic endowment (nature) or environmental factors (nurture). The specific genetic endowment of an individual is referred to as his genotype. The genotype is carried in each body cell of the person and tends to remain constant throughout life.

Genotype

Until recently, genotypic constancy was regarded as an immutable given.

---

1. Throughout the text the term *growth* will be used liberally as a synonym for development.

However, scientific advances have now made it possible to alter genetic endowment. Ausubel, Beckwith, and Janssen (1974) report that a number of researchers have demonstrated the feasibility of changing the genetic composition of developing embryos by combining two embryos from different sets of parents during the early stages of development. The offspring resulting from these combinations share characteristics of both sets of parents.

Experiments such as the above make it clear that the day when it will be possible to control genetic characteristics on a broad scale is close at hand. We may soon live in a world in which parents can specify height, eye color, hair color, and who knows, perhaps even genetic aspects of intelligence and personality prior to the birth of their children. Genetically transmitted disease and predispositions to disease may be all but eliminated in this new world. As is the case with vaccines today, the central barrier to the control of genetically transmitted disorders may be the problems associated with alerting the public to available genetic control services. The possibility of genetic control, of course, raises the issue of how such control should be used, what limitations should be placed on control, and who should be given decision-making power with respect to genetic influences. These issues are already the subject of extensive debate among contemporary social theorists.

The manner in which genotype controls development is, in the main, not directly observable. The effects of genotype must be inferred from the examination of overt characteristics. The term *phenotype* is used to refer to observable characteristics of the individual. Phenotype is, in part, a function of genotype, but it is also influenced by environmental factors. The heart of the nature-nurture controversy lies in the fact that it is difficult to determine to what extent the various aspects of phenotype are controlled by genotype and to what extent they are determined by environmental variables.

Phenotype

Environment influences phenotype in two ways. First, environmental conditions tend to have direct effects on behavior and other characteristics which are independent of the internal characteristics of the individual. A child may well scream at his mother when she steps on his foot regardless of his intellectual level or social or personal traits. In addition to determining actions and characteristics directly, environmental variables may influence the development of internal predispositions that frequently exert direct effects on overt characteristics or behavior. For example, a child may learn to scream at his mother during temper tantrums as a result of being rewarded by maternal attention for screaming behavior on previous occasions.

Ontogeny and phylogeny in development. Some developmental characteristics are common to all members of a species. Others are possessed by only some individuals in a species. Developmental acquisitions that are characteristic of all species members are called *phylogenetic* traits. Some familiar examples in humans are the opposable thumb and finger structure of the hand, which facilitates the use of tools, binocular vision, bipedal ambulation, and the capacity for language production and comprehension. Characteristics that vary among species members are called *ontogenetic* traits. Hair color, eye color, height, personality attributes, and IQ are some of the many examples falling into the ontogenetic category.

Phylogenetic traits are generally thought of as being genetically determined, and indeed, many common characteristics shared by a species are in all significant respects the result of genotypic influences. However, there are common characteristics determined by environmental as well as innate factors. Language

Determinants of phylogenetic traits

capability is a case in point. Basic language capability is a pan-human characteristic; but although the capacity for language development is genetically determined, the capability to produce and understand speech cannot develop in the absence of appropriate environmental stimulation.

*Determinants of
ontogenetic traits*

Some ontogenetic traits are determined entirely by genetic influences. Eye color and hair color are examples. Other ontogenetic characteristics, however, are the result of complex interactions between genetic and environmental factors. Intellectual performance, emotional reactions, and personality traits are included in the interaction category. Those traits resulting from interactive influences are generally the ones which have been of greatest concern in the socialization process and which have engendered the most heated debates in the nature-nurture controversy.

Developmental Theories and the Nature-Nurture Issue

During the early stages of the growth of developmental psychology as a science, the contribution of genotype to phenotype was depicted in extreme terms. Moreover, little distinction was made between ontogenetic and phylogenetic traits in assessing the role of genetics in determining overt characteristics. Early developmental theorists took the view that genetic endowment accounted for virtually all the significant aspects of development. This view, however, was soon challenged and to some extent counterbalanced by the behaviorist position that developmental differences in behavioral capabilities are generally learned. As we shall see, the polemical argument initiated in early theoretical conceptions persists in only slightly altered form today— despite some movement in the field to an interactive position stressing the combined contributions of nature and nurture to development. Moreover, socialization practices, particularly those applied in school settings, continue to be dominated by the early polemical version of the nature-nurture controversy.

The early biological model. The early biological model of development was initiated by G. Stanley Hall around the turn of the century. Hall's thinking was strongly influenced by Darwin's theory of evolution. For Hall, individual (ontogenetic) development was simply a reenactment or recapitulation of

*Hall's
recapitulation
· theory*

G. STANLEY HALL (1844-1924)   G. Stanley Hall was born into a New England farm family. His parents were poor and his upbringing reflected the stern puritanical traditions common in New England during the nineteenth century. Hall's initial ambition was to become a minister, and his first graduate degree was in divinity. However, his interest in psychology eventually led him to study with the eminent philosopher-psychologist William James and thereby to obtain the first doctorate in psychology offered by Harvard University. After receiving his degree, Hall pursued further studies in Germany in Wilhelm Wundt's laboratory, which was the first psychological laboratory ever to be established. Upon returning to the United States Hall served as a professor at Johns Hopkins University. In 1888 he was appointed as the first president of Clark University. Hall continued this position until his retirement in 1921.

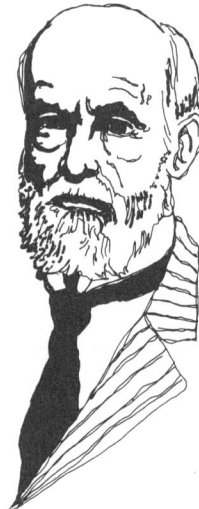

species development. Hall regarded the sequence of this recapitulation to be predetermined genetically, though he did recognize that environmental factors could influence behavior during the later stages of development (Riegel, 1972).

Hall's biological position was highly influential in shaping views on child development in the United States. Hall was an inspiring teacher and had a marked influence on those who were to become leaders in psychology in the generation ahead. H. H. Goddard, who introduced the Binet intelligence test into the United States and who was responsible for the long-held view that IQ measured innate intellectual ability, was one of Hall's students. Lewis Terman, who constructed the Stanford-Binet Intelligence Scale and thereby launched the testing movement in this country, also claimed Hall as his mentor. Finally, Arnold Gesell, who developed child-study research at Yale University during the first half of the twentieth century and whose books on age-related developmental capabilities are still widely read, was also a product of Hall's tutelage.

Hall's influence on developmental psychology and socialization

Hall's influence extended beyond professional psychology to the socialization practices of the home and of the school through child-study associations. The basic message Hall communicated to parents and teachers through the child-study movement was that adults responsible for guiding development should not attempt to interfere with genetically predetermined developmental progress. In 1901 Hall wrote:

> The guardians of the young should strive first of all to keep out of nature's way, and to prevent harm, and should merit the proud title of tenders of the happiness and rights of children. They should feel profoundly that childhood as it comes fresh from the hand of God, is not corrupt, but illustrates the survival of the most consummate thing in the world, they should be convinced that there is nothing else in the world so worthy of love, reverence, and service as the body and soul of the growing child. (Rippa, 1969, p. 325)

Hall's views on development provided a much needed corrective to earlier thought on the subject of child rearing. As indicated in the previous chapter, prior to the twentieth century, socialization practices were strongly influenced by the concept of original sin. The failure of a child to meet adult expectations was generally regarded as a moral lapse. For example, the child who did not succeed in school was typically chastised for his failure. Little recognition was given to the possibility that he might not have the genetic endowment necessary to succeed. The following description of student-teacher relationships by the well-known Swiss educator Johann Pestalozzi, at the end of the eighteenth century, illustrates the punitive attitude of educators toward student failure:

> At the close of school, those who had done well went up to him first, and said: "God be with you!" He held out his hand to each one replying: "God be with you, my dear child!" Then came those who had only done partly well, and to these he merely said: "God be with you!" without giving them his hand. Finally those who had not done well at all had to leave the room without even going to him. (Rippa, 1969, p. 89)

The pervasiveness of the assumption that scholastic ineptitude was based in the failure of the child to meet his educational responsibilities is underscored when one keeps in mind that Pestalozzi was one of the most progressive educational theorists of his age. He fashioned education after science, taking the position that knowledge was ultimately derived from direct observation of nature. In the area of social conduct, he sought to develop in children love and trust of humanity and of God. The punitiveness illustrated in the above quote was mild indeed compared to the floggings characteristic of the treatment of children in Pestalozzi's day.

Although Hall's recapitulation theory was not widely supported by later theorists, the idea that development was in large measure genetically predetermined continued to be a dominant theme in developmental psychology for several decades. Support for the position came first from animal research. The work of G. E. Coghill was particularly influential. Coghill (1929) conducted studies on the relationship between behavioral capability and morphological structure in the salamander. His research led him to the discovery of the principle of cephalocaudal development, which states that both morphological and behavioral development proceed from the head downward. In addition, he discovered the principle of proximodistal development, which states that morphological and behavioral development proceed from the trunk to the extremities. Coghill observed that the head of the developing salamander appeared before the tail and that spontaneous head movements occurred before spontaneous tail movements in the organism. Correspondingly, he found that the body of the salamander developed before its limbs and that the first movements of the limbs involved body movements, whereas subsequent limb movements were almost totally independent of body reactions. Coghill made the bold inference from these observations that experience had little or nothing to do with the development of behavioral patterns. Behavioral development, according to Coghill, was almost entirely the product of genetic factors. Coghill's findings received almost immediate support in research with humans through the work of Mary Shirley. Shirley (1931) found that in humans, as in the salamander, motor control begins in the head and gradually progresses to the feet. She, like Coghill, concluded that behavioral development was influenced little by experience.

Descriptive research on developmental sequence in the tradition of Coghill and Shirley was augmented by studies in which practice opportunities that might affect development were manipulated. The underlying assumption in all these studies was that insofar as experience affected development, additional practice would be beneficial and deprivation from practice would be detrimental in influencing development. In general, studies of practice effects supported the genetic viewpoint. Gesell and Thompson (1929), for example, found that providing special training in such skills as stair climbing had no discernibly beneficial effects on development. They worked with twins in their research. One twin was provided with early skill training. The other received no training; yet at a subsequent time the untrained child acquired skills with little practice. These results led Gesell and Thompson to conclude that motor-skill development was predetermined by genetic factors. As we shall discuss in detail in chapter 4, it is now clear that this conclusion was unwarranted. Gesell and Thompson apparently assumed that the twin who had received no special skill training had therefore not engaged in practice relevant to the task. This was clearly not the case, however. For example, the walking experiences of the untrained twin might well have had a beneficial effect on stair climbing.

Although early research provided support for the biological model of development, it is important to recognize that the model did not have its origins solely in research-related concerns. Developmental psychologist Klaus Riegel (1972) suggests that the biological view of development derived largely from political and economic circumstances existing in England in the nineteenth century.

During that period England had emerged as a dominant sea power. Individual opportunity in the fields of manufacturing and international trade was at a peak. Financial gain and social success were available on an unprecedented scale to those who were able to survive in the crucible of keen competition.

The biological model of development adopted in England during the nineteenth century mirrored the social and economic conditions of the day. As we pointed out earlier, the biological position had its origins in Darwinian theory. The Darwinian view of the survival of the fittest emphasizing the competitive selection of able individuals by a harsh environment was in close harmony with the prevailing circumstances surrounding financial success in nineteenth-century England.

Riegel (1972) suggests that when the concept of the successful survivor was translated into social terms, he turned out to be "the white, middle-class adult most likely engaged in manufacturing or business enterprises" (p. 130). Riegel goes on to assert that individuals and groups not falling in the successful category tended to be characterized in negative terms:

> Children are regarded as incomplete adults; old persons as deficient, criminals, mental defectives, colonial subjects, and non-white as far below the rank of white middle-class adults. (p. 130)

Contemporary versions of the biological model in the United States continue to identify "successful survivors" as well as individuals and groups that deviate in one or more ways from the characteristics of the successful survivor. Moreover, as in the past, deviant groups continue to be characterized in negative ways. For example, one of the characteristics of the successful survivor in contemporary society is a high level of intelligence. As we shall discuss in detail in chapter 5, research has shown that children from poor families tend to score lower on intelligence tests than children from middle-class families. From the standpoint of the biological model, these differences are regarded as genetically based. According to the biological view, the poor suffer economic deprivation at least in part because they are genetically intellectually inferior to the middle class.

The behaviorist model. The principal challenge to the biological model of development came from the behavorist position, which had developed within the psychology of learning at the beginning of the twentieth century. Behaviorism was a reaction to the mentalistic stance which had dominated psychological theory in Europe and the United States since the inception of psychological science. Prior to the establishment of behaviorism, introspective reports of conscious experience constituted the principal source of data in the field of psychology. Experimental subjects reported the images and thoughts which came into their consciousness under a given set of stimulus conditions. Reliance on such reports threatened the objectivity of psychological science. Experiments conducted in one laboratory produced radically different reports from experiments of a similar sort in another laboratory.

In 1913 John Watson dealt the death blow to the introspectionist psychology of the nineteenth century in his declaration *Psychology as the Behaviorist Views It.* Through this publication, behaviorism was born. Watson rejected both the study of mental processes, such as thinking and perceiving, and the method of introspection. In their place he advocated a science of psychology analogous to the natural sciences based on the study of observable behavior. This new science would commit itself to the description, prediction, and control of behavior.

JOHN B. WATSON (1878-1958)
John Broadus Watson received his Ph.D. from the University of Chicago in 1903. He remained at Chicago for five years after receiving his degree and then became a professor at Johns Hopkins University. His professorship at Johns Hopkins lasted for only twelve years. During this relatively brief time span Watson developed his ideas on behaviorism and communicated them to the scientific community. In 1920 Watson's career in psychology was terminated abruptly when he was forced to resign from Johns Hopkins because he had divorced his wife. After his expulsion from academic life, Watson pursued a successful career in advertising and gradually withdrew entirely from the field of psychology.

Behaviorism and the environment

Behaviorism represented a radical form of environmentalism which held that individual variations in observable action were entirely experientially based. Concerning experience Watson (1930) wrote: "Give me a dozen healthy infants, well-formed and my own specified world to bring them up in and I'll guarantee you to take any one at random and train him to become any type of specialist I might select—doctor, lawyer, artist, merchant-chief, and yes, even beggar-man and thief, regardless of his talents, penchants, tendencies, abilities, vocations, and race of his ancestors" (p. 104).

Genetics and behavior

Behaviorists did not and do not deny the influence of genetic factors. In their view, however, the central contribution of genetics has to do with phylogenetic

B. F. SKINNER (1904-)
Burrhus Frederic Skinner was born into a professional family in Susquehanna, Pennsylvania. He majored in English at Hamilton College and was elected to Phi Beta Kappa at that institution. His initial ambition was to become a writer. However, after a two-year effort to establish himself in that field, his interests turned to the study of psychology. He received his Ph.D. from Harvard University in 1931, taught for a few years in Minnesota and Indiana and then returned to Harvard where he has remained throughout his long and productive career. In his years at Harvard, he developed his views on behaviorism and on the application of behavioral technology toward the solution of significant social problems. A skillful writer, Skinner has been able to communicate his ideas effectively not only to the scientific and professional community in the field of psychology, but also to the general public. He stands today as the most articulate contemporary spokesman for the behavioral position.

rather than ontogenetic traits. More specifically, they take the position that genetic endowment determines the manner in which the environment influences behavior. They assert that the manner of environmental influence is essentially the same across individuals. For example, B. F. Skinner (1953), a most articulate contemporary spokesman for the behaviorist position, has asserted that in all individuals who are not severely structurally damaged behavior is controlled by the antecedent and consequent events surrounding it.

Antecedent conditions may evoke reflexive behaviors (i.e., automatic reactions to stimuli). For instance, a puff of air directed at the eyelid will invariably elicit a blinking response. Likewise, a light tap on the patellar tendon in the area of the knee produces a forward jerk of the lower leg.

Antecedent influences on behavior

Beyond their influence on reflexive reactions, antecedent events serve mainly as signals for the occurrence of action. For instance, a mother coming into a baby's room with a bottle may signal the experience of receiving food and thereby cue sucking reactions on the part of the infant. The mother and bottle do not automatically produce the sucking reflex, as may be evidenced by the fact that the sucking response does not invariably occur in the presence of mother and bottle.

The principal controlling influences on so-called voluntary behaviors, such as the act of sucking, are the consequences which ensue after the behavior has occurred. Consequent events that increase the probability of occurrence of the behaviors which precede them are called positive reinforcers. One of the main contributions of behavior theory has been to demonstrate that positive reinforcers can control an enormously wide range of behavior.

Consequent influences on behavior

Laboratory research conducted by Skinner and his colleagues demonstrated the powerful influences of reinforcing consequences on animal behavior (see, for example, Skinner, 1938; Ferster & Skinner, 1957). Following their successes with a variety of animal species, behaviorists began to work in a number of situations involving important practical consequences for society. For example, in an early and amusing effort to demonstrate the social relevance of behavioral science, Skinner trained pigeons in missile guidance (Skinner, 1960). He put his pigeons in a container which he presented to authorities in the armed services as a missile guidance system. The military was impressed with what it then regarded as the incredible capability of the system in the guidance field until Skinner opened the container and showed the perhaps wisely conservative military decision makers what was inside.

Applications of behaviorism

In the late 1940s, Skinner explicated his views on the use of behavioral principles in the practical affairs of human beings in *Walden Two*, a utopian novel which describes a small but complete society designed on the basis of behavioral procedures (Skinner, 1948). However, it was not until 1954 that Skinner turned his talents in earnest to the application of behavioral principles in the socialization of the young. In an article entitled "The Science of Learning and the Art of Teaching," Skinner (1954) faulted existing educational practice for its failure to make systematic use of reinforcement principles. He argued that the careful sequencing of instructional content coupled with immediate positive reinforcement for correct responses would eventuate in a significant enhancement of student learning. He further asserted that it was doubtful that teachers, given the numbers of students with which they had to deal, could provide the systematic sequencing and immediate reinforcement needed to enhance educational progress. With characteristic boldness, he suggested that the principal responsibility for instruction of the young be assigned to machines which could be systematically programmed to provide the needed sequencing of instructional content and administration of positive reinforcement. The programmed-instruction movement was initiated largely as a result of this suggestion.

While programmed instruction was still in its infancy, Skinner and his colleagues broke new ground in yet another area of social significance, the treatment of the mentally ill. In the middle 1950s a number of Skinner's associates applied reinforcement techniques with marked success in the control of "abnormal" behavior patterns (e.g., see Krasner & Ullmann, 1965). The use of Skinnerian techniques in the treatment of mental disorders came to be called behavior modification. Behavior modification spread quickly to concerns beyond mental illness. Some educational psychologists applied behavioral principles in instruction (e.g., Staats & Staats, 1963) while others used behavioral techniques to assist parents in the socialization of their children (e.g., Patterson, 1965).

Cultural influences on behaviorism

Behaviorism, like the biological model of development, has been influenced by cultural factors occurring outside of developmental psychology as well as by research and theory in developmental science. The cultural origins of behaviorism can be found in the rise of science and technology in Western Europe. Behaviorism shares the faith, which spread across Western culture during the last 500 years, that science coupled with technology holds the key to the betterment of human life. As we pointed out earlier, the initial aim of behaviorism was to develop a science of psychology analogous to the physical sciences. Behaviorism is an extension of the cultural belief that humans can gain control over nature through scientific study linked to the development of technological products designed to control environmental conditions.

Skinner (1971), representing the contemporary behavioral view, points out that although great strides have been made in the physical sciences, the science of behavior has lagged far behind. He goes on to assert that the need to develop a science of behavior commensurate in depth and scope with the physical sciences is critical. The physical sciences have gone far in fulfilling their promise of affording humans control over nature. As a result, the power which people now possess to alter natural conditions is awesome indeed. In Skinner's view, human development, particularly the ability to control the environment wisely, has not kept pace with advances in the natural sciences. Consequently, there now exists the serious threat that humans may destroy their environment and themselves through lack of intelligent management of the awesome power which they now have at their disposal.

Criticisms and rebuttals relating to the behavioral view

Critics of the behavioral position have argued that a commitment to behavioral science and technology represents a mechanistic and dehumanizing approach to child development and socialization (Silberman, 1970). They assert that the child is reduced to an automaton whose development is measured by industrial concepts, such as rate of productivity. Socialization institutions such as the public schools are analogous to factories responsible for producing products (graduates) according to a set of predetermined specifications.

Contemporary behaviorist Albert Bandura (1974) in his presidential address to the American Psychological Association traces criticisms of the behavioral position in part to the failure of behavioral theorists to emphasize the role which people play in interpreting and modifying their environment.

The central emphasis of behavioral science and technology has been on environmental control of behavior. In behavioral conceptions of socialization, socializing agents such as parents and teachers have typically played the role of the controlling environment. Children, on the other hand, have generally been assigned the part of the individual being controlled. The potential for conceptualizing the child in mechanistic terms within the environmental-control paradigm is clearly present.

Bandura points out that recent behavioral research and theory have demonstrated the role which people play in controlling their own behavior by interpreting and altering environmental conditions (e.g., see Mahoney & Thoresen, 1974). When viewed from this contemporary behavioral perspective, the child in the process of socialization is not merely a passive agent. Although he is controlled by his environment (e.g., parents and teachers), he also plays an active part in shaping the conditions around him. Moreover, the child can learn how to manage his environment in systematic ways to guide his own development.

The interactive stance. In the period between 1930 and 1950 a number of forces began to gather which eventuated in a fundamental change in the character of the nature-nurture debate. With the advent of the interactive position, developmentalists became concerned with the manner in which nature and nurture interacted to determine development. The movement toward an interactive stance in developmental psychology has been gradual and has been influenced primarily by theoretical arguments advanced in the areas of intellectual and social development.

The interactive view regarding intellectual development has been influenced by developmental investigations of intelligence-test performance and by laboratory investigations of intellectual growth carried out by the Swiss psychologist Jean Piaget and his colleagues. Both of these sources of influence suggest that intellectual growth results from the combined effects of genetic and environmental variables.

Early developmentalists in the United States conceived of intelligence as being determined entirely by innate factors. H. H. Goddard was largely responsible for this view. As mentioned earlier, Goddard was one of G. Stanley Hall's students and was a strong subscriber to Hall's notion that development in all areas was largely determined by genetic influences.

Intelligence testing and the interactive view

Over the years evidence began to accumulate suggesting that environmental influences played a role in determining intelligence as measured by standardized tests. Case studies often revealed large changes in the IQs of children who experienced significant alterations in their environment. For example, black children who moved from rural environments in the South to urban ghettos in some instances gained as much as forty IQ points (Klineberg, 1935). In addition, favorable changes in the economic or cultural character of an area were often associated with marked changes in the intelligence of the inhabitants of the area. For example, when the Tennessee Valley Authority was introduced into the rural South, IQs in that area rose sharply (Wheeler, 1932, 1942). Finally, a few field experiments (see, for example, Kirk, 1958) demonstrated that innovative educational programs could produce changes in IQ.

Recognition of environmental influences on intellectual growth brought shifts in research questions related to the nature-nurture debate. The earlier either-or issue gradually gave way to concerns about the relative contributions of hereditary and environmental factors to development and about the manner in which heredity and environment interact to determine development. As we shall discuss in detail in chapter 5, debate is still active and heated with regard to both of these issues. For example, Arthur Jensen (1970) has written:

The question to which scientists have sought an answer can be stated as follows:

How much of the variation among persons in a given population is attributable to differences in their environment and how much to differences in their genetic endowments? Numerous studies conducted by psychologists and geneticists over this last 40 or 50 years provide an answer to this question. The answer is unambiguous and is generally agreed upon by all scientists who have considered all the evidence on this question. This evidence strongly supports the conclusion that genetic factors are much more important than environmental influences in accounting for individual differences in IQ. How much more important? The evidence indicates that genetic factors account for at least twice as much of the variation in IQs as environmental factors. (p. 2)

Christopher Jencks and his colleagues take a different view concerning the relative contribution of genetic and environmental variables to development: "Our best estimate is that genes explain about forty-five percent of the variance in American's test scores, that environment explains about thirty-five percent, and that the tendency of environmentally advantaged families to have genetically advantaged children explains the remaining twenty percent" (Jencks et al., 1972, p. 66).[2] Jencks' last point requires comment. Jencks asserts that families who provide an advantaged environment for their children tend to be genetically advantaged. Thus, some children receive the double advantage of superior genes and a favorable environment for cognitive growth.

Recognition of the joint influences of both genetic and environmental variables fostered concerns about how nature and nurture combine to produce development. Jencks and his colleagues, for example, point out that genetic factors may influence development by affecting the kind of environment the individual experiences. For instance, genetically determined characteristics such as skin color may influence the kinds of opportunities which the child has for learning. These in turn may affect his cognitive development.

During the 1920s and 1930s when the intelligence testing movement was in its heyday, Jean Piaget was beginning his long and productive career of the study of intellectual development (Flavell, 1963). Piaget's impact on the interactive position has been in the specification of the ways in which nature and nurture combine to determine qualitative changes in intellectual functioning. His work will be discussed at length in chapter 6.

Piaget and the interactive view

Piaget describes development as occurring in a series of invariant stages, each characterized by a discrete set of mental operations used in organizing experience and adapting to the environment. He believes that the tendencies to organize experience and to adapt to changing conditions in the environment are genetically determined. However, the rate of developmental progress is assumed to be influenced by experience. In this connection he has written:

The proof of this limited character of the role of physical maturation is that, though the states of development we have described always succeed one another in the same, the natural and spontaneous character of their sequential development (each one being necessary for the preparation of the following one and for the completion of the preceding one) they do not, on the other hand, correspond to absolute ages; on the contrary, accelerations or delays are observed according to differences of social environment and acquired experience. Canadian psychologists working in Martinique, for example, using my own operational tests have discovered time gaps of up to as much as four years in this respect. (Piaget, 1970, p. 331)

---

2. Jencks and his colleagues include an extensive set of footnotes and appendices documenting the manner in which they arrived at their conclusions. The reader interested in an in-depth treatment of their work should consult the original text.

*JEAN PIAGET (1896-   )
Jean Piaget was born in Neuchâtel,
Switzerland. Piaget was introduced
to scholarly pursuits early in life by
his father, who was a professor of
medieval literature. By the time
Piaget was 15, he had already published papers in scientific journals
in the field of biology. One of these
eventuated in an offer of a position
in a museum which, of course, had
to be rejected since the precocious
Piaget was still in secondary school.
Young Piaget received his Ph.D.
in biology from Neuchâtel University at the young age of 21.
After postgraduate study in Paris,
he was appointed as director of
research at the Jean Jacques Rousseau Institute which is affiliated
with Geneva University. For many
years it has been Piaget's habit to
retreat to his Alpine farmhouse in*
*the summer time. There he does much of his writing. The result has been a remarkable
outpouring of some 30 books and hundreds of articles presenting what many theorists
regard to be the most revolutionary and insightful contributions to our knowledge of
child development to appear in the twentieth century.*

Piagetians advise parents and teachers attempting to promote intellectual
growth to adapt environmental influences to the developmental level of the
child. In practical terms, this means that those responsible for guiding development must begin their work by attempting to understand how the child presently
thinks. This suggests that they must value his understandings without incessantly
categorizing what he says and does as either right or wrong. Attempts to broaden
and deepen the child's knowledge should be based on his current understandings. In this connection, David E. Elkind (1974), an American authority on
Piaget, writes:

> . . . when we deal with (the child's thinking processes) we must not evaluate
> them as right or wrong but rather *value* them as genuine expressions of the
> child's budding mental abilities. When we deal with spatial, temporal, causal, or
> quantitative concepts, we need to explore the kinds of meanings children give
> to such terms. Such exploration reveals the level and reference frame of the
> child's understanding. More importantly, such exploration avoids the inhibiting
> suggestion that the child's incomplete (but partially correct) understanding of
> such terms is "wrong." A teacher who sees a child's productions as having value,
> as meaning something, avoids putting the child on the track of always seeking
> "right" answers. More importantly, perhaps, her orientation conveys to the
> child a sense of her attempt to understand him and her respect for his intellectual
> productions. (p. 125)

The introduction of social development as a significant content theme in
developmental psychology was a second major influence on the movement toward
an interactive stance. Research on social development deals with the manner
in which socializing agents in the culture affect the development of social behavior in the child. Interest in social development resulted largely from the
impact of Freudian psychology on developmental theory. Freud's influence was
slow to take hold in the United States. Freud had delivered a series of lectures
at Clark University in 1909. However, more than twenty years passed before
researchers in the development field began to take the Freudian point of view
seriously.

*Freud and the
interactive view*

Freud, whose work will be discussed further in chapter 8, formulated the
first comprehensive theory of socialization based on the interactive viewpoint

Freud, 1938). In the Freudian system the influence of nature was represented by the *id*, the seat of the instincts. Nurture was represented by the *superego*, which was comprised of internalized values instilled in the child by parents, and by the *ego*, the seat of rational thought. The id, in the Freudian scheme of things, was an unruly force generating energies which often urged humans to seek culturally forbidden pleasures related to sex and aggression. The gratification of instinctual impulses eventuated in the release of noxious tensions within the individual thereby producing a sense of well-being. However, unrestrained impulse gratification was thought to be destructive both to the individual and to society. Thus, desire (the id) had to be checked by conscience (the superego) and good sense (the ego).

*SIGMUND FREUD (1856-1939)
Sigmund Freud was born in Czech-oslovakia. However, he spent most of his life in Vienna. In 1881 he obtained a doctorate in medicine. His specialty was neurology, and for a number of years he conducted research on neuranatomy. In the course of his work, he discovered that many of the disorders he encountered were based in psycho-logical rather than organic prob-lems. This observation radically changed psychological and psychi-atric practice in the twentieth cen-tury. Before Freud introduced his views on mental illness, it was gen-erally assumed that mental dis-orders were caused by brain pathology. Freud was responsible for making mental-health profes-sionals aware that in many in-stances mental illness occurs largely as a result of experiential factors. Freud's theory of development was derived from his clinical observations. These observations led him to conclude that the most crucial ex-periences shaping an individual's life were those occurring during the early years of childhood. Freud was a prodigious worker. He wrote most of his many books and papers in the evenings after his daily work with patients had been completed. He was also a man of great personal courage. Despite repeated attacks and villifications by members of his profession, Freud held to his views and developed and elaborated his theories. No theorist has had a greater impact than Freud on psychological theory and practice in the twentieth century.*

Although the effects of nurture were recognized within the Freudian position, it was believed that environmental factors exerted their influence mainly in the early years of life. The manner in which parents raised their children in the early years was thought to be a crucial determinant of later development. In an effort to provide empirical support for the Freudian view, developmentalists launched a host of studies of early parenting practices, particularly those involv-ing feeding and toilet training. The results of these studies provided only limited support for the Freudian position (Caldwell, 1964). Nevertheless, the Freudian view had and continues to have substantial impact on socialization practices in this country. Parents receiving Freudian advice are admonished to breast feed their children to provide them with a lasting sense of security. They are told not to be too harsh in their demands during toilet training and to defer training until the child can communicate well enough to understand what is expected. It is reasoned that excessive demands in toilet training can destroy the child's confi-dence in his ability to perform tasks adequately.

*Interactionism and
genetic influences
on the environment*

The modern interactive position in social development has gone well beyond Freudian theory by considering the effects of innate characteristics on environ-mental determinants of the behavior of the child (Bell, 1968). Freud and his followers conceived of innate factors as direct influences on individual be-havior, but they did not emphasize the influence of innate variables on the environment which supported behavior. Today, interactive theorists hold that innate factors can produce highly significant influences on environmental variables which control specific behaviors. For example, sex, an innate characteristic, produces differences in the treatment of children which support the development of differential behavior patterns in boys and girls and men and women. While in some cases sex-related differences in behavior may be beneficial to the individual and to society, in other cases they do not have an entirely salutary effect. The stereotypes of the helpless female and the aggressive male, for example, insofar as they accurately depict male and female reactions, are qualities of questionable value. Yet society does much to foster passivity in girls and aggression in boys (e.g., see Bandura, 1969).

Contemporary interaction theory in social development includes focus on the identification of innate influences on environmental variables that affect behavior. The assumption is that the identification of innate influences and the environmental effects they create will serve as a basis for enabling the individual and society to control environmental effects to produce desired behavioral outcomes. For instance, the girl who is aware of social forces that may produce passivity and dependence in her behavior is presumably in a better position to control such factors than the girl who is not aware that her sex produces environmental conditions which may affect her actions.

Developmental Research and the Nature-Nurture Issue

In order for research to be classified as developmental, it must focus on changes which occur in individuals as a function of age (Ausubel & Sullivan, 1970). Some developmentalists study changes occurring as a function of age simply by describing individual characteristics and the relationships among them at different age levels. This has been the principal approach of those advocating a genetic stance regarding the determinants of developmental change. Other developmentalists study developmental change by experimentally manipulating environmental conditions to influence behavior at different age levels. This approach has been the principal tool of those advocating an environmentalist view regarding the determinants of development.

Descriptive methodology. The simplest form of descriptive research is a cataloging of individual characteristics. Data on individual characteristics may be obtained through direct observation of behavior. It may be gleaned from self-report measures such as questionnaire responses, or it may be obtained from test scores. Much early developmental research, for example, that coming from Arnold Gesell's laboratory at Yale, was descriptive cataloging. Gesell's approach was one of raw empiricism. He collected thousands of hours of film on child behavior which he and his research assistants subsequently coded and used to describe the characteristics of children.

Descriptive cataloging

Over the years developmentalists have tended to move away from simple cataloging. For some time now developmentalists using descriptive techniques have tended to focus on describing relationships among characteristics for which descriptive data have been collected. Much of the research on intelligence-test performance is representative of the relational form of descriptive study. For example, early studies attempting to assess the extent to which intelligence was genetically determined investigated the relationships among intelligence levels of related and unrelated persons. Similarities in IQs for sets of identical twins were studied and compared to IQs of fraternal twins, siblings, and unrelated individuals. A substantially higher degree of similarity in IQs was observed for identical twins than for other groups. This finding has generally been regarded as supportive of the view that IQ is largely genetically controlled (Guilford, 1967).

Research describing relationships

In general, descriptive research becomes developmental research when description involves differences in age. This can occur in two ways. In the so-called *cross-sectional* approach, individuals who differ in age are studied during the same time period. For example, a researcher might investigate similarities in IQs of 7-, 9-, and 11-year-old twins using a cross-sectional design. If this were done, groups of 7-, 9-, and 11-year-old children would all be tested within the same time period. In the *longitudinal* method, the same individuals would be studied at successive age levels. The famous Berkeley Growth Study (Bayley, 1949), which investigated changes in intellectual functioning of a group of individuals from infancy to the age of eighteen, is an example of the longitudinal approach. This investigation showed a high degree of relationship between intelligence during the early years and intelligence during adolescence. However, intellectual levels assessed during infancy had a much weaker relationship to later intelligence than was the case for childhood and adolescent intelligence.

There are advantages and disadvantages to both the cross-sectional and longitudinal approaches. The cross-sectional approach is much quicker than the longitudinal method. An assistant professor in a "publish or perish" university could become old and gray without ever being promoted if she put all of her research eggs in the longitudinal basket. On the other hand, factors besides age are more likely to influence cross-sectional research results than they are to affect longitudinal research outcomes. For example, one research finding from cross-sectional investigations, which was accepted rather uncritically in the developmental literature for some time, was that intelligence declines substantially in the later years of life. Investigations such as the following raised doubts about this conclusion. Draftees in World War II were given both the intelligence tests used in screening World War I and World War II G.I.'s. Soldiers evidencing average performance on the World War II test scored well above average on the World War I test (Tuddenham, 1948). These findings suggest that citizens now in their seventies might take comfort in the fact that they haven't slipped as much in intellectual power as they may have thought. However, at the same time they would have to admit that on the average they never were as bright as their sons.

Since the beginning of developmental psychology as a science, the descriptive approach has been the principal tool of researchers advocating the view that genetic factors control development. Early descriptive studies revealed marked regularities in patterns of development. These regularities were thought to be manifestations of the orderliness of nature which revealed the unfolding of genetically predetermined growth. Modern descriptive studies are much more sophisticated than their earlier counterparts and generally include complex measures of relationships among growth variables. Nevertheless, the descriptive method continues to be the principal approach used by advocates of a genetic stance (e.g., see Jensen, 1969).

There is nothing inherent in descriptive methodology which requires a genetic interpretation of development; and, indeed, many environmentalists have used descriptive techniques to good advantage. However, the descriptive approach is well suited to the genetic position in that it does not predispose the investigator to engage in environmental manipulations which might alter growth patterns.

Critics of descriptive methodology often point out that descriptive techniques do not lend themselves to the discovery of causal influences. To show that two events are related does not indicate causal connection between them. For example, age and physical growth are highly related, but age does not cause growth. Those arguing in favor of descriptive methodology point out that experimentalists may be overzealous in their willingness to attribute influences to environmental variables which have been manipulated in experiments. For example, Bowers (1973) argues that it is no more reasonable to look to the environment for cause in an experiment than to look to the subjects participating in the experiment. Even though experimental effects may be demonstrated, these are at least in part a function of the characteristics of the individuals in the study.

Experimental methodology. Over the years there has been a marked increase in the use of experimental methodology in developmental research. The experimental approach is intended to reveal the influence of some variable or set of variables on another set of variables. In the case of developmental research, the variables being influenced are generally child behaviors, whereas the ones responsible for the influence are environmental conditions.

Influence variables selected for study in an experiment are called independent variables to signify that they can be altered without affecting other relevant variables which might determine experimental outcomes in the investigation. Verbal praise is an example which has served as an independent variable in countless experiments. In most situations, it is reasonable to assume that praise can be manipulated without altering other variables. For instance, it would be possible to assign children to different praise conditions by a random procedure analogous to drawing names from a hat. If this were done, one could determine whether differences in praise affected some aspects of the children's behavior. *Independent variables*

There are unfortunately a number of highly important variables which can not be manipulated in an independent fashion. Age, sex, and skin color are among the more familiar of these. One cannot assign individuals by random procedure to different conditions and then assign the individuals in each condition an age, sex, or skin color. When an experimenter assigns individuals to experimental conditions according to age, sex, or skin color, he may inadvertently alter other conditions. For example, early research on language revealed sex differences in language skills during childhood (McCarthy, 1954); girls were found to be more advanced in language development than boys. These differences were initially attributed mainly to genetic variations; however, differences in child-rearing practices are now regarded as the central factor producing sex differences in language skills (Ausubel & Sullivan, 1970).

The variables being influenced in an experiment are called dependent variables. As indicated above, these are generally child behaviors. The behaviors selected may be chosen to reflect intellectual capabilities, social-interaction patterns, language skills, emotional reactions, and other characteristics deemed to be important in society. *Dependent variables*

Experimental research becomes developmental research when it involves manipulation of environmental conditions at different age levels (Ausubel & Sullivan, 1970). As in the case of the descriptive approach, developmental experiments may be undertaken using either longitudinal or cross-sectional designs. For example, one might study the effects of a particular set of instructional techniques on intellectual performance at different age levels. Studies of this sort have often revealed that different instructional approaches may be more efficacious at some age levels than at others. *Longitudinal and cross-sectional designs*

Experimental research is predisposed toward the environmentalist stance in that the application of experimental techniques generally involves the manipulation of environmental variables presumed to exert some influence on behavior. Thus, it is not surprising that experimental methodology tends to be favored by *Experimental research and the environmentalist stance* those taking an environmentalist position with respect to the determinants of growth. However, experimental research used in developmental studies is also well suited to an interactive position regarding the determinants of development. The developmental experiment, as we have pointed out, includes the manipulation of environmental conditions at different age levels. This type of experiment makes it possible to study the interaction between the environment and internal changes which may be genetically controlled and which are related to changes in age.

DEVELOPMENTAL PROCESSES

The term *developmental process* refers to structural and/or behavioral changes which occur within an individual as a function of time. Changes in physical characteristics (such as height, weight, or skeletal structure), intellectual functioning (for example, performance on tests of intelligence or creativity), social characteristics (for example, aggressiveness or independence), and affective reactions (for example, anxiety or joy) are all examples of developmental processes. In this section we shall present an overview of the general characteristics of developmental processes and their implications for socialization practices. Detailed consideration of specific processes will be given in chapters 3 through 10.

Stability in Developmental Processes

Stability is one of the most critical characteristics of developmental processes. Research on stability includes both investigations of situational and longitudinal consistency in individual characteristics associated with developmental processes. Interest in stability has been stimulated by the fact that evidence regarding stability has implications for arguments centering around the nature-nurture issue. For example, to the extent that it can be shown that intellectual or social characteristics such as intelligence or assertiveness are tied to specific situations, it becomes difficult to argue that such characteristics are controlled by genetic factors.

Early views on stability. Because of their assumption that development was genetically controlled, early developmentalists assumed a high degree of both situational and temporal consistency in growth for all characteristics. For example, with respect to situational consistency, it is only stretching the point slightly to say that early developmentalists would no more have expected a situational change in intelligence or personality than they would have expected to see a man change in height going from a restaurant to a drug store.

Early theorists had a fair amount of success in demonstrating stability in behavior. Most of the laboratory studies in early developmental psychology involved physical-growth characteristics and phylogenetic motor skills. These phenomena tend to be rather stable across situations and over time. Investigations of intellectual growth also revealed a substantial degree of temporal and situational stability. Intelligence-test performance of children was found to be quite consistent across tests and stable over long time spans (see Guilford, 1967).

Stability and the genetic stance Early theorists interpreted observed stability in physical and intellectual growth as supportive of their genetic views regarding the control of developmental change. They tended to ignore or discount disconfirming evidence showing some instability in growth patterns. Moreover, they went well beyond any reasonable interpretation of the empirical evidence in extrapolating their research findings for use in applied settings. For example, with regard to the issue of disconfirming evidence, early workers in the field of mental retardation used the following reasoning: they defined mental deficiency as a genetically based disorder (Masland, Sarason, & Gladwin, 1958). In those cases in which a child who had previously scored at a retarded level on an intelligence test subsequently attained a score in the normal range of intellectual functioning, it was assumed that the earlier test results were in error. The child was described as "pseudo–feeble-minded." The fact that this was a *heads I win, tails you lose* kind of argument didn't seem to trouble anyone very much. Similarly, with respect to the matter of extrapolation of research findings, no one questioned the reasoning that insofar as the development of motor skills (e.g., stair climbing of preschoolers) could not be accelerated through intensive intervention it followed that the development of intellectual and academic skills could not be significantly altered through training.

*Stability and
socialization*

The assumption of stability in early developmental theory suggested a passive, almost laissez-faire approach to socialization. Teachers and parents were led to assume that systematic attempts to alter growth patterns could not be successful. Children experiencing difficulty in school would probably always experience difficulty. Some children, described as "late bloomers" (Olson, 1959), did make unexpected gains, but these were not attributed to instructional intervention.

Contemporary views on stability. In modern developmental psychology, the temporal and situational consistency of intellectual, social, and emotional characteristics have become matters of great contention. For example, in the early 1960s Hunt (1961), using data from the intellectual-growth studies of early developmentalists, provided evidence suggesting that intellectual growth over time was not as stable as it had been purported to be and that inconsistencies in growth could be interpreted as arising from environmental influences. Hunt summarized data reporting changes of from 20 to 60 IQ points on intelligence tests. Although genetically oriented explanations had been offered with regard to these extreme variations, Hunt argued that environmental causes could not be ruled out.

*Stability and
intellectual
development*

The idea of consistency in social and emotional characteristics has come under heaviest attack by behaviorists. Behavioral researchers argue that there is little empirical support for the view that situationally stable emotional and social characteristics exist. Mischel (1968, 1973), for example, has gathered an impressive amount of evidence which indicates that, despite monumental research efforts spanning most of this century, there is little support for the view that social or emotional traits are stable across situations and over time. The child who is aggressive in one situation may be quite docile in another. The child who is anxious in one situation may be quite calm in another. Behaviorists assert that insofar as individual characteristics are situationally specific it is unreasonable to assume that such characterstics exert a controlling influence on behavior. A child is not outgoing because he is an extrovert or shy because he is an introvert. Nor does he get into fights because he is aggressive. What he does is controlled mainly by his environment and his past learning experiences.

*Stability of social
and emotional
characteristics*

Although the views of early developmentalists concerning consistency have been severely challenged by contemporary researchers, the debate regarding consistency is by no means over. As we shall see in subsequent chapters, there is an impressive amount of research suggesting a high degree of stability in intellectual performance. The evidence regarding consistency in social and emotional characterstics is, as Mischel points out, far less compelling. Nonetheless, the existence of social and emotional traits cannot be ruled out.

Contemporary views regarding stability in development imply a much more active approach to socialization than was advocated by earlier theorists. The debate among contemporary developmentalists is not whether socialization practices influence growth, but how to enhance growth through socialization in the culture.

Commonality versus Uniqueness in Growth

One of the most basic and important characteristics of developmental processes is that changes in such processes evidence a high degree of commonality across members of the same species. For example, in humans changes in height, weight, motor skills, patterns of social interaction, and so on all display a significant degree of similarity across individuals. For those interested in the establishment of a science of human development, this is indeed a fortunate state of affairs because without commonality in development it would be impossible to make generalizations about the nature of growth. Each individual would have to be considered separately from all other individuals. What scientists learned from observing the growth of one child could be of no help in understanding the growth of other children.

While it is true that there is a substantial amount of similarity in growth patterns across individuals, it is nonetheless a fact that there are marked individual differences in the rate and patterning of development. This fact underscores the need for adapting socialization practices to the unique developmental patterns of the individual. The need for such adaptation is particularly important to consider in social institutions, such as the public schools, which have tended to ignore the uniqueness of growth patterns.

Developmental norms. Since the inception of developmental psychology as a science, developmentalists have relied heavily on norms to reflect the commonality in developmental change. A developmental norm provides a standard against which to judge level of development with respect to a particular developmental process. For example, developmental norms can be used to provide standards for judging changes in height, weight, and intellectual performance, which occur as a function of age. Norms are constructed as follows. First, samples of individuals from each of several age groups are selected to be used as norm groups for the process under study. Then characteristics or behaviors related to the process being investigated are measured in each of the norm groups. The scores for each of the various norm groups on the measures which have been taken are used as standards against which to judge developmental progress.

Uses of norms Average levels of growth at successive ages are computed from norms to describe developmental changes with respect to particular processes. For example, developmental changes in height can be described by charting the average height of children at various age levels. Similarly, developmental changes in intelligence-test performance can be described by average test performance at various age levels. Developmental norms may also be used to describe individuals with respect to a developmental process; for example, a child might be described as being about the same height as the average 5-year-old or as having about the same intelligence as the average 7-year-old.

From a practical standpoint, perhaps the most significant fact about developmental norms is that they provide society with a basis for establishing expectations with regard to changes in the behavior and characteristics of children. Parents, for example, are invariably concerned with whether or not their children are developing "normally." Do they learn to sit up at the age that they are expected to acquire that skill? Do they walk and talk at the expected age?

Norms as standards (margin note)

How tall or heavy is the child with respect to his age-mates? Questions such as these weigh heavily on the minds of parents because information regarding a child's standing with respect to developmental norms can be of vital importance in making informed decisions as to how best to guide growth.

Individual differences in growth. Differences in rate of growth manifest themselves both among and within individuals. Just as people vary among each other in height, emotional reactivity, intelligence, and so forth, so also there are variations in level of growth with respect to various characteristics within the individual. Thus, a child may excel in reading and yet not do very well in math, or he may do well in academic and athletic endeavors, but perform poorly in art and music.

From the standpoint of child rearing, one of the most significant facts about individual differences in development is that they tend to increase with age. For example, as children grow older, their abilities become increasingly specialized. What may initially have appeared to be a slight difference between one form of competency and another may become a marked difference with the passage of time. A child, for instance, might initially show a slight degree of superiority in mechanical skills over verbal skills and over time display substantial variation in mechanical and verbal ability. Just as differences in developmental characteristics within the individual become more pronounced with age, so also differences among individuals increase over time. Figure 2–1 provides a graphic illustration of this fact in the area of reading (Olson, 1959). As the figure shows, differences in the reading abilities of the boys whose skills were recorded became greater with age. The phenomenon of age-related increase in individual differences has been recognized as a matter of extreme importance in child rearing for years.

Individual differences and age

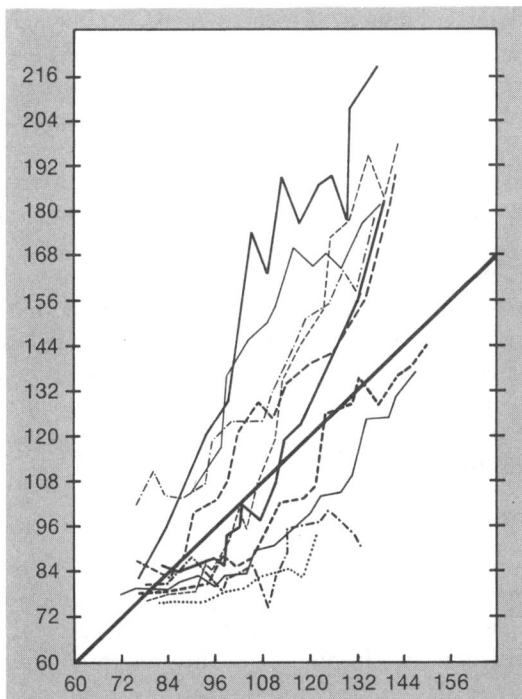

Individual growth curves in reading for ten boys. (From W. C. Olson, Child development. [2nd ed.] Boston: Heath, 1959, p. 147.)

Figure 2-1

Early developmentalists explained increasing variations in developmental characteristics as a manifestation of innate growth processes. The implication for family and school alike was that adults responsible for guiding development should adapt socialization practices to the immutable nature of the growing child. Parents were told not to "push" their children academically. They were counseled not to be alarmed at temporary lapses or retrogressions in academic progress. As figure 2–1 shows, the course of growth for the individual child over short time periods tends to be quite uneven, being characterized by sharp spurts and declines in progress. The school was justifiably castigated for its failure to adapt to individual differences. For example, theorists such as Olson pointed out the folly of assuming that academic progress occurs in stair-step fashion in the manner suggested by the grade-level approach to instructional grouping. Olson and others provided research indicating that differences in performance within a grade level invariably spanned several years and that the school's persistent attempts to homogenize abilities within grades was doomed to failure. Early researchers presented an abundance of evidence indicating that practices designed to reduce individual differences, such as retaining children because of lack of academic progress, were of questionable value and ought to be abandoned in favor of an adaptive approach to individual differences. In this connection Olson wrote:

> Curiously enough, whether the retention or failure rate is 10 percent or 50 percent, the same argument is heard: That standards must be maintained. The obvious answer—that the curriculum should be adapted to all the individual differences among children and to all the social needs of the community—has gained ground, though often slowly and with much opposition. (1959, p. 420)

Sadly, it must be said that several years after this statement was written, the effort to accommodate individual differences in the public schools has not progressed very far. Despite the availability of a rather well-developed technology for achieving individualization (Flanagan, 1970; Glaser & Nitko, 1971), most schools still follow the practices which Olson and his contemporaries ably discredited.

Contemporary researchers in child development have observed essentially the same findings regarding individual differences as those reported by early workers in the field. However, modern theorists tend to place greater emphasis on environmental factors in explaining individual differences than did early researchers. Most contemporary theorists take the position that learning can be maximized by providing the child with environmental stimulation articulated to his developmental level. For example, in the early 1960s Hunt (1961) advanced the idea that intellectual development could be maximized by matching environmental circumstances to the intellectual level of the child as reflected in Piagetian developmental theory.

Developmental Stages

In the main, developmental processes are characterized by continuous, gradual change occurring over relatively long time periods (Ausubel & Sullivan, 1970). Changes in height and strength, for example, tend to be continuous throughout childhood. However, there is, of course, an abrupt growth spurt during adolescence. Despite the high degree of continuity in development, there are marked discontinuities in growth for certain significant developmental processes such as social and cognitive growth. Accordingly, many developmentalists find it useful to describe development in terms of qualitatively distinct stages.

ARNOLD GESELL (1880-1961)
*Arnold Gesell grew up in the little
town of Alma, Wisconsin along the
bank of the Mississippi river. Gesell
was the eldest of five children in a
closely knit family. His mother and
father both valued education
highly, and Gesell was oriented
early in life toward a career in
teaching. He took undergraduate
training at Stevens Point Normal
School and graduated from
that institution in 1899. After
graduation Gesell taught high
school for two years and then attended the University of Wisconsin
where he obtained a bachelor of
philosophy degree. Upon complet-*
*ing his work at Wisconsin, he assumed a high school principalship. However, he stayed
in that position for only one year before deciding to pursue his Ph.D. in psychology at
Clark University under the tutelage of G. Stanley Hall. Hall had a great influence on
Gesell, but it was not until two years after he had received his doctorate that Gesell
finally determined to spend his life studying the development of children. Despite all of
his previous training he felt unprepared for this task because he lacked knowledge of the
physical bases and physiological processes underlying growth. To rectify this deficit he
decided to return once more to school. After five years of study beyond the doctorate
in psychology, Gesell obtained a medical degree from the school of Medicine at Yale
University. He remained at Yale until his retirement in 1948. In his laboratory he com-
piled the most complete descriptive record of children's development ever to be constructed.*

Age as a basis of stages. Early theorists, the prime example being Arnold
Gesell (1940), used age as a basis for defining developmental stages. Gesell described the behavior of children at successive age levels. Each age was considered
to represent a discrete developmental stage in the life of the child. Insofar as
Gesell considered behavior to be predetermined, age took on a quasi-causal
significance in determining behavior. For example, 3-year-olds, who were characterized as trusting, docile individuals who wanted to please and who placed
absolute faith in parental judgment, were thought to be trusting and docile because they were age three. More precisely, they were trusting and placid
because the genetically determined biological makeup which governed their
behavior was that of a 3-year-old.

Most modern theorists hold the view that age does not make a very good
criterion for establishing developmental stages (see, for example, Flavell, 1963
or Bijou, 1968). Age is not descriptive of changes in internal structures which
might exert a controlling influence on behavior. Nor does it serve as a reliable
indicator of significant changes in environmental conditions which might affect
behavior. For example, a child's age does not indicate the kinds of mental processes which he uses in organizing his experiences or in adapting to his environment, nor does his age specify environmental conditions which might influence
his actions. In regard to the latter, Bijou (1968) points out:

> A system of psychology using time as a causal variable can only describe inter-
> response relationships, can only describe behavior as a function of a conglomera-
> tion of unanalyzed conditions—biological, physical, and social. Most of us
> recognize this, yet now and then we find lapses in the literature. Behavior is
> attributed to an age or stage and a birthday is given magical qualities. There
> are, for example, educational films called: "The Terrible Two's and The Trusting
> Three's" and "Frustrating Four's and Fascinating Five's." (p. 422)

Structural change as a basis for stages. Some contemporary theorists, mainly
those inclined toward Piagetian or Freudian concepts, define developmental
stages in terms of hypothesized internal structures or states. For example, Piaget
delineates three broad periods of development: the sensorimotor period, the period of concrete operations, and the period of formal operations. Each of these

periods represents a qualitatively distinct mode of representing or conceptualizing experience. In the sensorimotor period the child represents his world mainly through physical acts. The objects in his environment are understood in terms of the actions which he takes with respect to them. Chairs are to sit on. Balls are to throw. Rattles are to shake. In the period of concrete operations, which is initiated with the onset of language, the child is able to represent concrete events with symbols. Objects in this period are designated by words. In the period of formal operations, the individual is able to represent not only concrete events, but also abstract possibilities, symbolically. He is able to conceptualize what would happen if conditions other than those present in the immediate situation were to exist.

Stages are not tied to specific age levels in theories such as Piaget's. Although there is some association between age and the period of development in which the child is most likely to be, there may be substantial differences among children in the age at which a transition occurs from one developmental period to the next.

The reason that theorists such as Piaget define stages on the basis of hypothesized internal conditions is that this strategy makes it possible to explain behavior within a given stage in terms of both environmental and organismic influences. Piagetians argue that when one does not consider internal functioning, there may be a tendency to treat children as though they apprehended things in the same way that adults do. David Elkind (1974) provides a delightful example relevant to this point:

> A few years ago . . . while driving with my son Paul, who was five years old at the time, he asked, "If we keep driving will we come to the end of the earth?" I started to reply that the earth was round and that no matter how far one traveled he would never reach the edge. I checked myself, however, realizing that there was no way to convey to a five-year-old that the earth was round. The roundness of the earth is, or at least was up until the advent of space flight, a non-perceivable fact. It is a logical deduction from certain sorts of evidence such as the disappearance of ships on the horizon or the shape of the earth's shadow on the moon. The young child cannot engage in that sort of reasoning nor accept such proofs. (pp. 35-36)

Elkind then answered the child's question as follows: "Well, when you come to the end of the land there is water and when you come to the end of the water you arrive at some more land" (p. 36).

Changes in interaction patterns as a basis for stages.   Behaviorists take issue with the strategy of defining developmental stages in terms of hypothesized internal conditions (Bijou, 1968). In their view this approach obscures the relationship between behavior and the stimulus conditions which control it. They suggest that when internal conditions are assigned causal roles in determining activities, there may be a tendency to overlook past learning and stimulus conditions in the immediate situation which may affect behavior.

As an alternative to the hypothesized internal-structures approach, Bijou and Baer (1961) have suggested that developmental stages be defined in terms of qualitative changes in the interactions that occur between the individual and his environment. Following Kantor (1959), they designate three broad stages of development: the foundational, basic, and societal stages. The foundational stage begins before birth and continues through infancy. The behavior of the child during this period is controlled mainly by reflexive reactions to environmental conditions. However, the uncoordinated exploratory movements of the infant do eventuate in situations in which rudimentary forms of behavior come under the control of the environmental consequences which they produce. The basic stage begins right after infancy and extends through childhood. The principal sources of influence on the child's behavior during this period are the interactions he has with his parents. The societal period is initiated when the individual begins to have large numbers of contacts with groups outside the family and continues throughout life.

The reactions of the child at any given period of development, according to the behaviorist view, will result from a combination of his biological makeup, his past experiences, and stimulus conditions in the immediate situation. Thus, for example, in determining how to answer the child in the example provided by Elkind, the behaviorist would want to know something about the boy's past learning with respect to the concept *round*. Could he, for example, identify round objects? Could he conceptualize imaginary round objects? On the basis of knowledge of past learning, the behaviorist would make a determination regarding how to use current stimulus conditions to move the child in the direction of comprehending that the earth is round and does not have an edge.

DEVELOPMENTAL PSYCHOLOGY AND SOCIALIZATION

Developmental psychology has played a key role in guiding the efforts of socializing agents since G. Stanley Hall initiated the child-study movement at the beginning of the twentieth century. Developmental concepts pressed into the service of socialization practice become tools used in the achievement of culturally determined socialization goals. Socialization goals change with changes in cultural values. Moreover, there is typically no general agreement as to precisely what the goals of socialization should be. Nevertheless, we feel that there is some justification in calling special attention to two broad categories of goals which appear to have emerged as major objectives of socialization in contemporary society: the development of individual competence and the development of responsible self-direction. As indicated in chapter 1, these goals have been expressed most forcefully in recent years by contemporary humanists. Humanists describe the goal of attaining competence as the development of the total individual including physical, intellectual, social, and affective development. They conceive of self-direction in terms of the responsible use of freedom.

The goals of developing competence and self-direction have been addressed within each of the three theoretical models of development presented in this chapter. In the following pages, we shall present the views of each developmental model as they relate to these two broad goals of contemporary socialization.

Developing Competence

Each of the major theoretical influences in developmental psychology has had an impact on contemporary socialization efforts to foster competence. The early biological model pointed out the need for the individualization of socialization practices and provided basic concepts to assist in the individualization process. The behavioral position generated knowledge concerning how to stimulate movement toward competence. The interactive stance, as reflected in Piagetian theory, provided a means for relating environmental influences to the developmental level of the child.

Competence and the biological model. As we have seen, the early biological model increased recognition of the need to accommodate individual differences

Competence and genetics

in efforts to foster physical, intellectual, social, and affective growth. The early view of genetically predetermined growth suggested that development could not be accelerated by environmental intervention. Even if intensive intervention appeared to produce developmental change, it was believed that whatever gains might occur would be only temporary. The child pushed beyond his capabilities might spurt ahead for a while, but eventually he would return to the pattern of development dictated by his genetic endowment. The only case in which intensive intervention might be effective was that in which a previous lack of appropriate developmental experiences had caused growth to be stunted. The presumed futility of trying to make the child be something that his genetic endowment did not permit him to be underscored the need for parents and teachers to learn something about the nature of growth and to gear their socialization efforts to the physical, intellectual, social, and affective characteristics of the children in their charge.

Developmentalists advanced two key concepts used by parents and teachers in meeting the individual needs of children: maturation and readiness. Although these ideas were advanced early in the history of developmental psychology, they continue to influence present-day socialization efforts. However, both terms have taken on altered meanings to accommodate contemporary thought regarding the nature of growth.

Maturation was defined by early developmentalists (e.g., Gesell, 1940; Olson, 1959) as developmental change controlled by genetic factors. The concept of maturation was advanced as a counterpart to the idea of learning. It served to remind parents and teachers of the possibility that behavioral changes in children might result from the operation of innate mechanisms. Maturation was believed to set limits on growth. Within those limits, learning could produce changes in behavior. Development was thought to result from the combined influences of maturation and learning.

Maturation

On the surface, early views on maturation and learning seem quite close to contemporary thought concerning these topics. However, there are profound differences. As indicated earlier, it is now recognized that innate mechanisms may affect the kind of environment which the individual experiences. It is also known that at least in certain limited circumstances environmental factors may influence genetic makeup, particularly in certain lower organisms. For example, in the fruit fly, variations in temperature during gestation influence the sex of offspring. In early developmental theory, maturation and learning were thought of as independent influences which each contributed to development. Today it is realized that maturation and learning interact with one another in determining growth.

Readiness

Early developmentalists believed that maturational factors limited the kinds of experiences which could be expected to produce effective learning in the child. If teachers and parents provided learning experiences which were beyond the limits imposed by maturational influences, learning would not occur. Moreover, in all likelihood the child would become frustrated and unhappy. Developmentalists introduced the concept of *readiness* to indicate the level of growth at which there was a match between the capabilities of the child and the kinds of learning experiences provided for him.

The concept of readiness was used most frequently in connection with early instruction in reading. Developmentalists were greatly concerned with what they perceived to be the dogged persistence of the schools to force children at age six to read whether or not they were developmentally ready to profit from reading instruction. Gesell (1940) commented on this state of affairs as follows:

The persistence of old tradition dictates that reading should be begun by the age of six years, despite the skepticism and even downright disagreement expressed by numerous recent investigators. . . . The attempt to force reading . . . frequently leads to temporary or permanent maladjustment and more or less serious disturbance of the course of normal school achievement. (p. 208)

The concept of readiness as it was articulated by early developmentalists suggested a passive approach to instruction. If a child was not learning, it was argued that he was not ready to learn. The possibility that the instructional approach used to teach him might be at fault was not considered, nor was it recognized that the manner in which instructional content was presented could be adapted to developmental level.

Jerome Bruner (1960) struck the first major blow at the traditional concept of readiness. Bruner argued "that any subject can be taught effectively in some intellectually honest form to any child at any stage of development" (p. 33). This argument suggested that traditional subject-matter structures be altered to match the developmental level of the child. For example, Bruner asserted that topics traditionally reserved for courses in advanced mathematics could be taught at the first-grade level if the content were presented in a manner appropriate to the developmental capabilities of young children. Bruner suggested a spiral approach to curriculum organization in which basic concepts would be presented in an elementary form at early stages of development and then periodically reintroduced in increasingly more complex ways at advanced levels of growth.

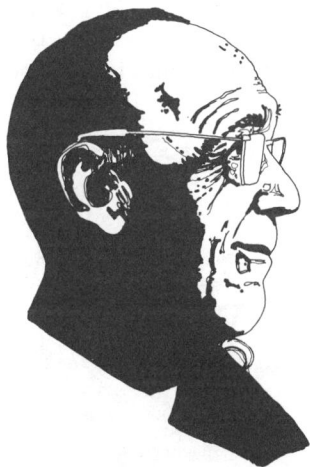

*JEROME BRUNER (1915-   )
Jerome Bruner is a native of New York City. He became interested in psychology while attending Duke University as a result of an incident which had little to do with academic interests per se. Bruner was threatened with expulsion from school for failing to attend chapel. William McDougall, an outstanding psychologist on the faculty at Duke, interceded in Bruner's behalf. Bruner subsequently worked in McDougall's laboratory and then went on to Harvard to attain his Ph.D. in 1941. During World War II Bruner conducted research for the Foreign Broadcast Intelligence Service, the Department of Agriculture, and the office of Public Opinion Research at Princeton University. Following the war he returned to Harvard where he* formulated his views on development and education. Bruner has conducted extensive research on the process of intellectual development and has written widely on matters pertaining to the education of the young. In 1962 the American Psychological Association formally honored Bruner with a distinguished scientific contribution award, and in 1969 he served as president of the association. Currently he is a professor at Oxford University.*

Whereas Bruner faulted early developmentalists for their failure to recognize that instructional content could be altered to fit the developmental level of the child, other contemporary theorists have pointed out that early workers in the field failed to recognize that readiness could be influenced by the child's learning experiences (e.g., see Ausubel & Sullivan, 1970). The use of readiness in contemporary developmental theory involves recognition of the importance of the match between developmental level and learning experiences. At the same time it includes the realization that developmental level may be significantly influenced by learning.

Competence and behaviorism. The principal contribution of behaviorism with regard to the development of competence has been to provide insight into the manner in which competencies are learned. One of the earliest behavioral contributions was to advance the state of knowledge concerning the control of emotional reactions. Behaviorists have long recognized that strong affective reactions are generally not under voluntary control and that they can significantly influence behavior. Acquiring the ability to control emotional responses and their effects on overt action is one of the most crucial accomplishments in the area of affective development.

Watson and Rayner (1920) demonstrated the control of emotional reactions in a classic study in which they conditioned and subsequently eliminated fear in an infant. Watson and Rayner conditioned Albert, an 11-month-old child, to fear small, furry animals by pairing the presence of a rat with a loud noise which frightened the child. The fear was subsequently eliminated by pairing the rat's presence with food. Since Watson's classic study, behaviorists have developed a variety of highly sophisticated procedures which have been applied to assist children and adults to gain control over their emotions (see Bandura, 1969).

In the 1940s, behaviorists turned their attention to problems of social development. During this period, John Dollard and Neal Miller (1950) advanced the view that personality characteristics, language behavior, and emotional reactions were learned in social situations. Learning was thought to occur mainly as a result of rewards for behaviors matching those modeled by adults, in particular, parents. Subsequently, Albert Bandura (1969) and his colleagues demonstrated that a large variety of social and cognitive behaviors could be learned simply through observing the behavior of others. For example, Bandura and his associates demonstrated that aggressive responses could be acquired simply by observing a model engaged in aggressive behavior.

ALBERT BANDURA (1925-) Albert Bandura received his initial academic training in Canada. In 1949 he earned his bachelor of arts degree from the University of British Columbia. He then went to the State University of Iowa where he received his Ph.D. in clinical psychology in 1951. Following graduation Bandura entered a postdoctoral internship program in clinical psychology at the Wichita Guidance Center in Kansas and then in 1953 joined the faculty at Stanford University where he currently is a professor. While at Iowa Bandura was exposed to behavioristic views of the learning process. He became convinced that mental disorders were often learned in social situations and has conducted extensive research demonstrating that both aberrant and normal behavioral patterns can be acquired through observation in social settings. Bandura's work has been a guiding force in the development of the social-learning point of view within behavioristic psychology. The American Psychological Association gave recognition to his contributions to psychology by electing him to serve as President of the Association in 1973.

The rather straightforward demonstration that a variety of significant human reactions can be acquired through observation has had profound implications both for psychological theory and for socialization practice. For example, the fact that aggression can be learned by observation has challenged long dominant Freudian assumptions that aggressive tendencies are innate and that the control of aggression requires the analysis of unconscious motives believed to determine overt action. The phenomenon of observationally induced aggression has also raised questions about the inadvertent socialization of aggression which may take place as a result of prolonged exposure to TV violence (see, for example, Surgeon General's Scientific Advisory Committee on Television and Social Behavior, 1972).

Developmentalists outside the behavioral tradition have generally scored behaviorists for their failure to deal with complex mental processes regarded as most crucial for the development of intellectual competence. During the initial period of development of the behaviorist position, this criticism was justified. Early rejection of the study of mental processes within behavioral psychology was followed by a long period in which little research of significance was done on intellectual functioning. It was not until the 1930s that the study of intellectual operations was reintroduced into the psychology of learning. During the 1930s some behaviorists began to recognize the possibility of inferring mental functioning from observable events. However, it was not until the late 1950s that psychologists within the behaviorist tradition began to study intellectual operations in earnest. Since that time, the science of cognitive learning has emerged from a relatively primitive state to a well-developed scientific discipline (Bourne & Dominowski, 1972). However, despite the recent advances made in the area of cognitive learning, advocates of humanistic socialization practices have continued to fault behaviorists for their failure to consider complex intellectual processes. For example, the Plowden report, which summarizes recommendations of a committee of educational experts concerning instruction in the infant and primary schools in England, asserts:

> Research into the ways in which children learn has produced, broadly, two interpretations of the learning process. One which is still dominant in the United States and is associated with the names Thorndike, Hull, Pavlov and Skinner among others, is essentially behaviorist. It is concerned with simple and complex operant conditioning, the place of reinforcement and learning, habit formation and the measurement of various kinds of stimulus-response behavior. Much of the more recent work derives from animal studies and its main relevance is to motor learning, though some work has been done on the learning of information, concepts and skills by children and adults. It does not offer very much direct help to teachers since, for the most part, the motives and sequence of children's learning are too complicated for analysis in terms of simple models. A second school of research, which is dominant in Great Britain and apparently gaining ground in the United States, is associated with the names of Baldwin, Isaacs, Luria, Bruner, and in particular Jean Piaget. This school is interested in discovering the ground plan of the growth of intellectual powers and the order in which they are acquired. One of its most important conclusions is that the great majority of primary school children can only learn efficiently from concrete situations as lived or described. From these situations, children acquire concepts in every area of the curriculum. (Central Advisory Council for Education, 1967, p. 192)

Contemporary theorists in the behavioral tradition (e.g., Gagné, 1970) argue that complex intellectual capabilities can be acquired through carefully sequenced instruction. Modern theorists hold that attainment of complex skills is based on mastery of subordinate skills. For example, in order to understand the rather simple rule: *round things roll,* the child must first understand the concepts *round things* and *roll.*

The first task in determining specifically what to teach the child to foster mastery of complex skills is to determine the hierarchical arrangement of subordinate skills required for complex skill mastery. Then it is necessary to identify the skills the child already possesses. Instruction begins at that level in a learning hierarchy which marks the point at which the child no longer displays mastery of requisite skills. For example, it would be pointless to try to teach a child to solve story problems in arithmetic if he could not count or if he did not realize that numerals represented numbers of things. Similarly, there would be no sense in expecting a young child to count objects if she could not point to each object to be counted once and only once. Without this skill she would count some objects more than once and thereby make errors.

The identification of hierarchically related sequences makes it possible for parents and teachers to take an active role in guiding the intellectual development of children. No longer must adults simply wait for the child to become ready for complex learning. They may now actively promote such learning by identifying the skill level of the child and providing hierarchically organized instruction with respect to skills the child is lacking.

Competence and the interactive position. Theorists who are proponents of the interactive stance hold that the combined influences of hereditary and environmental factors produce internal mental structures and character traits that determine an individual's level of intellectual, social, and emotional development. In the case of social and affective development, the traits acquired are, in general, presumed to exert a controlling influence on behavior. Thus, the development of competencies in the area of social and affective development overlaps greatly with the development of self-direction. We will discuss the interactive view regarding social and affective development in the section on self-direction.

Piaget's interactive view of intellectual development

Jean Piaget has been mainly responsible for fostering the interactive position regarding the development of intellectual competence in children. Piaget's interactive position is based on a fundamentally different view of the mind than that reflected in either the early biological model or the behavioral tradition. Piaget's formulation of mental functioning includes both internal and external mechanisms. The individual in Piaget's view acts upon his environment rather than reacting to it. He interprets his environment rather than simply reflecting experience in mirrorlike fashion. In Piaget's view the mind is like a creative artist. Artists do not simply copy nature, nor do they create their own inner vision of things independently from reality. Rather they relate the world around them to their inner experience.

The internal structures the child uses to interpret reality change as a function of age. Thus, it can be expected that the child's views concerning the nature of things will be quite different from those of the adult. According to the interactive view, the child does not simply copy what his parents and teachers convey to him about things. Rather he formulates his own views on the basis of the information provided to him. The tendency of children to construct their own version of reality is illustrated in the many charming and amusing "errors" which occur in their logic. The child who, upon learning that an uncle had spent some time in the Vietnamese war, says "Then he must be dead" conveys an original thought which is neither based exclusively on experience nor on innate makeup.

Development and discovery learning

The principal method advocated for promoting intellectual growth has been the discovery-learning approach to instruction. This approach requires that the child be given the opportunity to discover the nature of things for himself. In describing discovery learning, Piaget states:

The goal in education is not to increase the amount of knowledge, but to create the possibilities for a child to invent and discover. When we teach too fast, we keep the child from inventing and discovering himself. . . . Teaching means creating situations where structures can be discovered; it does not mean transmitting structures which may be assimilated at nothing other than a verbal level. (Elkind & Duckworth, 1973, p. 206)

Discovery learning will be discussed in detail in chapter 11. In brief, discovery learning involves presenting the child with a problem or instances of a rule and then providing him the opportunity to solve the problem or to discover the rule from the instances presented. For example, as the reader may recall, in the Socratic version of what is today called discovery learning, students were given examples of various types of virtue. From these examples, the students were led to the discovery of the nature of the virtues being studied.

Application of discovery-learning procedures in the Piagetian approach to socialization requires that the principles to be acquired through discovery be matched to the developmental level of the child. For example, according to Piagetians, it is pointless to try to teach a child abstract concepts by discovery, or by any other means, when the child is operating at a concrete level of thinking. The result of frequent attempts of this sort is that the child reinterprets what is being taught to conform to his existing intellectual structures. Thus, in the elementary school, terms like government, friendship, or religion may be translated to mean a building with a gold dome on top, someone to play with, and a club which meets on Sunday.

Developing Self-direction

As in the case of developing competence, each of the major theoretical orientations presented in this chapter has contributed to contemporary socialization practices aimed at promoting self-direction. The early biological view of development fostered recognition of the need for providing children a degree of autonomy in governing their own affairs. The behavioral approach revealed skills that could be acquired to achieve self-direction. The interactive stance suggested the possibility that internal predispositions and intellectual structures acquired as a result of the combined influences of hereditary and environmental factors may determine self-direction.

Self-direction and the biological model. The fundamental contribution of the early biological model to the development of self-direction lay in the assertion that the control of growth resided within the developing individual. Insofar as growth was a function of genotype, it was pointless to engage in efforts to manipulate development. Recognition of this fact, along with the rise of the democratic philosophy of socialization spearheaded by John Dewey, did much to set the child free from adult controls built into the home and the school. Parents and educators became more permissive in their interactions with their children. Children were given broader freedom than in the past to govern their own affairs. Moreover, they were accorded a new dignity in their relationships with adults. With the advent of the biological model of development, the child's behavior was regarded as a manifestation of the natural order of things. Parents and teachers were given the responsibility not only of guiding development, but also of understanding how it occurred. The child was not regarded as morally corrupt because he differed from the adult. What he said and did was taken seriously because it was a manifestation of natural processes.

Self-direction and freedom from adult control

Although the biological model did much to free the child from a harsh and often punitive adult world, many have felt that it often left the child without necessary guidance for learning. Behaviorists have been particularly strong in their criticism of those who fail to provide guidance for development. Skinner (1973) has ably expressed behavioral reservations regarding the guidance issue by tracing the idea of innate self-direction to the work of the French philosopher Rousseau:

> His name is Emile. He was born in the middle of the eighteenth century in the first flush of the modern concern for personal freedom. His father was Jean-Jacques Rousseau, but he has had many foster parents, among them Pestalozzi, Froebel, and Montessori, down to A. S. Neill and Ivan Illich. He is an ideal student. Full of goodwill toward his teachers and his peers, he needs no discipline. He studies because he is naturally curious. He learns things because they interest him.
>
> Unfortunately, he is imaginary. He was quite explicitly so with Rousseau, who put his own children in an orphanage and preferred to say how he would teach his fictional hero; but the modern version of the free and happy student to be found in books by Paul Goodman, John Holt, Jonathan Kozol, or Charles Silberman is also imaginary. Occasionally a real example seems to turn up. There are teachers who would be successful in dealing with people anywhere—as statesmen, therapists, businessmen, or friends—and there are students who scarcely need to be taught, and together they sometimes seem to bring Emile to life. And unfortunately they do so just often enough to sustain the old dream. But Emile is a will-o'-the-wisp, who has led many teachers into a conception of their role which could prove disastrous. . . . (p. 13)

Skinner's remarks constitute a justifiable criticism if one views the issue of self-direction versus management by adult authority as an either-or issue. While many early developmentalists seemed to view the issue in this way, most contemporary theorists tend not to pose the matter in such stark terms. Socialization in the home and in the school is now viewed by many as a task involving the blending of adult guidance with opportunities for responsible self-direction. Silberman (1970) expresses the modern view as it applies in educational settings:

> . . . freedom and structure are perfectly compatible; there can be, and indeed are, schools in which students have considerable freedom to set their own goals and follow their own interests, without the teachers in any way surrendering their responsibility to set external goals of their own. (p. 199)

Behaviorism and self-direction. The issue of self-direction has been by far the most significant source of disagreement between behaviorists and other developmentalists. Individual variations in human development, according to behaviorists, are controlled almost entirely by external forces. Genetic factors produce phylogenetic mechanisms which govern how learning occurs, but these mechanisms are essentially the same for all members of the species. Whatever variations may take place in behavioral patterns are attributed to experience.

Behaviorism and autonomous human beings
Developmentalists outside the behavioral tradition have argued that the environmentalist position of the behaviorists is an unjustifiable assault on human freedom and dignity which denies individuals the right and responsibility to govern their own behavior. Behaviorists do reject the idea of individual volition. They argue that insofar as humans are free to act in any way they choose, their actions cannot be studied scientifically. Science presupposes order. Human behavioral science presupposes order in human nature. Regarding this issue, Skinner (1971) writes in his book *Beyond Freedom and Dignity:*

> Autonomous man is a device used to explain what we cannot explain in any other way. He has been constructed from our ignorance, and as our understanding increases, the very stuff of which he is composed vanishes. Science does not

dehumanize man, it de-homunculizes him and it must do so if it is to prevent the abolition of the human species. To man qua man we readily say good riddance. Only by dispossessing him can we turn to the real causes of human behavior. Only then can we turn from the inferred to the observed, from the miraculous to the natural, from the inaccessible to the manipulable. (pp. 200, 201)

Notwithstanding the castigations of other developmentalists, the behaviorist position concerning order in human nature is not fundamentally different from that of developmental psychology in general. All developmentalists hold that behavior is governed in a lawful fashion. Differences in viewpoint arise only with respect to the locus of behavioral control. Developmentalists outside the behavioral tradition hold that individual variations in behavior are influenced by genetic factors. This view denies the existence of autonomous man just as the behavioral position does. Autonomous man is free from all influences, both innate and experiential. Behaviorists recognize the role of genetic factors in shaping species-wide behavorial reactions. However, they ascribe developmental uniqueness mainly to environmental influences.

Although behaviorists reject the idea of autonomous man, they do not reject the notion of self-direction. Self-direction from the behavioral standpoint is the self-management of internal and external stimuli which may influence behavior. Self-direction, according to this view, is not an internal force controlling action. It involves an interaction of internal and external factors. In this regard Carl Thoresen (1972) writes:

Self-direction and self-management of conditions affecting behavior

> Self-control is not conceptualized as a basic personality trait of the person, nor is it viewed as a force wholly within the person, such as "will power." Self-control viewed as individual action is best understood as a complex interaction of internal and external responses. Consistent with the basic humanistic premise, this behavioral view sees the ability to manage or control oneself as a valued human act. Every person is capable of learning self-control. Every person is also responsible or accountable for his actions. The concerns of humanistic psychologists for the individual . . . are well served by this behavioral perspective. (p. 15)

The internal behaviors involved in interactions which characterize self-direction are typically covert verbalizations and mental images. For example, a school-age child may say to herself, *If I take Carol's toy away from her, I may hurt her feelings* or, *If I don't study hard for my examination, I will get a low grade.* Verbalizations of this sort may exert a controlling influence on behavior.

External reactions involved in self-direction include responses which control environmental conditions which may influence behavior. For example, an adolescent may realize that he cannot study effectively when the television is on. In an effort to control his studying behavior he might do his studying in a room where there is no television.

Behavioral research on self-direction (see accounts by Mischel, 1968; Bandura, 1969; Mahony & Thoresen, 1974, for example) indicates that self-direction can be conceived as a set of learned acts. The implication for parents and teachers is clear. Fostering the development of self-direction does not necessarily mean simply leaving the child to his own devices. It may include assisting him to acquire skills useful in managing behavior in a responsible fashion and helping him to set goals which he may strive to achieve using self-management skills.

Self-direction and the interactive position. Theorists holding the interactive position view self-direction as a manifestation of internal characteristics shaped by innate forces and experience. Theorists (e.g., Allport, 1937; Freud, 1938; Erikson, 1950) who conceptualize social behavior as being controlled by internal traits or states within the individual have been mainly responsible for advancing the interactive position regarding the development of self-direction. As indicated earlier, the interactive position holds that genetic and environmental influences produce stable internal traits or dynamic structures which control behavior. Theories which assume the existence of structures presume that interactions between structures may produce states such as anxiety which can influence behavior.

ERIK H. ERIKSON (1902-   )
Erik Erikson was born in Frank-
furt, Germany. His initial aim was
to become an artist. However, he
was unable to support himself in
that field. He was introduced to
psychology quite by accident while
serving as a tutor for a family in
Vienna. The family was acquainted
with Sigmund Freud, and this asso-
ciation eventually led Erikson to
pursue a career in the field of psy-
chiatry. Erikson came to the United
States in 1933 and became the
first psychoanalyst in the Boston
area specializing in children's dis-
orders. During his years in the
United States he taught at several
universities including Harvard,
Yale, and the University of Cali-
fornia at Berkeley. Erikson's theory,
which is an elaboration of Freudian
developmental views, has attracted
wide attention in this country and has stimulated a great deal of the developmental
research conducted on psychoanalytic concepts over the last 40 years.

The trait-state view of self-direction

The development of self-direction from the trait or state point of view is effected primarily by child-rearing practices controlling the formation of traits and states. Erikson (1950) discusses the role of child rearing in instilling internal characteristics which guide behavior in the following passage:

> Man's "inborn instincts" are drive fragments to be assembled, given meaning, and organized during a prolonged childhood by methods of child training and schooling which vary from culture to culture and are determined by tradition. In this lies his chance as an organism, as a member of a society, as an individual. In this also lies his limitation . . . man survives only where traditional child training provides him with a conscience which will guide him without crushing him and which is firm and flexible enough to fit the vicissitudes of his historical era. (p. 90)

As implied in the above quote, the assumption of most trait-state theorists is that internal predispositions guiding behavior are firmly fixed during childhood years. Thus, the matter of child-training techniques is an issue of crucial importance. Suggestions concerning the manner in which training should be carried out vary with theoretical orientation. In most, though not all, theories of child rearing, techniques must be matched to level of development. For example, Erikson conceptualizes child growth in a series of stages. At the earliest levels of growth, the most significant experiences in the child's life involve feeding. Parents are admonished to provide sufficient affection and gratification of the child's food-related needs to insure the development of a basic sense of security and self-confidence which is presumed to last throughout life. At a somewhat more advanced level of development, the most crucial experiences in the child's life are related to cleanliness training. At this stage parents must avoid putting undue pressure on the child to master toilet-training skills. The mastery of cleanliness skills is regarded as the child's first major individual responsibility. Successful mastery is believed to underlie feelings of confidence in one's ability to master other sorts of tasks in later life.

The trait-state interactive stance regarding self-direction supports the long-held view in American society that behavior in a wide range of situations ought to be controlled by a thoroughly developed value system or philosophy of life. Research indicates that affective reactions such as values and attitudes can influence specific behaviors (Bandura, 1969). However, as indicated earlier, at present the evidence to support the view that people develop stable traits which control behavior in a wide variety of situations is far from compelling (Mischel, 1968). Our best guess at the present time is that people must take special care if they are to insure that what they do matches what they believe. The development of effective self-control is an unending responsibility.

The Piagetian view of self-direction

Outside of the influence of trait and state theories, Piagetian theory (Flavell, 1963) and derivatives from it (see Kohlberg, 1963, 1969) have made a major contribution to modern thought regarding self-direction. Piaget views self-direction as a cognitive act. Intelligence, for Piaget, is founded in innately governed action. Self-direction in a strictly cognitive sense is reflected in the child's innate tendency to organize his experiences and to adapt to his environment. Self-direction, however, also includes ethical control of behavior.

As part of the child's cognitive growth, he develops moral judgments which may serve as guides for ethical behavior. In the earliest phases of development, right and wrong are judged primarily in terms of the practical consequences of offenses and related sanctions imposed by adult authority. But as development progresses, the child begins to view morality in terms of the motives behind individual action and the social implications of antisocial behavior. For example, the young child regards the individual who accidentally breaks a group of dishes as more culpable than one who maliciously breaks a single cup in the course of committing a misdeed. On the other hand, the older child takes into account the motives behind and consequences of moral acts. Thus, for him breakage associated with a misdeed would be a more serious offense than accidental breakage.

According to the Piagetian position, socialization practices aimed at fostering self-direction must begin with an effort to understand how the child currently interprets experience. The teacher or parent must make an effort to provide the child with experiences appropriate to his developmental level. As in the case of promoting intellectual competence the basic approach for stimulating growth in self-direction is the discovery-learning method. Through discovery the child develops mental processes which enable him to make moral judgments which may serve to guide his actions (Flavell, 1963).

DEVELOPMENTAL PSYCHOLOGY:
A CHANGING SCIENCE IN A CHANGING SOCIETY

The material in this chapter depicts developmental psychology as a science which has changed rapidly during the brief period of its existence. It began with a strong commitment to the biological model of growth with its emphasis on genetic control of development. This approach, however, was soon challenged by the behaviorist position which suggested the importance of environmental factors in determining growth. Finally, when the science was only a few decades old, the interactive view with its recognition of both hereditary and environmental influences on development came on the scene.

As we have seen, changes in the character of developmental psychology have been accompanied by changes in views on socialization. The early biological model advanced a view of socialization that stressed the need for providing children with the freedom to pursue those interests and activities appropriate to their maturational level. The behaviorist position suggested an active approach to socialization emphasizing the need to identify significant skills to be acquired during the course of development and to teach those skills to the child. The interactive stance has offered the view that socialization ought to include provisions for adapting efforts to promote development to the needs, interests, and developmental level of the child. At the same time it has suggested the possibility of stimulating developmental progress through active socialization efforts.

The rapid changes which have occurred in the character of developmental science and in socialization practices related to that science have in part taken place because the method of science used in developmental psychology and other sciences makes it possible to determine the validity of assumptions made about growth quickly. In the prescientific era, society relied on tradition and philosophy to determine its views on development. The adequacy of the assumptions made about growth in many cases went unchallenged for very long periods of time. With the advent of science, empirical validation of assumptions about growth took its place alongside other societal forces in determining views on development.

Just as science has accelerated the pace of change in views on development and socialization, so also it has accelerated change in other aspects of society. The societal forces outside of developmental science which have influenced views on growth have been changing at an unprecedented rate. Developmental psychology in the present age is best viewed as a changing science in a changing society. At one and the same time, it is the product of social as well as scientific forces and it is an influence on social and scientific thought and practice.

SUGGESTED READINGS

Bell, R. Q. A reinterpretation of the directions of effects and studies of socialization. *Psychological Review*, 1968, *75*, 81-95.

Bijou, S. W. Ages, stages, and the naturalization of human development. *American Psychologist*, 1968, *23*, 419-26.

Bowers, K. S. Situationism in psychology: An analysis and a critique. *Psychological Review*, 1973, *80*, 307-36.

deMause, L. Our forebears made childhood a nightmare. *Psychology Today*, 1975, *8* (11), 85-87.

Elkind, D., & Duckworth, E. The educational implications of Piaget's work. In C. E. Silberman (Ed.), *The open classroom reader*. New York: Vintage, 1973.

Erikson, E. H. *Childhood and society*. New York: Norton, 1950.

Skinner, B. F. The free and happy student. *Phi Delta Kappan*, 1973, *55*, 13-16.

Watson, J. B., & Rayner, R. Conditioned emotional reactions. *Journal of Experimental Psychology*, 1920, *3*, 1-14.

Part Two

Biological and Physical Processes

3

In the Beginning: Biological Factors in Development

Instructional Objectives	Recognize or recall
	Compare and contrast
	Describe or demonstrate
	Evaluate

Lamarckian, "homunculus," and genetic explanations of the transmission of parental characteristics.

the definitions of somatic cell, germ cell, chromosome, gene, locus (as it relates to genes), zygote, mitosis, meiosis, homologous chromosomes, homozygous, heterozygous, phenotype, and genotype.

the process by which the DNA molecule can reproduce itself.

the contribution of "crossing over" to individual variation.

the contribution of Gregor Mendel to the science of genetics.

the process of transmission of sexual characteristics.

the process of sex-linked inheritance (with examples).

transmission processes and characteristics of

a. red-green color blindness	g. epilepsy
b. hemophilia	h. sickle cell anemia
c. phenylketonuria	i. Down's syndrome
d. Tay-Sachs disease	j. Klinefelter's syndrome
e. microcephaly	k. Turner's syndrome.
f. hydrocephaly	

the conception of monozygotic and dizygotic twins.

major events in the development of the embryo.

mechanisms for exchange of nutrients, oxygen, and waste substances between mother and fetus.

prenatal influences on development.

mechanisms involved in Rh incompatibility.

CHAPTER CONTENT

Transmission of human characteristics

    Conception

    Germ cells

    Mitosis

    Meiosis

    Mendelian concepts

    Genes and alleles

    Dominant and recessive traits

    Phenotype and genotype

    Sex determinations

    Sex linkage

Genetic and chromosomal defects

    Deleterious genes

    Effects of abnormal chromosomes

Untangling genetic and environmental influences

    Twin studies

Prenatal development

    Influences on prenatal development

Birth trauma

Premature birth

Implications

Strictly speaking, the beginnings of life start in the evolutionary history of human-kind, but that subject is beyond the province of this book. For our purposes, life begins with conception. The information considered here encompasses factors initiated by conception and ending when the child leaves the protective environment of the mother's body. Bear in mind, however, that the influences of events that transpire during this brief period may span the individual's life-time.

The major portion of this book is devoted to an examination of ways in which experience may influence development, but that focus should in no way be taken to minimize the importance of biological influences. Development is determined exclusively by neither biological nor by experiential factors. These determinants produce their influences primarily through their interactions, and not through the independent operation of either one or the other.

Interaction of biological and environmental influences

An oversimplified analogy may help to illustrate the ways in which biological factors and environmental circumstances may interact to produce an effect. From a healthy, properly fertilized chicken egg we expect a baby chick to hatch. But that can happen only if the egg is maintained within a given temperature range for a specified period of time. If the temperature is too hot or too cold, or if it is maintained for an insufficient period of time, the chick embryo inside the egg will die, and the anticipated hatching will never take place. The egg is useless, except in a few societies in which fertilized eggs are regarded as delicacies. In parallel ways, an individual with the biological equipment to become a brilliant scholar will have no chance of developing her intellectual potential if she is reared under conditions of extreme isolation and lack of intellectual stimulation. Similarly, under conditions of poor diet, an individual with the genetic potential for tallness would not achieve his full possible stature. Anthropologists have demonstrated that succeeding generations of Japanese and Chinese, for example, have attained greater physical stature than their forebears, and that this change has been associated with improved standards of health and nutrition (Hulse, 1965). The basic genetic composition of the population has not changed, only the observable manifestations of a genetic potential that was present all along.

TRANSMISSION OF HUMAN CHARACTERISTICS

There is no way of knowing when humans first discovered the relationship between sexual behavior and reproduction, but it must have been many thousands of years ago. Sometime in the early dawn of prehistory, people must have noted the resemblances of children to their parents and begun to put these and certain other facts together, though there are tribes that believe conception results from some kind of supernatural processes, or that females give birth to babies with no more than incidental help from males. Trobriand Islanders make such claims. To substantiate their theory that males have nothing to do with reproduction, they castrate their domestic boars and offer as evidence the fact that their sows continue to reproduce. Quite a convincing demonstration it seems, until one realizes that there are plenty of wild boars around whose attentions to the sows are in no way discouraged (Hulse, 1963).

Conception

Long before scientists identified the specific ways in which the genetic materials of a male and female combine to produce a new life, most peoples of the world had concluded that babies were conceived through the sexual union of a male and female, but they did not know the particulars of the process by which parental characteristics were transmitted. Lamarck, a French zoologist, promulgated the view that acquired characteristics of a parent could be passed to succeeding generations through the reproductive process. The long neck of the giraffe, for example, was explained as the result of successive generations of giraffes stretching their necks to obtain the leaves in tall trees, and passing their progressively elongated necks on to one generation of offspring after another. That explanation may sound more than faintly reminiscent of one of Kipling's tales about how the elephant got his long nose, but it was a seriously entertained proposition until it was demonstrated that the "germ cells" do not change as body changes take place through disease, aging, or other processes. Moreover, mounting evidence for natural selection as an important mechanism in species differentiation and change aided in dealing a death blow to the Lamarckian point of view.

*Lamarckian
theory*

*Union of male and
female germ cells*

Conception occurs when a male sperm enters an ovum, or egg, during its journey down one of the fallopian tubes to the uterus. If not penetrated by a sperm by the time it reaches the uterus, the ovum simply disintegrates. A new egg is produced in one of the female ovaries about each 28 days, usually about the middle of the menstrual cycle. Its trek down the fallopian tube takes about three to seven days. If it is penetrated by a male sperm during that period, conception has occurred and the development of a child has begun.

The sperm is infinitesimal in size. A single drop of seminal fluid may contain as many as one hundred million sperm (Scheinfeld, 1965). They could not even be seen until the invention of the microscope, and with the early instruments they could not be examined in detail. Upon seeing the human sperm for the first time, scientists thought they saw a tiny embryonic being, and with proper scientific gravity they give this being the name *homunculus* (little man). Another theory of hereditary transmission was born, and ". . . scientific papers appeared showing careful drawings of the little being in the sperm—although there was some dispute as to whether it had its arms folded or pressed against its side and whether its head had any features" (Scheinfeld, 1965, p. 4).

The "discovery" of homunculus suggested that what was transmitted in the male sperm was essentially a tiny version of the final product of birth.

The female ovum is a giant in comparison to the sperm, exceeding it in size by thousands of times. Yet even the ovum is smaller than a period on this page. Of the millions of sperm discharged in a single ejaculation by the male partner in the venture of procreation, only one penetrates the waiting egg. Once that penetration is accomplished, the outer coating of the egg hardens to prevent the intrusion of another sperm.

Germ Cells

The sperm and the egg, or ovum, are collectively referred to as *germ cells*, or gametes, and they differ in important ways from all the other cells in the body. Each of the somatic, or body, cells consists of 23 pairs of chromosomes for a total of 46, while each of the germ cells carries only 23 chromosomes, or one of each of the pairs.

Chromosomes

Chromosomes are the physical vehicles of the hereditary material (McClearn, 1970). Under a microscope they appear as strandlike bodies, and research has demonstrated that genes, the small particles of hereditary material, are arranged in a linear fashion along the length of the chromosomes.

Genes

Locus

Each gene has a fixed position or locus on the chromosome. These loci are identified by number for easy reference. For a long time the nature of the genes was unknown. They had never been seen, but their existence was hypothesized on the basis of observations of the regularities in biological transmission. We now know that a most important constituent of the gene is a chemical known as deoxyribonucleic acid (DNA). A major breakthrough in the understanding of heredity came about in 1958 when three scientists, J.D. Watson, F.H.C. Crick, and Maurice Wilkins, were able to show how the DNA molecule is constructed. All three received Nobel prizes for their discovery (Scheinfeld, 1965). The DNA molecule consists of two chains or strands which are held together by weak chemical bonds and which coil around each other in a double helix (see fig. 3-1). You can get an impression of the structure of the DNA molecule if you think of a rope ladder twisted along its axis from top to bottom. The weak chemical bonds are represented by the rungs of the ladder, the DNA molecule by the ropes. This discovery was important because it helped to explain how genetic

*Deoxyribonucleic
acid (DNA)*

Double helix

material can reduplicate itself. The DNA molecule can reproduce itself by "unzipping" itself along the weak chemical bonds represented by the ladder rungs. Each of the two strands then forms a new molecule of DNA.

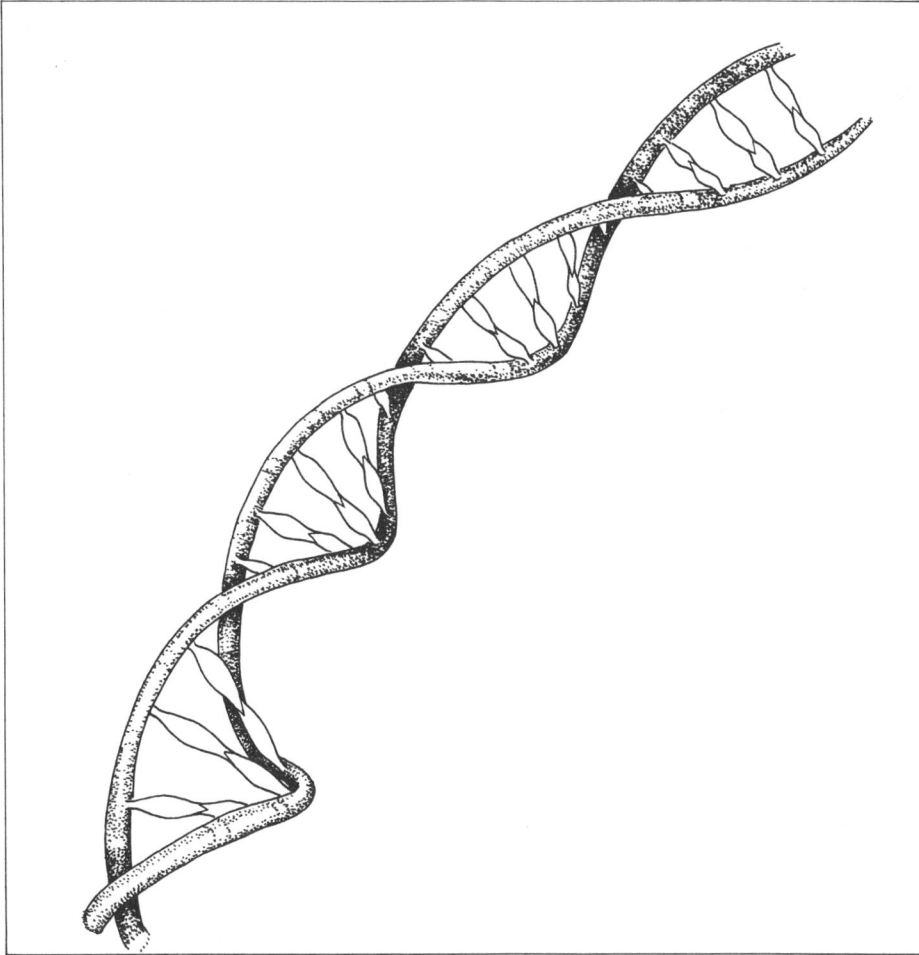

Artist's conception of the double helix.

Figure 3-1

Mitosis

When the male sperm penetrates the ovum, the 23 chromosomes and their constituent genes unite with the 23 chromosomes contributed by the mother. The fertilized ovum, called a *zygote,* begins to grow immediately through a process of cellular division called *mitosis.* Very briefly, the 46 chromosomes of the zygote, the first cell of the new individual's identity, split along their length, forming two daughter chromosomes. These daughter chromosomes are called *chromotids.* The chromotids then separate, and members of the chromotid pairs move to opposite poles of the mother cell. As the chromotids move to opposite sides of the original cell, the two halves of the cell pull apart as a new cell wall is formed to divide the original cell into two daughter cells (Fraser, 1966). Each of these daughter cells then redivides, and so on, and each new cell contains the duplicated original genetic contributions of each parent. We will examine the outcomes of this process shortly.

Zygote

Chromotids

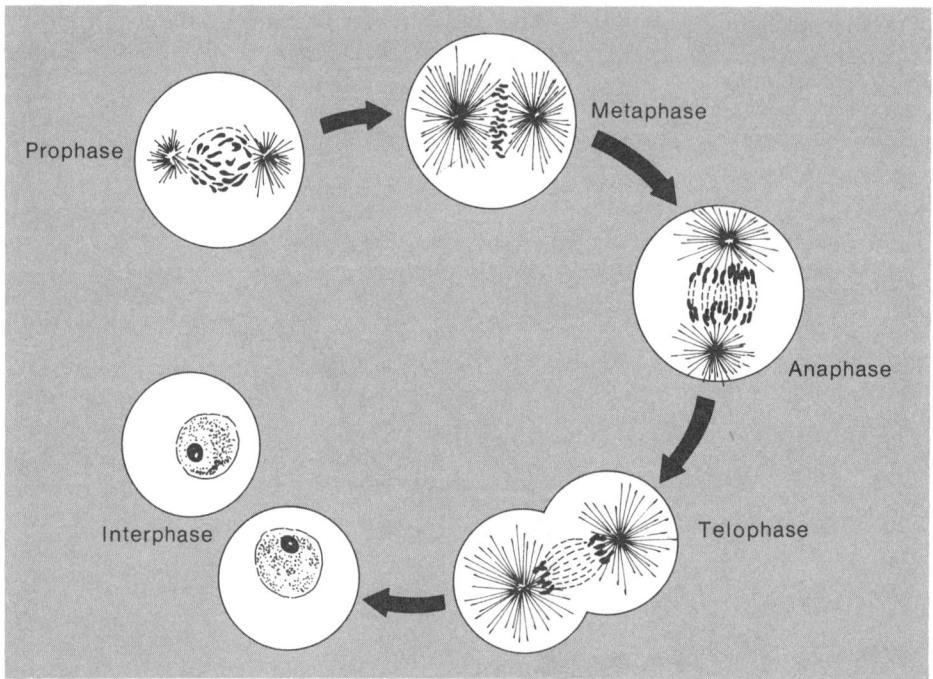

Figure 3-2 *Schematic diagram of mitosis, the process of reduplication in somatic cells.*

Since each body cell contains 23 pairs of chromosomes, clearly, some other arrangement is necessary for the process of cellular division in the gametes—otherwise the union of two sex cells would result in a cell with 92 chromosomes. How does it happen that the gametes contain 23 rather than 46 chromosomes?

Meiosis

All the body cells of the normal human being contain 46 chromosomes. That, however, does not mean that all the cells are identical. Within a short time after the zygote begins dividing into daughter cells, the cells begin to be differentiated or specialized. Some become muscle cells, others skin, and so on. The germ cells (gametes) are among those which develop for specialized functions. Thousands of gametes are created, beginning at puberty, through a process of cellular division and redivision of original germ cells which are present in the neonate when it is born. This process, called *meiosis,* is similar to mitosis in

Reduction division

the early stages of the division process. The essential difference is that after the chromotids move to opposite poles of the mother cell, the two representatives of each pair of chromosomes then separate and move to opposite poles of the newly formed cells. (The chromosomes that normally form pairs during meiosis

*Homologous
chromosomes*

are homologous chromosomes.) As they move away from each other, a new cell wall forms, creating two additional new cells (Stern, 1960; Fraser, 1966; Scheinfeld, 1965). An important aspect of this process is that the chromosomes are assorted entirely independent of each other during this division. Maternally or paternally derived chromosomes are in no way associated with each other as a unit during this assortment. In the human being, with 23 pairs of chromosomes, the number of possible combinations of chromosomes from this random assortment is 8,388,608 (Hulse, 1963). And even that does not begin to suggest the range of possibilities for differences in the hereditary material of individuals. The chances of two people ever being exactly alike is apparent when we

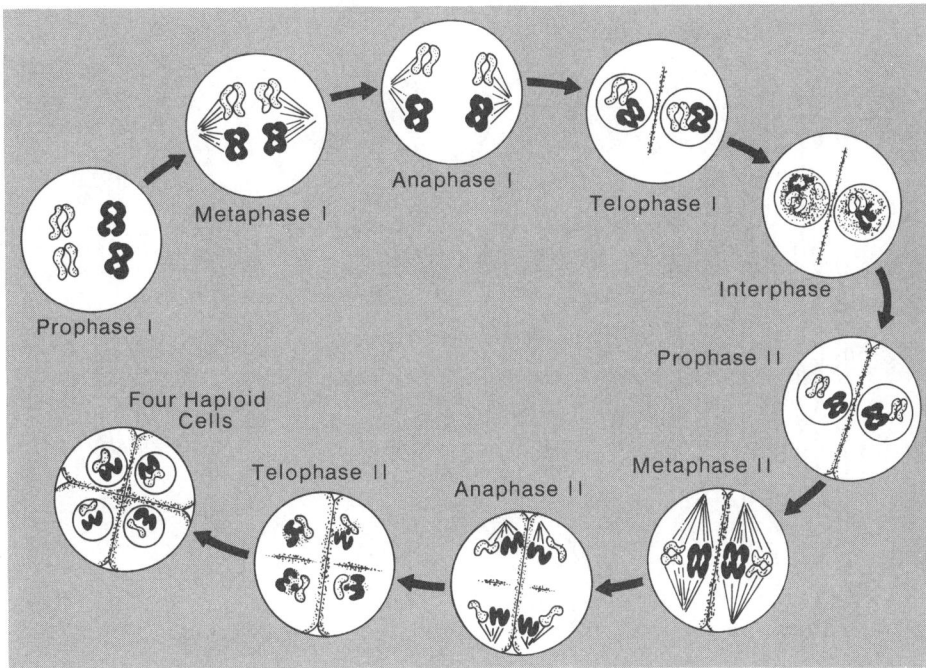

Schematic diagram of meiosis, the process of reduction division in germ cells.   **Figure 3-3**

recognize that the chance that one specific sperm of the 8,388,608 possible ones will combine with a specific member of the 8,388,608 possible eggs is less than once in about 64 trillion times (Scheinfeld, 1965).

The possibilities are really even greater than these figures suggest because of recombinations of genetic material that can result from crossing over. Early in the process of meiosis, when homologous chromosomes from the mother and father are lined up together, exchanges of genetic material may take place between maternal and paternal chromosomes. The result is that when the chromosome members of a pair (*homologs*) part company, they are no longer exclusively maternal or paternal in derivation. Meiosis, by creating new gene combinations in each generation, further adds to variety by redistributing genetic materials (Fraser, 1966; Hulse, 1963).

Crossing over

Homologs

Mendelian Concepts

Some of the most basic rules and concepts relating to genetic transmission were first discovered by Gregor Mendel, an Augustinian monk who was busily and carefully sorting, counting, and breeding pea plants in a monastery in Moravia early in the nineteenth century. His discoveries were published during his lifetime (1866), but their importance went unrecognized until his work was "rediscovered" around 1900 (McClearn, 1970; Hulse, 1963). Mendel observed a number of differences among pea plants: some have wrinkled seeds, while the seeds of others are round; some have green seeds and some have yellow. On some plants the flowers are in one position, while on other plants, in a different position. Luckily, the characteristics he chose to study were ones which were controlled by genes on different chromosomes of the pea plant (Hulse, 1963). Therefore, these characteristics were transmitted completely independently of each other, as you could deduce from what we have said about the independent assortment of chromosomes.

*Independent
assortment*

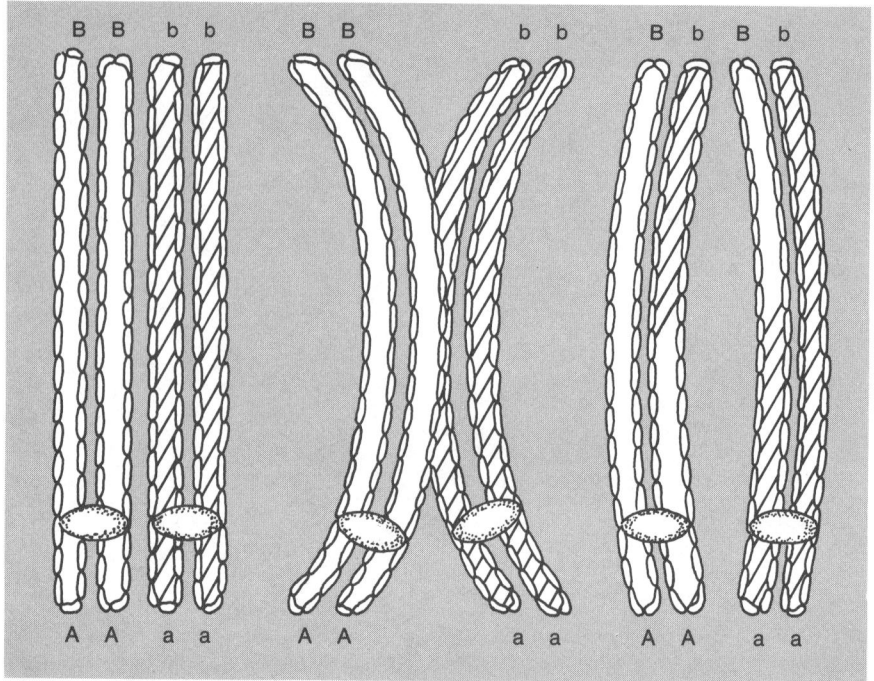

B B b b   B B   b b   B b B b

A A a a   A A   a a   A A a a

Figure 3-4   *Diagram depicting chromosomes exchanging genetic material during the process of crossing over.*

Genes and alleles. From his systematic observations of successive generations of pea plants, Mendel concluded that the determination of individual characteristics is controlled by hereditary material which he called *genes.* As we indicated earlier, to early scientists the genes were merely hypothetical entities.

The gene for a particular condition, such as color or smoothness-wrinkledness in the seed of a pea plant, may exist in alternative states. Some simple characteristics of organisms are controlled by single pairs of genes, one of which is contributed by the mother and the other by the father. These genes may exist
Alleles   in two or more alternative or contrasting states, which are called *alleles.* When an individual has two alleles (located on homologous chromosomes) for the
Homozygosity   same state (smoothness, let's say), the individual is said to be *homozygous* for that gene. If the individual inherits the allele for one state (smoothness, for example) from one parent and the allele for the contrasting form (wrinkledness,
Heterozygosity   for example) from the other parent, the individual is *heterozygous* for that gene. Homozygosity and heterozygosity are extremely important concepts in the understanding of hereditary transmission.

Dominant and recessive traits. Mendel found that some states are dominant, while others are recessive. The allele for yellowness in pea plants, for example, is dominant over the allele for greenness. Thus, if a pea plant receives the allele for yellowness from each parent plant, it will produce yellow peas. For convenience let us call that allele *A.* But it will also produce yellow peas if it receives the *A* allele from one parent, and the allele for green (*A'*) from the other parent because the dominant allele (*A*) masks the effect of the recessive allele (*A'*). Only if the offspring receives the recessive allele from each parent (*A'A'*) will it produce green peas. The green pea individual may only be homozygous for greenness (A'A'), while the yellow pea plant may be *either* homozygous (AA) or heterozygous (A A'). Just the same, the heterozygous plant has a fifty-fifty chance of passing the recessive allele on to an offspring. Thus, if two heterozygous individuals are mated, and each throws the recessive form of the allele, the offspring will be homozygous for the recessive trait and be different in appearance from both parents for that particular characteristic. Since each parent has a fifty-fifty chance of throwing the recessive gene, the chances of them both throwing the recessive gene for two specific germ cells that come together to form a union is one chance in four.

Phenotype and genotype. For the sake of simplicity we have been talking about pea plants rather than human beings because there are relatively few human characteristics that involve simple dominance and recessiveness and a single pair of alleles. Of course, there are some examples. Check to see if your ear lobe is attached to or detached from the facial tissue at the side of your head. Attached lobes are recessive; detached lobes are the dominant trait. Therefore, if your lobes are attached, you must be homozygous for the recessive allele. Attached earlobes reveal both your genotype and phenotype. If your earlobes are detached, you may be either homozygous or heterozygous for that trait. Detached lobes are your phenotype, but we can't tell from looking at your ears what your genotype is for that trait.

For many human characteristics there appear to be complex genetic interactions involved. What we commonly call intelligence, for example, cannot be attributed to the influence of a single set of alleles. Nevertheless, the concepts illustrated in these simple examples are vitally important to the understanding of mechanisms of biological inheritance. It should be clear from the illustrations offered above that an individual may possess, within his genetic makeup, qualities which are not observable because they are masked by other genes, and are therefore not open to observation. The genetic constitution of an individual, whether its effects are directly observable or not, is his *genotype*. The characteristics that can be observed, as a result of the effects of the individual's genetic constitution *and* his environment, is his *phenotype*.

*Genotype and
phenotype defined*

Sex Determination

Of the 23 pairs of chromosomes in a human body cell, one pair is notably different from all the others. The other 22 pairs are *autosomes*. The autosome pairs are equal in appearance and in other regards. The twenty-third pair, the sex chromosomes, are unequal in length. The longer member of the pair is designated the X chromosome, while the shorter member of the pair is the Y chromosome. Ova produced by females bear only X chromosomes, while males produce X- and Y-bearing sperm in equal numbers. As we noted previously, when human beings form gametes, each cell contains only half of the individual's chromosomes—one from each pair. Since the female has two Xs, every ovum she produces has one X chromosome. The male, on the other hand, has both an X and a Y chromosome, so when the reduction division of the meiotic process transpires, one of the newly formed sperm cells of each division will have an X chromosome, while the other will have a Y. If the sperm that reaches and fertilizes the ovum contains an X chromosome, an XX individual will be started on the way to life. Organisms carrying two X chromosomes (XX) are female. If a Y-carrying sperm penetrates the egg first, the resulting XY individual is a boy (McClearn, 1970; Scheinfeld, 1965).

*X chromosome
Y chromosome*

Sex Linkage

The genetic materials which are randomly assorted during meiosis are the chromosomes rather than the genes themselves. The X and Y chromosomes contain genes other than those that determine sex. Genes that are on the same chromosome are said to be linked, in the sense that genes on the same chromosome tend to be inherited as a unit. The closer together genes are on a chromosome, the less the likelihood that they will be separated by crossing-over processes. Since the X and Y chromosomes carry genes other than those that determine sex, the characteristics determined by these other genes are said to be sex-linked because they are inherited along with one's sex (Hulse, 1963; Fraser, 1966).

Color blindness   One example of a sex-linked characteristic is red-green color blindness. The gene for red-green color vision is carried on the X chromosome. Normal red-green color vision is dominant, while red-green blindness is recessive. If a woman is homozygous for the dominant allele, she will have normal color vision. She will also have normal color vision if she is heterozygous for the trait, having one dominant and one recessive allele. Only if she is homozygous for the recessive allele will a female have defective color vision. A male, on the other hand, has only one X chromosome, and therefore, only one allele for red-green color vision. The frequency of occurrence of color blindness in males is therefore greater because males have no allele for color vision on the Y chromosome to counter the effects of a color-blindness allele that might be transmitted on the X chromosome by the mother.

Hemophilia   Hemophilia is another well-known sex-linked characteristic. Hemophilia is a disease in which the blood-coagulating process fails to work properly because of the failure of a particular gene on the X chromosome. Hemophilia is famous not because so many people are afflicted by it—it is actually a comparatively rare disease. Rather it is well known because of the high station of some of those who have carried it. A single gene for hemophilia was passed on through Queen Victoria of England to the son of a Czar and Czarina of Russia, who in turn were preyed upon by the Monk Rasputin. Rasputin manipulated the Czar and his wife by holding out hopes of a magical cure for their son. It has been suggested that this episode may have played a vital role in bringing on the Russian Revolution (Scheinfeld, 1965).

GENETIC AND CHROMOSOMAL DEFECTS

There are a number of genetically determined defects which are not sex linked, as was the case with hemophilia and red-green color blindness. Some of these defects result from the influence of deleterious genes, and some result from chromosomal abnormalities.

Deleterious Genes

Phenylketonuria (PKU) is a genetically determined condition which leads to mental deficiency. It is inherited through a simple recessive gene which leads to a breakdown in the production of the enzyme required for the proper

Phenylalanine   metabolism of an amino acid called phenylalanine. There are now methods by which phenylketonuria can be detected through a urine test administered very soon after an infant's birth, and the mental retardation that results from the build-up of phenylalanine in the blood may be controlled, to a significant degree, by limiting the diet of afflicted infants to foods free of the amino acid phenylalanine. PKU develops when the infant is homozygous for the deleterious gene, but the presence of a single recessive gene may now be detected through chemical tests, and the knowledge that an individual carries the recessive gene for PKU may be of great value in genetic counseling (Reed, 1964; Scheinfeld, 1965; Stern, 1960).

Another genetic disorder which leads to intellectual impairment is *Amaurotic family idiocy*. There are several varieties of this disorder; the most common is *Tay-Sachs disease*, which results from a pair of recessive genes in the homozygous condition, and begins to show its effects in early infancy. It is a metabolic disorder which causes the nerve cells of the brain and spinal cord to swell with fat. The condition produces not only mental deficiency, but blindness and paralysis also result, and death usually ensues within a few years.

Microcephaly, a condition in which the brain and skull stop growing at an early age, causes severe mental retardation and generally results from a pair of recessive genes, though it may also occur as the result of other causes such as pituitary deficiencies or X-ray exposure during pregnancy.

Another genetically determined abnormality gives an appearance quite the opposite of the "pinhead" symptoms of the microcephalic. In the condition *hydrocephaly*, the skull becomes enlarged because the brain fills with abnormal amounts of cerebrospinal fluid. If untreated, it results in mental deficiency. The genetic factors operating in this condition have not been clearly identified. Hydrocephalics may often be treated successfully through provisions for draining off the excess fluid.

Epilepsy, a term encompassing a number of convulsive disorders, is popularly considered a genetic disorder. The etiology of the various forms of epilepsy is not clearly established, but the prevailing opinion of authorities is that epilepsy is probably not inherited as a specific disorder, but that a susceptibility to the disease is probably genetically inherited. Given this hereditary predisposition, the disease may or may not develop, depending on whether or not the individual is subjected to whatever environmental traumas are required to trigger the disorder.

Hereditary predisposition

The last example of the effects of deleterious genes to be discussed here provides an excellent example of the complex interactional effects of heredity and environment. Clearly, most of the normal individual differences in characteristics that we inherit from our parents have no specific adaptive advantage or disadvantage. Blue eyes, for example, have no adaptive advantage or disadvantage compared to brown eyes, and even though popular belief has it that blonds have more fun, there is no concrete evidence to suggest that fair-haired people have any reproductive advantage over their darker haired peers. Inherited, visible markers of racial or caste status, of course, may serve as cues which elicit discriminatory treatment from those who control the privileges and resources of a society, so in that way inherited characteristics and environmental encounters may interact to produce important psychological effects. But an even more clear-cut illustration of environmental-genetic interactions is provided by sickle cell anemia.

Sickle cell anemia is a disorder characterized by the formation of defective red blood cells. When an individual carries only a single gene for this condition, there is little ill effect on the individual, except that it could be dangerous under conditions of high altitude. But when an individual carries two genes for the condition, death usually occurs during early childhood.

The gene for sickle cell anemia is practically nonexistent in most populations, but it is found in almost 40 percent of certain African populations. The population distribution of this gene raises several interesting questions. First, why is it found in such concentrations among Negroes? Second, since its effects are so deleterious, why has natural selection not reduced its frequency in the gene pool of the Negro population?

The answers to these questions were revealed by a scientist named Allison (1955) who was able to show that when an individual carries a single sickle cell gene, he is afforded some protection from malaria. The populations in which the sickle cell gene is prevalent came from areas of Africa in which malaria, carried by anopheline mosquitoes, is common. Those individuals carrying a single gene for sickle cell have some resistance to the disease, and therefore have a reproductive advantage, which affords them the opportunity to pass their sickle cell gene on to their progeny. The unfortunate infant who receives a double dose of the gene, one from each parent, will probably not survive, but this liability to survival is somewhat balanced by the survival advantage of individuals with the protective single gene.

Adaptive advantage in heterozygous condition

Sickle cell anemia constitutes a serious health problem for blacks in the United States whose ancestors came from these areas of Africa, because the harmful effects continue to operate in an environment in which the single gene condition no longer offers a survival advantage (Scheinfeld, 1965; Stern, 1960; Boyd, 1956; Dunn, 1959).

Effects of Abnormal Chromosomes

Besides those developmental disorders that may result directly from the operation of deleterious genes or from the interaction between environmental conditions and genetically inherited predispositions toward specific developmental disorders, there are disorders that have their origin in abnormalities in the chromosomes.

Down's syndrome is a fairly common disorder that is caused by an abnormal condition among the chromosomes. A characteristic feature of this condition is small, slanting eyes with an inner fold of skin which gives the individual afflicted with this disorder an "oriental" appearance. The common name for the disorder, mongolism, is based on this external feature of appearance. Other external features characteristically associated with Down's syndrome are a large, often misshapen forehead, a flat and sunken nose bridge, small malformed ears, a fissured tongue, and hands and fingers which are frequently deformed. Intellectual functioning is severely impaired, which accounts for the historic term mongolian idiot, which once was applied insensitively to individuals with this condition. Children with Down's syndrome are frequently dwarfed, may have serious heart defects, and are especially susceptible to serious infections. Their life expectancies are therefore markedly reduced, although medical advances have dramatically improved the prognosis. The extent of these physical and mental abnormalities varies considerably from one afflicted individual to the next. In recent years educational innovations have demonstrated that Down's syndrome children can be taught academic and social skills formerly considered beyond their capabilities.

Mongolism

Individuals with Down's syndrome have 47 rather than 46 chromosomes. The disorder apparently results from having an extra member of the number 21 chromosome pair, but beyond that fact the exact etiology of the disorder has not been well established. The extra chromosome seems to arise from the failure of the number 21 chromosome to separate properly during meiosis. Mongoloid children can be born to mothers of any age, but the frequency of occurrence is disproportionately high among older mothers (Fraser, 1966; Reed, 1964;

Number 21 chromosome

Older mothers

Scheinfeld, 1965). Mothers between the ages of 45 and 49 are 10 times more likely to give birth to a child with Down's syndrome than mothers in the age range 15 to 25.

Aberrations sometimes occur in the X and Y chromosomes, occasioning abnormal development of sexual characteristics. One example is the *Klinefelter syndrome,* which is most common among individuals with an extra X chromosome resulting in an XXY genotype. In this condition male testes are not fully formed, are incapable of producing sperm, and deficiencies in the production of male hormones hinder the normal development of male secondary sexual characteristics.

In the *Turner syndrome,* the individual usually has only a single sex chromosome, and that one is an X. The lack of a Y chromosome to influence the development of male sex characteristics, or a second X chromosome to facilitate full development of female sex characteristics, results in the incomplete development of internal female sex organs (Scheinfeld, 1965; Stern, 1960).

These abnormalities, *Down's syndrome, Klinefelter syndrome,* and *Turner syndrome,* are just a few examples of atypical development that may result from a breakdown in the transmission of chromosomes.

UNTANGLING GENETIC AND ENVIRONMENTAL INFLUENCES

Obviously the development of an individual is influenced by both genetic and environmental influences, and by the complex interactions between them. How is it possible to determine which characteristics are influenced by heredity and which by environment, and in what degree? For many complex human attributes, such as intellectual capability, it is not at present possible to disentangle these influences precisely, but one widely used approach to provide approximations of the interactional effects of heredity and environment has been to study twins reared in different environments.

Twin Studies

Monozygotic
Dizygotic

Twins come about in two different ways. In one instance the twins arise from a single ovum. Shortly after an egg is fertilized by a single sperm, it splits and develops into two separate embryos. The resulting twins are identical, or monozygotic (MZ), since they have arisen from the same egg and contain exactly the same genetic material. Fraternal, or dizygotic (DZ), twins arise from a situation in which two separate ova are fertilized by separate sperm, giving rise to two zygotes that develop simultaneously. DZ twins are no more similar to each other in genetic constitution than are any other pair of siblings.

Differences in the development of MZ twins are most likely to result from environmental influences, while differences in DZ twins reflect the effects of both environmental and genetic influences (McClearn, 1970). Obviously, just because a pair of twins is reared in a single family does not mean that their environments are identical. But the environments of twins reared in a single family may be assumed to be more similar to each other than the environments of individuals reared in different families. On the basis of such reasoning, scientists have compared differences in individual characteristics, such as intelligence and personality, by comparing sets of fraternal and identical twins reared either in the same family or in separate family environments. Specific findings of investigations of this kind will be discussed in chapter 5.

PRENATAL DEVELOPMENT

Blastocyte

Ectoderm

Mesoderm

Endoderm

Trophoblast

Amniotic fluid

Placenta

Embryo

The ovum is en route down the fallopian tube to the uterus when it is fertilized by a sperm, thus becoming a zygote. Within ten to fourteen days the fertilized ovum, now called a *blastocyte,* becomes attached to the wall of the uterus. As cells continue to divide and redivide, they become differentiated into different layers. The outer layer of cells, the *ectoderm,* eventually develops into the outer layer of skin, nails, hair, the nervous system, and other specific tissues. The middle layer of cells, called the *mesoderm,* develops into the inner layer of skin, skeletal and muscle tissues, and organs of the circulatory and excretory systems. The *endoderm,* or inner layer of cells, develops into tissues of the respiratory organs, such as lungs, trachea, and bronchial tubes, and into various endocrine glands. These developments take place in the inner cell mass. The outer layer of the cell (trophoblast) is meanwhile developing into the tissues which will nourish and protect the embryo. These tissues, together with a membrane from the wall of the mother's uterus, form a sac filled with amniotic fluid, which serves to protect the embryo from shocks.

An umbilical cord forms, connecting the embryo to the uterine wall. This cord carries blood from the developing child to the placenta. Both the child's and the mother's bloodstreams are connected to the placenta, but they are separated by the cell walls of a semipermeable membrane within the placenta, a thick mass of tissue that develops within the uterus. (See fig. 3-5.) This membrane allows the passage of nutrient substances from the mother to the child's bloodstream and waste substances from the child to the mother's bloodstream, but prevents blood cells themselves from passing through. Thus, the bloodstreams of the child and mother remain separate.

The *embryo* itself begins to take shape within 18 days. Early growth is extremely rapid, and by about nine weeks facial features have begun to take form and arms, legs, hands, and feet have made their appearance, even though the embryo is still only about an inch long.

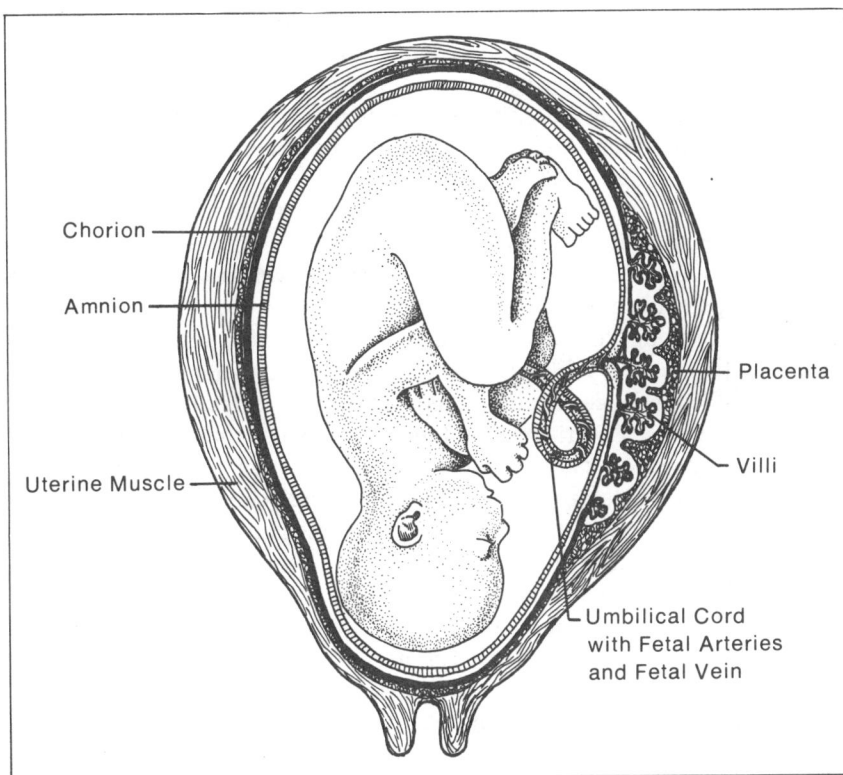

Diagrammatic representation of the relationship between a mature fetus and the placenta.   **Figure 3-5**

Beginning at about the end of the second month of development, the designation *fetus* is used to refer to the developing organism. During this period the rudimentary body systems become well developed and begin to function. The fetus becomes capable of responding to stimulation, and the development of differentiation of motor functions continues. By 28 weeks the organs and body systems of the fetus have become sufficiently well developed that it may be able to survive outside the protective environment of its mother's body if an appropriate environmental temperature is maintained, although development is still not complete. Body systems continue to develop and become refined until 40 weeks, when full-term birth normally occurs.

Fetus

Influences on Prenatal Development

Nutrition.   Since the developing fetus is entirely dependent upon its mother for the nutrient substances required for healthy development, it is very important that the mother have a nutritious diet. When people speaking from folk wisdom tell an expectant mother, "Remember, you're eating for two," they do not mean that the mother should eat twice as much. It does mean that she should eat food containing the vitamins, minerals, and proteins the fetus needs to develop into a healthy infant. These nutrients are passed on to the fetus through the semipermeable membrane in the placenta.

If the mother's diet is inadequate, the fetus gets more than its proportional share of whatever nutrients the mother consumes. Nevertheless, because the fetus is growing so rapidly, it may suffer more than the mother from the effects of malnutrition (Montagu, 1962; Pasamanick & Knobloch, 1966). Inadequate maternal nutrition increases the likelihood of stillbirth, spontaneous abortion, and development in the infant of disorders such as rickets and anemia. Mothers from lower socioeconomic backgrounds and from racial or ethnic groups that are overrepresented among low-income groups produce a disproportionate number of infants who suffer the effects of maternal malnutrition (Pasamanick & Knobloch, 1966; Montagu, 1962).

Drugs. Many expectant mothers are complacent about the possible effects of substances taken into their own bodies on the development of their unborn children. Perhaps this complacency arises in the belief that the filtering system in the placenta provides an effective barrier to protect the fetus against harmful substances in the mother's bloodstream. It has become increasingly clear that such a sense of confidence is unfounded. The most dramatic evidence of this comes from the tragic experiences of families in which mothers were taking a *Thalidomide* tranquilizing drug called thalidomide during pregnancy. "Thalidomide babies" were born with severe deformities of the extremities. Quite clearly, the filtering system between the mother and child's bloodstreams is not a completely effective barrier against the effects of harmful drugs.

Sedation Further evidence abounds. Excessive sedation of the mother during the last weeks before birth may result in permanent brain damage in an infant (Montagu, 1950). And with the increase in use of narcotic drugs among young women from all cultural and socioeconomic groups, there has been a marked increase in the number of infants born with drug addictions. All drugs affect *Over-the-counter* the human system in some way, and even "innocent," over-the-counter drugs *drugs* should be used with caution during pregnancy. Expectant mothers often are advised to avoid all unprescribed drugs during pregnancy. These include such common products as aspirin, reducing pills, and nose drops or sprays.

Tobacco It is easy to overlook the fact that tobacco, a widely used product in our society, is a drug which does apparently affect the developing child during the prenatal period. There are more stillbirths among smoking than nonsmoking mothers, and their babies have a greater chance of being low in birth weight and dying in infancy than those of nonsmoking mothers.

Radiation In some ways the wonders of medical technology are a mixed blessing. X-rays are not drugs, but they are considered here because massive doses of X-rays are often used therapeutically for disorders such as tumors or cancer. Mothers who have undergone such treatment have a much greater chance of having infants with physical or mental disabilities (Montagu, 1962). The potential dangers of exposure to X-rays is not limited to the prenatal period, for radiation may *Mutations* cause mutations in genetic material carried in the gametes (Scheinfeld, 1965; Montagu, 1962). Mutations are changes in the arrangement, qualities, or quantity of the genetic material, and they result in inheritable changes in the genotype *Deleterious nature* (Fraser, 1966). Mutant genes have a high probability of being deleterious, a *of mutant genes* consideration that should lead to greater caution in the use of X-rays and other forms of radiation that have become increasingly common in our culture. Irradiation may come from all sorts of unsuspected sources, including improperly shielded or defective home appliances, such as color television sets or microwave ovens.

Maternal disease. Any number of diseases may be of relatively little consequence for the unborn child of a mother who contracts them during pregnancy, but there are others that may be serious indeed for the developing fetus. Many infectious diseases, including syphilis, chicken pox, mumps, and tuberculosis, among others, may be transmitted through the imperfect barrier in the placenta to the developing child. *Rubella* (German measles) may also have particularly grave effects on the child if contracted during the first three or four months of pregnancy. Children whose mothers have contracted the disease during the first three months of prenatal development have a better than average probability (better than one chance out of ten) of being born with one or more of a variety of disorders, including intellectual impairment, severe defects in vision or hearing, and malformations of the heart (Greenberg, Pelliteri, & Barton, 1957; Montagu, 1962). Expectant mothers should take extreme caution to avoid exposure to rubella during the early months of pregnancy.

Toxemia is a disorder that strikes mothers of lower socioeconomic status more frequently than it inflicts middle-class mothers. Its symptoms are dysfunctions in the mother's kidneys and circulatory systems, accompanied by swelling in the mother's face, ankles, and hands, and heightened blood pressure. There is a heightened level of albumin in the urine, and sometimes headaches, blurred vision, and dizziness. Toxemia may have damaging effects on the developing fetus and if untreated may lead to severe complications and even death for the mother (Fleming, 1972). *Toxemia*

Very likely the overrepresentation of this disorder in women from lower socioeconomic backgrounds is due to lower nutritional status and limited access to prenatal medical care that would provide early identification and treatment of the disorder. *Socioeconomic differences*

Maternal activity and emotions. The activity level and emotional states of a mother may influence the development of the fetus, but these factors interact with other variables in exceedingly complex ways, making it difficult to identify clear-cut influences on fetal development. Abnormal emotional states, for example, may alter the mother's intake of food, thus affecting the availability of nutrients to the fetus (Montagu, 1962). Either excessive activity or fatigue on the part of the mother affect the pulse rate and activity level of the fetus by altering levels of lactic acid and carbon dioxide in the fetal blood (Montagu, 1962; Pasamanick & Knobloch, 1966).

Rh incompatibility. When most people think of blood types, they think of types A, B, AB, or O. The gene for type A blood, for example, produces a substance known as antigen A, the gene for type B produces B antigens. Both antigens are present in the blood of a person with type AB blood, but the gene for type O produces neither antigen. In addition to their characteristic antigens, A and B blood types also carry antibodies, or clumping substances, which combat any foreign antigen that may enter the bloodstream. Severe clumping reactions may occur if an individual receives a blood transfusion of any blood type which will be combated by the antigens of his own blood type.

The fact that blood incompatibility causes dangerous reactions creates some unique problems for fetuses whose hereditary blood substances differ from those of their mother. The blood substance involved is the Rh factor rather than one of the main blood-type substances. When an individual has either one or two of the dominant Rh genes, his blood type for this substance is *Rh-positive*. If instead the individual has two of the recessive Rh genes, his blood is of the *Rh-negative* type.

If a mother is Rh-negative, and the fetus is Rh-positive, having inherited the dominant gene from the father, the child may *in some cases* develop a serious disorder called erythroblastosis fetalis, which involves the destruction of red *Erythroblastosis fetalis* blood cells in the fetus. This is how it happens. If the filtering mechanism of the placenta is not functioning optimally, some of the Rh substance in the fetus may get through the filter into the mother's bloodstream. The mother's body reacts by manufacturing Rh-antibodies to combat the foreign material. Some of these antibodies then get back through the placenta into the fetal bloodstream, causing the red blood cells to agglutinate, or clump. The result is severe anemia and jaundice (Scheinfeld, 1965; Pasamanick & Knobloch, 1966). If an Rh-negative mother is having her first Rh-positive baby, the antibodies she produces are rarely sufficient to seriously harm the fetus. But with successive births of this type (every baby would be of this type if the father is homozygous for the dominant gene), the antigens accumulate in the mother's bloodstream and the attack on the fetal red blood cells may be sufficient to kill the child unless medical intervention replaces the infant's Rh-positive blood with Rh-negative blood (Scheinfeld, 1965).

*Medical
intervention*

BIRTH TRAUMA

Even if the infant comes equipped with a first-rate genetic constitution, has the advantages of good nutrition, and is free of the deleterious effects of drugs, disease, and other prenatal influences that may impair development, there are still dangers to be faced during the process of delivery itself. In the space of a very short time the fetus must leave the warm, dark, fluid environment of his/her mother's protective body to enter a world of light, noise, and all sorts of stimuli which impinge on the senses almost continuously. Never again in our lives do we undergo such a drastic environmental change as the one that must be endured by a child making the transition from fetus to neonate. (The term *neonate* refers to the first few weeks of life; by the time the child is a month old he is regarded as an infant.)

Anoxia

When labor is prolonged and difficult, anoxia, as well as physical injuries, are likely to occur. Anoxia, or lack of oxygen, may cause damage to cells in the brain stem, which may result in impairment of motor functions and in lower than normal development quotients on tests of infant mental ability. Most deliveries, however, are not difficult and protracted, and the stresses of the birth process are not beyond the ability of most infants to withstand trauma (Ausubel & Sullivan, 1970).

PREMATURE BIRTH

*Socioeconomic
differences*

As with other hazards of prenatal development and birth, premature birth is more common among economically disadvantaged populations than among middle-class groups. Again, this fact is probably associated with the lower nutritional and prenatal medical advantages of this group compared to that available to higher income groups. Premature birth may result from some of the conditions we have already discussed, such as maternal disease and Rh incompatibility (Ausubel & Sullivan, 1970). The premature infant is weaker than his full-term counterpart, and except for vision his sensory capacities are not as well developed.

Premature infants require a special environment with controlled temperatures during their early weeks, and special attention must also be given to diet.

*Prematurity
defined*

Infants who are under 5½ pounds at birth, or who are born before 37 weeks of gestation, may be considered premature. Premature babies generally lag behind full-term babies in motor behaviors during their early years, and babies

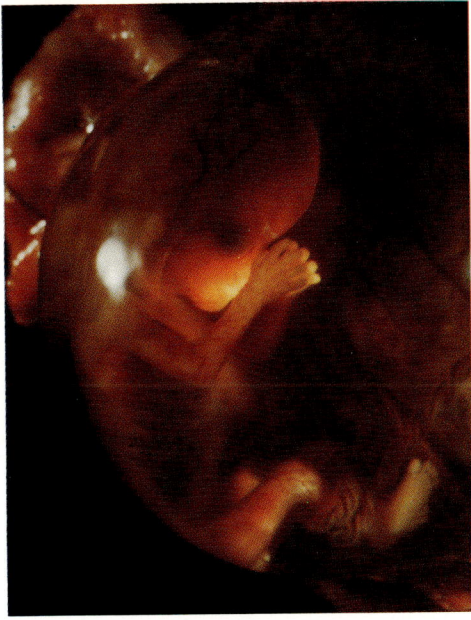

Prenatal Development

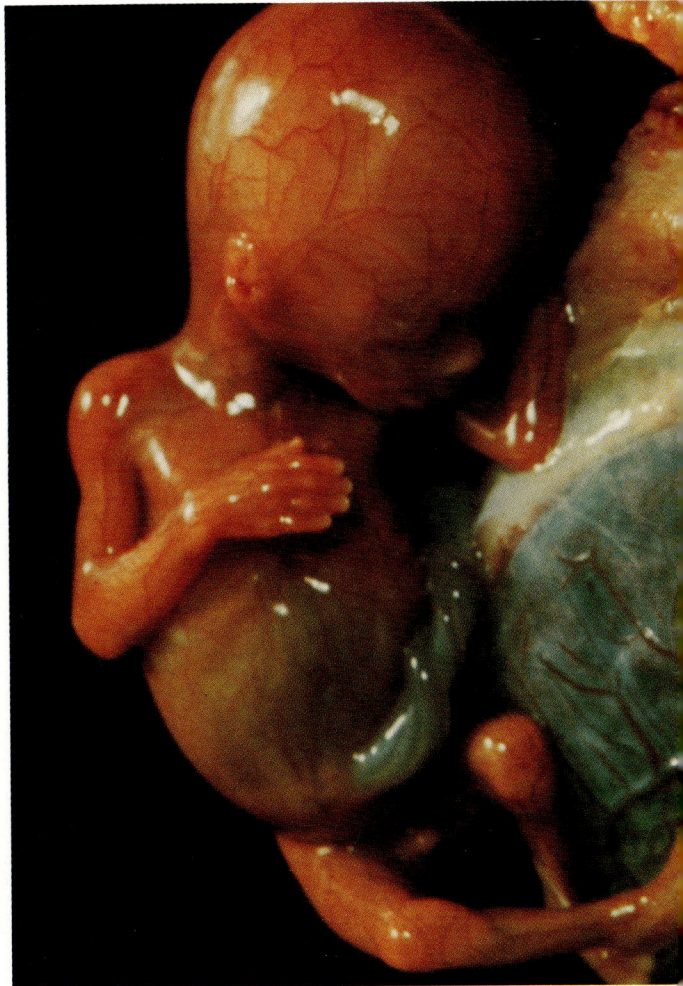

Children acquire motor skills through play.

who are extremely premature may continue to evidence impairment in attention, intellectual capacity, reading ability, and certain other behaviors (Ausubel & Sullivan, 1970).

IMPLICATIONS

The basic processes by which human hereditary material is passed from parents to children is relatively well known. But in humans, perhaps more than any other living creature, the interactions between environmental influences and genetic constitution are so complex that the exact extent to which heredity and environment influence important capacities, such as intellectual capability, can only be crudely estimated. The important question is not how much environment and heredity each influence development, but how they interact to produce their effects (Anastasi, 1958).

We have some clues to the interworkings of environmental and genetic factors from knowledge of the specific processes involved in the transmission of characteristics, such as sickle cell anemia which bears a strong evolutionary relationship to environmental factors. However, the processes involved in the inheritance of other human characteristics of immediate and general social concern are in all likelihood infinitely more complex than the sickle cell example, involving more than a single set of genes and patterns of genetic transmission and expression that are much more complex than the simple patterns of dominance and recessiveness, which are well established.

The fact that the genetic and environmental factors involved in the transmission of certain important human characteristics are not well established should not obscure the fact that there are many other characteristics for which the processes of hereditary transmission are well-mapped. This information is invaluable to medical practitioners and can be used to good advantage by genetic counselors (Stern, 1960). The obstetrician who knows that an expectant mother is Rh-negative, and that the father is Rh-positive, will be on the alert for signs of Rh incompatibility in the fetus and will be prepared to take therapeutic action if complications develop. Genetic counselors are able to advise prospective parents with family histories of a genetic disorder of the probability that a child

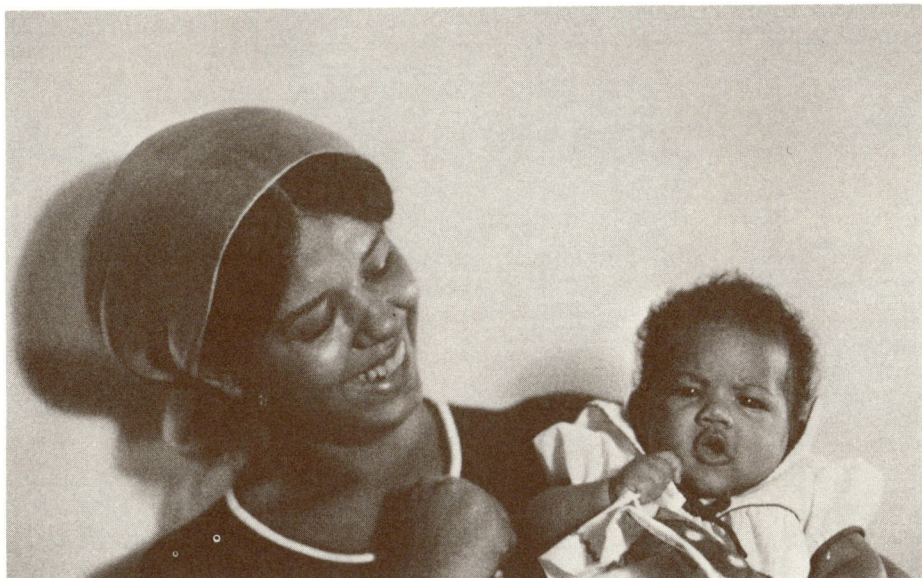

to be conceived would inherit the debilitating condition. Knowledge of hereditary processes may therefore be applied in ways that serve to reduce disabilities and mortality among the newborn. Unfortunately, these benefits are not equally available to all sectors of the population, and those who are least well equipped to cope with the financial hardships of disabilities may be disproportionately affected.

The facts of unequal access to conditions that promote healthy development are perhaps even more evident when one considers the effects of nutrition and environmental stress on prenatal development. Mortality rates and disabilities associated with substandard nutrition and poor prenatal care are substantially higher among families of lower socioeconomic status, and there are no figures available to index the social cost of that circumstance.

These factors also affect physical growth and psychomotor skills during later periods of development, as we shall see in the following chapter.

SUGGESTED READINGS

Birch, H. G. Health and the education of socially disadvantaged children. *Developmental Medicine and Child Neurology*, 1968, *10*, 580-99.

Bowes, W. A., Jr., Brackbill, Y., Conway, E., & Steinschneider, A. The effects of obstetrical medication on fetus and infant. *Monographs of the Society for Research in Child Development*, 1970, *35*, (4, Whole No. 137).

DuBos, R. Man overadapting. *Psychology Today*, 1971, *4* (February), 50-53.

Hardy, J. B. Rubella and its aftermath. *Children*, 1969, *16*, 91-96.

McClearn, G. E. Behavioral genetics: An overview. *Merrill Palmer Quarterly of Behavior and Development*, 1968, *14*, 9-24.

Scheinfeld, A. *Your heredity and environment*. Philadelphia: J.B. Lippincott, 1965.

4

Physical Growth and
Motor-Skill Development

Instructional Objectives	Recognize or recall
	Compare and contrast
	Describe or demonstrate
	Evaluate

the definition of physical growth.

the shapes of brain-, general-, and reproductive-growth curves.

the regulatory characteristics of growth.

procedures for measuring skeletal growth.

the central advantage of skeletal growth as a measure of physical development.

growth curves for height and skeletal development.

the major areas of the brain.

how brain growth occurs after birth.

procedures for measuring brain growth.

indices of reproductive growth.

the definition of puberty and its initiation in males and females.

the psychological consequences of early and late maturation for boys and girls.

the endocrinology of growth.

the relationship of growth to other indices of development.

the definition of the term *motor skill.*

Posner and Keele's specification of the stages in motor-skill enactment.

ontogenetic and phylogenetic skills.

the cephalocaudal, proximodistal, and massed-to-specialized activity trends in skill development.

research findings and uses for norms describing motor-skill development.

the relationship between motor-skill development and intellectual development.

ethnic and social-class variations in physical development.

the secular trend.

research findings examining genetically based variations in physical development.

the findings regarding activity and stimulation level and physical development.

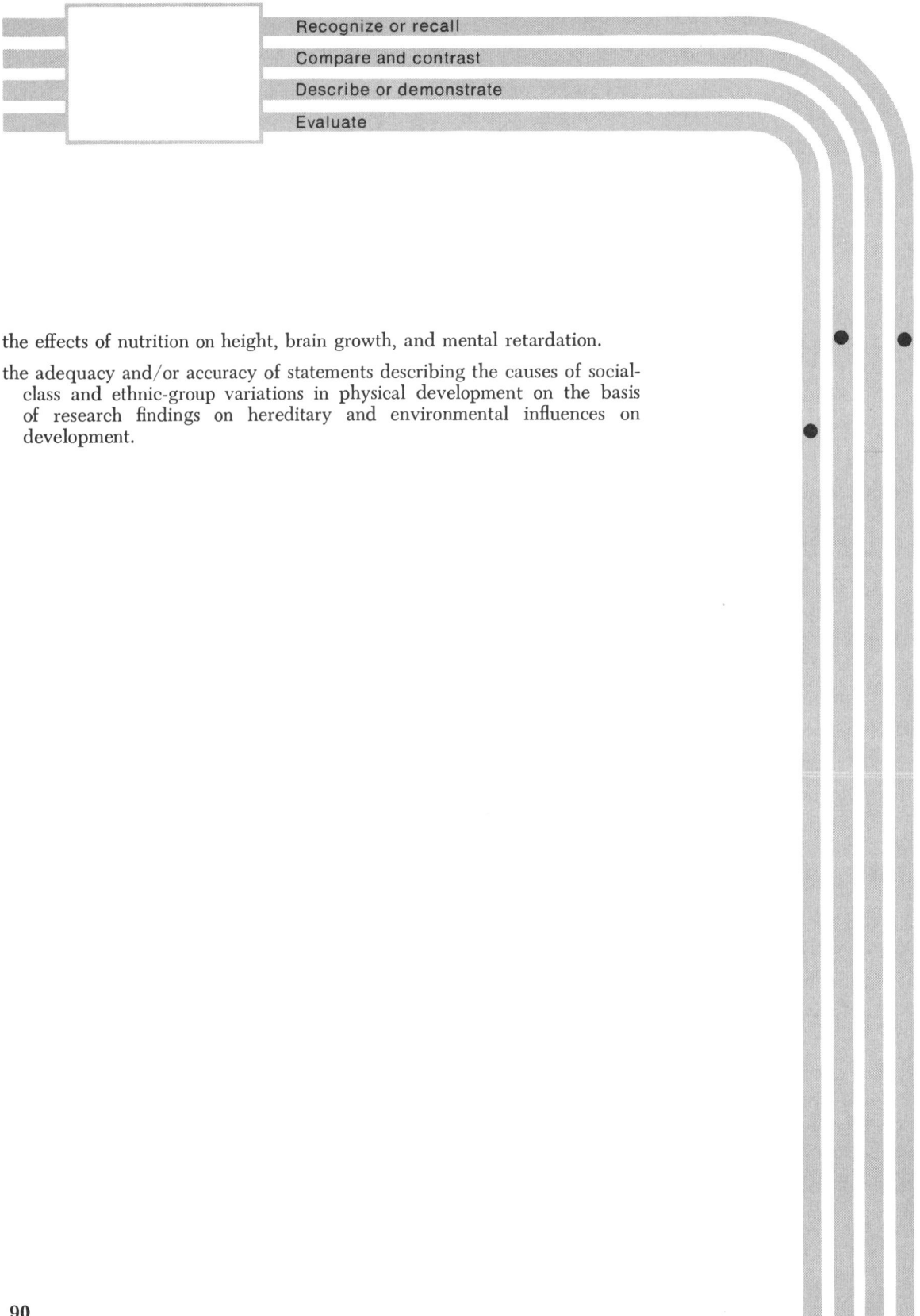

the effects of nutrition on height, brain growth, and mental retardation.

the adequacy and/or accuracy of statements describing the causes of social-class and ethnic-group variations in physical development on the basis of research findings on hereditary and environmental influences on development.

CHAPTER CONTENT

Nature of physical growth and skill development

    Physical growth

    Motor-skill development

Physical development and culture

    Cultural variations in physical development

    Heredity, environment, and physical development

Physical development, including body growth and the acquisition of skill in controlling body movements, is generally a source of concern and fascination for adult socializing agents and also, no doubt, for children. There are many reasons for this. One is the fact that physical development has practical consequences which affect persons involved in the development process. *I bought these pants three months ago and already he has outgrown them* says a bewildered mother. *Do you think I'll be big enough to play on the football team?* asks a boy grappling with the uncertainties of physical change. Familiar comments such as these illustrate the extent to which concerns about the physical aspects of growth permeate practical problems in everyday life.

In addition to its practical consequences, physical development is of interest because it may affect the attitudes of individuals toward one another and toward themselves. For example, consider a 7-year-old girl who observes with envy that her older sister is beginning to develop a mature figure. In an effort to bolster her own damaged self-esteem, she decides to improve upon nature by using an old undershirt as chest padding.

A third reason for interest in physical development is that it is a manifestation of underlying physiological processes which function in highly predictable ways. There is a remarkable degree of orderliness in physical development. As a result, it is possible to predict with some accuracy many of the kinds of changes that will occur in the course of growth. For example, one can determine when in the sequence of skill development a child will learn to sit up or to walk. Similarly, it is possible to predict with considerable accuracy how tall a child will be at successive ages.

The predictable character of physical development enables socializing agents to use indices of growth and skill acquisition as signals indicating the extent to which developmental change is occurring as expected. Radical deviations from expectations may indicate developmental problems requiring medical or other professional attention.

Physical development takes place in a cultural context. Over successive generations, cultural characteristics may influence genetic contributions to development by favoring the survival of individuals possessing certain genetic features. In addition, culture may produce environmental circumstances which can directly affect development.

In the present chapter, we shall discuss physical growth and skill development in their cultural contexts. First, we will describe some of the major concepts and research findings relating to physical growth and skill development. Then we will consider the cultural variations which exist in physical development and the genetic and environmental determinants of those variations.

NATURE OF PHYSICAL GROWTH AND SKILL DEVELOPMENT

To gain even a rudimentary understanding of physical development one must consider a number of questions. What kinds of patterns are characteristic of growth and skill acquisition? What are the relationships of growth and skill development to other developmental processes? Finally, what are the major types of growth and skills that are of concern in socialization? These are the topics to be considered in the following pages.

Physical Growth

Definition of growth

The term *physical growth* refers to the enlargement of various body structures during the course of development. The growth of physical structures in the body follows characteristic patterns. Moreover, different patterns exist for different types of growth. Growth patterns are regulated to a significant degree by internal mechanisms that preserve the orderliness of development by modulating the effects of temporary environmental conditions threatening to alter growth sequences. Physical growth is related to other developmental processes, but the relationships tend to be rather small.

General growth curve

Growth curves. Many measures of human physical growth reveal a highly predictable pattern which has come to be called the general growth curve. The characteristics of the general growth curve were first recorded over 200 years ago by Count Philbert de Montbeillard (Tanner, 1970). The count measured changes in his son's height from birth through the age of 18. The general pattern of growth which the count observed has been verified in numerous studies.

The shape of the general growth curve is shown in figure 4-1. As you can see, physical growth proceeds rather rapidly during infancy and the preschool years, then tapers gradually until about the age of 12. During adolescence there is a marked growth spurt.

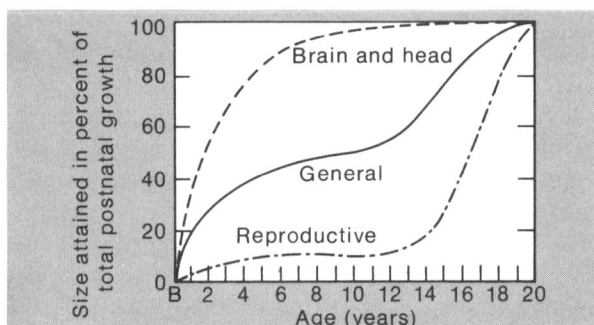

Figure 4-1   *Growth curves. The brain and head curve is an amalgamation of measurements of head size and neurological structures. The general growth curve includes measurement of overall body growth involving changes in characteristics such as height, body shape, and respiratory and digestive organs. The reproductive growth curve is made up of measures of changes in organs such as the testicles, ovaries, seminal vesicles, and fallopian tubes. (From R. E. Scammon, The measurement of the body in childhood. In J. A. Harris, C. M. Jackson, D. G. Paterson, & R. E. Scammon. The measurement of man. Minneapolis: University of Minnesota Press, 1930, p. 193.)*

The adolescent growth spurt is a primate characteristic not found in other forms of life. The functions that it serves are not precisely known. However, Tanner (1970) points out that it does provide a relatively long period of dependence on parents. This increases the amount of time available for socialization.

In the case of human beings, socialization time is a critical issue since human survival is heavily dependent on the social transmission of elaborate cultural patterns.

Although a large number of growth indices adhere to the general growth curve, there are some measures of physical growth which do not follow the general pattern. One of these has to do with neurological development. As shown in figure 4-1, the growth of the brain tends to progress quite rapidly during the childhood years. However, brain growth levels off before adolescence and does not display the adolescent spurt.

Brain growth

Figure 4-1 reveals that reproductive development is somewhat similar to general growth. However, reproductive growth during the childhood years tends to be minimal. Moreover, the adolescent growth spurt is much more pronounced for sexual growth than for general growth. A little boy or girl can change into a young man or woman in a short time. Parents then must quickly learn to change both their expectations of children and their child-rearing practices to meet new social, emotional, and intellectual needs associated with physical maturity.

Reproductive growth

Regulatory characteristics of growth. Not only does growth generally follow a highly predictable pattern, but also, if it is deflected by chance events from its initial course, it tends after a time to return once more to its original path. For example, consider the data on height shown in figure 4-2. The child whose growth is depicted in this figure went through two periods in which food inges-

Compensatory growth

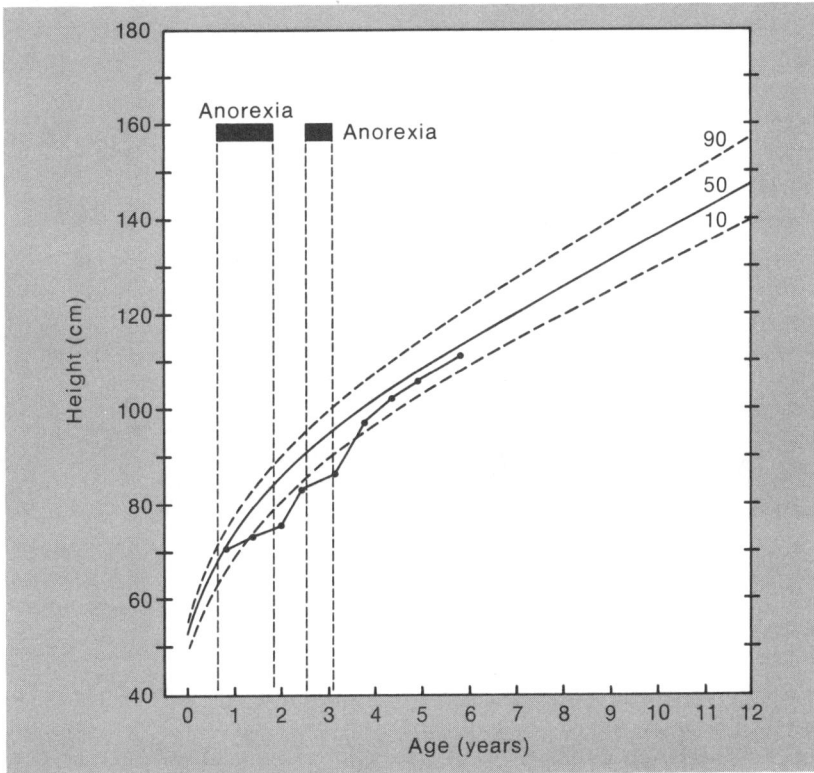

Two periods of catch-up growth following episodes of anorexia (i.e., loss of appetite) in a young child. The two dotted lines and the solid line between them indicate percentile ranks for height at successive age levels in the population. (From A. Prader, J. M. Tanner, & G. A. von Harnack, Catch-up growth following illness or starvation. Journal of Pediatrics, 1963, 62, p. 648.)

Figure 4-2

tion was greatly reduced. During these periods there was a marked decrease in his rate of growth. However, when his diet returned to normal, his growth rate accelerated to a sufficient extent to make up for the lost growth associated with low food intake (Prader, Tanner, & von Harnack, 1963).

Although there is a tendency for growth to return to its original trajectory, this tendency operates only within restricted limits. For example, when malnutrition persists over an extended time period, growth may be permanently retarded (Tanner, 1970).

Skeletal growth. During the course of development, cartilage in many areas of the body is gradually replaced by bone. For example, as shown in figure 4-3, there is a dramatic increase in the number of bones in the wrist between ages 3 and 13.

The shift from cartilage to bone can be used as an index of skeletal maturity. A radiograph (that is, an X-ray photo like the one in figure 4-3) can be used to reveal the amount and area of bone in a given body part.

Skeletal development follows the general growth curve characteristic of most physical changes which take place during childhood and adolescence. Growth is gradual and continuous during childhood. Then, during adolescence, there is a sharp spurt.

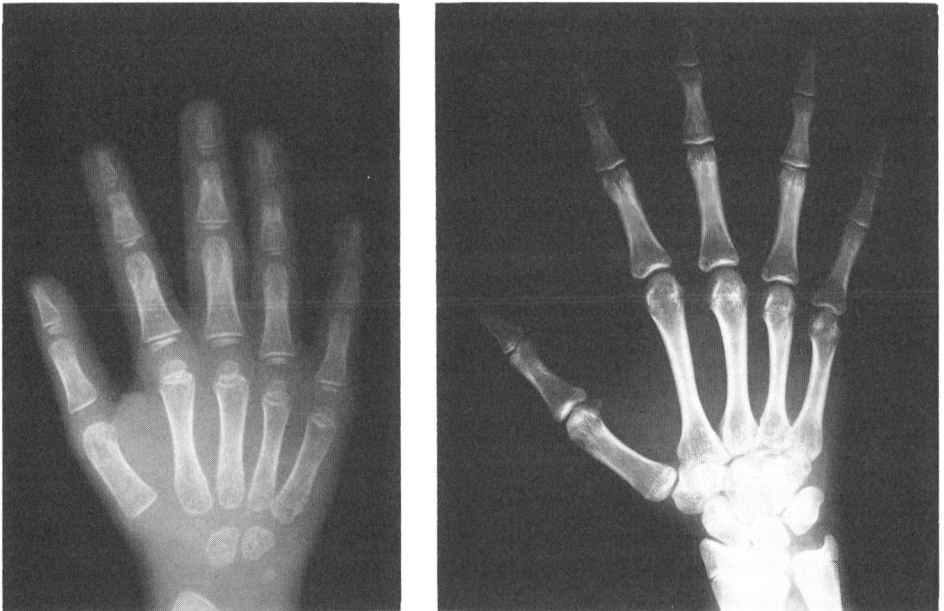

Figure 4-3 *Changes in skeletal development reflecting typical growth in a boy from ages 3 to 13 years.*

Skeletal development provides an excellent measure of physical development because it affords a scale of developmental progress which is common across individuals. Virtually all children eventually achieve the same degree of bone development. In this respect, skeletal growth is quite different from characteristics such as height and weight which vary greatly in fully mature individuals.

Growth in height. Developmental change in height is among the most familiar and useful indices of physical growth. One of the ways in which parents, teachers, and other socializing agents judge maturity is by assessing height. *You're getting so big*, a proud aunt or grandfather may say. Height serves as one of a number of cues signaling change in adult expectations for children. Thus, a mother, indicating a new behavioral expectation for her child, may comment *you're too big to be carried*.

Height, as we indicated in our discussion of Count de Montbeillard's son, follows the general growth curve. There is a gradual increase in growth during childhood followed by the adolescent growth spurt.

It is usually of some interest to both adults and children to find out that adult height can be predicted with substantial accuracy during the childhood years. By the time children are 9 years old, it is possible to predict their adult height within ±1½ inches 90% of the time (Tanner, 1970). In order to achieve this degree of accuracy, however, it is necessary to measure not only a child's current height and age, but also his skeletal maturity. These three variables are combined to predict adult height.

Growth of the brain. As figure 4-4 indicates, the brain can be described in terms of five major areas: the cerebrum, midbrain, pons, medulla, and cerebellum. The cerebrum, which is divided longitudinally into two hemispheres, is the largest part of the brain. Centers associated with thinking, memory, hearing, sight, smell, taste, bodily sensation, and the voluntary control of body movements are found in the cerebrum.

The five areas of the brain

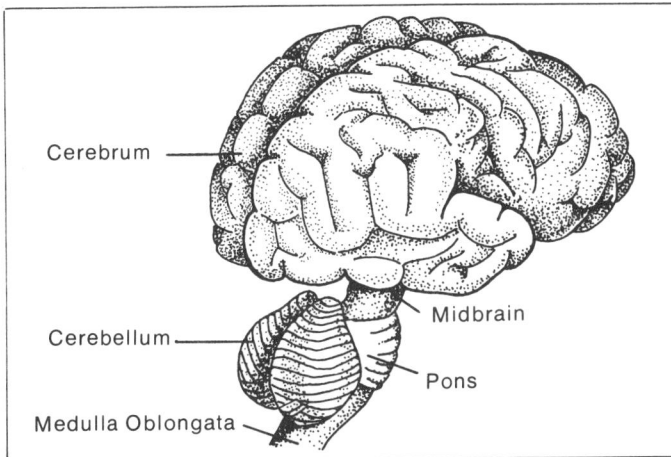

Component parts of the brain as seen from the right side. The parts are represented as separated from one another considerably more than is natural so as to show their connections.

Figure 4-4

The midbrain, pons, and medulla are those portions of the brain which carry neural impulses toward and away from the spinal cord. The midbrain transmits sensory impulses associated with sight, sound, touch, pain, and muscle sensations. It is the center controlling visual and auditory reflexes such as the turning of the head and eyes toward a visual stimulus. The pons serves as a bridge between the two halves of the cerebrum. The medulla connects the brain to the spinal cord. It controls life functions such as respiration and circulation.

The cerebellum, which lies behind the midbrain, pons, and medulla, is composed of two connected hemispheres. It, along with the cerebrum, plays a role in the voluntary control of movement.

As figure 4-1 shows, the brain grows rapidly during the childhood years. There is no adolescent growth spurt. By the time a child is 10 years old his brain will have attained 95% of its adult weight. The remaining 5% is achieved gradually during the later childhood and adolescent years.

*How the
brain grows*

The growth of the brain from birth through adolescence takes place through cell differentiation. It is believed that all or nearly all the cells in the brain are present at birth. However, after birth various parts of nerve cells grow. Moreover, sheaths that make the transmission of neural impulses possible are formed around nerve fibers.

*Measurement of
brain growth*

One way to measure brain growth is simply to plot changes in the overall weight of the brain. There are, however, other more sophisticated techniques. For example, with cell differentiation the density of neurons per unit of brain volume decreases. Thus, neuron density can be used as a measure of brain development.

*Differential rates of
brain development*

Different areas of the brain develop at different rates. For example, within the motor area, nerve cells controlling the movement of the arms and upper trunk develop ahead of those controlling the leg. As might be expected, the development of neural structures is prerequisite to behavior. Thus, the young child achieves control of the arms and upper trunk before mastering leg movements (Tanner, 1970).

*Reproductive
growth as organ
enlargement*

Growth of the reproductive system. Growth of the reproductive system is assessed mainly in terms of the enlargement of various organs which serve some function in the reproductive process. In the male, the testes, prostate gland, and seminal vesicles are among the principal measures of reproductive growth. In the female, uterine and vaginal growth are used in the assessment of reproductive development. Although bodily changes directly related to reproduction are mainstays in the measurement of reproductive development, other indices are also used. The growth of pubic hair is a familiar example.

Puberty

There are dramatic changes in reproductive growth at puberty. Initially, puberty referred to that period of growth marked by the development of pubic hair. However, current theorists tend to define puberty mainly in terms of the enlargement of the various organs related to reproduction.

In the male the first sign of puberty is an enlargement of the testes. Pubic hair begins to develop shortly after this enlargement. About a year later there is a marked acceleration in penis growth and in body height. The development of axillary and facial hair follows about two years after onset of pubic hair.

In the female puberty begins with the simultaneous development of the uterus, vagina, and breasts. Menarche, the first menstrual period, may occur a number of years after the initial growth process begins. Moreover, it may be as long as 18 months after menarche before pregnancy can occur.

*Variations in
developmental rate*

As shown in figure 4-5, there are marked individual variations in the rate of development of the reproductive system and attendant changes in other growth processes such as height (Olson, 1959). During adolescence it is not unusual to find vast developmental differences in size and sexual maturity among members of the same age group. A 14-year-old may have the development of a mature adult or may be most of the way along the developmental continuum or may be just beginning the adolescent spurt.

For boys, there is a definite advantage to early maturation. When compared to early-maturing boys, those maturing late tend to be rated as less poised, less physically attractive, more affected in their behavior, and more tense in so-

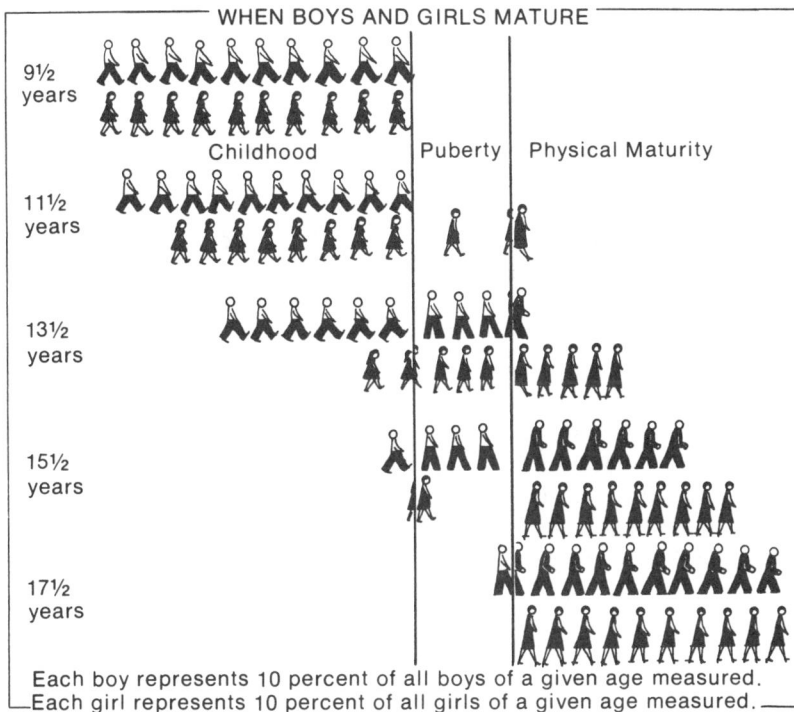

9½ years

Childhood | Puberty | Physical Maturity

11½ years

13½ years

15½ years

17½ years

Each boy represents 10 percent of all boys of a given age measured.
Each girl represents 10 percent of all girls of a given age measured.

Variability in sex maturation in boys and girls. (Adapted from A. V. Keliher, Life and
growth. *New York: Appleton-Century, 1938, p. 185.)*   **Figure 4-5**

cial situations. Morever, they tend to be restless and unpopular with their peers
(Jones, 1938; Jones, 1958; Jones and Bayley, 1950).

Late-maturing boys tend to score higher than early maturers on personality
tests measuring feelings of guilt, anxiety, depression, and inferiority. They also
have greater needs to be encouraged by others than is the case for early maturers (Weatherley, 1964). Finally, they tend to display negative self-esteem
and feelings of being rejected (Mussen & Jones, 1957).

The consequences of variations in maturation rate are more complex for girls
than they are for boys. In the upper elementary school early maturation seems
to be a disadvantage. For example, Faust (1960) found that peers tended to rate
physically less mature girls as having more desirable traits than physically advanced girls. However, this pattern changed for girls in the junior high school.

The endocrinology of growth. Growth is regulated to a large extent by the
endocrine glands (Tanner, 1970). The thyroid gland, the adrenal gland, the
testes, the ovaries, the pancreas, and the pituitary gland, all secrete hormones
that affect growth processes. For example, the development of the reproductive
system during adolescence is influenced by hormone secretions in the testes and
ovaries. In boys increased secretions of testosterone produce many of the specifically male characteristics which emerge during adolescence. Similarly, estrogen
secreted from the ovaries influences the development of many female
characteristics.

Most of the endocrine glands are controlled by secretions from the pituitary
gland, which is often called the master gland. For example, the secretion of thy-
roxine from the thyroid gland occurs in response to the emission of the thyroid-

stimulating hormone from the pituitary. Similarly, the pituitary produces gonado-trophic hormones which stimulate growth in the ovaries or testes.

The activities of the pituitary gland are governed by releaser substances which come from the brain. The releaser substances are in turn controlled by information from various parts of the body. For instance, increases or decreases in the amount of a given hormone in the bloodstream may signal the activation of releaser substances influencing pituitary secretions.

In addition to influencing the activities of the other endocrine glands, the pituitary plays a direct role in controlling physical growth. From about the tenth week after conception, the pituitary secretes a growth hormone which to a significant extent controls physical growth. The level of secretion of this hormone is particularly high before birth, which is to be expected in light of the rapid growth changes which occur during this period. Although physical development can be attributed to a major degree to the growth hormone, the causes of the adolescent growth spurt in body size are not yet known.

Individual differences in the rate of physical development are probably controlled by small differences in hormone secretion. However, which hormones are involved and how they function to regulate the tempo of development remain unanswered questions.

Growth and other indices of development. There is evidence that physical growth is to some extent related to a number of other developmental processes. However, the extent of the relationship between growth and other types of development is for the most part rather small. Thus, for every individual instance of correspondence across developmental processes, there are many instances of noncorrespondence. The physically immature boy or girl, for example, may be intellectually precocious and/or highly skilled in social situations.

Growth and ability

Despite the exceptions, there is a tendency for children who are physically advanced to score slightly higher on tests of intellectual ability than children who are relatively slow in developing physically. It has been shown that the intelligence of girls who have had their first menstrual period is likely to be higher than that of girls of the same age who have not yet experienced this event (Tanner, 1970). Similarly, large children tend to score higher on intelligence tests than small children throughout childhood and adolescence (Tanner, 1970). When differences in stature are great, differences in intellectual functioning can be quite substantial. For instance, Tanner (1970) reports a 9-point difference in intelligence-test scores between children at the seventy-fifth percentile and children at the fifteenth percentile in height.

It may be tempting to conclude from the above findings that physical growth plays a causal role in determining intelligence. However, growth and intelligence are related to other variables (for example, social class) which may control the observed relationship between physical development and intellectual functioning (Kaplan, 1972).

Growth and social and emotional development

Slow-growing children tend to score lower on measures of social and emotional development than do fast-growing children (Tanner, 1970). There are a variety of possible reasons for these findings. Late-maturing children may feel unsure of their capability to compete with their more mature age-mates. The boy who stands 4 feet 10 inches tall may be reticent to challenge the leadership claims of a classmate who is more than a foot taller.

Growth and skill development

Physical growth plays an important role in skill development just as it does in social and emotional development. Skills generally require certain minimal levels of growth. If a child lacks muscular strength, size, and skeletal maturity, his performance of physical skills may be inadequate. Developmental studies support this assertion. Research has revealed relationships between such growth variables as height and weight and effectiveness in performing complex skills (e.g., Chesquiere, 1958).

Motor-Skill Development

Motor skills are sequences of muscular movements which conform to predetermined standards of acceptable performance. For example, a child who upon taking a faltering step tumbled to the ground in a heap would be judged as lacking the skill of walking because his behavior did not meet accepted performance standards. On the other hand, a little one who waddled some distance before falling would probably be judged as possessing some walking skill.

Motor skills are made up of component sequences of action. Some skills are manifested by nearly all people. Others are possessed by some individuals but not by others. Those skills generally achieved by all persons tend to develop in invariant sequences which closely parallel the development of biological structures. On the other hand, specialized skills possessed by only a limited number of persons may develop in a variety of ways.

Component stages in motor-skill enactment. Although motor skills give the impression of being unified behaviors, there is evidence that they are, in fact, made up of a number of relatively discrete stages. Posner and Keele (1973) identify four such stages: preparation, decision, movement, and storage.

The first phase in the performance of a motor skill is the preparation phase. In this initial stage the individual readies himself to respond. Readiness may take the form of sensory alertness or motor preparedness to activate a particular set of movements.

Humans, like other animals, have the capability of selectively attending to various sensory stimuli (Gibson, 1969). In skill enactment, sensory alertness sensitizes an individual to signals triggering motor responses. Alertness of this kind has obvious survival value. The individual who can selectively attend to stimuli signaling possible danger and who can respond quickly to such stimuli has a greater probability for a long life than the individual who is insensitive to potential threats in the environment.

Motor preparedness associated with the preparation phase of skill enactment involves the readying of certain muscle groups for response. Readiness of this kind takes the form of mental preparations for action. The girl who, while walking down stairs, comes to a missing step that she has failed to notice will recognize that her muscles have been prepared to perform in an expected pattern which the missing step has suddenly rendered inappropriate.

The second phase in skill enactment is the decision stage. At this stage the brain directs appropriate muscle groups to respond. Decisions governing motor movements are made in a period called reaction time. This is the time interval between the onset of a signal to respond and the actual initiation of the response. For example, when a child is riding his bike and a friend suddenly cuts in front of him, the child must decide whether to try to change direction to avert a collision or to apply his brakes or to do both of these things. The time interval between seeing his friend and responding to this event is the reaction-time period. As this example shows, speed of reaction can be quite important. It might mean the difference between bent spokes, dented fenders, and bruised shins and nothing more than a brief moment of anxiety.

The third stage in motor-skill enactment is skill execution. During this phase

Children develop many ontogenetic skills through participation in sports.

the individual carries out the sequence of motor movements required in the skill.

The final stage in skill enactment involves the memory of skill performance. A child may recall what it felt like to execute a particular skill; he may remember the sights and sounds associated with skill execution or may retain words describing the enactment of the skill. The memory phase of skill performance plays a particularly important role in skill learning. If a child can recall the characteristics of accurate skill execution, he will be in a relatively good position to improve his skill performance on subsequent occasions.

In the early stages of skill development verbal recall can play an important part in skill learning (Posner & Keele, 1973). Sensory impressions such as the physical sensations associated with skill execution tend to fade from memory within a few seconds (Gibson, 1969). However, words can be recalled over an extended period. Thus, a child learning to hit a tennis ball may say to herself *keep a firm wrist* and thereby reinstate a behavior which otherwise might be forgotten.

Ontogenetic and phylogenetic skills. It is useful to distinguish between skills that are possessed by only some members of a species and skills that are manifested by nearly all species members. One reason for making this distinction is that these two kinds of skills serve different functions. A second reason is that the influence of genetic and environmental factors on skill development differs for these two types of skills.

Ontogenetic skills   Ontogenetic skills are skills possessed by some members of a species, but not by all members. For example, some children can ice skate, but there are many who cannot. Similarly, some children can swim, but there are others who have not acquired this skill. Even when an individual has achieved full maturity, he may lack many ontogenetic skills. Thus, a socially sophisticated, intelligent adult may fall while skating in a fashion not dissimilar to a toddler tumbling to the ground as he learns to take his first steps.

Ontogenetic skills enable individuals to perform specialized societal functions. In some cases they may involve leisure time activities as in those instances in which skills are used in games. However, in other instances ontogenetic skills are used in work-related activities such as operating a lathe, cutting hair, or performing surgery.

There is an abundance of evidence indicating that ontogenetic skills are strongly influenced by learning and motivation. If a child has adequate instruction in an ontogenetic skill, if he has opportunities to practice the skill, and if he is motivated to develop the skill, there is usually a good chance that he will achieve skill mastery (Ausubel & Sullivan, 1970).

Although ontogenetic skills are markedly affected by learning and motivation, they are also influenced by maturational factors. If a child lacks the neuromuscular capability to perform a skill, obviously he will not be able to learn it. There is no point in trying to teach an infant to ride a bicycle or roller skate. The infant simply does not have the physical capabilities to emit these kinds of behaviors.

Phylogenetic motor skills are skills which are possessed by all members of a *Phylogenetic skills* species who are not physically impaired. Prehension, the ability to grasp objects, is an example. Virtually all humans have the ability to pick up and hold objects with their hands.

Phylogenetic skills tend to enable the individual to emit behaviors which serve highly general and often extremely significant functions for the species. For example, developmental psychologist Jerome Bruner (1970) points out that prehension skills enable humans to make their intelligence have an impact on their environment. Prehension makes it possible for humans to use tools. Through

Children refine ontogenetic skills through practice.

the use of tools they shape their environment in accordance with the dictates of their intellects.

Parents encourage the development of phylogenetic skills.

The role of prehension as an instrument of the intellect in all likelihood was the result of gradual evolution. Regarding this point Bruner (1970) states:

> . . . it is the evolutionary direction of morphological change in the hand, from tree shrews through tarsiers through New World monkeys through Old World monkeys to men, that should reveal how the function of the hand has changed and, with it, the nature of the implementation of human intelligence. That change has been steadily in the direction of a very special form of despecialization. (p. 64)

Early developmentalists made a strong case for the view that phylogenetic skills were controlled almost entirely by genetic factors. For instance, as indicated in chapter 2, Gesell and Thompson (1929) demonstrated that practice had little effect on skills such as stair climbing. As we indicated in the discussion of their work, early developmentalists overstated the case for genetic control. This fact is illustrated in a study by Johnston, Kelley, Harris, and Wolf (1966) demonstrating that climbing behavior in preschool children can be increased when it is rewarded by adult attention.

Much of the learning of ontogenetic and phylogenetic skills takes place through play. During the preschool years children learn to climb, to jump, to slide, to swing, to run, and so forth as part of their many play experiences. Learning of this kind may occur in informal neighborhood settings. In addition, the elaborate playground equipment often found in public parks and school grounds may serve as a source of motor-skill development through play.

During the middle-childhood and adolescent years, children acquire many highly specialized skills through participation in games. Throwing and hitting a baseball, throwing and kicking a football, and shooting a basketball are some of the more familiar examples.

The kinds of play experiences that children engage in during childhood and adolescence are influenced by societal expectations, many of which are related

*Children acquire
motor skills in
the natural
environment.*

to sex roles. In the past girls have generally been encouraged to engage in more sedentary play activities than boys. Moreover, opportunities for physical development through participation in organized sports have been severely limited for girls. Recent mandates at the federal level of government should do much to improve opportunities for girls to develop motor skills. However, it seems likely that radical changes in sex-role expectations will be needed if girls are to have the opportunity to achieve their full potential in motor-skill development.

Sequence in skill development.   Early developmental research revealed that the acquisition of a number of humans' most fundamental phylogenetic skills generally follows a fixed sequence. Phylogenetic-skill development is usually described in terms of three sequential trends. One is the *cephalocaudal trend*

*Cephalocaudal,
proximodistal, and
massed to
specialized activity*

I CAN DO IT MYSELF.

described in chapter 2. The cephalocaudal sequence in motor-skill development refers to development proceeding from the head downward. Another developmental sequence mentioned in chapter 2 is the *proximodistal trend.* Proximodistal development is development proceeding from the central regions of an organism to the extremities. A third kind of sequence, which characterizes skill development, is the *mass activity to specialized activity trend.* This trend describes the change in skill development from highly generalized action involving large muscles to more specialized behaviors involving small muscles.

Sequential development in posture and locomotion

Mary Shirley's (1933) work describing the acquisition of posture and locomotion skills illustrates the sequential orderliness of skill development. As shown in figure 4-6, by the time a child is 1 month old he is generally able to raise his chin when in a prone position. At 4 months a child will probably be able to sit with support. When 7 months of age he may be able to sit alone and shortly after he will be able to stand alone. At 10 months the child will often be able to creep with his stomach off the floor. At this point he not only broadens his contact with the environment, but also becomes a minor threat to person and prop-

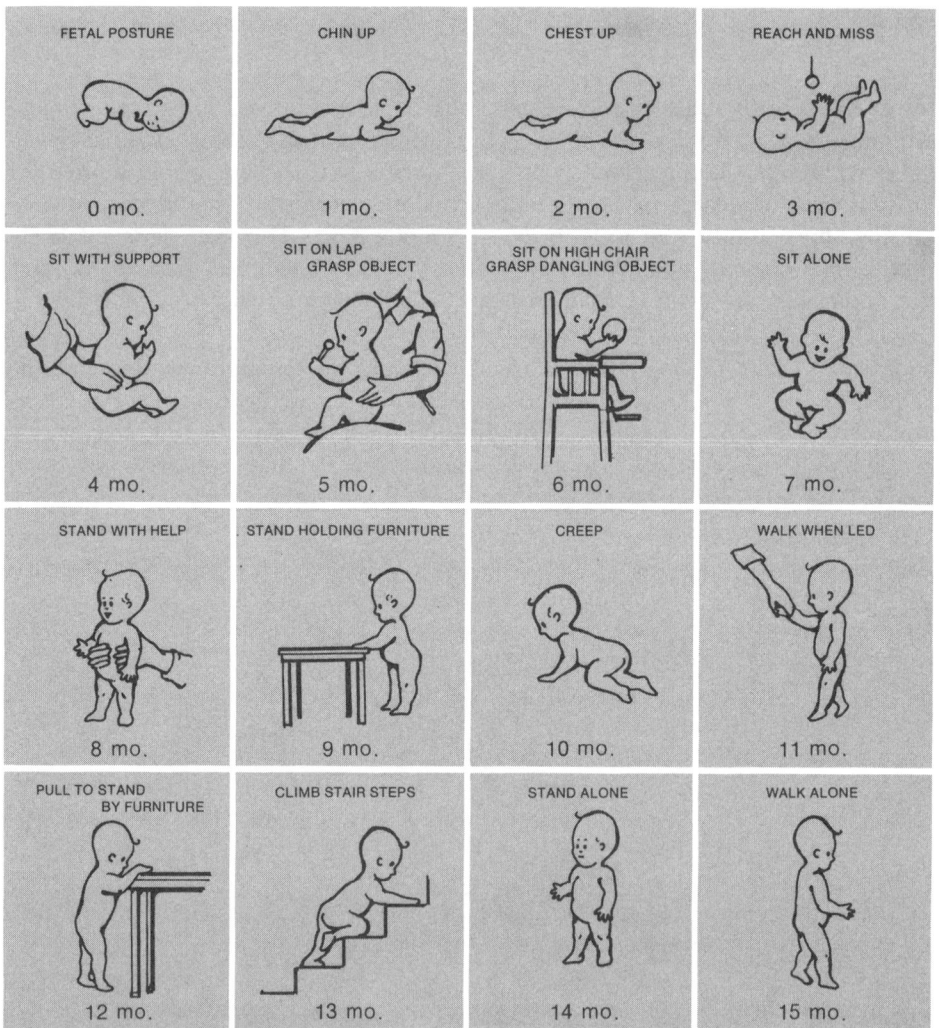

FETAL POSTURE	CHIN UP	CHEST UP	REACH AND MISS
0 mo.	1 mo.	2 mo.	3 mo.
SIT WITH SUPPORT	SIT ON LAP GRASP OBJECT	SIT ON HIGH CHAIR GRASP DANGLING OBJECT	SIT ALONE
4 mo.	5 mo.	6 mo.	7 mo.
STAND WITH HELP	STAND HOLDING FURNITURE	CREEP	WALK WHEN LED
8 mo.	9 mo.	10 mo.	11 mo.
PULL TO STAND BY FURNITURE	CLIMB STAIR STEPS	STAND ALONE	WALK ALONE
12 mo.	13 mo.	14 mo.	15 mo.

Figure 4-6   *The motor sequence. (From M. M. Shirley,* The first two years. Vol. II. Intellectual development. *Minneapolis: University of Minnesota Press, 1933, p. iv.)*

erty. The child can move with lightning speed from one breakable object to another, leaving a path of destruction slightly resembling that of a tornado. At 15 months the child will usually be able to walk. With this achievement his environmental horizons will be broadened still further and the problems associated with controlling his behavior become formidable indeed. Fortunately, he quickly learns to avoid most dangerous situations and to conform to many of the constraints imposed upon his physical curiosity and "free-wheeling" lifestyle by his parents. If this were not the case, no doubt the human species would not survive.

*Sequential
development in
grasping*

Another phylogenetic skill that reveals the sequential orderliness of development is visually directed grasping. During the early years of life children learn to grasp objects which they see. In the initial phases of development they will stare at an object but make no effort to reach it. When they are between 2 and 3 months of age, they will make unsuccessful grasping motions. By the time children are between 5 and 6 months of age, they will be able to make contact with the objects they are attempting to reach (White & Held, 1966).

Not only does the capacity to make contact with objects in the visual field follow an orderly sequence, but also changes in the manner of picking up objects take place in a predictable order. Halverson (1931) made detailed filmed records of the grasping behavior of young children. The sequence of development which Halverson discovered is shown in figure 4-7. When the child first becomes able to grasp an object, he simply squeezes it with his entire hand. At a somewhat more advanced stage, the child will grasp the object in his palm. At the most advanced stage of development, the child is able to grasp small objects with his thumb and two fingers.

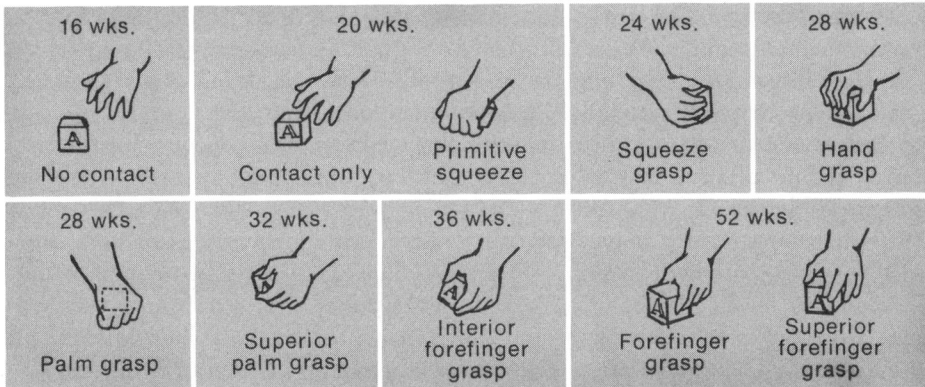

The development of prehension in the infant. (From H. M. Halverson, An experimental study of prehension in infants. Genetic Psychology Monographs, 1931, 10, 212-13.)   **Figure 4-7**

The progression of motor-skill development revealed by Shirley's observations follows the cephalocaudal sequence. Control of the head comes first. Then the child achieves mastery over the trunk. Finally, he learns to control his legs. The sequence in visually directed reaching and grasping follows the proximodistal developmental trend. Initial grasping efforts involve the control of the upper arm. Later the child masters movements of the hand. Finally, he achieves control of the fingers. The developmental sequences for both locomotion and visually directed grasping reveal a trend from mass activity involving large muscles to more specialized movements involving small muscles.

*Structural and
behavioral
development and
genetics*

Early developmentalists contended that the sequence of behavioral development followed the same sequence as that manifested by internal structures supporting such development. In addition, they held that the internal structures were controlled directly by genetic mechanisms. The behavior patterns of the growing child were thought to be in the main manifestations of a genetic blueprint which controlled action independently from environmental influences.

There is an abundance of evidence which supports the early developmental view of genetic control of behavior (see Thompson, 1954). For example, as pointed out earlier in the chapter, the development of neurological structures controlling the trunk and arms occurs before the development of structures controlling the movement of the legs. This is the same sequence as that described by Shirley in connection with locomotion. Clearly, genetic factors do influence motor development, but environmental conditions also play an important role in controlling motor-skill growth. For example, it is possible to accelerate the development of walking capability by providing early opportunities for practice. If a 1-week-old infant is held in a standing position, he will make a primitive reflexive attempt to walk. Normally this behavior disappears from the child's repertoire when he is about 2 months old. However, Zelazo, Zelazo, and Kolb (1972) demonstrated that it did not disappear in infants given practice in walking. They asked a group of mothers to spend 12 minutes per day providing practice in walking for their children from the second to eighth week after birth. The average age of walking for these infants was 10 months, which is over two months ahead of developmental expectations.

The discovery of orderly sequences in motor development and the attendant specification of age levels indicating the points at which the acquisition of individual skills might occur was greeted with great enthusiasm by parents and other socializing agents. Moreover, information of this kind continues to be widely used both in the home and in institutional settings responsible for the development of young children. Information regarding motor growth has achieved wide acceptance and use in part because it tells socializing agents whether or not a child is developing "normally." Development occurring ahead of schedule is generally a source of pride and hope for the future. Development occurring behind schedule often serves as a signal alerting socializing agents to possible growth problems.

Although norms for motor development do serve a useful function, they must be interpreted with caution. The rate (Shirley, 1933) and to some extent the sequence (Ames, 1937) of early skill development may vary among individuals. Moreover, early skill development is not predictive of later motor-skill accomplishment (Bayley, 1935). Knowing when a child learned to walk provides little information on the subsequent likelihood of skill mastery in baseball, swimming, tennis, or in other motor skills.

Motor-skills and intellectual development. A number of developmental theorists hold the view that there is a close relationship between motor development and intellectual growth. For example, Jean Piaget (1952), whose views will be discussed in detail in chapter 6, suggests that the earliest manifestations of intelligence are sensorimotor sequences. In Piaget's view, a child learns to represent environmental events through motor movements. A door opens and a child opens his clenched fist. The gesture is an intellectual representation of the event that he has just observed.

The assumed relationship between motor development and intellectual development has influenced the construction of a number of scales of infant intelligence. The earliest of these was a scale developed by Arnold Gesell (1925,

1928). One of the most widely used of current infant measures is the *Bayley Scales of Infant Development* (Bayley, 1969). Measures of infant intelligence tend to include a number of items dealing with motor development. The motor behaviors typically assessed involve such skills as body control, manual coordination, creeping, walking, and jumping.

One of the major functions of infant intelligence tests is to predict future intelligence. Generally, they have not been very successful in this. Regarding this point Kessen, Haith, and Salapatek (1970) comment:

> Their search has been for ways to foresee the later development of babies for practical (e.g., in justification of adoptive placement) as well as for theoretical reasons. But the literature supports the conclusion that, however well we may know the timing and sequence of many responses in the human infant as member of a species, we have not been able to devise procedures sufficient to the diagnostic and predictive task. (p. 306)

Although most of the literature fails to support the predictive value of infant scales, researchers have continued to study the predictive power of infant measures. Moreover, recent evidence suggests that the relationship between infant intelligence and intelligence in early childhood may be higher than has been previously suspected. Ronald Wilson (1974), using the Bayley Scales, found that knowledge of intelligence assessed at age 1½ years improved prediction of Wechsler intelligence-test scores obtained at age 6 years by about 20%. While this is not a large amount, it does suggest that there is some relationship between early intelligence assessed largely in terms of sensorimotor performance and later measures of intellectual capability.

PHYSICAL DEVELOPMENT AND CULTURE

One of the most significant facts to come out of developmental research is the pervasiveness of cultural differences in development. This is true for physical development as well as for other developmental processes. In this section of the chapter we shall examine some of the more significant cultural variations in physical development. Then we shall discuss the genetic and environmental factors that may influence development.

Cultural Variations in Physical Development

There are three major types of cultural differences in physical development. First, there are differences associated with ethnicity. People from different ethnic groups may differ markedly in physical growth and to some extent in motor-skill development. In addition to ethnic differences, there are social-class differences in physical development. Children from lower socioeconomic levels are generally behind children from higher socioeconomic levels in physical growth. Finally, for well over 100 years there have been differences in physical development occurring across generations. Children from middle-class backgrounds today are substantially more advanced physically than similar children of previous generations.

Ethnicity and physical development. Members of some cultures tend to be tall and thin while those with other cultural heritages tend to be short and stocky. Similarly, rate of motor-skill development occurs more rapidly in the early years in some cultural groups than it does in others.

Developmental patterns in two African tribes living in Rwanda illustrate ethnically related variations in physical growth (Hiernaux, 1963, 1964). One group, the Tutsi, tend to be tall and thin. The other group, the Hutu, are generally short and stocky. Throughout childhood the Tutsi grow at a faster rate than the Hutu, though both groups generally reach maturity at about the same age. Although the Tutsi and the Hutu share the same physical environment, the Tutsi, by virtue of being the ruling caste, are better nourished. This fact, of course, raises the possibility that the size differences between the groups may be at least in part environmentally based.

Geber's (1958) research comparing black children in Uganda with European children illustrates ethnic differences in motor-skill development. During the early years of life, Ugandan children tend to be well ahead of European children in motor-skill performance. On the first day after birth, Ugandan children can usually keep their heads from falling back when brought into a sitting position. Moreover, they will very likely be able to hold their backs straight. By the time the children are 6 weeks old, they will be able to control their heads regardless of body position. When 4 months old, they will be able to sit unattended. At 8 months they will be able to stand alone, and at 10 months they will be able to walk. On the average they will be about two to three months ahead of their European age-mates. These early developmental differences, however, will disappear in later years.

Social class and physical development. There are no important social-class differences in the development of motor skills (Ausubel & Sullivan, 1970). However, there are considerable differences in growth among social classes (Graffar & Corbier, 1966). Specifically, children from higher social strata tend to be taller at all ages than children from lower social-class groups. For example, in Britain the difference in height between children of fathers holding professional and managerial positions and those whose fathers are unskilled laborers is presently about one inch for 3-year-olds and two inches for adolescents.

To some extent social-class differences in height are perpetuated by customs of social mobility which favor the upward mobility of tall persons and the downward mobility of short persons (Tanner, 1970). Tanner reports that regardless of their social class, tall women tend to marry men who have more prestigious jobs than those held by the husbands of short women.

Sexual development, like height, is class related. Tanner (1970) reports that the typical lower-class girl in European countries reaches menarche from two to four months later than girls from the highest socioeconomic levels. A variety of factors may be contributing to class-related differences in sexual development. Among the most probable are differences in nutrition, sleep, and exercise occurring across social classes.

Developmental differences across generations: the secular trend. Over the past 100 years there has been a marked increase in the physical development of children at all ages. This increase is generally referred to as the secular trend in physical development. In most parts of the world the secular trend is still continuing. However, there is some evidence to suggest that for children in the higher socioeconomic classes of the United States, growth rate may have reached a maximum (Tanner, 1970).

The magnitude of the secular trend is shown in figure 4-8, which plots the heights of Swedish boys and girls in 1883 and 1938-1939. The secular trend starts shortly after birth and continues throughout childhood and adolescence. During

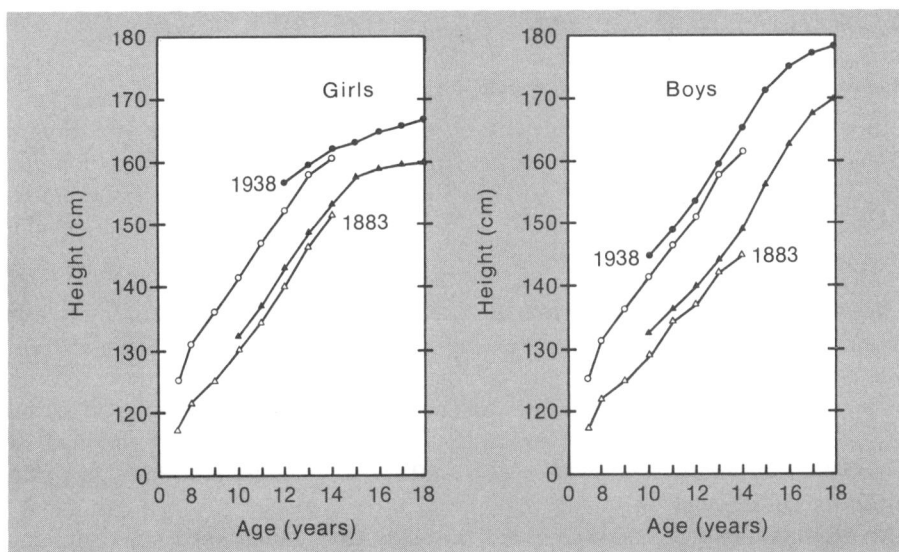

Secular trend in growth of height. Height of Swedish girls and boys measured in 1883 (lower curve) and in 1938-1939. Elementary schools 7-14, secondary schools 10-18. (From J. M. Tanner, Growth at adolescence *(2nd ed.). Oxford: Basil Blackwell, 1962, p. 144.)*   **Figure 4-8**

the beginning school years there is approximately a 1 to 2 centimeter difference in height across each decade. When children are between 10 and 14 years the difference for each decade is 2 to 3 centimeters (Tanner, 1970).

Adult height has also risen during the twentieth century, but to a smaller degree than height in children. Until recently full height was not reached until about the age of 25. Now it is usually achieved by the time an individual is 18 or 19 years old. It is for this reason that the magnitude of the secular trend is not as great for adults as it is for children. Nonetheless, there is a difference in height between contemporary adults and adults of earlier generations. The difference currently amounts to about 0.3 centimeters per decade (Tanner, 1970).

The secular trend is manifested in sexual development as well as in height. As indicated in figure 4-9, in the middle 1800s the typical age of girls in Norway at menarche was 17 years. By the 1950s it was approximately 13 years in a number of countries.

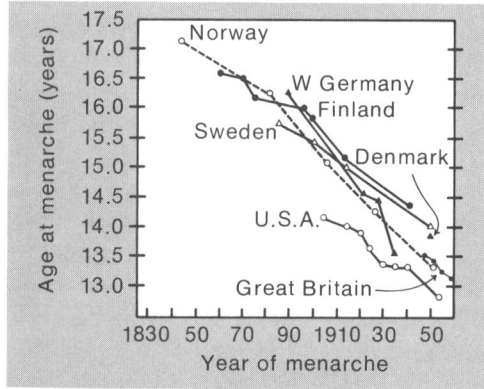

Figure 4-9   *Secular trend in age at menarche, 1830-1960. (From J. M. Tanner,* Growth at adolescence *(2nd ed.). Oxford: Basil Blackwell, 1962, p. 153.)*

Heredity, Environment, and Physical Development

Both genetic and environmental factors play a role in producing variations in physical development. The role of genetic influences is, no doubt, a dominant one. However, environmental conditions such as opportunity for activity, amount of available stimulation, and nutrition may also have profound effects on development.

Genetics and variations in development.   Without question genetic factors exert a dominant influence on physical development. They constitute a major determinant of both physical growth and motor-skill development. Insofar as genetic factors do influence physical development, they may impose limits on certain characteristics of a culture. For example, genetic influences on the physical size of people may influence the size of furniture, dwellings, clothing, and other cultural accouterments.

An abundance of research supports the view that genetic characteristics play a key role in determining physical growth. For example, in a typical case, identical (one-egg) twin girls are no more than two months apart in age when they reach menarche. On the other hand, sisters who are not twins may differ in age by as much as 10 months at menarche (Tanner, 1970).

Twin studies as evidence of genetic influences

Research on skeletal development also suggests the central role which genetic factors may play in determining growth. Reynolds (1943), for example, observed a higher degree of correspondence in the skeletal growth of identical twins than he found in the growth patterns of siblings.

As might be expected, studies of height reveal a strong genetic influence on growth. Identical twins are more similar in height than are siblings or parents and their offspring (Harris et al., 1930). Moreover, even though they do not share an identical genetic makeup, the degree of correspondence between siblings and between parents and their children is substantial.

Twin research suggests a strong genetic influence on phylogenetic motor-skill development. Stern (1949), for example, reported a greater degree of correspondence in the development of phylogenetic skills among identical twins than among fraternal (two-egg) twins.

Although genetic factors do play an important role in determining physical development, in the case of cultural variations in development, they do not exert their effects independently from the environment. As Darwin (1859) long ago pointed out, environmental factors very likely influence the selection of genetic traits in a given population. We can assume that environmental circumstances such as climate, physical terrain, and cultural characteristics favor the survival of certain genetic traits and discourage the survival of others. Given that environmental conditions do not change radically, genetic characteristics should conform increasingly to environmental demands over successive generations. Tanner (1970) suggests that despite recently high levels of population mobility we can still observe the effects of selection on growth characteristics in different populations. In this connection he writes:

Environment and natural selection

> The extent to which nutrition, climate, altitude, and other ecological conditions are the causes of the differences between populations is not known. We must presume that these ecological features originally governed the selection of growth-controlling genes and hence led to the emergence of the differences we see now. (p. 137)

Activity and environmental stimulation. Both the amount of activity engaged in by a child and the level of stimulation provided to the child may influence physical development. These two factors often covary in developmental environments. The child who is not receiving adequate stimulation may also lack opportunities for needed activity. Thus, he faces a double risk with respect to possible developmental impairment.

The potentially damaging effects of environments lacking in stimulation and opportunity for activity were first observed in studies of infants in institutional settings. An early investigation by Rene Spitz (1945) is one of the classics in the field. Spitz studied the effects of institutionalization of infants in a nursery and a foundling home. The nursery was a facility provided for the children of

Institutionalization and development

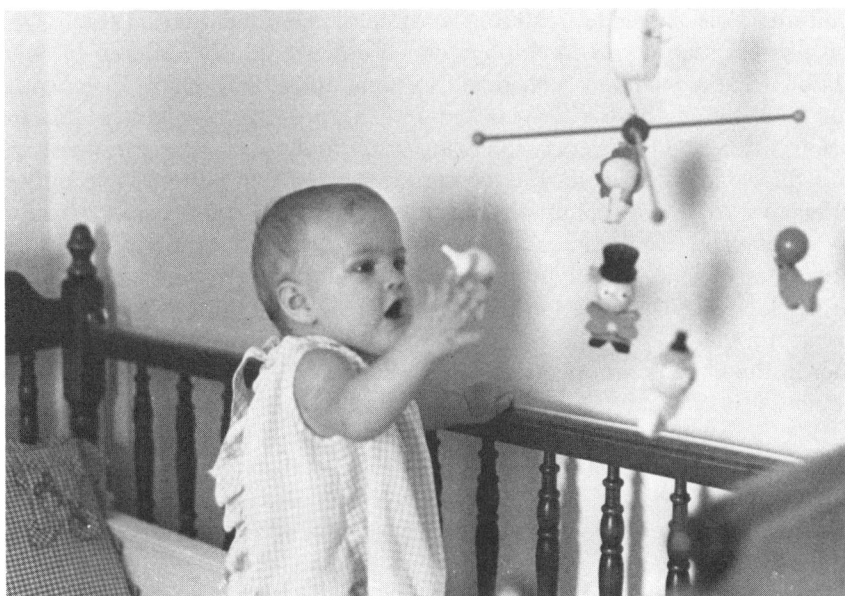

Visual stimulation invites motor response.

delinquent girls who were incarcerated in a local penal institution. The children in this setting had toys to play with. Moreover, they were subjected to a wide variety of environmental stimulation including social contact. They were cared for either by their mothers or by employees of the institution. The situation in the foundling home was quite different. Although the physical needs of the children were met adequately, they received very little stimulation and had little opportunity for movement. They had no toys and they were rarely held. The differences between these two groups of infants were profound. Not only were the foundling-home children retarded in both physical growth and motor-skill development, but they also suffered extensive social, emotional, and intellectual impairment.

Spitz interpreted the deficits which he observed as the consequences of a lack of mothering. However, other factors could have produced the observed differences. Differences in level of stimulation and opportunity for movement are two likely variables which may have affected the children's development (Thompson & Grusec, 1970).

Other studies of institutionalization have revealed findings similar to those reported by Spitz. Provence and Lipton (1962), for example, studied the development of children in a nursery which provided little stimulation and obtained results similar to those of Spitz. Dennis and Najarian (1957) observed children in a foundling home in Beirut, Lebanon. These investigators reported early impairment in infant intelligence which they attributed largely to deficits in motor skills. This impairment, however, was only temporary. By the time the children were 4 years old, their intelligence-test scores were within the normal range. Dennis (1960) studied the motor-skill development of children in three Iranian orphanages, two of which provided inadequate stimulation and opportunity for movement. The children in the two orphanages providing inadequate environments were retarded in motor-skill development. Moreover, the creeping stage, which normally precedes walking, failed to occur.

There have been a number of studies which have attempted to isolate the separate effects of stimulation and opportunity for movement on development.

Stimulation and development

Landauer and Whiting (1963) observed that adult height tended to be greater in cultures that subjected children to intensive stimulation in the form of physical stress than it was in cultures which did not subject children to stressful conditions. Stress included such practices as altering body features for cosmetic reasons, subjecting children to extreme temperatures, and subjecting children to abrasions. Adults in societies following such practices were observed to be two to three inches taller on the average than adults in cultures not subjecting children to early stress conditions. Factors other than stress could account for these differences. Environmental conditions such as the general hardships of life in stressful cultures might eventually produce tall, strong people through natural selection (Thompson & Grusec, 1970).

Extra stimulation may affect motor-skill development as well as growth. Earlier in the chapter we mentioned Geber's (1958) work revealing the extreme precociousness of Ugandan infants in motor-skill development. Geber suggested that this precociousness might have resulted from the abundance of extra stimulation which Ugandan infants receive during their early years. A Ugandan mother never leaves her child alone. When she does daily chores, she carries the infant on her back. She also sleeps with the infant and feeds him on demand. Geber suggested that the abundance of maternal stimulation which Ugandan infants receive could produce the high activity levels and attendant advancement in motor development frequently observed in these children.

Casler (1965) conducted an experiment on the effects of extra tactile stimulation provided to infants in an institutional setting. For a period of 10 weeks an experimenter provided the eight infants in the experimental group with 20 minutes of extra tactile stimulation. The experimental treatment involved saying the words "hello baby" every 60 seconds to get the child's attention. At the same time the experimenter touched the child. In a comparison group the experimenter said "hello baby," but did not provide tactile stimulation. Both groups declined in performance on a measure of infant intelligence. However, the experimental group of children performed significantly better than the control children on sensorimotor tasks measured by the intelligence scale.

Movement and development

A number of investigators have studied the effects of opportunity for movement on motor-skill development. For example, Spalding (1954) restricted the flight movements of swallows and observed a resulting impairment in flight capability. Dennis (1941) obtained similar results with another group of birds.

Dennis and Sayegh (1965) studied the effects of extra movement in children. As indicated earlier, Dennis and Najarian took the position that the intellectual retardation of infants raised in institutional settings was due primarily to lack of opportunity to develop motor skills measured on tests of infant intelligence. Dennis and Sayegh tested this hypothesis by providing institutionalized infants practice in sitting, watching, and manipulating objects. Infants given this kind of experience made significantly greater gains on a measure of infant intelligence than children in a comparison group who had not been given opportunities to practice basic motor skills.

The findings on level of activity and stimulation have special significance at the present time in American culture. As increasing numbers of young women enter the work force in American society, there will very likely be greater reliance on institutional facilities such as day-care services for the care of young children. The various studies of young children placed in institutional settings clearly indicate that the provision of adequate sensory stimulation and opportunity for motor movement cannot be left to chance. Societal institutions can provide adequate environmental conditions for the development of young children (Thompson & Grusec, 1970). However, there is no guarantee that they will unless specific provisions are made both for the implementation and evaluation of procedures to create environments that will stimulate growth.

Nutrition. Nutrition may play a highly significant role in determining physical development. Much of the early research on nutritional effects involved retrospective descriptions of growth variations associated with cataclysmic events such as war and depression. For example, Tanner (1970) summarizes data on *Height and weight* the height of children in Stuttgart, Germany from 1911 to 1953. These data are presented in figure 4-10. As you can see, there is a marked decrease in height toward the ends of World War I and World War II when the children in the city had inadequate food supplies.

Palmer (1935) studied three groups of Americans who were children during the Great Depression of the 1930s. One group involved children who were well-to-do and therefore well-fed during the depression years. The second group was comprised of children who were poor and remained poor throughout the depression, and the third group was made up of individuals who became poor during the depression. The first group was above average in height and weight. However, the second group was below average in these characteristics, and the third group dropped to below average on these growth measures.

Brain growth   There is evidence to suggest that malnutrition may affect brain growth as well as growth in height and weight. Winick, Rosso, and Waterlow (1970) reported results from autopsies of 16 Chilean and Jamaican children who died

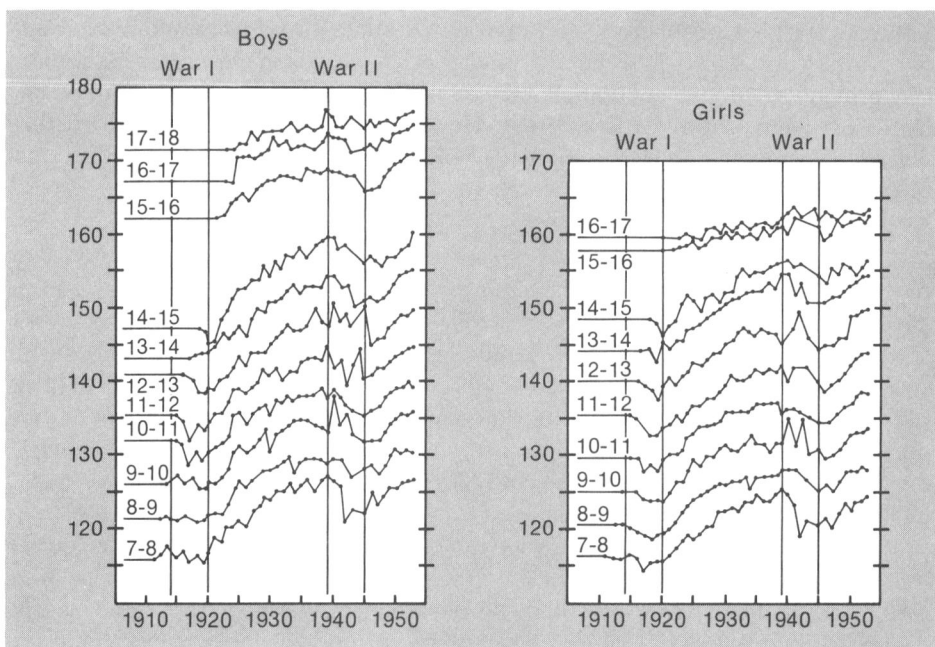

Figure 4-10   *Effect of malnutrition on growth in height. Heights of Stuttgart schoolchildren from 1911 to 1953. Lines connect points for children of same age and express secular trend and effect of war conditions. (From J. M. Tanner,* Growth at adolescence *(2nd ed.). Oxford: Basil Blackwell, 1962, p. 122.)*

of malnutrition before the age of two. All of these children had a substantially smaller number of brain cells than would be expected in a normal 2-year-old. Other autopsy studies have reported similar findings. Brown (1966), for example, summarized the results of autopsies assessing brain weight in over 1,000 Ugandan children. He found that brain weight was below normal for malnourished children.

Research findings on the relationship between nutrition and brain growth constitute one line of evidence suggesting that malnutrition may cause mental retardation. Recently there have been several studies which have investigated this possibility. Stoch and Smythe (1967), for example, matched 20 black infants living in South Africa and suffering from extreme malnutrition with children of the same age and sex who had not been subjected to an inadequate food supply. Both groups were selected from the lowest socioeconomic level in the culture. Stoch and Smythe estimated that the average intracranial volume was 13.7% less in the malnourished children than in their well-fed counterparts. Moreover, all the malnourished children scored substantially below the average for the well-nourished group on intelligence tests.

Nutrition and retardation

Warren (1973) has criticized studies of the influence of malnutrition on intelligence on methodological grounds. He argues that past research has failed to control for a number of variables other than nutrition that might affect intelligence. For example, malnourished children are often immobile for long periods of time. It may be that lack of movement results in restricted environmental stimulation which in turn impairs mental growth.

In the course of questioning conclusions from previous nutritional research, Warren cited preliminary data from a carefully controlled study being conducted by the Institute of Nutrition of Central America and Panama under the direction of R. E. Klein. These data suggested that:

> (a) nutritional and social variables largely overlap in accounting for psychological development; (b) malnutrition has a small unique effect, which could be temporary; and (c) motivational and attentional processes may be those affected. (Warren, 1973, p. 327)

It is too early to tell whether or not these preliminary conclusions are warranted. Thus, the extent of direct influence of malnutrition on mental retardation remains an open question.

In addition to the studies of malnutrition in children, there is research indicating that an inadequate diet in mothers may adversely affect child growth. For example, Burke, Harding, and Stuart (1943) observed a consistent relationship between protein consumption by expectant mothers during the last six months of pregnancy and size and weight of their infants.

Maternal malnutrition

Malnutrition in mothers during their own childhood years may also adversely influence the physical development of offspring. Women who have suffered early malnutrition tend to be small in stature. A fact of particular importance in this regard is that their pelvic areas tend to be small. Walker (1955) pointed out that infant mortality is higher in small women than in women of average size. Thomson (1959) observed an inverse relationship between mother's stature and fetal malformations and infant deaths. Montagu (1962) reported a relationship between stature and brain disorders in infants. Kaplan (1972) suggests that pelvic size may be a key factor in explaining the relationship between parental stature and brain disorders in infants. A small pelvis may increase the risk of birth trauma and attendant central-nervous-system damage to the child.

Although pelvic size might play a role in determining infant health, it should be pointed out that there are many other possible explanations for the observed disorders associated with stature. The mothers in the above studies tended to come from the lowest socioeconomic levels in society. They suffered from many problems other than small stature which could have contributed to infant disorders.

The cultural variations in growth described in the preceding section are all to some extent related to variations in nutrition. Growth variations associated with ethnicity, social class, and the secular trend all involve concomitant variations in dietary adequacy (Tanner, 1970). Thus, a child in the lower class is likely to be below average in growth and in nutrition. Similarly, ethnic groups which are below average on various indices of growth will also tend to have substandard diets.

The magnitude of the problem of providing adequate nutrition to the peoples of the world is immense. Warren (1973) suggests as a conservative estimate that one billion people on this earth go to bed hungry every night. Malnutrition is particularly severe in underdeveloped nations. In *The Limits to Growth*, Donella Meadows and her colleagues quote a 1970 United Nations' report which clearly illustrates the consequences of the food-shortage problem in underdeveloped countries:

> In Zambia, in Africa, 260 of every thousand babies born are dead before their first birthday. In India and Pakistan the ratio is 140 of every thousand; in Colombia it is 82. Many more die before they reach school age; others during the early school years.
> Where death certificates are issued for preschool infants in the poor countries, death is generally attributed to measles, pneumonia, dysentery, or some other disease. In fact these children are more likely to be victims of malnutrition. (1972, p. 57)

Meadows and her associates comment as follows on the magnitude of the food-shortage problem in nonindustrialized nations:

> No one knows exactly how many of the world's people are inadequately nourished today, but there is general agreement that the number is large—perhaps 50 to 60 percent of the population of the less industrialized countries, which means one-third of the population of the world. (1972, p. 57)

Food shortages are not limited to other countries. They exist in America as they do elsewhere. In 1968 the Citizens' Board of Inquiry into Hunger and Malnutrition in the United States published findings estimating that 10 million Americans were suffering from hunger and malnutrition. Who are these people? The answer, as might be expected, is that they are those at the lowest socioeconomic levels in society. Malnutrition in this country is a direct function of income (Citizens' Board, 1968).

The magnitude of world malnutrition and the developmental problems associated with it indicate an obvious need for massive social action. Although efforts have been initiated to deal with the problem of nutritional deficits (Kaplan, 1972), it seems likely that malnutrition will become even more severe in the years ahead than it has been in the past. As shown in figure 4-11, since 1650 world population has been expanding at an exponential rate. The capability of world food production to keep pace with the current rate of population expansion is open to serious question (Meadows et al., 1972).

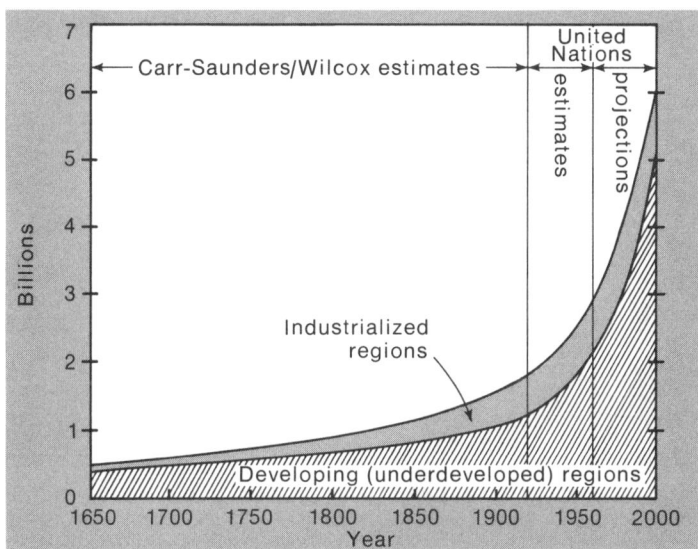

The exponential rate of population growth since 1650. (From D. J. Bogue, Principles
of demography. New York: John Wiley, 1969, p. 50.)   **Figure 4-11**

SUGGESTED READINGS

Dennis, W. Causes of retardation among institutional children: Iran. *Journal of Genetic Psychology,* 1960, *96,* 47-59.

Dennis, W., & Najarian, P. Infant development under environmental handicap. *Psychological Monographs,* 1957, *71,* No. 7.

Dennis, W., & Sayegh, Y. The effect of supplementary experiences upon the behavioral development of infants in institutions. *Child Development,* 1965, *36,* 81-90.

Geber, M. The psychomotor development of African children in the first year and the influence of maternal behavior. *Journal of Social Psychology,* 1958, *47,* 185-95.

Johnston, M. K., Kelley, C. S., Harris, F. R., & Wolf, M. M. An application of reinforcement principles to development of motor skills of a young child. *Child Development,* 1966, *37,* 379-87.

Kaplan, B. J. Malnutrition and mental deficiency. *Psychological Bulletin,* 1972, *78,* 321-34.

Shirley, M. M. A motor sequence favors the maturation theory. *Psychological Bulletin,* 1931, *28,* 204-5.

Tanner, J. M. Physical growth. In P. H. Mussen (Ed.), *Carmichael's manual of child psychology* (Vol. 1) (3rd ed.). New York: Wiley, 1970.

Warren, N. Malnutrition and mental development. *Psychological Bulletin,* 1973, *80,* 324-28.

White, B. L., & Held, R. Plasticity of sensory motor development. In J. F. Rosenblith & W. Allinsmith (Eds.), *Readings in child development and educational psychology* (2nd ed.). Boston: Allyn and Bacon, 1966.

Zelazo, N. A., Zelazo, P. R., & Kolb, S. Walking in the newborn. *Science,* 1972, *176,* 314-15.

Part Three

Cognitive Development

5

The Measurement of Intellectual Development: Psychometric Concepts in Contemporary Society

Instructional Objectives	Recognize or recall
	Compare and contrast
	Describe or demonstrate
	Evaluate

the meanings of norm-referenced assessment, IQ, and correlation.

the relationship of norm-referenced assessment of intelligence to societal thinking about intelligence in the twentieth century.

studies of the validity and reliability of intelligence tests.

the theory of general intelligence and the multiple-ability theory of intelligence.

the social consequences of describing children from different ethnic groups in terms of general intelligence.

the three dimensions in Guilford's structure of intellect.

implications of Guilford's model for socialization in contemporary society.

research on divergent production.

research findings on IQ similarity in related and unrelated persons.

research findings on the stability of intelligence from infancy through adolescence.

the critical-period hypothesis regarding the development of intelligence.

findings of research on the independent and combined influences of genetic and environmental factors on intelligence.

the findings and interpretations of research on the relationship between intelligence and social class.

the implications of research on intelligence and social class for socialization policies.

the findings and interpretations of research on intelligence and race.

the potential use of eugenics in controlling intelligence.

types of special-class placement used in adapting to individual differences in intelligence.

complaints of ethnic minorities regarding diagnostic labeling based on intelligence testing.

findings of the effects of diagnostic labels and assumptions about ability level on teacher judgment, teacher behavior, and student performance.

descriptions of socialization practices related to intellectual competence on the basis of existing research knowledge regarding hereditary and environmental influences on intelligence.

CHAPTER CONTENT

There is an old cliché in the field of psychology which asserts that intelligence is what an intelligence test measures. While this is not an entirely accurate statement, it is certainly the case that society's conceptions of intelligence and intellectual development are influenced by the manner in which intelligence is assessed. For most of this century intellectual growth has been measured by psychometric techniques initiated in the nineteenth century and developed technologically during the early part of the twentieth century. These techniques are among the most impressive accomplishments ever to come out of the field of psychology. They have enabled society to gain knowledge concerning the nature of intelligence, the characteristics of intellectual growth, and the diverse manifestations of intellectual competence in different individuals and social groups.

For many years psychometric theories and technology were accepted uncritically as accurate indices of intellectual capability. However, in recent years psychometric techniques have come under heavy attack. The reason for changes in attitude toward psychometric technology can be traced in part to changes in the character of society. Psychometric concepts were developed within the context of a society built upon the capability to discover natural and human resources and to apply those resources in productive channels. The intelligence test provided a useful tool in the effort to discover human resources. In recent years there has been a movement away from the former emphasis on resource discovery and use toward a conservation stance stressing the need to protect and to develop natural and human resources. The society in which psychometric concepts developed was a so-called "melting pot" society built upon the premise that varying cultural heritages should be blended into the cultural mainstream. In such a society, intellectual competence could be defined by tasks of importance in middle-class society. Today there is a movement toward a pluralistic society which values cultural diversity and stresses the protection of diverse cultural heritages. These changes in culture have created a need to reexamine psychometric concepts and their place in contemporary society and to interpret what we know of intellectual growth psychometrically in light of contemporary social views. The present chapter discusses psychometric concepts and the psychometric knowledge base as they relate to contemporary social themes.

PSYCHOMETRIC INTELLIGENCE FROM A SOCIAL PERSPECTIVE

Psychometric theories of intelligence assert that intelligence may be measured in terms of an individual's relative standing among his peers on an intelligence test. There are two variations of the psychometric position. One holds that intelligence is a general ability underlying effective performance in a variety of important life situations. The other takes the position that intelligence is comprised of a series of discrete abilities, all of which may enhance the effectiveness of individual performance at one time or another. Both the technology of the psychometric approach and the two major theoretical positions which have evolved from that technology have played a highly important role in shaping society's views on the nature of intelligence, on manifestations of intelligence in individuals and in societal groups, and on socialization practices intended to enhance intellectual growth.

Psychometric Technology and Its Social Implications

Over the past 100 years, psychometric theorists have developed an elaborate technology for measuring intellectual growth. Psychometric technology may be regarded as a set of tools which has enabled society to ask and to obtain at least tentative answers to some very important social questions related to intelligence. At the same time, psychometric technology may be thought of as a set of related points of view about intelligence which to some degree has predisposed society to ask the kinds of questions it has asked about the intellect and to adopt the socialization practices it has adopted with respect to intellectual development.

Norm-referenced assessment. The hallmark of psychometric technology is the strategy of describing individual intelligence in terms of group position. Today this strategy is referred to as norm-referenced assessment. The rudiments of the norm-referenced approach were developed by Francis Galton in the nineteenth century. His work has formed the cornerstone of psychometric technology. As a result, the effect of his ideas on socialization in Western culture has been monumental. Norm-referenced techniques have dominated theory and practice related to the measurement of intelligence during most of the twentieth century. They have shaped the great nature-nurture debate, they have provided the basis for what is known of ethnic-group and social-class differences in intelligence; and they have played a determining role in the design of socialization practices affecting intellectual development.

Galton led the Western world into the era of norm-referenced assessment by focusing on variability in intellectual performance among individuals rather than on average level of performance. Regarding the issue of variability, Galton (1869) wrote:

Galton's contribution to norm-referenced assessment

> It is difficult to understand why statisticians commonly limit their inquiries to averages, and do not revel in more comprehensive views. Their souls seem as dull to the charm of variety as that of the native of one of our flat English counties, whose retrospect of Switzerland was that, if its mountains could be thrown into its lakes, two nuisances would be got rid of at once. (p. 62)

Galton described variation in intelligence by referencing individual performance to group performance. An individual might be depicted as below average, average, or above average in a given group. With the development of testing technology during the first quarter of the twentieth century, it became common practice to construct norms for intelligence tests which could be used to specify individual performance in terms of group position. The process of norming is accomplished by administering test items to groups of individuals representing specified populations. The scores attained by individuals in these groups serve as norms for the test being developed. The performance of individuals who take the test after it has been normed is described by specifying their position in the appropriate norm group. For example, norms for the *Wechsler Intelligence Scale for Children*-Revised (WISC-R) were established by administering the Wechsler test to groups of children varying in age from six years to 16 years. The scores obtained for each of these age groups served as norms for the test. The intellectual performance of the children taking the test is described by referencing their scores to performance in the norm groups. For instance, the performance of a 6-year-old on the test would be described by specifying his position in the norm group of 6-year-olds.

IQ The term IQ (intelligence quotient) is generally used to denote norm-group position. The concept of IQ originally referred to the ratio of mental age (computed from the test score) to chronological age. However, the ratio IQ has been largely abandoned. In most of today's tests, IQ simply designates group standing. An IQ of 100 indicates average performance. Values above 100 denote above average performance, whereas those below 100 indicate below average performance.

Norm-referenced assessment and differences in intellectual functioning Galton's norm-referenced approach enabled him, and perhaps predisposed him and subsequently virtually all Western societies, to look for differences in intellectual performance. During the twentieth century, this emphasis on difference has become increasingly entwined with societal concerns regarding social-class, ethnic-group, and individual differences in intellectual development.

In the cases of social-class and ethnic composition, concern for differences has been translated into questions relating to differences in intelligence between lower-class and middle-class groups and to questions regarding differences between intelligence in whites and other ethnic groups. Findings related to questions revealing the existence of social-class and ethnic-group differences in intelligence raised further concerns. Do differences in intelligence contribute to differences in social station or are they a product of social station? Do differences in intelligence contribute significantly to differences in the level of and opportunity to enhance the productivity of the nation and to participate in the economic rewards attendant to productivity? Are social-class and ethnic-group differences in intelligence primarily determined by genetic or environmental factors? Finally, is the psychometric definition of intelligence too limited in scope to serve the needs of a pluralistic society? There may be significant cultural variations in the ways in which intelligence is cultivated and manifested. What is valued in one segment of society may not be in another. Many argue that it is not appropriate to impose standards for judging intelligence derived from the dominant middle-class culture on other groups in the social system.

Intelligence and selection Emphasis on differences has had its effect on societal thinking about individuals as well as about groups. Concern for individual differences has first of all fostered the development of a technology of selection supportive of a consumption-oriented approach to our human resources, which has to some extent paralleled our approach to natural resources. In the consumption-oriented approach, intelligence is regarded as a resource to be discovered. Individuals who possess this resource are assigned to positions presumably requiring a high level of intellectual competence and are rewarded economically and socially for accepting those positions and for carrying out the tasks required in them. The central agent in the discovery process is the school, and its principal tool is the test. John Gardner (1961) pointed out the school's role in the early 1960s:

> Our kind of society must make maximum use of the talent available. It needs desperately to find and train able individuals at many levels, and to an increasing degree modern educational systems are designed to accomplish that result. To the extent that they are not well fitted to achieve that end they are not modern. (p. 37)

Intelligence and adaptive socialization

Concern for individual differences has been manifested not only in the technology of selection, but also in a technology of adaptation to the individual. Indeed, the first practical test of intelligence, constructed by Alfred Binet around the turn of the century, was designed explicitly for the purpose of adapting socialization practices to the ability levels of children, particularly those children who were having difficulty in school. The Binet test was used to identify children who were having school problems because of a lack of intelligence. Binet's purpose in identifying children manifesting low intelligence was to avail them of special instruction designed to raise their intellectual level. Binet and his colleagues developed instructional methods which they called "mental orthopedics" for the purpose of raising the intellect. Regarding these Binet wrote:

> Having on our hands children who did not know how to listen, to pay attention, to keep quiet, we pictured our first duty as being not to teach them the facts that we thought would be most useful, but to *teach them how to learn*. We have there-fore devised . . . what we call exercises of mental orthopedics. . . . In the same way that physical orthopedics straightens a crooked spine, mental orthopedics strengthens, cultivates, and fortifies attention, memory, perception, judgment, and will. . . . (Tuddenham, 1962, p. 488)

Early developmentalists in the United States, most of whom were strongly influenced by G. Stanley Hall's views on the genetic determination of growth, generally did not share Binet's optimism about raising intellectual level. None-theless, they were strongly disposed to the idea of adapting socialization to ability level. Teachers and parents were advised not to push children beyond their intellectual capability. Activities in the school and in the home were designed to articulate to the child's intellectual level. For example, manufacturers of toys and games for children designed their products to match the average intellectual levels of children of various ages. This sound practice is, of course, still followed as a visit to any well-stocked toy store will reveal.

Most contemporary theorists are much closer in their thinking to Binet's position than to the views of the early developmentalists in this country. While they recognize that socialization practices ought to be adapted to intellectual level, they also believe that attempts should be made to increase intellectual capability. Unfortunately, although researchers have had some success in in-creasing intellectual competence in isolated instances, the nation has not yet developed the necessary technology to increase psychometric intelligence sys-tematically on a broad scale.

As the above discussion indicates, Galton's norm-referenced strategy has had an enormous influence on society's ideas about intelligence and on society's views concerning the nature of intelligence in groups and in individuals. The strategy of norm-referenced assessment, however, could not have had the impact that it has had without the development of an additional critical psychometric tool: correlational technology.

Correlational technology. As in the case of norm-referenced assessment, it was Galton who developed the basic rationale underlying correlational technology. Galton reasoned that relationships among phenomena could be measured by *Correlation* specifying in quantitative terms the extent to which the phenomena varied in the same way. For example, Galton felt that if fathers and sons tended to be about the same degree above or below average in intelligence, it ought to be possible to express that fact quantitatively. Galton asked a mathematician friend, Karl Pearson, to develop a quantitative index to represent relationships such as the degree of relatedness in father and son intelligence. Pearson constructed his famous index of correlation to meet Galton's needs.

The Pearson correlation statistic measures the extent of covariation between phenomena. The index has a range of from $+1$ to -1. The $+1$ indicates a perfect positive relationship, while the -1 represents a perfect negative relationship. Thus, if father and son intelligence varied in precisely the same way, the correlation expressing the extent of covariation between these two variables would be $+1$. If, on the other hand, bright parents had dull offspring and dull parents had bright offspring, and if this perplexing and unlikely state of affairs prevailed throughout the entire ability range, then the correlation between father and son intelligence would be -1.

Correlational technology provided a powerful tool which over the years has been used to establish the credibility of psychometric tests, to study genetic and environmental factors related to intellectual performance, and to investigate the nature of intelligence.

Intelligence testing became widespread in Western culture because correla-*Test validity* tional technology made it possible to present evidence of the credibility of intelligence tests. Before Binet had developed his test in France, J. McKeen Cattell had conducted extensive studies of mental capability in his laboratory in the United States. Initially Cattell's work attracted wide attention. Then Clark Wissler (1901) demonstrated that performance on Cattell's tests did not correlate to any significant degree with performance in school. Wissler's work and that of other investigators led professionals in the field to conclude that Cattell's tests did not really measure intelligence, for if they did they surely would have been related at least to some degree to school success. In contrast to Cattell, Binet wisely selected the items for his test in part on the basis of the extent to which they correlated with teacher judgments of school performance. Consequently his test in its completed form correlated highly with school success. The observed correlations between test performance and school performance were presented and widely accepted by professionals in the field as evidence of the validity of the claim that the test did indeed measure intelligence.

Validity studies today are much more sophisticated than those conducted by early researchers, but the fundamental rationale underlying validity claims has not changed. To the extent that test performance correlates with variables with which it ought to correlate, the validity of the test is presumed to be established.

Test reliability The issue of test credibility involves questions of reliability or consistency as well as validity. If, for example, intellectual level as measured by test performance changed capriciously from day to day, people would be unwilling to accept the claim that the test in question measured intelligence. Stability can be established by demonstrating a high correlation between test performance on two occasions. There are other forms of reliability and other ways to measure reliability, but in every case the stability of norm-referenced instruments is established by the use of correlation.

Correlational techniques have been widely applied in studies to determine the relative influences of genetic and environmental factors on intellectual performance. Studies of this sort require correlations between measures of intellectual performance taken on related and unrelated persons. Some investigations have assessed the relationships between intellectual levels of parents and their offspring. Others have dealt with the relatedness of intelligence among siblings and fraternal and identical twins.

*Correlation and
genetic influences
on intelligence*

Correlation has been the basic tool for studying the nature of psychometric intelligence. The mathematical techniques which have been developed for this purpose are quite involved, but they are all based on correlations. The fundamental question which researchers have asked in determining the nature of intelligence is to what extent various measures of ability correlate. To the extent that different measures are related to one another, it is assumed that they all measure the same ability. Insofar as measures do not correlate highly, it is assumed that they measure for the most part different abilities.

Psychometric Theories and Socialization

The application of correlational technology in studies of the nature of intelligence eventuated in two major psychometric theories of intelligence: the general-intelligence view and the multiple-ability view. Each of these has had some impact on socialization. However, the general-intelligence position has been more influential than the multiple-ability view.

The theory of general intelligence. The concept of general intelligence was first advanced by Charles Spearman (1904). It was ironic that Spearman should initiate the general-intelligence view since the correlational techniques which he developed to demonstrate the existence of general intelligence later served as the technological basis for multiple-ability theories. Nonetheless, Spearman's early work led him to conclude that ". . . all branches of intellectual activity have in common one fundamental function. . ." (Jenkins & Paterson, 1961, p. 72).

Spearman eventually included both general and specific abilities in his theory. Thus in the 1920s he wrote that individual measurements of ability:

Spearman

> . . . can be divided into two independent parts which possess the following momentous properties. The one part has been called the "general factor" and denoted by the letter *g*. . . . The second part has been called the "specific factor" and denoted by the letter *s*. (1927, pp. 74-75)

The idea of general intelligence holds that there is one common ability which underlies at least in part variations in performance on different kinds of intellectual tests. A given test may measure specific abilities in addition to general intelligence. Moreover, there may be variations in the extent to which a particular test measures general and specific abilities. However, insofar as there is some degree of correlation among the tests, it can be assumed that to some degree they all measure general ability.

The concept of general intelligence was thrust into the practical affairs of people as a result of the widespread use of the Binet test. This, too, was ironic because Binet believed that intelligence was comprised of a variety of abilities rather than one general ability. Binet regarded his test as a measure of an

The Binet test

individual's average level of intellectual functioning (Tuddenham, 1962). He included a variety of different types of intellectual tasks on his test ranging from memory for digits to the ability to recognize logical absurdities. He assumed that individual test scores reflected an overall level of performance with respect to the variety of specific abilities sampled by the measuring instrument. As indicated in table 5-1, which describes some items from the 1960 *Stanford-Binet Intelligence Scale*, the variety built into the original test by Binet has persisted in subsequent versions of the instrument.

The key factor in the Binet test that promoted the notion of general intelligence was the fact that intellectual level was described in terms of a single score. Eventually it was discovered that the various items of the Binet test did measure a great deal of the same thing. Moreover, the numerous tests which

Table 5-1   *Some examples of content from the 1960* Stanford-Binet Intelligence Scale

Subtest Name	Subtest Activity
Year 2	
Three-Hole Form Board	The child must place three forms into the correct recessed areas on a form board.
Delayed Response	The child must locate an object after it has been hidden under a box and the box has been screened from view for 10 seconds.
Identifying Parts of the Body	The child is asked to point to various body parts (for example, the hair) on a paper doll.
Picture Vocabulary	The child is asked to name 18 common objects pictured on cards.
Year 6	
Vocabulary	The child is asked to define words which range in difficulty from very easy to very difficult.
Differences	The child must be able to tell the differences between specific animals and objects, such as a bird and a dog.
Mutilated Pictures	The child is shown a series of pictures and is asked to determine which part is missing from each one.
Number Concepts	The child is given 12 blocks and is asked to count out a certain number of them. This is repeated for several different numbers.

have been patterned after the Binet have been found to a large extent to
measure one ability.

The representation of intelligence by a single test score has had enormous
practical consequences for views on socialization in that it has predisposed
educators and social-policy makers to compare the skills of different individuals
and groups along a single dimension. For example, consider the child who is
black and poor and who is described as less intelligent than the child who
is middle-class and white. Under the assumption of general intelligence, the
possibility that these two kinds of children may have different types of ability
which enable them to function effectively in their own environments is largely
ignored.

*General
intelligence and
socialization*

We know today that what has been described by psychometric theorists as
general intelligence is comprised mainly of verbal skills, which are highly prized
within the mainstream of middle-class society and which represent the kinds of
competencies that socializing agents within middle-class culture wish to cultivate
in the young. These verbal skills are related to school success, which is not at
all surprising given the premium which schools place on the mastery of verbal
material. Whether or not the awesome label of intelligence should be attached
to these verbal competencies is open to serious question. The term *intelligence*
is widely used when referring to test performance; however, some investigators
feel that the association of the label *intelligence* with tests of verbal ability should
be dropped (e.g., see Jencks et al., 1972).

The multiple-ability theory. The multiple-ability theory of intelligence holds
that intelligence is composed of a variety of specific abilities. Multiple-ability
research has revealed great diversity in intellectual capabilities and has shown
the relationship of diverse competencies to problem-solving activities. In so
doing it has contributed knowledge useful in implementing socialization practices
based on contemporary social themes recognizing the importance of problem-
solving skills in a society such as ours characterized by rapid cultural change.

L. L. Thurstone (1948) was the first theorist to develop an empirically based
multiple-ability theory of intelligence. Using Spearman's early work as a starting
point, Thurstone constructed the mathematical technique of multiple-factor analysis. This procedure enabled him to represent clusterings of correlations among
tests quantitatively. Thurstone applied multiple-factor analysis in investigations

*Thurstone's
primary mental
abilities*

*Intelligence involves more
than verbal skills.*

of a variety of different mental tests and after extensive studies concluded that intelligence was composed of seven primary abilities: verbal comprehension, word fluency, computational facility, spatial visualization, associational memory, perceptual speed, and reasoning ability.

Other investigators discovered additional abilities and thereby suggested that Thurstone's primary mental abilities theory was too limited in scope. Recognition of the limited scope of Thurstone's conceptualization of the intellect led J. P. Guilford (1967) to develop his comprehensive model of intelligence.

Guilford's model   Guildford's structure of intellect model, shown pictorially in figure 5-1, postulates the existence of 120 different intellectual abilities. Guilford conceptualized intellectual abilities in terms of three dimensions: operations, products, and contents.

Operations   The operations dimension classifies the kinds of mental operations which may be involved in performing intellectual tasks. Included here are cognition (i.e., perceptual recognition or knowledge about objects or events), memory, convergent production (i.e., problem-solving behavior which leads to one correct answer), divergent production (i.e., the generation of a variety of different ideas on a topic), and evaluation (i.e., the ability to judge objects or events against a standard).

Products   The second major dimension of the model is the product dimension. This dimension classifies the types of information upon which mental operations are performed. There are six product categories including: units, classes, relations, systems, transformations, and implications. Information units refer to elemental types of information. Intellectual responses producing units generate information without reference to any superordinate category. An example of a task involving the cognition of information units would be recognizing the letters of the alphabet. Classes refer to categories of information. Responses producing classes specify a superordinate category to which units of information belong. Sorting words into classes such as parts of speech is an example of a task involving the production of information classes. Relations refer to correspondences between things. The test item shown in figure 5-2 depicts a task in the relations category.

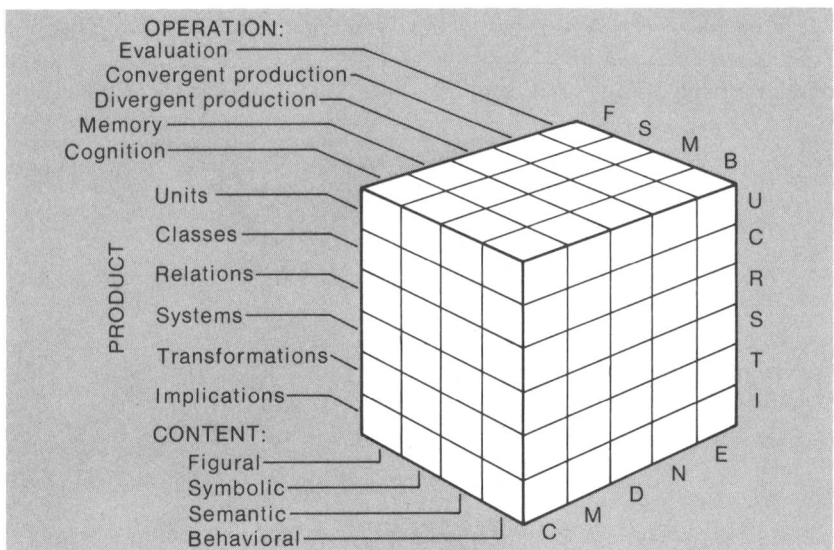

Figure 5-1   *Guilford's structure-of-intellect model. (From J. P. Guilford,* The nature of human intelligence. *New York: McGraw-Hill, 1967, p. 63.)*

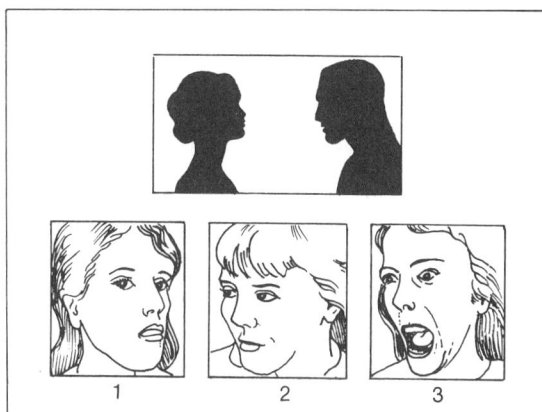

Figure 5-2

Which of the three female faces below most likely goes with the girl in silhouette, in view of the two postures? The skeptical expression of number 1 seems to satisfy the two related postures. The girl is not just thoughtful, nor is she agitated. (From J. P. Guilford, The nature of human intelligence. *New York: McGraw-Hill, 1967, p. 90. Silhouettes from Robert H. Knapp.)*

The item requires the individual taking the test to identify a social relationship revealed in the postures of two silhouetted figures. Systems are patterns of information. A familiar example of a task involving the production of information systems is that of recalling melodies. Transformations are changes in information. Figure 5-3 shows a task involving the cognition of a social transformation. The problem is to identify which of the three facial expressions in the lower half of the figure represents the greatest change from the expression in the upper half of the figure. Implications are information products which indicate what one expects to happen on the basis of available evidence. The cartoon in figure 5-4 illustrates a task involving the production of an implication. The problem in this example is to determine what is most likely to happen next to the individual shown precariously hanging from the rain gutter in the top half of the figure.

The third dimension of the structure of intellect model is the content dimen- *Contents*
sion. This dimension classifies the type of material upon which intellectual operations are performed. There are four content categories: figural content, symbolic

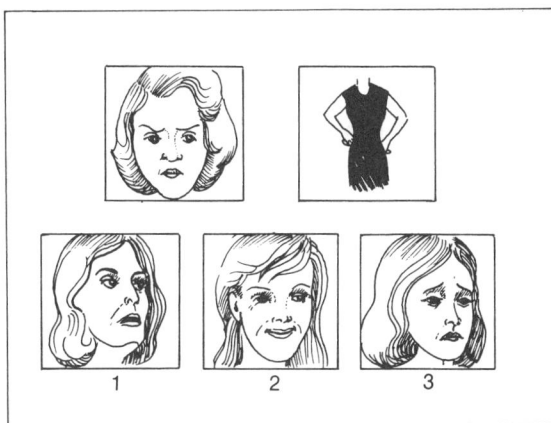

Figure 5-3

An item from Expression Exchange. Imagine the head at the top placed on the body at its right. Then decide which of the three heads below would change the behavioral meaning of the body most if it replaced the first head. (From J. P. Guilford, The nature of human intelligence. *New York: McGraw-Hill, 1967, p. 103.)*

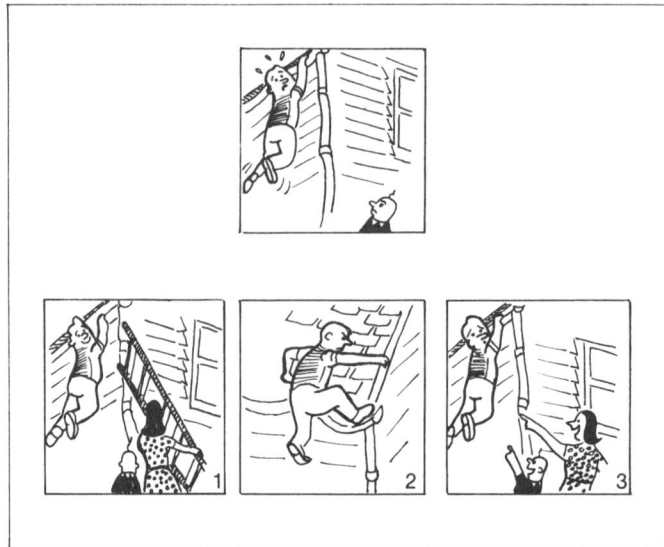

Figure 5-4   *An item from Cartoon Predictions. Starting with the scene above, state which of the three alternative scenes below is most likely to come next, all visible cues being considered and human nature being what it is. (From M. O'Sullivan and J. P. Guilford, Cartoon predictions. Orange, Calif.: Sheridan Psychological Services, 1965.)*

content, behavioral content, and semantic content. Figural content deals with the sensory qualities of objects (e.g., form, color, pitch). Symbolic content refers to material used as symbols in the culture (numbers and letters, for example). Semantic content deals with the meanings of symbols, objects, and events. Behavioral content refers to social actions and interactions such as those depicted in figures 5-2, 5-3, and 5-4.

Intelligence as problem solving

Guilford conceives of intelligent behavior as the coordinated application of intellectual operations on content to produce information products. In its highest form, intelligence is creative problem-solving ability requiring the use of all of the intellectual operations in the structure of intellect model. Cognition abilities are required to provide an adequate information base to solve problems. Memory is needed for the recall of information used in achieving problem solutions. Divergent production is useful in generating a variety of ideas which may lead to problem solutions. Convergent production abilities are useful at those points in the problem-solving process in which a single correct answer is required. Finally, evaluation abilities may be used in judging the adequacy of problem solutions and the methods used to attain them.

Creative problem solving may take various forms depending on the content of the material involved and the type of information product required. For example, artistic productions often require the production of figural systems and transformations. An artist preparing a sculpture may make a variety of sketches presenting alternative versions (i.e., transformations) of the overall pattern (i.e., system) of the figure to be produced. On the other hand, problem solving in the sciences may involve operations on symbolic and semantic material to produce a variety of types of information products.

Problem solving and cultural change

The structure of intellect model suggests a view of the intellect that relates well to contemporary societal needs. In slowly changing societies, such as those found in the pre-industrial period and in the early phases of industrial Western culture, the most widely used intellectual capabilities are those which enable the individual to amass necessary knowledge and skills to be applied in preestablished ways upon entering the adult work force. Modern technological culture is characterized by rapid change. In a culture of change, new challenges are continually arising. Here the central competency required is creative problem-solving ability. As Toffler points out, what is needed in our culture with its rapidly expanding knowledge base is:

> . . . not millions of lightly lettered men, ready to work in unison at endlessly repetitious jobs, . . . but men who can make critical judgments, who can weave their way through novel environments, who are quick to spot new relationships in the rapidly changing reality. It (the culture of change) requires men, who in C. P. Snow's compelling term, "have the future in their bones." (1970, pp. 402-403)

The structure of intellect and socialization

The structure of intellect model raises new possibilities for socialization practices designed to enhance creative problem solving. It suggests that efforts to promote the development of problem-solving capabilities might involve teaching children how to apply a range of intellectual operations in creative production. A substantial amount of work of this sort has been done on an experimental basis in the area of divergent-production abilities.

Research and applications relating to divergent production

Some of the early research on divergent production focused on the problem of determining whether or not divergent-production skills played an important role in creativity. A number of these studies revealed moderate relationships between divergent thinking and creative production. Jones (1960), for example, conducted a study with sixth grade children which investigated the relationships between measures of literary and artistic production and tests of divergent thinking. In this study, children's art work and written compositions were rated by expert judges. Tests of divergent thinking involving semantic content and figural content correlated significantly with measures of creative production. As might be expected, verbal-test scores were superior to figural scores in predicting creative writing. Conversely, figural-test results were superior to verbal scores in predicting artistic production.

Studies of the relationship between divergent thought and creativity were followed by a variety of research efforts to teach divergent-production skills. For example, Zimmerman and Dialessi (1973) demonstrated that fifth grade children's divergent-production capabilities could be increased through observation of a televised model. In their study, children watched an adult on television in the process of emitting divergent verbalizations. In one condition the adult model, whose task was to name unusual ways to use cardboard boxes, demonstrated the ability to generate many ideas in a short time period. In a 90-second interval the model generated 18 responses. In another condition involving the same task, the model generated only six responses in 90 seconds. Children who observed the rapidly responding model emitted significantly more verbalizations on a subsequent divergent-production task than did children who observed the model demonstrating a low verbalization rate.

Meichenbaum (1975), working with college students, demonstrated that divergent production could be enhanced by altering self-instructions. For example, he found that many of the students with whom he worked initially expressed negative comments about their own creative abilities. He used modeling to show students how they could replace self-criticism with verbalizations that might enhance divergent production. The model taught the students to practice saying such things as: *think of something no one else will think of; don't worry what others think; elaborate on ideas; free-associate; let ideas flow.* Rehearsal of statements such as these significantly improved divergent-production performance.

Not only has there been a substantial amount of research on divergent production, but also there has been a great deal written on ways in which socializing agents can use what is known about divergent thought to foster creativity (e.g., see Torrance, 1962; 1965). Despite the extensive literature which now exists on divergent thinking, what is known about the subject has not yet been widely applied in socialization practice. For example, one of the major ways in which socializing agents influence the intellectual behavior of children in educational settings is through the kinds of questions they ask. The teacher who says *In what year did the French Revolution begin?* directs the student to display simple cognition. On the other hand, suppose that a teacher were to say: *Charles Dickens opens his novel* A Tale of Two Cities *with the paradoxical assertion that the period just before the French Revolution was both the best of times and the worst of times. Would you think of as many ways as you can that the people in power during this period could have capitalized on the positive aspects of conditions of the day to forestall the blood bath which followed?* The teacher in the above illustration is calling for divergent production. The students are being asked to view history from a problem-solving point of view.

One of the authors participated in a study to determine the kinds of questions which teachers tend to ask students (Zimmerman & Bergan, 1971). The investigation involved teachers in both rural and urban schools scattered across the entire nation. It included a heavy concentration of schools using "open classroom" procedures which stress the importance of teaching students to be creative problem solvers. The disappointing finding was that the vast majority of teacher questions recorded required nothing more from students than the simple recall of information. Only a small percentage of questions called for divergent production. This is an unfortunate state of affairs since there is clear evidence that divergent thought can be enhanced through socialization efforts.

PSYCHOMETRIC INTELLIGENCE AND THE
NATURE-NURTURE DEBATE

During the first part of the twentieth century, it was generally assumed in this country that scores on intelligence tests were determined almost exclusively by genetic factors. Early developmentalists influenced by the biological model of development accepted the idea of genetic determination of intelligence uncritically. They advocated and to some degree were successful in promoting socialization policies and practices which stressed the need for parents and teachers to adapt their socialization efforts to the immutable and unique individual growth patterns of the child's developing intellect. However, as evidence of the potential influences on intellectual growth of the family, the school, and the cultural circumstances of the individual began to accumulate, the dominance of the genetic view began to weaken. As evidence of possible environmental influences on intelligence became more widely accepted, investigators turned their attention to the potential interaction which might occur between hereditary and environmental factors in determining intelligence. The interactive view which evolved from recognition of environmental influences suggested an active stance toward intellectual development which, while recognizing the need for adapting socialization efforts to individual differences in ability, also stressed the need to stimulate intellectual growth through active intervention procedures.

Investigations of Genetic Influences

In the early 1900s, H. H. Goddard, the psychological director of the Vineland Training School for the mentally retarded and a former student of G. Stanley

WELL, DAD, IS IT MY HEREDITY OR MY ENVIRONMENT?

Hall, translated Binet's writings on his intelligence test into English. Binet, as we have mentioned, was an environmentalist who believed that intelligence was comprised of a variety of abilities. Goddard, however, added his own views concerning the nature of intelligence to his translation of the material dealing with Binet's test. Goddard had been strongly influenced by the ideas of his former teacher, G. S. Hall, and by the writings of Spearman. Thus, Goddard described intelligence as measured by the Binet test as genetically determined general intellectual ability. In delineating his position Goddard (1920) wrote:

> Stated in its boldest form our thesis is that the chief determiner of human conduct is a unitary mental process which we call intelligence: that this process is conditioned by a nervous mechanism which is inborn: that the degree of efficiency to be attained by that nervous mechanism and the consequent grade of intelligence or mental level for each individual is determined by the kind of chromosomes that come together with the union of the germ cells: that it is but little affected by any later influences except such serious accidents as may destroy part of the mechanism. (p. 1)

Goddard's views rode on the coattails of the popularity of the Binet test and thereby established the genetic view of intelligence as the dominant explanation of intellectual performance in the United States for over a half century. The genetic view was further bolstered by empirical studies demonstrating high correlations among intelligence-test scores for closely related persons and by investigations demonstrating that one's relative standing among one's peers on an intelligence test tended to remain stable over long time periods.

IQ similarity in related and unrelated people. Guilford has summarized the results of 56 studies involving 113 groups of related and unrelated people. His data are presented in table 5-2. This table indicates a very high median[1] correlation (.88) for identical twins reared together and a high median correlation

Twin studies

---

1. The median is the midpoint in a distribution of scores. The median correlations given are the middle values obtained in the various studies reported in table 5-2.

(.75) for identical twins reared apart. As these statistics show, the IQs of twins raised together are not much more closely related than the IQs of twins raised apart. This fact has led some investigators to conclude that environment plays a rather minor role in determining intelligence. This conclusion, however, overlooks possible environmental effects on the relationship between the IQs of twins reared separately.

Twins have characteristics which may produce similarities in their environments even when they are not reared together. These characteristics may account for part of the similarity in their intelligence levels. For example, shared physical characteristics or personality traits of twins may affect the way in which parents, teachers, and society in general react to them. Twins who are exceptionally affectionate at an early age may receive more verbal stimulation from doting adults than twins who spend an inordinate amount of time crying and squirming. Verbal stimulation in turn may influence cognitive development.

No attempt was made in any of the twin investigations to determine the degree of similarity in the environments of twins raised together or apart. Thus, it is entirely possible that the environments of twins reared separately may have been quite similar. Whatever environmental similarity there may have been presumably would contribute to the observed similarity in their intellectual levels.

Another type of twin investigation bearing on the nature-nurture controversy is represented by studies comparing identical and fraternal twins. Fraternal twins differ in their genetic makeup whereas identical twins do not; yet twins of both types may have very similar environments. As indicated in table 5-2, the median correlation for fraternal twins reared together is .53. This is substantially lower than the correlation for identical twins reared together. This finding suggests that genetic factors may play a major role in producing the high degree of observed similarity in the IQs of identical twins. The validity of this conclusion, however, is dependent upon the assumption that fraternal and identical twins reared together will probably have equally similar environments. This assumption may be unjustified. There may be similarities in physical characteristics and personality traits for identical twins which produce environmental similarities that would not exist for fraternal twins.

Table 5-2   *Correlations in Intelligence among Related and Unrelated Persons* *

Kind of pairing	Number of groups	Range of correlation coefficients	Median r
One-egg twins, reared together	15	.76–.95	.88
One-egg twins, reared apart	4	.62–.85	.75
Like-sex twins, from two eggs	11	.44–.87	.53
Unlike-sex twins	10	.38–.66	.53
Siblings, reared together	39	.30–.77	.49
Siblings, reared apart	3	.34–.49	.46
Parent-child, parent-reared	13	.22–.80	.52
Foster parent with child	4	.18–.39	.19
Unrelated, reared together	7	−.17–.31	.16
Unrelated, reared apart	7	−.04–.27	.09

* From data provided by L. Erlenmeyer-Kimling, enlarged from data published by Erlenmeyer-Kimling and Jarvik (1963) as reprinted in J. P. Guilford, *The nature of human intelligence.* New York: McGraw-Hill, 1967, p. 352.

A number of studies of intelligence-test performance have investigated parent-child correlations in IQ, correlations for siblings, and correlations for unrelated persons. As table 5-2 shows, related people generally have IQs which are more closely correlated than are the IQs of unrelated persons. However, in absolute terms the IQs of related people other than twins are not very highly correlated. Even if one assumed that the entire observed relationship in intelligence between related people were controlled genetically, there still would be a great deal of unaccounted-for variation in observed intelligence. For example, it can be shown mathematically that for the median data in table 5-2 knowledge of a parent's IQ improves prediction of the child's IQ by only 27%. This leaves 73% of the variation in the child's IQ to be accounted for by errors in measurement, environmental influences, and genetic factors which do not manifest themselves in the parent's IQ score.

Parent-child studies

Overall what can one conclude from the massive amount of data which Guilford has so concisely summarized? First of all, the evidence suggests that genetic factors do play a significant role in determining intelligence-test scores. However, the exact magnitude of the contribution of genetic factors is difficult to estimate. The evidence also suggests that environmental factors play a part in determining IQ. Again, it is hard to determine precisely how big a part they play. Finally, even if one assumed that genetic factors determined observed relationships in intelligence completely, one could not predict individual intelligence very precisely because even closely related people may not have very similar IQs.

Stability in intellectual growth. A second type of evidence offered in support of the assumption of genetic control of intelligence involved studies of stability in intellectual growth. In these investigations stability was typically determined by correlating test performance of a group of individuals at successive age levels. The general finding in these studies was that intellectual level tended to remain highly stable over long periods of time. Results of the famous Berkeley Growth Study (Bayley, 1949) and Berkeley Guidance Study (Honzik, Macfarlane, & Allen, 1948) presented in figure 5-5 illustrate the findings generally obtained in studies of stability in intellectual growth. The data in figure 5-5 show the correlations between IQs measured at age 18 and IQs assessed at successive age levels from infancy through age 17. As the reader can see in the figure, by the time children reach seven years of age, their IQs correlate quite highly with intelligence measured at age 18.

*Research findings
regarding
stability*

Figure 5-5 shows that the correlations between intelligence measured in infancy and in the preschool years and intelligence assessed at age 18 are quite low. For example, the relationship between intelligence measured during infancy and intelligence at age 18 approaches 0. As pointed out in chapter 4, the relationship between intelligence measured in infancy and intelligence assessed during the preschool years is also relatively small. A number of investigators explained the low relationships observed at early age levels by suggesting that tests administered during the early years measured different abilities from those assessed during the school years. Hofstaetter (1954), for example, concluded that infancy and preschool tests of intelligence measured nonverbal capabilities whereas tests administered during the school years dealt mainly with verbal capabilities.

*Interpretations
of findings on
stability*

Some environmentalists came to a different conclusion about the source of the low correlations obtained at young age levels. They argued for a "critical period" view of intellectual development which suggested that environmental factors exerted their maximum effects on development at early age levels (see, for example, Bloom, 1964). According to this view, a child deprived of an appropriate

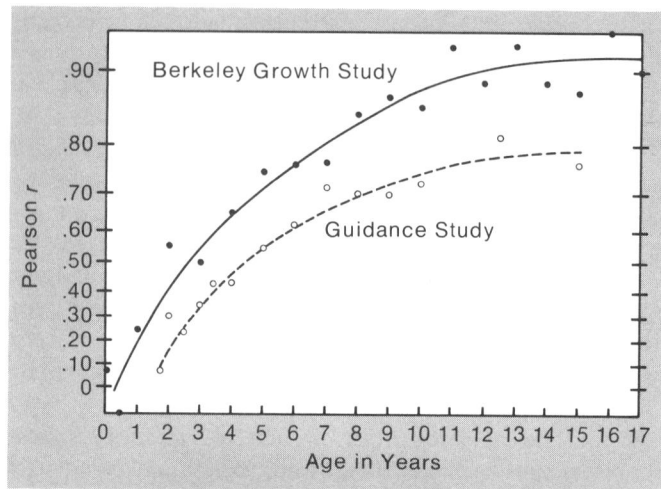

Figure 5-5   *Correlations of intelligence scores at age 18 with scores at successive earlier ages.
(From J. E. Jones, The environment and mental development. In L. Carmichael [Ed.],
Manual of child psychology. New York: Wiley, 1954, p. 639.)*

environment early in life would very likely be damaged intellectually. The
suggestion that intelligence was most vulnerable to influence in the early phases
of life was one of the major forces underlying the initiation of the massive Head-
Start program which was intended to raise the intellectual level of economically
disadvantaged children.

Further support for an environmental interpretation of findings of studies on
the stability of intellectual growth came from an examination of individual
changes in intelligence. Although in most instances intelligence does tend to be
highly stable over long time periods, in a small number of cases dramatic changes
in IQ have been observed as a function of age. For example, in 3 to 4% of the
cases in the Berkeley Guidance Study, IQ changes of the order of 60 points were
observed. Nativists explained these differences as manifestations of genetically
predetermined patterns of intellectual growth (e.g., see Goodenough & Maurer,
1942). Environmentalists suggested that alterations in the environment could
certainly be regarded as a likely source of changes of that extreme magnitude
(Hunt, 1961).

The studies of stability in intellectual growth, like the investigations of intelligence in related and unrelated persons, reveal evidence of both hereditary and
environmental influences on intelligence. The high degree of stability observed in
intellectual growth provides impressive support for the role of genetic factors in
determining intelligence. The low correlations obtained at young age levels and
the extreme changes in IQ observed in some individuals raise the possibility of
environmental influences on intellectual growth.

Investigations of Environmental Influences

Along with those studies designed primarily for the purpose of investigating
genetic influences on intelligence, there have been a large number of investigations directed at revealing environmental effects on intellectual growth. These
investigations have included assessments of cultural influences, family influences,
and school influences on intellectual development.

Cultural effects on intellectual development.   Studies of cultural variables affecting intellectual growth were among the earliest investigations of environmental

influences on intelligence. Investigations of cultural factors included case studies of changes in the intellectual levels of individuals who had migrated to a different cultural setting, changes in intellectual level associated with alterations in the cultural characteristics of a given location, and studies of changes in the intelligence of individuals who, because of institutional placement, had been deprived of cultural experiences.

Otto Klineberg (1935) conducted one of the most comprehensive early investigations of migration effects on intellectual growth. Klineberg set out to investigate the widely held assumption that the migration of large numbers of blacks from the South to northern cities was depleting the southern section of the nation of its most able black people. Differences in IQ between blacks in the North and blacks in the South had been well established, and it was generally assumed that the more able blacks from the then rural South were attracted to the potential opportunities for economic advancement in northern urban areas. Klineberg, however, found no evidence to suggest that blacks who left the South were any

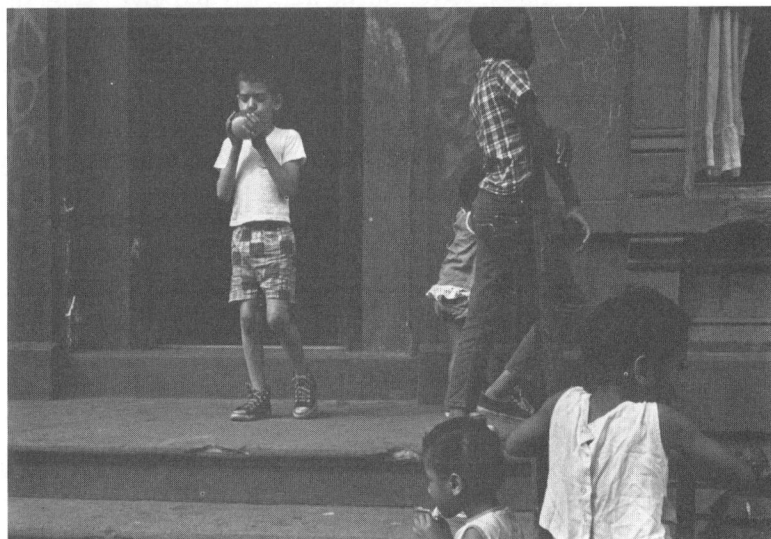

more able than those who remained. Rather, he observed a change in intellectual level associated with the amount of time spent in the North.

Klineberg's study had certain methodological flaws. However, it was subsequently replicated with greater methodological care by Lee (1951). Lee obtained IQ scores over a period of years on children in the Philadelphia public schools who had migrated from the South. He compared these scores with those of children raised from birth in Philadelphia. His findings confirmed those of Klineberg. Those children who had been in Philadelphia for an extended period had moderately higher IQs than they had attained when they had just entered the city. Moreover, after a number of years their intellectual levels were about the same as those who had been raised from birth in the city.

Similar kinds of results as those observed in migration studies have been found when the cultural characteristics of an area have undergone marked change. For example, Wheeler (1932) showed that children from east Tennessee who lived in rural areas largely isolated from the middle-class cultural mainstream had lower IQs than less isolated children. Ten years later, after the introduction of the Tennessee Valley Authority into the area, which was accompanied by increased road construction, increased availability of telephone communication, and the widespread introduction of the radio, the IQs of the children were markedly higher than they had been at the time of the previous study. This change could have occurred as a result of selective migration of able people into the area. On the other hand, it may also have resulted from an increase in cultural stimulation of the residents who had always lived there.

Studies of institutionalized children

Undoubtedly the most poignant investigations of the effects of cultural factors on intelligence are those which deal with the devastating influences on development of an inadequate environment early in life. As discussed in chapter 4, one of the most striking accounts of this kind of cultural deprivation was that rendered by Spitz (1945, 1946) and Spitz and Wolf (1947). These researchers studied the responses of children who had been separated from their mothers and placed in an institutional setting when they were infants. The infants initially reacted to the separation with agitation and irritability. Then they began to withdraw their attention from their surroundings. These symptoms disappeared if the infants were returned to their mothers. However, if separation continued, the infants deteriorated physically and mentally. Even though the children in the institution were adequately fed and given good medical care, 23 of the 88 children which Spitz observed died. In a ward of 26 children ranging between 18 months and 2½ years in age, only two could speak more than a couple of words, and only three could walk.

As pointed out earlier, Spitz concluded from his data that the effects which he observed were produced by maternal separation. This conclusion was certainly not warranted as there are a variety of possible causes for the retardation. For example, as we indicated in chapter 4, the institutionalized children may have received an inadequate level of sensory stimulation. It has been known for some time that cognitive functioning may deteriorate when individuals are deprived of sensory stimulation from the environment. Bexton, Heron, and Scott (1954) conducted the earliest of the so-called sensory deprivation studies. These researchers observed a marked deterioration in perceptual and cognitive functioning of college students who had been deprived of visual and auditory stimulation for a short time span.

Family influences on intellectual development. For most of this century, the potential influence of the family on intellectual development has tended to be largely overlooked. This state of affairs is understandable when one recalls that when the nation entered the era of universal public education, the major responsibility for educating all children in a society was transferred from the home and assigned to a social institution, the school. The task of promoting intellectual development under the system of universal education became the school's responsibility.

Intelligence, social class, and child-rearing practices

In the early 1960s, the primacy of the school's role in promoting cognitive growth began to be challenged. During this period Davé (1963) and Wolfe (1964) investigated the well-documented relationship between school achievement and social class. These investigators suggested that the relationship could be explained by differences in the child-rearing practices of middle-class and lower-class parents. They identified a number of practices which they felt would stimulate academic growth in children, including the extent to which parents read in the home and the extent to which they provided a variety of types of environmental stimulation to their children. Their studies revealed high correlations between these home variables and achievement in school.

Shortly after Davé and Wolfe conducted their investigations, Hess and Shipman (1970) carried out a classic study which also suggested that parental child-rearing practices could have a significant impact on intellectual growth. These investigators studied the teaching styles of middle-class and lower-class parents. Each mother who participated in their study was asked to teach her child to perform some simple tasks. For example, one task involved sorting plastic toys by color and function.

Hess and Shipman found marked differences in the ways in which middle-class and lower-class mothers instructed their children. Specifically, middle-class mothers tended to be much more elaborate and complete in their verbal instructions to children than did lower-class mothers. The following protocol provides an illustration of a middle-class mother's language patterns:

Parental teaching style may influence intellectual development.

"All right, Susan, this board is the place where we put the little toys; first of all you're supposed to learn how to place them according to color. Can you do that? The things that are all the same color you put in one section; in the second section you put another group of colors, and in the third section you put the last group of colors. Can you do that? Or would you like to see me do it first?" (Hess and Shipman, 1970, p. 182)

Here is an example of a lower-class mother's language for the same task:

"I've got some chairs and cars, do you want to play the game?" Child does not respond. Mother continues: "O.K. What's this?" (Hess and Shipman, 1970, p. 182)

Effects of socialization training on intelligence

Given the possibility that differences in child-rearing practices may influence cognitive development in children, is it feasible to attempt to alter parental practices and if one does alter them, will there be beneficial effects on intellectual growth? Gray and Klaus conducted a study which examined these questions. These investigators devised a training program to teach the mothers of economically disadvantaged preschoolers to stimulate intellectual growth in their children (Gray, 1971). The program was intended to foster attitudes and aptitudes related to school success. Attitudes selected for instruction included motivation to succeed in school activities, interest in school work, and persistence in participating in school-related tasks. Aptitudes involved the acquisition of perceptual discrimination skills and the development of language.

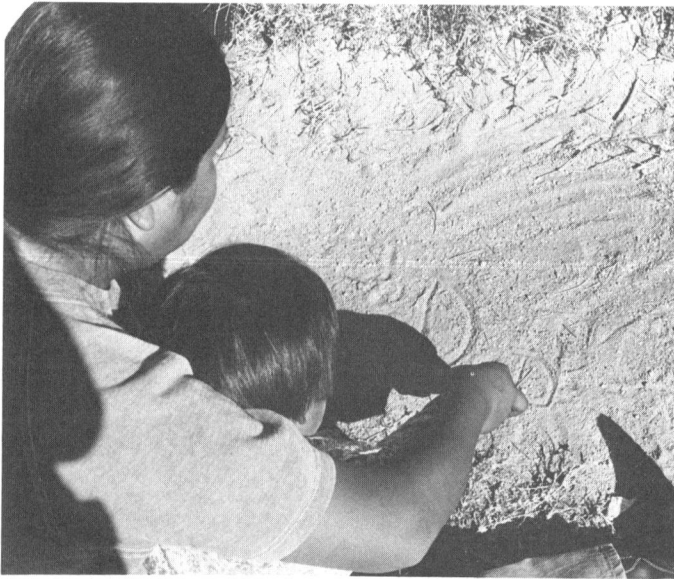

Children acquire intellectual capabilities through the kinds of interactions they have with their parents.

Gray and Klaus divided the children who participated in the study into experimental and control groups. Control-group children received no special instruction. On the other hand, the children in the experimental groups received instruction in a nursery-school setting during the summer. In this program the children were taught basic academic skills related to areas such as reading. For example, the teachers read stories to the children and encouraged them to look at the pictures in books and to tell what they thought was happening in a picture and what would be likely to happen next.

In the experimental condition, parents were trained by home visitors to work with their children during the fall following the summer program. The home visitors spent one hour per week in each child's home demonstrating procedures which parents were encouraged to implement in order to guide their children's cognitive growth. The home-visitor part of the study was in effect for only one year. However, the intellectual progress of experimental- and control-group children was evaluated periodically for several years. Over a six-year period the experimental groups performed consistently better than the control groups on the *Stanford-Binet Intelligence Scale*. However, there was some decline in IQ for both experimental and control children at the older age levels. School achievement levels also declined. Moreover, substantial differences in achievement observed between experimental and control children at early age levels disappeared by the time the children reached the fourth grade. These findings led Gray to conclude that an:

> . . . intervention program before school entrance simply cannot carry the entire burden of improving educability. An effective early intervention program for a preschool child, be it ever so good, cannot possibly be viewed as a form of innoculation whereby the child is immunized forever afterward to the effects of an inadequate home and a school inappropriate to his needs. (1971, p. 14)

Effects of schooling on intellectual development. During the early 1960s, amidst newly awakened social concern for the rights of all Americans to a quality education, the nation turned its attention to the comprehensive examination of its educational programs and at the same time launched a massive effort to improve the quality of education of economically disadvantaged children.

Interest in the assessment of educational programs evolved from concerns related to the inequality of educational opportunity between whites and minority-group children, which was tacitly assumed to exist by many social and educational theorists. The concern for inequality of opportunity was manifested in the following directive by Congress to the Office of Education in Section 402 of the Civil Rights Act of 1964.

> Sec. 402. The Commissioner shall conduct a survey and make a report to the President and the Congress, within two years of the enactment of this title, concerning the lack of availability of equal educational opportunities of individuals by reason of race, color, religion, or national origin in public educational institutions at all levels in the United States, its territories and possessions, and the District of Columbia.

This directive eventuated in the most comprehensive survey of the effects of schooling on cognitive skills ever undertaken. The survey was directed by James Coleman of Johns Hopkins University and was conducted on a sample of 4,000 schools involving 60,000 teachers and 570,000 school pupils. The results of this massive investigation were published in 1966 in a two-volume work which has come to be known as the "Coleman report" (Coleman et al., 1966).

The Coleman report

Coleman's findings constituted a seemingly devastating blow to the cherished hopes of those who believed that the quality of schooling was the key to the elimination of social and economic inequality long known to be associated with a lack of verbal skills of the sort measured by intelligence and achievement tests.[2]

The Coleman report distinguished between equality of educational input and equality of educational output. The surprising finding regarding input was that the schools of the poor and of ethnic minorities had instructional facilities and

---

2. The Coleman report focused on the examination of achievement test scores. Achievement tests are highly correlated with IQ. Many contemporary theorists hold that IQ tests and achievement tests measure a good deal of the same thing (e.g., see Jencks et al., 1972).

teaching staffs which, by available measurement standards, were of equal quality to those enjoyed by the white middle class. However, educational output, evaluated primarily in terms of achievement tests measuring verbal and numerical skills, was strikingly different for the poor and those from most ethnic minorities. With regard to the outcomes for ethnic groups, Coleman (1966) wrote:

> Thus, by the criterion . . . that the effectiveness of schools in creating equality of educational opportunity lies in making the conditional probabilities of success less conditional—the schools appear to fail. At the end of school, the conditional probabilities of high achievement are even *more* conditional upon racial or ethnic background than they are at the beginning of school. (p. 73)

In determining the source of ethnically based educational inequality, Coleman looked to the home:

> Altogether, *the sources of inequality of educational opportunity appear to lie first in the home itself and the cultural influences immediately surrounding the home; then they lie in the schools' ineffectiveness to free achievement from the impact of the home, and in the schools' cultural homogeneity which perpetuates the social influences of the home and its environs.* (1966, p. 74)

Reanalysis of Coleman's data

As would be expected, the Coleman report raised doubts in the minds of professionals. The report was written under tremendous time pressure, and many wondered if further analyses of the data might not reveal significant findings overlooked in the initial study. Almost as soon as the Coleman report appeared, a group at Harvard, under the leadership of Frederick Mosteller and Daniel P. Moynihan, undertook the task of reanalyzing the Coleman data. They published their findings in 1972 (Mosteller & Moynihan, 1972). Although the reanalysis produced many additional insights into the data, it essentially confirmed Coleman's earlier findings.

More recently Wiley and Harnischfeger (1974) have challenged the conclusions of the Coleman report and the Mosteller and Moynihan reanalysis of the Coleman data. They have asserted that both reports overlooked a crucial input variable, namely the number of days of schooling provided during the academic year. Their analysis of achievement in a small number of schools suggests that amount of schooling given in a year has dramatic effects on cognitive skills. The results of their small study have provided a promising lead which deserves further investigation. If their findings hold up in large-scale analyses of the sort conducted by Coleman, they will have significant implications for national policy dealing with the nurturance of intellectual development.

Head Start and the Westinghouse report

At about the same time that the comprehensive assessment of existing educational programs was undertaken, the nation initiated a number of large programs designed to stimulate the intellectual growth of poverty children. The most comprehensive of these was the national Head Start program. The Head Start program was designed primarily to enhance the cognitive skills of children through instruction provided at the preschool and kindergarten levels.

In the late '60s, the Westinghouse Learning Corporation (1969) published its evaluation of the effects of Head Start on intellectual development. The results were disappointing. The report concluded that neither year-round nor summer Head Start programs had any significant long-term impact on cognitive development.

Planned variation studies

The findings of the Coleman report and the Head Start evaluation suggested to some professionals in the field that it was not sufficient for the government simply to provide funds for educational programs to eliminate cognitive inequality between the economically disadvantaged and the economically advantaged. Attention would also have to be given to the kind of educational experiences provided for children. A number of studies were conducted in connection with this hypothesis. Joan Bissell (1970) of the Office of Child Development conducted an analysis of a number of small-scale investigations of different kinds of programs and concluded that highly structured preschool programs aimed at promoting specific cognitive skills (e.g., letter recognition, counting skills, and basic language skills) did have an effect on cognitive skills measured by IQ tests.

Unfortunately, small-scale investigations do not insure the feasibility of producing massive changes in cognitive skills. Perhaps the most blatant error in judgment which characterized the enthusiastic and optimistic socialization efforts of the 1960s was that of implicitly assuming that given sufficient financial resources, sound socialization practices would immediately be implemented. This assumption was faulty on two counts. First, we are not entirely sure what constitutes sound socialization practices with respect to the task of stimulating intellectual development. Second, we know very little about how to deliver scientific knowledge about socialization practices in a manner which will produce change in the behavior of socialization agents. Until we know more about the coordination of scientific knowledge with socialization practices and the delivery of scientific knowledge to socialization agents, it seems unrealistic to expect massive changes in the cognitive capabilities of children.

Independent and Combined Effects of Genetic and Environmental Variables

As the controversy over the contribution of hereditary and environmental factors to intellectual development ripened, it became apparent that intelligence should not be construed as resulting only from the independent influences of genetic and environmental conditions. The combined effects of these two variables could very well exert a powerful influence on intellectual growth over and above the direct contribution of either of them taken separately. Recognition of the combined influences of hereditary and environmental factors represents the central contribution of psychometric theories to what we have called the interactive stance of modern developmental psychology.

We shall describe two investigations of the independent and combined effects of genetic and environmental variables on intelligence. As you will see, these two reports have produced widely discrepant findings and both have generated a furor of controversy.

The Jensen position: IQ determined largely by genetic factors. In the late 1960s Arthur Jensen (1969) published an article in the *Harvard Educational Review* which jarred the sensibilities of the liberal social-science community. The article was entitled "How Much Can We Boost IQ and Scholastic Achievement?" In the course of 123 pages of intricate argument exploring the complexities of genetic theory and available evidence on genetic and environmental influences, Jensen answered his question by saying that educational efforts to boost IQ represent a misdirection of educational resources which might better be put to other uses.

Jensen suggested that variations among individuals in IQ can be described as a function of genetic variations, variations due to assortative mating (i.e., the tendency of people who have similar characteristics to mate with one another), variations in environment, combined variations involving hereditary and environmental factors, and measurement error.

Jensen presented evidence from a number of investigations that genetic factors constitute the principal source of variation in IQ among individuals. For example, he cited data presented by Burt (1958) which suggested that genetic influences account for between 77% and 87% of the variation in IQ of English children in the London area. The variation accounted for by the association between hereditary and environmental factors was estimated to be somewhere between 1% and 10%, a small figure indeed. Environmental effects were shown to account for only 6% of the variation in IQ scores.

The Jencks position: environment is important. In the late 1960s, Christopher Jencks assembled a group at Harvard to do a further analysis of cognitive inequality in America. The results of this effort eventuated in the publication of the book *Inequality: A Reassessment of the Effect of Family and Schooling in America* (1972). A part of this book dealt with the question of the independent and combined influences of hereditary and environmental factors on intelligence.

Jencks and his colleagues (1972) suggested that variations in IQ among individuals occur as a function of genetic variation, environmental variation, and the combined variation of hereditary and environmental factors. They analyzed three kinds of data in determining their estimates of the contributions of hereditary, environmental, and combined influences on intelligence. These included investigations based on parent-child correlations, investigations based on studies of children reared together, and studies of correlations among intelligence in children reared apart.

Jencks' estimates of the contributions of hereditary factors to IQ are substantially and consistently lower than those reported by Jensen. The reason is that the work which Jensen reports includes studies conducted in England. As Jencks and his associates show, English studies yield consistently higher estimates of the contribution of genetic factors to intelligence than do studies for populations in the United States. There are a number of reasons why this might occur. For example, there might be less environmental variation of the type affecting intelligence in Britain.

On the basis of several data analyses, Jencks and his colleagues estimate that in the United States genetic factors account for about 45% of the observed variation in IQ. Environmental influences amount to about 35% of the observed variation, and the combined influence of hereditary and environmental factors accounts for about 20% of the observed variation.

INTELLIGENCE IN CULTURAL SUBGROUPS

At various points in the preceding discussion of the nature-nurture evidence, we indicated that there are group differences in intelligence-test performance related both to social class and ethnicity. American cultural traditions have generally included the expectation that there will be substantial individual differences in intellectual capability based on differences in motivation and genetic endowment. However, group differences have not been expected. American traditions dealing with cognitive socialization are based on the premise that all Americans are entitled to an equal opportunity to develop their intellects. The existence of group differences in intelligence raises questions about the adequacy of the nation's commitment to providing equality of opportunity for cognitive growth to all segments of the culture. We now undertake to examine the basis for group differences in intelligence and their implications for socialization. As you will see, the nature-nurture debate has played a major role in shaping both views on group variations in intelligence and ideas about the kinds of socialization policies that should be developed to deal with such differences.

Intelligence and Social Class

Prior to the Industrial Revolution, societies in Western culture rigidly followed the practice of assigning social status on the basis of family membership. The result of this practice, no doubt, was that many individuals in society never developed or used their intellectual potentials to the fullest. As John Gardner (1961) has noted:

> Human societies have severely and successfully limited the realization of individual promise. They did not set out consciously to achieve that goal. It is just that full realization of individual promise is not possible on a wide scale in societies of hereditary privilege—and most human societies have had precisely that characteristic. There have been systems in which the individual's status was determined not by his gifts or capacities, but by his membership in a family, a caste, or a class. Such membership determined his rights, privileges, prestige, power, and status in the society. His ability was hardly relevant. (p. 3)

With the onset of the Industrial Revolution, Western culture experienced increased needs for people of capability. Moreover, the opportunity for reaping rewards from intellectual accomplishments increased as a function of mounting industrial productivity. In part as a result of increased needs and opportunities for people of ability and in part as a result of the scientific and democratic philosophies which gained increasing favor during this period, the practice of assigning status on the basis of family membership gradually began to wane.

It was against this background of social change that the concept of intelligence was born. Interestingly enough, the scientific concept of psychometric intelligence came into being long after the powerful forces for social change in Western society exerted their major effects regarding hereditary privilege. Nevertheless, since its inception the concept of intelligence has been linked intimately to social position.

Galton's early research. Research on the relationship between intelligence and social class goes back as far as Galton. In 1869 he published a volume, *Hereditary Genius: An Inquiry into Its Laws and Consequences,* which was to set the tone for research on intelligence and social class for the next century. In this volume Galton described a genealogical study of 300 families of high social station to determine the extent to which eminence was characteristic of a specific family line. For each of the families studied, Galton identified an illustrious family head who evidenced a degree of intellectual accomplishment achieved by one person in a million. His data indicated a decreasing likelihood of eminence as the extent of the relationship to the illustrious head decreased.

On the basis of his findings, Galton concluded that intelligence was controlled by hereditary factors. He also firmly linked the concept of intelligence to social position based on individual accomplishment. That linkage persists to this day and it has been validated in countless empirical studies. People who score highly on intelligence tests tend to get more education and subsequently to achieve a higher socioeconomic status than people who do not score well on such tests.

Contemporary research: Jensen and Jencks revisited. Although the relationship between intelligence and social position has been reliably demonstrated many

*Genetic influences
on intelligence and
social class*

times, the basis for the relationship has long been disputed. The nature-nurture issue has provided the central focus of debate. Some theorists, such as Jensen, suggest as Galton did that whatever benefits in social station may accrue to the intellectually superior are the result primarily of genetic influences. In this regard Jensen (1971) writes:

> Social classes as defined largely in terms of educational and occupational status are subject to differential selection for mental abilities. Since these have genetic as well as environmental components, they are transmitted to the offspring, and because of a high degree of assortative mating for mental traits in Western cultures the gene pools for different social classes will differ in the genetic factors related to ability. . . . It is now generally accepted by geneticists, psychologists, and sociologists who have reviewed the evidence that social class differences in mental abilities have a substantial genetic component. This genetic component should be expected to *increase* in an open society that permits and encourages social mobility. (pp. 40-41)

Social class, associative learning and conceptual learning

In addition to asserting that social-class differences in intelligence are in the main genetically determined, Jensen (1969) argues that a "unidimensional concept of intelligence is quite inadequate as a basis for understanding social-class differences in ability" (p. 109). Jensen holds that there are two types of ability. The most basic of these he calls associative learning. Associative learning involves the capability to acquire information in essentially a rote fashion. For example, one frequently used measure of associative learning is the ability to repeat a list of digits in the same order in which they were presented. Jensen's second type of ability is called conceptual learning. Tasks which require information to be classified or elaborated in some way illustrate conceptual learning. Most IQ tests are heavily weighted with tasks of this kind.

Jensen holds that both associative learning and conceptual learning are in large measure genetically determined. He argues further that conceptual learning is related to social class, but associative learning is not. On the basis of these assertions, he concludes that the education of lower-class children ought to emphasize associative-learning ability.

A number of investigators have challenged various aspects of Jensen's views on social class and intelligence. One of us directed a study which casts doubt on Jensen's assertions concerning the nature of associative learning (Bergan, Zimmerman, & Ferg, 1971). We asked fifth grade children to recall in order sets of digits and other similar stimuli. In one condition of the experiment, the items to be recalled were presented one at a time. In another condition, they were presented in groups of twos or threes. For example, one digit series included numerals such as *2, 1, 3, 2* and another involved combinations such as *21, 12,* and so forth. The surprising finding was that recalling groupings of digits turned out to be a separate ability from recalling single digits. Jensen wrote to us to congratulate us on our results and also to suggest that further analysis might have revealed a relationship between the two abilities we discovered. Such a relationship would, of course, support his concept of associative learning. Although it is possible that there could be some relationship between the two abilities we identified, our data suggested that the relationship would be so small that it would be of no practical significance.

Guthrie (1971) conducted a study which raises doubts about Jensen's view that instruction provided for lower-class children ought to emphasize associative learning. Guthrie taught lower-class and middle-class children simple grammatical rules analogous to the rule which calls for the use of the word *an* before nouns beginning with a vowel (e.g., *an apple*). In one condition of the experiment, he told the children the rules which were to be acquired. In a second condition, the children learned to apply the rules through rote memorization of examples of them. The first condition required conceptual learning in that the children had to classify word groupings in accordance with the rules to which they conformed. The second condition required associative learning in that during training the children were simply required to remember word sequences. Contrary to the predictions which would be made on the basis of Jensen's theory, Guthrie found that for both middle-class and lower-class children, experimenter verbalizations of the rules to be acquired facilitated learning to apply the rules.

Jencks and his colleagues challenged Jensen's genetic view regarding conceptual learning. Jencks believes that there is a substantial environmental influence operating in the case of the relationship between IQ tests and social class. In this connection he asserts:

Environmental influences on intelligence and social class

> Everyone who has studied the matter agrees that test scores have *some* genetic determinants, that there is *some* social mobility in America, and that test scores have *some* effect on a child's chances for mobility. It follows, then, that there must be *some* genetic differences between rich and poor. The real question is not whether such differences exist, but whether they are large or trivial. More specifically, the question is how much of the test score gap between rich and poor children is likely to be due to genes and how much is likely to be due to environment. (1972, p. 79)

Regarding this question Jencks concludes that "about 30% of the observed relationship between a father's occupation and a child's test scores is explained by genes, and that about 70% is environmental" (1972, p. 80).

In addition to challenging the genetic basis for the relationship between intelligence and social class, Jencks argues that the implicit assumption that intelligence contributes directly to the achievement of high social station may be inaccurate. Jencks suggests that the cognitive skills measured by intelligence tests are related to social class largely because they are related to educational attainment. The individual who is willing to spend many years in school is granted access to favored occupations. Insofar as scores on intelligence tests are related to educational attainment, they will necessarily be related to social class.

The Jencks position challenges the notion that intelligence and education contribute directly to job performance. Jencks asserts that it is possible that the central function of schooling is simply to provide credentials which serve as passports to desirable occupations. On this point, Jencks and his colleagues write:

Intelligence and job performance

> There is abundant evidence that employers prefer workers with more education to workers with less. . . . This may reflect real differences between people with a great deal of schooling and people with less schooling, or it may be an essentially arbitrary rationing system, whose primary function is to keep the number of people trying to enter high-status occupations in balance with the number of places. There is something to be said for both theories and very little evidence that allows us to choose between them. (1972, p. 182)

Other contemporary theorists, while recognizing that schools to some extent do serve merely as credential agencies, do not view the issue of credentials versus productivity in either/or terms. For example, Bowman writes:

> . . . schooling does in fact contribute to productive capability; the question is how

much of what schools do has this effect, how much of what we observe in earnings differentials is attributable to the use of schools as selection agencies or filters through which people pass. . . . What this is leading to . . . is a reexamination of just how schools do function in the career development process, including both direct training and learning effects and selection into opportunities for greater or lesser training and learning at work. (1974, p. 240)

Social class and socialization. The data provided by Jencks and his colleagues on the relationship between intelligence and social class suggesting the significant role which environmental factors can play in determining intellectual competence indicates the possibility of developing socialization policies and practices that can raise the level of cognitive skills in economically disadvantaged children. The failure of compensatory educational programs to succeed in increasing the intellectual competencies of the poor, coupled with the substantial amount of existing evidence indicating the importance of cultural and familial factors in determining intellectual competence, suggest a multi-faceted attack on the problem of increasing cognitive skills. Such an attack would require research to generate new knowledge regarding factors affecting cognitive development. Procedures would also need to be devised for communicating innovative socialization techniques to parents and teachers. Finally, efforts would be needed to identify specific cultural conditions that could stimulate cognitive growth and provisions would be needed at the community level to insure that those conditions prevailed.

The achievement of conditions which would enhance intellectual competence in the nation on a broad basis would require a massive research effort and a much greater coordination between research and socialization practice than has ever existed in the past. It seems doubtful that the nation is prepared at the present time to make the kind of resource commitment that would be required to achieve the lofty goal of broad-based enhancement of intellectual ability. There are those who question the value of such an effort, pointing out that intellectual competence has increased dramatically during the course of this century; yet we continue to have poverty, hunger, and a host of other social evils. Before any marked change in the existing level of commitment to the task of increasing cognitive skills can be expected, the nation will have to ask and answer the question: Would the quality of life of the people be improved by an increased commitment to the task of stimulating cognitive growth?

Intelligence and Race

The observed relationship between intelligence and social class has fostered debate on the closely related and highly sensitive issue of the relationship between intelligence and race. The debate on intelligence and race centers around the fact that there is about a 15-point difference between the average IQs of whites and blacks. The figure of 15 points itself is not in dispute, but the basis for it is. Some theorists, for example Jensen, suggest that racial differences may be largely genetically determined. Others hold that the environment is principally responsible for racial differences. Finally, practically everybody admits that nobody knows for sure the extent to which racial differences in IQ are genetically or environmentally determined.

Genetics,
intelligence,
and race

Heredity, environment, and race. Jensen has been the most articulate spokesperson for the group suggesting that genetics may make an important contribution to racial differences in intelligence. His position is that common sense and what research we have available at the present time suggest that there probably are genetic differences in intelligence between races. In this connection Jensen (1970) writes:

> It is hard to imagine that there have not been different selection pressures for different abilities in various cultures and that these pressures would be as great for intelligence as for many physical characteristics which are known to differ genetically among racial groups. (pp. 18-19)

Regarding research evidence from one study on intelligence and race Jensen (1970) states: "By assuming genetic equivalence (in the IQs of whites and blacks), one simply cannot make any sense out of the available data" (p. 21).

Although Jensen does feel that the available evidence favors a genetic interpretation of racial differences in intelligence, he believes that there is currently not enough evidence to make a definitive judgment on the issue. He favors an intensive research effort to determine the contribution of hereditary and environmental factors to racial differences in intelligence, and he faults environmentalists for refusing even to consider the possibility that racial differences may be genetically based. In regard to these points he states:

> In recent years . . . we have witnessed more and more the domination of ideologically motivated environmentalist dogma concerning the causes of large and socially important differences in average educational and occupational performance among various subpopulations in the United States, particularly those socially identified as racial groups. For example, the rate of occurrence of mental retardation, with IQ's below 70 plus all the social, educational, and occupational handicap that this implies, is six to eight times higher in our Negro population than in the rest of the population. According to research sponsored by the National Institutes of Health, as many as 20 to 30 percent of the Black children in some of our largest urban centers suffer severe psychological handicaps. Yet the Government *has* not supported, *does* not, and *will* not, as of this date, support any research proposals that could determine whether or not any genetic factors are involved in this differential rate of mental handicap. To ignore such a question, in terms of our present knowledge, I submit, may not be unethical—but it is, I believe, shortsighted, socially irresponsible, and inhumane. (Jensen, 1972, p. 6)

Environment, intelligence, and race

Those who favor the environmental interpretation of racial differences in intelligence suggest that skin color has been associated with differential treatment of whites and blacks and that these differences in environmental circumstances may have produced the observed differences in intelligence between whites and blacks. Gage (1972) expresses this view eloquently, likening the differential treatment of blacks and whites to a large and cruel experiment which in the end yields no definitive conclusions.

> American history since 1700 has designed and executed a massive experiment in which radical manipulations of the environment constituted the experimental treatment. One substantial fraction of the population was enslaved, literally, not figuratively. Then, after being freed, it was subjected to an elaborate, pervasive, systematic, and rigorously enforced set of social, political, economic, and educational discriminations. The treatment operated so as to impair the fabric of that fraction's familial and educational life. The experimental group was deprived of books and access to opportunities to hear standard English. Its workers were kept so physically tired by hard labor that they seldom could find energy for self-educative activities demanding intellectual effort. The experimental fraction was insulted, impoverished, made fearful, and instilled with self-hatred. In short, it would be difficult for psychologists . . . to plan an environment better designed to harm the average intelligence of an experimental group consisting of about a 10% sample of the nation's population. (pp. 311-12)

Gage goes on to point out that the experiment had one glaring flaw, the failure to assign subjects to experimental treatments by random procedure. All the subjects in the experimental group were of the same race. Thus, it is impossible to determine whether or not the effects of the experiment on intelligence and other characteristics were produced by the experimental treatment or by the race of the subjects. Gage then asks the obvious rhetorical question: "If we cannot be sure that the educational and economic inequalities of Negroes result from the grievous experimental treatment to which they have been subjected, should we leap to the conclusion that it was their genetic makeup?" (1972, p. 312).

Jensen's analysis of data on IQ and race

To give the reader some feel for the basis of the diverse views which currently exist regarding the subject of intelligence and race, we will describe briefly Jensen's (1970) analysis of a study of black elementary school children conducted by Kennedy, Van de Riet, and White (1963). Jensen points out that the variation in IQs among the black children in the Kennedy study is only a little over half as large as the variation in IQs for white children. He then suggests that a reasonable estimate of the contribution of genetic factors to the variation in white IQs is 80%. Finally, he points out that 80% of the total variation in white IQs (i.e., the amount of variation accounted for by genetic determinants) is larger than the total variation for black IQs. He concludes that since genetic factors alone account for more variation than there is in black IQs, blacks and whites could not possibly be genetically equal. Jensen recognizes that the heritability estimate of 80% might be questioned and that different results might be obtained with different samples of children. It is for these reasons that he advocates additional research studies.

Suppression of variations in intelligence

The heritability estimate of 80% is an especially critical parameter in determining the contribution of genetic factors to race differences in intelligence. As we have already noted, there are investigators who believe that 80% is much too high an estimate of the contribution of hereditary factors to intelligence in America. In the case of black IQs, that estimate may be even more inflated than it is suspected of being for the population at large. As pointed out in the Gage quote above, blacks have lived under oppressive conditions in this country for two hundred years. A significant aspect of this oppression has been a lack of opportunity to acquire competencies valued within the dominant middle-class culture and measured by IQ tests. When conditions are unfavorable for learning, the general result is a marked reduction in variation in performance. For example, take the extreme case of no learning at all. Under this condition there will typically be no variation in performance. It is only when society has taken some steps to promote learning that variations in performance begin to appear. Differences in interests and abilities combine with opportunities for learning to produce differences in performance. In the case of blacks, opportunities for the kinds of learning measured by IQ tests have been minimal. Accordingly, it is to be expected that variability in performance among blacks on IQ tests will be suppressed.

Racial differences and socialization. The debate over racial differences in intelligence has had profound effects on socialization for black children and for white children. Radical theorists favoring the genetic hypothesis regarding racial differences have advocated genetic control techniques for eliminating racial differences. Moderates have relied on the strategy of adapting instruction to the intellectual level of the individual child. In practice, adaptive instruction has typically been limited to placement of low IQ children in classes for the retarded. Finally, some theorists suggest that the use of IQ tests as a basis for identifying racial differences in intelligence ought to be eliminated.

In our view, the most frightening aspect of the debate on racial differences in intelligence is its relationship to the growing interest in eugenics which exists in this country. Eugenics is genetic engineering engaged in for the purpose of "improving" genetic endowment. Like any science, eugenics can be used for desirable or undesirable ends. For example, new genetic technology has made it possible to identify and to treat numerous genetic defects before birth. At the same time, innovations in the genetics field have made it possible to control who shall be born and what human characteristics shall exist. This kind of capability raises the questions of who shall control genetic engineering and for what purpose shall it be used.

Perhaps the simplest form of genetic control is sterilization. It may surprise the reader to learn that as of 1971,

> . . . 21 states had laws authorizing forced eugenic sterilizations of persons labeled as mentally defective. Minnie and Mary Alice Relf, 14 and 12 years old, are examples of Alabama's interpretation of the law. A white doctor performed tubal ligations on both of them when they went to a clinic, ostensibly for a "shot." (R. L. Williams, 1974, p. 41)

In addition to sterilization laws, the vast majority of states have genetic screening laws which either permit or mandate that hospitals screen newborns and children in utero for a host of possible genetic defects. As Ausubel, Beckwith, and Janssen (1974) point out, "Some of these laws can indeed help to anticipate and prevent serious diseases. However, they can also provide the opening wedge for a eugenics program" (p. 30).

Ausubel, Beckwith, and Janssen (1974) indicate that there are a number of scientists who feel that serious consideration should be given to expanding genetic control beyond disease prevention into the active manipulation of genetic endowment. They quote Bernard Davis, a professor of bacteriological physiology at Harvard, as suggesting the feasibility of a eugenics program:

> . . . aimed primarily at reducing the production of individuals whose genetic endowment would limit their ability to cope with a technologically complex environment. . . . At the present time . . . the climate of opinion is hardly receptive to any discussion of eugenics. But . . . times are moving rapidly: we do not have many decades before we will be forced to stabilize the size of the population, probably by accepting external restrictions on our freedom to procreate; and the step from quantity control to selective control may then not seem a large one. (p. 34)

While contemporary society may still be a long way from adopting eugenics as a strategy for eliminating mental defects related to race and social class, a number of theorists regard eugenics as a direct threat to the existence of ethnic minorities (e.g., see R. L. Williams, 1974).

The strategy of adapting instruction to individual differences in intellectual level has been the principal means employed by society for dealing with differences in intelligence including racial differences. Adaptive instruction based on intelligence-test performance is usually limited to children who score well below average on IQ tests. The general procedure is to label such children as educable mentally retarded and to place them in special education classes.

Adaptive education

There are two varieties of special-class placement: the self-contained class and the resource room. The self-contained class is generally a small class containing no more than 15 students. This type of class is an "all-day" class designed to provide for all the student's instructional needs. In recent years there has been some tendency to move away from self-contained special class placement toward temporary placement in a "resource room." In the resource-room approach, the child receives special instruction in the resource room for a part of the day and spends the remainder of the day in regular classes.

Special classes are taught by special education teachers. These individuals receive special training for working with "handicapped" children, including low IQ children. Thus, children placed in special education programs are presumed to have the double advantage of a small class, which permits the teacher to spend an extensive amount of time with each child, and a highly skilled teacher, who possesses special competencies not found in most regular classroom teachers.

Because special education classes are small and because they require teachers with special skills, they are expensive to operate. Most local schools do not have the money to implement a special education program. Consequently, such programs are generally supported in part by state funds. The typical procedure is for a local school district to establish a register of children eligible to receive special education services and to provide the state with figures on the average daily attendance of the children in special education classes. The state uses the figures provided as a basis for reimbursing the local school districts.

We mention the financial arrangements for supporting special education services because they have implications for the use of intelligence tests in the schools. In most states, in order for a school district to receive reimbursement for low IQ children, the children on the register must be labeled as mentally retarded. The assignment of that label requires, among other things, the attainment of a low score on an IQ test.

Criticisms of special class placement

Despite the fact that special education programs can provide high quality educational services to children, the practice of assigning children from minority groups to such programs on the basis of intelligence tests has come under heavy attack in recent years (Mercer, 1973). Thomas Oakland (1973) of the University of Texas, in his survey of the status of minority-group testing, describes the feelings of minority-group members regarding tests:

> They are justifiably angered when tests are misused to denigrate their dignity and are justifiably frustrated when tests are misused to severely limit their educational and vocational opportunities. They charge that tests reflect only middle-class values and attitudes and do not reflect children's linguistic and cognitive abilities and cultural experiences. Also, it is very evident to them that tests discriminate among individuals—usually against them because of their relatively lower socioeconomic status and minority group membership. To many, the use of tests is perceived as an attempt to maintain racially biased social order and institutional practices. (p. 295)

The key complaint of minority group members regarding intelligence testing centers around the issue of labeling children on the basis of their test scores. Critics of testing practices argue that to call a minority child mentally retarded is simply to have invented another of the seemingly endless ways to proclaim the inferiority of minority group members. In this connection R. L. Williams (1974) writes:

> Historically, when one group of people has wished to subjugate or exploit another group, they dehumanized them by ascribing derogatory characteristics to the subjects: animalistic, savage, emotional, over-sexed, lazy, unscrupulous and crazy, to name a few. It was also necessary to impugn the subjects' ability to deter-

mine their own destinies; they were described as child-like, immature, backward, simple-minded, illiterate, or of low intelligence.

The Black-White IQ controversy presents an analogous situation. When a people is labeled consistently as being of low-intellect or simple-minded, the respect among the general populace for their rights to life can and will erode to nothing. It has happened historically, and it has happened here. (p. 38)

The point which Williams and others have been trying to make has been difficult to communicate. One reason for the difficulty is that individuals from ethnic minorities do generally score lower on IQ tests than individuals from the white middle class. Since this is the case, it is quite easy to assume that labels, such as mentally retarded, assigned to minority-group members simply reflect the objective fact that a significant proportion of the members of minority groups have low IQs. This assumption, however, has been questioned.

Available evidence from a variety of sources suggests that ethnic minorities are different from the white middle class. This does not imply, however, that they are inferior to the middle class. As Cole and Bruner (1971) have noted:

In the present social context of the United States, the great power of the middle class has rendered differences into deficits because middle class behavior is the yardstick of success. (p. 874)

The fact that intelligence testing has indicated that minority-group members generally receive lower scores than members of the middle class indicates that individuals from minorities are often not adept at certain verbal skills prized by the middle class. It certainly does not suggest that significant numbers of them are retarded. This is a value judgment imposed by society.

The plight of the ethnic minorities regarding the testing-labeling issue raises questions regarding socialization policies and practices affecting all individuals in the society. Is it necessary to assign derogatory labels to children in order to provide instruction adapted to their individual intellectual needs? The assignment of labels can damage a child's pride in himself and injure his confidence in his ability to succeed. Moreover, it may affect teachers' expectations of the child in the area of learning. Regarding the last point, Kenneth Clark (1969), the first black president of the American Psychological Association, wrote:

. . . I find myself constantly thanking God that when I was in the Harlem public schools nobody knew I was culturally deprived. I'm afraid that if they did know I would not have been taught on the grounds that being culturally deprived I wouldn't be able to learn. (p. 36)

The question of the justifiability of the kind of fear expressed by Clark regarding teacher expectations has been the subject of vigorous research in recent years. Rosenthal and Jacobson (1968) stimulated scientific concern regarding the potential effects of teacher expectancies on children's behavior. They concluded that teachers' assumptions about a child's ability level affected later academic achievement. However, subsequent analyses of their research revealed significant methodological flaws which cast doubts on the validity of the findings (Barber & Silver, 1968; Thorndike, 1968; Thorndike, 1969). Moreover, efforts to replicate the Rosenthal and Jacobson research with adequate methodology have yielded mixed results (Claiborne, 1969; Kester, 1969; O'Connell, Dusek, & Wheeler, 1974).

Some investigators have attempted to identify specific differences in the way in which teachers treat students assumed to differ in ability levels. For example,

Beez (1968) found that teachers taught more to students described as high in ability than to students described as low in ability. Similarly, Good (1970) observed that students believed to be of low ability were given fewer opportunities to respond in class than were students thought to be high in ability.

As in the case of studies assessing expectancy effects on pupil achievement, research on teacher behavior has produced mixed results. For example, Alpert (1974) found no evidence to suggest that assumed ability level affected teacher behavior toward students. She studied teaching procedures in high- and low-ability reading groups and concluded that the quality of instruction was as good in low-ability groups as in high-ability groups. She suggested possible experimenter bias as one reason for discrepant findings between her research and earlier studies. The experimenters rating quality of instruction in the Alpert study were unaware of the ability levels of the groups that they were observing, whereas this was not the case in earlier research.

Diagnostic labels and teacher judgments of children

Whether or not teachers' assumptions about ability affect their behavior toward children remains an open question. Likewise, whether or not teacher expectancies influence student achievement is still an unsettled issue. However, it seems fairly certain that teacher assumptions about student characteristics affect their judgments of students' future prospects. Moreover, the use of diagnostic labels plays an important role in influencing teacher views about students. Herson (1974) studied the effects of diagnostic labels on teacher judgments of the probable degree to which hypothetical students labeled in various diagnostic categories would be psychologically incapacitated. Teachers rating students assigned labels such as marginally retarded or emotionally disturbed presumed a greater degree of incapacitation than did those who were only provided a description of the child's behavior. For example, in comparison to those receiving descriptions, teachers in the labeling group were more likely to rate the child's prognosis as poor, his condition as having a predetermined and adverse course, and his effects upon his peers damaging.

Given the questions which have been raised concerning the potentially harmful effects of labeling, is it appropriate for the states to provide financial rewards to local school districts in the form of special education reimbursements for assigning derogatory labels to children? Would it be feasible to reimburse individualized instruction of the sort provided through special education without the requirement that labels be assigned to children?

Questions such as these are being raised with increasing frequency. The answers to these questions will clearly have an enormous effect on the concept of intelligence and on socialization policies and practices related to that concept.

INTELLIGENCE AS A CULTURAL INVENTION

Psychometric intelligence is an invention of culture shaped by cultural needs and at the same time influencing cultural practices. As we have seen, psychometric concepts have had a remarkable effect on our ideas about the nature of intelligence and intellectual development, on our thinking about the contributions of heredity and environment to intelligence, and on our views concerning differences in intellectual capability among cultural subgroups. All of these matters in turn have affected our socialization efforts to increase cognitive growth.

The effect of psychometric intelligence on society is all the more remarkable when we reflect on the fact that everything might have been quite different if Galton had not made his pioneering explorations into norm-referenced testing and correlational technology. For example, we might have been less concerned with differences between individuals and groups and more concerned with finding out what people who are intelligent do that makes them intelligent. Of course, it could be argued that society needed and still needs a technology that provides information about differences, and that if Galton had not been the one to initiate the development of that technology, someone else would undoubtedly have done it. In any case, it is important to keep in mind that psychometric principles are points of view and that there are other ways of asking and answering the question *What is intelligence?*

SUGGESTED READINGS

Alpert, J. L. Teacher behavior across ability groups: A consideration of the mediation of pygmalion effects. *Journal of Educational Psychology,* 1974, *66,* 348-53.

Ausubel, F., Beckwith, J., & Janssen, K. Stimulus/response: The politics of genetic engineering: Who decides who's defective? *Psychology Today,* 1974, *8* (1), 30-44.

Bergan, J. R., Zimmerman, B. J., & Ferg, M. Effects of variations in content and stimulus grouping on visual sequential memory. *Journal of Educational Psychology,* 1971, *62,* 400-404.

Bissell, J. S. *The cognitive effects of pre-school programs for disadvantaged children.* Washington, D.C.: National Institute of Child Health and Human Development, 1970.

Gray, S. W. Children from three to ten: The early training project. *Early Education Papers and Reports* (Vol. 5, No. 3). Nashville, Tenn.: George Peabody College for Teachers, Demonstration and Research Center for Early Education, 1971.

Guthrie, E. R. Relationships of teaching method, socio-economic status, and intelligence in concept formation. *Journal of Educational Psychology,* 1971, *62,* 345-51.

Herson, P. H. Biasing effects of diagnostic labels and sex of pupil on teachers' views of pupils' mental health. *Journal of Educational Psychology,* 1974, *66,* 117-22.

Hess, R. D., and Shipman, V. C. Early experiences and the socialization of cognitive modes in children. In M. W. Miles and W. W. Charters, Jr. (Eds.), *Learning in social settings.* Boston: Allyn and Bacon, 1970.

Hunt, J. McV. *Intelligence and experience.* New York: Ronald Press, 1961.

Jensen, A. R. How much can we boost IQ and scholastic achievement? *Harvard Educational Review,* Reprint Series No. 2, 1969, 1-124.

Jensen, A. R. The heritability of intelligence. *Engineering and Science,* 1970, *33* (6), 1-4.

Mercer, J. R. *Labeling the mentally retarded.* Berkeley: University of California Press, 1973.

Oakland, T. Assessing minority group children: Challenges for school psychologists. *Journal of School Psychology,* 1973, *11,* 294-303.

Williams, R. L. Stimulus/response: Scientific racism and IQ—The silent mugging of the black community. *Psychology Today,* 1974, *7* (12), 32-100.

6

The Process of
Intellectual Development

the three types of covert behaviors which behaviorists describe in relation to thinking.

ways of assessing covert behavior.

influences among the environment, covert behavior, and overt behavior.

the definition of the terms *concept, rule,* and *rule-governed behavior.*

the advantages afforded by the use of rule-governed behavior in the symbolic representation of environmental occurrences.

the definition of abstract thinking.

abstract thinking, problem solving, and rule-governed behavior.

theoretical views on how rule-governed behaviors are acquired.

discrimination and generalization.

conservative focusing and successive scanning.

the meaning of the terms *modeling, imitation,* and *mimicry.*

Gagné's eight types of learning.

Gagné's account of how conservation of volume is acquired and the implications of his account for teaching.

the application of behavioral principles in solving social problems associated with cultural change and diversity.

behavioral rebuttals to humanist criticisms of behavioral socialization.

Piaget's views on the manner in which intelligence develops and the two types of changes which occur in intellectual functioning during the course of development.

the functions, contents, and structures of intelligence as described by Piaget.

Piaget's views on how intellectual development occurs.

intellectual functioning during the sensorimotor period.

the findings of laboratory research on sensorimotor development.

intellectual functioning during the subperiod of preoperational thought.

intellectual functioning during the period of concrete operations following the preoperational subperiod.

the meaning of the term conservation and laboratory research on conservation.

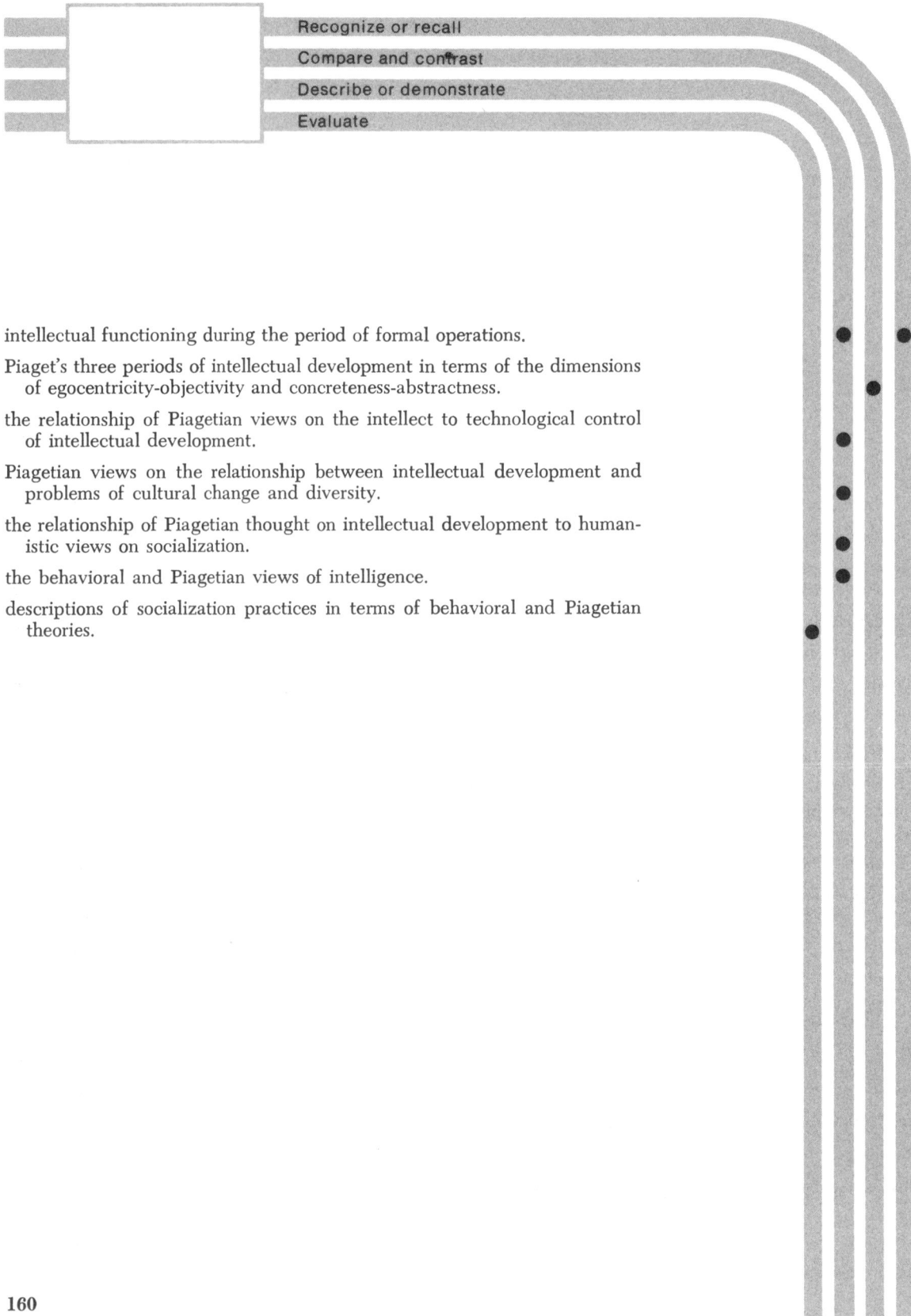

Recognize or recall

Compare and contrast

Describe or demonstrate

Evaluate

intellectual functioning during the period of formal operations.

Piaget's three periods of intellectual development in terms of the dimensions of egocentricity-objectivity and concreteness-abstractness.

the relationship of Piagetian views on the intellect to technological control of intellectual development.

Piagetian views on the relationship between intellectual development and problems of cultural change and diversity.

the relationship of Piagetian thought on intellectual development to humanistic views on socialization.

the behavioral and Piagetian views of intelligence.

descriptions of socialization practices in terms of behavioral and Piagetian theories.

CHAPTER CONTENT

As a young child and his mother were walking together in the late afternoon, the child looked back at the long, moving shadow which he had cast upon the sidewalk and then turned to his mother to say: "Look, that boy come too." The mother could not help smiling. From an adult point of view, the charm of the child's remark lay in the fact that it implied equal status among the shadow and the walkers. The shadow was described as though it were a person with the attributes and capabilities characteristic of such a living being. Perhaps his mother's smile seemed perplexing to the child. If he did indeed view the shadow as a living being whose tagging along was of some interest but in no way amusing, he would have been puzzled. It is also possible that he had at least rudimentary knowledge of the properties of shadows, but lacked the language skills to express his views on shadows in a precise way. In any case, the example illustrates that the child's conception of the world may be strikingly different from that of the adult. Recognition of this fact constitutes the starting point for theory and research on the process of intellectual development.

When used to describe intellectual development, the term *process* refers to changes in intellectual functioning which occur across the long span of growth and to the events which produce such changes. The specification of the process of intellectual growth requires a description of alterations in the nature of intellectual functioning which occur with development and the identification of those genetic and environmental influences which promote intellectual growth.

Currently there are two major theoretical accounts of the process of intellectual development: the behavioral view and the constructionist position advanced by Jean Piaget and his followers. The present chapter discusses these two positions and their implications for socialization in contemporary society.

INTELLECTUAL DEVELOPMENT FROM
THE BEHAVIORAL PERSPECTIVE

Throughout the long history of Western culture, people have developed elaborate conceptions detailing what the intellect is and how it functions. The views of society regarding thinking processes are contained not only in scholarly treatises on the intellect but are also carried in our language. Through their incorporation into speech, ideas about the nature of intellect have become implicit in the verbal behavior of virtually every individual in Western society.

The view which our culture has advanced regarding the nature of intellectual functions holds that intellectual activities are the province of the mind, an executive agent within the individual responsible for controlling action. The idea of the controlling mind is carried by our language in expressions which ascribe the causes of action to the individual rather than to the circumstances in which he finds himself. Personal pronouns are the principal carriers of the notion of individual control of action. Thus in response to the question *Why are you doing that?* we might say *Because I want to*. The phrase *I want to* assigns responsibility for action to the individual while giving no recognition to environmental conditions which might influence behavior.

Society recognizes that the controlling mind is not an absolute power, which undoubtedly enhances the credibility of the idea of mind. Thus we say *I've got to get better control of myself* or *I can't seem to help myself*. Expressions such as these give recognition to the possibility that someone or something other than *I* might have an influence on behavior. Nevertheless *I* is regarded as the principal controlling agent so far as human behavior is concerned.

It was quite natural that science, which came into being long after our basic conceptions of human nature had developed, should be influenced by the concept of the mind as a controlling agent. And so it was that scientists interested in the study of the intellect went in search of *I*. They reasoned that if they were to find out why people did the things that they did, they would have to find out who *I* was and what *he* or *she* was like.

Prescientific conceptions depicted *I* as a homunculus, a little man who resided inside the head. This view, however, was eventually abandoned. It became obvious that if one presumed the existence of a little man inside the head, one was faced with the problem of explaining the behavior of two beings rather than one. Virtually all scientists agree that this was an unnecessary duplication of effort.

Although the notion of a homunculus was given up, the basic idea of a controlling mind has hung on with what behaviorists regard as dogged persistence. Modern versions of the concept of mind are much more sophisticated than the early homunculus view. They generally conceive of the mind not as a being, but as a structure or set of structures inside the individual. Thus, it is not uncommon to run across phrases such as the *mental apparatus* or *intellectual structure* in contemporary psychological literature.

Behaviorists take the position that to speculate about intellectual structures is to engage in useless fantasy. Their view is that *I* is a will-o'-the-wisp, or at best a mythological character who, like Icarus, Odysseus, and Captain Marvel, should be accorded the status of a hero of a bygone age and be left to sleep and slowly decay in the language which so long ago brought him to life.

For the behaviorist, intellectual processes are behaviors controlled by the environment and by the genetically determined physiological makeup of the individual. Intellectual behaviors differ from other behaviors in two ways. The first is that they often occur in covert form. The second is that they fall into categories of action which society has designated as intellectual.

Intellectual Functioning as Covert Behavior

The world of the intellect is generally regarded as a private world hidden from the view of others. For example, thoughts are typically described as occurring inside the head where they cannot be observed by outsiders. Behaviorists recognize the private nature of intellectual activity by suggesting that intellectual behaviors typically occur in covert form.

In describing thinking as covert action, behaviorists have attempted to reinterpret structuralist descriptions of modes of thought from a behavioral standpoint. In addition, they have made extensive efforts to deal with the problem of observing covert behavior so that it can be subjected to scientific study. Finally, they have challenged the structuralist assumption that thought controls action and have offered in its stead the view that the environment plays an important role in controlling thinking processes and the overt behaviors related to them.

Modes of thinking as covert behaviors. As shown in figure 6-1, there are three generally recognized modes of thinking:

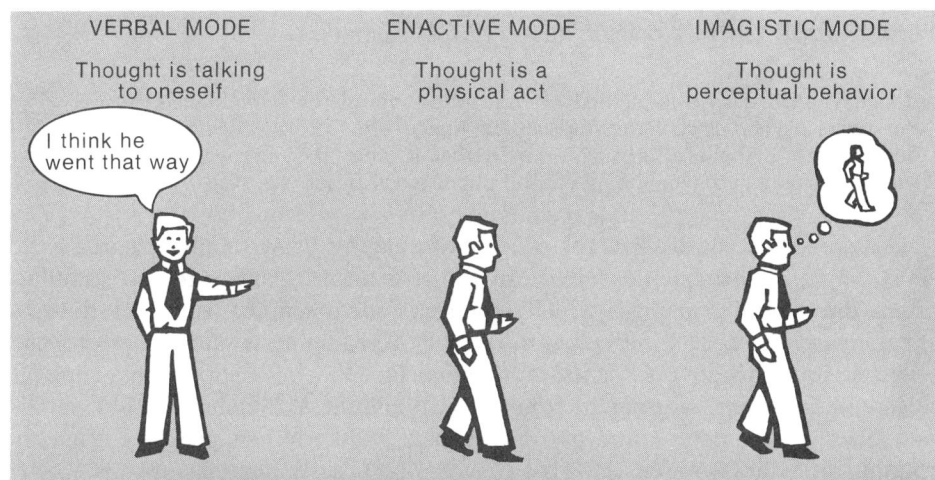

| VERBAL MODE | ENACTIVE MODE | IMAGISTIC MODE |
| Thought is talking to oneself | Thought is a physical act | Thought is perceptual behavior |

I think he went that way

Modes of thought as covert behaviors.   **Figure 6–1**

the verbal mode, the enactive mode, and the imagistic mode. Behaviorists characterize each of these three kinds of thought as covert action.

It is widely recognized that many of our thoughts occur in verbal form. The structuralist position assumes that verbal thought exists as an object of the mind. We give credence to this view in such expressions as *I can't seem to get that idea out of my head.* As far as the behaviorist is concerned, there is no idea in the head. The only thing there is behavior.

In the behavioral view, verbal thought is the act of talking to oneself. In some cases covert verbal behavior actually involves subvocal movements of the vocal musculature. However, in other instances there may be no involvement of the musculature. In these instances, inner speech occurs entirely within the central nervous system.

Behaviorists take the position that covert verbalization has its origins in

The verbal mode

overt speech. Young children often carry on dialogues with themselves out loud. However, parents eventually find this kind of behavior disturbing and attempt to eliminate it. As a consequence of previous parental efforts and the vigorous rebuffs which can be expected from peers, adults rarely talk to themselves loudly enough to be heard by others. Nevertheless, it is quite certain that adults engage in almost continuous covert verbalization. We recognize this fact in expressions, such as *a penny for your thoughts*, that we use when we attempt to make the covert verbalizations of another individual overt.

The enactive mode

Behaviorists and structuralists have no quarrel regarding the enactive mode of thought. Enactive thinking is by definition behavioral since it refers to physical acts which the individual may engage in to represent objects and events in the environment. Covert acts used in thinking are generally reductions of more easily observable behaviors. For example, a person may "think" about looking for a lost object in an adjacent room by looking in the direction of the room. In this case the behavioral sequence of looking toward the room, walking into the room, and then engaging in search behavior is reduced to the initial act of looking.

The imagistic mode

Seemingly, the most difficult mode of thought to conceptualize in behavioral terms is imagistic thought. The concept of imagery has traditionally been regarded as within the bastion of structural theory; and structuralists have taken great pains to fault behaviorists for failing to deal with the imaginal life of the individual. On this point Skinner (1974) remarks:

> Behaviorism has been accused of "relegating one of the paramount concerns of the earlier psychologists—the study of the image—to a position of not just neglect, but disgrace." I believe, on the contrary, that it offers the only way in which the subject of imaging or imagining can be put in good order. (p. 82)

Behaviorists do not disavow the concept of imaging. They simply disagree with the structuralists' explanation of it. For the structuralist, an image is a stimulus within the mental apparatus which represents some sensory aspect of the external environment. The individual in the act of imagining is said to perceive an image existing within the mental apparatus. For the behaviorist, imagining is perceptual behavior. No mental stimulus is required. As Skinner (1974) points out, "Seeing does not require a thing seen" (p. 86). When people engage in imaging behavior, we often say that they see or hear things that are not really there. The words *not really there* indicate our belief that what is seen or heard is not in the environment. Why should we assume that it is anywhere else?

The observation of covert behavior. One of the advantages of conceptualizing thinking as behavior is that it characterizes intellectual activities as tangible events which can be observed and thereby subjected to objective, scientific study. In practice, of course, it is not always easy to gain access to covert behaviors. However, it is almost invariably possible to attain at least indirect knowledge about covert actions. Moreover, there is a growing technology which has already greatly enhanced our capability to observe covert action directly.

Self-report

The most common indirect way to attain knowledge of covert behavior is, of course, to ask the individual to report his covert actions. We do this routinely with such questions as *What are you thinking?* Of course, there is always the danger that the individual will report his covert actions inaccurately. This generally happens when the individual's own self-interests favor a report which departs from what has actually occurred. For example, when a menacing mother says to her child: *You were thinking of breaking your brother's toy, weren't you?*

the answer may well be *no*. Sometimes inaccurate reports occur when the person is asked to report on things about which he has no knowledge. A frequent example of this may be observed in the angry parent who, in the wake of a misdeed, says to a child: *Why did you do that?* Sometimes in this kind of situation a young child will systematically search for answers in an attempt to please the parent. Thus, he or she may say: *It was a mistake.* If that answer does not achieve the desired parental response, the child may go on: *I wasn't thinking.* Eventually the child will find some explanation that is at least minimally satisfactory.

Although self-report continues to be the most common procedure for gaining access to covert intellectual behavior, advances in electronic technology have made it possible to observe manifestations of a variety of types of covert behavior in the individual directly. For example, the occurrence of covert verbal behavior can be observed by amplifying the movements of the vocal muscles. The procedure is a relatively simple one. Small microphones designed to pick up bioelectric signals from the vocal chords are placed on the surface of the neck. The microphones feed the impulses which they receive into an electromyograph which translates the bioelectrical impulses into an observable signal.

Observation of physical manifestations of covert behavior

Observations of subvocal speech can be useful in a number of ways. For example, they can assist in improving reading speed. Covert verbalization during silent reading may retard reading rate. Often a reader is unaware that he is subvocalizing. A tone signal from an electromyograph can alert the reader to his covert verbal behavior and thereby assist him to eliminate it (Karlins & Andrews, 1972).

Direct observation of covert behavior is as yet not practical on a broad scale, but it is fast becoming so. The rapidly growing technology which is developing under the rubric of biofeedback may soon provide broad segments of the population with the technological tools to observe a wide range of covert intellectual and emotional behaviors. Biofeedback research suggests that with observation, particularly self-observation, people will gain greater control of their internal actions than was ever believed to be possible.

Covert action and behavioral control. As illustrated in figure 6-2, the concept of covert behavior to some extent transfers the control of overt actions from the environment to the individual. Behaviorists recognize the fact that one behavior may influence another (Mahoney & Thoresen, 1974). When a behavior has been emitted, it may serve as a stimulus controlling other actions. If the initial behavior happens to be covert, it can be said that the individual has controlled his or her own actions.

In some cases covert control will take the form of a stimulus which serves as a signal or cue for the occurrence of behavior. For example, a child may say to himself: *It's getting dark, I had better get home for supper.* A covert verbaliza-

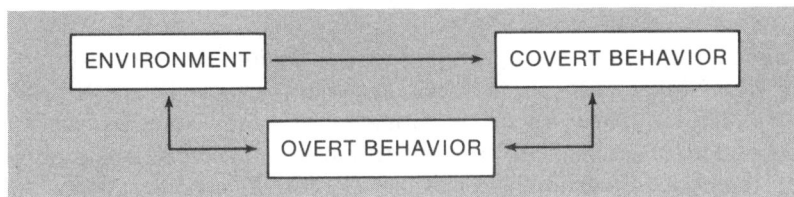

Influences among the environment, covert behavior, and overt behavior. Arrows indicate potential directions of influence.

Figure 6–2

tion such as this may serve as a signal for the overt behavior of walking home. Sometimes covert control will follow the behavior which it affects. For instance, if a child has broken one of her toys, she might covertly charge herself with stupidity. The child's castigation of her own behavior and, of course, the loss of the toy could serve to lessen the likelihood of toy-breaking behavior on future occasions.

Although the concept of covert control does to a degree place the control of action inside the individual, it does not lock control irrevocably within the person. Covert behavior, like other behavior, is subject to direct environmental influence. For instance in the example given earlier of the child who told himself to go home for supper, an overt event, the darkness, could be described as a signal for the covert verbalization *I had better get home for supper.* We have in this instance a chain in which an overt stimulus, darkness, served as a signal for a covert verbalization, *I had better get home,* which in turn served as a cue for an overt act, going home.

In many cases individuals are unaware of influences on either their covert or overt behavior. It is this fact that leads to alternative interpretations regarding behavioral control. An individual may say to himself *Why did you do that?* and come up with any number of answers. The answers are themselves covert behaviors which may be influenced by a variety of covert and overt stimulus events.

Our explanations of our actions and the conditions which actually control what we do are relatively independent of one another. A father may say that he has spanked his child because of the child's transgressions when in fact the act was perpetrated out of anger. A mother may force a child to go to bed at an excessively early hour arguing that the child needs his rest when in reality it is the mother who needs a few moments of peace and quiet.

Identifying conditions controlling behavior
Behaviorists hold that the determinants of behavior can be identified through the discovery of relationships between stimulus events and behavior (Mischel, 1973; Skinner, 1974). For example, consider the case of a second grade girl having difficulty in reading. The child's older sister had difficulty too, and it is suspected that there may be some genetically determined retardation in the development of the mental apparatus which is responsible for the reading problem. Observation reveals that poor oral reading is generally followed by extra attention in the form of special individualized help from the teacher. In addition, the teacher indicates that the child's father, who is a busy professional person and who spends very little time with his daughters, has given his evenings to work with his little girl on reading. No one, including the little girl, suspects that an intellectual process such as reading could be influenced by environmental factors such as teacher and parental attention. Yet the consistent relationship between these environmental events and reading behavior suggests that the possibility of environmental control be considered. When teacher and parent attention is made to depend on good reading rather than on poor reading, the reading problem disappears.

Stories such as this one have appeared in the behavioral literature so frequently that they have almost taken on the character of time-worn clichés. Nevertheless, the point which they make continues to have great significance for socialization practices related to intellectual growth. Although intellectual acts may control behavior, there are often links between intellectual behaviors and the environment. From the behavioral standpoint, one of the principal tasks of those responsible for guiding development is to find those environmental links and to assist the child to use them to enhance intellectual growth.

Intellectual Functioning as Rule-Governed Behavior

Most of the intellectual activities that are generally classified by developmentalists as manifestations of intelligence fall in the category of rule-governed behavior. Phenomena outside the rule-governed category, that is processes related to perception and memory, are sometimes included in the domain of intelligence. However, more often than not developmentalists (e.g., see Flavell, 1963; Piaget & Inhelder, 1973) make distinctions among perception, memory, and intelligence and, accordingly, this is the practice which we shall follow.

Rules and rule-governed behavior. A rule is a set of specifications which describes relationships among phenomena. One of the most familiar types of rules is the concrete concept, which is a rule for classifying things. For instance, the concept *cow* is the rule which specifies the characteristics animals must possess to belong to the category *cow*.

Rule-governed behavior is behavior that conforms to a rule. For example, when an individual emits the same response to a variety of different examples of a category, he or she is evidencing rule-governed behavior. If, for instance, a child says *gogie* upon seeing her own dalmatian and then points to the neighbor's collie and says *gogie*, her behavior is conforming to a rule, in this case a rule permitting her to classify a certain category of animal.

Rule-governed behavior can, of course, be much more complex than that of dog naming. Indeed, many of people's greatest achievements, their ability to communicate with others through language and their accomplishments in the arts and sciences, can be construed in large measure as examples of complex rule-governed behavior. This is one of the reasons why rule-governed action can be classified within the domain of intelligence development.

Rules and the behavioral representation of the environment. One of the most significant facts about rule-governed behavior is that it provides us with a means to represent our environment symbolically. When, for example, a child names a class of objects in the environment, the name can be used as a symbol for the objects being named.

Rule-governed behavior used in symbolic representation gives people a powerful tool for dealing with environmental complexity. When children represent concrete objects with acts, images, or words, they are no longer required to consider the specific and often highly intricate characteristics of the objects being represented. Their behavior need only produce the symbols for the objects, which are usually much less complex than the objects symbolized. When, for example, a child says the word *horse*, he or she does not have to recreate the mane, the tail, or other physical characteristics of the animal. All that the child must recreate is the word.

Rule-governed behavior and environmental complexity

The reduction in complexity effected through symbolization makes it possible for individuals to process more environmental information than they otherwise could. For example, when individuals are confronted with problem-solving tasks, they are often required to consider a great deal of information about the environment simultaneously, and in many cases they will need to recall large amounts of information which they have acquired in the past. The ability to represent environmental events with symbols greatly reduces the complexity of problem-solving tasks because it reduces the complexity of the information with which the individual must deal during the problem-solving process.

In addition to its advantages relating to environmental complexity, rule-governed behavior may be quite useful in enabling the individual to apply past learning in new situations. When a child has learned to represent a given set of objects or events symbolically, she may apply previously acquired rule-governed behavior to represent new instances of the category to which the rule applies. This capability greatly enhances learning efficiency. For example, when a child acquires concepts such as near and far, above and below, and in back of and in front of, she may apply these concepts in judging relationships among objects she has never seen before. If this were not the case, learning would, indeed, be a very tedious process.

Of course, symbolic rule-governed behavior does not always lead to increased learning efficiency. The child may upon occasion overgeneralize in his or her application of a rule and thereby make erroneous judgments concerning experiences. A child who had recently acquired the concept *post office* offers an amusing illustration of this fact. One morning, after having been to the local post office, the child asked if his father was getting ready to leave for the post office. The boy's mother said that daddy was going to his business office, not to the post office. The boy's parents thought little about the incident until the same question arose the next morning. Again the mother explained and the boy seemed satisfied. Nevertheless, the confusion persisted. Finally the mother said in exasperation, "When are you going to learn that daddy does not work at the post office?" In a remark expressing not only his newly acquired knowledge of the concept *office*, but also his judgments about the world of work, the boy quipped, "I know! He's just going to that old business office."

Rule-governed behavior and abstract thinking. Older children gradually acquire the capability to manipulate symbols to produce hypothetical conditions which may or may not exist in the real world. For example, in response to the question *What would happen if the nation were suddenly to run completely out of oil?* a child approaching adolescence would probably be able to identify many of the plausible eventualities even if he or she were unfamiliar with the volumes of adult nightmares which have accumulated in recent years on the subject of oil reserves.

The capability to manipulate symbols as though they were concrete conditions is frequently referred to as abstract thinking ability. From a behavioral standpoint, abstract thinking is rule-governed behavior. Thus, an adolescent description of the consequences of an ultimate energy crisis would be regarded as an example of rule-governed verbal behavior. A description of this sort would differ from simpler forms of rule-governed behavior, such as identifying categories of objects, because it would involve higher order rules expressing relationships among concepts representing possible rather than actual conditions. For example, a statement such as *smog would be reduced* involves three concepts: the concept of *smog*, the concept of *reduction*, and the concept *would be* which expresses the inferential character of the statement.

Abstract rule-governed behavior is of enormous importance in the guidance of human affairs because it frees people from the present and permits them to conceptualize both their past and their potential future. Humans use abstract rules to interpret the past and to transmit the records of such interpretation from generation to generation. By this means they are able to profit from the learning history of previous generations to an extent not possible for any other animal species. Humans use abstract rules to forecast alternative possible futures and to assess the likelihood of their coming to pass. In this way they are able to gain at least some long-range control over their own destiny.

Rule-governed behavior and problem solving.   One of the most useful applications of rule-governed behavior is in the area of problem solving. Problem solving is a form of rule-governed behavior, distinguished from other varieties by the fact that it requires rule discovery (Gagné, 1970).

Problem solving is initiated by the posing of a problem, that is, by the specification of what it is that needs to be discovered. In some cases, problem posing is a fairly obvious matter. When a plumber sees a leaky faucet, he or she knows that it has to be fixed. Similarly, when a government economist receives information that the nation is suffering from raging inflation, he or she knows that something ought to be done to deal with the problem of inflation. In some instances, of course, recognition that there is a problem to be solved requires great intellectual sensitivity (Guilford, 1967). Recognition of the need to raise the level of consciousness in the nation regarding the extent of discrimination against women in employment is a case in point.

After a problem has been posed, the problem solver generally must go through a series of steps to achieve problem solution. For example, a young child faced with the problem of gaining access to an out-of-reach cookie jar must find something, e.g., a chair, to stand on in order to extend his/her reach. Then the child must place the chair in the appropriate location with respect to the cookie jar. Next he/she must stand on the chair. Only after these steps have been taken, can he/she reach into the jar and extract its culinary delights.

The final act of problem solution and the steps leading to problem solution are rule-governed behaviors. The problem-solver's task is to find the right combination of rules to achieve solution. Solution is achieved when he has discovered a new rule which relates all the various rules applied in the steps taken toward solution (Gagné, 1970). For instance, problem solution in the cookie jar example would require application of rules such as *standing on an object will extend one's reach* and *chairs are examples which fall into the category of things that can be stood upon.* These rules would have to be applied in the comprehensive rule: *if I stand upon the chair I will be able to reach the cookie jar.* Of course, it is unlikely that a young child would be able to verbalize any of these rules, but his behavior nevertheless would have to conform to them before he could get any cookies.

As children grow older, they will learn to solve problems which require symbolic (usually verbal) specification of rules. At the onset of adolescence, the powerful tool of abstract rule-governed behavior will enter into this kind of problem solving enabling them to solve problems of enormous complexity.

The capability to solve complex problems is a key factor underlying humans' ability to survive in varied, complex, and rapidly changing environments. In many forms of animal life, a slight modification in environmental conditions can eventuate in extinction of the species. In contrast, humans have been able to survive in outer space and on the ocean floor. Their habitats have covered the entire spectrum of climatic conditions from extreme heat to bitter cold. There can be no doubt that problem solving has played the central role in making these impressive feats of adaptation possible. In consequence, it is not surprising that many theorists representing a variety of theoretical persuasions describe problem solving as the highest form of intellectual functioning (e.g., see Gagné, 1970; Guilford, 1967; Piaget, 1973).

How the Development of Rule-Governed Behavior Occurs

As shown in table 6-1, there are a variety of views regarding the manner in which rule-governed behavior is acquired. Some theorists have taken the position that rules are learned by the process of discriminating among classes of stimuli. Others have described rule acquisition as hypothesis testing in situations requiring rule discovery. Some theorists have stressed the role of social factors in rule learning. Finally, some theorists regard rule acquisition as a complex form of learning which is the product of simpler forms of learning.

The various explanations which have been advanced regarding rule learning need not be construed as competing positions representing mutually exclusive views on the subject of rule acquisition. Rather, they represent alternate means by which the development of rule-governed behavior can take place. Consequently, knowledge of each of these views may be useful in guiding intellectual development.

Discrimination

Learning rules through discrimination and generalization. Imagine a yellow-eyed cat staring intently at a bird cage containing a canary. When the canary is removed, the cat stops watching, but when the bird is returned once more to his perch, the cat resumes his watchful gaze. We say that the cat has discriminated the canary because he responds differentially to the presence and absence of the bird.

In contrast to structuralists, behaviorists generally explain the acquisition of this sort of discrimination behavior in terms of environmental conditions rather than in terms of changes in internal intellectual structures. Thus, a behaviorist would argue that the discrimination behavior of the above cat is explained more adequately by the animal's learning history with birds than by the operation of

Table 6–1   *How Rules Are Acquired*

Types of Rule Learning	Descriptions of Types
Learning by discrimination and generalization	Rules can be acquired through the discrimination of categories of stimuli
Learning by hypothesis testing	Rules can be discovered by testing assumptions regarding relationships among environmental phenomena
Social learning	Rules can be learned by observing rule-governed behavior in a model
Cumulative learning	Rules can be acquired as a result of learning sets of hierarchically related skills

internal intellectual mechanisms. More specifically, he would very likely assert that bird watching is generally a function of bird catching. Similar arguments would, of course, be advanced to explain human discrimination behavior. Thus, for example, girl watching could easily be substituted for bird watching in any of the currently thriving male chauvinist groups in our culture. But that's getting far ahead of our story. For the moment we must return to our cat.

Generalization

Suppose we observe that the cat looks in the direction of the cage not only when the canary is there, but also when any small bird is on the perch. We can now say that the cat's discrimination behavior has generalized so that at the very least it includes all the varieties of small birds which have been placed in the cage.

Presumably, if one varied the characteristics of the creatures in the cage to a sufficient degree, gradually a point would be reached at which the cat no longer displayed the same kind of watching behavior that he had in the past. For example, bird size might gradually be increased to the point that a large hawk was placed on the perch. Under this condition the cat might yowl and hide or at least pace nervously back and forth. The point at which the cat's response changed would define the limits of the category represented by the watching behavior.

The cat in this example demonstrates a rudimentary form of rule-governed behavior in that through the combined use of discrimination and generalization he responds differentially to different categories of objects in his environment. In this regard, his behavior is essentially the same as that of the small child described in an earlier example who evidenced rule-governed behavior by applying the verbal label *gogie* to the various breeds of dogs which she encountered in her neighborhood.

Discrimination learning as rule learning

Rule learning based on discrimination and generalization may occur in a number of ways. The most common behavioral description of the process, which has been documented in countless studies, holds that discrimination takes place when responses to one category of stimuli are reinforced while responses to another category of stimuli are not reinforced. The assumption underlying this classical view of rule learning is that non-reinforcement will produce a gradual diminution in response rate which will eventually lead to non-response to one category of stimuli. On the other hand, reinforcement will maintain a high rate of response to the other category (Hunt, 1962).

Discrimination learning and reinforcement

Throughout the course of development, children may learn vast numbers of rules through discrimination and generalization. Stimulus conditions and behavioral consequences will determine what categories of objects will be represented by rule-governed behavior. Thus, in the early years of life, children will invariably acquire concepts such as fork, knife, and spoon. If they live in a cold climate, they will learn to differentiate between mittens and gloves. As they are given increasing responsibility for their own care, they will learn the concepts of right and left, which they will apply in a variety of tasks ranging from putting on shoes to learning to read. They probably will not acquire the capability to distinguish between an oak leaf and a maple leaf at a very early age even if they live in a region where these trees abound. The reason has little to do with the difficulty of learning these concepts. Rather it involves the fact that there are generally no special consequences in the environment which accrue as a result of identifying oak leaves and maple leaves. If a child lived in a society in which gathering acorns and making maple syrup were widespread activities, he would very likely acquire the concepts of oak leaf and maple leaf quite early in life.

Rules acquired through discrimination and generalization

Learning rules through hypothesis testing. Although much of the rule learning occurring early in life may take place through discrimination and generalization, the acquisition of rules in older children and adults generally involves other, more complex behavioral processes (Kendler, Kendler, & Wells, 1960). As children develop, they learn techniques which enable them to acquire rules more quickly and efficiently than would be possible if rule learning were based solely on discrimination and generalization. These techniques generally take the form of covert intellectual behaviors which must be inferred from observations of the rule-learning behavior of the child.

One of the major ways in which older children and adults acquire rules is by hypothesis testing. Hypothesis-testing behavior is most apparent in situations calling for rule discovery. For example, when a high school student is given the problem of identifying an unknown substance in chemistry class, she must test a series of hypotheses to discover the rule identifying the substance with which she is dealing. Hypothesis testing, however, is not specifically limited to situations calling for rule discovery. For example, a child asked to write a list of spelling words ten times may test a series of hypotheses to find the rule for completing this onerous task as quickly as possible. The many children who write the first letter of a spelling word ten times, the next letter ten times, and so on, until they have completed their assignment, show evidence of this kind of unexpected hypothesis testing.

The hypothesis-testing view of rule acquisition was developed by Jerome Bruner and his colleagues working outside the behavioral tradition (Bruner, Goodnow, & Austin, 1956). Since its inception, it has received support in a variety of carefully designed laboratory studies (e.g., see Restle, 1962; Bower & Trabasso, 1964; Levine, 1962). The idea that people test hypotheses during rule acquisition was derived from the assumption that humans are active learners attempting to discover the nature of their environment through encounters with it. As we have seen, the behavioral position is that people's actions, including intellectual functioning, are controlled by environmental events, particularly those events which occur as direct consequences of behavior.

Despite the fact that hypothesis theory developed outside of the behavioral tradition, behavioral psychology has had no trouble accommodating the hypothesis-testing view of rule learning. For the behaviorist, hypothesis testing is simply learned problem-solving behavior under the control of environmental consequences. The principal consequence affecting such behavior is, of course, the achievement of problem solution. As Skinner (1974) remarks, "A person has a problem when some condition will be reinforcing but he lacks a response that will produce it. He will solve the problem when he emits such a response" (p. 111).

Strategies In a rule-discovery situation an individual will generally test a series of hypotheses which conform to an overall strategy. The strategy typically is not stated.

Moreover, in many cases an individual will not be able to describe the strategy used even when asked to do so. Fortunately, however, the strategies can be inferred through careful observation of the sequence of hypotheses which the individual tests.

Bruner et al. (1956) identified a number of strategies which can be used in rule-discovery situations. One of the most effective in the typical rule-learning task is the conservative-focusing strategy. To get some feel for this strategy, imagine two boys fishing for trout in a clear, fast-running stream. One boy casts his line repeatedly into the water and observes fish after fish darting toward the hook, but then stopping and turning away. Meanwhile, the other boy is catching fish to the degree that he is approaching his limit for the day. "You ought to change your bait," says the successful fisherman. "I don't think it is the bait," replies the frustrated angler. At this point we shall endow both boys with a seemingly unnatural degree of scientific curiosity which we shall explain by assuming that the discussion regarding fishing success has reached such heated proportions that it has eventuated in a wager of substantial size. Thus, together the boys begin to advance hypotheses concerning the factors which might influence trout catching. Of course, it could be the bait. On the other hand, the unsuccessful fisherman may have selected a hook which was too big, or perhaps he placed his sinker too close to the hook thereby alerting the trout to the danger associated with attempts to get the bait.

Conservative focusing

If the boys were to approach their bet about trout catching in a systematic way, that is by using the conservative-focusing strategy, they would test their hypotheses one at a time by varying one characteristic of the successful fishing approach while holding all other characteristics constant. For example, they might begin by altering the position of the sinker. If they continued to catch fish, they would know that sinker position was not relevant. They then might change bait. If they no longer caught fish, they would know that bait was relevant. However, they would still have to determine the relevance of hook size. They might find that both hook size and bait affect trout catching.

The conservative-focusing strategy is, of course, the experimental method of science which is indeed a powerful tool in rule discovery. Bruner and his associates have shown that the method of science is also a method of thinking which can be used by people in rule discovery occurring in everyday life.

Young children would not be nearly as scientific in their approach to rule discovery as the boys in our fishing example. However, Bruner and his colleagues have identified another strategy which does involve a degree of systematization and which often approximates the behavior of young children in rule-discovery tasks. This is the successive-scanning strategy. A child using a successive-scanning strategy concerns himself with one hypothesis at a time in the same way as that required by the focusing strategy. However, he does not take the trouble of insuring that characteristics associated with other hypotheses are held constant. For example, a 7- or 8-year-old child might test the hypothesis that hook size was a key factor in trout catching and at the same time change bait. The successive-scanning strategy is obviously much less efficient than the focusing strategy. A young child would have to test many more hypotheses to come up with a definitive answer regarding the essential factors associated with trout catching than would the older child using the focusing strategy. However, the scanning strategy does have the advantage of being simpler to implement than the focusing strategy. The child using the scanning approach need consider only one factor at a time. It is this fact which probably accounts for the tendency of young children to apply the scanning technique.

Successive scanning

Hypothesis testing is an almost continuous activity in childhood and undoubtedly accounts for much of the rule learning which occurs from the age of three or four throughout life. Parents and teachers are often unaware of the hypotheses which children advance in their efforts to acquire rules. However, children's hypothesis frequently come to light after the fact in many of the surprising and charming things which they say. For example, a young child who had just fallen off the swing and had the "wind knocked out of him" announced upon regaining his voice, "I'm still living." Clearly he had made certain assumptions about the effects of falling off the swing. Or consider a boy who said to his mother just before going to bed, "Mom, is the world upside down at night?" Obviously, he had been making weighty assumptions about the nature of things in his environment even though there was nothing in his previous behavior to lead the mother to suspect that her child had ever thought about the spatial orientation of the earth.

Rule acquisition through social learning. Despite the fact that a child may learn many rules through hypothesis testing, hypothesis testing probably does not account for the lion's share of rule learning which occurs in the course of development. If it did, the child would be deprived of the vast reservoir of rules amassed within the culture. As Skinner (1974) points out, ". . . not much can be learned in a single lifetime, and an important function of a culture is to transmit what others have learned" (p. 111).

Observational learning

Social-learning theorists take the position that much of the rule learning which occurs during development is acquired through observation (Bandura,

Children acquire intellectual capabilities through observation.

1969). The child observes someone in the environment (for example, a parent or teacher) who models behavior consistent with rules which the child is attempting to acquire. Although the child may not reveal that a rule has been acquired at the time of observation, subsequently the child may imitate the observed behavior, thereby giving evidence of learning.

In some cases modeling which eventuates in observational learning takes the form of behavioral enactment of the rule to be acquired. For example, a teacher may say to a child *We write our stories this way* and then demonstrate the linear left-to-right sequencing customary in written communication. Sometimes modeling may be in the form of a verbal description of a rule, as when a first-grade teacher says: *Remember, when two vowels go walking, the first one does the talking*.

Imitation, like modeling, may occur in either behavioral or verbal form. Thus a child might demonstrate the "walking-vowels" rule by reading words such as *goat* and *leaf* aloud. Or the child might be asked to state the rule verbally upon seeing double-voweled words.

Whether children imitate a model behaviorally or verbally, their imitated responses must go beyond exact duplication of the model's actions before it can be assumed that a rule has been acquired. Imitation implies more than a monkey see, monkey do kind of mimicry. It indicates the ability to generalize from observed behavior displaying a rule to new instances of the rule.

The issue of whether or not people can in fact acquire rules by observation has been a subject of heated debate among rule-learning theorists. Critics of the social-learning position have asserted that although people can mimic, they cannot learn rules by imitation. A number of experiments have cast doubt on the validity of this criticism (Zimmerman & Rosenthal, 1974). For example, Rosenthal, Zimmerman, and Durning (1970) found that children can acquire rules governing their question-asking behavior as a result of observing a model in an experimental setting. For instance, these investigators demonstrated that children who observed an experimenter asking causal questions were able to imitate that type of question without duplicating the exact verbal behavior of the experimenter-model.

Imitation and mimicry

Not only do children acquire rules through observation, but also they may acquire strategies which can be used in rule discovery by observing the behavior of models. For example, in a developmental study of rule learning in third, fifth, and seventh grade children, Laughlin, Moss, and Miller (1969) demonstrated that children can be taught rule-learning strategies through observation of a model. The effectiveness of modeling instruction, however, is influenced by the developmental level of the child. Thus modeling of a strategy which involved a systematic approach to rule discovery analogous to that required in conservative focusing was found to be more effective at the fifth grade level than it was at either the third or seventh grade levels. Seventh graders used the strategy extensively without instruction, but it was difficult for the third graders to acquire the strategy even when they had been exposed to appropriate modeling.

Observational learning of strategies

The demonstration that rules and rule-learning strategies can be acquired through observation raises the possibility that modeling may be a key factor in explaining how the home and the school affect the intellectual development of the child. Parents and teachers model rules and rule-learning strategies extensively during the course of the day. Even when they are unaware that their behavior is influencing children, observational learning may be occurring.

Rule acquisition through cumulative learning. One of the long-standing difficulties which has plagued behavioral efforts to detail a plausible explanation of intellectual functioning involves the well-established fact that there are developmental differences in intellectual capability. Behaviorists claim that intellectual functioning is environmentally determined. It would seem from this point of view that all individuals ought to react in the same manner to environmental stimulation. As we have illustrated in a number of instances, this is not the case. For example, recall that Laughlin, Moss, and Miller (1969) found that it was difficult to teach a particular rule-learning strategy to third graders.

Development and learning history

In the main, behaviorists have attempted to explain developmental differences by falling back on the concept of learning history. The behavioral argument in essence is that differences in individual capability are largely a function of differences in past experience. Of course, the physiological makeup of the individual may play a determining role as well. An infant, for example, is not physically equipped to perform most of the behaviors displayed by an older child.

Developmentalists outside the behavioral tradition have been highly critical of the concept of learning history, arguing that it is a catch-all phrase which behaviorists use to explain phenomena which cannot be dealt with effectively from a behavioral viewpoint. Critics assert that to say that developmental differences in behavior occur because of learning history provides little or no information of any value since the critical variables in learning history which might affect behavior are not specified. Robert Gagné (1968, 1970) has constructed a cumulative-learning model which attempts to detail the critical characteristics of learning history as they relate to the development of intellectual competence. Gagné takes the position that learning tasks differ in complexity and that the more complex forms of learning, such as rule learning, are dependent upon simpler varieties of learning. Insofar as an individual has not acquired the skills associated with the mastery of a simpler form, he or she will not be able to master the more complex types.

Gagné asserts that observed developmental differences in intellectual functioning arise in part as a result of variations in the mastery of skills which are prerequisite to the attainment of competencies associated with the higher forms of learning. He does not rule out the traditional developmental position which assigns developmental differences in intellectual capability to maturational factors. However, he does believe that there would be substantial advantage to a fuller explanation than has occurred in the past of the effects of cumulative learning occurring over long time spans.

Gagné's eight types of learning

Gagné distinguishes eight types of learning. The simplest variety is signal learning, which is Gagné's name for traditional Pavlovian conditioning. In signal learning, a cue is paired with another stimulus which has the power to evoke a reflexive reaction. In the Pavlovian studies of conditioning in dogs, the cue was generally a bell which was paired with meat powder which in turn evoked a salivation response. After a time the dogs in Pavlov's studies learned to emit the salivation response when the bell was presented even in the absence of meat powder.

The second type of learning which Gagné distinguishes is stimulus-response learning, which is essentially operant conditioning. Stimulus-response learning involves the presentation of a cue which serves as a signal for the occurrence of a response which is subsequently reinforced.

Both signal learning and stimulus-response learning involve only one response. The next three varieties of learning which Gagné identifies involve chains of stimulus-response associations. Type 3, which is called chaining, requires the learning of a set of responses in sequence. Learning to tie shoes is a familiar example of a chaining task which children are required to master. Tying one's shoes

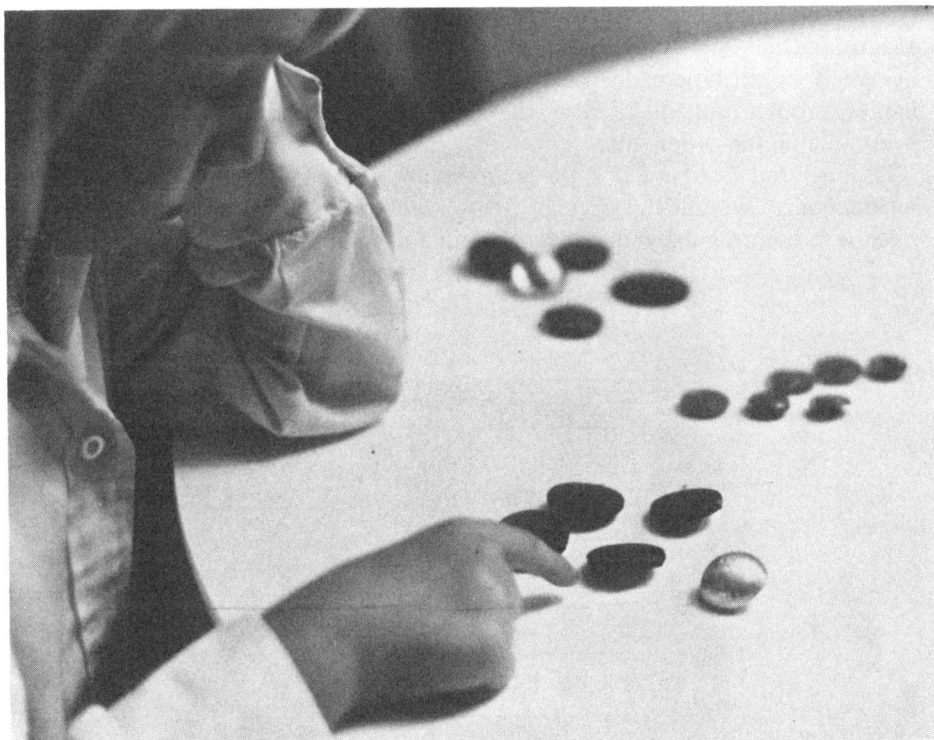

*There are generally several prerequisite forms of learning associated with the acquisition
of complex rule-governed behaviors. The child in this picture is learning the concepts
of more, less, and same, which are necessary in making judgments about the equality
and inequality of sets of objects.*

involves a series of motor movements. Each movement is a response which in
turn serves as a stimulus for the next movement.

Verbal association is Gagné's fourth type of learning. Verbal association is
chaining which is verbal in character. Gagné distinguishes verbal association
from chaining because in verbal association the learner often emits covert responses which mediate between stimuli and responses in a chain. For example, a
young child might learn to identify the word *look* by commenting to himself
that the two *o*'s in the word look like glasses.

The fifth category of learning which Gagné identifies is multiple-discrimination
learning. This category refers to the capability to distinguish among individual
stimuli in a set. Learning to identify sets of sight words or letters of the alphabet
are familiar multiple-discrimination tasks faced by the school-age child.

Gagné's sixth type of learning is concrete-concept learning. Gagné uses the term
concrete concept to refer to what we have described as a simple variety of rule
learning, namely acquisition of the ability to classify concrete objects. The verbal
labeling behavior of young children offers perhaps the most familiar example of
this form of learning. Learning to name the countless objects in the environment,
including houses, dogs, and cars, is a consuming pastime of the young child.

Gagné's seventh type of learning is rule learning. Gagné reserves the term *rule*
for learning which involves the specification of relationships among concepts. For
example, consider the rule *round things roll*. This rule specifies the relationship
between two concepts, *round things* and *roll*. Presumably the reason for distinguishing between concrete concepts and rules involving relationships among

concepts is Gagné's view that the acquisition of concrete concepts is prerequisite to learning rules specifying relationships among concepts.

Gagné's eighth type of learning is problem solving. As indicated earlier in the chapter, problem solving requires the application of subordinate rules in the discovery of a higher order rule.

As illustrated in figure 6-3, the varieties of learning which Gagné has identified generally, though not in every case, represent increasingly complex forms which are hierarchically dependent upon one another. Thus, problem solving

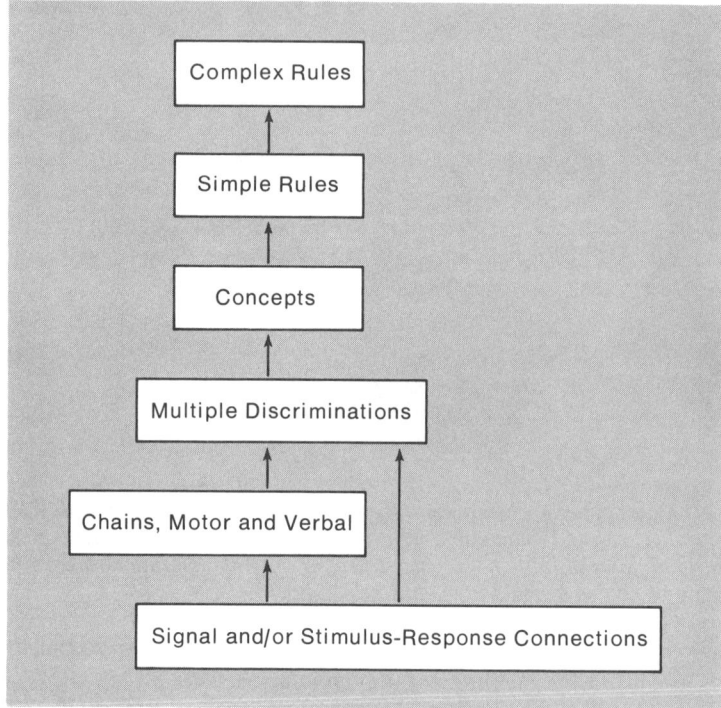

Figure 6–3   *A general sequence for cumulative learning. (Adapted from R. M. Gagné, Contributions of learning to human development.* Psychological Review, *1968, 75, 182. Copyright 1968 by the American Psychological Association. Reprinted by permission.)*

requires previous rule learning. Rule learning in turn is dependent upon concrete-concept learning. The acquisition of concrete concepts is based on the ability to make multiple discriminations. Multiple-discrimination learning in some cases depends upon verbal association and chaining. Finally, verbal associations and chaining require stimulus-response learning and in a few instances signal learning.

Cumulative learning and conservation

Gagné's cumulative-learning view provides a potentially powerful tool for explaining why intellectual development proceeds as slowly as it does and, perhaps, for taking steps to accelerate growth when that course of action seems desirable. Gagné's analysis of a task which Piagetians call conservation of volume illustrates the application of his approach to the explanation of intellectual

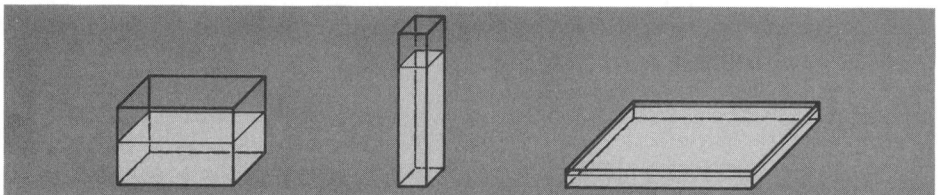

Figure 6–4   *Materials typically used in conservation of volume tasks.*

development. The conservation task requires the child to judge whether or not water poured into a tall, thin container is equal to what it was when it was held in a short, wide container. The materials typically used in conservation tasks are illustrated in figure 6-4.

As we shall see later in the chapter, Piagetians argue that the ability to

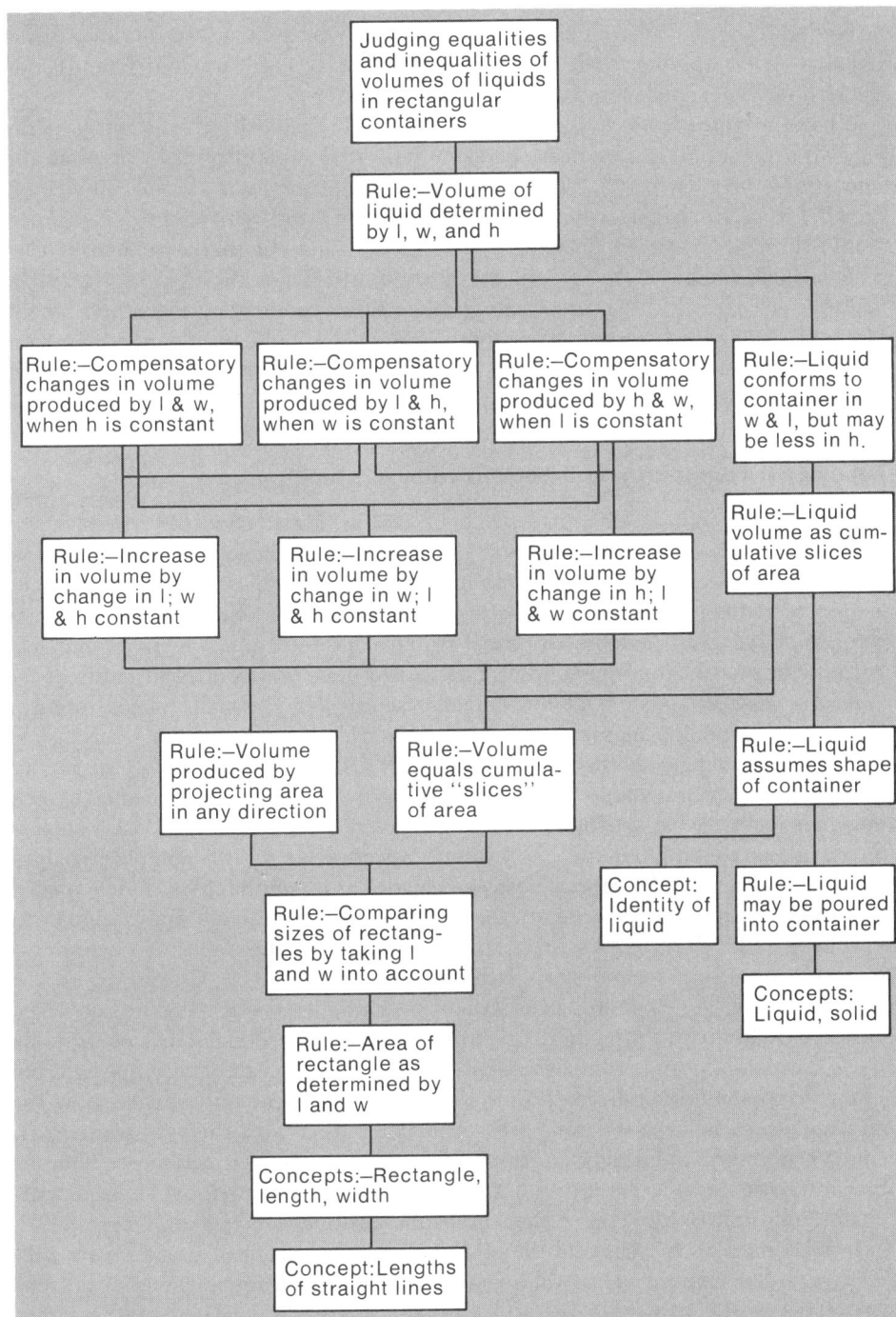

A *cumulative learning sequence pertaining to the development of nonmetric judg-* **Figure 6–5**
ments of liquid volume. (From R. M. Gagné, Contributions of learning to human development. Psychological Review, *1968, 75, 184. Copyright 1968 by the American Psychological Association. Reprinted by permission.)*

conserve volume is a developmental ability which evolves as a result of the formation of intellectual structures based on the biological makeup of the individual and his interactions with the environment. Gagné's account, which is illustrated in figure 6-5, is much more explicit. He describes conservation as the result of cumulative learning. In general, what the analysis in figure 6-5 suggests is that the child cannot comprehend the three-dimensional measurement of volume until he understands the two-dimensional measurement of area. Likewise, he will not be able to comprehend the measurement of area until he understands uni-dimensional concepts such as length.

What one gains from an analysis of the sort illustrated by this example is not only an explanation of how a particular intellectual capability develops, but also some guidelines as to what to teach a child in order to foster his intellectual growth. Gagné suggests that parents, teachers, and curriculum developers would do well to specify in concrete terms the kinds of intellectual tasks they believe children ought to be able to accomplish. Then these tasks should be analyzed to reveal the prerequisite skills necessary for task accomplishment. Next the skills which the child currently possesses should be identified. Instruction should then be targeted toward the development of those capabilities which the child needs to acquire to master those tasks which have been identified as critical for intellectual growth.

Behavioral Technology and Socialization in Contemporary Society

As we pointed out in chapter 1, one of the principal concepts to shape the character of contemporary culture is the idea that science and technology hold the key to human progress. Since the inception of science as a point of view and a form of human endeavor, advocates of the scientific method have maintained a fundamental faith that the empirical study of physical phenomena would lead not only to increased understanding but also to increased control of nature.

As the scientific movement developed, science was given the major responsibility for advancing our understanding of natural phenomena while the task of control was assigned to technology. Although faith in science as a tool for advancing the state of human knowledge has remained high, the theme of technological control has become somewhat sullied in recent years. Technology has brought us polluted air and water, overcrowded cities, computerized invasion of privacy, and weapons with the capability to annihilate all living species. Nevertheless, it can be argued that technology has solved many significant problems and that it can assist in solving the problems which have accrued as by-products of past technological achievements.

As indicated in chapter 2, the behavioral perspective is part of the larger cultural tradition asserting faith in both science and technological control. Behaviorism has its origins in seventeenth-century empiricism. The empiricist philosophy extended scientific faith in the power of empirical study to the view that all knowledge is derived from sensory experience. From this perspective, the content of one's intellect is a direct function of one's experiences. The behavioral position that intellectual functioning is determined by environmental conditions is an outgrowth of the empiricist position.

In keeping with the cultural theme of technological control based on scientific discovery, behaviorists argue that a technology of behavior is essential not only for attaining the goal of a better life, but also for the survival of the human species. From the behavioral standpoint, one of the most critical issues of modern life is the fact that we have developed a powerful technology based on achievements in the natural sciences, but have lagged far behind in technological development in the social sciences. Humans use highly sophisticated technologies in such areas as physics, chemistry, and biology to control nature.

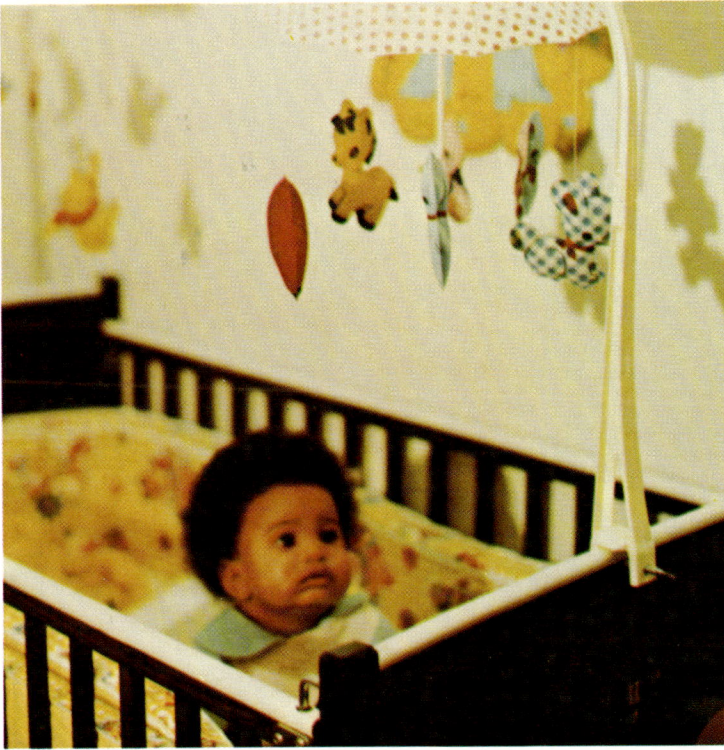

Environmental stimulation influences intellectual growth.

Behaviorists assert that if we are to control wisely, our own level of development must be increased. Regarding this line of reasoning, Skinner (1971) argues:

> What we need is a technology of behavior. We could solve our problems quickly enough if we could adjust the growth of the world's population as precisely as we adjust the course of a space ship, or improve agriculture and industry with some of the confidence with which we accelerate high-energy particles, or move toward a peaceful world with something like the steady progress with which physics has approached absolute zero (even though both remain presumably out of reach). But a behavioral technology comparable in power and precision to physical and biological technology is lacking, and those who do not find the very possibility ridiculous are more likely to be frightened by it than reassured. (p. 5)

During the last two decades, behaviorists have made extensive efforts to develop a behavioral technology of the sort for which Skinner has called. These efforts, although still in their infancy, have produced impressive results in such fields as mental health, education, and child development.

The emerging technology of behavioral socialization in the main has taken the form of systematic environmental control. The intent is to intervene in an active way for the purpose of shaping development. Intervention involves first of all the control of reinforcers, modeling stimuli, and cues which may affect behavior. In addition, intervention includes the careful sequencing of learning tasks from the simple to the complex in the manner recommended by Gagné.

Ultimately, the use of behavioral principles in socialization will probably depend upon the extent to which the philosophy and science of behaviorism articulate to the demands of life in contemporary society. Among the most important forces shaping contemporary culture are the rapid cultural change created by technological progress, the extensive cultural diversity that has characterized our nation from its inception, and the rise of humanistic concerns stemming from the threat of dehumanization produced largely by technology. If behaviorism is to be an effective tool for socialization, it must articulate to these cultural themes.

Behavioral socialization and cultural change. As we have noted previously, the modern technological society in which we live is a society characterized by rapid cultural change. The accelerated rate of change in contemporary life creates continual demands for adaptation on the part of the individual. Modern people must adjust to changing living patterns, changing work requirements, continuous physical mobility, and changing values. Social theorists (e.g., see Toffler, 1970) argue that in order to adapt to the level of change which exists in contemporary culture, society must place greater emphasis on the development of problem-solving skills than it has in the past.

Behaviorists take the position that through the application of behavioral technology humans' intellectual capabilities can be altered to meet the demands of a changing society. As we have demonstrated, behaviorists argue that higher forms of intellectual functioning, such as problem solving, may be developed by systematic instruction in prerequisite capabilities related to less complex varieties of learning. As the technology of behavioral control is refined, it should be possible to develop a level of problem-solving capability in the populace which has not generally been achieved in the past.

Behavioral socialization and cultural diversity. America is a nation built by immigrants, and in consequence cultural diversity has been a part of our society since its inception. Diversity has been both a societal characteristic and a social problem. Suspicion, hatred, and persecution of various ethnic groups have a long-standing tradition in American culture.

For a period of time, we Americans attempted to deal with the problem of cultural diversity through a melting-pot concept of socialization. This concept, however, failed to solve the problem of diversity. Despite assertions that all ethnic groups would eventually blend into one cultural mainstream, Americans continue to live in a highly varied social system.

Beyond the undeniable fact that the melting-pot solution to the problem of cultural diversity did not achieve its purposes, it unfortunately must be said that from the standpoint of socialization the melting-pot concept has produced some very unfortunate consequences. In part because of the melting-pot idea, American society has tended to judge all individuals on the basis of a single set of value dimensions constructed to conform to the characteristics of the dominant middle-class culture. For example, in the area of intellectual development children have been judged on the basis of tests of middle-class verbal skills. As was pointed out in the previous chapter, substantial social class and ethnic differences have been observed in tests of intellectual performance. There can be no doubt that such differences are associated to a degree with the kinds of skills the tests measure.

Cultural diversity and intellectual competence

As the nation has begun to move away from the melting-pot concept of socialization toward a stance which values cultural diversity, increasing numbers of people have begun to question the justifiability of the practice of measuring intellectual competence in terms of verbal skills prized by middle-class society. As indicated in the previous chapter, the emerging issue is essentially this: To what extent is the concept of intelligence simply one of the many extant tools for denigrating the characteristics of those groups which differ from the middle class?

Behavioral technology and middle-class values

Behaviorists have not concerned themselves with the legitimacy of judging all children in accordance with value dimensions which reflect middle-class cultural characteristics. They have simply assumed that observed differences have resulted from environmental influences and that such differences can be eliminated through the application of behavioral technology.

For those many individuals both within the middle class and within ethnic minorities who take the position that it is essential for all children to develop middle-class intellectual capabilities, behavioral technology offers an option which should be given serious consideration. There is, however, a significant danger associated with the behavioral approach. The high degree of environmental control required by behavioral technology may reinforce the long-established tradition of placing excessive amounts of control in the hands of middle-class socialization agents. When this occurs, as it often does in educational settings, children from ethnic minorities are placed in an inferior and vulnerable position vis-à-vis adults from the middle-class. Under these conditions, children's pride in their own language, their sense of cultural identity, and their belief in their own intellectual competence may all suffer serious damage.

Of course, there is nothing endemic in the behavioral position which demands that it be implemented in a way which will produce cultural denigration. It is, as it purports to be, a technology. As scientists and engineers never tire of reminding the lay person, technologies are neither good nor bad in and of themselves. They may, however, produce good or bad consequences depending upon how they are used.

Humanist criticisms of behaviorism

Behavioral technology and humanism. As we have indicated previously, humanists have generally regarded behaviorism as inimical to their views. With respect to the issue of intellectual functioning, they have faulted behaviorists for their failure to deal with complex mental processes and for their denial that humans' intellects direct their actions. As might be expected from a consideration of their criticisms of the behavioral conception of the intellect, humanists have serious reservations about the behavioral technology of socialization as it applies to intellectual development. They question the idea that intellectual development can be enhanced through stringent environmental control, and they argue that behaviorists have failed to consider the growth of the self-directive functions of the child's intellect.

Behaviorists assert that the validity of the criticisms humanists have directed against them can be questioned. As we have shown in the description of rule learning, behaviorists do deal with complex intellectual actions, and they do recognize that intellectual behaviors play an important role in directing behavior. As for the criticisms of the behavioral technology of socialization, it can be argued that these grow out of an overly narrow conceptualization of the relationship between people and their technological environment. Behavioral technology is intended to create an environment which will control and thereby enhance intellectual growth, but it also must be pointed out that people developed behavioral technology. Their relationship to technology is cyclical in character. Technology enhances intellectual capability. Then people use their newly acquired capability to develop additional technology to gain increased control of themselves and their environmental circumstances.

Behaviorist rebuttals

INTELLECTUAL DEVELOPMENT FROM THE PIAGETIAN PERSPECTIVE

Having examined the basic principles of the behavioral position regarding intellectual growth and the relationship of those principles to socialization in contemporary society, we will now turn attention to the constructionist view of intellectual development which has been fashioned over the last 40 years by Jean Piaget and his colleagues. Piaget's constructionist view is an extension of the structuralist tradition which has dominated conceptions of the intellect during most of recorded history. In the Piagetian position, the mind, or rather its contemporary surrogate the intellectual structure, is given a position of primacy in controlling behavior. Intellectual structures control how people think and thereby exert some influence over what they will do. However, in contrast to earlier structuralist views, Piaget does not conceive of intellectual structures as independent of environmental influences. Indeed, in the constructionist view the individual forms intellectual structures through his or her interactions with the environment. The biological makeup of the individual determines the manner in which interaction occurs, but the kinds of environmental encounters which the individual has determine when structures will develop.

Intelligence as the Construction of Knowledge

In Piaget's view, people are not the passive recipients of information. Rather they construct knowledge as a result of their encounters with the environment. Piaget holds that the manner in which knowledge is construed changes as a function of development. The developmental changes which occur first involve a movement from subjective, personalized representations of reality to objective representations of experiential phenomena, and second, include movement from concrete representations toward the development of abstract thinking capabilities.

From personal to objective knowledge. In the early stages of any given level of development, knowledge is highly subjective. The developing individual fails to distinguish between his own construction of things and the objective

Egocentrism

reality of the phenomena which he experiences. Piaget uses the label *egocentrism* to describe this failure. Egocentrism manifests itself in different ways at different periods of development. For example, in the earliest stages of life it takes the form of a failure to distinguish between imagistic experiences and the objects which give rise to them. At a somewhat more advanced level of growth, egocentrism may show itself in the child's inability to distinguish between his own intellectual representation of things and the way things actually are.

Objectivity

As development within a given period progresses, the child's conception of reality becomes increasingly objective. The source of objectivity is the individual's increasing knowledge of his own intellectual functioning. The more the child learns about the way in which he construes reality, the more able he becomes to appreciate the limitations of his own perspective.

As the child moves from one qualitatively distinct developmental period to the next higher period, he will acquire new intellectual capabilities which initially he will not thoroughly understand. As a consequence, new forms of egocentrism will emerge. Thus at each new developmental level, the child must not only acquire new intellectual competencies, but also must gain some understanding of the nature of his intellectual capabilities so that he can make objective judgments concerning experiences.

From concrete to abstract knowledge. During the initial stages of development, the individual's knowledge of the world tends to be closely tied to immediate concrete events. In the earliest stages of development, attempts to acquire knowledge take the form of efforts to gain an accurate conception of objects in the physical environment. For example, one of the principal developmental accomplishments of the young child is the discovery that objects endure over time.

At advanced developmental levels the individual's concepts become increasingly free from concrete circumstances. With the development of language the child acquires a powerful tool for representing environmental events symbolically. As indicated earlier in the chapter, as the child approaches adolescence the capability to use symbolic representation will be refined to the point that the individual will be able to represent hypothetical events. At this point, the child's thinking processes become to a large extent independent of concrete conditions.

Piaget's Analysis of the Intellect

As illustrated in table 6-2, Piaget distinguishes three fundamental characteristics

Table 6–2 *Characteristics of the Intellect*

Names	Descriptions
Functions of intelligence	innate tendencies to organize and adapt to the environment
Contents of intelligence	behavioral manifestations of intelligence
Structures of intelligence	organizational properties of intelligence

of the intellect: function, content, and structure. The functional characteristics of intelligence define the manner in which the intellect operates on the environment. Intellectual contents and structures refer respectively to intelligent behavior and the mental mechanisms underlying it.

The functions of intelligence. The functions of intelligence are genetically determined modes of action which control the kinds of interactions which the individual has with his or her environment. Intellectual functions determine how the child makes developmental progress. They provide the motivating force underlying intellectual growth, and they control the kinds of changes in intellectual functioning which take place during the course of development.

One primary function of intelligence is the innate tendency to organize experience. In Piaget's view, this tendency is the motivating force underlying intellectual development. The child's propensity for structuring experiences manifests itself in his continous efforts to interpret events even when he lacks the necessary skills or information to do so adequately. For example, the young child who says *He finded his jacket* shows evidence of having made an active and rather impressive attempt on his own to organize language in terms of rules. If the child were a passive learner, he would only utter those sentences which he had heard others produce. He would not attempt to establish his own rules for constructing language. *Organization*

In order for children to utilize their propensity for organization, they must be free to act upon the environment, to advance hypotheses and to test them by manipulating objects in their surroundings. With regard to this point, Piaget states,

> Experience is always necessary for intellectual development. . . . But I fear that we may fall into the illusion that being submitted to an experience (a demonstration) is sufficient for a subject to disengage the structure involved. But more than this is required. The subject must be active, must transform things, and find the structure of his own actions on the objects. (Elkind & Duckworth, 1973, p. 207)

Despite the fact that Piaget holds that the child has an innate tendency to act upon his environment, he also recognizes that the developing child is influenced by his environment. In recognition of this fact, Piaget suggests that the tendency to adapt to environmental conditions is a major function of intelligence. Through adaptation, the child increases his knowledge about the environment and about his own intellectual functioning. In addition, the child acquires new ways to represent environmental conditions. Adaptation, then, provides the means by which the child moves from egocentrism to objectivity and from concrete to abstract thought. *Adaptation*

The contents of intelligence. The contents of intelligence are the specific behavioral capabilities of the individual. For example, when a child displays the capability to name objects or to solve a particular kind of mathematical problem, he is evidencing behavioral competencies which are part of the contents of his intelligence.

Piaget's many observations of the mental functioning of children have led him to conclude that the contents of intelligence are variable across situations. The level of capability which the individual displays will be determined in part by the specific type of task which he is performing. For example, an individual who is clearly able to perform an algebraic problem of a given degree of complexity may be unable to solve the same problem when it is presented in geometric form. The obvious source of this kind of variability in performance is of course differences in experience with different kinds of tasks.

The structures of intelligence. The term *intellectual structure* refers to the organizational properties of intelligence. Piaget, like other structural theorists, assumes that there is some form of systematic arrangement of elements within the mental apparatus limiting the kinds of intellectual capabilities which an individual can display behaviorally.

Piaget's position differs from that of early structuralists in that he assumes that intellectual structures are created as a result of interactions with the environment. The early structuralist view, which can be traced at least as far back as early Greek civilization, asserted that intellectual structures were innate givens. Plato's concept of innate ideas is an example of this view. The notion of a pre-formed intellect offered at least some explanation as to how people could know reality, but it did little to enhance people's knowledge of the relationship between the environment and the intellect. Piaget's assertion that intellectual structures emerge as a result of environmental encounters gives recognition to the role of interactions between the individual and the environment in promoting intellectual growth.

How Intellectual Development Occurs

One of the most compelling arguments for a constructive theory of intellectual development is that in many instances children do not learn when they are passive recipients of information from the environment. David Elkind (1974) reports an interesting Piagetian anecdote which illustrates this fact. While talking with a young boy, Piaget happened to ask how the lake of Geneva was formed. The boy responded,

> . . . "There was a giant who stood on the mountain holding a huge boulder above his head, and when he saw his enemy below he threw the boulder at him and this made a great hole in the ground. Then it rained and filled the hole full of water and that is how the lake was made." (p. 59)

After expressing tactful appreciation of the boy's yarn, Piaget explained in some detail that the lake had been formed by melting glaciers in the area. A few months later, Piaget ran into the child again and asked if the boy remembered their previous conversation about the lake. The boy assured the grandfatherly Piaget that he did indeed remember the conversation whereupon Piaget asked him to recount once more how the lake was made: "The boy replied, without a trace of malice or guile, 'Well, there was a giant who stood on the mountain, holding. . .'" (p. 69). If intellectual development cannot be accounted for entirely in terms of environmental input, how does it occur?

Developmental progress through accommodation and assimilation. As we have already indicated, the intellectual functions, organization and adaptation, are responsible for producing developmental progress. Organization provides the motivational force underlying developmental change while adaptation is the vehicle through which developmental progress occurs. Adaptation may take two forms: accommodation and assimilation.

Accommodation   Accommodations are adaptive changes occurring in the manner in which the individual acts on the environment. During the course of development, the child will encounter many situations in which previously acquired ways of representing or reacting to experience will not be adequate to meet new environmental conditions. Under these circumstances the child must change the way in which he represents environmental events.

At the simplest level, accommodations to the environment take the form of changes in the character of physical acts used to represent reality. For example, at some point in the life of an infant a rattle becomes not merely something to look at when it is placed within view, but rather an object that can be grasped. Learning to grasp the rattle requires an accommodation on the infant's part in that he must act upon the environment in a new way. This new way of behaving toward the rattle constitutes a new meaning for the object.

At advanced levels of development, accommodations may take the form of changes in symbolic representations of reality. For example, at some point during the preschool years, the child will discover that numbers are not merely words used in rote counting but rather are symbols representing quantities of things.

Assimilation

After accommodation has taken place and the child has acquired a new mode of representing experiences, he may apply his newly developed intellectual competencies in a variety of situations and thereby enrich his knowledge of the world. Piaget uses the term *assimilation* to refer to the acquisition of new information which can be represented by an existing intellectual structure.

Play offers a good illustration of assimilatory behavior. For instance, after engaging in the serious task of acquiring the capability of representing a rattle as a graspable object, an infant might well play with a variety of objects in the crib, holding each one and cooing with delight. In engaging in this kind of play, the infant would have assimilated new objects to a previously acquired cognitive structure.

Equilibrium and disequilibrium in development. Piaget takes the position that although development is in some respects occurring continuously, there are nevertheless dramatic qualitative shifts in the level of development which occur across relatively long time intervals. These qualitative changes in development take the form of significant alterations in the manner in which children represent their experiences. Changes which occur in the mode of representing reality are initiated by perceived inadequacies in previous methods of representing experience. Developmental change is completed when the individual acquires a new set of intellectual structures which will permit him or her to represent experiences in an adequate way.

Equilibrium

For the most part, intellectual functioning within any given level of development represents what Piaget calls a state of equilibrium. That is, the intellectual structures which the child uses to represent environmental conditions are in harmony with the information extracted from the environment. For example, at some point after a child has learned to talk, she will acquire the ability to count things. Her rudimentary counting skills will provide her with a variety of useful information about things in her surroundings. Insofar as this is the case, we can say that the child is in a state of equilibrium vis-à-vis her environment.

Disequilibrium

The child enters a state of disequilibrium when his mode of representing reality is no longer adequate to the conditions which he faces. Figure 6-6 provides an illustration of this state of affairs in the area of number concepts. Although the child in this cartoon has rudimentary counting skills, he does not have a grasp of the fundamental mathematical fact that a whole must remain unchanged despite variations in the patterning of the parts.

"Why did you cut my squash in half, Mommy? Now I
have TWICE as much to eat."

Figure 6–6 *Intellectual functioning of a child in a state of disequilibrium. (The Family Circus
by Bil Keane, reprinted courtesy The Register and Tribune Syndicate, Inc.)*

A child's failure to recognize the invariance of wholes may be revealed in a
variety of surprising and amusing behaviors. For example, if you ask a kindergarten child if there are more boys or more children in his class, the child would
probably say that there are more boys in the class if boys outnumber girls. Or, to
take an example which closely parallels that in the cartoon, consider the case of a
young boy who complained to his mother that he wanted two cookies instead of
the one he had been given. The mother simply broke his cookie in half much to
the child's satisfaction.

The child in a state of disequilibrium is a problem solver. He does not, indeed
according to Piaget he cannot, acquire the knowledge he needs by being told
what he so obviously does not know. For example, it would do no good to tell a
child who was not already aware of the fact that wholes must remain invariant.
Nor would it be of any value to tell a child that there are really more children in
the class than there are boys since in all likelihood he would simply make the
same kind of erroneous judgments of things in other analogous situations.

In Piaget's view, the child learns those things requiring significant modifications in intellectual structures by discovery. The learning occurs slowly since it
requires repeated and thorough examination of the phenomena under consideration. In the absence of discovery, learning does not occur at all. Like the boy
who stubbornly asserted that the lake of Geneva was formed by a stone-throwing
giant, the child who is deprived of the opportunity to discover the nature of things
for himself will continue to represent things as he has in the past.

Periods of Intellectual Development

As indicated in table 6-3, Piaget conceives of intellectual development in terms
of three broad periods: the sensorimotor period, the period of concrete operations,
and the period of formal operations. These three periods describe a progressive
movement from subjective to objective thought and from concrete to abstract
thought. During the first period of development, the child learns to represent the
concrete world through his own physical actions. Toys, for example, may be
represented as objects to grasp. A bottle, on the other hand, may be represented
as an object to suck. During the period of concrete operations, the child represents the concrete world with words. Finally during the period of formal opera-

tions, the individual's concepts are freed from concrete experience. At this stage the individual is able to consider hypothetical experiences which have no correspondence in reality. In each of these three periods, the child's initial conceptions are highly subjective. However, in the course of progress through a given stage, the child becomes a more and more objective thinker.

The sensorimotor period. The first major period of intellectual development is the sensorimotor period. This period describes the developmental accomplishments of the child occurring for the most part before the onset of language. The sensorimotor period normally extends from birth to about two years of age. During this brief span of time, the child acquires the necessary capabilities to conceptualize experiences through his actions.

The most fundamental intellectual accomplishment of the sensorimotor period is the acquisition of the ability to recognize objects as discrete entities free to move in space and stable over time. Piaget assumes that objects are initially regarded only as perceptual experiences. They have no spatial existence for the child when they are not in view, nor do they endure over time since the instant that they disappear from view they cease to exist perceptually.

Object recognition

In order to learn that objects exist in space and time, a child must learn to distinguish between objects and his perceptions of them. In Piaget's view, the child makes this kind of distinction as a result of changes in the manner in which he acts in the presence of the things around him. In the initial phases of life, the child makes very little attempt to adapt to the presence of objects in the environment. However, he very quickly learns to follow objects with his eyes, and then to look in the direction of an object. At a much more advanced level, the child will learn to search for things which have disappeared from view, thereby giving clear evidence of recognition of the fact that the object endures even when it is not present perceptually.

The child's inability to distinguish objects from percepts constitutes the earliest form of egocentrism. Reality for an infant is what he sees and hears. Through

Periods of Intellectual Development

Table 6–3

Period Names	Major Period Accomplishments
Sensorimotor Intelligence (ages 0–2 years)	The child learns to represent concrete experiences through physical acts.
Concrete Operational Intelligence (ages 2–11 years)	The child learns to represent concrete events with symbols and rules. During the first half of this period, called the subperiod of preoperational thought, the child learns to use symbols. During the second half, the child learns rules to relate concrete objects.
Formal Operational Intelligence (ages 11 or 12 throughout life)	The child acquires abstract thinking ability.

the infant's physical interactions with the things represented by his images, he gradually learns that objects exist independently of his perception of them. This realization is the earliest achievement of objectivity in intellectual functioning.

Causality

As a child begins to learn that objects have an existence which is independent of his experience, he will also begin to realize that the things which happen in the environment must have a cause. Consistent with his initial tendencies toward egocentrism, the child assumes at first that his own thoughts control environmental happenings (Piaget, 1954). In many, if not all, cultures, this belief may persist in various forms even into adult life. The practice of voodoo provides an example. The adult who believes that by sticking a pin in a doll he will be able to cause harm to an enemy is not very different in his belief system from the child who takes the position that what he thinks will control what will happen.

The first disconfirming evidence to the child's view that thought controls environmental events comes when the child learns that his own actions can affect what happens in the environment. Piaget (1952) recorded an observation of this kind of discovery in the following account of his daughter's behavior:

> At age three months and five days, Lucienne shakes her bassinet by moving her legs violently (bending and unbending them, etc.), which makes the cloth dolls swing from the hood. Lucienne looks at them, smiling, and recommences at once. . . . The next day, I present the dolls: Lucienne immediately moves, shakes her leg, but this time without smiling. Her interest seems intense and sustained. (pp. 157-58)

Toward the end of the sensorimotor period, a child will become quite adept at controlling objects by physical acts. As he gains skill in this regard, he will develop a thorough knowledge of the fact that events have physical causes. However, the child's knowledge will be restricted to nonverbal forms of intellectual functioning. When he acquires language, he will have to learn once again in a different way that thinking does not control the events which take place in the environment.

Laboratory studies of sensorimotor intelligence

Piaget (1952) developed his ideas concerning sensorimotor intelligence on the basis of observations of his own three children. In view of the limited number of children that he observed and the necessary lack of control associated with observation conducted without benefit of laboratory facilities, one might expect a significant amount of inaccuracy in Piaget's descriptions. However, a substantial amount of laboratory research conducted with great care and ingenuity has provided general support not only for Piaget's descriptions of child behavior during the sensorimotor period, but also for his interpretations of sensorimotor sequences (Harris, 1975).

Laboratory studies of sensorimotor behavior have focused heavily on the analysis of Piaget's views concerning object recognition. As indicated above, Piaget points out that in the early phases of life (birth to two months) a child does not adapt to objects in his environment. For example, he does not visually search for objects that have disappeared from view. Piaget (1954) argues that the reason for this is that objects lack permanence for the young child. According to this view, an object out of sight ceases to have a location and thus there is no reason to search for it. Perhaps there is another explanation. Maybe the infant simply fails to see that the object has disappeared, or maybe he cannot remember the object when it is out of sight.

Bower (1967) demonstrated that infants are able to perceive the disappearance of objects. Infants in his study were assigned to one of five conditions. In the first of these, a sphere was slowly covered by a screen. In the second, the sphere, which was a projected image, was gradually made to fade from view.

In the third condition, the sphere shrunk instantaneously to nothing. In the fourth condition, the sphere was covered instantly by a screen. The fifth condition was a control condition in which the sphere remained in its original position. Bower measured the sucking responses of infants in each of the five conditions. Sucking was less disrupted in conditions one and five than in the other conditions, suggesting that infants respond differentially to different types of disappearance.

Bower's (1967) research also indicated that at least for brief periods infants do remember objects that have disappeared. Bower found that sucking responses that had been suppressed during the disappearance of an object were restored to full strength when the object reappeared within five seconds after it initially vanished from view.

Bower's findings are supportive of Piaget's views in that they rule out two possible alternative explanations for the lack of visual-search behavior in infants. Research with older infants (three to nine months) provides more compelling evidence for Piaget's position. Piaget (1952) asserts that at about the beginning of the third month of life the child shows rudimentary search capability in that he or she will anticipate the future position of a moving object. This assertion has been corroborated in a number of laboratory investigations (e.g., see Nelson, 1968).

Although the child does engage in rudimentary search behavior, Piaget argues that the infant does not recognize that objects have permanence in space and time. This is shown by the errors that the child makes in search behavior. Bower (1971) provides data which is supportive of Piaget's position regarding errors in visual search. Bower found that infants observing an object going behind a screen would look toward the other end of the screen in anticipation of the object's movement to that point. This would seem to imply that the infants assumed that the object continued to exist while it was behind the screen. However, Bower conducted a number of additional experiments which demonstrated that infant search behavior is not based on the assumption of object permanence. One of these involved the observation of a toy train. As shown in figure 6-7, if the train typically went in one direction and then reversed its path, the infants looked to the point to which the train customarily moved rather than where it actually was. They did this even though the train was in full view as it moved in the opposite direction from the point where the infants expected it to arrive. Bower suggests that infant search behavior is guided by a cognitive rule which holds that if an object has been found in a given location in the past it will appear in that location again. The application of this rule in the train experiment implies that the infants had not yet achieved the concept of object permanence. Presumably, if the infants had assumed that they were dealing with a permanent object, they would have determined its location by watching it as it moved rather than by shifting their gaze away from the object to a relatively distant point where it had appeared in the past.

When infants are about five months old, they begin to search for missing objects not only with their eyes, but also with their hands. Initially search will be restricted to moving an object placed in the hand into the visual field (Bower, Broughton, & Moore, 1970; Piaget, 1952). However, before children are a year old many will uncover an object which has previously been observed as it was being covered (Harris, 1971).

Piaget asserts that children fail to engage in manual search for hidden objects during the middle part of the first year of life because they assume that objects do not have a location when out of view. A simpler explanation would be that children lack the motor skills necessary for manual search. However,

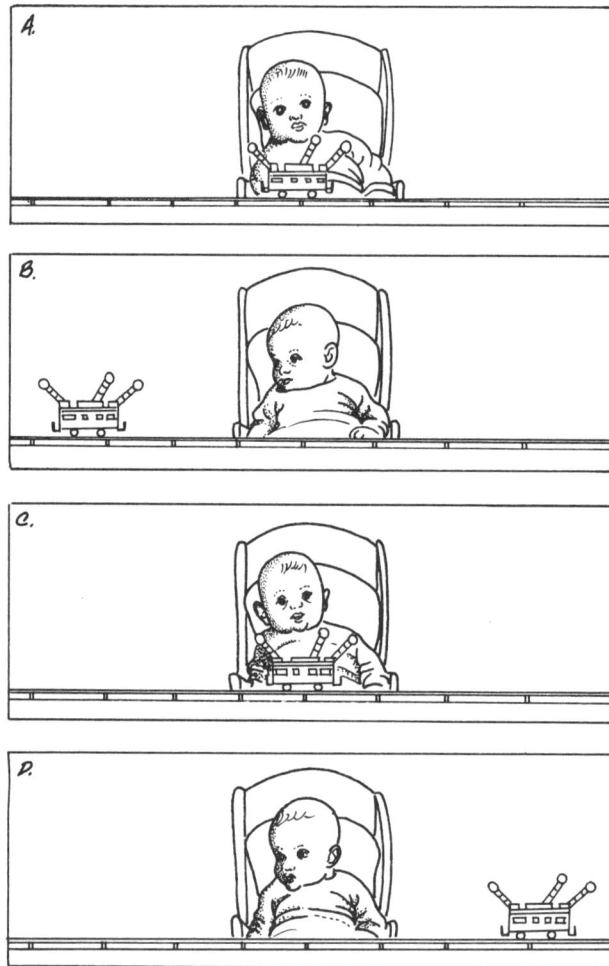

Figure 6–7   *A child's observation of a moving train. "The disappearing train confirms the hypothesis that infants 12 weeks old do not watch a single object when the object is at first stationary, then moves and stops. They do not follow the moving object from place to place but rather apply a cognitive rule that can be stated: 'Object disappears at A; object reappears at B.' In the experimental test the infant sat watching a toy train with flashing lights at rest in the middle of the track (a). After 10 seconds the train moved to the left and stopped (b) and remained there for 10 seconds before returning to the center again. The cycle was repeated 10 times. On the next cycle (c, d) the train moved slowly to the right and stopped. If the infant had been following the moving object, he would have looked to the right, but if he had been following the hypothesized cognitive rule, he would have looked to the left in the place where the train had stopped before. Every 12-week-old infant tested made the error predicted by the hypothesis." (From T. G. R. Bower, The object in the world of the infant.* Scientific American, *1971, 225, p. 36. Copyright © 1971 by Scientific American, Inc. All rights reserved.)*

Gratch (1972) observed that 23 out of 24 six-month-old infants were able to successfully retrieve an object placed under a transparent cloth, though infants of that age will not search for an object which they have observed being placed under an opaque cloth.

Even after a child is able to retrieve a hidden object, it is still doubtful that he recognizes that the object is an enduring entity. Piaget (1954) observed that if an infant watches an object being hidden first in one place and then in another, the infant will tend to look for the object in the initial hiding place. This observation has been partially confirmed by subsequent research. What apparently happens in the case of more than one hiding place is that the child engages in some accurate search at both locations, but has a tendency to err in favor of the initial hiding place (Bower & Paterson, 1972).

After a child has passed his first birthday, search behavior becomes increasingly accurate and sophisticated. By the time he is between 14 and 16 months old, he will probably be able to find a hidden object even when it has been placed in a container and moved from one hiding place to another (Kopp, Sigman, & Parmelee, 1974). At this stage, the behavior of the child suggests that he does indeed conceive of objects as relatively permanent entities enduring across different locations and different times.

The subperiod of preoperational thought. The acquisition of language marks the end of the sensorimotor period and the onset of the next major period in the child's intellectual development, which is the period of concrete operations. The period of concrete operations is initiated by a lengthy subperiod called preoperational thought. This subperiod begins at about the age of two and may last until the child is as much as seven years of age (Flavell, 1963).

Symbolic thought

The central task accomplished by the child during the subperiod of preoperational thought is the acquisition of the ability to represent concrete experiences through the use of symbols (Piaget, 1951). At first the child's symbolic representations take the form of private signs whose meanings are known only to him or her. Later, the symbols used will be primarily words, the meanings of which are, of course, shared by others.

In Piaget's view, children learn to represent the environment symbolically through their actions. Thus, the first private signs which children construct are overt behaviors. For example, a child may represent a falling object by dropping her hand, or she may represent the act of eating by moving her lips. Eventually the overt acts which the child uses to stand for events will be internalized as perceptual images of actions she has taken in the past. These images enable the child to represent the environment with internal mental mechanisms.

It is only after the individual has learned to represent reality imagistically that he or she begins to use words to stand for things. According to Piaget, the acquisition of language does not cause the child to think symbolically. It is a sign that symbolic thinking has already developed. The principal thing which the child learns through language acquisition is a way to label concepts which are already possessed in imagistic form.

Preoperational egocentrism

With the development of language, a new form of egocentrism becomes apparent in the thinking of children. They fail to distinguish clearly between properties of their symbolic representations of reality and the characteristics of objects in the environment. The following protocol from one of Piaget's experiments illustrates children's difficulties in this regard:

Have words got strength? -*Yes.* -Tell me a word which has strength? -*The wind.* -Why has the word "wind" got strength? -*Because it goes quickly.* -Is it the word or the wind which goes quickly? -*The wind.* (Piaget, 1963, p. 45)

The reemergence of the problem of object stability constitutes another example of preoperational egocentrism. For the preoperational child, variations in the context in which an object is observed may lead to the presumption of an entirely new object. The following example illustrates this.

Seeing the baby in a new bathing suit, with a cap, J. asked: *"What's the baby's name?"* Her mother explained that it was a bathing costume, but J. pointed to L. herself and said: *"But what's the name of that?"* (indicating L.'s face) and repeated the question several times. But as soon as L. had her dress on again, J. exclaimed very seriously: *"It's Lucienne again,"* as if her sister had changed her identity in changing her clothes. (Piaget, 1951, p. 224)

As the above examples illustrate, the child's ability to represent experiences symbolically soon leads to a variety of erroneous judgments about the nature of things. Gradually the child will discover the inconsistencies in his thinking patterns and once again make a dramatic surge toward a higher level of intellectual functioning.

The period of concrete operations. The period of concrete operations, excluding the preoperational subperiod, extends from approximately seven years of age to 11 years of age. During this period children acquire rules which enable them to use previously developed symbolic capabilities to represent environmental occurrences in a logical fashion (Flavell, 1963).

Classifying relationships

The central achievement of the latter phase of the period of concrete operations is the acquisition of the ability to classify concrete objects in terms of their relationships with other objects. The ability to conceptualize relationships among objects makes it possible for the child to make logical judgments. For example, whereas for the preoperational child it might seem quite reasonable that two cookie halves were greater than one whole cookie, a child in the advanced phase of the concrete operational period would not be so easily fooled. Similarly, when parents tell him that a 200-pound Santa Claus is going to come tumbling down their chimney on Christmas eve, he is bound to question the credibility of the adult view of things.

Conservation

The child achieves the capability to classify relationships among objects through the development of conservation of the whole. Conservation of the whole requires recognition that a whole must remain unchanged despite variations in the arrangement of its parts. For example, the advanced concrete-operational child will recognize that pouring liquid from a tall, thin container into a short, wide container doesn't change the overall quantity of liquid available (Piaget & Inhelder, 1941). Similarly, the child will know that increasing the overall length of a row of sticks by increasing the distance between each stick doesn't alter the number of sticks present (Piaget, 1952), and he or she will realize that rolling a long, thin lump of clay into a ball doesn't change the amount of clay that there is (Piaget & Inhelder, 1941). All of these facts seem obvious indeed, but the preoperational child fails to recognize them. Thus, one must conclude that the deductions required are not as simple as they might initially appear to be.

Piaget (1950) argues that the achievement of conservation requires that the child be able to consider all the elements which produce a whole at the same time. For instance, in order to conserve liquid, a child must recognize that the whole is determined by the height, breadth, and the width of the container. If he considers only one of these dimensions, for example, height, he is bound to come to the conclusion that a change in that dimension will result in a change in the quantity of liquid in the container. This is the basic flaw in the thinking processes of the preoperational child. He conceptualizes wholes in terms of only one dimension at a time. Thus, for example, the reason that the child falls into such logical traps as asserting that there are more boys than

A young child participating in a conservation-of-volume task. Notice the surprise which she shows when she observes that the liquid stands at a higher level in the narrow container than it does in the wide container. (From J. R. Bergan, & J. A. Dunn. Psychology and Education: A Science for Instruction. *New York: Wiley, 1976. Reprinted by permission.)*

children in his class is that he cannot conceive of the concept *children* as being made up of both boys and girls simultaneously.

The development of conservation represents a giant step forward in children's reasoning ability enabling them to comprehend basic forms of both quantitative and verbal logic. For example, the development of conservation makes it possible for children to comprehend basic arithmetic operations. The equations involved in addition, subtraction, multiplication, and division all require that a child conceptualize a whole in terms of more than one constituent part. Similarly, verbal deductions require conservation. In order for children to comprehend syllogisms of the general form: *All collies are dogs; Lassie is a collie; therefore Lassie is a dog even if she does sleep in your bed,* the child must be able to conceptualize the concept *dog* as including both collies and Lassie.

As the above examples imply, conservation ability enables a child to advance from his earlier egocentric thinking patterns to a new level of objectivity. The rules which he has learned for conceptualizing relationships among objects make it possible for him to differentiate between his mode of representing things and the way in which things in the environment actually are. And so it is that children learn that words have no magical power over things, that dreams are not the same as reality, and that teddy bears and rabbits do not live in houses. The following comment by a 9-year-old who had been frightened by a bear while camping in a national park illustrates the objectivity of the concrete-operational child quite adequately: "I wish that the bear's visit had been a nightmare. It would have been safer that way."

A large amount of laboratory research has been undertaken to examine Piaget's views on conservation as they relate to the period of concrete operations. Initial work in the area focused on replicating Piaget's studies under tightly controlled laboratory conditions. Results of replication efforts have been generally supportive of Piaget's descriptions of conservation behavior in children (Reese & Lipsitt, 1970).

Much of the recent research on conservation has sought to detail specific factors underlying conservation skill. For example, recent research has revealed that conservation is in part a function of language capability. Children participating in conservation tasks are generally required to have knowledge of the meanings of words such as *same* and *more*. A child may be asked if the liquid in a tall, thin container is the same or more than it was when it was in a short, wide container. To answer this kind of question the child must comprehend the relational terms used by the experimenter. Siegel and Goldstein (1969) observed that young children generally do not comprehend the meanings of relational terms. Harasym, Boersma, and McGuire (1971) found a correspondence between the ability to conserve and the extent of comprehension of relational terms.

Another factor which apparently influences conservation is the perceptual characteristics of the conservation tasks. Pufall and Shaw (1972) conducted a study which provides general support for Piaget's view that the non-conserver bases his or her judgments on the perceptual features associated with the conservation task. In their study children were asked to judge whether two rows of dots were the same or whether one row had more dots than the other. Young children tended to base their judgments on differences in the length of the rows or on differences in the closeness of the spacing of the dots.

LaPointe and O'Donnell (1974) conducted a study which clarifies the role of both language skills and perceptual factors in conservation. In their study children were asked if two rows of beads were the same or if one row had more beads than the other. If children answered these questions inconsistently, it was assumed that they did not comprehend the language used in the experiment. For example, if a child confirmed that two rows were the same and then went on to assert that one row had more beads, it was hypothesized that the child did not really understand what was being asked. Some children were consistently incorrect in their responses. If they said that two unequal rows were equal, they would also respond that one row had no more beads than the other. The behavior of these children suggests that lack of conservation is not entirely a problem of lack of language comprehension. Some children responded correctly on both trials. These children evidenced conservation behavior.

Results of the LaPointe and O'Donnell study are shown in figure 6-8. Inconsistent responses indicating a lack of language comprehension decreased steadily with age. Consistently incorrect responses increased and then decreased. This finding resulted from the fact that many children acquired the language skills necessary to emit a consistent response before they learned to conserve. Thus, at age four the decrease in inconsistent responding was accompanied by an increase in consistently wrong responses. The results for consistently correct responses indicate a steady rise in conservation between ages two and five.

Results of the LaPointe and O'Donnell study suggest that both language comprehension and perceptual features of the conservation task affect performance. Children below the age of four cannot conserve because they do

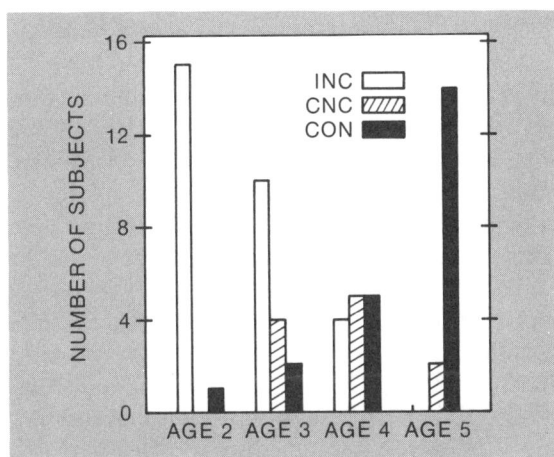

Number of subjects who answered either inconsistently (INC), consistently but non- Figure 6–8
*conservingly (CNC), or conservingly (CON) on one randomly picked conservation trial.
(From K. LaPointe, & J. P. O'Donnell, Number conservation in children below age
six: Its relationship to age, perceptual dimensions, and language comprehension. Developmental Psychology, 1974, 10, p. 426. Copyright 1974 by the American Psychological Association. Reprinted by permission.)*

not understand the questions that they are asked. Most children aged four and
over have the necessary language skills to respond correctly. However, many
4-year olds and some 5-year olds do not conserve. LaPointe and O'Donnell
observed that these children tended to respond on the basis of perceptual cues
(i.e., the overall length of the rows and the spacing between the individual beads).

You probably noted that conservation in the LaPointe and O'Donnell study
occurred at a much younger age than that suggested by Piaget's observations.
This discrepancy reflects a difference in the criteria used to establish conservation. Piaget required the children in his studies to justify their equality judgments.
LaPointe and O'Donnell required only a yes or no response regarding the
equality or inequality of the rows of beads. When they asked for justification, they
found that no children below the age of five could conserve. LaPointe and
O'Donnell argue that insistence upon verbal explanation may obscure the
existence of conservation in young children. They interpret their results as
suggesting that many young children have the ability to conserve but lack the
skill to express their ability verbally.

A number of studies have suggested that it is possible to accelerate the
development of conservation. For example, Halford and Fullerton (1970) trained
children to discriminate between numerically matching and nonmatching sets of
objects and thereby enhanced conservation responses. Zimmerman and Rosenthal
(1974) used a modeling procedure to increase conservation. In their study a
model emitted conservation responses while being observed by children. Children
who watched the model displayed significantly more correct responses than a
control group on a subsequent conservation task.

Behavioral theorists (e.g., Zimmerman & Rosenthal, 1974; Siegler, Liebert, &
Liebert, 1973) have assumed that the results of some training studies are
damaging to Piaget's position. They suggest that the acceleration of development
negates the validity of Piaget's view of the process of development. Piaget (1970)
does not share this assumption. He believes that development can be enhanced
through experience. He asserts that the order of progression through develop-

mental stages is invariant, but he does not deny that it is possible to enhance progress from one stage to the next. It should also be pointed out that investigators sympathetic to Piaget's views have criticized many of the training studies on methodological grounds. For example, Turiel (1973) points out that many of the studies have used inadequate criteria as evidence of developmental progress. Moreover, the stability of changes produced in some of the training studies is open to question. Finally, in some cases the children being trained were probably at a transitional stage and therefore might have shown improvement without training.

Despite the above criticisms of training studies, the results of training research do suggest that developmental progress may be made in ways other than those described by Piaget. For example, the Zimmerman and Rosenthal study indicates the possibility that stage transition may occur through observational learning rather than only through discovery learning.

The period of formal operations. Although the intellectual achievements which take place during the concrete operational period represent a truly remarkable advance in a child's intellectual functioning, he will gradually encounter problems which cannot be solved on the basis of applications of his available intellectual structures. And so, once again he will find himself facing circumstances which lead to conflicting and obviously inaccurate judgments concerning the nature of things.

Children in the period of concrete operations have developed intellectual structures which enable them to perform logical operations on the concrete objects in the environment, but their ability to use the rules of logic to explore possible realities in addition to actual realities is highly limited. Thus, they simply cannot solve those problems which require the conceptualization of alternative possible hypotheses.

Formal operations and abstract thinking

During the period of formal operations, thought is at last freed entirely from the concrete. As children approach adolescence, they acquire the abstract-thinking patterns which will characterize their intellectual functioning for the remainder of their lives. At this stage of development, they are able to represent the full range of hypothetical realities which might exist with respect to a given situation.

Formal operations and problem solving

The intellectually mature person to emerge during the period of formal operations is a problem solver. When circumstances require it, he or she is capable of asking the question: *What might have caused the conditions which I now observe?* Moreover, he or she is able to advance a systematic set of hypotheses which represent possible causes for the occurrences observed in problem-solving situations.

Piaget's research on formal operations

In investigating thinking at the formal operational period, Piaget and his colleagues utilized tasks derived from a number of the great discoveries of science. Inhelder and Piaget's (1958) study of Archimedes' law of floating bodies can be used to illustrate their findings concerning thinking in the period of formal operations. Youths participating in the study were presented with several buckets of water and a variety of objects. Their task was to classify the objects on the basis of whether or not they would float in water. Then they were asked to state the rule which governed floating.

In order to discover the law of floating bodies, the participants in the study had to advance a set of hypotheses which were by no means apparent in the concrete stimuli they were presented. Included among these were the possibilities that the weight of an object determined whether or not it would float, that the volume of the object controlled its potential for floating, and that the weight of the object compared to the weight of an equal volume of water determined floating.

The following protocol illustrates the reasoning of a child who successfully grappled with the problem of the law of floating bodies.

> Why do you think this key will sink? *-Because it is heavier than water.* -This little key is heavier than water? (The bucket is pointed out.) *-I mean the same capacity of water would be less heavy than the key.* -What do you mean? *-You put them* (metal or water) *in containers which contain the same amount and weigh them.* (Inhelder & Piaget, 1958, p. 38)

Note that the child in this example solved his problem without actually testing the hypothesis which he advanced. This illustrates the fundamental capability acquired in the period of formal operations, the ability to reason about possible realities without actually having to observe a concrete example of those realities.

Egocentrism and formal operations

Although the period of formal operations represents the highest level of intellectual achievement, it nonetheless initially eventuates in the emergence of a new variety of egocentrism. Specifically, the individual's powers of abstract thinking lead to an inflated view of the capabilities of his intellect. In Inhelder and Piaget's (1958) words,

> The indefinite extension of powers of thought made possible by the new instruments of propositional logic at first is conducive to a failure to distinguish between the ego's new and unpredicted capacities and the social or cosmic universe to which they are applied. In other words, the adolescent goes through a phase in which he attributes an unlimited power to his own thoughts so that the dream of a glorious future or of transforming the world through Ideas (even if this idealism takes a materialistic form) seems to be not only fantasy but also an effective action which in itself modifies the empirical world. (pp. 345-46)

Eventually, of course, as the adolescent gains increased experience in the adult world, idealistic egocentrism fades, and he or she achieves a more realistic view of the role of thinking processes in guiding the affairs of humanity.

Constructive Intelligence and Socialization in Contemporary Society

As we have shown, the picture of a human being to emerge from the Piagetian theory of intellectual development is that of a problem solver who, through interactions with the environment, not only discovers knowledge, but also develops complex intellectual structures which enable him or her to interpret experiences in increasingly effective ways. Although Piaget rejects the early structuralist view of a preformed intellect, he nonetheless assigns the major responsibility for intellectual functioning to biological characteristics of the individual. The intellectual structures which arise over the long course of development come into being as a result of humans' innate tendencies to organize and adapt to the phenomena which they experience. The environment plays a role in the development of intellectual structures, but it is not an active role. Environmental factors merely set the occasions for the development of intellectual structures.

The Piagetian view of human intellectual growth suggests quite a different approach to socialization than the technology advocated by behaviorists. From the Piagetian point of view, the principal task of parents and teachers attempting to promote intellectual development is to provide opportunities for children to learn by discovery. In the early phases of development, discovery learning must

Discovery learning

be closely tied to concrete objects in the environment. Children must be given the opportunity to manipulate things with their hands, to see how they work, and to represent them symbolically through their actions. At the most advanced levels of development there is less need for concrete experience. Nevertheless some contact with concrete phenomena will be essential for gaining new information about objects in the environment and for testing hypotheses related to problem-solving activities.

In order to provide appropriate discovery-learning experiences for children, parents and teachers must have knowledge of the stage of intellectual development at which the children in their charge are operating. They may attain such knowledge by observing children at work and at play and by soliciting their interpretations of how things in the environment function. On the basis of knowledge of a child's level of development, socialization agents can arrange the environment so as to provide a broad range of activities which the child may pursue to further his or her own intellectual growth.

As in the case of behavioral technology, presumably the long-term viability of the Piagetian approach to socialization will depend on the extent to which it meets the needs of contemporary society. As a consequence it will be useful to examine the question of how the Piagetian views of intelligence and socialization relate to salient themes which have emerged in contemporary culture.

Constructive intelligence, science and technology. The theme of controlling human development through technology based on scientific discovery is totally absent from Piagetian thinking. People have created science and technology. They do not control them. They are the products of their mental activity.

One might then ask: Why study intellectual development? So far as Piaget is concerned, the principal reason is that such study provides information about the nature of knowledge (Flavell, 1963). In Piaget's view, knowledge is not information stored in books on library shelves; it is a manifestation of human thought. Thus, to understand the nature and origin of knowledge, one must understand the nature and origin of human thinking.

Although advances in science and technology cannot in themselves eventuate in the control of the intellect, they do provide important opportunities for the advancement of intelligence. As we have pointed out, in Piaget's view individuals develop their intellects through the process of discovery. The extent of intellectual discovery, however, is limited by the kinds of problems which the environment provides for the individual to solve and by the breadth of information which the individual can bring to bear on the achievement of problem solutions. Thus, science and technology, and for that matter all other forms of knowledge, are catalysts to intellectual growth. They permit people to deepen their understanding of themselves and their environment, and they make it possible for them to increase the level of their intellectual functioning.

Despite the fact that Piagetian theory does not advocate the development of a technology of intellectual growth, it certainly does provide an abundance of information about the types of environments needed to foster intellectual development. In a sense, this information can be regarded as the basis for a kind of technology, but it is a technology which lacks many of the characteristic attributes normally associated with the idea of technology. There is, for example, no specification of a product to be produced, nor is there any significant degree of concern for efficiency. For example, the idea of maximizing intellectual growth, which is implicit in behavioral technology, is not a particularly important concern for Piagetians. In this connection Piaget (1973) remarks,

Technology and developmental environments

> . . . should passage from one stage of development be accelerated or not? To be sure, all educaton, in one way or another, is just such an acceleration, but it remains to be decided to what extent it is beneficial. It is not without significance that it takes man much longer to reach maturity than the other animals. Consequently, it is highly probable that there is an optimum rate of development, to exceed or fall behind which would be equally harmful. (pp. 22-23)

Constructive intelligence and cultural change. Piagetians have been highly sensitive to the dominant themes which have arisen from living in a rapidly changing culture. They are well aware of the need for adaptation to change and for problem-solving skills necessary to cope with change.

To meet the challenges of a changing culture, Piagetians have proposed radical alterations of contemporary socialization practices, particularly those practices which have traditionally characterized the operation of our educational institutions. Specifically, they suggest that the long-standing tradition of concentrating instruction on the acquisition of verbal knowledge and the memorization of factual information be abandoned. Piagetians would have children spend less time memorizing facts and more time questioning the validity of facts. And of course, they would provide many more opportunities than now exist in the schools for children to learn by discovery. On the last point, Piaget (1973) remarks,

> The first . . . (condition of intellectual training) is, of course, the use of active methods which give broad scope to the spontaneous research of the child or adolescent and require that every new truth to be learned be rediscovered or at least reconstructed by the student, and not simply imparted to him. (pp. 15-16)

Constructive intelligence and cultural diversity. As we have pointed out, the major issue to emerge from the relationship between intelligence and cultural diversity has had to do with observed differences in intellectual functioning among different ethnic groups in the society. Piaget places very little emphasis on group differences or for that matter individual differences in intellectual capability. He assumes that the stages of intellectual development which he has identified are universal; and, while there may be variations in the rate at which different individuals or cultural groups pass from one stage to the next, these differences are not matters of primary concern to Piaget.

The matter of central interest is that of how children think at various stages in their development. Piaget has only marginal interest in the extent to which one individual or group of individuals thinks better than another. There is no attempt to label individual differences in intelligence, and consequently there is no emphasis on assertions that one group is inferior or superior intellectually to another. Accordingly, within Piagetian theory, there are no arguments about genetic differences among groups, nor are parents and teachers told that compensatory efforts must be made to make up for inadequate child-rearing practices in the home.

Some might argue that the Piagetian stance, or rather lack of stance, regarding group differences is tantamount to blatantly ignoring one of the major social problems of our times. On the other hand, there are those who would point out that the Piagetian viewpoint has the distinct advantage of not denigrating the intellectual characteristics of ethnic groups outside the mainstream of middle-class culture. Moreover, the lack of concern which Piagetians display for group and individual differences in intelligence does not in any way affect their deep commitment to the task of promoting intellectual development in children. From the Piagetian standpoint, the task of promoting intellectual growth requires that parents and teachers know the stage of development at which the child is functioning. On the basis of this information, they can construct a learning environment appropriate to the child's level of growth. There is no compelling need for them to be concerned about the extent to which his level of growth is more or less advanced than that of some other child.

Constructive intelligence and humanism. Socialization theorists within the humanistic tradition generally consider Piagetian theory to be a useful psychological model for guiding the development of the intellect (Silberman, 1970). Humanists look upon people as self-directed problem solvers; and, of course, this view is quite compatible with the Piagetian position regarding intellectual functioning. About the only reservation humanists have concerning Piagetian theory has to do with the fact that it is limited largely to the consideration of intellectual growth. Thus, for example, Piaget has little to say about the affective side of human nature. The humanist concern for the development of the "whole person" requires psychological theory dealing with all developmental processes, not just with intellectual processes.

Humanists not only support the Piagetian view of the intellect, but they also are staunch advocates of Piagetian ideas concerning the socialization process. One of the main reasons why Piagetian socialization practices are attractive to humanists is that Piagetian procedures provide children with the opportunity and responsibility for directing their own learning. In the discovery-learning approach advocated by Piaget, children control how they will interact with the environment and thereby how they will learn. A second reason for the attraction of humanists to Piagetian techniques is that Piagetian socialization practices foster respect between adults and children during the course of socialization. Parents and teachers using Piagetian procedures tend not to be placed in the position of continually criticizing children for their wrong answers, nor do they often find themselves facing the onerous task of forcing children to acquire knowledge that they do not want. For example, the familiar "drumming in" of information through tedious drill is rarely observed in Piagetian socialization efforts.

Although the Piagetian approach is attractive from a humanistic standpoint, some theorists outside the humanistic tradition have reservations about Piagetian socialization practices. These reservations all center around the extent to which agents of socialization should assume responsibility for the development of the child. The essential argument is this: Teachers and parents must assume the major responsibility for controlling the learning of children. Children do not have the wisdom to guide their own development, and as a result they must be given a substantial amount of supervision.

*Criticisms of
Piagetian
socialization*

Piagetians do not dispute the need for adults to assume responsibility for guiding intellectual growth. What they do dispute are the far-reaching attempts of adults to control in a systematic way every phase of children's thinking and learning. So far as Piagetians are concerned, such attempts are unworkable.

BEHAVIORAL INTELLIGENCE VERSUS CONSTRUCTIVE INTELLIGENCE

The behavioral-intelligence and constructive-intelligence positions clearly represent fundamentally different views of the nature of the intellect with basically different implications for socialization. The behavioral position holds that intellectual behavior can be acquired by direct environmental influence and that the most efficient way to promote intellectual development is to teach intellectual behaviors directly. For example, one may teach a rule-learning strategy by modeling the strategy for the learner. The constructionist view asserts that intellectual structures develop out of the efforts of the individual to construct knowledge from his or her encounters with the environment. For example, in attempting to discover physical laws, a child may gradually acquire new intellectual structures representing a higher level of intellectual development than he had previously attained. According to the constructionist view, the best way to promote intellectual growth is to provide the child with opportunities to learn by discovery.

Given the fundamental differences between the behavioral and constructionist approaches, two questions arise: Which position provides the most adequate representation of intellectual development and which position offers the most adequate guide to socialization practice?

Despite a superfluity of rhetoric from advocates of both theoretical positions, there is no compelling evidence as to which view of intellectual development is most adequate. Moreover, it is doubtful that compelling evidence will be forthcoming. The behaviorist and constructionist positions represent different world views rather than competing scientific theories (Reese & Overton, 1970). The behavioral position starts with the assumption that the environment controls behavior. The constructionist view starts with the assumption that behavioral control resides within the individual. Neither theory is designed to test these assumptions. Rather the experimentation carried out within each theory is intended to provide evidence regarding the nature of development assuming the validity of the basic assumption underlying each theory. For example, to show that the individual acquires new intellectual capabilities and attendant intellectual structures as a result of environmental encounters in no way tests the belief that the child constructs knowledge from interactions with the environment. Analogously, to show that certain manipulations in the environment eventuate in behavioral change does not prove that behavior is ultimately under environmental control.

The issue of which theoretical position constitutes the most adequate guide for socialization is plagued by essentially the same difficulty as that of deciding which position offers the most adequate account of development. There is no compelling evidence that a behavioral approach to socialization produces results which differ in any substantive way from a discovery approach (Nuthall & Snook, 1973).

If one is to choose between the behavioral and constructionist positions, one must do so on other than empirical grounds. Many people have chosen between the two approaches, usually for philosophical reasons. However, particularly from the standpoint of socialization practice, there is something to be said for not giving one's allegiance to either view exclusively. First, insofar as one maintains an open mind regarding theories of intellectual growth, one can make effective use of the abundant storehouse of knowledge generated by both positions. Those who become ardent advocates of one position or the other may fall into the trap of discounting the knowledge generated by the view which they have disdained. Another reason for utilizing both theoretical positions is that such utilization promotes a balance in socialization practice. A parent or teacher who never let a child learn anything for himself would be both a tyrant and a bore. While no thoughtful behaviorist would advocate such excessive control, it is a fact that applications of behavioristic principles in socialization have in some instances occasioned excesses in the realm of adult control. Analogously, a parent or teacher who insisted that children learn everything by discovery would surely produce a highly inefficient and chaotic learning environment. While no thoughtful Piagetian would support such anarchy, it is nonetheless true that applications of the discovery-learning approach to socialization have upon occasion degenerated into chaos. Thus, even though the behavioral and Piagetian positions are opposing views, each has a contribution to make to socialization and to our understanding of the nature of intelligence.

SUGGESTED READINGS

Bower, T. G. R. The object in the world of the infant. *Scientific American*, 1971, *225*, 30-47.

Elkind, D. *Children and adolescents: Interpretive essays on Jean Piaget* (2nd ed.). New York: Oxford University Press, 1974.

Gagné, R. M. Contributions of learning to human development. *Psychological Review*, 1968, *75*, 177-91.

Gagné, R. M. *The conditions of learning* (2nd ed.). New York: Holt, Rinehart and Winston, 1970.

Inhelder, B., & Piaget, J. *The growth of logical thinking from childhood to adolescence.* New York: Basic Books, 1958.

Piaget, J. *The construction of reality in the child.* New York: Basic Books, 1954.

Piaget, J. *The child's conception of the world.* Totowa, N. J.: Littlefield, Adams, 1963.

Siegler, R. S., Liebert, D. E., & Liebert, R. M. Inhelder and Piaget's pendulum problem: Teaching preadolescents to act as scientists. *Developmental Psychology*, 1973, *9*, 97-101.

Skinner, B. F. *Beyond freedom and dignity.* New York: Knopf, 1971.

Skinner, B. F. *About behaviorism.* New York: Knopf, 1974.

Zimmerman, B. J., & Rosenthal, T. L. Conserving and retaining equalities and in-equalities through observation and correction. *Developmental Psychology,* 1974, *10,* 260-68.

7

Language Development

Instructional Objectives	Recognize or recall
	Compare and contrast
	Describe or demonstrate
	Evaluate

the acquisition of language through operant conditioning.

the application of shaping in early language learning.

the relationship of language learning to rule learning.

Bandura's view and Skinner's view of the manner in which modeling influences language development.

Gagné's cumulative-learning view of language development.

the meaning of the phrase *language acquisition device* (LAD).

Chomsky's justification for the LAD.

Chomsky's views on the role of the environment in language development.

statements describing how language is acquired from the standpoint of behaviorism and/or Chomsky's nativist position.

the behavioral view and Chomsky's position concerning the manner in which language is acquired.

the mand, the intraverbal operant, the tact, and the autoclitic.

Chomsky's definition of grammar.

the three components of grammar.

the definition of the term *phoneme*.

universal and specific grammar.

deep and surface structure.

rules of formation and transformation.

the meaning of the term *transformational grammar*.

conclusions from research findings in transformational grammar.

Brown's specification of sentence characteristics related to language development.

roles conveyed by sentences.

Brown's first two stages of language development.

the relationship between grammatical relations observed in Brown's Stage I and Piaget's sensorimotor development.

the effects of parental expansions of children's speech on their language development.

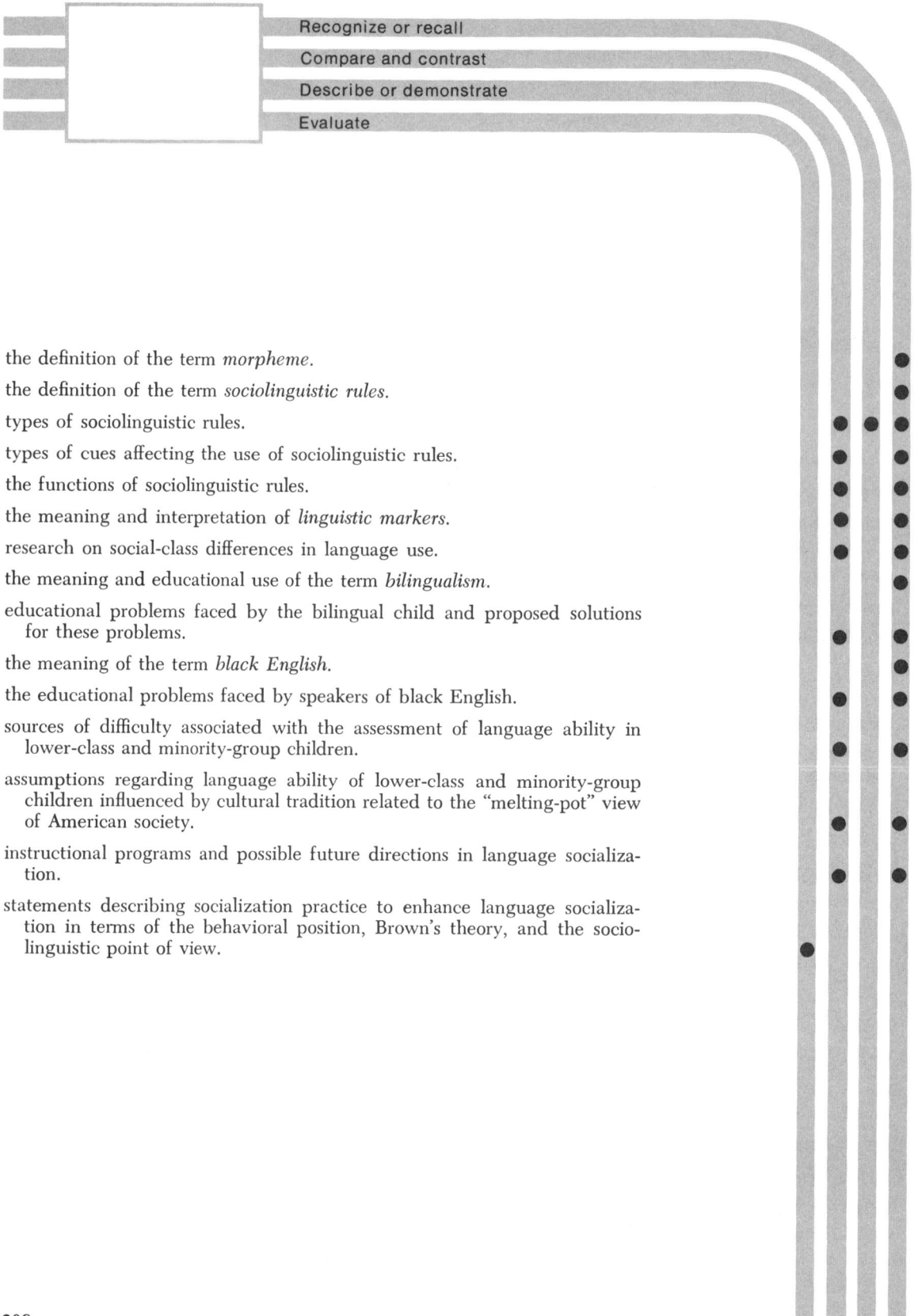

the definition of the term *morpheme*.

the definition of the term *sociolinguistic rules*.

types of sociolinguistic rules.

types of cues affecting the use of sociolinguistic rules.

the functions of sociolinguistic rules.

the meaning and interpretation of *linguistic markers*.

research on social-class differences in language use.

the meaning and educational use of the term *bilingualism*.

educational problems faced by the bilingual child and proposed solutions for these problems.

the meaning of the term *black English*.

the educational problems faced by speakers of black English.

sources of difficulty associated with the assessment of language ability in lower-class and minority-group children.

assumptions regarding language ability of lower-class and minority-group children influenced by cultural tradition related to the "melting-pot" view of American society.

instructional programs and possible future directions in language socialization.

statements describing socialization practice to enhance language socialization in terms of the behavioral position, Brown's theory, and the sociolinguistic point of view.

CHAPTER CONTENT

How language is acquired

    The behaviorist viewpoint

    Chomsky's nativist position

What is acquired through language development

    Language development as the acquisition of operants

    Language development as the acquisition of grammar

    Brown's stages of language development

    Language development as the acquisition of sociolinguistic rules

Guiding language development in a culturally diverse society

    Language in cultural subgroups

    Societal interpretations of linguistic diversity

    Language socialization strategies

Recall, if you will, the opening scene from Shaw's (1953) *Pygmalion:* a summer night, quite late, and torrents of rain falling in sheets upon the London streets. A group is huddled under the portico of St. Paul's Church. Among them is the flower girl, Eliza Doolittle yowling "Ah-ah-ah-ow-ow-ow-oo" and Professor Higgins wincing "Heavens! what a sound!" as he busily takes notes on her speech. Soon Higgins strikes up a conversation with a stranger who, through dramatic convenience, turns out to be none other than the famous expert on Indian dialects, Colonel Pickering. As the two men talk, Higgins, in one of his frequent fits of braggadocio, lays down the assertion upon which the play is built:

> You see this creature with her kerbstone English: the English that will keep her
> in the gutter to the end of her days. Well, sir, in three months I could pass that
> girl off as a duchess at an ambassador's garden party. I could even get her a place
> as lady's maid or shop assistant, which requires better English. (p. 228)

Shaw's lines raise fundamental issues around which much of the research and socialization practice related to language development turn. To what extent is it the case, as Shaw through Higgins claims, that the ability to speak the Queen's English is a learned capability? Assuming that language is in all significant respects a learned competency, what is the nature of that competency? Can we assume, as Shaw does, that a bath now and then, the provision of some reasonably stylish clothes, and the ability to make well-formed English sentences can transform an individual from the lower-class to the middle-class? Put in another way, to what extent is language a correlate of social and cultural factors? Finally, can the systematic application of principles of language science during limited instructional time periods effect significant alterations in language performance?

HOW LANGUAGE IS ACQUIRED

There are those who assume, as Shaw apparently did, that language is indeed a learned ability. On the other hand, as you may have grown accustomed to expect after repeated encounters with the nature-nurture controversy, some theorists argue that language capability is largely genetically determined.

The Behaviorist Viewpoint

Consistent with their position regarding other developmental processes, behaviorists have been the main proponents of the environmentalist stance regarding language development. Behaviorists view language skills in the main as a form of rule learning. The basic mechanisms by which language is acquired include operant conditioning, learning by observing the behavior of a model, and cumulative learning.

Language development through operant conditioning. B. F. Skinner (1957) set forth the operant view of language learning in his classic book *Verbal Behavior.* The standard form of operant language learning involves a cue which serves to signal the occurrence of a response followed by reinforcement. The initial cue derives its properties as a signal as a result of repeated association with reinforcement. Thus, in the early phases of learning, the initial signaling function is absent from the operant paradigm.

Shaping

In the first phases of development, operant learning takes place in a process called *shaping* which controls the acquisition of speech sounds. A little later in development, operant events occur in discrimination learning through which the child acquires such abilities as learning to name objects.

During the first year of life, children emit many and varied sounds. Parents are generally quite interested in the unintelligible babblings of their children and often tend to become nearly euphoric over the most primitive approximations to adult speech. *She said ma-ma. Did you hear that?* says a mother or father beaming at an infant. Behaviorists assert with some experimental support (e.g., see Rheingold, Gewirtz, & Ross, 1959; Weisberg, 1963) that the repeated reinforcement of vocal behavior in infants increases the probability that the behavior in question will occur on future occasions.

During the early phases of development, parents tend to be quite liberal regarding the range of vocal behaviors which they reinforce. However, as children grow older, parents become more selective in rewarding vocalizations. As a result, the broad range of sounds initially produced by the child is gradually narrowed to the point that it begins to reflect mainly the vocal patterns of his or her parents. This process of selectively reinforcing successive approximations to a desired response is called *shaping.*

Object naming

Near the end of the first year of life, reinforcement practices will turn increasingly toward the reward of speech sounds emitted in the presence of objects in the environment. *Doggie. Yes, that's a doggie,* a mother will say as she smiles at her child who has just said *oggie.* Of course, if the child calls the animal a hat, the parent is not likely to give such a positive reaction. Recalling the discussion of rule learning in chapter 6, you will recognize that the language learning of the child being described here is an example of learning through discrimination and generalization. As indicated in chapter 6, when reinforcement is given for responses emitted in the presence of one class of objects and withheld for responses emitted to other classes of objects, the child will learn to discrimi-

nate the class of objects which has been reinforced from other classes. By this means, words gradually begin to represent categories of things.

As discussed in chapter 6, what the child actually learns through discrimination are rules for categorizing classes of objects. Language learning, from the behavioral point of view, is to a great extent rule learning. The rules which the child may acquire in the course of language development will include rules regarding the kinds of sounds which may be used within the language, rules specifying the meanings of words, and rules governing the patterning of words into phrases, sentences, and larger units of discourse.

Language development through observational learning. Although much of the child's early language learning may involve shaping and discrimination, these processes are by no means the only mechanisms for stimulating language learning. As in the case of other forms of rule learning, the child may learn many linguistic rules by observing the linguistic behavior modeled by parents.

Brown and Fraser (1963) have found that during the early phases of language development, the child will be unable to imitate much of the linguistic behavior of his parents accurately. For example, two- and three-year-old children tend to simplify the utterances which they imitate in much the same fashion as an adult guarding his pennies in a telegram message. The "little words" such as *the, of,* and *an* tend to be omitted. However, both the word order and the words designating objects, people, and actions (that is, the *who did what to whom* words) tend to be expressed in children's imitative speech. For example, in response to the sentence *I showed you the book*, one child in the Brown and Fraser study said, "I show book." *Failures in imitative language learning*

One obvious question raised by the Brown and Fraser study is how does modeling affect new responses. It is possible that children don't imitate certain classes of words because they only imitate linguistic patterns they already have in their repertoire of linguistic behaviors. This possibility carries with it the currently controversial assumption that people cannot acquire novel responses through observation alone.

Some behaviorists (e.g., Bandura, 1969) hold that individuals can acquire totally novel responses as a result of observing the behavior of a model. This is a hard position to prove. It has been convincingly demonstrated in a number of instances that people can learn to emit a response in a novel stimulus situation *The novel response controversy* simply by observing a model emit the response (e.g., see Bandura, 1965). However, there are other aspects of the novel-response issue which must be considered in evaluating the position that new responses can be acquired solely through observation.

One factor bearing on the novel-response controversy, which is particularly important from the standpoint of language development, has to do with the type of sensory stimulation emitted by the model and its relationship to the required response. In the case of language learning, a child sees his parents' lips move and hears the language which the parents produce. However, in order to imitate what he has seen and heard, he must use his vocal musculature. The child presumably acquires little or no information regarding the operation of the vocal musculature through observation of his parents. Thus, it is difficult to see how the child could learn to imitate language simply by observing their language behavior (Skinner, 1957).

Of course, if the response to be imitated were already in the child's repertoire of linguistic capabilities, then he presumably would be able to imitate parental language without difficulty. This, so far as Skinner and his supporters are concerned, is the key to explaining the relationship between modeling and imitation.

According to the Skinnerian view, the child acquires a repertoire of linguistic responses through parental reinforcement. Of course, the child must be capable of emitting a response before it can be reinforced. The function of reinforcement is to bring the response under environmental control. After a response has been brought under environmental control through reinforcement, it can be placed under the control of modeling stimuli (Baer & Sherman, 1964).

The ability to imitate modeled behavior constitutes a highly important factor affecting the efficiency of language learning. Even if we assume that the child must already have responses to be imitated in his linguistic repertoire, he can learn to apply his linguistic behaviors in new combinations and in new situations through observation of the behavior of others. Moreover, new applications of this sort can often be acquired within a single learning trial. This kind of one-trial learning provides a sharp contrast to the slow and cumbersome learning required in the case of shaping and discrimination.

Language development through cumulative learning. Gagné's (1970) model, discussed in chapter 6, suggests that certain language skills are acquired through cumulative learning. As you shall see, Gagné's analysis of language learning represents something of a departure from the Skinnerian view described above. Whereas Skinner describes such tasks as learning to name objects largely in terms of discrimination and generalization, Gagné divides tasks such as object naming into a number of subtasks, each requiring a special form of learning.

In Gagné's view, initial language learning occurs through operant conditioning in the manner described by the Skinnerians. As a result of early operant learning, the child acquires simple stimulus-response connections which enable him or her to emit speech sounds signaled by environmental cues and followed by reinforcement.

Stimulus-response learning

After simple stimulus-response connections have been acquired, they are combined into chains. Gagné suggests that the earliest efforts of the child to name objects in the environment require chaining. For example, as shown in figure 7-1, the act of identifying a ball can be depicted as a two-link chain. In the first link, the stimulus (ball) elicits a nonverbal observing response. The act of observing provides internal cues, for instance sensations from muscles and joints, which elicit the overt verbal response, *ball.*

Chaining

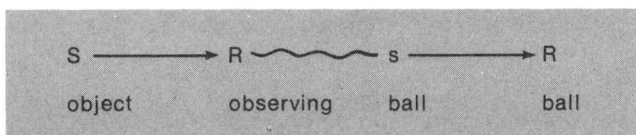

Two-link chain used in object naming. S stands for an overt stimulus; R, for an overt response; s, for an internal stimulus. Arrows indicate that a response is being elicited. The wavy line shows that a response produces an internal stimulus.

Figure 7–1

Throughout the course of language development, children will acquire countless verbal chains, many of which will be much more complex than the simple two-link chain described here. For example, they will learn to count and to say the alphabet. They will learn verbal conventions such as *Fine, thank you. And how are you?* As they come in contact with the media, they will learn stylized speech (*my fellow Americans, distinguished guests, ladies and gentlemen*). Hopefully, through reading they may acquire the language patterns of great writers and thinkers, past and present.

Although acquisition of the simple two-link chain permits children to name objects, it does not insure that they will be able to distinguish among the various objects which they encounter or that they will be able to apply the correct labels to the objects in their experience. Multiple-discrimination learning is required for the accomplishment of these tasks.

Multiple-discrimination learning

In multiple-discrimination learning, the child is confronted with a large number of different objects, all of which have different names. The acquisition of simple verbal chains is prerequisite to multiple-discrimination learning in that a verbal chain is required to name each of the objects which the child must learn to name. However, the ability to emit verbal chains will not by itself necessarily insure effective multiple-discrimination learning.

There are two major problems associated with making multiple discriminations. First, an individual must learn to distinguish among both the objects to be discriminated and the language sounds used to label the objects. Many of the objects for which labels must be acquired are frustratingly similar to one another. For example, every elementary school teacher is familiar with the difficulties involved in teaching children to distinguish between letters such as p and q. Language sounds are also similar enough to cause confusion for the child. The little boy who asked his mother if Clifford Columbus was going to discover America tomorrow illustrates among other things the problems which may arise in distinguishing among language sounds.

In order to learn the complex discriminations which may be involved in distinguishing among objects or sounds, the child must learn to extract distinctive features from the stimuli in his or her environment (Gibson, 1969). For example, in learning to make discriminations between letters such as p and q, the child must focus on the position of the circle with respect to the line. The ability to extract distinctive features may occur as a result of repeated experience with stimuli. However, it can be enhanced by calling attention to distinctive features in various ways, for example by naming them (Bergan, 1972).

The second major problem involved in making multiple discriminations has to do with the interference of learning occurring at one time on learning occurring at another time. As is well known, when people have many new things to learn, they will often forget things learned previously. Such forgetting is widespread in language learning throughout life. The problems in remembering the meanings of words not frequently used is a case in point. The time-honored method for forestalling forgetting is practice. Language learning provides ample opportunity for practice in that people talk to others or to themselves during most of their waking hours.

Concept learning

After children have acquired multiple discriminations, they have the necessary prerequisites for concept learning. As we have indicated previously, in concept learning the individual classifies objects in the environment into categories. As discussed in chapter 6, children's first concepts will be representations of concrete things. However, as development progresses, children become increasingly free from concrete phenomena in their thinking so that by the time they reach adolescence they are capable of the kind of abstract thought required in complex problem solving.

Chomsky's Nativist Position

Shortly after Skinner (1957) had completed his comprehensive exposition of the behaviorist position in *Verbal Behavior,* Noam Chomsky (1959) wrote a devastating critique of Skinner's work, asserting that behaviorism could not adequately account for language acquisition. After having summarily dismissed the behavioral explanation of language learning, Chomsky went on to elaborate his own view that language learning requires prior knowledge of language rules, knowledge innately built into humans but not into other species (Chomsky, 1968).

The LAD and universal rules

The language acquisition device. Chomsky uses the term language acquisition device (LAD) to describe the individual's innate knowledge of linguistic rules. Chomsky holds that there are certain rules which apply to all languages and certain rules which are restricted in their application to a specific language. The LAD is comprised of those rules which have universal application. For example, it is known that there are a limited set of distinctive features of speech sounds which can be used in the formation of a language. Specific languages are comprised of subsets of distinctive features selected from the larger universe of possible features. In Chomsky's view, the learner has innate knowledge of the distinctive features of speech. His or her task is simply to discover which sounds are used in the particular language he or she will be required to learn.

The infinity of possible utterances

Chomsky bases his argument for the existence of the LAD on several observations related to the nature of language and language learning. First, Chomsky notes that the number of possible utterances available in any given language is infinite. This is easily shown by considering the fact that it is possible to create an infinite string of grammatical verbalizations by embedding clauses within a sentence. For example, if one were fool enough to want to do it, one could say *What Bill expected was what John wanted which was why Susan objected to what Martha felt she ought to say to Allen regarding when the period should come in this endless string of nonsense.* Of course we could go on, but it is a virtual certainty that our capacity to generate embeddings of this kind would quickly extend beyond your interest in reading them.

Chomsky suggests that insofar as language does allow an infinite number of verbal utterances, language acquisition cannot be explained in terms of habits acquired through conditioning. Regarding this point, he remarks,

> The idea that a person has a "verbal repertoire"—a stock of utterances that he produces by "habit" on an appropriate occasion—is a myth, totally at variance with the observed use of language. Nor is it possible to attach any substance to the view that the speaker has a stock of "patterns" in which he inserts words. . . . Such conceptions may apply to greetings, a few clichés, and so on, but they

completely misrepresent the normal use of language, as the reader can easily convince himself by unprejudiced observation. (Chomsky, 1968, p. 118)

Chomsky suggests that what is needed to explain the capacity of language to produce an infinite number of utterances is the assumption of a finite set of rules from which the infinite number of possible utterances can be produced. The LAD is assumed to contain the finite set of rules necessary for language production.

A second observation which suggests the need for the LAD has to do with the creativity of speech. Chomsky points out that people almost never say exactly the same thing twice. He argues that the degree of variety in human speech provides strong evidence suggesting that linguistic utterances are not acquired through conditioning processes.

The LAD and linguistic creativity

In fairness to Chomsky's opposition, it should be noted that Skinner is well aware of the novelty in human speech patterns and he has a simple explanation for it. People say what others reinforce them for saying. Audiences generally don't like to hear the same thing more than once, so speakers tend not to repeat themselves. They simply combine previously acquired habits in new ways appropriate to the controlling stimuli in the existing situation (Skinner, 1957).

A third factor which suggests the need for a language acquisition device has to do with the fact that the child is simply not given enough information to acquire the linguistic rules which he or she eventually masters. For example, consider the following pair of sentences:

The LAD and learning opportunity

> *John is easy to please.*
> *John is eager to please.*

These sentences are apparently the same in grammatical structure. Yet they are quite different as can be easily seen by transforming them in the following manner:

> *It is easy to please John.*
> *It is eager to please John.*

Chomsky has demonstrated that there are rules which explain why the first transformation is permissible and does not alter the meaning of the sentence and why the second transformation is not permissible. Virtually all competent speakers of English know these rules in that they quickly recognize that the first transformation is appropriate whereas the second one is not. How do speakers of English learn such rules? Chomsky asserts that it stretches the imagination beyond the pale of common sense to assume that rules of this sort are acquired by conditioning processes and the imitation of parental speech patterns.

The LAD and hierarchical rule application

A fourth aspect of language which supports the need for the LAD has to do with the way in which language rules are applied in the production and comprehension of speech. Chomsky argues that language rules used to generate sentences must be applied in a hierarchical sequence. First, a rule specifying the general character of the entire utterance to be spoken is enacted. Then a rule designating the major subdivisions of the utterance (that is, the subject and the predicate) is put into operation. Next the major subdivisions are subdivided further. Finally the utterance is transformed into the pattern which is actually spoken.

One line of argument which suggests that hierarchical sequencing of some kind is required in language use has to do with the fact that in many cases the meaning of a sentence is not communicated until the very end of the sentence. For example, consider the following: *What I am looking for is a pair of pajamas.* It is not clear what the speaker is talking about until the final word has been uttered. Presumably the speaker knew that he was going to say something about pajamas before he ever opened his mouth. Thus he must have had some conception of the entire sentence in mind before he began to speak.

The LAD and language as a human characteristic

A final characteristic of language which suggests the need for the LAD is the uniqueness of language as a human characteristic. Chomsky suggests that no other species has the capability to generate an infinite number of novel speech patterns. He is, of course, aware of the work which has been done in attempting to teach chimpanzees to use language. In an oblique reference to these efforts he quips:

> One expositor of Cartesian philosophy, Antoine Le Grand, refers to the opinion "of some people of the East Indies, who think that Apes and Baboons, which are with them in great numbers, are imbued with understanding, and that they can speak but will not for fear they should be employed, and set to work." If there is a more serious argument in support of the claim that human language capacity is shared with other primates, then I am unaware of it. (Chomsky, 1968, p. 102)

The limited role of the environment. Although Chomsky goes to great lengths to build a rationale for the view that the ability to use language requires a LAD built in by innate mechanisms, he does recognize that the environment plays a role in language acquisition. However, he suggests that the role is a limited one. In this regard, he points out that despite the fact that there are marked individual differences in the ability to use language, which can be attributed in part to individual heredity and in part to environmental factors, the degree of similarity in language competence among individuals and groups is far greater than has been traditionally recognized. In this connection he writes:

> As participants in a certain culture, we are naturally aware of the great differences in ability to use language, in knowledge of vocabulary, and so on that result from differences in native ability and from differences in conditions of acquisition; we naturally pay much less attention to the similarities and to common knowledge, which we take for granted. But if we manage to establish the requisite psychic distance, if we actually compare the generative grammars that must be postulated for different speakers of the same language, we find that the similarities that we take for granted are quite marked and that the divergences are few and marginal.

What is more, it seems that dialects that are superficially quite remote, even barely intelligible on first contact, share a vast central core of common rules and processes and differ very slightly in underlying structures, which seem to remain invariant through long historical eras. (Chomsky, 1968, p. 79)

Exactly what does the environment contribute to language learning? It determines the specific language the individual will acquire, including the special rules which apply to that language and no other. Moreover, since there are certain clearly discernible cultural variations associated with most languages, the environment will determine the subvarieties of a given language which will be learned. Thus, in the case of English, for example, it will determine whether a speaker is likely to say *He be comin in a minute* or *He'll be here shortly*. Similarly it will determine whether a speaker is likely to say *Why you try an make me talk like a damn haole* [1] as opposed to *Why are you trying to make my speech patterns approximate standard English?* Clearly, linguistic variations, such as those given in the examples here, are fraught with enormous social significance, but the basic content of the messages communicated is not greatly different across the dialectic variations illustrated. This fact, of course, supports Chomsky's point that after all languages and dialects are much more similar than has been traditionally recognized.

Environmental contributions to language development

WHAT IS ACQUIRED THROUGH LANGUAGE DEVELOPMENT

Having discussed the mechanisms which have been proposed to specify how language is acquired, we may now examine the question of what the child acquires in the course of language development. As you shall see, the answers which have been given to this question are varied indeed. Behaviorists hold that the child learns a set of operant verbal behaviors during development. Chomsky asserts that the child acquires a grammar which enables him or her to relate language sounds to meanings. Roger Brown, an eminent psycholinguist, has carried out longitudinal research suggesting that the child acquires syntactic and semantic rules. Finally, sociolinguistic theorists have pointed out that the child learns rules which relate speech to the social context in which it occurs. Although the various views regarding what is acquired through language development represent widely differing perspectives, they should not necessarily be looked at as competing perspectives since each makes a unique contribution to our understanding of the nature of language behavior.

Language Development as the Acquisition of Operants

Skinner (1957) asserts that traditional analyses of language in terms of sound patterns, word meanings, and syntactic structures do not provide a particularly useful way to conceptualize what is learned in language development. The problem with traditional analyses is that they do not specify the environmental factors controlling speech. For example, to say that a child's remark such as *I wish I had a cookie* is made up of a subject, a verb, etc., is to miss the point entirely that the child is probably attempting to get someone, his audience for the moment, to give him a cookie.

In an attempt to overcome what he perceives to be the inherent weakness of traditional language analyses, Skinner has conceptualized linguistic utterances as operant verbal behaviors. As shown in table 7-1, he distinguishes four basic verbal operants: the *mand,* the *intraverbal operant,* the *tact,* and the *autoclitic.*

---

1. *Haole* is a word used by Hawaiians to refer to Caucasians.

The mand. A mand is a verbal operant in which the verbal response of the speaker is reinforced by a characteristic consequence. For example, if a speaker says *pass the butter*, the reinforcement which will characteristically follow his utterance will be that he will receive some butter. Mands often take the form of imperative statements such as *pass the butter.* However, they also include questions (*What time is it?*) and exhortations (*Please don't wipe your dirty hands on the tablecloth*).

Table 7–1   *Verbal Operants Acquired in Language Development*

Operants	Definitions	Examples
Mand	a verbal operant in which a response is reinforced in a characteristic way	Pass the butter.
Intraverbal	verbal behavior under the control of verbal stimuli	horse and buggy
Tact	a verbal operant signaled by an object or property in the environment	That is a ball.
Autoclitic	a verbal operant involving behavior based upon other verbal behavior	I think I should ride my bike.

The mand is generally initiated by a state of deprivation within the speaker. The individual who emits a mand may be hungry, thirsty, or just in need of information. Mands may also be prompted by the presence of aversive stimulation. For example, consider the father who after being repeatedly pestered by his daughter requested in grim jest, "Go play in traffic."

The mand is intended to produce reinforcement for the speaker. However, it does little for the listener. Accordingly, the speaker may go through a variety of ploys to disguise the mand or to mollify its harshness. For example, a young child said to a woman standing nearby, "I wish I had an ice cream cone like that." Consistent with his most fervent hopes, she responded: "Would you like a bite?" Sometimes the mand is even more subtle than the young child's disguised request. For instance, a speaker may say: *It certainly is hot in here.* Hopefully the listener would reply with a comment such as *Let me open a window.*

Sometimes a speaker will attempt to make up for the lack of reinforcement provided for the listener by preceding a mand with listener reinforcement. *Be a good boy now and go to bed.* The implication, of course, is that if the child does not go to bed he is not being a good boy. In other instances, the speaker will engage in a form of barter with the listener. *Get your pajamas on and I'll read you a story,* says a mother offering an attractive "deal" to her child. Finally, very often compliance with a mand will be followed by reinforcement for the listener. *Thank you* says the hungry child who has just received an extra helping of French-fried potatoes.

The intraverbal operant. The second type of operant which Skinner asserts is acquired in the course of language development is the intraverbal operant. The intraverbal operant is made up of verbal behavior under the control of verbal stimuli. There are several varieties of intraverbal operants. Reading, in the limited sense of vocalizing words presented visually, and writing, that is transcribing language, are two of the most familiar. In addition to these, Skinner includes verbal chains and verbal imitations of language models as intraverbal operants.

Intraverbal operants are always elicited by a verbal stimulus. This is obviously the case in imitative verbal behavior. Here, of course, the eliciting stimuli are the verbal utterances emitted by the model. In the case of verbal chains, the initial term serves as the first eliciting stimulus. From there on each link in the chain has an effect on subsequent links. In reading, the eliciting stimuli are the printed words, and in writing, they are words to be transcribed.

Eliciting intraverbal operants

Although Skinner assumes that intraverbal behaviors have in every case been acquired by being reinforced, after they have been acquired they are generally not under the control of reinforcement. For example, whereas a child may have initially been reinforced for imitating the behavior of an adult model, after a repertoire of imitative responses has been developed, control of imitation may be transferred to the eliciting stimulus, namely the model's behavior.

Intraverbal operants and reinforcements

Intraverbal operants may seem to have a machine-like quality in that they are habits which occur almost automatically. For example, verbal chains such as *horse and buggy, bread and butter,* and *over the hill* have a thoughtless quality to them. It is as though they are not emitted by a speaker at all, but rather by a recording machine that has no conception of what it is saying. Of course, in some cases effective language use requires almost automatic adherence to form. Greetings are a case in point. In most instances, however, verbal behavior must be innovative in character if effective communication is to occur.

Automatic character of intraverbal operants

Although intraverbal behaviors play their most obvious role in language in the production of seemingly automatic speech patterns, they also serve an important function in novel communications. Intraverbal operants provide raw material from which the rules of language which are used to produce new utterances may be extracted. For example, after learning a set of verbal chains such as *dog runs, boy runs, cat runs,* a child may generalize the application of the word *runs* to other communications. In so doing, the child has, of course, acquired an important language rule which will substantially expand the flexibility of his or her speech patterns.

Intraverbal operants and novel communications

The tact. One of the most crucial elements in any theory of language is the manner in which it explains the relationship between language and meaning. Most language theories take the position that words are symbols that are related to the phenomena for which they stand through thought processes of one kind or another. For example, a word may be related to a mental image which in turn represents an object in the environment. Skinner takes issue with traditional views of meaning on essentially the same grounds on which he faults traditional language theory in general, namely its failure to specify the environmental variables which control the manner in which verbal behavior is used to refer to environmental phenomena.

The tact serves the function of describing meaning from the behavioral standpoint. A tact is a verbal operant signaled by an object or property in the environment. For example, when a child sees a ball, he may say the word *ball*. Fortunately, he will not say the word every time he sees a ball, which demonstrates the fact that the object being referred to is only a signal. It does not actually control the occurrence of the naming response.

Audience and the tact

What does control the occurrence of the tact? Generally it is the behavior of the speaker's audience. For example, a parent may mand the occurrence of a tact by saying: *What is that?* Parents and teachers delight in manding tacts. For instance, many studies have shown that in any given period of instructional time teachers ask many more questions than their students. Moreover, the kinds of questions they ask often tend to require naming responses which are characteristic of the tact (e.g., see Zimmerman & Bergan, 1971). Presumably the reason that adult socialization agents mand tacts so frequently is that it is reinforcing to them in their attempts to meet their educative responsibilities.

In some cases tacts are reinforcing because they enlarge the audience's contact with the environment. When two children are hurrying home for supper just after dark and one says *What was that sound?* the other might respond *It's only a frog.* His tact provides reassuring information about the environment to his frightened companion.

Just as tacts are generally initiated by the audience, so also are they reinforced by the audience. When a mother says *What is this?* and her child responds *moo-moo* or *choo-choo* or whatever, the mother will often say something like *Yes, that's very good.* Similarly in adult conversation a listener may respond to needed information and *I really appreciate your telling me* or *I'm glad to know that.*

Generalizations of the tact

After a tact referring to a property of an object has been acquired, it may be generalized to new instances of the class of objects containing that object. As we have pointed out in a number of places previously, as this occurs the individual is in the process of acquiring a concept or classification rule.

Keeping the basic requirements for learning classification rules in mind, we may consider a second kind of generalization of the tact. Skinner (1957) provides the following charming example. A child drinking soda water for the first time remarked that it tasted "like my foot's asleep" (p. 92). What we have here is an example of metaphor. We can now see that metaphors may be produced by essentially the same processes as concept learning. In both cases, the verbal response is generalized to a new stimulus on the basis of common properties of the new stimulus and the stimulus to which the response was initially emitted. The common property in the case of the child's metaphor was the tingling sensation which she or he felt both after slightly prolonged immobility of the foot and after drinking soda water. The only difference between a metaphor and a concept is that in the case of the concept, the verbal community of which the speaker is a part specifies what the common properties defining categories are. In the case of metaphor, the speaker selects common properties indicating the similarity among phenomena.

The ability to emit behavior in accordance with classification rules and the ability to produce new rules through the use of metaphors provide the fundamental behavioral repertoire essential in describing what has traditionally been called meaning. For Skinner, the meaning attached to an environmental phenomenon is defined by the probability that a given verbal response will occur in the presence of that phenomenon given appropriate stimulation from the speaker's audience to bring forth the response. The role that concepts and metaphors play in defining meaning is to extend the definition of meaning to cover cases other than the simple naming of objects. Concepts extend the notion of meaning to cover categories of objects. Metaphors extend the definition of meaning beyond conventional classification into the realm of private and innovative meanings which may expand humans' conceptualization of their environments.

The autoclitic. The verbal operants which we have discussed to this point suggest a rather passive role for the speaker vis-à-vis his environment. In the main, the speaker is, as Skinner puts it, an interested bystander whose utterances are controlled largely by his audience. Of course, although we have not made the point explicitly in this chapter, the speaker may serve as his own audience by talking to himself. Under these circumstances he may exert some control over his own verbal behavior. However, the kind of control which the speaker can achieve in this way is limited in that it does not determine in any precise way the form or specific content of verbal discourse.

The mand, the intraverbal, and the tact are, in Skinner's (1957) view "the raw material out of which sustained verbal behavior is manufactured. But who is the manufacturer (p. 312)?" Skinner suggests that this question cannot be answered by falling back on the supposition of an internal controlling agent. Rather, he argues that "Part of the behavior of an organism becomes . . . one of the variables controlling another part" (1957, p. 313).

The type of verbal operant which Skinner calls the autoclitic has the necessary properties to serve the function of controlling other verbal behavior by the speaker. Autoclitic verbal behavior is verbal behavior "which is based upon or depends upon other verbal behavior" (Skinner, 1957, p. 315). Autoclitic verbalizations have the special property of influencing the listener's interpretation of other verbal utterances. For example, if a girl says *I want bread,* she conveys one meaning to her audience. On the other hand, if the child inserts the word *no* between *want* and *bread,* she changes the meaning of the sentence markedly.

In some cases autoclitics may describe or interpret the speaker's verbal behavior. For example, a child may say *I should ride my bike on the sidewalk-I think I should,* indicating his uncertainty about his bike-riding beliefs to his audience. Or an adult may say *I hope you won't take offense if I tell you this, but your socks are inside out,* suggesting that his observation is intended to be informative rather than derisive.

Some autoclitics qualify the meaning of verbal utterances. Negation, as in the example *I want no bread,* is a case in point. Assertion, of course, represents the other side of the qualification coin. The speaker who says *By George, it is a green bear* conveys not only a rare phenomenon, but also that *he* is asserting that the phenomenon exists.

From the standpoint of the speaker's control of his own verbal behavior, the most important class of autoclitics includes those which deal with the formation of grammatical structures. Applications of what are traditionally regarded as the rules of grammar serve an autoclitic function in that they modify the interpretation of a verbalization by a listener. For example, when a speaker adds an *s* to the word *boy,* he has modified the meaning of what has been conveyed to his audience. Similarly when he inserts a conjunction between two clauses, as in *John went, but Bill didn't,* he changes the message by adding the implication that Bill was probably expected to go even though he did not go. Finally, and most important, when a speaker changes the order or arrangement of words as from *Will he come* to *He will come,* he may substantially change the meaning of his utterance.

The production of verbal behavior is made possible in part by the application of grammatical autoclitics. In Skinner's view, the speaker may initiate a segment of verbal behavior with a relatively primitive grouping of words. For example, a hungry boy might upon seeing food say to himself covertly *potatoes, want*. To make his verbal behavior an effective communication from the standpoint of his audience, he reverses the order of the words and adds *I*. In deference to the exigencies of polite form, he replaces *want* with *would like* and adds *some* and *please*. What his audience hears, then, is *I would like some potatoes, please*.

Construction of verbal behavior

As we have seen, critics of the behavioral position often chide behaviorists for assuming that verbal behavior is merely a collection of habits. The verbal behavior described in the above example is not simply a string of verbal phrases acquired by habit. It represents a construction based on successive modifications of an initial covert utterance. Observations of modifications of verbal patterns may be readily observed in the behavior of writers who frequently alter the initial approximations to the final form of a written segment. In the case of oral communication, modifications often escape observation. However, they may be inferred from the many hesitations which occur in extended oral communication. Moreover, the need for alterations may be verified in the ungrammatical combinations and blunders which occur in spoken language.

Language Development as the Acquisition of Grammar

Whereas behaviorists conceptualize language largely in terms of its relationship to a controlling environment, Chomsky and his followers conceive of language competence mainly in terms of the operation of a system of rules represented within the individual. In Chomsky's view, the environment exerts virtually no control over the operation of language rules. In this connection he states,

> . . . the normal use of language is . . . free from the control of detectable stimuli, either external or internal. It is because of this freedom from stimulus control that language can serve as an instrument of thought and self-expression, as it does not only for the exceptionally gifted and talented, but also, in fact, for every normal human. (Chomsky, 1968, p. 12)

The rules which people acquire to make language production and comprehension possible enable them to relate sequential patterns of word sounds to meanings. The totality of rules of this kind constitutes what linguists call *grammar*. Grammar, then, is not just a set of conventions defining proper language forms. Rather, it is a description of the rules with which people think.

Grammar defined.   Chomsky defines grammar as a system of rules which specifies the sound-meaning relationships for a language. As indicated in table 7-2, a grammar has three components: a phonetic component, a semantic component, and a syntactic component.

The phonetic component of grammar

The phonetic component of a grammar is comprised of those rules which specify the types of sounds used in the language, the organization of sounds into speech units called phonemes, and the segmentation of phonemes in extended utterances.

Phonemes are the smallest categories of sound which the speakers of a language are generally able to distinguish. To get some feel for the concept of phonemes in a language, it may be convenient to think of the sounds associated with letters of the alphabet. If one could assume that each letter stood for a unique sound category in the language, then letters would be phonemes. Actually, of course, letters do not provide an accurate catalogue of unique classes of language sounds. For example, the letter *c* may be pronounced with a *k* sound as in the word *can* or it may be said with an *s* sound as in the word *cereal*.

Speakers are generally not aware of the distinctive sound characteristics of the various members of a class of sounds defining a phoneme. For instance, in English the sound of the letter *p* is aspirated in some cases and not in others.

The Three Components of Grammar

Table 7–2

Component	Definition
Phonetic	rules governing the sounds used in a language
Semantic	rules for assigning meanings to words
Syntactic	rules governing the arrangement of words into larger units

Unless you have made a study of phonetics, you are probably unaware that you sometimes emit a puff of air from your lips as you pronounce the letter *p*. However, you can easily demonstrate the fact for yourself by lighting a match and pronouncing the word *spin*, which does not call for aspiration, and the word *pin* which does. The match should go out when you say *pin* but not when you say *spin*.

There is a general point to be gleaned from the match demonstration. First it includes the obvious fact that there are rules which govern the production of speech sounds, and second the more subtle observation that even though speakers may faithfully enact phonetic rules, they are often unaware that they are doing so.

The semantic component of a grammar is responsible for representing the meanings of linguistic units. From a linguistic point of view, meaning is defined in the main by specifying the defining attributes of words or word combinations. The heart of the semantic component of a grammar is a lexicon, a kind of dictionary which classifies verbalizations in terms of their defining attributes. For example, a word such as *knife* might be classified in terms of its grammatical properties as a common noun. In addition, it might be characterized by the physical attributes implied, such as sharpness. It also could be described in terms of function—cutting. Finally, it might be characterized in terms of the emotional reactions it elicits. *The semantic component of grammar*

The syntactic component of a grammar is comprised of those rules which determine the arrangement of words into phrases, clauses, and sentences. The syntactic component specifies how the parts of a sentence, the nouns, verbs, prepositions, articles, and so on, are put together. For example, there is a basic syntactic rule with which you are no doubt familiar that indicates a sentence can be formed from a noun phrase (the subject of the sentence) and a verb phrase (the predicate of the sentence). *The syntactic component of grammar*

In Chomsky's view, the syntactic component of a grammar serves the very special function of providing the mechanism for relating language sounds to meanings. As we have seen, syntax supplies the structure of a sentence. Chomsky assumes that after structure has been supplied, sounds and meanings may be attached to it. For example, syntax may specify that a sentence will begin with a noun phrase. The phonetic component represents this phrase with sounds, for example, *the dog*. The semantic component attaches meaning to the phrase indicating, for instance, that the noun refers to a four-legged, fur-bearing, barking mammal frequently referred to by the cliché, man's best friend.

Universal and specific grammar.   Chomsky argues that all three components of a grammar include rules which apply to all languages and rules which are specific to a given language. The phonetic, semantic, and syntactic rules which relate sound to meaning in all languages comprise what is called the universal grammar. These are the rules which Chomsky assumes to be innately given and which make up the language acquisition device discussed earlier in the chapter. The rules which are unique to a given language make up the specific grammar of the language. The acquisition of the rules of specific grammars is subject to environmental influence.

There was a time in the history of linguistic science when the idea of a universal grammar was seriously questioned. Languages are seemingly quite different from one another; and accordingly, it is not surprising that many theorists assumed that each language was comprised of its own unique set of rules. However, contemporary linguists and psycholinguists have been able to identify a number of rules which apparently do apply across all languages. For example, all languages contain rules for specifying a subject and a predicate in a sentence. As we mentioned earlier in the chapter, all languages are constructed from a universal set of distinctive phonological features. Finally, all languages include terms which convey meanings such as the concept of an agent who initiates action, the action taken, and the recipient of the effects of action.

Deep and surface structure.   Chomsky assumes that there are two levels or types of syntactic structures in a grammar. He bases this assumption on the fact that the meaning of a sentence cannot always be interpreted from its surface appearance. For example, consider the sentence *They are visiting dignitaries.* It is impossible to tell precisely what this sentence means from its appearance. It could mean that a group of people have the status of being dignitaries from another place. On the other hand, it could indicate that a group of individuals are going to visit another group of people who are dignitaries.

Chomsky argues that the discrepancy between appearance and meaning requires that there be two sets of syntactic structures, one to relate syntax to meaning and the other to relate syntax to sound. The structure which relates syntax to meaning is referred to as the deep structure of the sentence. In the example above, the deep structure would serve the function of representing either one or the other of the possible meanings of the sentence, depending on which meaning was intended. The surface structure would produce the sentence in the pattern in which it finally appeared.

Rules of formation   *Rules of formation and transformation.*   The deep structure of a sentence is generated by what Chomsky calls rules of formation. As shown in figure 7-2, rules of formation are hierarchically sequenced. First, a rule is applied which generates a noun phrase (NP) and a verb phrase (VP) for a sentence (S). At this point, we have a gross representation of the fact that the sentence will be composed of a subject and a predicate. Next the noun phrase is divided into its components, which in the example given include an article (T) and a noun (N).

At the same time, the verb phrase is broken into its constituent parts including a verb (V) and a noun phrase (NP) which serves as the object of the sentence. Finally, that noun phrase is separated into an article (T) and a noun (N).

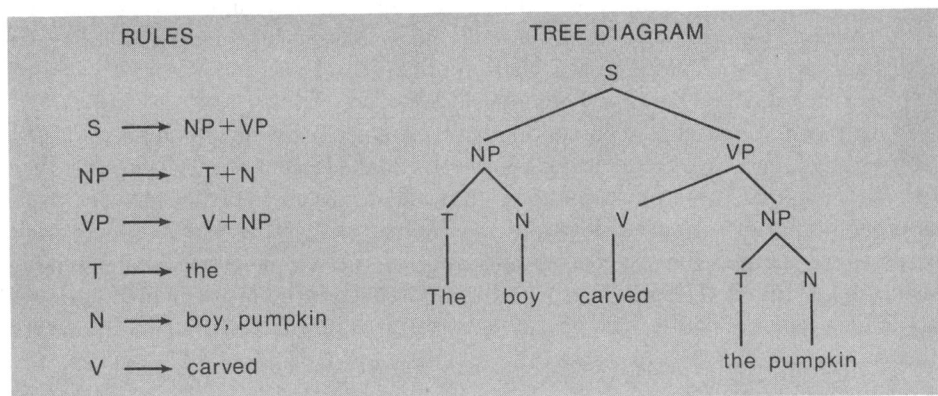

```
RULES                              TREE DIAGRAM
                                         S

    S  ⟶  NP+VP
                                 NP                VP
   NP  ⟶    T+N
   VP  ⟶   V+NP            T      N      V          NP

    T  ⟶    the
                              The   boy   carved    T      N
    N  ⟶  boy, pumpkin

    V  ⟶   carved                                the  pumpkin
```

An example of a set of rules of formation. S stands for sentence, N for noun, P for phrase, V for verb, and T for article. Arrows indicate that symbols on the left can be rewritten in the forms given to the right of the arrows. The tree diagram on the right reveals the hierarchical structure of rules of formation.

Figure 7–2

In the simple example given in figure 7-2, the surface structure and the deep structure are identical. Thus, only rules of formation are required to represent the utterance as it will finally appear. However, as already indicated, in many instances the deep and surface structures in a sentence will not be identical. In such cases, it is necessary to apply rules of transformation which convert deep structures into surface structures. For example, suppose that one wished to make a question out of the sentence in the above example. In order to accomplish this, a rule would have to be added which placed the word *did* at the beginning of the sentence. This rule would be a transformational rule because it would transform the deep structure of the sentence.

Rules of transformation

Rules of transformation fulfill a variety of different functions. Sometimes they are used to convert a statement into a question. Sometimes they are used to convert a sentence from the active voice (*Polly ate the apple*) to the passive voice (*The apple was eaten by Polly*). Finally, sometimes they are used in relating an ambiguous surface structure to a deep structure which conveys a definite message.

Chomsky's recognition of the fact that the meaning of a sentence does not always coincide with its surface appearance and his conceptualization of how the deep structure articulated to meaning is transformed into surface appearance constitute a singular achievement in linguistic science. In recognition of the role which rules of transformation play in relating deep structure to surface structure, Chomsky's grammar is often referred to as transformational grammar.

The psychological reality of transformational grammar. Chomsky's assertions about deep and surface structure and about the rules of formation and transformation presumed to generate these two kinds of syntactic structures constitute a theory requiring empirical validation. During the 1960s, psycholinguists began to conduct extensive investigations into the psychological reality of deep and surface structure.

Early research suggested that something approximating Chomsky's notions of deep and surface structure probably do exist within the individual. For example, it was found that the auditory perception of sentences seemed to be affected by the deep and surface structures of sentences (Fodor & Bever, 1965; Garrett, Bever, & Fodor, 1966; Bever, 1970, 1971). More specifically, it appeared that people mentally grouped words into phrases sometimes in accordance with surface structure and sometimes in accordance with deep structure. In addition, early studies suggested that grammatical structure affected memory (Miller & Isard, 1964; Savin & Perchonock, 1965).

More recent research on perception and memory reviewed by Johnson-Laird (1974) has failed to support the Chomsky position. Recent studies indicate that the meaning conveyed by a sentence may affect psychological processes such as perception and memory. However, it is not at all certain that it is necessary or useful to assume the psychological reality of a deep structure which relates syntax to meaning. Despite these findings, Chomsky's theory remains a viable possibility and no doubt will be the subject of vigorous research in the years ahead.

Brown's Stages of Language Development

Chomsky's theory specifies the grammatical rules defining language competence in a mature, ideal speaker. Even if one assumes, as Chomsky does, the existence of an innately determined set of rules governing language production and comprehension, one must recognize the obvious fact that the rules controlling language do not operate in the young child in the same way that they do in an older individual. Language and the grammatical rules by which it is generated are acquired over an extended period of time. In order to guide development effectively, it is important to know not only the grammatical competencies which the individual amasses at the end of development, but also the capabilities which he or she acquires along the way.

Empirical studies of the acquisition of language rules, as you might expect, have been of relatively long-standing concern in developmental psychology. However, early research in the field assumed that the grammatical rules the child mastered were simply adult rules of grammar. Contemporary psycholinguists now recognize that during the course of development a child acquires his own rules to guide language production and comprehension. Of course, child grammar must lead ultimately to the acquisition of adult grammar. Nonetheless, the child's rules are worth considering in their own right. If we are to understand what the child comprehends, why he speaks as he does, and what he is capable of learning at any given period of development, we need to know the rules which the child uses in controlling his speech patterns.

Roger Brown and his colleagues at Harvard University have conducted an extensive program of research on the development of language rules in young children. Brown (1973) holds that during the course of development children learn a hierarchically related set of rules based on certain fundamental characteristics of sentence structure. Brown describes the acquisition of language rules in terms of stages. At each stage of development, the child's major achievement is the mastery of a new set of rules related to one of the basic characteristics of sentences which Brown has identified. In the discussion which follows, we shall describe the sentence characteristics which Brown has specified as being critical to development, and we shall detail the two stages of language development which Brown has outlined as of the time of this writing.

Roles conveyed in sentences   *Sentence characteristics related to language development.* The first sentence characteristic that Brown suggests as having special significance for development has to do with the types of roles served by the people, places, things, and so on described in sentences. A sentence conveys information about the roles of the individuals and/or other phenomena which it describes. These roles are analogous in character to familiar social roles such as husband, wife, or teacher in that they indicate what is expected of the occupant of the role. However, the roles described by sentence structure are much more general in scope than social roles. For example, one of the major roles which may be conveyed in a sentence is the role of agent. An agent serves the function of producing a change in another object or being. For instance, in the something less than fascinating proclamation *The boy hit the balloon*, the boy is functioning as an agent.

Table 7-3 gives examples of roles conveyed in sentences. In addition, it provides sentences illustrating each type of role. From a brief analysis of the table, you can easily infer that the roles conveyed by sentences define basic categories of meaning. The acquisition of rules enabling the child to convey basic meanings represents what is perhaps his or her most fundamental and significant linguistic achievement.

A second sentence characteristic of importance for language development involves the fact that sentences contain grammatical units which modulate or alter information conveyed about basic sentence content. For instance, the articles

Modulation of sentence information

Some Semantic Roles Played by Noun Phrases in Simple Sentences   **Table 7–3**

Role	Definition	Examples
Agent	Someone or something which causes or instigates an action or process. Usually animate but not always, an agent must be perceived to have its own motivating force.	*Harriet* sang. *The men* laughed. *The wind* ripped the curtains.
Patient	Someone or something either in a given state or suffering a change of state.	*The wood* is dry. He cut *the wood*.
Experiencer	Someone having a given experience or mental disposition.	*Tom* saw the snake. *Tom* wanted a drink.
Beneficiary	Someone who profits from a state or process, including possession.	*Mary* has a convertible. This is *Mary's* car. Tom bought *Mary* a car.
Instrument	Something that plays a role in bringing about a process or action but which is not the instigator; it is used by an agent.	Tom opened the door with *a key*. Tom used *his knife* to open the box.
Location	The place or locus of a state, action, or process.	The spoon is in *the drawer*. Tom sat in *the chair*.
Complement	The verb names an action that brings something into existence. The complement, on a more or less specific level, completes the verb. This use of the word "complement" is not, incidentally, its most common use in linguistics.	Mary sang *a song*. John played *checkers*.

From W. L. Chafe, *Meaning and the structure of language.* Chicago: University of Chicago Press, 1970 and from R. Brown, *A first language: The early stages.* Cambridge: Harvard University Press, 1973, p. 8. Reprinted by permission.

in the sentence *The boy hit the balloon* indicate a specific boy and a specific balloon. If the sentence had been changed to *That boy,* even greater specificity would be indicated. Articles, prepositions, and inflections (for example, adding *s* to form a plural) are among the major grammatical constructions which modulate basic sentence content. The acquisition of these grammatical structures makes it possible for the child to add precision to his or her communications with others.

Sentence modalities

A third sentence characteristic related to language development involves the fact that sentences come in a variety of modalities defined by variations in word order. The declarative, interrogative, and imperative forms of sentence construction are familiar examples. During the early stages of language development, children are not capable of using all the various sentence modalities, though they may well express meanings which call for variations in modality. For example, a child may say *Mommy sock* to indicate the declarative assertion *That is my mommy's sock* or to convey the imperative *Mommy, put on my sock.* Acquisition of the capability to use modality adds a further dimension of precision to the child's communications.

Embeddings

A fourth characteristic of sentences associated with language development is that sentence complexity can be increased by embedding one clause or sentence within another. For example, a child may say *I hope I will get a balloon,* or after having received his balloon, he might tearfully say *Whoever popped this balloon must replace it.*

The capability to use embeddings such as the above represents an obviously advanced achievement in language development. When the child has learned to use embeddings, he or she can say many more things in many different ways than he or she could previously. However, Brown notes that embeddings do not seem to add any new dimensions to the basic meanings conveyed in sentences. For example, the clause *Whoever popped this balloon* functions in the role of agent for the complex sentence of which it is a part. In this connection, it occupies essentially the same role as the word *boy* in the simple sentence *The boy hit the balloon.*

Coordination in sentences

The final sentence characteristic which Brown asserts as having special importance for development involves increases in sentence complexity associated with the coordination of simple sentences or propositions. The ability to tie sentences together with coordinating conjunctions enables the child to express relationships among the statements he or she makes. The kinds of relationships expressed can range from a simple joining of thoughts which somehow seem as though they ought to go together as in *Carol went to the store and Alice went for a walk* to subtle linkages such as *Carol hit Bob even though Alice told her not to do it.*

Age and Stage I

Stage I: semantic roles and grammatical relations. Brown calls the first stage of grammatical development the stage of semantic roles and grammatical relations. The central achievements to occur at this stage are the acquisition of a set of meanings which convey basic roles occupied by the persons or things described in sentences and a simple grammar which expresses relationships among the meanings which have been acquired.

There is no set age at which children typically pass through Stage I, or for that matter any of the other stages which Brown has specified. Children vary widely in the age at which they attain the competencies associated with a given stage. For example, one of the children studied by Brown and his colleagues entered Stage I sometime before she was 18 months old. Other children had not achieved a comparable stage of development until they were 27 months old.

The language capability that defines Stage I is the ability to put two words together usually for the purpose of forming what might be described as a primitive sentence. For example, children functioning at Stage I may say things like *All broke, More taxi,* or *Pants dry.* Expressions such as these can be readily translated into sentences such as *It is broken, I want a longer ride in the taxi,* and *My pants are dry.*

It is a fact of some interest that parents generally do expand the two-word utterances of children into complete sentences. For some time it was thought that expansions of this kind served a training function. However, the currently available research evidence suggests that expansions do not materially affect a child's speech patterns (Cazden, 1973).

The grammar the child learns at Stage I is comprised of a set of meanings which are expressed in the two-word utterances he or she uses in communication. These meanings include basic roles such as agent and object. As shown in table 7-4, the roles are joined in two-term relations. For example, the role of agent may be related to action in a two-term utterance such as *Mommy do.* Similarly the role of possessor may be related to possession in a verbalization such as *Adam toy* which may be translated to mean *Adam's toy.*

Stage I and sensorimotor development

Surprisingly, the content of the utterances expressed in the simple relations of Stage I corresponds quite closely to the major developmental achievement of Piaget's sensorimotor period. What the young child talks about are the impor-

Two-Term Relations Acquired in Stage I   **Table 7–4**

Two-Term Relations	Relations Described	Examples of Relations
agent and action	an instigator initiates a process	Adam pull
action and object	a process affects someone or something	Break cup
agent and object	an instigator and object in interaction	Adam ball (as in Adam kicks the ball)
action and location	action eventuates in a change in place	Put table (as in Put it on the table)
entity and location	something in a place	Lady home (as in The lady is home)
possessor and possession	a relation between a being and that which belongs to the being	Daddy chair (meaning Daddy's chair)
entity and attributive	specification of an attribute of something	Yellow block
demonstrative and entity	naming objects	See ball

tant things which he or she learned before being able to talk. As you will recall, the central accomplishment of the sensorimotor period is the recognition that objects endure both over time and across different spatial locations. The simple grammatical constructions which develop during Stage I presuppose the existence of objects which endure despite changes in space and time. For example, an utterance involving location such as *Where ball* conveys the child's knowledge that there is a ball which endures despite the fact that it is absent from his or her immediate sensory experience.

Age and Stage II   *Stage II: grammatical morphemes and the modulation of meaning.* Brown has labeled the second major developmental stage he has investigated the stage of grammatical morphemes and the modulation of meanings. The term *morpheme* indicates the smallest sound unit to which a meaning is attached. The phrase grammatical morphemes and the modulation of meaning refers to the fact that in Stage II the child acquires small grammatical units (articles, prepositions, and so on) which he or she uses to alter the meanings of sentences.

Children enter Stage II when they begin to utter sentences which are generally three words in length rather than two. As in the case of Stage I, there is no fixed age at which children pass through Stage II. One of the children which Brown studied was only 21 months old when she began to acquire Stage II constructions. On the other hand, other children participating in the research were between 2½ and 3 years old when they began to acquire Stage II morphemes.

Grammatical morphemes   The acquisitions which occur at Stage II reveal the hierarchical complexity of language development. Children acquire grammatical morphemes after they achieve the ability to verbalize the relations of Stage I because they must be able to express the meanings learned during Stage I before they can be expected to modulate them. The hierarchical complexity of language learning explains the obvious, yet puzzling fact that young children do not simply learn language by imitating their parents. They cannot imitate many of the things their parents say because they have not acquired prerequisite competencies for such imitation.

Language Development as the Acquisition of Sociolinguistic Rules

To this point we have considered language rules as though they were largely independent of the social context in which they are applied. But, of course, language rules are not independent of social context. When Shaw's (1953) Eliza Doolittle says, "Nah then, Freddy: look wh' y' gowin, deah" (p. 219), she conveys quite a different message from a social standpoint than she would have conveyed if she had said: *Now then Freddy: look where you are going dear.*

In the present section we shall discuss those sociolinguistic rules which relate language to the social context in which it occurs. First we shall consider the general nature of sociolinguistic rules. Then we shall discuss the social variables which may serve as cues for applying a given set of sociolinguistic rules. Finally we shall outline the functions which sociolinguistic rules may serve for a speaker and listener.

The nature of sociolinguistic rules. Sociolinguistic rules specify linguistic alterations associated with variations in social factors. Alterations may be phonological, semantic, syntactic, or some combination of these. For example, Labov (1966) has recorded phonological variations associated with social factors in speakers from New York City.

As is well known, city living often produces definable phonological patterns. In the case of speakers from New York, these patterns are quite distinctive. One of the idiosyncrasies of New York speech is the failure to pronounce the letter *r* as in the sentence *Dat's Ian's cah* which may be translated *That's Ann's car.*

The failure to pronounce *r* is related to the social setting in which the letter is spoken and the social class of the speaker. Lower-class speakers tend to omit the *r* more than middle-class speakers, and all speakers tend to omit the *r* more in informal settings than in formal settings.

Similar examples to the phonological illustrations may be easily found for semantic and syntactic structures. The use of special vocabulary as in *Be cool, man* provides a familiar semantic alteration used by young people mainly in informal settings. A pattern such as *He be the one* as opposed to *He is the one* illustrates a syntactic feature which may vary as a function of social factors.

There are four broad categories of sociolinguistic rules. Each category defines a specific style of communication in the language.

*Categories of
sociolinguistic rules*

The most basic class of rules is that which defines the *formal style* of speech within the language. Formal style is generally used on ceremonial occasions, in public gatherings involving discourse among acquaintances or strangers, and in a variety of written communications, such as nonfiction books and magazine articles.

Another major class of sociolinguistic rules produces *colloquial styles* within a culture. Colloquial styles tend to vary from region to region. They are generally used in informal settings involving discourse among close acquaintances, friends, or relatives. The defining characteristic of colloquial style is that it is not regarded as the standard form of the language by the majority of speakers.

A third category of sociolinguistic rules includes those rules which generate *slang* or vulgar speech. The defining feature of vulgar speech is that it is regarded by most speakers as at best improper and at worst repulsive. Of course, there are occasions when slang or vulgar expressions are accepted. If this were not the case, presumably this category of language would cease to exist. The young child does not always get his mouth washed out with soap for his linguistic improprieties. When he is with peers in informal settings, vulgarities may be rewarded.

The final category of sociolinguistic rules defines *nonstandard dialects* within a culture. In American culture, there are a variety of nonstandard dialects including Cajun, which is a version of French spoken mainly in areas of the Southeast, Chicano, which includes a variety of speech patterns spoken by Mexican-American groups, and black English, which is a dialect spoken mainly by lower-class blacks living in urban ghettos.

The defining feature of a dialect is that it includes a set of language rules characteristic of a particular cultural subgroup. Dialects are used mainly in speaking to other members of the cultural subgroup which has established the dialect. However, of course, in those many cases in which the speaker has not mastered the standard form of the language, dialectic forms may be used in conversing with individuals outside the cultural subgroup with which the dialect is associated.

*Consistency in the
application of
sociolinguistic rules*

Sociolinguistic rules not only specify that certain language styles should be applied in certain social contexts, but they also require that linguistic features prompted by social variables be applied in a consistent fashion. For example, a sentence such as *Dat cadenza at dee end of dee first movement of Beethoven's second concerto for piano and orchestra be really cool* would strike a listener as being very strange indeed. The mixture of dialectic and informal speech patterns and rather technical musical terms is jarring to the ears.

One of the problems faced by speakers of nonstandard dialects is that they generally do not apply standard language forms in a consistent way. Contrary to what might be expected, they usually have all the standard speech patterns in their linguistic repertoires, but they do not use the standard forms on all occasions in which they are required. In this connection, Ervin-Tripp (1972) points out:

> Labov, McKay, Henrie, Kernan, and indeed everyone who has collected considerable samples of speech of dialect speakers have found that the full range of most standard forms will appear *some time* in their speech. That is, the problem of standard speech is in most cases not that the form is outside the repertoire but that the speaker *cannot maintain a consistent choice* of standard alternatives and not make slips. (p. 136)

Social variables related to language. There are a variety of social variables which may trigger the application of different sets of sociolinguistic rules. Some of the examples given in the preceding paragraphs illustrate that one of these is the social setting in which language is spoken. A boy generally speaks in a different tone of voice and uses a different set of expletives in church than he does on a baseball diamond.

Although many of the linguistic alterations which occur as a function of setting are well known to most speakers, others are not. In some cases, failure of *Situational* individuals and groups to be aware of situational effects on language have had *influences* *on language* disastrous consequences. For example, for many years it was assumed that

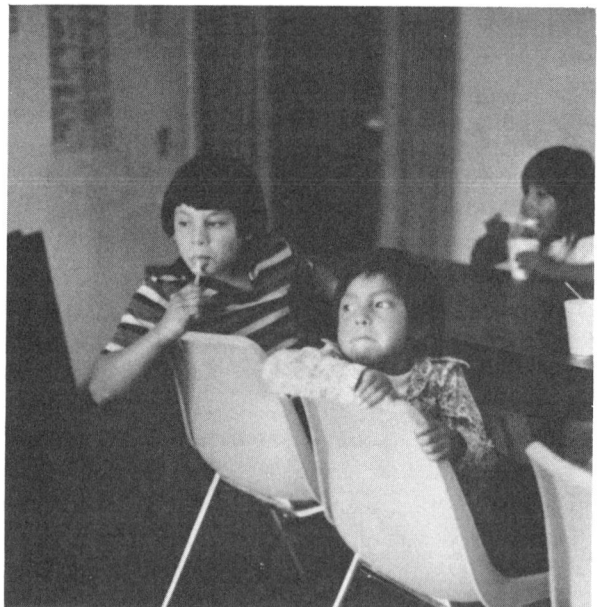

Language style may vary with the setting.

lower-class black children suffered from "verbal deprivation," which manifested itself in a lack of language output. It is now recognized that the presumed failure of black children to do much talking was simply a function of the fact that samples of their speech were collected in formal testing settings. Outside of the testing situation, verbal deprivation is hard to find. Regarding this fact Susan Ervin-Tripp (1973) comments,

Recent investigators such as Labov and Cohen . . . in Harlem and Eddington and Claudia Mitchell in San Francisco and Oakland have recorded natural interaction. All have found that Negro lower class speakers are highly verbal in terms of speech frequency. Both adolescents and children engage with great skill in verbal games for which they have complex traditions. "Controlled situations" may, in fact, obscure the very skills which have been most developed within a particular group. (p. 351)

A second social variable which may prompt alterations in language use is the social position or status of the participants in a conversation. For example, people are more likely to address an older person or an individual of high status or authority as Mr. or Ms. than they are to apply a title of this sort to a peer.

Language and the social position of participants in conversation

Social status may signal variations in dialect as well as alterations within the standard form of a language. For example, Houston (1969) found greater use of standard English by black children being interviewed by an adult authority than was observed in samples of the children's language taken in classroom interactions.

As already indicated, the cultural affiliation of the participants in conversation is a social variable which may prompt alteration in language use. Individuals from the same cultural subgroup may use the speech patterns of that group when speaking to one another, whereas they might tend to use the standard language patterns of the larger culture when conversing with someone outside of their own particular subgroup (Ervin-Tripp, 1973).

Language and the cultural affiliation of conversation participants

The use of language patterns associated with a particular subgroup communicates the fact that the listener and speaker share certain social meanings which are not shared by outsiders (Labov & Cohen, 1967). These shared meanings may create a sense of solidarity between speaker and listener, a feeling that each understands the other in a way not possible for those who do not belong to their particular subgroup.

Functions of sociolinguistic rules. Sociolinguistic rules serve many important functions in communication. One of these is to convey information to the listener regarding his or her social relationship to the speaker. For example, a child may use a vulgar expression in conversing with peers to affirm that he is part of the peer culture. Similarly, an adolescent girl may call a teacher by his or her first name to show that she does not recognize the teacher's authority. Conversely, a teacher may encourage students to use his or her first name to break down social barriers related to the assumption of teacher authority on the part of students.

Linguistic rules and social relations

Sometimes sociolinguistic rules are used to convey the speaker's attitude toward the listener. For example, an adult may use a familiar form of address such as *dumpling* or *sweetheart* to show affection for a child. Contrastingly, a child may hurl an insult at a playmate by applying appellations such as *fatso* or *dum-dum.*

Language and affect

One of the most important functions of sociolinguistic rules is to convey information about the speaker's social and/or cultural identity. Certain features of speech serve as *markers* which indicate the speaker's social and cultural affiliations to the listener (Labov, 1966). The omission of the *r* in the speech of New Yorkers is an example.

Linguistic markers and cultural identity

A somewhat surprising fact is that even though a speaker may emit linguistic markers in less than half of his vocalizations, listeners generally conclude that markers are emitted all the time. In other words, most listeners draw stereotypic conclusions about a speaker's language patterns even when those patterns are highly inconsistent with respect to the presence of markers.

Unfortunately, the stereotypic conclusions which listeners draw regarding speech patterns drastically color their views of speaker characteristics which have no direct relationship to language. In this connection Ervin-Tripp (1972) writes:

> It turns out to be the case . . . that listeners tend to give categorical judgements, as Labov first pointed out. They will judge intelligence, ambition, and honesty just from "accent." They do not react to frequencies reliably but . . . tend to pick out the "lowest" ranked social feature . . . as an indicator of the speaker's social ranking. . . . (p. 141)

Ervin-Tripp's remarks illustrate clearly the far-reaching implications which sociolinguistic rules may have when they are used to establish the cultural identity of a speaker. People use sociolinguistic rules to determine cultural affiliation and on the basis of that information alone they are often willing to make obviously unwarranted assumptions about personal characteristics.

GUIDING LANGUAGE DEVELOPMENT IN A CULTURALLY DIVERSE SOCIETY

One of the most significant manifestations of cultural diversity in America is the diversity which exists in language patterns. Although English is the dominant language in our society, Americans speak many other languages, including Spanish, French, Hawaiian, Chinese, Japanese, and a number of Indian languages. Moreover, as we have already noted, there are a variety of dialects spoken. There is even a pidgin language which is still widely used in Hawaii.

If we are to establish effective socialization practices for guiding language development, we must understand both the kinds of linguistic diversity which exist and the nature of the various types of diversity. On the basis of this understanding, we must establish a rationale for interpreting linguistic variations. Finally, we must develop socialization strategies for guiding language development in accordance with our interpretations of language differences.

Language in Cultural Subgroups

Linguistic diversity is related to two cultural variables: social class and ethnicity. It is generally true that different linguistic patterns prevail in the lower class than in the middle class. Likewise, it is usually the case that language varies across ethnic groups. Social class and ethnicity are not entirely independent of one another with regard to their effects on language. Ethnically related linguistic diversity tends to occur mainly in the lower class. When individuals from ethnic minorities move from the lower class into the middle class, they tend to adopt the language patterns of standard English.

Language and social class. There is a variety of experimental evidence supporting the view that there are differences in children's language related to social class. In general, the experimental findings suggest that lower-class children use fewer linguistic devices than middle-class children to make their meanings explicit. For example, Hawkins (1969) found that lower-class children tended to use pronouns in situations in which middle-class children often used nouns. The use of the pronoun precluded the insertion of modifiers which might amplify

Class differences in the use of linguistic devices

what the child intended to say. For example, a lower-class child might say *He picked it up.* In contrast, a middle-class child might say *The boy in the blue hat picked it up.* The phrase *in the blue hat* can be used to modify the noun *boy*, but it would not very likely be used with the pronoun *he*.

A second finding of the Hawkins study was that lower-class children tended to use pronouns which did not take the listener's point of view into account, whereas this was not the case for the middle-class child. For example, a lower-class child asked to describe the content of a picture might say *She threw it.* Use of the pronoun *she* requires that the listener be able to see the picture to determine who *she* is. A middle-class child describing the same picture might say *The girl threw the ball and it broke the window.* The pronoun *it* in this sentence would be easily interpreted by a listener without the necessity of seeing the picture.

Basil Bernstein (1968, 1972) has constructed an elaborate theory which characterizes social-class differences in language development and attempts to explain their origins. Bernstein's analysis of speech patterns in middle-class and lower-class families led him to describe social-class differences in speech in terms of a restriction-elaboration dimension. His research suggests that lower-class speech tends to fall in the restricted category, whereas middle-class speech generally reflects the elaborated category. Bernstein attributes observed class-related differences in category of speech to differences in the functions which speech serves in middle-class and lower-class families.

The restricted language code of the lower-class family is characterized first of all by a tendency to use concrete as opposed to abstract terms. One example of this emphasis on the concrete may be found in concern for the accomplishment of physical tasks. Sentences such as *Brush your teeth* or *Take out the garbage* illustrate the concreteness of sentences related to physical accomplishments.

The restricted language code

A second characteristic of the restricted code has to do with Bernstein's observation that lower-class families generally fail to be concerned with the motives and intentions of those with whom they speak. A lower-class mother is more likely to say simply *Get the paper for your father* than she would be to say *Your father looks tired. I'll bet he would appreciate it if you brought him the paper.*

A third feature of the restricted code is that it tends to emphasize social status as a standard for guiding behavior. For example, a lower-class mother might well attempt to stop her son from crying by saying something like *Boys don't cry* indicating that the child's behavior is inappropriate in light of his sex role. On the other hand, a middle-class mother might attempt to dissuade crying by saying *Billy will be so disappointed if he sees you crying.*

Bernstein suggests that middle-class language patterns are defined by an elaborated code described by characteristics which are essentially opposite to those of the restricted code. Thus, the language of the middle class tends to be abstract rather than concrete. It includes the exploration of motives and intentions, and it is person rather than status oriented.

The elaborated code

Bernstein argues that class-related differences in language use derive from differences in the functions which language serves in the middle class and lower class. Bernstein asserts that lower-class families are generally directly involved in many tasks demanding physical labor. Decision making requiring knowledge of others' intentions and motives is at a minimum. Moreover, there is little need to view things in an abstract way. On the other hand, the demands of middle-class life require decision making based on abstract concepts.

Class-related differences in language functions

There is a need to understand people's motives and to deal with them as persons rather than in terms of their social position.

Whether or not Bernstein's characterization of social-class differences in language is accurate and thus whether or not his explanation for the origin of presumed differences is valid are questions which will undoubtedly be the subject of research and controversy for some time. Many investigators feel that the assumption that lower-class language follows a restricted code is unwarranted. Another possibility is that lower-class groups simply apply different rules in the production and comprehension of language than the rules used by the middle class (Cazden, 1970).

Bilingualism. Significant numbers of American children do not speak English as their first language. The vast majority of these speak Spanish. However, there are many children who speak one of a variety of other languages including Chinese, Japanese, French, or one of the many Indian tongues.

The definition of bilingualism

Technically speaking, when a child speaks two languages, for example, Spanish and English, he may be described as bilingual. However, bilingualism and monolingualism are not either/or conditions. Some children classified as bilingual for educational purposes actually speak little or no English. Others speak both English and the language of their homes fluently. Finally, there are some who speak only English. Children in this group are sometimes classified as bilingual strictly because of their ethnic backgrounds.

Educational problems of the bilingual child

Bilingual children often face serious educational problems. Insofar as they do not speak English well and because English is almost invariably the language of instruction in the schools, they may have difficulty profiting from the instruction which they receive.

Early efforts to deal with the educational problems of the bilingual child were based on the rather naïve and, as it turned out, probably inaccurate assumptions that children should be discouraged from speaking the language of their homes in school and that every effort should be made to teach them to speak English as quickly as possible. Educational efforts to solve the language problems faced by the bilingual child have been notoriously ineffective. Many contemporary theorists argue that the central difficulty with past educational approaches to the problem of bilingualism was that in discouraging the use of the child's first language, educators conveyed the attitude that the child's language and by inference his culture were inferior to the language and culture of the middle class. For example, Ervin-Tripp (1973) points out that English-speaking children living in Canada where they are required to learn French have no difficulty mastering the second language. She then asks:

> If this could happen, why do Chicanos have problems in our California schools? Since the overt linguistic circumstances seem entirely parallel, it seems to me the differences are social. In the Montreal environment, English-speaking children have no sense of inferiority or disadvantage in the school. Their teachers do not have low expectations for their achievements. Their social group has power in the community; their language is respected, is learned by Francophones, and becomes a medium of instruction later in the school. (p. 92)

Many educators now suggest that what is needed to overcome the educational problems of the bilingual child is bilingual-bicultural education. Such education is designed to enhance the cultural identity and traditions of bilingual speakers

Bilingual-bicultural education. The teacher in this classroom shows that she values the cultural heritage of the children. Note the use of materials related to ethnicity in the classroom displays. (Courtesy Behavior Associates, Tucson, Arizona).

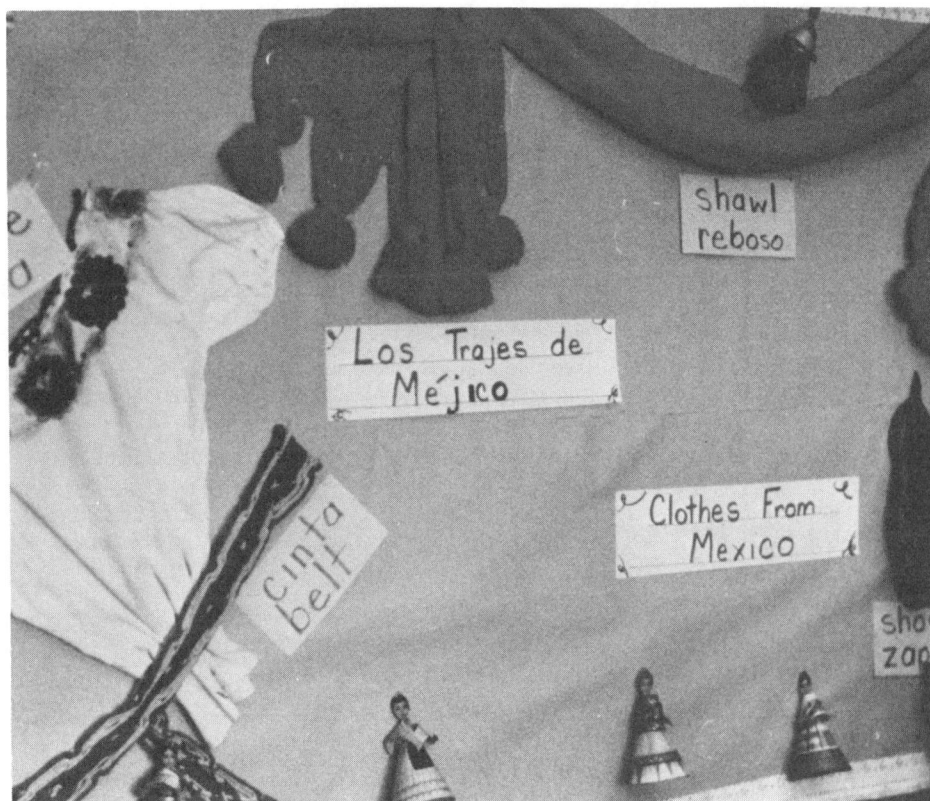

by (1) including instruction conducted in the first language of the child as well as in English and (2) incorporating the cultural traditions of the child's home as well as middle-class traditions into the curriculum.

Nonstandard dialects: black English. Nonstandard dialects are variants of the phonological, semantic, and syntactic features of a language. Dialects are related partly to the region of the country in which the speaker lives. However, they are also culturally determined. The nonstandard dialect which has been studied most in this country is black English, a dialect spoken mainly by lower-class blacks living in urban ghettos. Although black English is by no means representative of all the characteristics associated with nonstandard dialects, it nonetheless can serve as an adequate example reflecting many of the problems faced by children who speak a nonstandard dialect.

The reader can get some feel for the characteristics of black English from the summary of some of its syntactic features which Baratz (1969) has provided. As shown in table 7-5, these features include among other things omission of linking verbs as in *He goin'*, omission of the possessive marker as in *John Cousin*, and substitution of *be* for *is* as in *He be here*.

Speakers of black English face severe educational problems similar to those of the bilingual child. Like the bilingual child, the child who speaks black English is likely to find that the language he or she speaks at home will be denigrated by the school. The issue of denigration is probably even more significant

Educational problems faced by speakers of black English

for the speaker of black English than it is for the bilingual child in that in many cases black English may not be valued by members of the child's own culture.

Unlike the bilingual child, the speaker of black English does not face the problem of receiving instruction in what to him or her is a foreign language. However, dialectic differences between black English and standard English may nevertheless cause serious learning problems. For example, there are phono-

Table 7–5   *Some Syntactic Differences between Standard English and Black English*

Variable	Standard English	Black English
Linking verb	He is going.	He goin'.
Possessive marker	John's cousin.	John cousin.
Plural marker	I have five cents.	I got five cent.
Subject expression	John lives in New York.	John he live in New York.
Verb form	I drank the milk.	I drunk the milk.
Past marker	Yesterday he walked home.	Yesterday he walk home.
Verb agreement	He runs home.	He run home.
Future form	I will go home.	I'ma go home.
"If" construction	I asked if he did it.	I ask did he do it.
Negation	I don't have any.	I don't got none.
Indefinite article	I want an apple.	I want a apple.
Pronoun form	We have to do it.	Us got to do it.
	His book.	He book.
Preposition	He is over at his friend's house.	He over to his friend house.
	He teaches at Francis Pool.	He teach Francis Pool.
Be	Statement: He is here all the time.	Statement: He be here.
Do	Contradiction: No, he isn't.	Contradiction: No, he don't

Reprinted with permission from Baratz, J. C. Teaching reading in an urban negro school. In J. C. Baratz and R. W. Shuy (Eds.), *Teaching black children to read*. Washington, D.C.: Center for Applied Linguistics, 1969.

logical differences between black English and standard English which may make it difficult for the black child to learn to read. One of these differences involves the fact that consonants at the end of words are often simplified in black English. This results in the production of black English homonyms which do not exist in standard English. For example, *past* and *pass, mend* and *men,* and *wind* and *wine* are three pairs of words which are pronounced the same way in black English, but not in standard English. Phonological variations, such as the ones given in these examples, make it more difficult for the child who speaks black English to use phonics to sound out words than it is for the child who speaks standard English.

At present there is no satisfactory solution to the educational problems of speakers of black English. Some thought has been given and experimentation done in rendering instruction in black English. But this approach is generally regarded as being of little value since it does not lead to a solution to the fundamental problem of teaching the child to read standard English.

Societal Interpretations of Linguistic Diversity

Failure to comprehend the nature of variations in language among different cultural groups has led society to misjudge the language competencies of lower-class and minority group children. As we have indicated, the problem of misjudgment has had its most severe consequences in education. In effect, the schools have told children who speak languages and dialects other than standard English that their languages are inferior and should not be used. In addition, in many cases there has also been the implication of intellectual and cultural inferiority.

Ignorance regarding language competency may stem from two sources. The first is the kinds of tests used to measure language performance, and the second is the set of cultural traditions which has led teachers and other socialization agents to make unwarranted assumptions about language variations in different cultural subgroups.

Language competence and test performance. Many contemporary language theorists feel that test performance may not always be an accurate gauge of language competence (e.g., see Ervin-Tripp, 1973). In the case of lower-class or minority group children, tests may convey serious misinformation about language. Such misinformation constitutes a significant problem because of the aura of objectivity which surrounds the use of tests. The fact that testing practices include precautions to insure objectivity makes it easy to overlook other potential shortcomings.

The minority child's interpretation of testing situations

One source of difficulty with the use of tests with minority group and lower-class children involves the fact that such children may misinterpret the nature of the testing situation. For example, a child who has not been taught to answer questions simply to demonstrate his capability to do so may decide to answer only those questions which he feels will convey needed information to his listener. Ervin-Tripp (1972) reports an example of this. An experimenter testing a child's language ability asked him to describe where he lived. The boy waved his thumb and said that he lived "over there." A little later the experimenter's husband asked the same question. The boy responded, "You go down the stairs, turn left, walk three blocks. . . ." (p. 143). What prompted the markedly different quality in these answers? The experimenter had been to the child's house and therefore did not need detailed directions to get there. The experimenter's husband, however, had not been to the child's house and, thus, presumably needed the detailed information he was given.

Cultural bias in tests

Another potential source of test-related misinformation about language competency stems from possible cultural bias in test items. Testing practices in the schools have been under attack for years regarding the issue of cultural bias. A number of contemporary theorists take the position that there is indeed a significant amount of bias in language-test items. For example, Elsa Roberts (1971) found that 24 out of 33 items on one of the subtests of the *Illinois Test of Psycholinguistic Abilities* (a widely used test of language development) called for different linguistic constructions in different subcultures. She also analyzed the vocabulary subtests from four commonly used mental ability tests and found approximately 30% of the items to be subculture specific.

Language competence and cultural tradition. America is a nation built by vast migrations of people, first from foreign lands and later, within the country, from east to west. The migrations came in waves. When new groups moved into an area, they were viewed with hostility and suspicion by those who had already settled in their location. The language and customs of new settlers served as signals to those in the established culture eliciting hostility and repressive action.

Schools were given the responsibility of preparing those from "inferior" backgrounds for entry into the societal mainstream. A part of this responsibility included language instruction. Speaking a "foreign" language was generally strictly forbidden. Many states actually went to the extreme of passing laws prohibiting foreign language instruction in the schools. Perhaps many of these might still be on the books if it weren't for the fact that laws of this kind were ruled unconstitutional in the 1920s (Kopan, 1974).

In light of the cultural traditions which stimulated socialization efforts related to linguistic diversity, it is not surprising that many educators as well as other socialization agents should assume implicitly that the language patterns of lower-class and minority group children were deficient. Insofar as the nation has begun to recognize the value of cultural diversity, the time is ripe for action to change the conception of socialization agents regarding linguistic diversity. Regarding this point, Ervin-Tripp (1973) argues that a concerted effort needs to be made to make socialization agents aware of the nature of linguistic diversity. She suggests that socialization agents be given systematic training exposing them to the language and customs of cultural subgroups with whom they have contact. In addition, she favors a kind of sensitivity training in which socialization agents could be made aware of their own preconceptions and misconceptions about the language of children from different cultural backgrounds.

Language Socialization Strategies

Research efforts aimed at identifying socialization strategies for enhancing language development have almost invariably focused on lower-class and/or minority group children. Experimental efforts to promote language development in these cultural subgroups generally begin with the assumption that the language which the child would acquire or has acquired in the natural course of development is inferior. Accordingly, experimental intervention is almost always aimed at forestalling the ill effects of the child's natural language environment. From what we have said in the previous section, it seems certain that basing socialization in language on the assumption of language inferiority is unfortunate. Nevertheless, the socialization techniques which have been developed and the outcomes they have produced in experimental programs are of interest.

Structured intervention during the infant and preschool years. Genevieve Painter (1971) describes a tutorial program designed to enhance the language and cognitive skills of young children from economically disadvantaged homes. Painter argues that systematic intervention beginning during infancy and extending through the early preschool years can forestall linguistic and cognitive deficits which might otherwise accrue in the disadvantaged child.

In the Painter program, female tutors worked with infants and toddlers one hour a day, five days a week for a year. Although specially trained tutors were used in the experiment, Painter assumes that the techniques applied could be taught to parents.

Painter advocates beginning language training before the child utters his first word, usually when he is about 10 months old. The first instructional task is to teach him to imitate the acts of others. This is accomplished by a variety of means, including the familiar bye-bye game in which an adult waves to the child and says *bye-bye* hoping that the child will wave back. When and if the child does, he is reinforced with smiles and praise.

When the child is about one year old, he is taught to imitate sounds. One way in which this is accomplished is by imitating the child's babbling. Hopefully, the child will get the idea that he can imitate adult language just as the adult can imitate his language.

At about the age of 14 months, the child is encouraged to identify and to name objects. For example, he might be encouraged in identification by a question such as *Where is the cup?* Naming may be elicited by similar questioning, for example, *What is that?*

When the child is about 16 months old, he is encouraged to verbalize his needs and wants. For example, when he attempts to ask for something by pointing, as children frequently do, he is encouraged to verbalize the request.

Sometime between the ages of 18 and 24 months, the child is helped to construct elaborated sentence structures. One of the ways in which this is accomplished is by having the child tell stories.

At about the age of 24 months, an effort is made to develop skill in conducting internal dialogues for the purpose of guiding problem-solving efforts. One technique used to promote verbal problem solving is to verbalize the steps necessary to accomplish a task such as putting a puzzle together.

Painter reports a 10-point IQ advantage for children in her program as compared to children who did not receive tutorial training. While this is an impressive result, it should be pointed out that it is unlikely that it can be attributed entirely to the language program. As indicated earlier, the children received cognitive training as well as language training. An additional fact of importance is that the children were about 2½ years old at the time of testing. The test which they took (the Stanford-Binet) is largely nonverbal when it is used with children of that age. It seems improbable that it would be particularly sensitive to language learning.

Evaluation of Painter's program

Directed instruction in the school years. Osborn (1968) reports a training program designed to develop language skills in black economically disadvantaged elementary school children. Osborn based the design of this program on presumed language deficits of speakers of black English. Among these were a failure to understand the use of the negative in sentence constructions, incorrect production of plurals, and omission of short verbs, i.e., variants of the verb *be*.

Osborn's program employed a "pattern drill" approach in which language concepts to be acquired were framed in sentence structures like the following:

Osborn's pattern-drill approach

> *This is a* _____.
> *This is not a* _____.

Correct responses were modeled for children and correct answers on the part of the child were reinforced.

Osborn reports a significant IQ advantage for children who participated in the program as compared to children who did not. Although the IQ results are impressive, it should be mentioned that the Osborn program, like many others, is based on a partial misconception of black English. For example, speakers

Evaluation of Osborn's program

of this dialect are generally well aware of the use of negatives in sentences as indicated by the fact that they can comprehend them when they are spoken in standard English. They simply express negatives differently from the way in which speakers of standard English express them.

Instruction in the development of an elaborated code. Gahagan and Gahagan (1970) describe an educational program intended to develop an elaborated language code in young economically disadvantaged children. The program was based on Basil Bernstein's theory which, as you will recall from our earlier discussion of his work, asserts that the speech of lower-class families is characterized by a restricted code whereas the speech of middle-class families makes use of an elaborated code.

Elaboration skills

Gahagan and Gahagan's efforts to develop an elaborated code focused on such skills as teaching the child to render effective explanations of procedures to others and assisting him to describe the feelings and intentions of others. For example, explanation was fostered by having two children converse through a screen. One child was asked to build a structure which the other child could not see. Then he described what he had built so that his companion could build one like it. Picture description provides an example of a task designed to assist the child to discern the feelings and intentions of others. In this task children were asked to describe the feelings of characters shown in pictures.

Evaluation of the Gahagan program

Gahagan and Gahagan (1970) report that children who participated in the program performed in a superior fashion on a variety of measures of language skill. These measures included highly specific tests designed explicitly for their research as well as standardized measures of language performance.

Socialization and the assumption of language inferiority

Future directions in language socialization. In light of the research and theory which has been presented in this chapter on how language is learned and on what is acquired during language development, certain directions seem likely in socialization efforts of the future. First, hopefully we can look for the development of socialization strategies which will not begin with the assumption that the learner's language is inferior. Certainly it would be possible to develop such strategies. For example, when a speaker of standard English learns a second language such as Russian or German, he or she is not required to look upon English as an inadequate means of communication. What will probably be required in order to avoid the assumption of inferiority is the incorporation of the child's primary language and his or her culture into instruction. Such incorporation is already being attempted in many programs.

Observations for language instruction

A second possible future trend in language socialization is that as more becomes known about what children learn when they acquire language, the objectives of language-learning programs will become more precise. The Gahagan and Gahagan program foreshadows this welcome trend. We might expect other programs to spring up, for example to teach the verbal operants which Skinner has identified, or to promote the development of language rules such as those discovered by Brown in his developmental research.

Adapting to the child's language skills

Not only is it likely that programs will become more explicit in their objectives, but also it can be hoped that they will do a better job than they have in the past of taking into account what the child already knows. For example, a bilingual child comes to the language-learning tasks which confront him in school with a well-established set of learning strategies for interpreting phonetic, semantic, and syntactic structures. These strategies determine how he will approach language learning in the educational setting. Obviously, if instruction is to be maximally effective, it is essential to know what the child's existing strategies are.

A final trend which we can expect in the area of language socialization is increased explicitness in evaluative measures. IQ tests, which as we have pointed out are often used as measures of language learning, are not satisfactory for this purpose. The central difficulty with them is that they do not explicitly relate what has been taught to what has been learned. As the objectives of language-learning programs become more precise than they have been, we can expect the development of tests specifically targeted toward the measurement of program objectives. Consequently, there will probably be less need to fall back on inappropriate IQ measures.

Explicitness in the evaluation of language instruction

SUGGESTED READINGS

Baratz, J. C. Teaching reading in an urban Negro school. In J. C. Baratz & R. W. Shuy (Eds.), *Teaching black children to read.* Washington, D.C.: Center for Applied Linguistics, 1969.

Bernstein, B. A socio-linguistic approach to socialization with some references to educability. In J. J. Gumperz & D. Hymes (Eds.), *Directions in sociolinguistics.* New York: Holt, Rinehart and Winston, 1972.

Cazden, C. The neglected situation in child language research and education. In F. Williams (Ed.), *Language and poverty: Perspectives on a theme.* Chicago: Markham, 1970.

Chomsky, N. A review of *Verbal Behavior* by B. F. Skinner. *Language,* 1959, *35,* 26-58.

Chomsky, N. *Language and mind: Enlarged edition.* New York: Harcourt Brace Jovanovich, 1968.

Gahagan, D. M., & Gahagan, G. A. Talk reform: Explorations in language for infant-school children. *Primary socialization, language and education* (Vol. III). Sociological Research Unit Monograph Series, B. Bernstein, Director. London: Routledge and Kegan Paul, 1970.

Houston, S. A sociolinguistic consideration of the black English of children in Northern Florida. *Language,* 1969, *45,* 599-607.

Labov, W. *The social stratification of English in New York City.* Washington, D.C.: Center for Applied Linguistics, 1966.

Painter, G. A tutorial language program for disadvantaged infants. In C. S. Lavatelli (Ed.), *Language training in early childhood education.* Urbana, Ill.: University of Illinois Press, ERIC Clearinghouse on Early Childhood Education, 1971.

Part Four

Social and
Personal Development

8

Theoretical Perspectives in Social and Personal Development

Instructional Objectives

Recognize or recall
Compare and contrast
Describe or demonstrate
Evaluate

evidence of differential valuing of intellectual and affective qualities.

contemporary and Renaissance meanings of humanism.

Renaissance naturalism and contemporary phenomenology.

Christopher Jencks' views on the development of social competence.

functions and interrelationships of id, ego, and superego in psychodynamic theory.

interaction between the social environment and psychodynamic processes in the socialization process.

factors contributing to fixation.

sequence and characteristics of psychosexual stages.

relationships between Freud's theory and the culture of his time.

Freud's theory of psychosexual development and Erikson's psychosocial theory.

the psychodynamic explanation of conscience formation.

Piaget's and Kohlberg's explanations of moral development.

characteristics of moral judgments at each of Kohlberg's levels and stages.

Kohlbergian and cultural relativist views of moral development.

variables influencing the probability of imitative learning and responding.

four types of outcomes that may result from observation of models.

learning and performance, and the conditions that influence each.

the definitions of discrimination and generalization.

conditions contributing to generalization and discrimination.

the social learning theory explanation for the development of social behavior.

organismic and field theories of development.

psychodynamic, social learning, and phenomenological theories and their social utility.

CHAPTER CONTENT

Social competence and social values

Valued competencies reexamined

Humanistic influences

Competence and occupational status

Theoretical perspectives

Psychodynamic theory

Cognitive-developmental theories

Social-learning theory

Phenomenological theories

Social utility of theoretical perspectives

Psychodynamic perspectives

Cognitive-developmental perspectives

Phenomenological perspectives

Social-learning perspectives

Members of every society seem to have customary ways of characterizing their kindred beings according to the qualities which are displayed in their behavior. Moreover, in any given culture some human qualities or traits are valued and respected, while others are subjected to scorn. This point was well elaborated by the anthropologists Clyde Kluckhohn and Dorothea Leighton (1958) in their ethnography on the Navaho:

> The way of life which is handed down as the social heritage of every people does more than supply a set of skills for making a living and a set of blueprints for human relations. Each different way of life makes assumptions (and usually somewhat different assumptions) about the ends and purposes of human existence, about what human beings have a right to expect from one another and from the gods, about what constitutes fulfillment or frustration. Some of these assumptions are made explicit in so many words in the lore of the folk; others are tacit premises which the observer must infer by finding consistent trends in deed and word. (pp. 216-17)

Many of the qualities which Navahos value in their kin are similar to those which most middle-class Americans also profess to value—qualities such as truthfulness, the ability to get along with others, dependability and helpfulness—although the rationale for valuing these traits may differ from one society to another.

At a later point we shall identify some of the theoretical issues relating to whether the notion of personality traits is a misleading or useful concept for understanding the development of social behavior. For now it is sufficient to say that people do attribute certain characteristics to their fellows, and the task of this chapter is to summarize some representative theories which attempt to explain how these qualities develop.

Every culture has institutions, both formal and informal, which are charged with the responsibility of teaching the skills of the culture—of preparing children to perform the various roles they will be required to play in society. This is the process of socialization. In explaining the process of socialization, some theories stress mechanisms assumed to be inherent in human biological nature. Other theories emphasize the role of the social environment as the shaper of behavior, while others emphasize the interactive nature of the process. Some theories stress unconscious motives while others emphasize awareness and decision making. All these points of view emerged in a particular cultural context, and all have implications for socialization practices intended to promote the acquisition of competencies which seem to be important to children's development in contemporary society.

*Differential
emphasis in
theories of
socialization*

SOCIAL COMPETENCE AND SOCIAL VALUES

Among the skills and qualities which may be acceptable in a society, usually there are some which are valued more highly and bring greater prestige than others. In our culture we give verbal sanction to a number of characteristics we hope children will acquire as a result of their socialization. Boy Scouts, for example, learn that they are to be helpful, friendly, courteous, kind, and so on, but when one examines the amount of time spent in direct efforts to influence the development of various skills and qualities in our children and youth, it is obvious that far more attention is given to the cultivation of intellectual skills than to providing for social and affective growth and well-being.

The roots of the value system which influences this preferential attention to intellectual development over affective relationships and social competencies can be discerned early in the history of Western society. The reader may remember that Plato categorized the qualities which made up human nature according to different kinds of motives which were thought to be located in various regions of the body. Humans' appetites, feelings, and desires resided in the belly; drives such as courage and endurance were located primarily in the breast or heart; and the intellect reposed in the head. Plato's philosopher-kings, the highest expression of man, were ruled primarily by the intellect. People who were dominated by other qualities were relegated to roles of lesser significance. Those disposed to act primarily on the basis of their appetites, or affective qualities, were fit only to be workers, while those with courage and endurance were suitable to be fighters. These qualities were thought to be hereditary, and fixed from birth. Humans' possession of reason was what made them distinctly different from lower life-forms, and great value was attached to the cultivation of this characteristic. This view of human nature was absorbed by Christian tradition (Butts, 1955).

*Differential valuing
of intellect
and affect*

Valued Competencies Reexamined

In contemporary times, we have witnessed varied reactions against this stress on intellectual accomplishment which dominates the Western value system. This discontent is expressed in many forms. Expressions of dissonance include the anti-intellectualism of some contemporary youth, who often turn to efforts to cultivate the life of feelings and interpersonal relationships. Another expression is the contemporary interest in mysticism and in the religious thought of the Near and Far East. It is expressed in the "return to nature" movement, which may involve agricultural communes, the use of organic foods, and the rejection of "unnatural" cosmetics. It is seen also in the phenomena of sensitivity training and encounter groups, and in a plethora of publications and organizations which focus on "humanistic" concerns. "Humanist" has become a term of self-reference for individuals and organizations interested in "righting the balance" in social priorities. Humanistic influences cut across the various theoretical explanations for social and emotional development.

Humanistic Influences

It may be instructive to recall that the use of the term *humanism* represents a significant departure from the historic meaning. One pre-Renaissance scholar, John of Salisbury, advanced a rich array of arguments favoring humanistic training over practical or "synthetic" education. True education was humanistic education, which ". . . required a thorough grounding in the classics, in order to obtain knowledge, develop critical judgment, and discriminating taste, and acquire the mature understanding necessary to the contemplative mind" (Butts, 1955, p. 158).

Renaissance values   Humanists of the Renaissance valued reading, writing, and rhetorical exposition as the most notable accomplishments of humanity. Through these literary achievements the highest forms of the intellect could be cultivated. Greek and Latin literature provided the standards for emulation and appreciation. Therefore, "The best subject matter was considered to be not religious doctrine or the secrets of nature, but the style and content of the ancient classics" (Butts, 1955, p. 179).

These facts make it clear that in the early Western tradition of humanism, the qualities of people which were most valued were those which involved disciplined intellectual accomplishments. Even the concern for architectural and literary aesthetics was highly intellectualized, and beauty was not to be found in mundane, everyday experience. The quotation cited above, however, also contains the hint that this point of view was in competition with alternative values. Humanists looked to the classics for authority, while religious authority and Aristotelian philosophy guided the scholastics of the period. But soon an emerging science, based on inductive methods, turned to the investigation of nature for authoritative knowledge. This was a significant movement, and one which was greatly influenced by the discovery of the Americas. R. Freeman Butts (1955), a social historian, noted that:

Naturalistic
philosophy   Exploration and acquaintance with the primitive societies to be found in the Americas prompted interest in the "natural man" and the unspoiled "noble savage." Montaigne was struck with the fact that untutored savages with no ancient religion or "civilized" heritage could show such qualities as courage, honor, and integrity. The feeling grew that nature could produce a purer and better form of moral conduct than an oversophisticated civilization could. (p. 177)

This "spirit of naturalism" came into sharp contrast with the prevailing conceptions of human nature. Turning again to Butts' (1955) analysis:

The spirit of naturalism began to say that human nature had qualities for potential goodness within itself. The example of aboriginal native Americans led some to stress the fact that primitive peoples could be good without the benefits of civilization and religion. (p. 178)

These thoughts represented a growing opposition against the prevailing pessimistic conceptualization of human nature and provided a growing climate of opinion which anticipated the naturalistic philosophy later made prominent by Rousseau in the eighteenth century. It is also a point of view that is almost

Naturalism and   identical to the present-day persuasion of phenomenological psychologists and
phenomenology   educators that humans are, by nature, good.

The curious paradox in all of this is that during the Renaissance the events which led to the growth of an inductive naturalistic science were associated with a growing concern for social, emotional, and moral qualities of humanity. The concerns of Renaissance humanists were quite unlike those of contemporary humanists, who often fault science for our society's excessive concern for linear, analytic, intellectual processes, at the expense of a balanced regard for human social and emotional well-being.

What both the old and the new humanists seem to have in common is a commitment to cultivate those qualities they consider to be the most worthy expressions of human nature. Those qualities appear to many observers of contemporary society to be placed in jeopardy by the conditions imposed by a technological and highly urbanized environment. Under conditions of accelerating social change, it is not entirely clear just what qualities and capabilities will be most functional in the future, but then neither is there a consensus of opinion regarding the capabilities which are most desirable for contemporary functioning.

*Old and new
humanists*

Competence and Occupational Status

One hallmark of success in our society is the occupational status that one attains. In the past, it was widely assumed that the skills needed to function in an industrial society were intellectual, largely of the sort measured on intelligence tests (Vernon, 1965). There is cause to call this assumption into question. After spending three years reanalyzing the massive data collected by James Coleman and his associates (1966) for the now famous *Equality of Educational Opportunity Survey*, Christopher Jencks (1972) and his colleagues concluded that neither occupational status nor successful performance within an occupation are much influenced by intelligence. They state that:

> Our best estimate is that, all other things being equal, men who rank in the top fifth of the genetic distribution end up with occupational status five to eight points above the mean, while those whose IQ geneotypes are in the bottom fifth end up five to eight points below the mean. Differences of this magnitude are relatively small. Fourteen points is the difference between a dentist and a newspaper reporter or between a locomotive engineer and a fireman. (p. 188)

If intellectual competence, as measured by conventional tests, is not a good predictor of occupational success, what *are* the important capabilities? This is a question of some practical importance, yet there are no firm answers. Jencks (1972) and his associates addressed this issue in the following words:

> . . . neither parental status nor IQ scores explain most of the variation in occupational status and income. Yet we find it hard to believe that all of this variation is due to luck or chance. Experience suggests that there are personality differences between people who end up in high- and low-status occupations, and also between people who have high and low incomes. We believe, though we cannot prove, that these cognitive traits explain part of the variation in adult success.

> Social scientists have written dozens of volumes trying to specify what the traits might be: "need achievement," "the Protestant ethic," "future orientation," "respect for authority," "empathy"—the list is almost endless. (p. 131)[1]

*Qualities of
successful adults*

---

1. Jencks and his colleagues include an extensive set of footnotes and appendices documenting the manner in which they arrived at their conclusions. The reader interested in an in-depth treatment of their work should consult the original text.

Few people would feel disposed to argue that occupational status is the most important criterion for a happy and rewarding life, but work is one of the major settings in which adults are called upon to apply their social competencies. Therefore, as restricted a criterion as it is, occupation nevertheless is one observable indicator of an individual's success in coping with the social environment. Furthermore, at least for occupation and probably equally so for other sectors of social relationships, it seems clear that there are other competencies which are at least as important as intelligence. People must learn to function in a variety of different relationships with others, and a variety of interpersonal competencies are important in carrying out those relationships.

THEORETICAL PERSPECTIVES

Four "families of theory" will be summarized here to provide a representative cross-section of theoretical explanations for social development. Psychodynamic, cognitive-developmental, social learning, and phenomenological theories are discussed.

Psychodynamic Theory

Out of his clinical experience in the prudish Victorian culture of Vienna, Sigmund Freud (1856-1939) formulated a theory that pictured man as ". . . a dynamic system subject to the laws of nature. . ." (Hall & Lindzey, 1970, p. 170). Freud thought and wrote profusely for over 40 years and had a profound influence on thinking in child psychology. A few of the major points of his theory which bear most directly on social development are summarized here.

Freudian psychodynamic theory. Freud believed that personality was composed of a three-part structure. These major elements, the id, ego, and super ego, were mentioned briefly in chapter 2.

Id

The *id* is the basic energy source of the personality and provides the base from which the ego and the super ego are later differentiated. The id seeks immediate gratification of its instinctual wishes and impulses. The instincts are primarily sexual and aggressive in nature, and one's personality and character are formed as the instinctual wishes and impulses of the id are shaped and moderated by forces in the environment of the developing individual. This theory assumes that early socialization experiences are of utmost importance because the personality characteristics resulting from this molding process are very enduring and influence the individual's behavior and adjustment across a wide variety of different situations.

*Importance of early
socialization*

*Enduring
personality states*

The id has no knowledge of the world of reality outside the mind. It is impelled by instinctual energies which, if left unrestrained, would continually run afoul of conditions in the real world. The ego acts to delay gratification until objects and occasions appropriate for the discharge of tension are found. The ego tests reality to determine appropriate times, places, and objects for tension reduction, thereby making judgments and serving as the "executive" of the personality. It decides both which instincts will be satisfied and the manner in which they will be relieved.

Ego

The ego must mediate the demands of the id, the super ego, and conditions in the external world. Since these are frequently in conflict, it is no simple task to serve in this executive capacity. Ultimately, the ego's reason for being is to find ways to satisfy the instincts of the organism.

The super ego is the last component of the personality to be developed. It serves as the conscience by representing the values and moral standards of society. The super ego is formed as social standards, particularly as they are represented in the behavior of parents, are internalized or incorporated into the personality system. The super ego is the structure of the personality which enables the individual to exercise self-control—to resist temptation. Such a set of functions naturally afford the opportunity for conflict and opposition between the id and super ego.

Since the id is activated by instincts that are sexual and aggressive in nature, it is often frustrated because such impulses generally come into conflict with the prevailing norms of society. The personality is pictured as being in a state of continuous conflict, as the impulses of the id are blocked by social conventions *Conflict among* and prohibitions. Over time the child gradually learns to inhibit instinctual *personality* desires and conform to social convention. As the child internalizes the values of *components* society, the conflict continues to rage, but overt confrontations are reduced and the strife begins to take place among the components of personality, the id, ego, and super ego, resulting in anxiety. Anxiety produces painful tension, and an important part of the developmental process involves the characteristic ways in which individuals come to cope with tension by avoiding or reducing anxiety. These characteristic modes of adjustment are referred to in psychodynamic theory as defense mechanisms, which will be discussed in chapter 10.

The important point to be explored here is how psychodynamic theory conceptualized the process of social development. How, within this framework, can we explain individual differences in the development of competencies for functioning in social situations? Freud postulated a series of developmental stages, each of which was characterized by a unique set of requirements for the personality to adapt to biological and societal influences.

According to Freud, the child passes through a series of psychosexual stages characterized by differing tasks of adjustment. Freud believed that bodily pleasure is centralized primarily in different erogenous zones at different stages of *Psychosexual stages* development. Each stage of development, therefore, offers unique opportunities for gratification or for frustration of the pleasure-sensation motives that dominate that particular stage.

The first three stages of psychosexual development are collectively referred to as the pregenital stages. In Freud's work with neurotic patients, he found the problems often seemed to be associated with experiences of early childhood, and he came to believe that ". . . *the first few years are decisive for the formation of personality*" (Hall & Lindzey, 1970, p. 50).

At any given stage, a developing personality may become fixated. If, for example, the pleasure-seeking associated with any one of the early psychosexual stages is blocked or frustrated, sexual impulses may be arrested at that stage of *Fixation* development. In other words, the individual's future adjustment may be dominated by the unresolved problems of that period. Since fixation may result from either overindulgence or deprivation of the sexual impulses associated with each stage of development, and other people are involved in the gratification or frustration of these sexual instincts, the child's early socialization experiences are *Overindulgence* crucially important determinants of the development of his character. *and deprivation*

During the oral stage, which encompasses the first year or so of life, the mouth is the zone in which pleasurable sensation is centered. During this period the infant is totally dependent upon her caretakers, and their relationships with *Oral stage* her are thought to have lifelong influences. The infant receives gratification first by sucking and later by biting and chewing. Psychodynamic assumptions about the relationship of experiences during this stage to later development are illustrated in the following statement:

. . . Oral incorporation (as in sucking and taking in milk in the first oral period) becomes the prototype of such pleasures as those gained from the acquisition of knowledge or possessions. The gullible person (who is "easily taken in") is fixated at the oral, incorporative level of personality. The sarcastic, bitingly argumentative person is fixated at the second oral period—the sadistic level associated with biting and chewing. (Mischel, 1971, p. 34)

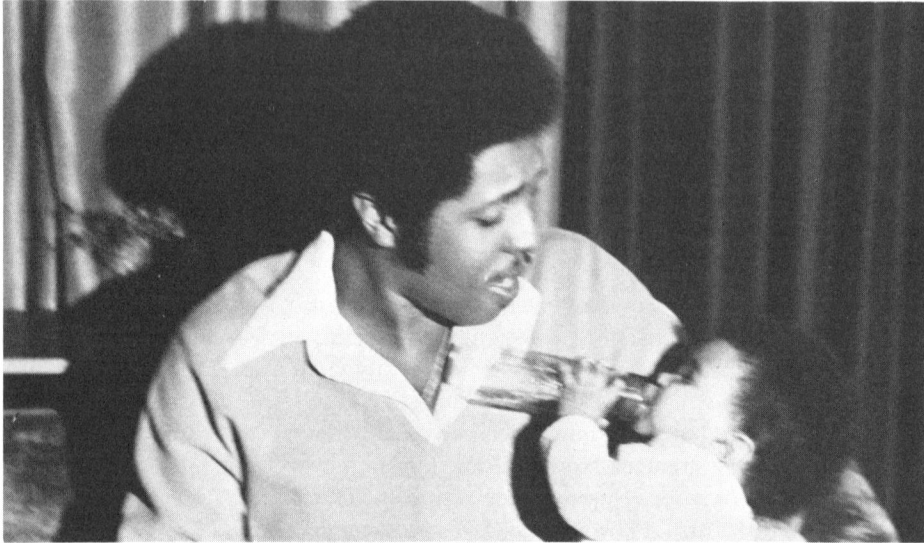

Some people continue to debate the virtues of bottle versus breast feeding.

Anal stage

While the child's relationship to the environment during the oral stage is exclusively a dependent one, his first experience with a requirement to control an impulse comes during the anal stage. For the young child, expulsion of feces produces a pleasurable feeling of relief. But during the second year, at least in most Western cultures, he is confronted with a requirement to postpone this gratification. The way in which the child is trained may have a pervasive influence on later behavior, at least according to this point of view. If a mother is severe and strict in her toilet training practices, the child may hold back his feces. Not only may he become constipated, but this "retentive" reaction to training may generalize to later modes of functioning such as stinginess. On the other hand the child may react rebelliously, by releasing feces at inappropriate times. Later manifestations of the "expulsive" traits to which this behavior may generalize may include cruelty, messy disorderliness, temper tantrums, and the like. Conversely, the child whose mother praises him for producing feces may come to see this as an extremely important activity. He may later become creative and productive.

During the later part of the anal stage, pleasure is thought to result from the retention of feces. Fixation at this stage may result in traits such as stinginess, precision, and orderliness. Persons with these qualities are often thought to be well-suited for professions requiring meticulous attention to order and detail, such as accounting.

Phallic stage

Sexual and aggressive impulses associated with the genital organs play the prominent role in the drama of psychosexual development during the phallic stage which extends from about the third through the fifth year. Masturbation and an active fantasy life provide for gratification and set the scene for developmental conflicts which must be resolved. Male children are thought to love their mother, who satisfies most of their needs during the early years, and to resent their father, who is seen as a rival for the mother's affection. Freud thought that little boys developed an incestuous desire for their mother during this stage, and that they feared they would be castrated by their father in retribution. Fear of castration, Freud supposed, resulted from the child's perception of the female as a castrated male, and from direct threats of castration as punishment for masturbation.

Oedipus complex

A boy faced with this uncomfortable state of affairs would repress his sexual desire for his mother and his hostility toward his father. To reduce his anxiety concerning possible castration, the boy would try to "be like" his father, or to identify with him. Through identification with his father the boy can, according to Freudian theory, experience some vicarious satisfaction of his sexual desires for his mother. The boy substitutes a tender affection for his mother for the original incestuous impulses, and through the resolution of this conflict the standards of the parents and society are finally incorporated into the super ego.

The equivalent process for girls follows a different course. Freud believed that it constituted a traumatic experience for a girl to discover that boys possess a protruding penis—an organ which she lacks. This discovery leads to transfer of love from the mother to the father. The girl would like to share his organ, which is an object of her desire. She has no reprisal to fear from the mother, as was the case for the boy and his father, so girls do not develop castration anxiety. Nevertheless, their sexual desire for the father is modified by realistic barriers to the consummation of such a desire.

The successful resolution of the Oedipus and Electra complexes of this period presumably leaves ". . . a host of deposits in the personality" (Hall & Lindzey, 1970, p. 53).

Electra complex

Toward the end of the phallic stage, there is a period of reduction in overt sexuality. This is the latency period.

Latency period

In the pregenital years love is narcissistic, or directed toward the self. Eventually love impulses are rechanneled, and the adolescent becomes capable of loving others for altruistic reasons. By the genital stage, the individual has completed the transition ". . . from a pleasure-seeking narcissistic infant into a reality-oriented, socialized adult" (Hall & Lindzey, 1970, p. 53).

Genital stage

Freud's theory is clearly a product of its time. His notion of psychic energy was consistent with the principle of the conservation of energy. Energy could be transformed from one form to another, as for example from physiological to psychic energy and vice versa, but energy was never lost. In Freud's mind there was no reason to think that there was any essential difference between the energy expended in muscular effort and respiration, and energy involved in thinking, remembering, and similar activities. A common energy source, food, could be channeled to multiple uses.

Cultural context of Freud's theory

The kinds of human problems which stimulated Freud's theorizing were also firmly imbedded in the cultural context of middle-class Viennese culture of the late nineteenth century. Given the prevailing repressive social attitudes toward sexual expression, it is not surprising that many of his patients appeared to suffer the results of traumatic experiences in that area. His theory was based upon relationships between parents and children in a very restricted population. Bronislaw Malinowski (1927), a well-known pioneer anthropologist, was quick to point this out and to show that the Oedipus complex, which Freud assumed was universal, did not exist in societies having socialization roles different from those of the population on which Freud's observations were based. In matriarchal societies, the mother's line of biological ancestry is emphasized in such functions as naming, succession, and inheritance. In societies organized in this manner, it is common to find relationships quite dissimilar to those of Western societies, which tend to emphasize patriarchal patterns. For example, a child in a matrilineal society may be disciplined by his mother's brother rather than by his biological father. The father is more likely to play the role of companion and teacher. This is the case in many American Indian cultures, and it was true of the Trobriand Islanders, who were studied by Malinowski. Malinowski took great delight in showing that boys in Trobriand society did not develop classical patterns of Oedipal hostility toward their fathers as would be expected if Freudian theory reflected basic human nature rather than the specific outcomes of cultural conditioning. From the evidence offered by Malinowski, it appears that a boy's hostility toward his father may be related to disciplinary practices in Western societies rather than to a "complex" developing out of competition for the sexual attention of the mother.

Freud has also been taken to task of late because his theory reveals a male chauvinist orientation. From a contemporary perspective, it is true that his theory seems to demean the position of women, but his point of view undoubtedly reflects the prevailing attitudes of his time.

Neo-Freudian points of view. Just as Freud's theoretical perspective emerged from his clinical experiences, so did a number of his followers propose modification in his position as a result of their own experiences in conducting psychotherapy. Most of the neo-Freudians gave more attention than Freud had to social influences on development. The theories of neo-Freudians, such as Carl Jung, Alfred Adler, Erich Fromm, and Erik Erikson, were based on humanistic conceptions of human nature, and of all the latter-day psychoanalytic theorists, Erikson's (1963) ideas have probably had the greatest influence on the psychology of child development.

Like Freud, Erikson (1963) thought that human development proceeds through a number of stages. The fact that he called these psychosocial rather than psychosexual stages underscores a basic difference between his theory and Freud's. Like Freud, Erikson (1963) thought that each stage poses unique problems for the individual to solve, but for Erikson these problems were primarily psychosocial crises resulting from the ever-widening range of social encounters with which the developing individual must cope. The adequacy of a person's solution to the problems posed by the social environment at each of eight stages has a determining influence on how adequate a person one will become.

Psychosocial crises Table 8-1 shows the psychosocial crisis associated with each stage and indicates the optimal outcome, which should result if the crisis is successfully resolved.

A few examples will serve to show the source of Erikson's stages in Freudian theory, and to identify Erikson's elaborations in terms of social crises and outcomes.

Trust vs. mistrust In the oral-sensory stage, for example, the child's basic attitudes of trust or mistrust are formed through the way in which her needs, largely associated with sensations of the oral zone, are satisfied in regular and predictable ways. From a satisfactory resolution of the crisis of this stage, the child will develop attitudes of hope and drive, which should serve her to advantage in future social encounters. The social contacts of the child during this stage are limited almost exclusively to the mother or other caretakers who satisfy the child's needs for oral incorporation and biting.

Autonomy vs. shame Basic trust must be established before the crisis of the second stage can be met successfully. The second psychosocial crisis involves learning to deal successfully with the episodes of toilet training. The relationship to Freud's anal stage should be obvious. The child who learns to control herself emerges from the experience with a sense of autonomy, while the unsuccessful child will experience a sense of shame. The outcomes of this stage, if successfully resolved, set the stage for development of competencies of self-control, or willpower.

The danger in the third stage is that the child, in his exuberance over new powers of locomotion and thought, will develop a sense of guilt over his goals and acts. The child who resolves the crisis of this stage successfully should emerge with a sense of direction and purpose.

Initiative vs. guilt

Given the successful resolution of the third stage, the child is ready to face the challenges of the years which Freud saw as a period of latency. Rather than a period of inactivity as Freud's formulation suggests, these are the years in which the child must face the competitive world of formal schooling. Peers exert an increasingly important influence during this period. The child must master the tasks which face her in a widening sphere of social relationships during this

Industry vs. inferiority

"Look Mom, no hands." Erikson believes that feelings of competence lead to industry in later life.

period in order to overcome feelings of inferiority. If the child is successful in this, she will develop habits of industry and a sense of competence.

The reader may see, from an inspection of table 8-1, that Erikson conceptualized development as a life-long process in which important developmental events were not confined to early childhood. Neither did he think that a satisfactory solution to the developmental crises of each stage would forever insure the individual against new conflicts and changing conditions. Development was, to Erikson, a continuous life-long process. One of his major contributions was to describe developmental processes of the elementary school years, the latency period which was largely ignored in Freud's writings. Erikson studied socialization practices in various societies in an attempt to conceptualize his stages in a form that would be applicable cross-culturally. Perhaps as a result, his formulations seem more relevant to common experiences than do Freud's examples. Many of Erikson's concepts, such as the identity crisis of adolescence, have become popular ways of designating familiar developmental challenges.

Identity crisis

Cognitive-Developmental Theories

The practice of defining social relationships in terms of morality has a relatively long tradition in the short history of the social sciences. The social sciences were once considered the moral sciences, and early twentieth-century theorists

Table 8–1   *Erikson's Stages of Psychosocial Development*

STAGE AND AGE	PSYCHOSOCIAL CRISIS	OPTIMAL OUTCOME
I Oral-sensory (1st year of life)	Trust vs. Mistrust	Basic trust and optimism
II Muscular-anal (2nd year)	Autonomy vs. Shame, doubt	Sense of control over oneself and the environment
III Locomotor-genital (3rd through 5th year)	Initiative vs. Guilt	Goal-directedness and purpose
IV Latency (6th year to start of puberty)	Industry vs. Inferiority	Competence
V Puberty and Adolescence	Identity vs. Role Confusion	Reintegration of past with present and future goals, fidelity
VI Early Adulthood	Intimacy vs. Isolation	Commitment, sharing, closeness and love
VII Young and Middle Adult	Generativity vs. Self-absorption	Production and concern with the world and future generations
VIII Mature Adult	Integrity vs. Despair	Perspective, satisfaction with one's past life, wisdom

From W. Mischel, *Introduction to Personality*, Holt, Rinehart and Winston, Inc., 1971, p. 39. Used by permission.

thought that morality was the key to understanding social development (Kohlberg, 1964). Such was certainly the case with Freud, who considered the development of a sense of guilt to be of primary importance in the evolution of human culture. Recall that according to the psychoanalytic viewpoint summarized in the previous section, the developing child incorporates the standards of his parents and society into his emerging conscience. The superego is formed as the child internalizes societal standards, which then serve to dictate behavior in diverse situations.

Inconsistencies in ethical and moral behavior.   Research on the moral behavior and judgments of children fails to bear out the psychodynamic assumption that generalized internal states produce consistent behavior across varied situations. One of the most ambitious studies of the moral behavior of children was carried out by Hartshorne and May (1928) several years ago. These investigators contrived an ingenious array of tests of lying, cheating, and stealing. These tests were administered in diverse settings, including school classrooms, athletic contests, Sunday school, and the home. In their responses to paper and pencil tests, children gave fairly consistent statements of opinion on moral issues. The degree of consistency in their opinions dropped considerably, however, when equivalent forms of the same tests were administered in different settings, such as the classroom, at home, or at Sunday school. The investigators concluded that their data did not support the notion that behavior is governed by a generalized code of ethics. Rather, it appeared as though children varied their behavior to suit the situation. Burton (1963) reanalyzed Hartshorne and May's data and highlighted moderate consistencies which revealed a weak common factor. Nevertheless, such a weak relationship fails to account for very much of the variation in behavior in temptation situations. Thus, Burton's results do not change the interpretations of the original Hartshorne and May study, but rather serve to point out that an individual's reactions in a variety of temptation situations are not entirely random (Mischel, 1968). Although Hartshorne and May's studies used preadolescents, more recent research with 5-year-olds (Rau, 1965) supports the finding that the tendency to cheat or not to cheat depends more upon situational factors than upon a generalized moral trait of honesty.

Situational influences

Decision-making in moral conduct: The case for cognitive explanations. Some research evidence has been interpreted to suggest that where consistency is found in moral conduct, the consistency may result from decision-making capabilities of the individuals involved rather than from fixed behavioral traits or generalized moral conscience. This interpretation (Kohlberg, 1964) may explain why honesty seems to be related to situational factors, and why the degree of risk in being caught in a dishonest act is an important determinant of whether or not one will yield to influence.

Risk as a cognitive influence

Findings on moral development have also failed to reveal age-related increases in moral or socially constructive behavior, such as altruism or responsibility. One possible interpretation for the fact that moral conformity is not much different in later life than in early childhood is that moral character develops very early in life. Such an interpretation would be consistent with the psychoanalytic assumption that the basic structure of the superego is well established by about the age of five. On the other hand, some psychologists have argued that while the form of moral conduct and judgment may show little systematic change with age, the reasons underlying the decision-making processes may change systematically with increasing age. Younger children, for example, may conform to social expectations because they fear punishment or reprisal for transgression. An older child may base her behavior or judgment on moral beliefs (Kohlberg, 1964).

Age-related factors in decision making

Cognitive theorists believe that this is indeed the case, and that children progress through a number of irreversible stages in the kinds of decisions they make. These stages are considered to be universal insofar as children would not be expected to skip a stage or reverse the order in which they pass through any adjacent set of stages. The stages are thought to be applicable to all cultures. Nevertheless, cognitive-stage theorists should not be accused of naïvely assuming that children progress through these stages simply as a result of maturational unfolding. The basic character of the cognitive-stage theory orientation is captured in the following quotation from Kohlberg (1964).

The "stage" approach to understanding such responses characteristic of an age group involves the analysis of their underlying thought structures found in different age groups in order to define the general direction of development. Such "stages" are then used to understand developmental differences among children of a given age and to isolate major social and intellectual influences upon development.

It seems obvious that moral stages must primarily be the products of the child's interaction with others, rather than the direct unfolding of biological or neurological structures. The emphasis on social interaction does not mean, however, that stages of moral judgment directly represent the teaching of values by parents or of their direct "introjection" by the child. In the theories of moral stages . . . parental training and discipline are viewed as influential only as a part of a world or social order perceived by the child. (p. 395)

Role taking and cognitive growth

In cognitive-stage theories the process by which children come to comprehend the social order is social participation and role taking. They must learn to take the role of others toward themselves and toward the group. The two most prominent cognitive-stage theorists are Piaget, whose pioneer thinking has inspired the majority of research on moral development, and Lawrence Kohlberg, who, with his associates, has elaborated on Piaget's basic ideas concerning stages of moral development and extended the theory through systematic research.

Piaget's stages of moral judgment. Piaget's ideas about moral development center primarily on the child's judgments concerning morality, justice, and ethics. Actual moral behavior is dealt with only secondarily (Flavell, 1963). The mechanisms accounting for the child's rational morality are presumed to be the same as those involved in rational thinking in general. John Flavell (1963), a major Piagetian scholar, provides insight into the nature of the interaction between the child and his environment which engenders the development of rational moral judgment:

Peer interactions

> It is clear that the mechanism which Piaget holds responsible for the development of a rational morality is exactly the same as that which he thinks engenders rationality in general. . . . Both morality and logic are fired in the crucible of the spontaneous give and take, the interplay of thought and action, which takes place in peer-peer interactions. The precepts, logical and moral, which parents and other adults impose upon the young and egocentric mind are compliantly accepted but at the same time simplified and distorted. It is only through a sharing of perspectives with equals—at first other children, and later, as the child grows up, adults— that a genuine logic and morality can replace an egocentric, logical, and moral realism. (p. 296)

Two examples of Piaget's ideas about stages of moral judgment will be provided here to illustrate his theory. One area of children's moral judgments that Piaget studied was their notions about rules. He identified three stages, the first of which is not very interesting because at this stage rules simply are not much of a part of the child's world. In the second stage, the child regards the rules of a game as immutable and eternal. Rules are thought to be given by parental or divine authority. The interesting thing about this stage is that while the child believes that rules are absolute and should not be violated, in her actual behavior she violates them at almost every turn, not seeming to notice the discrepancy between what she says and what she does.

In the third stage, the child tends to believe that rules are subject to change and remain in force only if others agree to abide by them. The interesting development here is that while maintaining a relativistic attitude toward rules, the older child will obey the rules rather scrupulously—quite the reverse of the situation in stage two.

A second interesting area of moral judgment, and one which has been given a good deal of attention by American psychologists, has to do with changes in the basis for moral judgments. Piaget postulates two stages of moral judgment: objective and subjective morality.

Children in the age range from about three through eight will most likely judge an act on the basis of its objective consequences, while older children are more likely to make subjective judgments which take the motive behind an act into consideration. Piaget and his associates have studied the moral judgments made by children of various ages by presenting short stories which portray a situation in which harm was done, and asking the child to render a judgment concerning which of the two stories represented the naughtier act. One of the authors prepared a video tape to demonstrate for students in child development courses the varying reactions of children of different ages to stories similar to those used by Piaget and his colleagues. Two large pictures of children were cut from a mail order catalog and introduced with names given to them by one of the children who was interviewed. Pointing to each of the pictures in turn, the interviewer said,

*Objective and
subjective morality*

> *This is Ronny and this is Jimmy. I'm going to tell a story about each of them. You listen carefully so when I finish you can tell what you think about what these boys did. Ronny, here, (point) wanted a cookie before supper. He knew he wasn't supposed to have one, but when his mother was out of the room he climbed up and tried to get a cookie out of the cookie jar. As he was reaching for a cookie he knocked over one of his mother's best cups and broke it.*
>
> *Now Jimmy here (point) did something different. His mother wanted some help in setting the table. Jimmy was helping, and when he was carrying dishes to the table he tripped and dropped all the dishes. He broke five of his mother's best cups.*
>
> *Now, you tell me which of these boys you think was naughtier. Which one did the worst thing?*

True to Piaget's theory, the 3-year-old girl on the video tape responded as one would expect.

Holly:	*Now what was this boy's name?*
Interviewer:	*Ronny.*
Holly:	*And how many cups did he break?*
Interviewer:	*He broke one of his mother's best cups.*
Holly:	*And what was this one's name?*
Interviewer:	*Jimmy.*
Holly:	*And how many did he break?*
Interviewer:	*Five. He broke five of his mother's best cups.*
Holly:	*Then this boy, Jimmy, did the badest thing, because he broke five cups, and this other boy only broke one, and five is more than one.*

In contrast, consider the following responses of a 7-year-old to the same stories.

Paige:	(With great assurance) *Well, this boy* (Ronny) *did the worse thing, because he was disobeying his mother. Even though he broke only one cup what he did was a worse thing than this other boy, because*

Jimmy was trying to do the right thing. He was helping his mother. Maybe he should have been more careful, but at least he was trying to do something good.

The older child based her judgment on the motives or intentions of the child who did the damage. The preschool child, on the other hand, responded like a moral realist and judged the seriousness of the offense on the basis of the amount of damage done—an objective criterion.

Piaget acknowledges that his stages of moral judgment represent a general sequence, and that a wide range of individual variation is found in the actual responses of children.

Basic assumptions   *Kohlberg's stages of moral development.* Three basic assumptions are implicit in Kohlberg's ideas about the development of moral judgment in children and youth (Rest, 1974). These assumptions have been identified as "structural organization," "developmental sequence," and "interactions." Structural organization refers to ". . . general, internalized conceptual framework and problem-solving strategies" (Rest, 1974, p. 242). The assumption about structured organization is that as people grow and develop, their cognitive competence increases. The operations and rule systems which underlie competence become more differentiated and elaborated. The more complicated later structures develop out of the structures of the lower stages. Therefore,

*Invariant sequence
of stages*

> . . . the developmentally earlier "lower" stages are prerequisites of the "higher" stages; the more complicated higher stages deal more effectively with problems of wider scope and greater intricacy than do the lower stages. Hence stages are *sequenced* in a certain order because the earlier are less difficult and are attainable before the later stages. Higher stages are said to be "better" than lower stages in the sense that the higher structural organizations can do a better job in analyzing problems, tracing out implications and integrating diverse considerations. (Rest, 1974, p. 243)

Kohlberg contends that few people ever reach the highest stage and that appropriate training can stimulate development through the stages. The importance of knowing the course and sequence of development is that it should guide the design of curriculum materials that would match instruction with the child's developmental status.

The child is not viewed as a passive receiver of experience. According to cognitive-stage theories, the child reacts to and interprets experience on *Interactional* the basis of his previously developed intellectual structures. The interactional *process* process by which the environment influences the child and in which he constructs his reality is described as follows:

> As the child notices certain regularities in the environment and establishes behavioral patterns that interact effectively with the environment, we say that the child has built up certain cognitive structures. As the child encounters new and different experiences which cannot be understood adequately or reacted to in terms of established structures, the child seeks to revamp his way of thinking. The new experience interacts with previously established cognitive structures to prompt the search for more adequate structures. Once a new "program" is found which can successfully "compute" the new situation, the program becomes a part of the person's repertoire. Therefore, the essential condition for the cumulative elaboration of cognitive structure is the presentation of this search-and-discovery process for more adequate ways to organize experience and action. (Rest, 1974, p. 245)

James Rest (1974), the author of the above statement, makes an analogy between the intellectually developing organism and a self-programming computer. The perceptive reader who recalls the discussion of assimilation and accommodation from chapter 6 should not miss the close parallel.

Kohlberg believes that the stages of moral development are universal, and he attributes that universality to certain consistencies in human social arrangements (Adkins, Payne, & O'Malley, 1974). One of Kohlberg's tactics for studying children's thinking about right and wrong involves telling a story that presents a moral dilemma. From the differing types of responses given by children of different ages, Kohlberg and his associates make inferences about the character of moral decisions made by children in various developmental stages. The following is one of the better known examples of his "moral dilemmas."

Moral dilemmas

In Europe, a woman was near death from a special kind of cancer. There was one drug that the doctors thought might save her. It was a form of radium that a druggist in the same town had recently discovered. The drug was expensive to make, but the druggist was charging ten times what the drug cost him to make. He paid $200 for the radium and charged $2000 for a small dose of the drug. The sick woman's husband, Heinz, went to everyone he knew to borrow the money, but he could only get together about $1000 which is half of what it cost. He told the druggist that his wife was dying and asked him to sell it cheaper or let him pay later. But the druggist said: "No, I discovered the drug and I'm going to make money from it." So Heinz got desperate and broke into the man's store to steal the drug for his wife. Should the husband have done that? (Kohlberg, 1963, pp. 18-19)

Follow-up questioning explored the children's reasoning behind their judgments.

From children's reactions to dilemmas such as this, Kohlberg has hypothesized three levels of moral judgment: preconventional, conventional, and a postconventional, autonomous, or principles level (Turiel, 1973; Kohlberg & Turiel, 1971). Each of these levels is further divided into two stages.

*Levels of
moral judgment*

At the preconventional level, culturally prescribed standards of good and bad are the basis of moral conduct. These standards are interpreted on the basis of the probable consequences of action, for example, reward, punishment, and the exchange of favors.

*Preconventional
level*

In stage one of the preconventional level, the child's orientation is one of unquestioning obedience to authority and avoidance of punishment. A child operating at this level might respond to the story about Heinz and his dying wife by stating that it was wrong for Heinz to steal the drug, *or* that it was the proper alternative for him to steal it. Illustrative reasons supporting each of these judgments on the part of a stage one child have been reported by Rest (1973).

The man was right to steal the drug: *It isn't really bad to take it—he did ask to pay for it first. He wouldn't do any other damage or take anything else and the drug he'd take is only worth $200, he's not really taking a $2,000 drug.* (Italics added, p. 92.)

It was wrong for him to steal the drug: *Heinz doesn't have any permission to take the drug. He can't just go and break into a store—maybe break through a window or break the door down. He'd be a bad criminal doing all that damage. That drug is worth a lot of money, and stealing anything so expensive would really be a big crime.* (Italics added, p. 92.)

Stage two is labeled the "The Instrumental Relativist Orientation." At this stage, right actions are those which will work to one's own benefit or bring some reward.

Some elements of fairness and reciprocity are present, but always in terms of "you scratch my back and I'll scratch yours," rather than reciprocity based on justice, gratitude, or loyalty. The stage two child who believes that Heinz should steal the drug might say,

Heinz isn't really doing any harm to the druggist, and he can always pay him back. If he doesn't want to lose his wife, he should take the drug because it's the only thing that will work. (Italics added, p. 92.)

The other side of the argument at stage two might go something like this:

The druggist isn't wrong or bad, he just wants to make a profit like everyone else. That's what you're in business for, to make money. Business is business. (Italics added, p. 92.)

Conventional level

At the conventional level, there is an element of loyalty to family, group, or nation that goes beyond a concern for immediate consequences. Stages three and four fall within this level. Stage three is perhaps best characterized by a "Good boy—nice girl" orientation. One earns approval by being "good" or "nice," and behavior is frequently judged on the basis of intentions. The child at this stage who believes that it is right for Heinz to steal the drug might say;

Stealing is bad, but this is a bad situation. Heinz isn't doing wrong in trying to save his wife, he has no choice but to take the drug. He is only doing something that is natural for a good husband to do. You can't blame him for doing something out of love for his wife. You'd blame him if he didn't love his wife enough to save her. (Italics added, p. 92.)

The child who judges stealing the drug to be wrong might respond in the following manner if she is operating at this level:

If Heinz's wife dies, he can't be blamed in these circumstances. You can't say he is a heartless husband just because he won't commit a crime. The druggist is the selfish and heartless one in this situation. Heinz tried to do everything he really could. (Italics added, p. 92.)

The major orientation in stage four is "law and order," a theme which dominated the political campaigns in the United States in the late 1960s. "Right" behavior at this stage consists of ". . . doing one's duty, showing respect for authority and maintaining the given social order for it's own sake" (Kohlberg & Turiel, 1971, p. 415). The stage-four child might respond to the story about Heinz and his wife as follows, if he thinks it justifiable to steal the drug:

The druggist is leading a wrong kind of life if he just lets somebody die. You can't let somebody die like that, so it's Heinz's duty to save her. But Heinz can't go around breaking laws and let it go at that—he must pay the druggist back and he must take his punishment for stealing. (Italics added, p. 93.)

On the other side of the argument, a "stage-four" child might condemn the theft by saying,

It is a natural thing for Heinz to want to save his wife, but it's still always wrong to steal. You have to follow the rules regardless of how you feel or regardless of the special circumstances. (Italics added, p. 93.)

At the postconventional or autonomous level, the individual attempts to define moral values and principles apart from the sanctions of authoritative groups or persons with which he is affiliated. At the first stage of this level, stage five, there is a social contract orientation. The relativity of personal values and opinions is recognized, and procedural rules for attaining concensus are stressed. "The result is an emphasis upon the legal point of view, but with an emphasis upon the possibility of changing law in terms of rational considerations of social utility (rather than rigidly maintaining it in terms of Stage four law and order)" (Kohlberg & Turiel, 1973, p. 416). Respect is important, but it is assumed that respect is based on reason rather than emotion (Kohlberg & Turiel, 1973; Rest, 1973).

At this stage an illustrative argument favoring theft of the drug would be as follows:

> *Before you say stealing is wrong, you've got to really think about this whole situation. Of course, the laws are quite clear about breaking into a store. And, even worse, Heinz would know there were no legal grounds for his actions. Yet, I can see why it would be reasonable for anybody in this kind of situation to steal the drug.* (Italics added, p. 93.)

And the side of the argument against the theft of the life-saving drug:

> *I can see the good that would come from illegally taking the drug, but the ends don't justify the means. You can often find a good end behind illegal action. You can't say Heinz would be completely wrong to steal the drug, but even these circumstances don't make it right.* (Italics added, p. 93.)

Kohlberg's sixth stage is called "Universal Ethical Principle Orientation." Self-chosen principles, conforming to the principles of logical comprehensiveness, universality, and consistency, define "right action." The principles are abstract and ethical rather than moral roles. They are not concrete prescriptions, such as the Ten Commandments, but rather are ". . . universal principles of justice, of the reciprocity and equality of the human rights, and of the respect for the dignity of human beings as individual persons" (Kohlberg & Turiel, 1973, p. 416). One loses self-respect if she fails to maintain moral principles.

At this stage, an argument favoring the theft of the drug might go something like this:

> *Where the choice must be made between disobeying a law and saving a human life, the higher principle of preserving life makes it morally right—not just understandable—to steal the drug.* (Italics added, p. 93.)

The other side of the argument might go like this at stage 6:

> *There are so many cases of cancer today that with any new drug cure, I'd assume that the drug would be scarce and that there wouldn't be enough to go around to everybody. The right course of action can only be the one which is consistent with Heinz's sense of justice to all people concerned. Heinz ought to act not according to his particular feelings to his wife, nor according to what is legal in this case, but according to what he conceives an ideally just person would do in this situation.* (Italics added, p. 93.)

Kohlberg claims that his sequence has been validated in both urban and rural environments in the United States, Great Britain, Taiwan, Yucatán, and Turkey. The sequential pattern of development does not seem to be related to formal religious belief systems, but differential rates of development have been found in different cultural and educational settings. For example, the rate of stage development seems to be more rapid for urban than for rural children.

Kohlberg and his associates do not agree with sociological (Durkheim, 1961), psychodynamic (Freud, 1960), behaviorist (Aronfreed, 1968; Eysenck, 1960), or social learning theories (Berkowitz, 1964; Bandura, 1969; Maccoby, 1968), all of which conceptualize moral values and judgments as being derived directly from the rules and sanctions of the culture. The cognitive-stage theorists instead hypothesize that development results from the individual's continuing attempts
Equilibrium   to achieve equilibrium. Turiel (1973) puts it this way:

> . . . if the individual's existing structure is inadequate to deal with events encountered, the resulting state of heightened disequilibrium (manifested in conflict and confusion) could lead to compensatory activity. In such a case the feedback of the new information could result in transition to a new stage. (p. 737)

Consistent with this reasoning, Turiel (1973) has advanced a possible cause for the cross-cultural differences which have been noted in developmental rates of moral judgment. He suggests that faster rates of development may be found in those cultures in which the social environment presents the individual with more conflicts and discrepancies.

Kohlberg and his associates quite clearly do not subscribe to the idea that the worth of a particular form of moral judgment depends upon the degree to which it conforms to the social sanctions and values of the culture in question.
Cultural relativity   This point of view is the concept of cultural relativity, which anthropologists have done much to promote by describing the integrated nature and functional interrelationships of belief systems and other components of a given culture. In contrast to the concept of cultural relativity of values, which is a widely accepted notion in the social sciences, cognitive-stage theorists steadfastly maintain that the higher in the stage hierarchy a form of moral judgment is, the better it is.

The idea that "higher is better," when "higher" means "associated with older age levels," is often accepted without question. One might pause to consider that, in general, the development of urban American children seems to proceed at a relatively fast pace, implying perhaps that urban social conditions facilitate more development. However, considering the problems associated with interpersonal relationships among people in our large cities, it might be wise to defer assigning "better" and "poorer" value labels to different kinds of moral judgments until more valid evidence is available. The authors recall that one feature of the reasons given by Navahos for actions toward others is that:

> The Navaho never appeals to abstract morality or to adherence to divine principles. He stresses mainly the practical considerations: "If you don't tell the truth, your fellows won't trust you and you'll shame your relatives. You'll never get along in the world that way." (Kluckhohn & Leighton, 1946, p. 218)

Such a mode of judgment would place the Navaho at about stage two, in the preconventional level of Kohlberg's hierarchy of stages of moral development. But in a period of real moral dilemma in American culture, actions based on the practicality represented in the Navaho's ethical reasoning could scarely be faulted.

Implications of cognitive stage theories of moral development. Kohlberg and Turiel have anticipated that some people might be displeased with the "elitist ring" of their conclusion that the stage six mode of moral judgment is most desirable. Whatever one's personal reactions to the "Kohlberg point of view," the implications of the theory are clear. The most common pattern of moral judgment in the United States, Great Britain, Israel, Mexico, and Tawian, is stage four. Less than ten percent of teachers or college graduates use stage six morals. Kohlberg and his colleagues, therefore, advocate that moral education be undertaken, using a developmental model based on their research, with the aim ". . . to stimulate the upward development of all children, to Stage six if possible" (Kohlberg & Turiel, 1971, p. 440).

Social Learning Theory

A third explanation of how the developing individual acquires his capabilities and preferred modes of dealing with other people is offered in social learning theory, which has been most comprehensively articulated by Albert Bandura at Stanford University. Psychologists whose work is guided by social learning theory accept most of the concepts and principles of operant psychology, but feel that by itself Skinnerian behaviorism is inadequate to deal with the complexities of human learning and development. The social learning point of view is sometimes called "cognitive behaviorism," suggesting that the theory does attempt to deal with processes "within the organism," which cannot be observed directly and which must, therefore, be inferred from overt behavior.

Observational learning. Anyone who has ever spent much time watching children has noticed that they learn a great deal by watching the behavior of other people and then imitating them. Adults also learn by observing behavioral models. It is doubtful, for example, that anyone could ever learn to play tennis solely through the lecture approach. Through observation and imitation we can learn large "chunks" of complex behavior all at once, or through the same processes we can learn to put skills that we have already mastered together in new configurations. It would take a very long time for humans to learn their native tongue or parliamentary procedure if all new behavior had to be learned through behavioral shaping—the reinforcement of successive approximations to a target behavior. While we do unquestionably learn some aspects of our social behavior through slow behavioral shaping, much more of it is learned through observation.

Influences on observational learning. But children do not just go about willy-nilly imitating the behavior of every model they see. Research has identified certain variables that may influence whether or not a witnessed behavior will be imitated.

A number of variables influencing the likelihood of imitative responding relate either to the characteristics of the model or to what the observer sees happen (behavioral consequences) to the model. First, the likelihood that an observed behavior will be imitated is increased if the model is reinforced for her behavior. For example, in one preschool a particular time was set aside each day for "free choice." Children usually chose to work with activities such as blocks and puzzles at this time, and the "attractive" picture books and other printed materials were left to idle on the shelves. The teacher and her aide thought the children would enjoy the books once they "got used" to them, so

Characteristics of the model

Consequences to model

one child was called aside before free choice time and asked to please go to the book area for a while. When he complied, the aide joined him at the table, commented favorably on his choice of the book activity and interacted warmly with him, calling attention to pictures, asking and answering questions, and so on. Almost immediately other children joined them at the book table and received their share of attention. This is an example of a deliberate informal application of a social learning principle.

When a model is seen punished for a behavior, the probability that an observer will imitate that behavior decreases. The effect is the opposite of positive reinforcement of the model. In our discussion of aggressive behavior in the next chapter, we will provide illustrations to show how reward or punishment of a model's transgressions influence the aggressive behavior of young observers, and how little correspondence there may be between children's actual behavior and their verbalized moral judgments.

Nurturance   Nurturance or rewardingness is another variable which is likely to influence the imitative learning or performance of an observer. The results from various studies of the role of nurturance in observational learning are not perfectly consistent, but generally they suggest that a child is more likely to imitate the behavior of a model with whom he has had warm, supportive interactions than he is to imitate a model whose relationship with him has been neutral. This has been demonstrated experimentally (Bandura & Huston, 1961), and through naturalistic studies, which are generally congruent in their findings that boys who have had nurturant fathers are more likely than boys with contrasting relationships to adopt the roles and characteristics of their fathers (Mussen, 1961; Payne & Mussen, 1956; Sears, 1953).

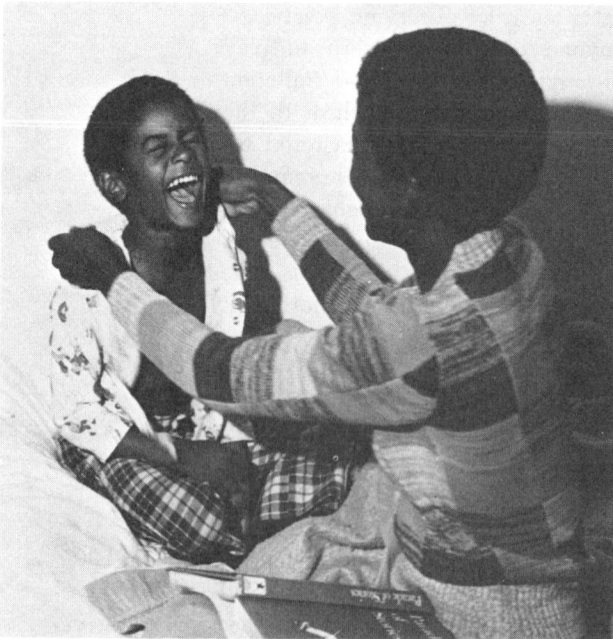

Nurturance is an important quality in the relationship between children and adult models.

In every person's environment there are "scarce resources," or desirable commodities to which he does not have free access. Recall from our earlier discussion that Freud believed that boys identified with or tried to "become like" their fathers because of their fear of reprisals (i.e., castration) growing out of rivalry over the mother in the Oedipal situation. John Whiting, who was interested in articulating psychodynamics and learning theory, conceptualized the rivalry between parent and child more broadly to include a range of valued resources, such as food, attention, and so on. Whiting assumed that since the child cannot compete for these resources directly, she must do it through fantasy and by pretending to be the parent (Mischel, 1971). An interesting question then becomes: Does the child identify with the parent because he wants to consume these resources or because he wants to control them? A number of studies have been addressed to this question. One very complex experiment (Bandura, Ross, & Ross, 1963) involved, among other things, exposing children to situations in which they observed adults either consuming or controlling a variety of attractive games and treats or as neutral (powerless) observers. After the various combinations of relationships among onlookers, controllers, and consumers were established, the child's behavior was assessed in a game situation to determine the degree to which the child imitated the distinctive behaviors of the various models. In general, the result was that the powerful adult, the controller of resources, was most influential. An interesting sidelight to this experiment was that when an adult male model was merely an onlooker, and the controller was a female, boys nevertheless seemed to attribute power to the male figure in spite of the powerless role he played in the experiment. We will comment further on this and related findings when we discuss sex-typing in the following chapter.

*Consumption
vs. control
of resources*

The conclusion to be drawn from this line of research seems to be that power over resources, rather than consumption of resources, is an important model characteristic which may facilitate observational learning.

Among the characteristics of a model which may vary is the prestige or social reputation which she enjoys. Every parent who has ever tried to persuade a child to eat spinach by calling attention to Popeye's love for this somewhat unpopular food must intuitively know that the prestige or status of a model

Social reputation

*Prestigeful models
exert vicarious influences
on children's interests.*

bears an important influence on behavioral adoption. This fact has been born out by several investigations, but perhaps most vividly in a study carried out by Duncker (1938) many years ago. Duncker first tested children's initial food preferences and found that they chose a pleasant tasting chocolate with lemon flavoring over a medicinal tasting sweet substance. The children were then told a story in which the hero, Eaglefeather, violently disliked a pleasant tasting food similar to that chosen by the children in their initial preference, and relished a food similar to that which the children did not especially care for. In reaction to these exciting stories and the exploits of the hero, children reversed their preferences in successive tests. Preference for the new food was maintained for a period of time by simply recalling the story briefly at subsequent tests.

More than likely, every reader can think of instances in which he or she has encountered this variable, the influence of a prestigious model, in operation. One of the authors has a young son, who, at the age of six, became an avid fan of a youthful musical group which was enjoying tremendous national popularity at the time. When he learned that the members of this musical family were devoted members of a particular religious group, he declared his intention to begin attending their church. This example is made even more telling by the fact that the author's son had previously attended that same church with family friends on a number of occasions, found it not to his liking, and declared his intention never to go again. As a postscript to this story we should note that many prestigious models come and go in the life of a six-year-old, and the influence, so far, appears to have been transitory.

Similarity of model

Sex

Observers are generally most susceptible to the influence of models whom they perceive to be similar in some way to themselves. Sex is perhaps the most obvious basis for identifying similarities and differences between models and observers. Maccoby and Wilson (1957) presented films depicting different interpersonal behaviors of boy and girl adolescents to seventh graders, and one week later gathered information to determine recall of behaviors displayed in the films and to identify which of the filmed models the subjects expressed a preference for. The boys and girls in the study tended to be better able to recall the behaviors of the characters of the same sex as their own than of the opposite sex, and they also identified with or expressed preference for the same sex character. In another film presentation, the socioeconomic class of the character was a variable of interest, and it was found that children preferred the model of the social class to which they aspired.

Age and ethnicity

Other dimensions of model-observer similarities and differences which have been found to influence the probability of observation learning include age (Hicks, 1965) and ethnic status (Epstein, 1966).

Obviously, if one is to learn through observation, she must pay attention to the relevant behavioral stimuli. The evidence suggests that similarities between the model and observer is an important variable because perception of similarity affects attentional processes. Various attributes of models become distinctive because in everyday life people are rewarded for emulating the behavior of some models but not for imitating models with contrasting characteristics. We will pursue this matter further later in this chapter, but here it is sufficient to say that observers learn to identify model characteristics that signal a high probability of reinforcement and attend closely to these cues (Bandura, 1969). The observer is more likely to notice and imitate the behavior of those models than she is to emulate the behavior of models whose characteristics are associated with a low probability of reinforcement.

Probability of reinforcement

Even under what may appear to be identical stimulus conditions, there is great individual diversity in acquisition of the modeled responses. Previous social learning experiences of the observer undoubtedly account for these individual differences. Given the complexity of the experiences involved in the learning history of any individual, it should not be surprising that research findings relating to the relationship between *observer characteristics* and response acquisition under modeling conditions are not completely consistent. Nevertheless, there is clear evidence that observer characteristics such as dependency, self-esteem, level of competence, socioeconomic status, and racial identity, and sex are associated with susceptibility to modeling influences (Bandura, 1969).

Take dependency for example. Other things being equal, highly dependent children are more likely than less dependent children to adopt the behavior of a model (Bandura & Walters, 1963). A possible reason may be that dependency, at least in some forms, is associated with a history of relatively infrequent reinforcement. The child who has been on a very thin reinforcement schedule may be more likely to adopt the behavior of a model, if he expects to be rewarded for so doing, than the child who is relatively well satiated on approval. This supposition is supported by the fact that imitative responding is facilitated by reinforcement to the observer, contingent on his matching the behavior of the model.

Learning and performance. There are some behaviors we know perfectly well how to perform, but do not engage in, or at least we do not do them very often. It is useful, therefore, to distinguish between those modeling effects which result in the learning of new responses or capabilities, and those which only increase or decrease the probability that we will perform a behavior learned sometime in the past. Social learning theorists often distinguish among differing classes of outcomes that may result from the influence of models. First, a person may learn entirely new response patterns simply through observation of the behavior of a model (Bandura & Walters, 1963). As we said earlier, relatively "large chunks" of behavior may be acquired for the first time in this manner. There are, however, other times when the observed behavior of a model will merely serve as a cue, which elicits or "occasions" a behavior already within the repertoire of the observer. People who smoke, for example, often find themselves pulling out a cigarette and lighting up, "without thinking about it" when they see a companion take a cigarette. The children in an earlier example were quite capable of sitting at the book table and turning pages, but they did not do it until they saw another child doing it.

Behavioral acquisition

Behavioral cuing

There are also behaviors which are not performed because they are inhibited. Under ordinary circumstances most people refrain from performing certain acts which are considered inappropriate, or which have been negatively sanctioned by the individual's family, church, or the larger society. However, when one sees these behaviors displayed by others, the observer may become disinhibited. The reader might easily identify this as the "all the other guys were doing it" effect of modeling. The story of the pillar of the small community who becomes a temporary "boozer" and woman chaser while attending a convention in a distant city is all too familiar. Certainly not all conventioneers become so disinhibited when released from the restraints of their daily lives, but it happens often enough to provide a compelling illustration of the disinhibition effects of modeling. A multitude of illustrations come from the rebellious years of the 1960s. Many a compliant and "well-behaved" college student found herself shouting profanity at officials, destroying property, and doing other things in the company of protesters, which she would never have done on her own.

Disinhibition

Inhibition

On the other side of the same coin, behavior may be inhibited through the influence of models. If an individual is given information that others do not behave in a certain way in a given situation, he is likely to also refrain from that behavior, even though it may constitute a common act for him in other settings.

Of these various types of modeling effects, only the first example constitutes learning. All of the other effects, eliciting, inhibition, and disinhibition, merely involve performance. The distinction between learning and performance, and the conditions which influence each, is important in social learning theory. Moreover, this distinction also involves the important question of whether or not reinforcement is essential to learning.

Reinforcement in learning and performance. Operant psychologists maintain that learning cannot take place in the absence of reinforcement. Social learning theorists, on the other hand, contend that reinforcement is not a necessary condition for learning to occur, although it may constitute an extremely important influence on performance. Suppose, for example, that a parent had "taught" a young child some self-maintenance behavior, such as buttoning his shirt, or a teacher had taught a list of new vocabulary words to a third grader. How could one determine whether the child had learned the desired behavior?

One could give a test, but the toddler may get her mother's attention by "failing the shirt-buttoning test," even though she knows perfectly well how to do it, or the third grader may find that it takes more effort than he is willing to spend to write out the meanings of the new vocabulary words. One way that has been used successfully to sort out learning and performance in laboratory studies, and which could be used to equally good advantage in the home or school, is to introduce incentive conditions designed to "motivate" the child to perform as well as she is able. Bandura (1965) tested this procedure by showing children a film in which an adult engaged in certain unique aggressive acts. Different groups of viewers saw different versions of the film. In one version the adult was punished for aggressive acts, in another there was no consequence for behavior, and in one film the children saw the model rewarded for his transgressions. As we might expect, the children who saw the model punished for aggressive responses imitated the behavior less than the children in either of the other two viewing conditions. Could one conclude from this outcome that the differences noted in the imitative behavior of the three groups of children reflected differences in what they learned from the films? Bandura took the study one step further to find out. He offered attractive incentives to the children for reproducing the model's behavior and found that differences originally found among the three viewing groups disappeared. From this he concluded that children in all of the original viewing conditions *learned* the unique behaviors displayed by the model equally well, but their original *performance* was influenced by the consequences associated with the model's behavior. It can further be concluded that the original learning took place *without reinforcement*.

Generalization and discrimination. Of all the stimuli which bombard our senses, some go unnoticed while we respond in quite predictable ways to others. Furthermore, it is not necessary to learn a new response to each unique instance of those stimuli to which we do respond. Without this economy in learning, it is difficult to imagine how survival would be possible. The processes by which we learn to respond to classes of stimuli and to react differentially to other classes of sensory information are referred to as generalization and discrimination. These processes, which we discussed in chapter 6, play an important role in learning to respond to the physical and social environment. As we drive our automobiles we discriminate between red lights and green lights and make differential responses to these stimuli. Luckily, it is a decision that requires little thought. If we respond to these stimuli as society says we should, we avoid possible aversive consequences. The color of the traffic signal, through learning, becomes a discriminative stimulus, or "cue," which signals the appropriateness of a particular behavior.

Discriminative stimulus

Children are differentially reinforced for attending to and emulating certain behaviors of models in their environments. Traditionally, little boys have been reinforced more for imitating the behavior of their fathers than that of their mothers. In fact, the behavior of an entire general class of models—males, turns out to be more appropriate for emulation than the behavior of mothers and other females. Children also learn to discriminate between those situations in which a given behavior may be appropriate, and another situation in which behavior in the very same response class may be inappropriate. One should not hit his little sister, but it is OK to return aggression in kind when the object is the neighborhood bully. There are numerous examples of behaviors which are appropriate for one sex but not the other, at one age but not another, in one

Differential reinforcement

Environmental variations produce differences in life space.

setting but not another. In the following chapter we will discuss the ways in which cultural and social influences contribute to this situational specificity in behavior, especially as it relates to aggression, sex-typing, and age-appropriate behavior.

Phenomenological Theories

A number of theories, variously referred to as wholistic, organismic, phenomenological, self-theories, growth theories, and cognitive field theories, while differing in important ways from one another, share a cluster of characteristics which have exerted a powerful influence on thought about child development. A discussion of two representative points of view within this orientation will provide a flavor of the way in which theories within this tradition have influenced conceptions of human development.

Gestalt psychologists: Wertheimer, Kohler, Koffka

Kurt Lewin's field theory. Kurt Lewin was born in Prussia and received his training in German universities. He was associated with Max Wertheimer, Wolfgang Kohler, and Kurt Koffka, the founders of Gestalt psychology, at the University of Berlin before coming to the United States, where he held posts at various universities during the 1930s and 1940s. The influence of Gestalt psychology, which stressed the importance of the interrelationships of elements within a whole and regarded the isolated study of parts within a system as reductionistic, is clearly seen in Lewin's work.

Life space

One of Lewin's concepts which has influenced the thinking of developmentalists and educators who attempt to use psychological information as a guide to curriculum development is his idea of life space. Life space includes all the individual's psychological reality—all of the facts which may, in any way, determine the individual's behavior. Life space includes the person and her psychological environment. Behavior, then, is a function of the interaction between the person and his psychological environment. Beyond the psychological environment is the physical world. This physical environment is not part of the life space, although the boundary between the psychological environment and the nonpsychological environment—those stimuli and facts which have no influence on the individual's behavior—is a permeable one. That is, the two environments can influence one another—once irrelevant facts in the nonpsychological environment may become relevant.

Those forces that influence behavior, in Lewin's view, are not need states or enduring personality traits, but the facts in the psychological environment, as they are perceived by the individual. He does not look back to the child's history for explanations of behavior (Hall & Lindzey, 1970; Baldwin, 1967).

*Individual
perceptions*

This is a very brief summary of only one of Lewin's major concepts, but it illustrates some of the assumptions which have had an influence on thinking in child development and education. Lewin's work stimulated extensive research in social psychology, where investigators attempted to alter the life space of individuals by trying to influence perceptions about the self, others, and events (Mischel, 1971). Research in psychological ecology owes its origins to Lewin, and whether the reader knows it or not, the curriculum which guided your own instruction in the early grades was probably constructed, in part, around the notion of life space. Anyone who learned to read with a basal reader should recall that the primers included only those characters who would be found in the stereotyped life space of the 6-year-old child—the immediate members of the family. As you progressed through the first, second, and third level readers, new characters were introduced—community helpers, people who live on a farm, and so on. Presumably this widening life space, as presented in the pages of the reading texts, was correlated with the expanding life space— the new social relationships and increasing differentiation of the person and the psychological environment—of the developing child. To a great degree this organization persists, in spite of the dramatic increase in "facts" which television has introduced into the psychological environments available to children.

*Psychological
ecology*

One important aspect of life space is that environmental forces act on the individual in the total life situation as he or she perceives it. These forces may attract an individual toward or away from a given situation. In one interesting investigation following the Lewinian tradition, Barker, Friesnen, and Williams (1970) contrasted student participation in extracurricular activities in large and small high schools. They found that even though the large consolidated high school offered a greater number of activities, or behavior settings, a smaller proportion of the students actually participated in these settings than was the case in the small school. According to this analysis, in the small school there was greater environmental press to participate in a variety of behavior settings because there is a lower practical limit on the number of individuals required to make a given activity possible. Students appear to be more likely in the small school to perceive their participation as important to the group, and a larger proportion of the student population is likely to be pressed into some kind of leadership responsibility. This study is worthy of particular note since one of the main reasons given for consolidating schools is so that a wider range of academic and extracurricular offerings can be provided than would be possible in a small school. The Barker and Gump study gives reason to question this assumption since even the variety of settings in the large school was only slightly greater than the small school had to offer, and the provision of just more settings may be of dubious value if the psychological environment fails to influence students to participate in what are presumably learning situations.

In summary, in the Lewinian view, it is the present psychological situation and the individual's perception of it that determine behavior—not the ghosts of the past. In any attempt to explain behavior and development it is the total situation that must be understood, rather than isolated elements within it.

Organismic theories. Kurt Goldstein, an eminent neuropsychiatrist, is often identified as the leading exponent of organismic theory (Hall & Lindzey, 1970). The organism behaves as an integrated whole rather than as a series of parts. If an individual is healthy, his behavior will be well integrated, consistent, and coherent. No component of the organism can be understood when abstracted and isolated from the whole.

From these brief comments, you can quickly see a major similarity between the field theory, discussed earlier, and organismic theories. A major distinction is that Lewin's theory was strictly psychological, while Goldstein was concerned with the entire biological organism. The relationship between these points of view is stressed in Hall and Lindzey's (1970) statement that:

> Organismic theory has borrowed many of its concepts from Gestalt psychology, and the two viewpoints are on the friendliest terms. Organismic psychology may be regarded as the extension of Gestalt principles to the organism as a whole. (p. 299)

Sovereign motive

A basic tenant of the organismic point of view is that one motive dominates human behavior. This sovereign motive is called self-actualization or self-realization. It means that the individual strives continually to realize her potentialities—what she can become she must become. Life is given a unity of purpose through this motive.

Abraham Maslow, Carl Rogers, and others who fall into this tradition assert that people are innately good and are always striving to enhance themselves. Behavior is purposeful in this sense, and if people do not always "do good" it is only because of an inadequate environment. Civilization imposes conditions which block the path to self-fulfillment and self-actualization. The parallels between this point of view and the ideas of Rousseau, which we discussed earlier, are too obvious to require elaboration.

Concept of self

As with Lewin's theory, it is not objective reality that determines behavior, but rather the individual's subjective perception of reality. One's perception of the nature of "his self" is therefore extremely important, and the concept of "the self" becomes the central organizing focus for some phenomenologists (e.g., Rogers, 1959). The individual's perception of her own adequacy or inadequacy is considered a major determining factor in behavior.

SOCIAL UTILITY OF THEORETICAL PERSPECTIVES

All the theories summarized here attempt to identify ways in which the situations and events encountered by the developing child influence his capabilities to deal effectively with the social environment. Although the theories differ from each other in important ways, each seems to offer some contribution to the improvement of conditions under which children are socialized. All offer insights, yet they differ in the degree to which their constructs, processes, and principles are amenable to scientific inquiry. The utility of a theory is governed, at least in part, by the degree to which the theory can be empirically validated and translated into principles which can be manipulated to produce desired outcomes.

Psychodynamic Perspectives

The reader may already have discerned a quality of indirectness and circularity in psychodynamic theory. According to the personality dynamics of Freudian theory, if an adult displays a certain trait, compulsive acquisition of possessions for example, it could be because she was overindulged during the oral stage, *or*, if that were not the case, it could be because she was unduly frustrated in her "incorporative" efforts at that period of development. Actual behavior plays an enigmatic role in the theory because it cannot be interpreted as a direct expression of an individual's inner state. Unconsciously, a behavior may serve to conceal one's true nature. For these and other reasons, Freud's theory would be difficult to prove or disprove. A necessary quality of a good theory is that it be testable, and as richly imaginative and creative as the psychodynamic explanations for development are, they cannot be validated in any comprehensive way. *Verifiability*

Perhaps it is unfair to expect that Freudian theory be judged on the basis of requirements for empirical validation which no comprehensive behavioral theory of its vintage could pass. On the plus side of the ledger, Freud's theory has undoubtedly promoted a more humanistic and considerate treatment of children. The importance of children's very early experiences are emphasized, and the possibility that ill-considered socialization practices may have life-long and possibly irreversible consequences has had a significant influence on child rearing and education. Freud's theory is based on the assumption that maturational changes in the organism dictate personality dynamics which, in turn, dictate the nature of the developmental problems which must be resolved in each stage of development. But in spite of its maturational orientation, Freud acknowledged the important role of the environment, and social influences were given even more attention by the neo-Freudians. The psychodynamic theories recognize that the social environment often imposes unrealistic and arbitrary requirements for conformity and that the consequences may be seen in maladaptive behavior and human suffering. Socialization practices in the home and formal education have both undergone some liberalization as a result.

There are some who feel that liberalization has gone too far—that it has resulted in permissiveness and that permissiveness leads to a poorly developed sense of social responsibility. Freudian influences have also been criticized because many parents have become fearful of the responsibilities of parenthood. They have come to believe that their mistakes as parents may cause irreversible psychic damage to their children. *Permissiveness*

If behavior is thought to be caused, in a very pervasive way, by early experience, individuals can excuse themselves from any responsibility for their own behavior. Leonard Bernstein and Stephen Sondheim captured this impression colorfully in the Broadway musical *West Side Story*. In the song "Gee, Officer Krupke!" the members of a street gang sang:

> Dear kindly Sergeant Krupke,
> You gotta understand,
> It's just our bringin' upke
>   that gets us out of hand.
> Our mothers are all junkies,
> Our fathers are all drunks.
> Golly Moses, natcherly we're punks!

The possibilities for guiding self-directedness with a view that holds remote antecedent experiences to have such profound and long-lasting effects seem limited at best. *Remote antecedents*

Cognitive-Developmental Perspectives

The cognitive-developmental point of view is also influenced by maturational concepts. The influences of the social environment are not simply incorporated directly into the decision-making and judgmental processes. Social experience stimulates the elaboration and differentiation of cognitive structures, but the nature of structural organization is such that development must pass through a biologically predetermined sequence of stages.

The theory provides a dynamic view of the cognitive processes involved in social development, and it makes the important point that the organism does not passively assimilate raw experience—but rather must act upon her experi-

*Construction
of reality*
ence. The child does not simply react to the external stimuli that constitute "reality." Rather, he constructs his own reality.

Kohlberg's view would encourage educators to systematically stimulate the moral judgment of young people to facilitate the progression to higher levels of functioning. Dramatic jumps across stages are, however, not to be expected.

While the dynamic interactional stance taken by cognitive developmentalists does take the complexity of human development into consideration, its utility is somewhat limited by the fact that the developmental processes postulated in Piaget's theory are rather vague and difficult to operationalize. Therefore, no clearly established strategies are established for selecting experiences which are just sufficiently discrepant from existing intellectual structures to stimulate development. Nevertheless, a number of moral education programs have been designed and carried out, using Kohlberg's refinements of Piaget's theory as it pertains to moral judgment (Rest, 1974).

Phenomenological Perspectives

Phenomenological views of development are avowedly humanistic. Phenomenologists are concerned with trying to see the developing individual "whole," and generally hold strongly negative opinions of behavioral approaches that seem to treat people in a mechanistic manner. A problem with this orientation, from the standpoint of science and society, is that insurmountable restrictions are placed on empirical investigation when objections are raised to the isolation and operationalization of key variables and well-specified desired outcomes. Moreover, no social application of developmental principles can restructure the total environment. Utility demands that variables with the greatest probability of having a facilitating influence be selected to guide the design of environments to promote human growth and development.

Some of the most promising approaches to the empirical study of environmental influences on development, within the phenomenological orientation, come out of the Lewinian tradition (e.g., Schoggen & Schoggen, 1971). These developments are discussed in chapter 12.

Social Learning Perspectives

Social learning theorists are engaged in empirical investigations of those sources of social influence which directly affect development. Their work has provided valuable insights into the nature of those variables most likely to lead to changes in individuals' learning and performance. The principles of social learning theory have been shown to exert a direct influence on the acquisition and performance of socially desirable behaviors and on the elimination of behaviors which are socially dysfunctional. A number of these findings are reviewed in the following chapter.

With the phenomenological orientation, social learning theory shares a concern for the present instead of seeking remote antecedent explanations for behavior. Both points of view give emphasis to situational influences on behavior. Common sense would tell us that there is at least some generalization of behavior across diverse situations, but evidence presented earlier in this chapter suggests that situational factors have a marked influence on behavior. Social learning theorists (e.g., Mischel, 1968; 1973) are attempting to identify those variables in the learning history of the individual and in the immediate content of behavior which may determine whether individual characteristics or features of the situation exert a greater influence on behavior in a given condition. This information could help to promote generalization learning where it would be advantageous, and to guide discrimination learning where differential responses to similar situations would be warranted.

Social learning theory has grown out of the behavioral tradition, but it takes into account internal mediational and representational processes. Therefore, it can be considered a cognitive rather than a mechanistic theory. It is distinguished from the cognitive-developmental theories by the fact that instead of beginning with molar, descriptive concepts of behavioral change, it attempts to build from a number of smaller, well established principles, toward a more comprehensive, integrated set of principles. That is not to say that all developmentalists who espouse this position are free of simplistic notions of what is required to enhance development to any socially significant degree.

In conclusion, children must develop skills required in carrying out the social transactions required in their society. The skills, or social competencies, which a society values, change with time and circumstance. Contemporary humanists in American culture have argued for consideration of a broader range of human capabilities than our social institutions have tried to foster in the past. In a heterogeneous society it is natural that different groups will assign differential value to different competencies.

In this chapter we have identified some of the changes that seem to be taking place in conceptualization of what competencies might contribute to successful functioning in a contemporary American society. We summarized various theories which attempt to explain how the organism acquires the competencies required to function in her culture. In the following two chapters, we shall pursue this matter further by specifying some of the specific social and personal capabilities which are important to the individual and society, and by presenting the results of empirical investigations designed to identify the conditions that influence the development of these competencies.

SUGGESTED READINGS

Bandura, A. *Social learning theory*. New York: General Learning Press, 1971.

Combs, A. W. (Chairman). American Association for Supervision and Curriculum Development Year Book Committee, *Perceiving, behaving, becoming*. Washington, D.C.: National Education Association, 1962.

Elkind, D. *Children and adolescents: Interpretive essays on Jean Piaget*. (2nd Ed.). New York: Oxford University Press, 1974.

Erikson, E. H. *Childhood and society*. New York: W. W. Norton & Company, Inc., 1963.

Flavell, J. H. *The developmental psychology of Jean Piaget*. Princeton, N.J.: Van Nostrand, 1963.

Kohlberg, L. Stage and sequence: The cognitive-development approach to socialization. In D. A. Goslin (Ed.), *Handbook of socialization theory and research*. Chicago: Rand McNally, 1969, 347-480.

White, R. W. *Lives in progress*. New York: The Dryden Press, 1952.

9

The Development of
Social Competence

Instructional
Objectives

Recognize or recall

Compare and contrast

Describe or demonstrate

Evaluate

the limitations of equating social competence with intellectual capability.

reasons IQ scores are still regarded by some educators as the most important index of competence.

four problems in specifying components of social competence.

the distinction between capability and performance, and the influence of situational variables on each.

arguments for and against the "bag of virtues" approach to the identification of social competencies.

the definition of egocentrism.

the evidence for and against the proposition that very young children are highly egocentric.

the limitations of studies of children's play behavior in nursery school settings conducted with children from professional family backgrounds.

the definitions of solitary play and parallel play.

the reasons that the name of a category of behavior (such as cooperation or aggression) is a poor index of whether or not the behavior represents a social competency.

the factors which restrict the range and complexity of peer relationships among young children.

the behaviors regarded by Harriet Rheingold as early manifestations of sharing behavior.

the factors which may influence attention span among young children.

the implications for planning of preschool activities of information or factors affecting attention span.

the task requirements of cooperative activity among children.

an experimental analogue of competition and cooperation.

the results and generalizations of the series of studies of competition and cooperation conducted by Millard Madsen and his associates.

the life conditions that may facilitate or impede the development of competitive and cooperative behavior in children reared in rural and urban environments.

the societal implications of socialization of competitive behavior in the contemporary development milieu of the United States.

the definition of altruism.

Recognize or recall

Compare and contrast

Describe or demonstrate

Evaluate

hypotheses and findings relating to cultural and social-class differences in altruistic behavior.

the influence of reinforcement practices on altruistic sharing among young children.

the vicarious conditioning of positive affect.

the definition of empathy.

the influence of modeling and admonition on children's behavior and on their evaluations of generous and miserly models.

the results and conclusions of Yarrow, Scott, and Waxler's study of children's learning concern for others.

the advantages of using multiple criterion measures as exemplified in the Yarrow, Scott, and Waxler study of learning concern for others.

advice, based on knowledge from research, for parents who wish to guide the development of altruism in their children.

arguments for and against the proposition that children of elementary school age or younger lack empathetic role-taking ability.

the research underlying Piaget's assumptions regarding the age at which capacity for empathy develops.

the correlates of leadership.

the relationship of leadership to situational requirements.

the frustration-aggression hypothesis as it relates to aggression.

social learning theory, psychodynamic, and drive reduction theory accounts of aggression.

the processes by which aggressive impulses may be reduced according to psychoanalytic and drive reduction theory.

the definition of catharsis, displacement, and sublimation.

the limitations of punishment as a means of controlling aggressive behavior in children.

the conclusion that children whose parents use physical punishment display relatively high rates of aggressive behavior because they learn from this experience to use aggression as a means of dealing with problems.

the dependency of effects of punishment on the context in which it occurs.

possible side effects of punishment as a control procedure.

recommendations on the control of aggressive behavior, to be used by parents or teachers.

the social and cognitive variables that influence cross-situational specificity and consistency in behavior.

282

CHAPTER CONTENT

On top of a group of wind-swept, isolated mesas in northern Arizona, the Hopi Indians have eked out a living for hundreds of years. One of their villages, Old Oraibi, is the oldest continuously inhabited community in the United States. In order to have survived for so long in this harsh environment, it has been essential that people work in harmony with one another and with nature. So pervasive is that theme that it has been called the "Hopi Way." If any man acts selfishly, taking more than he needs to sustain life, the entire universe may be set off balance. Although the Hopi Indians have long valued cooperation to an extent that stood in sharp contrast to the individualistic explorers and pioneers who first encountered them, the early white invaders expressed in their journals a greater respect for the Hopi than for the other Indian groups encountered on the trek westward. This was apparently because the Hopi were agriculturalists, carefully cultivating their poor land for the meager return it would yield, and their industrious agrarian way of life seemed somewhat more "civilized" to the early adventurers than the hunting and gathering habits of the Plains Indians. One early anthropologist (Beaglehole, 1937), who studied this group, reported that those Hopi people who deviated from group norms by preferring laziness to economic self-sufficiency were subjected to "merciless ridicule."

Cultural and situational differences in valued social competencies

The Navahos, a neighboring group, has until the present time maintained hostile relationships with the Hopi, but within their own society the Navaho expect their members to exercise sobriety and self-control. In spite of frequent violations of these expectations, which seem to stem in substantial measure from the stresses and strains of acculturation, individuals who function effectively in their relationships with fellow Navahos should exercise these self-controls. The extent of the value placed on self-control is exemplified by the fact that "Women are praised when they do not cry at desertion by their husbands or 'too much' at the death of children" (Kluckhohn, 1962, p. 170).

Contrast this emphasis on constraint and self-control to the characteristics required for effective functioning among the Iatmul of New Guinea. In this group it is important to be assertive if one is to get by. Margaret Mead (1940), a veteran anthropologist, reported that among these people "an individual's safety lies in getting angry first, in asserting his will over others, before they assert theirs against his" (p. 102).

The Navaho, in sharp distinction, follow the principle that "one good turn deserves another." This was convincingly illustrated by Kluckhohn (1962), who reported that "some of the Ramah Navaho refused attractive employment as United States Army scouts against Geronimo on the grounds that the Chiricahua and Mescalero Apache had behaved kindly to them during the time of the Fort Summer captivity" (p. 171). Hospitality and generosity are also highly praised, and generosity is valued to the extent that if one has nothing else to give to the starving, even one's sacred corn pollen should be given freely.

These are only a few examples of the kinds of behaviors which are differentially valued, and which have varying degrees of utility for social functioning in diverse cultural groups. Among every group there are some qualities and capabilities which seem to give those who possess them an advantage over others in coping with their social and physical environment, and in obtaining whatever privileges and commodities are valued in their culture. Chapter 1 identified examples of some of the human qualities which have been considered important in the social history of our own young nation. In the present chapter, we will discuss the development of those social capabilities which seem to contribute to the ability of people to cope with the interpersonal requirements of their culture. Recall that in chapter 8 we indicated that there is now some evidence that social competencies may be just as important in life success, perhaps even more critical, than the intellectual skills which have been emphasized traditionally. Here we will deal with some of the parameters of those competencies, the conditions which facilitate their development, flexibility, and durability.

THE DIMENSIONS OF SOCIAL COMPETENCE

The topic of this chapter is a *fuzzy* one to conceptualize. At the present time, there seems to be no widely agreed upon view of just what capabilities and habits contribute to the effectiveness with which one deals with the social environment. Neither is there any single unifying theory providing a comprehensive explanation of how social competencies are developed by individuals, or what conditions determine whether an individual will utilize those skills of which she is capable. This topic has been of sufficient recent concern that in 1973 the Office of Child Development, a component of the U.S. Department of Health, Education and Welfare, commissioned a conference of noted authorities on child development who were assembled with the aim of defining "social competency" (Anderson & Messick, 1974). This section of the present chapter draws heavily upon the work of that conference.

Early attempts to conceptualize social competence

The conference on social competence represents only one of a number of continuing individual and group attempts to cope with the complexities of defining social competency. The longevity of this effort may be illustrated by recalling that Plato attempted to deal with this question by categorizing sense and intellect as two separate aspects of human ability. Other qualities were gradually added by other writers who thought about the qualities constituting ability, until by the fall of the Roman Empire, the list of candidate capabilities included such factors as memory, imagination, invention, speech, attention, and measurement.

It was left to the faculty psychologists, whose work was discussed in chapter 5, to generate a really impressive list of abilities which were presumed to constitute the capabilities of humankind. Spearman, the dean of faculty psychologists, highlighted the commonplace ways in which abilities are inferred from behavior by describing Fagin's treatment of Oliver Twist on the occasion of the boy's attempted escape. According to Spearman's reading of Dickens:

Here is a typical picture of mental life in one of its most acute phases . . . Fagin *sees* Oliver, *remembers* his attempt to escape, *thinks* of punishing him, *notices* the club, *marks* the boy shrinking away and breathing quickly, *perceives* him stagger under the blow, [and so on]. Fagin also becomes *angry* at what the boy has done, *entertains a desire* to punish him, relishes the anticipation of him writhing in pain, *seizes* voluntarily the club and actually *uses* it. (1927, p. 2, italics added [cited in Anderson & Messick, 1974, p. 283])

Spearman categorized the processes employed by Fagin in this episode as "cognition" and "conation and affection." His assertion that these processes cannot be treated apart from one another has been little heeded, as witnessed by the common practice of educators to dichotomize educational objectives into affective and cognitive domains. In actual practice, however, the artificial dichotomy itself is not as serious as the fact that few policy makers pay much attention to any but the cognitive outcomes of instruction. The educational implications of this issue will be addressed directly in chapter 10, but for now it is appropriate to examine statements by two prominent psychologists who have had a role in the effort to give professional guidance to public policy.

The first of these statements was made in 1968 by Edmond Gordon, a prominent psychologist who played a central role in devising the Head Start program which began in 1965. Gordon said, *Neglect of social competence*

> Although the goals of education tend to be stated in broad terms, when we come to assess education it is always to cognitive development and academic achievement that we first look for evidence of change. Too often we either stop with those first results or turn with less rigor to look at other areas either as a second thought or as a rationalization for our failure to find more impressive evidence in the cognitive domain. (1969, pp. 13-14 [cited in Anderson & Messick, 1974, p. 283])

Four years later Edward Zigler, a professor of developmental psychology who became the first director of the federal government's Office of Child Development, amplified this common lament:

> It may come as a surprise to the Nation that this preschool program was not mounted in hopes of dramatically raising IQ scores. . . . Rather, the creators of Head Start hoped to bring about greater *social competence* in disadvantaged children. By social competence is meant an individual's everyday effectiveness in dealing with his environment . . . his ability to master appropriate formal concepts, to perform well in school, to stay out of trouble with the law, and to relate well to adults and other children. (italics added [cited in Anderson & Messick, 1973, p. 283])

As these statements indicate, intellectual performance, usually conceptualized as general intelligence, or IQ, has dominated thinking about competence. Because IQ is a gross, undifferentiated measure incorporating many aspects of functioning, some educators continue to argue for its use as the principal index of effective performance. The development of cognitive and linguistic skills which are heavily weighted in IQ assessment is of obvious value in dealing with the physical and interpersonal environments. But since the development of linguistic and intellectual ability has been treated in previous chapters, the present discussion will focus on those capabilities and modes of responding which enable the individual to relate effectively with others. Chapter 10 will deal with competencies enabling one to manage his own behavior. First we shall explore the pros and cons of differing approaches to the identification of the dimension of social competence. One of the most serious obstacles faced by the panel of experts who tried to assist the Office of Child Development defining the meaning of "social competence in young children" was the lack of agreement among educators and *Prominence of the IQ* social scientists about what variables should be included in the mapping of the domain.

The panel members were united in their rejection of general intelligence as the sole mark of competence, but a number of specific problems had to be confronted in moving beyond that consensus toward a definition of social competence. Some of these problems are directly relevant to the present discussion.

Values and competence

First, not all traits are universally admired, as the illustrations which introduced this chapter show. One society may stress cooperation, while the dominant theme in another may be aggressive independence. Beyond that, even within a single cultural group some behaviors may be valued or highly functional in some situations, and dysfunctional or subject to scorn in other situations. Therefore, any meaningful discussion of specific competencies must in some way specify the groups of people and the types of situations in which the behavior in question does indeed function as a social competency.

Typical and maximum performance

Second, people do not always employ the competencies they possess. This situation is not unlike that depicted in the story about the agricultural extension agent who asked a local farmer why he never attended the educational meetings to learn about new agricultural methods. The farmer's sage reply was that he already knew more than he could put into practice. Those readers who prefer more hard data than that provided in this anecdote might consider Labov's demonstration of the influence of situational variables on the language production of black ghetto children as discussed in chapter 7, which amply demonstrates the situational specificity of some behaviors. Lest it be thought that situational variables are limited in their influence to disadvantaged children, it should be noted that in an earlier experiment Arthur Pearl (personal communication) sent people holding doctoral degrees to be interviewed by street gangs, and found them to be notably nonverbal—displaying the same kinds of language limitations which have been described as linguistic characteristics of disadvantaged children. Such information clearly cautions that any discussion of competence should distinguish between capability and actual behavior, and between typical and maximum performance.

Bipolar dimensions of competence

Third, some competencies may be best categorized as bipolar dimensions. Behaviors such as extroversion-introversion and rigidity-flexibility are representative of such dimensions. Part of the problem is that there is often little agreement concerning what specific behaviors represent the various points on such a dimension.

Age-related distinctions

A fourth issue to be dealt with is the fact that various behaviors may have differential utility or social sanctions at different points on the age range.

With these considerations in mind, we shall turn to an examination of the development of some classes of behavior which may be considered candidates for selection as social competencies.

A SHOPPING LIST OF COMPETENCIES

Lawrence Kohlberg (Kohlberg & Mayer, 1972), whose views on moral development were summarized in chapter 8, has voiced strong objections to the "bag of virtues," "shopping list," or Boy Scout handbook approach to the identification of competencies. Some of his reservations have merit and have been discussed in the previous section. Specifically, he feels that it is difficult in such an approach to deal with multiple and often conflicting ideals, and that different characteristics are likely to have differential value depending upon the age of the individual in question. Presumably Kohlberg would prefer to discover a universal developmental sequence of social competencies similar to, or perhaps as an elaboration of, his developmental sequence for moral development. Unfortunately, any such comprehensive scheme would have to be so general as to render it useless as an explanation of the development of social competency, or as a guide to those who hope to facilitate the development of social competence in growing children. Such an approach evades the crucial task of identifying circumstances influencing the development of specific competencies required by a society for effective functioning. Neither does it identify ways in which people learn to engage in these behaviors flexibly, depending on when and where they are useful and appropriate. If one goes shopping for a product, she should do so with the appropriate uses of her selections in mind. Similarly, the society that places a high value on cooperation may do so with the reservation that there are some circumstances in which it may work against one's interest to cooperate. In this chapter, we shall therefore explore the development of a number of interpersonal behaviors and capabilities which, at least under certain circumstances, the culture deems desirable and may wish to select out for development. There are other behaviors which society attempts to restrict to a limited number of situations in which the behaviors in question are socially approved and constructive. The categories of behavior to be considered include play behaviors, which may serve as the roots of social competence, cooperative and competitive behavior, altruism, role taking, and leadership. Aggressive behavior and its control will then be discussed, followed by a general consideration of developmental conditions that apply to all of the classes of behavior considered.

The Roots of Social Competencies

Many of the roots of children's ability to interact and form interrelationships with others seems to emerge from play. These roots may well lie in a type of play which emerges in infancy in American children. Early social responses develop from interactions between the baby and caretaking adults or doting friends and relatives in the infant's immediate environment. Most readers have surely seen adults tickling a baby, "cootchi-cootchi-cooing" at him, and vibrating their lips against his belly. At least to the bystander, these activities seem intended at least as much to amuse the adult with the infant's responding coos, gurgles, and random movement of limbs, as to give pleasure to the baby. It seems clear that mutual pleasure may be derived from these adult-initiated interactions, and babies soon learn to tease their parents or other caretakers in return. We should recall, however, that such stimulation has not always been the norm in American society, and at times it has been negatively sanctioned by professionals in child care. John B. Watson, whom the reader will remember from chapter 2, advised parents not to joggle and otherwise stimulate the baby during the early months of its life. Additional evidence that the relationships developed in social-affective play are conditioned by cultural norms rather than representing universal stages of development is found in the descriptions of parent-child relations in other cultures. Japanese parents, for example, are prone to soothe their babies, and attempt to avoid stimulation.

Stimulation of infants

A prominent feature of children's early relationships with others is their egocentric orientation. Young children tend to conceive of all phenomena, interpersonal and physical, as centering on themselves. Piaget has reported various expressions of the egocentric perceptions of young children including their apparent inability to take the perspective of another person. In relationship to the physical environment, a child's egocentric point of view may be seen in such questions as, "Why does the sun follow me?" At least in part, this tendency

Egocentrism

to consider only one's own perspective may originate in the child's dependence on adults for nurturance (Ausubel & Sullivan, 1970). For most American children the provision of nurturance is a one-way process, with adults giving care and attention, and the child receiving. Swift (1964) has reported that:

> Under atypical conditions, however, where children become emotionally dependent on each other instead of adults, egocentricity is less marked. Thus, studies of children who are reared together as orphans and kibbutz children indicate less sibling rivalry and stronger identification with one another. (cited in Ausubel & Sullivan, 1970, p. 330)

When not involved in having their physical needs met, toddlers and preschoolers are preoccupied with the objects they are using or want to use, and their relationships with peers are likely to involve attempts to protect or obtain such possessions (Ames, 1952). Be cautioned, however, that the observations upon which most of the descriptive conclusions about the development of social behavior have been made on middle-class children, often coming predominantly from the homes of college professors and other professional families. It seems highly likely that even at such early ages, interrelationships among peers have been strongly influenced by the culture. American society is very materialistic in its orientation, and places a high value on things. A multimillion dollar industry is based on our fascination with objects designed to keep children entertained. In a culture where the "things" children play with are largely the natural objects which are in plentiful supply in the environment, it seems doubtful that early peer relationships would focus on the rivalrous behaviors required in the acquisition and defense of possessions.

As children gain the freedom of movement that comes from walking, the nature of their social interactions with peers changes.

In traditional descriptions of ages and stages of development, the period from about 18 months to 2½ years of age is often referred to as toddlerhood. The toddler typically develops a number of new social capabilities. Included among these are the development of solitary play, parallel play, and cooperative play.

The 1930s and 1940s were decades of intensive study of children's behavior in nursery school settings. The data from these studies were translated into descriptions of characteristic developmental patterns of young children, and were largely derived from observations of children in nursery school settings operated by universities. The degree to which this information is representative of children other than those from families of similar professional status, or of children from other cultures, is questionable. These limitations on the generalizability of data describing the developmental progression of social behaviors in young children should be kept in mind when this information is considered.

Early responses to peers

Children begin to attend positively to their peers at about 30 months of age, but generally positive responses occur only after initial conflicts have been resolved. Conflicts among children one year or more of age generally involve disputes over play materials. One can well imagine that such conflicts over playthings may be a function of the fact that in nursery school settings there are often highly desirable toys that are available in limited supply. There is not a tricycle or wagon for every child, nor is there likely to be space and materials for more than a very few children at a time to play with items such as floor blocks. Typical observations found in the literature may therefore be limited in their applicability to situations very much like the ones in which the original observations were made.

Even though children do begin to respond to one another from early infancy on, they remain more responsive to adults than to other children for quite some time. It has been suggested that this may be because adults attend to and respond with nurturance to the young child with greater regularity than do the child's peers (Hartup, 1970).

Most of the young child's social relationships with peers take place in the context of play, or at least what is perceived as play by adult observers. The toddler, viewed from the perspective of the normative-descriptive studies which had their heyday in the 1930s and 1940s, enters first into a solitary, or onlooker, stage in his relationships with peers. The role is that of a bystander, looking on at the play of other children. Very soon the child takes on a style of interaction that has been characterized as parallel play. At this stage children seem to want and seek out the company of peers, but an observer gains the impression that the children are playing *alongside* rather than *with* one another. Children may be seen playing with blocks or toy cars or large wheeled toys, such as wagons and tricycles; but even though they are actively engaged with the same toys or activities, there is little reciprocal exchange. Conversations of an analogous nature may also be the norm, with the children talking on the same topic, but with little by way of response to the content of their peer's messages. One child may be overheard to say *My dog got lost last night. We looked for him in the car.* His playmate, rather than asking if the lost dog had been found, or some other response to the first child's message, might reply that *I have a dog. He's a puppy.*

Solitary play

Parallel play

The studies which produced the descriptions and classification of parallel play and conversation have not been directly challenged through the systematic observation and description of social relationships of contemporary children or children from social class and ethnic groups differing from those who were studied in the decades before the turn of the century. Nor have comparisons been made of children's interactions in diverse settings. Informal child watching has led many observers of contemporary American children to conclude that parallel play is not such a common phenomenon even in middle-class toddlers as the older literature suggests. The authors and their students have witnessed countless children, 2½ years old, engaged in lively exchanges bearing little resemblance to classical descriptions of parallel play.

Harriet Rheingold (in press) has also called into question these earlier observations and interpretations of young children's behavior which emphasize their dependency and egocentric orientation. She reports that children 12 months of age or younger engage in sharing behavior. The children observed by Rheingold often took the initiative in making their mother a partner in their play, and they often did so by sharing. By 18 months of age children apparently do a great deal of sharing, which takes at least three forms at this early stage of development. Young children may share by *showing* an object to another person. They share by *giving* an object to their mother, and by *playing with* an object given to the mother while it is still in contact with her.

Rheingold considers sharing to be an important developmental milestone in the lives of young children. Not only do children share with their mothers, but they also share with their fathers, and even with strangers. The conditions which foster the development of these early forms of sharing have not yet been well defined, but apparently such a simple thing as adding colorful objects, such as posters or mobiles, to the environment increases the amount of *showing* a child does. Modeling and reinforcement processes undoubtedly also play a role in the development of sharing responses.

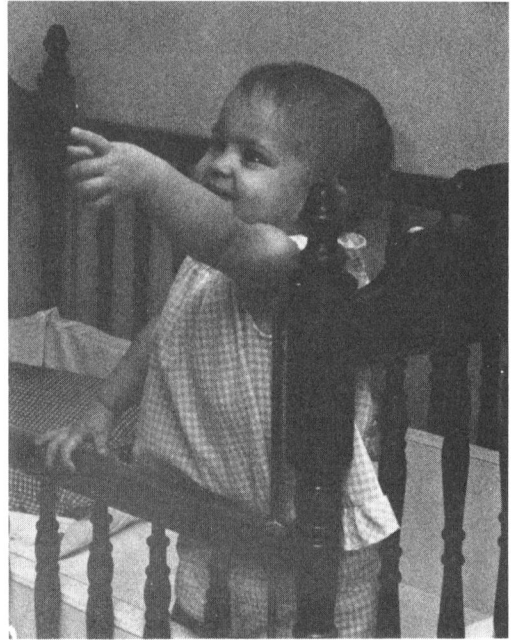

*Showing is an early milestone
in the development of
sharing behavior.*

From her study of literature on sharing among other species and in various cultures, Rheingold has come to speculate that sharing has an adaptive advantage for the human species. It seems to be a valued response in all cultures, and while parents of most higher organisms give to their young, reciprocal sharing is apparently confined to the human species. A truly significant paradox is therefore, what conditions in a child's experience lead to the decline of sharing responses, so that a year or so after a child has taken delight in showing or giving to another, parents and preschool teachers find it necessary to teach children to share.

As children progress from toddlerhood to preschooler, and into the early elementary school years, their social relationships become increasingly more varied and complex. As social participation increases, so do a number of pro-social behaviors such as cooperation, and to a lesser degree, altruism. At the same time, they engage in more competition, rivalry, and aggression. The increase is not necessarily of a cumulative or additive nature, however, because it has been observed that following an increase in aggression from the ages of two to four, aggression then tends to decline (Hartup, 1970). Moreover, the picture of the child becomes ever more complex as sex differences and other culturally conditioned elaborations of behavior come into play.

It is not always possible to designate whether an activity, such as cooperation, represents a social competency just by naming or even describing the behaviors involved. Behaviors that are advantageous in one situation may be dysfunctional in another.

For example, a number of conditions contribute to highly competitive behavior among college students. When grading is based on a "curve," or the relative performance of a student in reference to other members of the class, it is usually to the student's advantage to behave competitively. Scarce resources, such as scholarships and admission to high quality graduate programs, are contingent on out-performing one's reference group. In contrast, the ability to contribute to a set of common goals as a member of a cooperating group may be more highly valued in a work setting such as engineering.

Responses which are socially valued when performed by adults may be negatively sanctioned for children and youth, or vice versa. In many traditional cultures it has been expected that youthful members of the society should listen to and appreciate the wisdom of their elders. Young people in such cultures are expected to refrain from voicing their opinions. Even in American society, many children are raised with regular reminders that *children should be seen and not heard*, an admonition which according to adult caregivers often goes unheeded. On the other hand, most groups permit certain behaviors in young children that are negatively sanctioned for adults. In our society, young children may express their affection toward peers of the same sex without shame, but at the very least such expressions among adults bring raised eyebrows—even in the most liberal geographic areas.

Psychologists have contrived a variety of ingenious arrangements designed to identify the conditions influencing the development of social behaviors, and to identify groups and individual differences in the incidence of them. Information on differences among groups is often useful in stimulating the generation of hypotheses regarding the general manner in which the natural social environment influences the development and expression of social behavior. Studies involving the experimental manipulation of conditions in order to see how specific variables affect behavior help to identify and specify the specific means by which the natural environment influences the development of social competencies. *Naturalistic and experimental research*

Changes which occur in children's interrelationships should not be considered the simple results of increased age and maturity. Abilities which are prerequisites for complex social relationships are dependent on the interaction of biological maturation and knowledge and skills gained from experience. Preschool children have a great deal to learn, and while they accomplish it in an astonishingly short period of time, the complexity of peer relations among very young children is restricted because they are still learning many of the prerequisite skills. Motor skills, for example, are not sufficiently developed in very young children to permit them to engage in some kinds of joint play activities (Ausubel & Sullivan, 1970). Visualize the awkwardness with which two young children building a playhouse attempt to position a long board in place and nail it to uprights. *Maturation and experience*

Other factors limiting the nature and complexity of peer relationships among young children include cognitive immaturity, language limitations, a limited attention span, and ignorance of rules and norms (Ausubel & Sullivan, 1970; Hartup, 1970). *Factors limiting social relationships*

Prominent among the cognitive factors which may restrict early peer relationships is the young child's inability to take the perspective of others. Young children generally seem little aware of the feelings and needs of others. They are often little aware of group expectations, and have yet to learn to assume different roles as the situation dictates. Much of the dramatic play which is an integral part of traditional nursery school programs is undoubtedly motivated by the intent to facilitate the development of understandings and perceptions involved in role taking. Such experiences are thought to assist the child in progressing from his egocentric orientation toward more socially aware interaction.

Children master the forms of their language very early and are able to generate all the necessary utterances to communicate their ideas. They tend to forget, however, that others do not have psychic powers, or any other means of access to their private thoughts. Therefore, they often fail to provide sufficient explanatory information to make their wishes and intents clear to others. These limitations are also related to the cognitive egocentrism described by Piaget.

It has also been postulated that children may lack an adequate span of attention to sustain group interaction (Ausubel & Sullivan, 1970). This may be the case in some instances, but the notion that young children have short attention spans has probably been grossly oversold. We have seen children as young as two and one-half years old spend periods of time up to an hour engrossed in an activity. From a very early age attention span is specific to situations, and children will often persist for exceedingly long periods of time at activities which truly interest them. The widely held notion that all activities for preschoolers must change every few minutes to accommodate their short attention span is a part of the child development folklore which has had a pervasive influence on advice given to parents and on programs for preschool children.

Cooperation and Competition

It may seem a paradox that as children tend to display more cooperative behavior as they grow older, so does the incidence of competitive behavior increase. Those psychologists who described the developmental progression of children in the 1930s and 1940s (Gesell & Ilg, 1943) noted that competitiveness becomes an increasingly common mode of social interaction as young children "internalize" the competitive norms of American society. The competitiveness of preschool and kindergarten children is often expressed

> by grabbing materials from others, cornering a supply, making favorable comments about their own work, withholding assistance, increasing their work output, and showing great persistence. (Ausubel & Sullivan, 1970, p. 342)

The cognitive and social demands of these behaviors appear to be less complex in some ways than those involved in cooperation at this young age. Cooperation among peers requires that children be able to communicate effectively with one another, that they be able to subordinate their own interests for the collective good of a group, that they be able to take different roles, and that they understand the advantage to be gained from cooperative action (Wolfle & Wolfle, 1940, cited in Ausubel & Sullivan, 1970).

Distinctions between competition and cooperation

The basic difference between competition and cooperation, aside from possible differences in the skills and knowledge required of the individuals involved, centers on the relationship between individual effort and goal attainment (Deutsch, 1962). In a competitive endeavor one can attain his goal only at the expense of others involved in the activity. Each individual acts in a manner which increases her chances of attaining a goal, and simultaneously reduces the chances that other children with whom she is involved will attain their goals.

In contrast, when individuals behave in a cooperative manner, the efforts of each individual are oriented to a common goal of the group. Individual efforts are so related that in increasing one's chances of achieving a goal, that individual also increases the chances of other members of the group to achieve the same goal. Cooperative behavior also seems to have consequences which go beyond the immediate realization of a desired goal. Members of a group of cooperating individuals seem to get to like one another better as a side effect of cooperation, and they become willing to do things for one another (Deutsch, 1962).

Marble Pull Game: A device designed to measure cooperative and competitive behavior in young children. (Adapted from M. Madsen. Developmental and cross-cultural differences in cooperative and competitive behavior of young children. Journal of Cross Cultural Psychology, *1971, 2. By permission of the publisher.)*

Figure 9–1

A number of laboratory analogues of cooperative and competitive behavior have been developed to study the group differences in cooperative and competitive behavior, and to identify age-related changes in the nature and incidence of these activities. One of the analogues, which has proved useful in the study of cooperative and competitive behavior, is the marble-pull game devised by Millard Madsen (1971). The marble-pull game consists of a rectangular plank to which short table legs may be attached. The game board stands at a comfortable height for children who play while seated on small chairs. Positioned at the midpoint of the board at each end is an eyelet through which a string may be passed. Just in front of the eyelet is a hole in the game board, with a cup attached beneath it to hold any marbles which fall into the hole. The game is played by two children at a time. A plexiglass marble holder is placed in the middle of the board, and a string attached to each end is threaded through the eyelet at the ends of the board. When a marble is placed in the marble holder, it is possible for the players to pull it toward the hole at their own ends of the board. If the marble holder passes over one of the holes in the game board, the marble will fall from the opening in the bottom of the holder into the cup of whichever child has pulled the holder to his or her own end of the board. The interesting feature about this apparatus is that the two halves of the marble holder are held together with magnetic inserts. Therefore, whenever the children pull against each other with much force, in an attempt to get the marble to their marble cup, the marble holder breaks at the midpoint and the prize rolls into a groove at either side of the game board. The players must therefore choose between competition and cooperation. This feature makes it impossible for either child to win any marbles through competition because neither child wins the marble when the holder comes apart. Competition is therefore maladaptive—that is, it is impossible to win by competing with the other player.

Laboratory analogues

In a typical experiment, pairs of children (players) are seated at each end of the game board. They are told that this is a game in which they can get marbles. The experimenter demonstrates by placing a marble in the marble holder and pulling it along with one of the strings until it falls into one child's cup. The demonstration is then repeated with the holder being moved in the opposite direction so that the marble then falls into the second child's cup. The children are told that they can keep all the marbles that drop into their cup, and they will play for ten marbles (ten trials). The children are not informed that the marble holder will break apart if they pull against each other simultaneously. Whenever the holder comes apart and the marble rolls into a groove, the marble is removed and the children are told that neither of them gets it because it did not fall into a cup.

This game, and others like it, have been used to study cross-cultural and developmental differences in children's cooperation and maladaptive competition. In one such study (Madsen, 1971) this game was used with Mexican children from a small village (population 800) in Mexico, and with Anglo-American children from a large city (Los Angeles, California). In this study, Madsen contrasted not only rural Mexican with urban Anglo-American children, but he also made comparisons across ages by using samples of children who were in the age ranges 4-5, 7-8, and 10-11.

The findings from this study might come as something of a surprise to many Americans. We might think that children would quickly see that they could win nothing by competing, and that some cooperative strategy in which each could win part of the marbles would be to their mutual advantage. We might also guess that older children would come to that realization more quickly than would younger children, and there are at least a few ethnocentric Americans who might expect that American city children, with all the advantages of urban sophistication, would do better than Mexican children living in an isolated rural environment.

If you expected any of those things to happen, you were wrong. Anglo-American children in the 4-5 year age group obtained more marbles than either of the other two groups of American children. The cultural differences were even more striking than the age differences. When the averages for all of the pairs of subjects in both the 7-8 and 10-11 year age groups were compared, it was found that the Mexican children obtained a dramatically larger number of marbles. The children were then given instruction in playing the game cooperatively, following their first ten uninstructed trials. Then they played for an additional ten trials. Even after instruction in a cooperative strategy, a very large percentage of the Anglo-American pairs of children failed to get *any* marbles on the majority (62 percent) of their trials.

Urban-rural differences A most interesting picture begins to emerge from a series of studies like this one, which have compared children from different cultures and differing age levels. Madsen (1967) compared children from a rural Indian village in Mexico with both middle-class and poor children from a large city in southern Mexico and found that both the poor urban and the rural children were more cooperative than middle-class urban children. Another study (Shapira & Madsen, 1969) found children reared in an Israeli kibbutz, a rural communal settlement, to be more cooperative and less competitive than Israeli urban middle-class children. All these studies show a consistent trend for children to become more competitive with increased age, but the differences among children reared in different sociocultural environments are striking. In general, urban children seem to be more competitive and less cooperative than rural children. Since the child-rearing practices employed by the parents of these various groups of children were not directly assessed in any of these investigations, and no direct information on instructional practices in the schools were collected, we cannot reach a definitive conclusion about how these group differences came to be. We are not left to speculate entirely in the dark, however. Madsen's original interest in cooperation and competition in Mexican children reared in differing environments was stimulated by hypotheses which he arrived at by reading the ethnographic accounts of anthropologists. Oscar Lewis (1961) studied the village of Tepoztlan, about 60 miles south of Mexico City, in 1943. In 1956 he visited the village again and found that the most notable change to have taken place was a shift from an agricultural to a nonagricultural economy. The village had become a popular tourist spot during his absence.

Parental sanctions

Along with the change from agricultural to nonagricultural enterprises, Lewis noted changes in typical child-rearing practices. During his first visit he had observed that parents freely used physical punishment and fear to promote passive and submissive behavior. Impulsiveness, curiosity, aggression, independence, and competition were actively discouraged. Thirteen years later Lewis found parents treating their children with much greater indulgence and permissiveness.

Lewis's observations were remarkably consistent with those gathered by the Romneys (Romney & Romney, 1966) who studied a Mexican Indian barrio which was part of a larger town (Juxtlahuaca) in southern Mexico. Barrio children who were considered old enough to reason (five or six years old) were scolded if they tried to order other children around, and in general there were negative sanctions and contingencies for an individualistic achievement orientation. When children from the barrio went to the central school where they found themselves among a much more individualistic, aggressive, and achievement-oriented group of children from the nonagricultural section of town, they had difficulty adjusting.

Cultural task requirements

Judging from these descriptions, one might expect children reared under agrarian conditions to behave with less individualistic aggressiveness than urban children whose upbringing has valued and reinforced those qualities. Moreover, in an agrarian environment, especially where agriculture has not become a technological industry, cooperative action has a high functional value in everyday life. Descriptions of rural and village life in many cultures have identified a variety of ways in which individual advantage is closely tied to group advantage. People must cooperate in order to accomplish jobs too large to be done by individuals. Common examples are the cooperative harvesting of crops, group road-building efforts, and the barn-raising parties popularized in historical and fictional accounts of the American frontier.

A very conscious effort to promote cooperative group action is made in Israeli kibbutzim (Spiro, 1965). Even the techniques for formal instruction in the kibbutzim deemphasize competition, since grades and examinations are seen as undesirable. This emphasis contrasts with practices of urban parents and teachers, who are more likely to stress and encourage competition.

The thing about all of this that should give American parents and educators pause for reflection is that this evidence seems to show that the more closely groups approximate the urban, middle-class status, which has come to represent the norm in American society, the more competitive and less cooperative the children seem to turn out. This is suggested not only by experimental studies, but also by the descriptions of social interaction developed by trained observers. Not only does competitiveness seem to increase with age, and along a rural to urban continuum, but the form and degree of competitiveness and rivalry is so extreme as to have become maladaptive. It seems a reasonable hypothesis that:

> . . . in the developmental milieu in the United States, competition is rewarded to such an extent that United States children generalize a competitive strategy to situations in which it is nonadaptive. (Kagan & Madsen, 1971, p. 38)

For middle-class Anglo-American children, rivalry and competition are apparently so valued and reinforced that children are even willing to take a loss in their own absolute gain in experimental game situations, in order to lower the gains of their peers. By the age of eight, boys appear to be even more willing than girls to sacrifice their own absolute gains in order to reduce the gains of a peer (Kagan & Madsen, 1971).

Maladaptive competition in American society

While Americans have traditionally valued individualism and encouraged competition in educational and economic pursuits, there are significant problems facing Americans as a group. These problems are of such magnitude as to demand cooperative endeavors requiring well-developed interpersonal competence on the part of individuals who join together in groups to seek common goals. The problem seems especially serious for minority-group members, who appear to be much influenced by the highly individualistic, competitive orientation of American society. Jackie Kimbrough (Kimbrough et al., 1974) and her associates have argued convincingly that excessive individualism and competitiveness holds great perils for the black community. She has argued that the long-term viability of oppressed peoples depends on the development of effective political, social, and economic organizations. She further states that

> Among Black community groups, the development of effective organizations to deal with community problems has been impeded by vulnerability to the American ethic of competitiveness. (Kimbrough & Bikson, 1972)

Without doubt, both the requirements of the present and the future will require competence in group effort and the willingness of individuals to apply their abilities to a group outcome.

Altruism

Unusual indeed are the parents or teachers who do not occasionally nag their children to share with or give aid to a sibling or peer. Over the past few years, there has been an increasing expression of social concern over a similar issue, but one which is of broader and of more long-range social significance. The focus of this concern is an apparent growing unwillingness on the part of Americans to get involved by coming to the aid of others. A tragic caricature of this tendency was dramatized one night in March 1964. On that evening, at least 38 neighbors in a New York City apartment watched a young woman being stabbed to death. It took her assailant more than half an hour to murder her, and not a single witness so much as lifted the telephone to call the police. There could have been no misunderstanding of what was going on. From the victim's struggle and her cries of terror it was perfectly clear what was happening to her, yet no one made the slightest move to help in any way. This classic example of the lack of altruism has been called the Genovese case, after the murdered girl,

Kitty Genovese (Milgram & Hollander, 1964; Rosenthal, 1964). The case received a great deal of publicity and triggered a torrent of speculation in the press and among psychologists about the causes of such lack of altruism.

Events such as these, increasingly common in contemporary society, have stimulated research on the development of altruism and on the conditions which elicit and maintain it. How do children develop into caring people who will aid their fellows in distress and those who are less fortunate? What are the conditions most likely to assure that the capacity to help will be employed? These are the kinds of questions to which this research has been addressed.

As it has been defined by those who have attempted to study it scientifically, altruism refers to action that is freely directed to the well-being of other people. *Altruism defined* It involves behaviors such as sharing, helping, aiding, and donating.

The tendency to behave toward peers in altruistic ways increases with age over the preschool years, but much less dramatically than other forms of interpersonal relationships. This hesitant development of altruistic action is often considered another manifestation of the egocentric orientation of young children (Hartup, 1970). Changes in altruistic behavior may be related to the developing ability to take the point of view of another person, which seems to increase directly with age (Fry, 1967). A number of studies have demonstrated that altruistic behavior, such as sharing and generosity, also increases with age (Handlon & Gross, 1959; Midlarsky & Bryan, 1967; Ugurel-Semin, 1952). Sharing is sometimes postulated as the basis of the later development of a generosity value (Fischer, 1963).

Ugurel-Semin studied sharing among Turkish children at different age levels. The children were confronted with a task in which they had to work out a strategy for sharing an odd number of nuts with another child. The younger

children, those from four to six years old, tended to keep the extra nut for themselves, while by the age of eight there was a tendency to divide the nuts evenly
and give the extra one to the experimenter. Older children were likely either to
give the extra nut to the other child or to give it to the experimenter. At least
with this population of children it was also found that the children from larger
families tended to be more generous than those from smaller families (Ugurel-
Semin, 1952).

There are a variety of reasons suggested to explain why sharing and generosity
increase with age. The most direct explanation is that the older child has had
a longer period of time, and thus more opportunities, to learn the values of the
culture. An alternative explanation postulates that this change results from a predetermined sequence of stages of moral judgment (Kohlberg, 1963). The change
involved in this instance is explained by Kohlberg's notion that the basis for
moral judgment shifts from one based on hedonistic concerns to the "good boy"
morality, in which social approval influences judgments.

Altruism and SES Investigators have also wondered if there are differences in altruism among
members of different socioeconomic classes. Unfortunately, the only study of
social-class differences in altruism in children younger than adolescents is badly
flawed (Doland & Adelberg, 1967), and no clear conclusions can be drawn. It has
been hypothesized that children from an economically favored background
would be more likely to practice generosity than poor children, because the
middle-class children would have had more opportunity to observe generosity
practiced by others, and that they would have received in the past more reinforcement for practicing generosity themselves. Unfortunately, the poor children
who were studied were mostly black and the middle-class children were white.
All of them were expected to share with a white child. Clearly then, conditions
were not comparable for the two groups studied. Moreover, the basic hypothesis
does not seem reasonable. One of the authors has had numerous opportunities to
observe poor Mexican-American children in school situations where some treat
was distributed. The number of children who insisted on taking their treat home
to share with brothers and sisters was truly impressive. It seems much more
reasonable to suppose that the value of sharing is transmitted according to the
cultural norms which are dominant in the child's home. This assumption finds
support in research showing that family values are reflected in the altruistic
behavior of their children. Families which practice altruism and give support
to the expression of affect are most likely to produce children who have concern
for others. Children from families which stress competition and which are concerned with the satisfaction of their status needs seem to engage in less helping
behavior (Bryan & London, 1970).

*Incentives
and altruism* Beyond such general information about family characteristics which may influence altruism, little is known about the specific mechanisms by which altruism
is developed in children. Most of the empirical studies on children's altruistic
behavior have been addressed to eliciting succorant behavior rather than to
identifying how such behavior is learned (Bryan & London, 1970). Reinforcement
practices, for example, might be expected to increase the strength of altruistic
behavior, since reinforcement practices have been demonstrated to be effective
in influencing such a wide range of social behaviors. It is interesting to learn,
then, that social approval, praise, approving pats and hugs, and the like do not
seem to be effective in influencing children to sacrifice *material goods* (Fischer,
1963; Midlarsky & Bryan, 1967). It appears that such social reinforcement may
be most influential in influencing children when the acts involved are relatively
effortless, or involve no material cost or sacrifice on the part of the child. While

social reinforcement appears to have little effect on altruistic behavior in children, material incentives do influence their sharing. Three- and four-year-old children are apparently willing to share their marbles when reinforced with bubble gum, but not in response to verbal reinforcement (Fisher, 1963).

Altruistic behaviors in young children may also be enhanced through the vicarious conditioning of positive affect (Aronfreed, 1968). Imagine a situation in which a child gives some valued commodity, such as candy, to another person —say a parent. Visualize further that when the parent receives the candy he gives expressions of joy and performs some act designed to bring about positive affect in the child-donor—say giving the child a hug and a smile. The assumption is that the pleasure of the recipient of the child's donation will come to elicit positive affect which on repeated occasions has been associated with such expressions of pleasure. Children may then in the future sacrifice something which they like in order to produce joy in the recipient, which presumably makes them feel good themselves, and therefore functions as a reinforcer for generosity. This general hypothesis has been substantiated in a number of studies (Bryan & London, 1970). In this manner the child seems to develop empathy—the capacity to find pleasure in the pleasure of another person, and empathetic affective experiences such as this seem to play an important role in promoting altruistic acts on the part of children. It has been shown that when children were instructed to think happy thoughts, that is, to experience positive affect, sharing increased. Thinking sad thoughts had the effect of decreasing affect (Moore, Underwood, & Rosenhan, 1973).

Affect and altruism

Empathy and altruism

One of the most powerful ways of influencing the development of altruism in children seems to be through the provision of models displaying such behavior themselves. Since most adults attempt to influence children by giving them direct verbal instructions or by preaching about the value of helping others, it is interesting to contrast the relative effects of *telling* children how they should behave, as compared with providing them with *opportunities to observe* others performing desired acts. One study (White, 1967) is especially interesting because it examined the long-range consequences of differential attempts to influence altruism. Admittedly "long-range consequences" in this context means only over a few days period of time, but even this is a decided improvement over most laboratory studies of altruistic behavior in which outcomes are assessed only immediately following the experimental manipulation. In this study the fourth graders who participated played a bowling game in which they could win gift certificates. They could behave in an altruistic way by donating some of their winnings to an orphanage. Some of the children were instructed to donate half of the gift certificates they won in the bowling game to an orphanage. Others observed a model donate his winnings, and then they had an opportunity to donate in the presence of the model donor. Another group of children observed the model and then had a chance to donate, but they were not watched. The control group neither received instructions nor observed a model-donor. When left alone to play the game and donate immediately after the initial sessions, the children who donated the most were those who had been given the direct instruction to donate to the orphanage. The results of the experiment suggested that the children who were given a direct instruction to donate did so during the *initial* test session, apparently accepting the instruction as a rule of the game. The longer term outcomes, however, showed greater charity, especially among girls, among those children who watched a model donate, and then themselves had an opportunity to donate while being observed. This study should serve to remind us that the effects which seem most powerful immediately after an experi-

Models and altruism

ment may not be those that are most durable. This study and several others have also demonstrated that behavioral example is a much more effective way of influencing children's self-sacrificing behavior than are commands or moral exhortations (Bryan & London, 1970). The generality of findings relating to the effectiveness of behavioral example has been demonstrated with studies cutting across a wide variety of settings, diverse populations, and different kinds of tasks. It has been shown consistently that altruistic behavior can be significantly increased through the provision of models who display examples of the desired behavior.

If we ask the question *Are children more likely to behave as they are told, or as they see others in their environment behaving?* the answer clearly favors modeling. The old admonition *Do as I say and not as I do* is a loser. Yet one often hears parents instruct their children to do just that. Beyond the fact that children are clearly more apt to do as they see their parents do than they are to follow instructions, are there any other effects of lack of consistency between what models actually do and what they profess? This is an important question, because the hypocrisy of the older generation is often given by young people as a reason for abandoning their values. This question has been addressed in an interesting and important series of studies (Bryan, 1970). These investigations are important because in real life children are probably exposed to more situations in which there is inconsistency between what people do and what they say than to situations in which words and deeds are congruent. In order to study the effects of consistency and inconsistency between the practicing and preaching of models, some children were exposed to models who preached charity but practiced greed. Other children were exposed to models who preached greed, but in fact behaved in a charitable manner. In these experiments, the children played a bowling game in which they could win something of value so that they would have something of worth to contribute. Both adult and peer models have been used in these studies. The adult models were presented live, and the child models on videotape. The children observed the model playing the bowling game. The model who practiced charity placed one-third of his winnings in a canister each time he won. The models who practiced greed simply took their winnings with them upon leaving the room, in the case of live models, or conspicuously placed the winnings in their pockets in the case of models presented via videotape. Some models practiced charity but preached greed, others practiced greed while preaching charity, while other charitable and greedy models practiced what they preached. Preaching charity involves making statements such as *It is good to give to the poor children* or *I am going to give to the poor children* or *One should give to the crippled children* or some other statement to that effect. Those who practiced greed made the same statements, except that a negative was inserted into the appropriate position in the sentence. The preacher of greed would say something like *It is not good to give to the poor children* or *I am not going to give to the poor children*.

The interesting and consistent finding from this series of investigations is that when a model preaches charity but practices greed, or vice versa, the children's own behavior is influenced by what the model does and not what he says. Their opinion of him, however, is influenced more by what he says than by what he does. To children in grades two through four the hypocrisy does not seem to be apparent. In fact, the model who preaches charity but practices greed is likely to be evaluated as having been more generous than was the case. Consistency, or the lack of it, seems not to effect the child's own self-sacrifice, honesty, or evaluations of the model. Moreover, when interviewed about the value of charity,

Showing concern for others is a form of altruism.

most children agreed that one should give, although few of them did so. Bryant summarizes the outcomes of these studies by saying that:

> From these and other studies, it is clear that behavior is affected by modeling, but apparently neither boys nor girls are affected in their behavior by the exhortations of the model. Moreover, it is becoming clear that the cognitions of the young child concerning his social responsibilities, as indicated by his preachings and by his reactions to transgressors, bear only slight relationship to his behavior. It does appear, however, to be a just world as one can be assured that children's standards for consistency for others do not exceed those they hold for themselves. (Bryan, 1970, p. 72)

These conclusions are consistent with those from a very ambitious study of learning concern for others in preschool children (Yarrow, Scott, & Waxler, 1973). Preschool children ranging from three and one-half to five and one-half years of age were given training in giving help to a person or animal in distress. Unlike typical laboratory studies, in which subjects are often exposed to a very brief experimental treatment, one at a time, in this research small groups of children (six to eight in a group) were exposed to different training procedures under real-life conditions of a nursery school. The intervention was spread over a two-week period of time, with different groups of children being exposed either to a high-nurturant or low-nurturant adult who modeled sympathetic helping behavior. Nurturance meant that the adult caretaker initiated friendly interactions with children, offered them help and support freely, expressed confidence in the children's abilities, was sympathetic and protective, and responded to their bids for attention.

The training for part of the sample was carried out with symbolic materials, such as pictorial and diorama representations of distress situations. Other children were trained with both symbolic and behavioral situations of distress. The effects of training were assessed after two days and again two weeks following training. The children's recollections of the experiment and their concepts of helping were assessed six months later.

The results of this experiment are very instructive for a number of reasons. Most studies of altruism in young children involve a single measure of experimental effect. Normally this measure is an experimental analogue designed to represent the real-world situation under consideration. A game-like format is usually employed. The assumption that the experimental task will influence behavior in the same way as conditions in the natural environment remains unexamined. The assumption that children will respond to a situation presented as a game in the same way they would react to the real-world counterpart is also open to question. Confidence in the generalizability of principles is enhanced when congruent outcomes from naturalistic and experimental research is accumulated, and when the information yielded by varied measures of the same class of behavior is in agreement.

*Multiple
assessments*

In Yarrow's study of learning of social concern in young children, multiple assessments, both symbolic and behavioral, were used. Had only the symbolic measures been used, the conclusions would have been quite different from those which were obtained. The training had a significant effect on symbolic altruism, and the degree of nurturance of the adult model had no influence on outcomes in the symbolic situation. When measured in realistic encounters with distress, however, the highest degree of helping behavior was displayed by those children who had prolonged experiences with nurturant adults who modeled giving assistance in both live and symbolic situations. The effects of the training proved to be durable, and the main results of this study, which involved middle-class white children, were for the most part replicated with another sample who were primarily black children from low income families.

From this and related research it seems evident that children may respond differently to symbolic situations than to real situations in which someone or something is in distress. Not only are outcomes likely to differ depending on the kinds of measures used, but the effects of training seem to be stronger when training employs behavioral situations as well as symbolic ones. One cannot assume that what is learned in an abstract situation will automatically generalize to related situations in the natural environment of the home, neighborhood, or classroom.

In spite of the incompleteness of our knowledge about the development of altruism, the existing knowledge does offer some wisdom for parents, and probably for teachers too, on the basis of evidence accumulated so far. This wisdom has been well stated in the following quotation.

If one were to extrapolate from the findings of this study to child rearing, one might conclude that the parent who is an altruist in the world but is cold with his child reaps a small harvest in developing altruism in his child. Further, the parent who conveys his values to the child didactically as tidy principles, and no more, accomplishes only that learning in the child. Generalized altruism would appear to be best learned from parents who not only try to inculcate the principles of altruism, but who also manifest altruism in everyday interactions. Moreover, their practices toward their children are consistent with their general altruism. (Yarrow, Scott, & Waxler, 1973, pp. 255-56)

Pets may play a role in children's learning to show concern for others.

There remains the question of why consistency between the provision of principles and modeling of altruism made no difference in the Bryant studies, but produced an additive effect in the Yarrow investigation. The answer may lie in that fact that the provision of symbolic examples in the Yarrow study involved more than a simple verbal admonition. Helping actions were represented in relation to symbolic situations, which may more clearly communicate to young children than words alone.

Role Taking

In the early days of Head Start, large numbers of preschool teachers were needed in a very short period of time to staff the new program. Many of the people who were hastily recruited into the training program for Head Start teachers either had some previous teaching experience with older children or in traditional nursery school settings. At least this was true of one community with which the authors are familiar. Very few of the new teachers had experience working with children other than those from middle-class circumstances. In many training programs, the newly appointed Head Start teachers were encouraged to establish housekeeping or dramatic play corners, in which children could play out various family and community roles. One teacher found that this provision for dramatic play worked all too well for her liking. A tiny preschool boy approached the entrance to the play area staggering and swaying in a manner that quite accurately depicted the unsteady gait of a home-bound daddy who had had too many drinks. A petite little girl who was already in the house grabbed a toy broom with reflexive quickness and drove the "homecoming" fellow away amid a stream of words in a language which the teacher was thankful not to comprehend. This was too much of a slice of life for this particular pedagogue, and a good deal of persuasion was needed to entice her not to dispose of the housekeeping equipment and abandon the dramatic play business for good.

Whether the children in this episode were identifying with the feelings of the parents whose roles they portrayed or whether they simply imitated specific behavioral forms they had witnessed is not a debatable point, since we have no further information on these particular children. The important point is that role taking does appear to be a capability required in the exercise of many forms of prosocial behavior. It seems to be inherent in acts such as cooperation and altruistic interaction. That does not mean that children's increasing ability to take roles *causes* altruistic behavior, but since changes in role taking and altruism occur in concert with one another, it appears that they are functionally related in some way (Hartup, 1970).

Age and role taking: conflicting views Piaget believes that the young child's egocentric orientation makes it impossible for him to take the roles of others. Moreover, very young children show great respect toward older children and tend to accept the laws and rules which they pronounce as immutable (although they may violate them at practically every turn). Furthermore, very young children show great respect toward older children, but as they grow older they gain greater equality with their interaction partners. They participate increasingly in applying rules and in making decisions concerning the modification of rules. This process is thought to assist the child in coming to a new notion of what rules are all about. As we showed in chapter 8, younger children tend to regard rules as absolute, as though they were handed down by divine authority. Participation in the application and modification of rules presumably assists the child's movement to the next stage of development (Piaget, 1932; Hoffman, 1970).

At the same time, another process which enhances the child's competencies for peer interaction is taking place. This process involves the learning of mutual role taking. The youngster learns, for example, that she is an individual, different from her peers in many ways. At the same time she learns that in many situations she thinks and feels as others do. The consequences of action may be similar for herself and others, and yet viewed from their differential vantage points these consequences seem very different. The development of this awareness contributes to the learning of mutual respect, which is required for the understanding of rules of interaction and for the development of respect toward rules as products of group agreement.

The ability to take roles, to put oneself in another's place, and to view things from the other person's perspective helps the child to understand the feelings of others. This is considered a major factor in the development of the child's ability to treat others according to the "Golden Rule" (Piaget, 1932; Hoffman, 1970), and Piaget and his followers believe this development is not generally completed until adolescence, or middle childhood at the earliest. Many other investigators do not agree with this conclusion.

Supporters of Piaget continue to argue that because children are so bound by their own egocentrism, they do not develop role-taking abilities until early adolescence (Chandler & Greenspan, 1972). Other investigators (Borke, 1971, 1972) counter this argument by saying that children develop emotional role-taking abilities when they are as young as three years of age. The reason that earlier investigators failed to reveal this, they claim, is that children's response capabilities are very limited. Young children's failure to display empathetic role taking in earlier studies has been a function of the situations used in testing, which were not appropriately designed to elicit those forms of role taking which are within the range of the young child's behavioral repertoire. By somewhat exaggerated analogy, it would seem ridiculous to argue that children do not develop psychomotor abilities until adolescence, on the basis of a test for psychomotor abilities that uses gymnastic performance on the high-low bars as the criterion.

The weight of recent research and theory on this issue seems to support Borke's position that age-appropriate forms of role taking are indeed manifested in very young children (Hetherington & McIntyre, 1975). Flavell (1973) has developed a model which postulates that the development of perceptual role-taking abilities follows a hierarchical stagelike sequence. At the earliest stage the child is not even aware that others have visual experiences. From that point of unawareness he gradually moves through a series of four stages to a level in which he can represent, first in qualitative and then in quantitative terms, how a perceptual array appears to another peer. There is some empirical support for this model (McIntyre, Vaughn & Flavell, 1973). This ability to represent the perceptions of another person is at least logically prerequisite to empathetic role taking.

Perceptual role taking

Additional support for the view that young children can take roles is provided in studies of children's communications. By the age of four, children adjust the form and style of their speech for different listeners (Gleason, 1973; Hetherington & McIntyre, 1975; Shatz & Gelman, 1973). On balance, the evidence at this point seems to indicate that Piaget's conclusions were influenced by the complexity of the tasks used in his investigations (Hetherington & McIntyre, 1975).

Role taking and communication

Leadership

Leadership refers to an individual's capability to influence the norm-setting and activities of others in a group in which there are differentiated roles (Hartup, 1970). For most parents and other caretakers of children, an implicit goal of socialization is that the children in their charge develop qualities that will enable them to assume positions of leadership in interactions with their peers, and that they also become able to make appropriate contributions to group goals when they occupy positions as followers. Yet though most parents may entertain hopes that their own children will attain positions of influence, folk belief has it that "leaders are born, not made." What then are the characteristics of children who seem to naturally ascend to leadership positions in their groups, and can these qualities be developed through experience, thus countering the assumption that leadership qualities cannot be acquired through learning and experience?

Most of what is known about leadership in children relates to the first of these two questions, while the literature of child development is conspicuously silent on the second issue. Experimental studies of leadership among adults and college students abound (Stogdill, 1974), but aside from some significant research on peer group dynamics among adolescents (cf. Sherif & Sherif, 1964), we know little about the conditions under which children may arise to a challenge and assume leadership status.

The major portion of the available information on this important topic comes from descriptive research based on systematic observation of children in play groups (cf. Partin & Newhall, 1943), and from a multitude of studies correlating leadership status with personality, intellectual, and demographic variables, such as social-class membership. In this section we will consider the knowledge of leadership in children's groups provided by research information on the correlates of leadership.

Events or characteristics that are correlated have a systematic relationship to each other, but the fact that characteristics are correlated does not mean that one causes the other. A number of characteristics of individuals are correlated with leadership or the ability to influence others. For example, there is a rather small, but statistically significant, correlation between IQ and leadership status. But IQ accounts for a very small proportion of the variance in leadership status. That bit of information probably seems obvious to those readers who are careful observers of the national political scene.

Children who emerge as leaders are also generally perceived by their peers as sociable and competent with reference to group functions and objectives. Other qualities which seem to enhance a child's chances of exerting leadership influence, especially among boys, are superior strength in relation to their age-mates, athletic ability, aggressiveness, and assertiveness (Ausubel & Sullivan, 1970). Among boys, height is also correlated with leadership. How many short men have you seen become successful politicians?

An important and consistent relationship that has been found in a number of studies is the association between popularity and leadership. Studies of the relationship between these two qualities have yielded correlation coefficients between .50 and .80, with most of the studies yielding correlations in the low .70's (Hartup, 1970). These are among the highest correlations obtained between leadership and other variables. Even then, the relationship between popularity and leadership accounts for only about 25% to a little over 50% of the variance in these characteristics. That leaves about half or more of the variance in these qualities unexplained, and prompts us to ask what other influences account for the remainder of this variability, and how stable leadership status is across situations.

These findings do suggest that some of the characteristics influencing popularity may also enhance the individual's chances of becoming a leader in her group. Other things being equal, children who are sociable, friendly and outgoing—those qualities which influence popularity—would have a better chance to assume leadership than children without these qualities. But groups differ in their goals and functions, and the child who displays competence in the skills required to achieve group ends is more likely than a child lacking those competencies to emerge as a leader (Kobayashi & Saito, 1958). Competence in performing those functions characteristic of the group then surely accounts for some of the variance unaccounted for by the relationship between popularity and leadership.

Children also differ in their specific skills for exerting influence on others, and different children employ different strategies. Observations of young children in nursery school settings have revealed that some young leaders achieve their status through strategies of force—by bullying their peers around. Others use the early counterparts of skills of diplomacy, and influence their peers through suggestion and compromise. Some of these differences in style may be seen in excerpts from the conversations of children identified for their "artful" style of influence, or for their contrasting mode of "forceful" influence (Partin & Newhall, 1943).

Diplomat
"Joan, you can give me a ride on the back of yours [kiddy car] and Lawrence can give me a ride on the back of his." Or in the dramatic play situation in-

volving a circus: "Gwendolyn, what do you want to be with the wagon?" "Helen, what do you want to be?" "Do it some more, Helen."

Bully

"Are you doing what I tell?" "Don't put it down." "Stop, we have to go to the battery shop. Come in and say you want a battery." (Partin & Newhall, 1943, p. 521)

It was found that the bully represented in these conversation excerpts was restricted in his influence to relatively few children. He concentrated his influence on "his gang," while the artful diplomat exerted leadership over more children.

There is a degree of cross-situational stability in leadership among children (Hartup, 1970). This seems particularly true during the preschool and elementary school years. Then, after a period of less stability than seems to be associated with the rapid changes of the pubescent period, some stability in leadership patterns seems to be regained. This cross-situational stability probably results, at least in part, from the influence of popularity on leadership choices. But as children become more sophisticated they come more and more to make leadership choices on the basis of the functional requirements of the situation rather than upon popularity and friendship (Ausubel & Sullivan, 1970). Leadership becomes very specific to situations. The leader in athletics may not be the one looked to for guidance in planning a group study project.

Cross-situational stability and specificity

The fact that situational specificity of leadership is a function of the task before the group came through graphically to one of the authors, who spent part of the period during which this book was being written in a beach community on Monterey Bay in California. His children, having come from the desert, had little previous experience with the ocean. They took to life by the sea with gusto and spent a substantial amount of time fishing and crabbing from the wharf. One undersized child, who almost seemed to live on the wharf, was exceedingly knowledgeable about things such as what bait to use, what size hooks were appropriate, how often to pull up your crab net, what kind of fish you had when you were lucky or skillful enough to catch one, and all sorts of related things that are important to fledgling fisher-persons. The boy's influence was unchallenged among the temporary peer groups which sprung up on the wharf. Yet his language was ungrammatical, his academic prowess moderate, and his leadership, therefore, limited to the seaside.

It is most unfortunate that the bulk of our knowledge of leadership rests upon studies which describe the status quo. There is a tremendous need for field experiments in which conditions are manipulated to identify specific means by which parents and educators might expect to facilitate the development of those interpersonal and situational skills which enhance children's opportunities to experience group roles both as contributing members and as leaders. One way to develop children as leaders might be to assure that they experience a variety of situations in which opportunities are provided for the exercise of leadership skills. Such opportunities may constitute necessary but not sufficient conditions. Through direct instruction and role playing it seems quite possible that children could learn to exercise the competencies required of group leaders. Beyond a need to identify means of teaching the competencies required of leadership, it is probable that in a pluralistic society children from various population groups may have unique skills and abilities which could contribute to group objectives. Virtually nothing has been done to identify ways in which these resources

can be used to maximum group advantage. We will explore these issues further
in our discussions of institutions of socialization in chapter 12.

Aggression

Under certain circumstances aggression may be perfectly appropriate social
behavior, but under other conditions it is inappropriate and runs counter to
social goals. A considerable amount of contemporary social concern is concentrated on inappropriate expression of aggression, a concern accompanied by a
high interest in the identification of those conditions which promote violence
and aggression, and those measures which may be effective in its control.
Whether there has actually been an increase in aggression against persons
and property, or whether what we have witnessed simply reflects more effective
reporting and the effects of instant mass communication is not at issue here.
What is at issue is that large numbers of Americans *perceive* an increase in
aggression, regard it as one more sign that their country is "going to hell in a
handbasket," and have elected numerous public officials on the basis of their
promises to do something about it. Citizens are concerned, and with what little
optimism they have left, some look to psychology for some information that
may prove useful in righting the situation. If the current situation is out of hand,
how can the children being reared now be guided to develop into nonaggressive
adults, or who at least can channel their aggression into socially approved
activities?

A reflection of the profession's response to this kind of concern comes in the
form of a recent *Review of Child Development Research* (Caldwell & Ricciuti,
1973) which had as its central concern the influence of child development
research on social policy, and which featured an integrative review on "The
Control of Aggression" by a noted authority in the field (Berkowitz, 1973).
Aggression, it turns out, is a very complex phenomenon. In this section we will
present some of the information on this complex topic which has emerged from
research and theory on the causes of aggression, and the conditions which may
prove useful in its control.

Frustration-
aggression
hypothesis

Causes of aggression. Until very recently the frustration-aggression hypothesis
dominated theorizing and research on aggressive behavior (Dollard et al., 1939).
This hypothesis is reflected in the Freudian conception of the perpetual conflict between humans' inner instincts and the frustrating barriers which social
realities place in the way of the expression of these impulses. It is also
evident in drive-reduction learning theory. Dollard and his associates contended
that:

1. all frustrations increase the probability of an aggressive reaction, and
2. all aggression presupposes the existence of prior frustrations.

Aggression was considered the natural, unlearned response to frustration. The
research generated by the frustration-aggression hypothesis has therefore been
primarily concerned with the effects of frustration on aggression, the ways in
which aggressive responses to frustration may be inhibited, sublimated, displaced
to persons or objects other than the frustrator, or diffused through fantasy activity.
Under the influence of this hypothesis, studies of child rearing were launched in
an attempt to identify the kinds of frustrations presented to growing children
in various societies and to determine the influence of these events on adult
character (Whiting, 1941). Since frustration was assumed to be the primary
factor influencing the expression of aggression, little was done to reveal the
mechanisms by which complex patterns of aggressive behavior are learned.

Pro-social development takes many forms.

The main contentions of the frustration-aggression hypothesis failed to deal with the fact that people learn many, if not most, of their complex aggressive response patterns under nonfrustrating conditions. The social learning point of view mentioned in chapter 8 postulates that aggression is learned under much the same conditions as other behaviors. Social-learning theorists stress that patterns of aggressive behavior are often learned under conditions where the intent to inflict injury is absent. Soldiers and hunters, for example, ordinarily perfect their skills through hours of target practice, and boxers learn their skills with punching bags and sparring partners where their main intent is certainly not to inflict injury on an offending source of frustration (Bandura, 1969).

This is not to say that frustrating circumstances cannot lead to aggressive responses. The record clearly shows that frustration may in many cases be at least a contributing factor. It is only that the original proposition is "too simple and too sweeping" (Berkowitz, 1973, p. 97). Nevertheless, the frustration explanation for aggression has a common-sense appeal which makes it the explanation of choice among many lay people. The means by which aggression may be expressed and controlled, as seen within the framework of the frustration-aggression hypothesis, therefore warrant consideration here, along with the ideas suggested by alternative points of view.

Expression and control of aggression. From Freud's point of view, personality is based on a dynamic energy system. With regard to frustration and aggression, frustration is thought to lead to the buildup of a reservoir of accumulated aggressive urges. Every reader has surely heard everyday expressions of this point of view. A teacher, for example, may explain to a visitor that a child who displays an unusually high frequency of aggressive behavior has a lot of "pent-up aggression." The assumption is that aggressive impulses must be let out regularly, or a really violent outburst might be expected. Aggressive behavior is presumably the natural outlet for this accumulated force. Situations evoking this explanation need not be even so extreme as that of the child in the previous example who periodically abuses those about him. It is often assumed that confining activities such as normal school work are unnatural, and over a period of time a number of small frustrations gradually add to the reservoir of aggressive urges which must be given periodic release through such means as physical activities at recess.

Dollard and Miller (1950) have a similar conception of the role of aggression in releasing accumulated inner forces, although their explanations are phrased in drive-reduction learning theory rather than psychoanalytic terms. In fact, much of their work represented an attempt to explain psychoanalytic observations and concepts within a drive-reduction learning-theory framework. According to the frustration-aggression hypothesis, frustration results in the accumulation of pent-up aggressive impulses, as we said before. Catharsis is the process by which *Catharsis* this pent-up energy can be drained off or dissipated. Direct aggression against the cause of one's frustration is, of course, one way to reduce the accumulated aggressive urges. For a number of reasons this is not always possible or prudent. Catharsis may therefore take many forms, including displacement, sublimation, and fantasy.

It may, for example, be unsafe, or at least unwise, for an adult to aggress *Displacement* directly against her boss, or for a child to release his aggression directly toward a parent or teacher. The drive theory of aggression therefore postulates that aggression may be *displaced* from the real or perceived source of frustration to "safer" targets. The result is often the familiar scapegoating phenomenon. A mid-management level employee whose goals have been blocked may take his frustrations out against his subordinates at work, or against his wife, children, or pets when he gets home. Children who are angry at their teachers or parents may "take it out on" a nonthreatening target, such as a younger sibling or peer. Entire groups of people who collectively hold powerless positions may be singled out as the source of one's woes. Some psychologists have suggested that displacement is the basis for racial prejudice and the aggressive scapegoating patterns often associated with it. The differences between the direct discharge of aggression and the elaborations which come with displacement and other cathartic processes are diagrammed in figure 9-2.

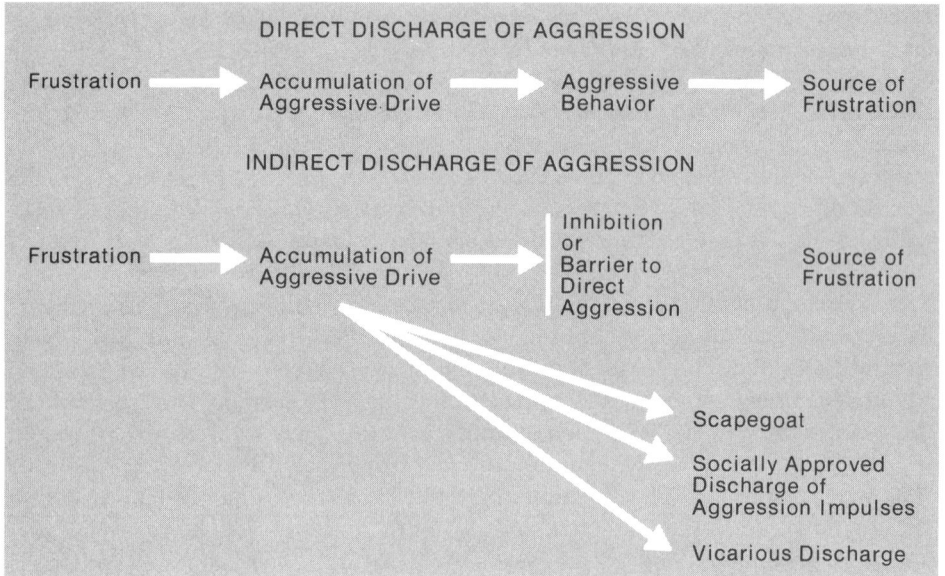

Figure 9–2   *Psychodynamic and drive-reduction conceptions of aggression.*

Procedures based on the displacement concept are sometimes prescribed as a means of reducing the inappropriate aggression of "acting out" children in schools and other child care settings. Punching pillows, for example, may be provided, and children are encouraged to give these inanimate objects a good pounding whenever aggressive urges come upon them. The evidence, however, does not seem to justify this procedure. The research shows that the frequency of aggressive behavior may increase under these conditions, rather than decrease (Bandura, 1969). It appears that about all this procedure may accomplish is to teach the child that aggression is an appropriate way to deal with problems, and aggression seems to generalize to other targets and situations.

Sublimation   Perhaps a better way to control aggression, from the drive-reduction point of view, is to channel aggressive energy into some constructive, socially approved activity. This is the process of sublimation, another form of catharsis. Aggressive energy can presumably be dissipated through such activities as enlisting in social causes or participating in sports. Illustrative of this point of view is William Menninger's (1948) claim that "competitive games provide an unusually satisfactory social outlet for the instinctive aggressive drive. . ." (cited in Berkowitz, 1973).

Sad to say, there is no conclusive evidence that competitive athletics do in fact reduce aggressive behavior. On the contrary, the evidence suggests that such activities are more likely to lead to even more aggression than they are to reduce it (Berkowitz, 1973). Any decline in overt aggression that seems to occur in association with the channeling of energy into socially approved pursuits may not be due to any cathartic process at all. Rather, as an individual becomes involved in an interesting activity, he is likely to cease to brood about real or imagined injustices he has suffered. It may simply be that the passage of time results in the dissipation of anger rather than that aggressive energies are channeled into the alternative channels.

Some writers have proposed that catharsis can be achieved through participation in fantasy activities. Those who subscribe to this view claim that reading *Fantasy* about violence or seeing it in sports or portrayed in films and on television will drain off the accumulated aggressive impulses of readers or viewers. At a common-sense level, anyone who has ever observed the audience at a hockey match might be inclined to have reservations about that assumption. Beyond common-sense judgment, while some of the research on this issue has shown no influence on aggressive responses resulting from the viewing of violence on television, most of the laboratory studies have demonstrated that increased aggressive responses in children may be induced by exposure to violence committed either by live or filmed models (Bandura & Huston, 1961; Bandura, Ross & Ross, 1961; Berkowitz, 1973). Investigations of imaginative play have shown that play with aggressive toys is likely to lead to an increased likelihood of open aggression rather than "draining off" aggressive urges presumably built up in the children (Berkowitz, 1973; Feshbach, 1956; Mallick & McCandless, 1966).

On balance, the rather large amount of available research on the effects of observed violence seem to justify Berkowitz's (1973) conclusion that

> rather than reducing aggression, filmed aggression can increase the likelihood that people in the audience will act aggressively themselves, and can teach them just how the violence should be carried out and even that some aggression is morally permissible. (p. 110)

If methods of controlling children's behavior through approaches based on the catharsis model are likely to be ineffective, or may even result in the increase of aggressive behavior patterns, what alternatives are open to parents, teachers, nurses, and others who hope to help children develop socially adaptive ways of dealing with problems that occur in interpersonal relationships? The first measure to occur to many people in caretaker roles is to punish the child *Punishment* for aggressive behavior, in spite of the fact that punishment is undoubtedly the least approved method according to advice columns written by psychologists and psychiatrists for popular magazines. There are good reasons for reservations about the use of punishment to control aggression, but the case is often oversimplified.

Parents who use frequent punishment to control their children's aggressions tend to produce children who are physically aggressive (Bandura & Walters, 1963). When parents model aggression as a means to their ends, children are likely to learn that physical aggression is an effective means of obtaining what one wants. The situation is not quite so simple as it appears on the surface, though. Various writers have pointed out that those parents who use punishment to control their children often possess other characteristics as well, which may have a contaminating influence on the relationship between children's aggressive behavior and the control procedures used by their parents (Berkowitz, 1973). For example, one investigator (Becker, 1964, cited in Berkowitz, 1973) has reported that parents who use physical punishment are also those who are least likely to provide positive reinforcement for appropriate behavior. They are also apt to display a generally hostile attitude toward their offspring and encourage their children to "stand up for their rights" in their relationships with other children.

There are additional issues which complicate the use of punishment as a control mechanism. Timing, for example, is crucially important. Berkowitz has concluded from the research on the timing of punishment that "we evidently would do far better to punish or rebuke a would-be aggressor immediately after he initiates his violent activity than after he completes his attack and achieves his aggressive goal" (p. 117). After all, once the goal has been attained, the goal-directed aggressive behavior has been reinforced, and whatever suppressing effects the punishment might otherwise have would be attenuated or canceled out.

The consistency with which punishment is administered is also important. Inconsistent punishment appears to contribute to further aggressive behavior. The reason seems to be that most children at least occasionally get their way by behaving aggressively. Aggressive behavior is therefore likely to be maintained on an intermittent reinforcement schedule, and behavior maintained on such a schedule is notoriously difficult to get rid of. This conclusion is supported by laboratory experiments (Walters & Brown, 1963) as well as by casual observation in the natural environment. Also, noncontingent punishment, or punishment which is delivered in such an inconsistent manner that the child has difficulty discriminating those behaviors which are not likely to be punished from those that are, is likely to lead to anxiety (Deese & Hulse, 1967).

Punishment is not a unitary stimulus having a uniform and predictable effect whenever it is used. Its effects are influenced by the context in which it occurs. Punishment may therefore be an effective control technique for some parents but not for others. Both naturalistic (Sears, Maccoby, & Levin, 1957) and laboratory studies (Parke & Walters, 1967) suggest that punishment seems to be an effective technique for mothers who are warm and affectionate toward their children, but not for mothers who are generally cold and hostile (Sears, Maccoby, & Levin, 1957).

From the many studies of conditions influencing the effects of punishment, it is clear that it can be a quick and effective suppressor of behavior under certain conditions. It can, however, have the unfortunate side effects of producing anxiety, avoidance of the punishment agent, and engendering more aggressive behavior which may generalize to new situations. As a general rule, aggression begets aggression, and it seems therefore very clear that punishmnt should be used with caution.

Nonpunitive control measures

Berkowitz (1973) has suggested a number of nonpunitive measures for controlling aggression, based on his extensive studies of this topic. Since aggression is often maintained because it gets attention and obtains results for the aggressor, it is often advisable to simply avoid responding to the aggression. Nonresponsiveness has been demonstrated to be effective in reducing such aggressive types of behavior as children's tantrums (Brown & Elliot, 1965) and hyperaggressiveness (Redel & Wineman, 1957). Ignoring aggressive behavior can have its limitations, though, because nonresponsiveness can be interpreted as an indication of approval or lack of parental concern, and extreme permissiveness can foster aggressive behavior in children (Becker, 1964). Berkowitz (1973) suggests that if aggressive behavior persists, the child should be quickly removed from the situation that instigated aggression, and that this action be combined with an explanation of why the behavior was wrong. Consistency is of utmost importance.

Eliminating aggressive behavior by ignoring it may be a very slow and risky way to control violent or otherwise aversive behavior in children, first, because the behavior is likely to be maintained by positive reinforcers not under the adult's control, and second, because there are times when the most determined parent may have trouble withholding attention consistently. It is easy to understand the good intentions of the parent who resolves not to give in to her offspring's demands for candy or rides on the mechanical horse on the next trip to the supermarket, but we can sympathize with her when she has trouble following through. Imagine a child having a tantrum in the aisles of the store, rolling about on the floor, kicking the cereal boxes from the shelves. It is awfully hard to ignore that behavior, especially when the other shoppers are congregated at either end of the aisle staring at you and your troublesome tot. The parent is in a real bind, because once she gives in, the tantrum behavior will become more intense and persistent on the next occasion.

A probable solution to this dilemma, suggested by social learning theory and research, is to strengthen or elicit responses that are incompatible with aggression (Bandura & Walters, 1963). The child going to market can be given a task for which she accepts responsibility, with reinforcement to be contingent upon her carrying it out.

Moreover, feelings such as guilt, shame, or sympathy may also have a suppressing effect on aggression. Calling attention to the harmful effects of aggression on innocent persons, for example, may serve to reduce the likelihood of violence.

The observation of aggression, whether live or filmed, may lead to the imitation of violence by the observers. A number of studies have shown, however, that defining or labeling witnessed aggression as "bad," "immoral," or "unjustified" may inhibit subsequent aggression (Berkowitz, 1973).

Research has also shown that those parents who have well-socialized and self-controlled children are those who are likely to reason with their offspring when disciplining them. Reasoning seems to help children learn to anticipate the consequences of their actions for themselves and others. When parents reason with their children, explaining the harmful effects of their behavior on others and identifying alternative ways of dealing with the situation that instigated the misbehavior, the children are likely to use reasoning (Berkowitz, 1973).

Behavioral examples can also be provided to teach appropriate modes of responding and dealing with problems. It is probably best to use positive examples of behavior to be emulated, rather than to call attention to examples of behavior to be avoided (Bandura & Walters, 1963). Behavior may be temporarily suppressed through examples of the punishment of forbidden behaviors, but the effects are generally short lived and the longer range consequences may be that previously unthought of behaviors become available for later aggressive acts.

A last and most important point to note is that aggression may be reduced by making aggression-evoking stimuli unavailable. Stimuli which have been associated with aggression can elicit aggressive responses under certain circumstances. To a person who was not angry, for example, a gun would not be likely to elicit an aggressive act, but given the readiness produced by anger, the situation may be quite different. Research has shown that giving children toy guns to play with increases aggressive responses in other play situations (Feshbach, 1956). The presence of weapons in the environment can affect adults and adolescents similarly (Berkowitz & LePage, 1970). As Berkowitz so aptly puts it,

> An angry person can pull the trigger of his gun if he wants to commit violence, but the trigger (i.e., the sight of the gun) apparently can also pull the finger, or otherwise elicit aggressive reactions from him, if he is ready to aggress and does not have strong inhibitions against it. (p. 132)

SOCIAL AND COGNITIVE INFLUENCES

To this point the present chapter has presented information on some of the ways in which children learn to interact with each other and with adults. We have stressed characteristic peer interactions, and some of the conditions which influence the development of the capabilities and favored ways of responding which are involved in these relationships. Clearly, the changes which occur in children's social behavior are closely tied to the development of other capabilities, such as cognitive and sensory-motor skills, and the ability to control impulses (Hartup, 1970). We turn now to a closer examination of those social and cognitive processes directly influencing the development and expression of social behaviors such as those which have been discussed in this chapter.

The social behaviors discussed in this chapter are often regarded by lay people and by some psychologists as aspects of personality. The teacher says, "Sean is an aggressive child," and "Ralph is uncooperative." Mary's mother is concerned about her "selfishness." As we indicated in chapter 8, trait and psychodynamic theorists regard such behavior as the result of internal dispositions which exert generalized influences on behavior. Trait theorists assume that these internal dispositions lead to consistency in the behavior of an individual, and influence him to behave in a consistent fashion across diverse situations. The literature clearly indicates that there is less cross-situational consistency in people's behavior than this view would suggest. Yet behavior is not random and under certain conditions people may behave in similar ways in different situations. Walter Mischel (1968, 1973) has carefully conceptualized some of the social and cognitive factors which may help to explain why behavior is often specific to situations, but may generalize across situations under certain conditions. Some of the ideas which he has brought to bear on this question are explored in this section.

Discrimination   What are the psychological processes which determine whether behavior will be consistent in varying situations, or whether it will be specific to situations? One important factor is surely the process of discrimination. While the lack of consistency in behavior across situations has often been attributed to faulty instruments or rating procedures used in the assessment of behavior, a more likely interpretation, one favored by social-learning theory, is that the situational specificity found in behavior is simply an accurate reflection of the fact that from an early age children learn to discriminate between those situations in which a given mode of behavior will be socially approved, reinforced, or at least not punished, from those situations in which the opposite contingencies would obtain.

Inconsistent, or situationally specific, behavior is regarded by some writers as a bad thing. The implication is that unless an individual behaves consistently he "lacks moral fiber," or is "two-faced." Quite the contrary, there are often very good reasons for behaving differently in one situation than in another, and the children who for some reason cannot discriminate the difference may find themselves in real difficulty. Moos (1968, cited in Mischel, 1973) has forwarded the persuasive proposition that

> . . . diminished sensitivity to changing consequences (i.e., indiscriminate responding) may be a hallmark of an organism coping ineffectively. In fact, indiscriminate responding (i.e., "consistent" behavior across situations) tends to be displayed more by maladaptive, severely disturbed, or less mature persons than by well-functioning ones. (p. 258)

Discrimination learning is an important component of the development of all the social behaviors considered in this chapter. If the information and contingencies provided by the environment are relatively consistent, children soon learn to discriminate between those situations in which a given behavior is appropriate, and those in which it is not. They learn that physical aggression is strongly disapproved in some situations, in relationships with younger siblings for example, but approved and encouraged in certain sports and games. Hopi Indians may be highly cooperative among themselves, but cooperation is not automatically extended to members of other groups. Experience has shown them that the consequences of cooperation with the white man may be to lose more than you gain.

Various behaviors are differentially reinforced for boys and girls, with the result that differences in sex-role behaviors begin to emerge very early. In middle-class American society, for example, it has been the custom to begin to discourage dependency behaviors in boys at a rather early age, but to encourage dependency in girls. The dependency simply shifts from parent to spouse. This pattern still prevails, but may be undergoing rapid change. Some behaviors are approved for adults but disapproved for children, so there are discriminations based on situational differences that are based on age status. Sometimes people become confused when the cues associated with different situations are unclear. When an approved behavior for adults has been strictly punished during childhood, the new age-appropriate behaviors may be inhibited. Years ago Ruth Benedict (1938) pointed to such problems associated with the cultural conditioning of sexual behavior in American society. Such problems were presumably absent in societies having more consistent expectations across age levels.

Another factor influencing the consistency or inconsistency of behavior is the set of *expectations* an individual has acquired through previous experience. *Expectations* Children learn to expect given consequences in given situations. Their behavior is likely to be consistent across situations if the expected consequences for the behavior are the same for both situations, and different if anticipated consequences are dissimilar. If a young boy has received approval for his participation in conversations at home, but at school he has experienced aversive consequences for talking out, he may be a chatterbox with his family, and shy and silent at school.

The consequences associated with particular behaviors do not have invariant, *Values and* objective values. Different individuals place different subjective values on given *consequences* consequences of behavior. Children may work hard in one situation for which they have learned to place a high value on success, but may fail to apply themselves at another kind of task in which success has little subjective value for them. Teachers of Yaqui Indians in Arizona and in the state of Sinaloa in Mexico often criticize their charges for failure to apply themselves to their studies. Presumably both countries are moving toward greater appreciation of cultural pluralism, but the stereotype of the "lazy Indian" may still be heard. Yet the same children exert tremendous physical energy and endure for days with little sleep to play their designated parts and fulfill their obligations in the religious observances of the Easter season. The subjective values associated with academic and spiritual activities are of quite different orders. For a Mexican-American child in school, to take another illustration, approval from a Spanish-speaking adult of the same ethnic group may provide a more powerful incentive than similar approval coming from an Anglo-American (Garcia & Zimmerman, 1972).

These are only a few examples of the kinds of expectations which may influence a child's behavior. Whether or not he cheats on a test may depend on his estimate of the likelihood of being caught, or what the probable consequences might be if he is caught.

Many aspects of an individual's experience are idiosyncratic. Others may be shared to a degree among members of a particular cultural group. Idiosyncratic behavior patterns may be expected to the degree that stimuli have different acquired meanings for individuals with different learning histories. While the phenomenon of discrimination may lead to situation-specific behavior associated with individuals' differential expectations regarding the consequences of behavior in distinguishable situations, the companion process of generalization leads to similar behaviors in different situations where individual experience leads to the expectation of similar outcomes.

Generalization

These considerations deal with the manner in which stimulus conditions, the individual's perception of them, and the subjective value she places on them influence the situational specificity or cross-situational consistency of behavior. An obvious but important fact, which has not been made explicit so far, is that given these stimulus conditions, the individual must be able to perform the behavior in question. One of the major means by which social competencies are acquired is by observation. By observing both live and filmed models, and through the symbolic models provided in printed media, new capabilities can be acquired. The sorts of things which can be learned observationally cover an impressive range of diverse classes of behaviors and concepts, from simple motor behaviors, gestures, and mannerisms, to conceptual principles essential for linguistic capability and intellectual problem solving, to social and moral conventions which guide conduct.

Performance capability

The repertoire of cognitive and social capabilities which children acquire through behavioral example provide the raw material for the construction of new behaviors. The concept of behavioral construction emphasizes the active manner in which the individual organizes and transforms acquired information and capabilities, and constructs his reality. Obviously, the realities constructed by individuals are not completely idiosyncratic. On the basis of experiences which are widely shared within particular groups, members of these groups construct realities which are more similar to those of their cultural kin than to those of out-group members. These shared aspects of constructed realities provide the cultural themes and world views which differ from group to group (Mischel, 1973).

Behavioral construction

Just because an individual *can* construct a particular behavior gives no assurance that she *will* perform as she is capable. Children may be capable of constructing the behaviors required to achieve a group objective in a cooperative activity, and yet they may refuse to do it. Children learn to hit, bite, kick, and scratch at an early age, yet parents and teachers may feel relieved that most children refrain from employing these skills of aggression most of the time. Incentives are useful in determining what behavior an individual is capable of constructing, as distinguished from the behavior he typically displays. When a teacher tells a classroom full of children that they should try their hardest and do their best on

Incentives

a test, it would be foolhardy to assume that such an admonition would have the universal effect of calling forth maximum performance from all children. Remember that the function of an incentive is determined by its subjective value to the individual. For example, group incentives may be most effective for children whose native culture emphasizes group effort for group advantage, whereas children whose culture stresses individualistic competition may be most influenced by individual incentives (Kubany, 1971). These matters will be considered in greater detail in chapter 10. For the present, it is sufficient to say that the performance which children typically display may not be indicative of what they are capable of doing. The provision of incentives provides a means of distinguishing between typical performance and competence.

By employing those principles which seem clearly to lead to the development and the expression of social competence, it seems highly likely that a larger proportion of children could be helped to develop effective skills for social interaction. As matters stand, this aspect of development is largely left to chance, while the efforts of caretakers and educational planners are concentrated on facilitating cognitive development. A rich resource of psychological principles lies virtually dormant.

SUGGESTED READINGS

Bandura, A., Ross, D., & Ross, S. A. Imitation of film-mediated aggressive models. *Journal of Abnormal and Social Psychology,* 1963, *66,* 3-11.

Becker, W. C. Consequences of different kinds of parental discipling. In M. L. Hoffman and L. W. Hoffman (Eds.), *Review of child development research,* Vol. 1. New York: Russell Sage, 1964.

Benedict, R. Continuities and discontinuities in cultural conditioning. *Psychiatry,* 1938, *1,* 161-67.

Bryan, J. H. Children's reaction to helpers: Their money isn't where their mouths are. *Journal of Social Issues,* 1972, *28,* 61-73.

Gallimore, R., Boggs, J. W., & Jordan, C. *Culture, behavior, and education.* Beverly Hills, Calif.: Sage Publications, 1974.

Madsen, M. C. Developmental and cross-cultural differences in the cooperative and competitive behavior of young children. *Journal of Cross-Cultural Psychology,* 1971, *2* (4), 365-71.

Mischel, W. Toward a cognitive social learning reconceptualization of personality. *Psychological Review,* 1973, *80,* 252-83.

Yarrow, M. R., Scott, P. M., & Waxler, C. Z. Learning concern for others. *Developmental Psychology,* 1973, *8,* 240-60.

10

The Development of Personal Competence

the definition of attachment.

Bowlby's theory and the conditioning explanation for the formation of attachments.

Harlow's research on attachment.

the phenomenon of imprinting.

the definition of critical periods.

the attachment hypotheses of the cognitive interpretation of "fear of strangers" and "separation protest."

the definition of:
a. unconditioned stimulus.
b. unconditioned response.
c. neutral stimulus.
d. conditioned stimulus.
e. phobic reaction.
f. higher order conditioning.

the conditions contributing to the direct and vicarious acquisition of emotional reactions.

the relationship among physiological, cognitive, and social influence on emotional states.

psychoanalytic and conditioning explanations of phobias.

Maslow's hierarchy of needs, drive reduction, and psychodynamic explanations of motivation.

the needs postulated in Maslow's hierarchy, in order of their prepotency.

Hunt's theory of motivation inherent in information processing.

the role of conditioning in the development of achievement motivation.

socialization practices designed to develop intrinsic motivation for intellectual pursuits.

achievement motivation and affiliation motivation; the socialization practices and the probable social consequences associated with each.

the assumption that children with high N ach. are superior in school achievement to children with high N aff.

Mischel's approach to the study of ego strength and approaches using measures of indirect signs.

direct and vicarious influences on gratification preference patterns.

evidence for the influence of cognitive variables on delay of gratification.

the definitions and examples of impulsiveness and reflectiveness.

	Recognize or recall
	Compare and contrast
	Describe or demonstrate
	Evaluate

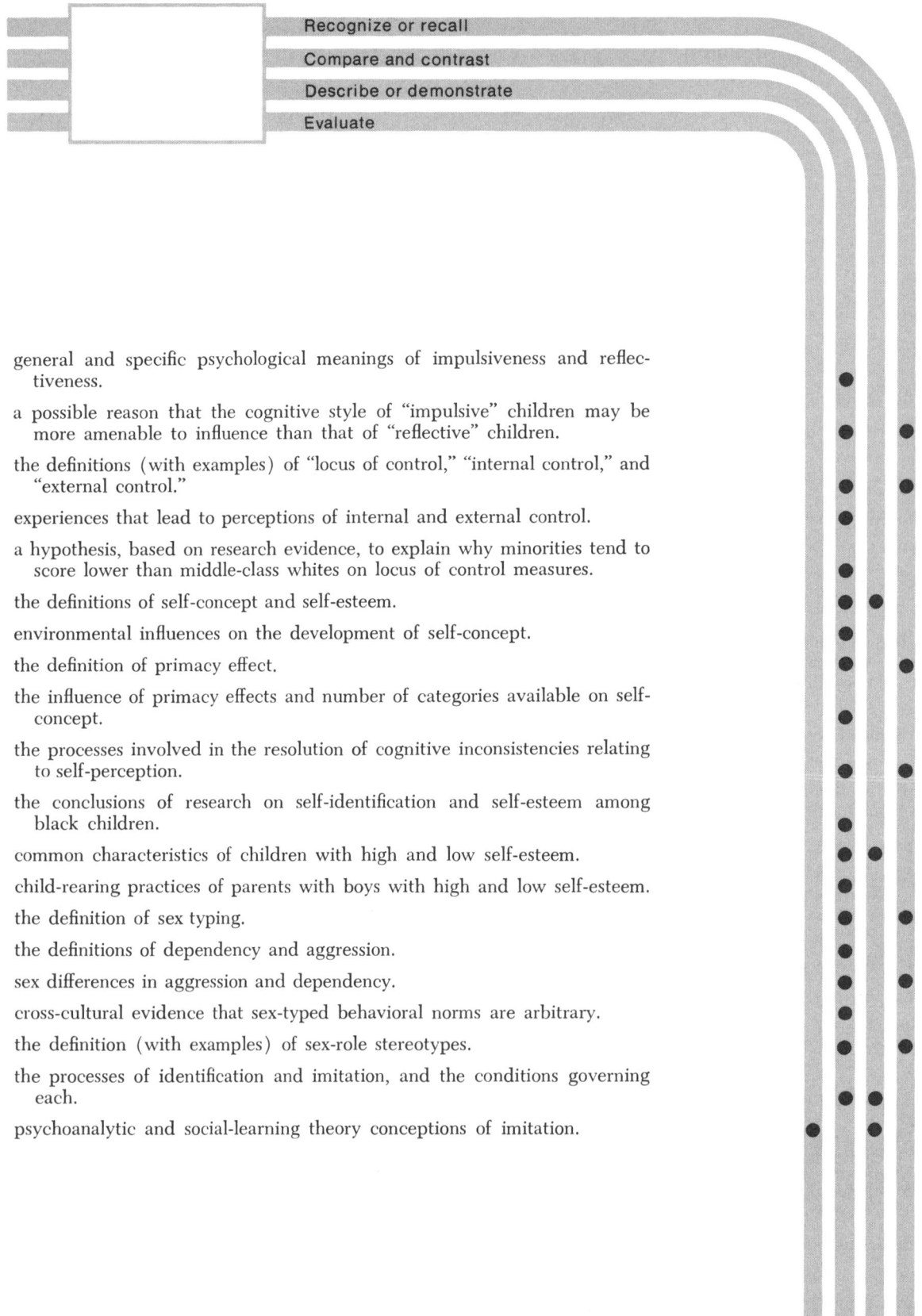

general and specific psychological meanings of impulsiveness and reflectiveness.

a possible reason that the cognitive style of "impulsive" children may be more amenable to influence than that of "reflective" children.

the definitions (with examples) of "locus of control," "internal control," and "external control."

experiences that lead to perceptions of internal and external control.

a hypothesis, based on research evidence, to explain why minorities tend to score lower than middle-class whites on locus of control measures.

the definitions of self-concept and self-esteem.

environmental influences on the development of self-concept.

the definition of primacy effect.

the influence of primacy effects and number of categories available on self-concept.

the processes involved in the resolution of cognitive inconsistencies relating to self-perception.

the conclusions of research on self-identification and self-esteem among black children.

common characteristics of children with high and low self-esteem.

child-rearing practices of parents with boys with high and low self-esteem.

the definition of sex typing.

the definitions of dependency and aggression.

sex differences in aggression and dependency.

cross-cultural evidence that sex-typed behavioral norms are arbitrary.

the definition (with examples) of sex-role stereotypes.

the processes of identification and imitation, and the conditions governing each.

psychoanalytic and social-learning theory conceptions of imitation.

CHAPTER CONTENT

Emotion

    Attachment

    Mechanisms of emotional development

Motivation

    Drive theory

    Maslow's hierarchy of needs

    Competence motivation

    Motives in information processing

    Achievement motivation

    Affiliation motivation

Self-regulation and impulse control

    Delay of gratification

    Impulse and reflection

    Locus of control

Self-concept

    Formation of self-concept

    Self-esteem

Sex-typing

    Dependency and aggression

    Sex-role stereotypes

    Sex-typing processes

Many people in this country find little pleasure in life. That is a distressing fact, but given the adversities which may strike during a lifetime most of us probably feel it is inevitable that some people should come to have little to gladden their hearts. The condition is less easy to dismiss when we see children who are tearful, anxious, persistently sad, and without joy. Yet there are such children, who by virtue of their poor choice of parents, race, social class, or school, have little chance for the carefree state of mind which epitomizes childhood. Well-balanced emotional development constitutes one personal competence which seems to contribute to effective interpersonal behavior. Children whose mental life is dominated by anxieties, hatreds, and fears have their energies drained away from productive pursuits, and the quality of their lives is depleted.

A well-balanced emotional development, then, constitutes a competence which should enable children to enjoy the good things that life sends their way, and to avoid being immobilized by the crises they encounter. How then do children learn to love? How do they learn to fear? What are the mechanisms by which the experiences handed one by the social environment result in the development of a capacity to feel sadness at the misfortune of another? In this chapter we shall explore information relevant to these questions.

There are other intrapersonal competencies which may enhance the growing child's capacity to enjoy the fruits of society, and to contribute productively to its well-being. The child must develop a motivational system which will influence him to expend effort at those pursuits beneficial to himself and others with whom he is associated. To be free of capricious influences the child must develop capabilities and response modes which increasingly enable him to regulate his own behavior in a socially responsible manner. The child must also develop an identity. He must know who he is and generally accept and value the self he discovers. He should know the appropriate behaviors associated with the social roles he occupies, such as his age and sex, but he, and perhaps for emphasis we should say *she*, must learn not to be unduly limited in her choices by arbitrary and socially stereotyped role expectations.

Like emotional development, these topics, motivation, self-regulation, self-concept, and sex-typing, designate areas of development which are relevant to intrapersonal competence. The conditions which facilitate or hamper the development of these competencies are embedded in our social institutions. We turn now to the first of these, emotion.

EMOTION

Emotions play an important role in the conduct of human affairs. They probably provide the spice that makes life not only palatable but at least occasionally, delectable. But emotion connotes psychic pain as well as pleasure. Substantial economic and human resources in contemporary United States society are devoted to the production and consumption of experiences designed to heighten various emotional states. The country and western music which increased in popularity during the 1970s depicts the everyday sorrows, woes, jealousies, and angers of "the common person," and evokes in many listeners vicarious emotional states. Songs like Bobby Bare's "Daddy, What If," evoke sentimental responses from many listeners, and when Bobby Jr. sings "Daddy, what if I stopped loving you . . . ," a few fans are even moved to tears. In the mid 1970s the movie industry turned to catastrophic and fearful events such as shipwrecks, earthquakes, and skyscraper fires to attract vast audiences. People, it seems, will pay good money to experience sorrow, fear, joy, and the entire spectrum of emotions in between.

While it has been traditional to speak of the pleasurable emotions as those which we try to prolong, and unpleasant emotions as those we try to avoid or terminate (Ausubel & Sullivan, 1970), even this common sense distinction requires qualification. Most assuredly, we try to avoid the fear that comes from walking dark streets that are frequented by muggers, but the "spook houses" that grace the concessions at community fund-raising events would soon be out of business if children did not actively seek a little fear. As with other aspects of development and behavior we have considered, situational influences must be taken into account.

The development of emotional maturity of the sort that would enable people to exercise their talents and to engage in affective relationships with other people, free of the debilitating effects of anxiety, is clearly important for the quality of life. For Freud (1963) it was the overriding goal of development. Yet there is no single theory which adequately integrates the phenomena that seem to influence the development of those qualities we call emotions. Moreover, even cogent definition of emotion is difficult, with most formal definitions merely substituting one abstraction for another. Emotion involves subjective states, such as love, hate, joy, depression, sorrow, fear, and euphoria. This brief list by no means exhausts the terms used by psychologists and lay people to designate subjective states. Emotion also connotes physiological arousal involving the autonomic nervous system, and a general lowering of response thresholds. Beyond this, the concept of emotion may best be elucidated at this point by providing examples of reactions that are considered emotional or affective, and by identifying some of the conditions which seem to influence the development of such reactions.

Attachment

One of the important events in the life of a young infant is the attachment that it forms for its mother and other significant caretakers. Many writers consider this attachment to be essential to the optimal emotional growth of the child. Attachment is defined as ". . . an affectional tie that one person forms to another specific person, binding them together over time" (Ainsworth, 1973, p. 1). Children who have experienced insufficient interaction with a mother figure are said to suffer from maternal deprivation. The long-term effect of prolonged and severe deprivation of maternal interaction during infancy and early childhood appears to be an inability to ". . . establish and maintain deep and significant interpersonal relations—that is, an inability to become attached" (Ainsworth, 1973, p. 53). A note of reservation should be added, however, because this conclusion is based primarily on research with children reared in institutions, and the institutional environment may present other inadequacies in stimulation for developing children which may contribute to the observed results of institutionalization.

Attachment defined

Maternal deprivation

A conditioning explanation. The traditional interpretation of an infant's attachment to its mother has it that the infant experiences pleasant sensations when its mother is present. These sensations have been thought to be related primarily to the reduction of tissue tension, especially hunger and thirst. When the baby is distressed, its mother appears and the discomfort of being hungry, wet, or thirsty is reduced. The pleasurable states resulting from the reduction of physical discomfort is regularly and predictably associated with the presence of the mother. Through a conditioning process, the pleasant feelings that formerly resulted from the reduction of physiological tensions come to occur in response to the mother's presence alone. Eventually, because of the similarity of the mother to other people, the love or attachment a child feels for its mother is presumably generalized to other people.

Harlow's research. Such a process may indeed account for some portion of the attachment process, but Professor Harry Harlow's experiments with rhesus monkeys have cast considerable doubt on the viability of this explanation. Over a period of years, Harlow and his colleagues conducted a number of ingenious experiments designed to discover how baby monkeys learn to love their mothers, and what happens when the conditions necessary for the development of affectional systems are absent (Harlow & Harlow, 1966; Harlow & Zimmerman, 1959). In an attempt to examine the hypothesis that the affectional tie of a baby to its mother is based upon feeding, these researchers constructed two types of mother surrogates for the young monkeys (see figure 10-1). One mother surrogate was made of wire and had fashioned into its chest a receptacle into which a feeding bottle could be inserted. The other type of mother was identical to the first, except that it was covered with terry cloth.

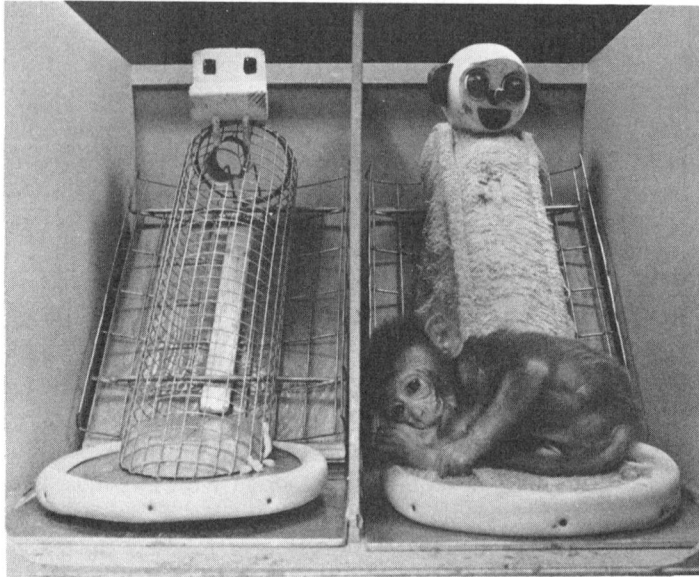

The baby monkeys had access to both mothers, but some were fed only on the wire mother, while others were fed by the cloth mothers. Harlow found that even the infants who were fed by the wire mother exclusively spent most of their time on the cloth mother, cuddling and clinging to her. They went to the wire mother who fed them only when they were hungry.

From this result it might be concluded that the infants developed a stronger affective tie to the mother who gave them tactile comfort, than to the one who fed them, but one type of evidence does not provide an adequate test of a hypothesis. A second set of tests was therefore designed to assess the infant monkeys' love for their mothers. A fear stimulus was constructed to frighten the baby monkey. What happens when an infant is frightened? It becomes tense and rigid and runs to cling to its mother if possible. That is just what Harlow's infant monkeys did. When confronted with a fearful mechanical contraption which moved, clattered, and flashed, the infants ran to their mother—not the mother who fed them—but to the cloth mother. Clinging to the mother visibly reduced the baby monkeys' tension. They clung less desperately to the terry cloth mother, relaxed their muscular tension, and some even made approach movements toward the fear stimulus, or made threatening vocalizations toward it.

Testing the affective bond

Another test of the affection of these infant monkeys for their surrogate mothers involved a situation in which a plexiglass barrier was placed between the infant and its cloth mother. A fear stimulus (see figure 10-2) was positioned between the baby and the mother, providing a stringent test of the infant's attraction to its mother. In order to get to its mother and gain whatever security she could offer, the baby had to pass near the fear stimulus. Babies who had been reared with a cloth mother ran right to the mother, even though to do so required that they approach the fear stimulus. Not only did they relax after their

initial clinging, but after being comforted by contact with the mother they left her side, engaged in exploratory behavior, and even examined and manipulated the fear stimulus.

Anxiety reduction and exploration

To young monkeys who had never known a cloth mother, the presence of one provided no relief from fear at all. Apparently, if young monkeys are deprived of the opportunity to exercise their clinging responses and to obtain tactile comfort during the early months of their lives they never develop the capacity for attachment at all. It would be risky to generalize directly from these experiments with monkeys to the development of attachment and affection in human infants, but

Typical response to cloth mother in the modified open-field test. (From H. F. Harlow & R. R. Zimmerman. Affectional responses in the infant monkey. Science, 1959, 130, 422. By permission of the publisher and Harry F. Harlow.)

Figure 10–2

Contact comfort may be important to a child's development.

early experience does seem to be important to human as well as to monkey infants.

Evolutionary basis for attachment.   There are differing opinions about the basis for the attachments which infants form for their caretakers. Some regard this development as being simply due to the nature of social interactions between the infant and those who care for him. Others (Ainsworth, 1973; Bowlby, 1969) propose that the roots of attachment are biological in nature. Bowlby (1969) maintains the position that human attachment behavior can be comprehended only within the context of Darwinian evolutionary principles. Briefly stated, attachment is seen as a genetically determined biological safeguard which has the effect of sustaining parental care throughout the period of immaturity. Attachment behaviors promote proximity, which serves to protect the infant from danger and enhance his chances of survival (Stayton, Ainsworth, & Main, 1973). Fear of separation is a natural cue to danger. In speaking of Bowlby's views on this, Stayton, Ainsworth, and Main (1973) have indicated that while situations such as separation are not in themselves dangerous,

> . . . they have been associated so frequently with dangerous situations throughout the evolutionary history of a species that fear behavior in response to them has been selected as advantageous for survival. For the human, as well as for a variety of other species, being alone is one natural clue to fear. (p. 213)

Imprinting.   Nature has provided various ways of keeping babies near their mothers. Consider the phenomenon of imprinting, for example. Greylag goslings and certain other species of fowl approach, follow, and become imprinted on the first moving object that enters their gaze during the first few hours after hatching. Thereafter the young fowl will follow their "mother," even if she does nothing for them by way of providing comfort or nourishment. But some fowl, mallards for example, will not unquestioningly accept the first living being they meet as their mother. Konrad Lorenz (1952), a famous comparative ethologist, learned that mallard ducklings have much more stringent criteria for choosing their parents. Lorenz found that infant mallards will accept as foster parents only those beings which have vocal expressions very similar to the mallard. Their demands do not end there, for they also refuse to pay attention to objects beyond a certain height. Lorenz found that tiny mallards would imprint on him if he uttered the appropriate sounds, while situated in a crouched position. As Lorenz (1952) tells it,

> This was not very comfortable; still less comfortable was the fact that the mallard mother quacks unintermittently. If I ceased for even the space of half a minute from my melodious "Quahg, gegegegeg, quahg, gegegegeg," the necks of the ducklings become longer and longer corresponding exactly to "long faces" in human children—and did I then not immediately recommence quacking, the shrill weeping began. As soon as I was silent, they seemed to think that I had died, or perhaps that I loved them no more; cause enough for crying! (p. 42)

In keeping with his obligations as a good foster parent, and in the interest of science, Lorenz subjected himself to this ordeal for hours on end. On one occasion he was leading his waddling charges through the garden when he glanced up to see a row of "dead white faces" staring over the fence at him. Their horrified expressions could be forgiven,

> For all they could see was a big man with a beard dragging himself, crouching, round the meadow, in figures of eight, glancing constantly over his shoulder and quacking—but the ducklings, the all-revealing and all-explaining ducklings were hidden in the tall spring grass from the view of the astonished crowd. (p. 43)

If the methods of the comparative ethologist [1] seem out of character with the descriptive and experimental modes of child study which we described earlier, a word of explanation from Lorenz (1952) may set things in perspective.

> The comparative ethologists' method in dealing with the most intelligent birds and mammals often necessitates a complete neglect of dignity usually to be expected in a scientist. Indeed, the uninitiated, watching the student of behavior in operation, often cannot be blamed for thinking that there is a madness in his method. It is only my reputation for harmlessness, shared with the other village idiot, which has saved me from the mental home. (p. 40)

Fortunately for the developmental psychologist it is not usual or customary to go to such lengths in the study of children's behavior. And fortunately for the survival of young mallards and kindred fowl, the first living being they encounter displaying the requisite visual and auditory qualifications is likely to be their mother.

Some 13 hours after hatching, ducklings no longer imprint. After that any object that is different from the attachment object will be avoided, amid calls of distress. From studies of imprinting, the conclusions of investigations such as Harlow's, and the findings that have been based on observations of children

---

1. An ethologist is a scientist who studies the behavior of animals in search of behavioral characteristics that are common to all members of a given species.

An infant reacts with pleasure toward her father, and with fear to a stranger. Intensity of fear reaction may depend on the degree of discrepancy in appearance between the stranger and familiar adults.

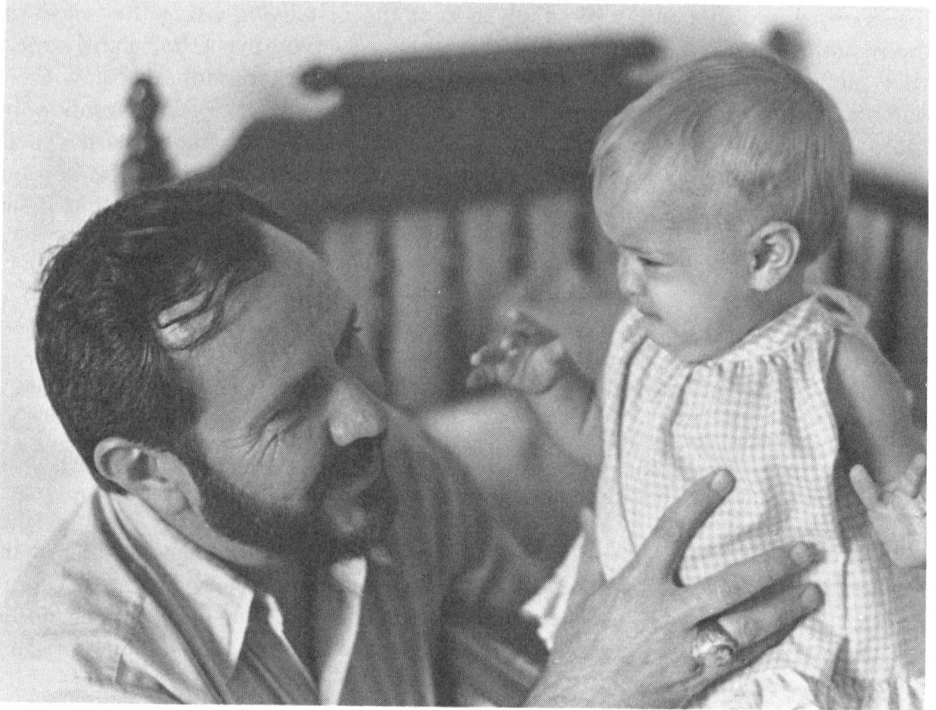

Critical periods

reared in institutional environments, some writers have concluded that for human children as well as species lower on the phylogenetic scale there are critical periods during which certain experiences must be made available to the children or certain aspects of development will never occur at all. The critical period hypothesis has often been applied (Yarrow, 1964) to explain the known relationship between maternal deprivation and future difficulties in forming permanent attachments. It is sometimes assumed that maternal deprivation will result in permanent impairment of the capacity to form relationships. This is probably overstating the case. The opportunity to form early attachments may be very important to an individual's future capacity to form close relationships with others, but it has not been demonstrated that the effects of limited opportunities to form early attachments are *irreversible* (Ausubel & Sullivan, 1970).

Fear of strangers. Mothers or other principal caretakers are rewarded by their infants by a variety of smiles, vocalizations of "pleasure," and other approach behaviors. During the early months these behaviors are also extended rather indiscriminately to others besides the mother or other principal caretakers. But not for long. Who has not seen a father embarrassed at the fact that his own infant cries when handed to him by the mother, or the hurt look of a grandparent whose overtures toward the infant are greeted by sobs and other signs of distress? This change is a significant development in the infant's relationships with other people (Morgan & Ricciuti, 1969). Fear of strangers emerges toward the end of the first year of life, usually sometime between eight and 10 months of age, and for that reason is sometimes referred to as "eight month anxiety" (Spitz, 1965).

Eight month anxiety

Some theorists, especially those with psychoanalytic leanings, have interpreted fear of strangers as evidence for the attachment bond between an infant and its mother. Current evidence does not seem to support this view since it is not at all clear that all infants who show signs of strong attachment to their mothers consistently display any fear of strangers (Ainsworth, 1973). Theorists with a cognitive orientation hypothesize that the fear results from the discrepancy between the child's established cognitive schemata and the unfamiliar objects represented by strangers. Many theorists of this persuasion appear to reject the view that at least some fears result from classical conditioning processes, an explanation which we will discuss later in this chapter. Rather, they see fears emerging spontaneously as new experiences present discrepancies from the memory traces or schemata earlier established for familiar object classes (Paradise & Curcio, 1974).

It seems clear that whatever the relationship between specific experiential and internal events that lead infants to come to fear strangers, the development must be mediated by individual differences which may include temperament. *Temperament* Not all infants show fear of strangers, and those who do differ in the intensity of their reaction. The role of temperament variables in the development of fear of strangers is suggested in Bronson's (1972) findings that strong distress reactions to startling events among three- and four-month-old infants were related to the early onset and maintenance of more intense reactions to strangers among older infants (cited in Paradise & Curcio, 1974). Clearly, cognitive development alone is not a sufficient condition for the development of fear of strangers in infants (Paradise & Curcio, 1974).

Separation protest. A second form of emotional reaction develops toward the end of the first year of a child's life. Beginning at about 10 to 12 months of age

Infant responses to separation from a parent vary. Some cry; others attempt to avoid separation by following.

and reaching a peak at about 15-18 months is a pattern in which children show signs of protest when their mother leaves the room, After this period the incidence of separation protest tapers off. The most obvious evidence of the child's distress is crying, and it is commonly believed that crying upon separation gives evidence of the child's attachment to its mother. Psychoanalytically oriented

Attachment hypothesis

theorists (Spitz, 1965) have generally regarded both separation protest and fear of strangers as different aspects of the same process—one in which the child becomes attached to its mother. A substantial amount of evidence now exists, however, to demonstrate that while both types of emotional reactions occur at about the same period in a child's development, they have independent courses of development and the onset of fear of strangers and separation protest do not coincide (Ainsworth, 1973). Moreover, it has been shown (Spelke et al., 1973) that even though babies spent much more time with their mothers than with their fathers, the children cried just as much when their father left them alone as when their mother did. More surprising perhaps was the fact that children with fathers who customarily interacted a great deal with them cried less when left alone by their father than did those children who had low rates of interaction with their fathers. It was conjectured that high levels of interaction with both parents may have led to cognitive advancement in these children.

Cognitive interpretations

Cognitive interpretations have been advanced as alternatives to the attachment hypothesis. One interpretation is that separation protest is a reflection of the child's level of cognitive development, and that it occurs because the mother's departure represents an event which he cannot assimilate or act upon. According to Piaget (1954), an infant is unable to search for an object which has disappeared until he reaches the fourth sensorimotor period. If this were true it would be expected that separation protest would relate to the child's development of object permanence. There is at least some tentative support for this position (Lester et al., 1974). The assumption is that separation protest begins when the infant has sufficient cognitive maturity to have a hunch about the location of the departed caretaker, but is unable to act on his thought or is frustrated in his attempts to recover the missing person (Lester et al., 1974; Spelke et al., 1973). There is some indirect evidence that infants who are cognitively precocious may be more prone than less cognitively advanced children to protest upon separation from a caretaker.

Criteria for separation protest

Crying or whimpering are ordinarily used as criteria for separation protest. Either in home or laboratory settings the mother leaves the room and the child is observed to see if he cries or whimpers. Crying and whimpering, however, are not the only possible behaviors which might be taken as signs of the child's protest over being separated from his mother. In one study (Stayton, Ainsworth, & Main, 1973) it was found that those infants who were capable of locomotion attempted to follow the mother about twice as frequently as they cried when the mother left the room. They were also more likely to greet the mother with pleasure upon her return than to cry when she left. Thus, while the evidence is indirect, it does

Positive reactions to separation

seem that children's reactions to separation represent attempts to regain proximity to her, and that these attempts are as likely to be active as passive.

The development of separation protest seems to follow a similar pattern of development across widely differing cultures, although the age of onset has been reported to be slightly earlier in Guatemalan (Lester et al., 1973) and Ugandan (Ainsworth, 1967) infants. It is possible that the earlier onset of separation protest in these societies may occur because separation represents a more discrepant event to infants in these societies. In Guatemala most children are reared in a one-room house, and infants are likely to be near their mothers most of the time. In

Uganda where infants are carried on their mother's backs most of the time separation may be an even more unusual event.

These facts describe some of the common manifestations of attachment, fear of strangers, and separation anxiety. We have also explored some of the hypotheses which have been investigated in attempts to identify the processes involved in the development of these emotional reactions. This leaves unanswered some questions of major significance in contemporary American society. What, for example, are the effects of long-term and short-term separation? Our social institutions are clearly evolving in a direction that is likely to result in frequent and sometimes protracted separations between mothers and their children. Are day-care arrangements of various types adequate substitutes for family care when it comes to the fostering of healthy social and emotional development? These and related questions will be addressed in our discussion of the institutions of socialization in chapter 12.

Mechanisms of Emotional Development

Beyond the fact that attachment bonds between children and their principal caretakers begin to form during the first year of life, and that toward the end of the first year many children develop a fear of strangers and perhaps a bit later express distress or engage in efforts to recover a caretaker from whom they have been separated, what else can be said about the development of emotions and affect in young children? Years ago Watson (1919) postulated that infants come into the world already equipped with three innate emotions: rage, fear, and love. These emotions could be evoked, it was assumed, by restraint, in the case of rage; by loud noises, in the case of fear; and by stroking, in the case of love. Those assumptions are now clearly recognized to be without foundation. Neonates will respond to noxious stimuli with excitement, as evidenced by crying and mass activity (Ausubel & Sullivan, 1970), but this excitement is undifferentiated—that is, it cannot be reliably identified as an expression of any particular subjective state, such as anger or fear. Unless they are aware of the stimuli which evoked the excitation state in question, observers are unable to agree on the specific emotional states of neonates (Sherman, 1927a; 1927b). Emotions appear to become differentiated as the infant matures as the result of various mechanisms governing the learning of affect.

Differentiation of emotions

Classical conditioning. There are many stimuli which are naturally aversive. Electrical shocks, for example, are none too pleasant, and touching a hot stove will produce pain in any child with a normal neurological system. Such events are unconditioned stimuli; that is, they produce their effects without any prior learning. The behavior produced by the unconditioned stimulus is an unconditioned response; in the case of touching a hot stove, this may be withdrawal, fear, and visceral excitation. If a previously neutral stimulus is paired with the unconditioned stimulus, the neutral stimulus will eventually evoke the same response as the unconditioned stimulus. The neutral event thus becomes a conditioned stimulus, capable of evoking the original response of fear, anxiety, or withdrawal.

Unconditioned stimuli

Unconditional response

Neutral stimulus

Conditioned stimulus

If a child hears the word *hot* at the same time she experiences the painful stimulation of touching the stove, the word *hot* alone may come to elicit the fear, avoidance, and withdrawal behaviors originally occasioned by touching something hot.

The often told story of Albert and the rat (Watson & Raynor, 1930), which we reported in chapter 2, nicely illustrates how this process works in the development of emotions. Not only was Albert conditioned to fear the rat, but his fear

generalized, so that he displayed fear reactions to a range of stimuli which had one thing in common with the rat—they were furry. The stimuli to which his fear generalized included cotton, fur coats, wool, and animals other than the rat. Such a generalized fear is considered a phobic reaction. Once a conditioned stimulus has been established, the response it elicits can be conditioned to occur in response to some new neutral stimulus which is paired with the first *Higher order* conditioned stimulus. This is called higher order conditioning.
conditioning

Just as in aversive classical conditioning the unconditioned stimulus is some pain-producing event, unconditioned stimuli may also be linked to pleasurable stimuli. Undoubtedly, many pleasurable emotions are conditioned in just that way. Sights and sounds, for example, which have been regularly associated with pleasure-producing experiences often produce visceral changes and mental images which people interpret as "happy feelings."

Operant conditioning. Operant conditioning also plays a role in the shaping of behavior associated with emotion or affective states. Simply speaking, behaviors which are followed by consequences that are favorable to the individual who performed the behavior are strengthened; that is, they are likely to occur more often under similar circumstances. The consequences which function to increase the *Reinforcing events* strength or probability of the behavior are reinforcing events. The child who was described in the last chapter—the one who threw a tantrum in the aisle of the supermarket—might be considered to be expressing emotion through particular behaviors. When his mother attends to his "emotional outburst" by arguing with him, buying him candy, or letting him ride the mechanical horse in order to quiet him down, she is reinforcing his tantrum behavior.

Vicarious influences. While many emotional reactions may be learned through processes of operant or classical conditioning based on direct experience, emotions may also be acquired vicariously through observation. Direct and vicarious conditioning are both based on the same principles, but whereas in direct conditioning the learner herself experiences the pleasure or pain-producing stimulus, in vicarious conditioning it is someone else who is subjected to the stimulation. The usual course of events is that a model experiences the painful or pleasurable stimulation, and his affective expressions serve as arousal stimuli for the observer (Bandura, 1969). The emotional state of another person cannot be observed directly, but it can be inferred both from the nature of the experi-*Live models* ences being undergone by a model, and by the model's behavioral cues which connote emotional arousal. A model may evidence painful stimulation by wincing, crying, or verbalizing feelings of pain. A model experiencing joy will smile, laugh, perhaps even jump up and down in the inane fashion of television game show contestants. Although the experience is vicarious, it appears that those cues which signify emotional response acquire the capacity to evoke similar affective responses through the same processes by which negative or positive valence is established through direct experience. Affective social cues alone acquire the power to produce emotional reactions in observers (Bandura, 1969).

A young child in school thus does not have to directly experience the shame that might come from violating a sex-role norm of his peer group. If she observes others being ridiculed by the group for such deviations, she may experience shame in a similar situation even though her infraction might not be observed.

Vicarious influences on children's emotional development are not limited to observations of live models either. Emotional responses may be learned through

the observation of models presented in movies, on television, or even in symbolic   *Symbolic models*
materials, such as books, which transmit information about the consequences
of certain behaviors. Not only do certain social cues acquire emotion-evoking
properties through observation, but values, tastes, and preferences are influenced
to a considerable degree through the same process. We will return to the implications of this fact in chapter 12.

Differentiation of emotions. This brings us to another point. The reader may
wonder why we have not by this time described the course of development of
specific emotions, such as joy, anger, jealousy, hate, sorrow, and so on. Clearly,
emotions involve the physiological activation and visceral arousal which is
mediated by the autonomic nervous system. But do the physiological changes
associated with various emotions differ from one another? Can the physiological   *Physiological*
correlates of differing emotional states be discriminated from each other? In sum,   *correlates*
is there any way one can tell from the physiological patterns of arousal that are
associated with emotions just which emotion is being experienced? The answer
might surprise you. But a moment's reflection on a commonplace example may
serve to show that the answer makes sense.

What happens when a child is confronted with a frightening event? Most
likely muscles become tense, heart rate increases, and the heart pounds. As a
matter of fact, that is also just about what happens when one experiences a strong
positive emotion, like joy, rapture, or ecstasy. One of the authors is reminded
that not long ago his children were looking forward to a visit from their grandmother, who invariably came bearing gifts. On the evening before her arrival the
7-year-old son said, "Dad, I'm just so excited I can hardly wait. It feels like my
heart is going to come out of my chest." Doubtless we have all experienced such
strong positive emotions, but the lion's share of them seem to be reserved for
childhood.

This example illustrates what physiological and psychological studies have
shown. The various emotions people experience are not accompanied by a
comparable range of physiological response patterns (Bandura, 1969). In short,
whether an individual feels that he is experiencing joy, anger, or jealousy, a

common physiological arousal mediates the various forms of emotional behavior and the diverse affective states which the individual experiences.

How then does one know whether she is angry or elated? Her emotional state is identified primarily on the basis of external stimuli, not on the basis of internal cues (Bandura, 1969). In a situation that signals danger, for example, the visceral arousal one experiences is interpreted as fear. If the situation is one in which one's desires are thwarted, the physiological signs may be taken as anger. Weddings are supposed to be happy occasions, so naturally the mother of the bride interprets her tears as tears of joy.

In summary, emotional states do result partly from physiological arousal, but social and cognitive variables play a crucial role in the identification of the subjective state, and even in judging the intensity of the emotion. We think it strange indeed when the intensity of an adult's outbursts of anger seem unrelated to the seriousness of the event to which she is responding, yet such behavior is often witnessed in children. It is not necessarily the intensity of the visceral arousal that tells the individual how angry she is. Rather it is the combination of social cues and cognitive considerations which provide an index of the seriousness of the event to which the offended party rises to anger. Children must *Cultural meanings* learn to identify these environmental cues and the cultural meanings attached *of behaviors* to them. The point is nicely illustrated by ethnographic examples of some of the varied ways in which feelings are expressed in various cultural settings. For example:

> A Masai warrior honors a young man who looks promising by spitting in his face, an Andaman Islander greets a visitor by sitting down on his lap and sobbing his salutation tearfully, a scolded Chinese schoolboy takes a reprimand with cheerful grinning as a sign of his respect, and to show anger Navajo and Apache Indians lower the voice instead of raising it. (Opler, 1967, cited in Mischel, 1971, p. 259)

Other examples abound. Among many Indian groups it would be a sign of disrespect for a child to look an adult in the eye while talking to her. It has been observed that teachers who are unaware of the meaning of this behavior in the child's culture interpret the avoidance of eye contact as being sneaky, or trying to hide something, an interpretation which they bring from their own cultural background. The meanings attached to the various forms of behavior are culturally defined.

Anxiety

Anxiety is a form of emotional response which warrants special consideration because it has received a great deal of attention in psychological theory and research, and because it is a concept which is frequently called upon by lay people to explain behavior. People often interpret their states of arousal as anxiety, and they commonly explain poor performance with such explanations as "I was too anxious to concentrate." From one point of view anxiety may simply be regarded as a learned fear (Mischel, 1971), while in psychodynamic conceptualizations a principal source of anxiety is thought to be the conflict among the components of personality, the id, the ego, and the superego.

Psychodynamic views. The anxiety created by personality dynamics centers around the resolution of conflict between biological impulses and the social con- *Defense* ventions prohibiting their direct expression. The individual copes with the *mechanisms* anxiety and relieves the painful tension created by it by developing defense mechanisms. Presumably the internal conflicts which prompt these modes of adjustment go unrecognized by the individual who employs them.

One of the defense mechanisms, *sublimation,* we referred to previously in our discussion of indirect release of accumulated aggressive impulses. The basis for sublimation often involves a sexual motive which creates anxiety because to even think of it is unacceptable. The individual may sublimate or transform his unacceptable impulses into some socially acceptable form, such as athletics.

In *projection,* the child's unacceptable impulses are attributed to someone else, whereas in *denial* unacceptable impulses or knowledge which evokes anxiety is simply denied. If a child learns that a parent has committed a serious crime or moral infraction, for example, the child may simply convince herself that it is not true. Denial is a particularly easy defense mechanism for the young child to employ because ". . . he is not yet upset by violating the demands of reality testing" (Mischel, 1971). As the child becomes more cognitively mature it is more difficult to deny the objective facts, so a more satisfactory defense may be recourse to *repression.* In repression an anxiety-provoking cognition may be removed from consciousness.

Projection and denial

Repression

A *reaction formation* serves to disguise an id impulse and make it acceptable to the ego. Citizens who mount campaigns against pornography are often accused of employing this defense, on the assumption that they are unable to admit their own preoccupation with sexual matters, and thus express their impulses by waging a battle against what represents their unacceptable interests.

Reaction formation

Regression involves reverting to a mode of behavior which was formerly acceptable, but which has become age-inappropriate. For example, a preschool child may feel that he is being displaced when a new baby comes into the home. He cannot express anxiety directly, so he may readopt old behaviors which formerly won him the love and affection of his parents.

Regression

Rationalization is a defense known to all of us. When the motives for our behaviors are unacceptable to our "conscience," anxiety is created. The anxiety may be reduced by substituting socially acceptable reasons for the behavior and convincing ourselves that these are the real reasons.

Rationalization

Displacement is another of the defense mechanisms which was previously discussed as a mode of catharsis in the reduction of aggressive urges. Displacement is also used in the sense of displacing emotional responses from their actual source to some other object. For example, an Eskimo might dream that he was hunting, and when confronted with a dangerous animal, such as a bear, his rifle failed to fire. A psychoanalytic interpretation might be that the rifle was symbolic of the penis, and that the dream reflected fear of impotence (Honnigmann, 1954). Such an interpretation seems to overlook the fact that in a society in which one must depend upon his weapons for both food and defense, the possibility that a weapon might fail during a dangerous encounter might be a much more realistic source of anxiety than fear of impotence. Nevertheless, such symbolism plays an important role in psychoanalytic interpretations of behavior, and childhood phobias are frequently explained on this basis. According to this view, a girl might fear snakes not because of the anxiety-provoking qualities of snakes per se, but because they constitute a symbolic representation of masculine sexuality. How else could an irrational snake phobia be explained if it is known that the girl has had no direct experience with snakes?

Displacement

Anxieties as learned fears. An alternative to the psychodynamic view of anxiety has already been discussed. Anxieties are fears which are learned through direct and vicarious experience. Babies come into the world with no fear of snakes, spiders, rodents, or any of the other assorted creatures which function as fear stimuli for countless numbers of people. Most of these fears seem to be acquired through vicarious conditioning. For the young child a spider is a neutral stimulus, but when the child witnesses its mother display overt signs of fear and distress upon encountering a spider, the child may come to experience similar fears of spiders.

Naturally not all anxieties are acquired vicariously. Direct experience with aversive stimuli, especially trauma, may result in enduring fears and phobias. A child who is attacked and injured by a dog, for example, may develop a phobia that could last a lifetime if subsequent learning does not demonstrate that the vast majority of dogs are unlikely to attack. Not only is the child likely to fear dogs, but her fear may generalize to other stimuli present in the situation in which she was attacked. If the attack transpired in an alleyway, the child may subsequently fear and avoid alleyways with similar characteristics. Such fears and avoidance behaviors are extremely resistant to extinction because the individual avoids situations involving the fear-producing cues, and she is therefore unlikely to have the opportunity to learn that such situations may not eventuate in aversive consequences.

MOTIVATION

Given a range of options, why do people do the things they do? Why does an adult choose to watch a situation comedy on television rather than a special documentary? Why does a 10-year-old listen to a rock and roll radio station rather than the local country and western station, or vice versa? Why do some students seem motivated to do well in school while others could care less about academic success, but seem very concerned about doing the things that meet the approval of the peer group? All these questions deal with motivation. Given the almost infinite range of possibilities, why do people try to do some things, even at the expense of great effort, while other possibilities go unheeded?

For the neonate the answer seems relatively simple. The newly arrived infant has a few needs which must be satisfied if he is to survive. These needs are primarily biological in nature, and include such necessities as food, thirst, elimination, and sleep. Before long, however, to varied degrees, individuals begin to march to different drummers, and an intriguing problem of psychology is to discover how differences in motivation come to be.

Drive Theory

One major theory of motivation has already been touched upon. According to drive-reduction theory, painful stimulation or deprivation of physiological needs *Primary drives* gives rise to a drive which activates behavior. Primary drives are those based on innate needs, such as the need for nourishment, water, and oxygen. Even the satisfaction of these primary needs involves some learning. The sucking response, though innate, improves with practice, for example. Miller and Dollard (1941) proposed that any strong external stimulation may become a drive if it is sufficiently intense. Loud noises, for example, may motivate behavior. As various social influences impinge on the young organism, the basic nature of these drives becomes somewhat altered, As neutral events are paired with the *Secondary drives* reduction of drives, secondary drives develop. Love or affection presumably develop through the pairing of neutral stimuli with stimuli which result in the reduction of physiological needs, and play an increasingly prominent role in motivating behavior as the organism matures. Moreover, basic needs, such as the drive for nourishment, become elaborated. While American children are developing a taste for "Captain Crunch," or some other sugar-coated cereal, Arunta children of the desert areas of northern Australia may be developing a preference for certain varieties of grubs. In the view of drive-reduction learning theorists, a variety of secondary drives develop on the basis of their association with the satisfaction of the primary drives.

Another approach to the question of what conditions motivate behavior is based on lists of needs which presumably require satisfaction in a diversity of cultures. Murray, for example, generated a list of 28 needs which presumably are not directly tied to physiological drives, but are encountered in a broad spectrum of cultures. These psychogenic needs (Murray, 1938) include abasement, achievement, affiliation, aggression, autonomy, deference, dominance, harm-avoidance, and twenty additional motives.

Psychogenic needs

The obvious difficulty with such lists is that there is no reasonable stopping place for them—that is, we could go on generating new needs as long as it is possible to think of labels for classes of goal-oriented behavior. Moreover, such listings do nothing to explain the processes involved in motive formation. Nevertheless, a number of theorists have postulated several needs which are presumably innate and are not derived through association with the reduction of specific physiological needs. Among the postulated needs which have received attention are the growth motives proposed by organismic or phenomenological theorists, curiosity or exploratory drives, competence motives, and motives inherent in information processing. Affiliation needs and achievement needs have also received a great deal of attention. These latter two categories of needs are not considered innate, but rather result from conditioning processes.

Maslow's Hierarchy of Needs

Abraham Maslow (1968), one of the most prominent of American phenomenologists, argued that both the psychodynamic and learning theory views of motivation distort the unique nature of human goal-directed behavior. According to his view, both drive-reduction learning theory and psychodynamic psychology see behavior as originating in deficits. Hunger, for example, is a deficit which must be satisfied in order that tissue tension may be reduced, and the need state of the organism brought back into balance. Similarly, in psychodynamic theory accumulated urges must find a channel for discharge in order that the organism may achieve homeostasis. Maslow did not argue that physiological needs play no role in human motivation. He simply believed that as the human child develops, physiological drives account for less and less of the individual's motivated behavior. The basic moving force in human behavior is considered the innate motive for growth, to become better than one is, to reach one's potentialities, and to become self-actualized. Maslow's theory of motivation depicts how this motive is articulated to other needs.

Deficit motives

Homeostasis

Maslow (1943) proposed that needs are related to each other in a hierarchical fashion. These needs, which include physiological needs, safety needs, need for love and belonging, need for esteem, need for self-actualization, and needs to know and understand, are represented in figure 10-3. These needs form a hierarchy because those at the base must be relatively well-satisfied before needs at the next higher level can influence behavior. Each level of need, then, is prepotent over the next level. Once a need has been relatively well-satisfied, it no longer serves as a motivator, and needs at the next level take over.

Principle of prepotency

Physiological needs include oxygen, liquid, food, and rest. These needs are especially important motivators in young infants, and of course may dominate the behavior of adults as well in cases where essential commodities such as food

Physiological needs

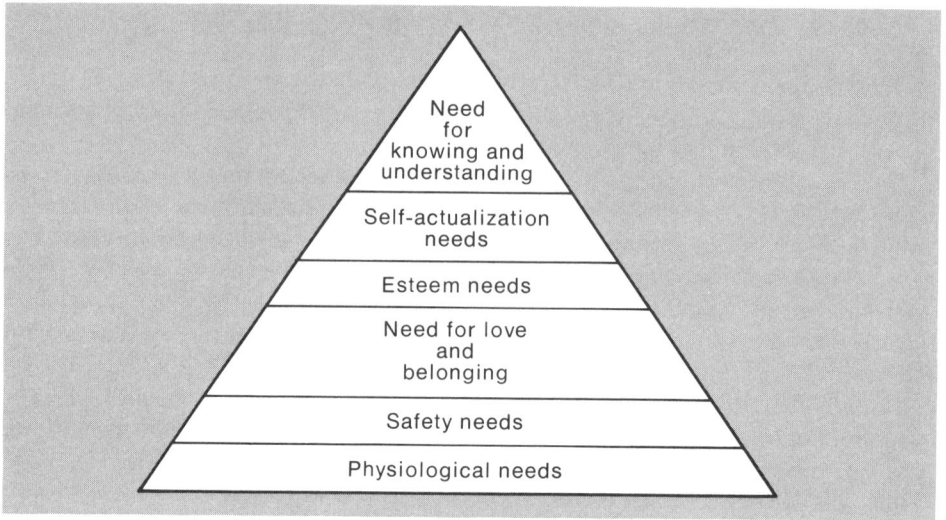

Figure 10-3 *Maslow's motivational hierarchy. Needs at each level in the hierarchy are prepotent over those at the next higher level.*

and water are in short supply. Maslow assumed that for people in our society the physiological needs are generally adequately satisfied, and that they therefore instigate a minor portion of most people's behavior. In recent years we have come to recognize that hunger even in the United States may be more widespread than is popularly believed, so physiological needs may not play quite such a minor role as Maslow believed. Many children go to school hungry. If that physiological need is prepotent over higher order motives, we should not be surprised if intellectual curiosity is not the primary motivating force among such children.

Safety needs   Safety needs in children are demonstrated by their preference for predictable routines rather than disorder. Safety needs exert the dominant influence on behavior in instances where the individual perceives danger. In a young child, for example, this may be when she is separated from a familiar person. A child who has been separated from her parents in a crowded store may be motivated only to find her mother, once the fact of separation is recognized. All the attractive objects and toys on display suddenly lose their attraction. When the lost parent is found, we usually see the young child clinging desperately to the parent for at least a brief period of time. Safety needs may also have a dominant role in directing behavior of adults in situations of war or natural catastrophe, and Maslow speculated that for some people religion serves to satisfy the need for safety, while for others science may fill that role.

Love and belonging   The need for love and belonging is a social motive. It involves a desire for affectionate relationships of various sorts and for affiliative relationships with social groups.

Esteem needs   People seek recognition from others that they are a worthwhile person. This reflects *esteem needs*. Such recognition leads to feelings of confidence and worth, in short, to self-esteem, which is essential to progression to the next level of needs.

Self-actualization   The need for self-actualization is the need to become all one has the potentiality to become. Self-actualization may be expressed through many different kinds of pursuits, and those who achieve self-actualization are presumably among the healthiest in our society.

Need for knowledge and understanding   The need to know and understand reflects a motive to seek knowledge, information, and relationships. One who is motivated by this need would presumably pursue knowledge for its own sake and seek to systematize and organize knowledge.

The concepts incorporated in Maslow's hierarchy are not well operationalized. Any two observers might be hard-put to agree that an individual's behavior is motivated by esteem needs, or by a need for self-actualization. Therefore, the validity of the theory is practically impossible to assess. Nevertheless, the theory is provocative, and in a very general sort of way it has implications for child rearing and education. If a child's positive affective relationships with others have been few or unstable, or if he has little reason to believe that he is accepted and well regarded by other people, it would be understandable if his behaviors were primarily directed to matters other than intellectual curiosity and school work.

Competence Motivation

In a stimulating paper originally published in 1965, Robert White proposed that traditional views of motivation—those which are derived from Freud's psychoanalytic theory or from drive-reduction theory—are unable to account for many of the most common examples of human behavior. He pointed out that children engage in a great range of activities, beginning with sucking and grasping and visual exploration, moving on to crawling and walking, and on to language, exploration, and curiosity, which apparently have no implicit drive-reduction function, and are not explained by personality dynamics. He suggested that what these and doubtless other activities have in common is that their development represents a fundamental desire for competence, or to have some *effect* on the environment. Behavior that is involved in an infant's learning to grasp, hold, and let go of an object, for example, is not random behavior. Rather, says White:

Effectance motivation

> It is directed, selective, and persistent, and it is continued not because it serves primary drives, *which indeed it cannot serve until it is almost perfected*, but because it satisfies an intrinsic need to deal with the environment. (1959, p. 318)

White believes that those behaviors which cannot be adequately explained by traditional theories of motivation all have a common biological significance; through the enactment of these behaviors the child learns to interact effectively with her environment. Playful and exploratory behaviors serve this end, and White feels that such activities must be motivated in their own right. This motivation which moves the individual toward competency is designated "effectance" motivation to characterize the feeling of efficacy which it produces. Such a motive is especially important to humans and other "higher animals" where little of the behavior is innate, and so much must be learned in order to deal with the environment and survive.

Motives in Information Processing

Clearly, play makes a significant contribution to the development of competence, and we would be hard put to explain the behavior of a boy throwing rocks into a pond to watch the ripples flow, or dragging a stick along a picket fence on the basis of primary drive reduction. But White's theory does not deal with the fact that some children display much more curiosity than others. Nor does it offer an explanation for why a situation which may elicit playful exploratory behavior from one child may evoke no response from another. Hunt (1960) has theorized that the reason lies in the motivating qualities of the act of information processing itself. Hunt's ideas were very much influenced by Piaget's work. Following Piaget, he proposed that schemata or intellectual structures are formed through the interaction of maturational processes and experience. When the child encounters objects or events which are congruent with his established schemata, those events are readily incorporated, or assimilated. Even if the encountered event is not identical to those which led to the formation of existing schemata, they will be interpreted on the basis of the cognitions which the child *Elaboration* has already acquired, and therefore they can be assimilated. Schemata grow and *of schemata* become elaborated on the basis of slight discrepancies between contemporary and previous experiences. However, if a new experience is too discrepant from previous ones, there will be no "cognitive template" to fit it, and therefore the child will be unable to assimilate it. Not only will assimilation be impossible, but attempts to deal with experiences which are excessively discrepant from those *Cognitive* represented in existing cognitive structures cause discomfort and negative moti- *avoidance* vation, or a desire to withdraw from the situation. Moreover, the child may fail even to attend to an object or event that is highly incongruent with those represented in her schemata. The assumption is that the discrepant object or event cannot attract the child's attention or elicit exploratory behavior unless it is somewhat familiar to her. On the other hand, when the same old objects or events are encountered repeatedly, with no variation on the theme, the fit with existing schemata is perfect, no accommodation is necessary, and after a time *Boredom* the child's response will be one of boredom. When the match between an experience and established cognitive structures is only slightly discrepant, the *Optimal match* task of accommodation will not only be within manageable proportions for the child, but the problem-solving process itself will also have motivational qualities. People, presumably, find information processing innately satisfying when the discrepancy between a present experience and existing schemata is appropriate.

Hunt calls this the problem of the "match." In order for information processing *Optimal* to be innately satisfying, there must be an appropriate match, or optimal degree *discrepany* of discrepancy, between a new experience encountered by the child and the cognitive structures he has already developed. This idea was seized upon by many compensatory education programs in the late 1960s. The unsuccessful experiences which many children from poverty and/or minority group backgrounds encountered in the formal educational system were assumed to result from the fact that they were reared in intellectually impoverished environments. Presumably, their family environment failed to provide experiences required to develop the intellectual structures which adequately "matched" the instructional experiences characteristically provided as part of the school curriculum. This point of view led to the widespread adoption of a "deficit" interpretation which attributed the poor school performance of children who were poor or culturally different from middle-class white children to inadequate child rearing. Thus, while the concept of the "match" does not dictate a deficit interpretation, this has been the most common interpretation, and programs aimed at remedying the deficiencies have been generated from coast to coast. Some writers have accordingly come to denounce this and related concepts as the "social science base for institutional racism" (Baratz & Baratz, 1970).

Achievement Motivation

While the motivation to accomplish the normal developmental tasks of childhood and to act upon the environment are important, our society also places considerable emphasis on other kinds of accomplishments. For example, many people have aspirations for their children to do well in school, and later in entrepreneurial enterprises. In psychology, a good deal of attention has been directed at discovering just what factors influence children to want to achieve, even in the absence of obvious extrinsic rewards. It has often been assumed that children develop a motivation to achieve if their parents have stressed early independence and actively reinforced achievement behavior. A well-known study by Winterbottom (1958) is often cited in support of both of these assumptions. Winterbottom studied achievement motivation in eight-year-old boys. Boys were dichotomized into groups displaying high or low achievement motivation on tasks which have conventionally been used to assess achievement motivation (*n Ach*). The general procedure for measuring *n Ach* is to present pictures which portray people in ambiguous situations. The pictures are purposefully made ambiguous, and respondents are asked to tell or write a fantasy story about the picture. The content of the stories is analyzed for references to achievement goals, concerns with achieving personal success, obstacles to the achievement of success, statements about achievement needs, and evaluation of performance against some "internal" standard of excellence.

Independence training and reinforcement

n Ach

Winterbottom found that the mothers of boys with high need for achievement, as judged by the scores on their fantasy stories, made earlier demands on their sons for independence and excellence than did mothers of boys with low *n Ach*. Moreover, when the boys with high achievement motivation met maternal expectations, their mothers reported using physical affection in response to the boys' accomplishment more frequently than did mothers of the less motivated boys. However, the weight of evidence from more recent research indicates that direct training for achievement is what contributes most to the development of achievement motivation, not general independence training (Zigler & Child, 1973). Illustrative of the evidence for this conclusion is a study by Rosen and D'Andrade (1959) who used situational tasks to assess the actual behavior of parents toward their children, rather than using parents' responses to questionnaires as the data base on interactions between parents and children. These researchers found that parents of children with high need for achievement held higher aspirations and expectations for their sons' performances than did the parents of boys with comparatively low *n Ach*. The patterns of mothers and fathers differed somewhat from one another. Fathers of boys who were high in *n Ach* engaged more than fathers of low *n Ach* boys in both independence and achievement training, while the mothers of the boys with high need for achievement were more dominant and expected less self-reliance from their sons than did mothers of boys with lower scores on *n Ach* measures. However, they were more likely than the mothers of low-achievement boys to reward success and punish failure.

Parental aspirations and expectations

This study and others which seem to confirm it provide a key to the processes involved in children's acquisition of achievement motivation. It appears that some children come to feel pride in their academic accomplishments because parents have reinforced such success. Others feel no such sense of satisfaction because parents have never reinforced such success. Through conditioning processes, when one class of events which functions as a reinforcer (such as praise from a parent) is paired with the child's success at a particular type of task, success alone on such tasks will acquire reinforcement value. Since direct reinforcement for academic success is sure to be delivered on an intermittent basis, simply because the socialization agent cannot be present each time such success is achieved, achievement behaviors are likely to be maintained for a long time in the absence of any external reinforcement. The observer is likely to interpret the child's behavior as evidence of intrinsic motivation, or to judge that

*Motivation to develop
intellectual competence may be
enhanced when parents obviously
value intellectual-performance.*

the child is evaluating her own performance on the basis of internal standards of excellence. Even the child's preference for academic over competing tasks depends on the types of activities which the parent has habitually reinforced at home (Swanson & Henderson, in press).

Affiliation Motivation

n Aff

Some students of American society feel that the trend in American society is away from the tendency to behave on the basis of internal standards, and toward a tendency to be motivated by a desire to "fit in," to be accepted by the group (Riesman, 1954). There are some other societies which appear to be much more *"Other-directed"* "other directed" than our own. Research has been conducted to examine the *society* relationship of academic success to both achievement motives (*n Ach*) and affiliation motives (*n Aff*).

On the basis of research in "mainstream" American society, we expect to find higher achievement among children high in *n Ach* than among children with low motivation to achieve. The expectation is strengthened by the fact that there is even some cross-cultural research (McClelland, 1961) showing a positive relationship between achievement themes represented in the folklore of a society and the entrepreneurial activities of members of the society. Thus, high *n Ach* seems to have a widespread relationship to actual achievement-oriented pursuits typical in the society. There are notable exceptions, however, that are just beginning to be uncovered. For a number of years now Ronald Gallimore and his associates (Gallimore, Boggs, & Jordan, 1974; Gallimore & Howard, 1968) have been studying Hawaiian-Americans, their socialization practices, and their schools. The initial findings of members of this group, based on 30 months of field research and participant observation in a Hawaiian community, provides some vivid insights into Hawaiian motivation.

While it is popularly held that Hawaiians are deficient in all sorts of areas . . .
essential to "successful" living, such generalizations are nearly always based on
an *economic* frame of reference and ignore the importance attached . . . to *human
relationships*. If one can depict Hawaii's other ethnic groups as achievement-
oriented in social and economic terms, then one must view Hawaiians as affiliation-
oriented. By this we mean that most Hawaiians will choose to honor a commitment
to a friend, provide aid to another person, seek out situations of good fellowship,
and so forth, *before* they will choose personal economic gain. (Gallimore &
Howard, 1968, p. 10)

Comparisons of Hawaiian boys with other ethnic groups in Hawaii on the
usual projective measures of *n Ach* and *n Aff* support this observation (Gallimore, Boggs, & Jordan, 1974; Sloggett, 1970). These findings are of particular
interest, because both high and low achieving Hawaiian boys had lower *n Ach*
scores than Japanese and Filipino-American boys, even though the high achieving
Hawaiian boys were from a school which selected them on a competitive state-
wide basis for their high academic potential and accomplishment. This suggests
that some motive other than *n Ach* might influence achievement in this particular
cultural setting. The deficit explanation clearly is not viable in the case of the
Hawaiians. If this is the case, what does motivate those Hawaiians who achieve?
Among the Hawaiians studied by Gallimore and his associates, it appears that
need for affiliation rather than *n Ach* is the relevant motive. The evidence suggests that *n Aff* does not operate as a general internalized disposition—we have
already dismissed that possibility as unlikely in previous discussions of personality
traits. Rather, external cues may operate to activate behaviors that are labeled
affiliative since affiliative responses are highly probable because of the values
inculcated in Hawaiian culture. The role of situational factors in influencing
success striving is nicely illustrated in an example provided by Gallimore and his
associates. In Japanese culture, according to one anthropologist, success striving
is usually motivated by the individual's concern about how others will react,
rather than because of any satisfaction of internal needs. The pursuit of purely
personal satisfaction, so greatly valued in American society, would be viewed by
Japanese as a "sign of excessive immoral egoism" (DeVos, 1968, p. 359, quoted in
Gallimore et al., 1974, p. 251).

SELF-REGULATION AND IMPULSE CONTROL

Most people think that children and adults should be able to regulate their own
behavior, to resist temptation, and to deny themselves immediate gratification
in order to obtain future rewards of greater consequence. The popular term for
such self-control is willpower. To some psychologists it is ego strength. An
important component of willpower or ego strength is the ability to delay gratification.

Ego strength

Delay of Gratification

Most, if not all, of the significant rewards available in our society require the
socialization of "enormously complex chains of deferred gratification patterns"
(Mischel, 1974). Many people today may feel that the Puritan ethic discussed in
chapter 1 carried the practice of self-imposed delay to unhealthy extremes, but
it is hard to imagine an individual achieving any satisfactory degree of success
and adjustment, even in the less demanding social institutions of today, without
developing some reasonable degree of voluntary postponement of gratification
for the sake of more distant but more substantial gratification. Walter Mischel

and his associates have been pursuing an intriguing line of research aimed at identifying the relationship between delay of gratification and other qualities of willpower or ego strength, and at discovering the processes involved in the development and expression of gratification delay.

Projective tests

Measurement of ego strength. Traditionally, ego strength has most often been inferred from indirect evidence. For example, children's responses to Rorschach inkblots are taken as external "signs" or "clues" to internal personality dispositions. Since the inkblots are totally ambiguous—they represent nothing in themselves—it is assumed that an individual's interpretation of them reveals something about her internal "states." It is assumed that the individual is unaware that she is revealing herself, and information about her hidden personality dynamics are therefore able to slip out past her defenses.

Information derived from such sources has not proved especially valid for the prediction of actual behavior. Other types of tasks involving overt behavior other than verbal responses have been devised. A typical task is one in which a child performs a motor behavior in response to some standard instruction. The child might be asked to draw a line slowly, or to pull a toy truck slowly by drawing on a string. Children differ in the degree to which they can follow these instructions by inhibiting their impulse to perform these motor acts rapidly.

Motoric inhibition

Even though these measures do involve overt behavior other than verbal statements, they have not proven valid as indirect measures of the kinds of self-regulation behaviors which are of primary interest to a parent or nursery school teacher. These people are more likely to be interested in whether or not a child can inhibit the impulse to aggress against another child, or his ability to sustain effort at a task in anticipation of some positive consequence in the future. Mischel has taken a very direct approach to the study of the school-and-society-relevant ability and inclination of children to sustain effort for future rewards.

Gratification patterns. Mischel's (1974) work on delay of gratification has revealed two contrasting preference patterns among children in various different cultures. The usual arrangement for assessing these patterns is to give children an opportunity to choose between two rewards, one of which may be obtained immediately and another more valued or more substantial reward for which they must work or wait. Some children are prone to select the smaller, more immediate rewards. At the opposite pole are children who usually delay gratification in order to obtain the more valued reward. These children, in contrast to those who opt for immediate gratification, are more apt to be high on achievement motivation, to be more trusting and socially responsible, to have higher aspirations, be brighter and more mature, and to display less uncontrolled impulsivity. "This extreme pattern resembles what has been called the 'Puritan character structure'" (Mischel, 1974). It is most often found in middle and upper socioeconomic classes and in cultures which are highly achievement oriented.

Immediate and future rewards

Mischel wisely cautions that excessively high patterns at either end of the delay of gratification continuum may be "maladaptive" in their extreme forms. Emotional restriction and perpetual postponement of gratification might characterize a person with excessively "high-delay" patterns, while persons identified as juvenile delinquents or psychopaths often display excessive "low-delay" patterns.

Maladaptive gratification patterns

Influences on gratification patterns. Even though there are a number of characteristics which are interrelated and might be referred to collectively as "ego-strength," this does not deny what we have said repeatedly about the relative situational specificity of such qualities. The correlations among these qualities are statistically significant, but low from a practical point of view which takes into consideration the vast amount of variation which is not explained by the association among these characteristics. In order to predict whether a given individual would choose an immediate or delayed reward on a given occasion, one would have to know a good deal more than what that individual's preference has been on past measures. Among the important factors to be considered are learning history and cognitive and situational influences.

A piece of research which Mischel (1974) carried out with lower-class blacks in Trinidad provides a nice illustration of the influence of situational factors on delay-of-gratification. These people often showed preference for the smaller but more immediate rewards offered by a white "promise-giver." Mischel explains that these people lived in a culture in which immediate gratification was commonly modeled and rewarded. Moreover, they had plenty of past experience with promises broken by whites. But under a different set of circumstances, many were willing to give up immediate gratification in favor of deferred satisfactions when they had the opportunity to plan ahead for future events, such as religious activities and feasts, when these events were under their own control. Clearly, gross generalizations about cross-situational "impulsivity" are unwarranted (Mischel, 1974).

Situational influences

Vicarious as well as direct experiences influence gratification preference patterns. Bandura and Mischel (1974) have demonstrated that children's self-imposed delay of gratification patterns are influenced by the patterns they see displayed by prestigious models. Presumably, by observing the model's behavior the child acquires information about the positive consequences which may be associated with delay of reward, and comes to expect similar positive consequences for adopting the pattern displayed by the model. Expectancies are very important determinants of a child's willingness to defer gratification. As the example of differential gratification-delay patterns among blacks in Trinidad suggested, whether or not a person is willing to delay reward for greater good fortune promised at a future time depends on expectations, and in the case under consideration particularly, this depends on feelings of trust. Trust, in turn, is dependent not only on the individual's history of prior reinforcements for waiting, but also on the past history of promise keeping on the part of the promise-giver. Rare is the parent or teacher who does not occasionally hear a child say "You always promise that, but you never do it." We might be well advised on these occasions to remember the degree to which gratification delay depends on trust in the promise-giver, which in turn depends on expectations based on promises fulfilled.

Vicarious experiences

Expectancies

Trust

Mischel has asked a second question. Once the individual has made a decision to delay gratification, how can she follow through with that intention? One thing seems clear. The individual's cognitions play a vital role in freeing the individual from the control of immediate stimuli. But how?

Because trust seems an important factor in gratification delay, it seemed at first to Mischel and his co-workers that delay might be more probable if the child could see the relevant reward. In that circumstance his doubts about the ultimate availability of the delayed (but more valued) outcome might be allayed. The actual results of research on this question (Mischel & Ebbesen, 1970) were exactly the opposite of what the investigators expected. When the delayed rewards were actually in view, delay of gratification decreased quite dramatically.

These unexpected findings set the researchers to wondering what the children did while waiting for their rewards. To explore this question the children were placed in the most difficult of all situations—one in which both the immediate and delayed outcomes were right before them. A device called "Mr. Talk Box" was placed in their presence, and the children were observed through a one-way mirror. "Mr. Talk Box," a tape recorder in disguise, introduced itself and cheerfully announced to the young subjects:

> Hi, I have big ears and I love it when children fill them with all the things they think and feel, no matter what. (p. 267)

In brief, what Mischel discovered was that the children evaded temptation by inventing elaborate self-distraction techniques. They sang, talked to themselves, invented games with their hands and feet, and even tried to go to sleep. Mischel sums it all up nicely in a statement that should evoke empathy in every reader. He says, "These tactics, of course, are familiar to anyone who has ever been trapped in a boring lecture" (p. 267).

Cognitive distraction

Given these clues from the children, the next step was to determine more specifically how cognitive distraction works to help children to delay gratification and raise their degree of tolerance to frustration of the sort involved in being faced with the temptation of rewarding objects. Mischel and his associates found that when desirable foods, such as marshmallows or pretzels, were placed before the children, instructions which got the children to think about the rewards substantially reduced the period of time they were able to defer gratification, while thinking about fun things, like finding frogs, enhanced gratification delay. Moreover, thinking happy thoughts facilitated delay of gratification more than thinking sad thoughts.

Cognitive transformations

Mischel (1974) has explored the influence of cognitive variables on delay-of-gratification further, discovering that the effects of a stimulus on a child's delay patterns can be influenced dramatically by cognitive transformations. A child who can sit alone on a chair waiting for a reward for less than half a minute on one occasion before terminating his waiting for a less desirable but immediately available reward, can on another occasion wait for a very long period of time. Under one condition children were instructed to think about the consummatory properties of the reward objects. That is, they were to think of the salty taste and crunchiness of the pretzels, or how soft and chewy the marshmallows would be and how sweet they would taste. Children were unable to wait much at all under that type of cognitive transformation, even though the rewards were not physically in view.

Consummatory properties

Non-consummatory qualities

In contrast, when children were given instructions intended to get them to think about non-consummatory qualities of the reward objects, a strikingly different result was obtained. For example, if the children imagined the pretzel sticks as thick brown logs, or if they thought of the marshmallows as puffy white clouds, they could delay gratification for very long periods of time (see figure 10-4). Indeed, they could outwait the graduate-student experimenters.

In summary, a number of individual differences in characteristics such as intelligence, imagination, and cognitive styles (such as impulsivity—reflectiveness) undoubtedly influence children's abilities to delay gratification. But in spite of these individual differences, a child's preference patterns can be influenced considerably by controlling situational and cognitive variables. Mischel's research on delay of gratification provides an excellent example of social learning theorists' attempts to understand the complex, interrelated influences of individual differences, environmental factors, and cognitive processes on the development of self-regulation.

Cognitive transformations.

Figure 10-4

Impulse and Reflection

We have already alluded to impulsiveness and reflectiveness—another dimension of self-regulation on which children may differ. These concepts refer to the degree to which children tend to respond slowly and reflectively or with quick impulse under conditions of uncertainty. This dimension, proposed originally by Jerome Kagan (1965a), is variously referred to as cognitive style or conceptual tempo. *Reflective children, as compared with impulsive ones, take longer and are more deliberate and careful in considering various alternative choices on a measure designed to assess impulsiveness and reflection. They also tend to make fewer errors in their choices than impulsive children. The task which is most often used to measure reflection—impulsiveness is the *Matching Familiar Figures Test* (*MFF*), which has been shown to predict performance on certain school-relevant tasks such as reading recognition (Kagan, 1965b). An illustration of the type of item used in the *MFF* is shown in figure 10-5.

Cognitive style

The *Matching Familiar Figures Test* involves a number of drawings of familiar objects. For a given item the child is shown a picture of a particular object, such as a teddy bear, and six smaller pictures. Only one of the smaller drawings is identical to the standard. The other pictures all differ from the standard in some minor way. The child's task is to select the one drawing which is identical to the standard. Responses may be scored both for the time a child takes in responding, and for the number of errors she makes.

Modification of cognitive style. Cognitive style is sometimes regarded as a relatively stable disposition of children. In fact, it has been found that the impulsive–reflective dimension of cognitive style may be stable for periods as long as a year (Kagan, 1965b). It has become clear, however, that children's predilection to respond to situations of uncertainty in a reflective or impulsive manner is amenable to influence. In one study (Riseberg, Parke, & Hetherington, 1971) children who were high on the impulsive dimension were exposed to films of models who behaved reflectively, and the children who were highly reflective were exposed to models who behaved impulsively. The reflective models exposed to *MFF* items responded with deliberation, taking an average of about a half a

Figure 10-5   *Type of Item Used in the* Matching Familiar Figures Test.

minute to make each selection, while models who displayed impulsiveness took only about one-third of that time to make their choices. Various combinations of scanning strategies and verbalizations of the process by which the model made his decisions were also depicted, both singly and in combination, with different groups of impulsive and reflective children.

Differential response to social influence   The major finding was that children displaying impulsive cognitive tempo could be influenced through observation of a model to respond more slowly and to make fewer errors. Reflective children who were exposed to the impulsive model increased their error rate. But the most intriguing finding was the paradoxical fact that reflective children who observed the impulsive models showed an *increase* in response time instead of the expected decrease. Latency of response, responding slowly, that is, and errors, were both related to intelligence. The investigators speculated that these results may indicate that impulsive children are more susceptible to influence than are children whose cognitive style is more reflective, possibly because the reflective child has experienced more successes in problem-solving situations and may have higher self-esteem as a result. The increased response latencies of the reflective children could result from a conflict between the strategies which were successful for them in the past and the apparently successful behavior of the model.

General and specific meanings. There are some important cautions to be held in the mind while considering the conclusions that might be drawn from the many studies on impulsive and reflective cognitive style. The concepts impulsiveness and reflectiveness have general as well as specific psychological meanings. Teachers, social workers, lay people, and even some psychologists use the term *impulsivity* in the broad sense of having little emotional control, taking unwise risks, and so on (Block, Block, & Harrington, 1974). Concern has been expressed that the terms *impulsive* and *reflective* have excess meaning—they connote behavior which may have little or nothing to do with the responses assessed in the *MFF* tests. The developer of the test insists that he has exercised appropriate caution in his own discussion of the concept (Block, Block, & Harrington, 1974; Kagan & Messer, 1975; Block, Block, & Harrington, 1975), but whether that is the case or not, the social fact seems to be that the meanings of the impulsive and reflective designations for conceptual tempo have been broadly misunderstood. For example, developers of programs for young children have at times assumed that the *MFF* test could be used to assess everything from tasks very much like those incorporated in the *MFF* itself, which may be appropriate enough, to impulsive aggression—an interpretation without any justification whatsoever. The lack of appropriate and reliable instruments for the assessment of children's socio-affective behavior constitutes a most distressing problem for programs charged with the care and education of children. The social significance of this problem will be elaborated in chapter 12.

*Validity of
conceptual
tempo measures*

In brief, children display differences in the care and speed with which they react to certain kinds of tasks in which there is high response uncertainty. Those who take more time to make their decisions tend to make more accurate responses. Children's cognitive styles can be influenced however, and fortunately, if we consider reflection to be better than impulse, impulsive children seem to be more easily influenced than reflective ones. It appears that a reflective style may lead a child to more frequent successes, which in turn may facilitate the development of self-esteem. The degree to which this is the case is not clear, because both reflective style and self-esteem are also related to intelligence.

Locus of Control

We have already seen that self-regulation is greatly influenced by expectations about the kinds of outcomes, good or bad, that may occur as consequences of behaving in a particular way. Julian Rotter's (1966) ideas about expectancies have stimulated a great deal of research on locus of control. There are some people who seem to believe that the things that happen to them are largely the result of their own behavior. Others seem to attribute things that happen to them to forces that are beyond their control. Those who generally see a contingent relationship between their behavior and the rewards or misfortunes that befall them are said to have "internal control." Those who see no connection between their own behavior and the rewards that come or fail to come to them are said to perceive control as "external." Naturally, a person who perceives control as internal is more likely to take specific action which she thinks may earn her the reward than an "externally controlled" person who thinks that obtaining the reward depends more on fate or luck than on his own effort.

Internal control

External control

Skill vs. luck. A number of laboratory studies have placed children in situations in which rewards could be manipulated to make it seem to some children that rewards they received were due to their skills, while to other children the rewards appeared to result from luck or chance, rather than as the outcome of

*Laboratory
research*

skilled performance. The results of these studies are quite congruent. They show that when people think the outcome of a task is controlled by the experimenter, by luck, or by some other conditions outside their control, reliance on past experience to guide behavior is reduced. The individual learns little—or perhaps the wrong things (Rotter, 1966). It seems that children are most likely to develop presumptions of externality of control under conditions where the relationship between their actions and their successes or failures are either unclear or inconsistent. Apparently it is very important to provide children with opportunities to experience success which results from their own skills and efforts, and to provide feedback that makes the relationship between behavior and outcome highly discernible.

Measurement of locus of control.   Differences in children's tendencies to interpret their successes and sorrows as the result of either chance or their own efforts and skills have been measured in various ways. Rotter's original instrument for measuring internal and external control perceptions, the I-E (Internal - External) Scale, was not suited for use with young children. Therefore, a number of investigators have attempted to develop downward extensions which would be appropriate for use with elementary and high school (e.g., Crandall, Katkovsky, & Crandall, 1965) or preschool (e.g. Stephens & Delys, 1973) children.

One of those instruments, the *Intellectual Achievement Responsibility* (IAR) *Questionnaire* (Crandall, Katkowsky, & Crandall, 1965) illustrates the types of items used to obtain responses from which inferences about locus of control are drawn. While Rotter's original instrument was intended to measure generalized expectancies, the IAR Questionnaire was developed to predict school achievement and striving behavior. It is purported to be suitable for children from third grade up. The distinctly academic focus of the instrument is evident in the following sample items from the IAR Questionnaire.

If a teacher passes you to the next grade, would it probably be

a. because she liked you, or
b. because of the work you did?

If you forgot something you heard in class, is it

a. because the teacher didn't explain it very well, or
b. because you didn't try very hard to remember?

Suppose you didn't do as well as usual in a subject in school. Would this probably happen

a. because you weren't as careful as usual, or
b. because somebody bothered you and kept you from working?

Suppose you became a famous teacher, scientist, or doctor. Do you think this would happen

a. because other people helped you when you needed it, or
b. because you worked very hard?

*Internal control,
sex, and achieve-
ment*

There is some evidence that boys who score high on the "internal-control" dimension of this measure do score higher on reading and arithmetic measures than do "externals," and that they spend more time in free play activities of an intellectual nature. The same does not appear to hold true for girls.

Individual differences and situational influences. Some efforts to measure locus of control have only assessed the degree to which expectancies of success result from one's own action or from external forces. Work by Mischel, Zeiss, and Zeiss (cited in Mischel, 1974) has shed additional light on the relationship between individual differences in children's expectations by measuring locus of control expectancies separately for positive and negative events. For one thing, there was little relationship between children's locus of control for positive events, and their locus of control with respect to negative events. Scores reflecting belief in internal control of positive events were labeled $I+$. Belief in internal control of negative events was labeled $I-$. Not only were $I+$ and $I-$ essentially unrelated to each other, but when the scores for $I-$ and $I+$ were correlated with delay of gratification, differential relationships were found. In situations in which goal-directed behavior could result in a positive outcome, $I+$ (but not $I-$) was related to persistence. In those situations where behavior could present a negative outcome, $I-$ was related to persistence but $I+$ was not. These results suggest that children's beliefs about locus of control may have some influence on their goal-directed behaviors, but the effects of these beliefs are moderated by conditions such as whether the outcome being waited for is a positive event or the prevention of negative outcomes, and whether the child's expectancy is to control positive events or negative events. Both expectancies concerning control of consequences and the specific goal-directed behaviors which may be influenced by locus of control perceptions seem to be highly specific.

These findings should caution against the assumption that highly generalized perceptions of internal or external control influence behavior across diverse situations. Lower-class people, for example, generally score more toward the external end of the locus of control dimension, and blacks appear more external than whites. Such a pattern is what one might expect given the orientation of most locus-of-control instruments toward expectations which have to do with outcomes like "success," influencing governmental decisions, school grades, and the like. If social barriers reduce the chances that individual effort will lead to "success" or policy influence, for example, it seems reasonable that a belief that control is external, and somewhat beyond one's own influence, could be a reasonably realistic representation of the environment. It is likely, however, that there are other areas of life in which the contingent relationship betwen effort or skill and outcomes may be clear for poor people and members of minorities. This possibility requires further exploration.

SELF-CONCEPT

It has already been necessary on several occasions to speak of *self-concept*. Few psychological concepts are granted the degree of credibility that has been afforded the notion of self-concept in the eyes of the general public. It makes perfectly good sense to most people to believe that in order to do well in school, in social relationships, or in any number of other pursuits, people must have positive feelings about themselves. The fostering of positive feelings about self is an important goal of most social and educational programs for children, and is likely to be the goal of highest priority in the preschool and early grades. Like other psychological concepts which have popular appeal (IQ is another such concept), the complexity of the self-concept and its relationship to other aspects of human behavior is often overlooked.

Self-concept refers to the beliefs, feelings, attitudes, and personal qualities which a person views as salient characteristics of herself (Coopersmith & Feldman, 1974; Walker, 1974). Many psychologists believe that those beliefs and assumptions about one's own nature which form the self-concept are ". . . persistent and enduring features of the individual's psychological experience" (Coopersmith & Feldman, 1974).

A unitary or situation-specific trait

In popular usage, the self-concept is usually regarded as a unitary self-evaluative trait. Caretakers of young children often say that a particular child has a *good* or *positive* self-concept, or that another child has a *poor* self-concept. A moment's reflection should suggest that rarely are things so simple as that. One child may have a very positive view of himself as a competent reader, but recognize that he has difficulties in mathematics. Another child in school may feel inadequate in a number of academic subjects, but eagerly look forward to recess where her athletic abilities give her a chance to excel and be a leader.

Measurement of self-concept

Self-concept is commonly thought of in terms of evaluative self-judgments, but not all aspects of self-concept involve judgments of worth or ability. Components of the self-concept include a notion of what one looks like, and other personal characteristics, to which judgments of worth may or may not be applied. Perhaps this is best understood by considering the characteristics commonly taken into consideration by instruments designed to measure self-concept. Most such instruments involve self-report, which may require a respondent to identify himself with a particular description, or to rate the degree to which statements are judged to be descriptive of his own characteristics. The *Lipsitt Self-Concept Scale*, for example (Johnson & Bommarito, 1971), employs 22 trait descriptive adjectives. Each adjective is preceded by the phrase "I am. . . ." The subject rates the degree to which the statement describes her. The adjectives employed should give the reader some idea of the diversity of qualities which may be considered components of self-concept. The adjectives used in this scale include friendly, happy, kind, brave, honest, likable, trusted, good, proud, loyal, cooperative, cheerful, thoughtful, popular, courteous, jealous, obedient, polite, bashful, calm, helpful, and lazy. Even the Boy Scout law pales by comparison to such a list. Other scales include still additional qualities, such as physical ability, attractive appearance, and work habits (cf., Sears, cited in Johnson & Bommarito, 1971).

Formation of Self-Concept

The formation of self-concept appears to take place in much the same way as other kinds of concepts are acquired. Both objects and events have attributes or properties which can be discerned by an observer. Every object or class of events has some characteristics which are similar to those of other objects and events, and some which are typical of the object or event under consideration. Information about one's own attributes comes from environmental feedback. The physical environment provides some kinds of information about one's performance. When a child learns to ride a bike, swim, or even build structures with blocks, the directly observable outcomes of her acts provide feedback on the proficiency of the performance (Coopersmith & Feldman, 1974). At an even earlier age perhaps, children get feedback in the form of the reactions of significant others in their environments, i.e., parents, siblings, and other caretakers, about how they are regarded by other people. Their own self-images and evaluations may directly reflect the evaluations they perceive in the reactions of significant others in the environment (Mead, 1934).

Environmental feedback. From environmental information, the individual begins to form an impression about the kind of person she is. People make remarks about how attractive a child is. If she begins to talk at an early age, and if she says things that seem clever or sophisticated for her age, people are likely to comment on it in her presence. If a child learns to throw and catch a ball at an early age, people may communicate in various ways that she is precocious in physical abilities. On the basis of such information the developing child begins to get some idea of what kind of person she is, at least as this information is provided within the scope of physical and interpersonal experiences. But information must be simplified in some fashion in order to be used. As Mischel has put it, ". . . self-concepts, like impressions of other aspects of the world, involve a synthesis and organization of a tremendous amount of information" (Mischel, 1971, p. 411). It is a matter of simple information reduction. One cannot deal with all the discrete information available, and therefore, some means of reducing the incoming information to a relatively small number of categories seems necessary. Two factors which seem to influence the use of incoming feedback are primacy of information, and the number of categories available for coding environmental input.

Influences on use of feedback

It is commonplace knowledge that first impressions may override the effects of later information. Children form impressions about themselves from the information provided by the reactions of people and physical events in the environment. Information available from such feedback is categorized, and the early impressions or categories into which an individual classifies environmental input may well influence her perceptions of future events (Mischel, 1971). Once categories or impressions are formed, future feedback may well be overlooked if it is contradictory to initial impressions, whereas information which is congruent with established categorizations will be used to substantiate early impressions. The categories of information on self generated by an individual may then have a constraining effect on subsequent information (Mischel, 1971), or act as a filter through which subsequent information is screened (Coopersmith & Feldman, 1974). This phenomenon is referred to as a primacy effect. In the present context it means that the earliest images of oneself serve to bias or selectively channel later information (Mischel, 1971).

Early impressions

Primacy effect

A second factor which may influence children's use of the information available from environmental information is the number of categories available to the individual for the organization and classification of incoming information. Dornbusch and his associates (Dornbusch et al., 1965) demonstrated the influence of the categories available for classification of individual characteristics by having children describe each other. In some cases one child described two other children. In one of the other conditions two children gave independent descriptions of a third child. The most interesting finding was that there was more similarity among a single child's descriptions of different children, than there was overlap in the descriptions of a single child rendered by independent child observers. It appeared that children's categorizations and descriptions were more dependent on their own perceptions and on their own implicit categories for the classification of observed characteristics than on the objective qualities of the child being perceived. Similar processes undoubtedly operate in the organization and classifications of children's own self-perceptions. With increased maturity, most concepts change from relatively global and undifferentiated to more differentiated impressions. It has been demonstrated that similar developmental changes take place in self-evaluations. Mullener and Laird (1971) demonstrated that with increased age, people tend to give increasingly more variable ratings across content areas when they evaluate themselves. This development parallels the development of other cognitive products, but in the case of self-

Available categories

Global and differentiated concepts

concept, it is not clear from the available evidence to what extent the progression from global to more differentiated self-concepts is due to an increasing capacity to form differentiated impressions, and to what extent it is due to increasing complexity and specificity in the feedback associated with performance as children grow older. It seems most likely that both factors are important. There are probably age-related differences in the complexity of information which individuals receive about themselves, and there are probably at the same time developmental changes in cognitive capabilities involved in the formation of differentiated self-impressions (Mullener & Laird, 1971).

Resolution of cognitive inconsistencies. While primacy effects result in selective attention to information about self which is congruent with earlier impressions, there appear to be other factors whch also contribute to a relatively consistent impression of one's own nature. Certainly not all of the information available about one's self is consistent. As Mischel puts it (1971), someone may steal on one occasion, lie on another, perform a charitable act on a third occasion, while cheating on a fourth. Yet that person may consider himself basically honest and moral. How can such inconsistency in behavior be resolved with a self-impression that obviously ignores many of the facts? It seems to be a general rule of cognitive activity that information is simplified and cognitive inconsistencies reduced so the information may be dealt with (Mischel, 1971). It is impossible to deal independently with each separate bit of available information, and it is difficult for an individual to hold two ideas that are discrepant. Festinger (1957) main-

*Cognitive
dissonance* tains that when an individual is confronted with two ideas that are psychologically dissonant, or inconsistent with each other, he reduces the dissonance by reinterpreting the facts in such a way as to make the two ideas more consistent with one another. This seems to be particularly true with reference to information about an object so important as the self. Compatibility may thus be imposed on discrepant cognitions.

Self-esteem

Self-esteem is a concept which is closely related to self-concept; indeed, some writers use the terms interchangeably (cf., Mussen, Conger, & Kagan, 1974). There is, however, an important distinction between self-concept and self-esteem because self-esteem involves a *judgment about the self-concept* (Coopersmith & Feldman, 1974). A child may have a concept of her physical appearance that includes being dark-skinned, speaking Spanish, and having a preference for Mexican food. These qualities may not affect her self-esteem until she begins to learn that these qualities are valued, or devalued, among the significant others with whom she has relationships. It is not likely that a child with these qualities of self would learn that such characteristics may elicit negative reactions from certain significant others such as teachers and peers until she enters school. In that context the salience and consistency of negative evaluations from others may be great enough to overcome the primacy effects of positive evaluations in the home and neighborhood settings.

*Self-esteem
and achievement* *Expectancies.* Some writers assume that a positive self-concept and high self-esteem lead to superior performance. Coopersmith and Feldman (1974), for example, suggest that ". . . positive self-concept and high self-esteem are likely to result in higher achievement, and more negative beliefs and feelings are likely to be associated with underachievement or failure" (p. 194). Cause and effect are often confused, however, and although some studies may be cited (e.g., Watten-

burg & Clifford, 1964) which suggest that high self-esteem predicts school achievement, the bulk of the available evidence seems to favor a different emphasis (Bandura, 1969; Mischel, 1971). As an outcome of experiences, children apparently develop expectancies relating to the outcomes of their performances at different kinds of tasks. As a rule, these investigations place children in a situation in which feedback about the quality of one's performance can be manipulated. When individuals have received positive feedback about their performance, they tend to expect to be successful in their next encounter with a similar task. Feedback that suggests that performance has been inadequate leads people to expect to be unsuccessful in future trials with the task. Moreover, the expectancies formed in one situation have a good chance of generalizing to related situations. The likelihood that generalization will take place depends on the degree to which the two situations are perceived as likely to lead to similar outcomes (Mischel, 1971).

Individual differences.   Expectancies are not the only factors to influence changes in self-esteem that might come about as a result of success experiences, however. Individuals differ in their concerns about avoiding failure and in their achievement striving, and these factors have an influence on the degree to which success or failure experiences will influence self-esteem. Gelfand (1962), for example, administered success and failure experiences in an effort to determine the influence of such experiences on self-esteem. As predicted, success had the effect of increasing self-esteem, while failure experiences lowered it, but Gelfand also found that people who were rated low in self-esteem were more easily influenced to conform than those who were rated high, and regardless of the initial level of self-esteem, those who were exposed to failure were more susceptible to later influences than those who experienced success. Presumably, people who are low in self-esteem want very much to please, and are thus more easily influenced than those who are confident in their abilities. Thus there seems to be a relationship between dependency and low self-esteem. But whatever the initial level of self-esteem, failure experiences may influence individuals to attend more closely to future environmental cues than do success experiences.

*Susceptibility
to influence*

Locus of control and self-esteem.   Locus of control also seems to be related to self-esteem. People appear to differ in the degree to which they believe that they either possess or lack the power to control what happens to them. As we indicated earlier, individuals who tend to interpret environmental events as consequences of their own actions are said to believe in internal control. Those individuals who see events as resulting from events beyond their control are classified as believing in external control. The authors of one study (Epstein & Komorita, 1971) assumed that external control, or a belief that one is powerless to attain personal goals, would be associated with low self-esteem. Their prediction that children with high self-esteem would be more internal than low self-esteem children was confirmed. They were also interested in children's interpretations of success and failure experiences, which were experimentally manipulated. They found that children were more likely to attribute failure than success to external causes. This study, which was conducted with lower-class black boys, has some rather interesting implications. As the authors put it:

> Insofar as a negative self-image is characteristic of an ethnic group exposed to rejection and conspicuous deprivation, this image gives rise to the belief that one's successes and failures are due to forces beyond personal control. (p. 7)

Disenfranchised groups. There is evidence, however, that the self-images of children of groups which have been traditionally disenfranchised may have undergone significant changes over the past 30 or so years. Some of the early evidence relevant to the development of self-esteem of black children was originally inferred from situations in which children were presented with both black and white dolls and asked to respond to the following requests (Clark & Clark, 1947, p. 169).

1. Give me the doll that you like best.
2. Give me the doll that is a nice doll.
3. Give me the doll that looks bad.
4. Give me the doll that is a nice color.
5. Give me the doll that looks like a white child.
6. Give me the doll that looks like a colored child.
7. Give me the doll that looks like you.

This task was administered to children three to seven years of age. With age, children become increasingly accurate in their self-identification, but it was interesting that 61% of the 3-year-olds misidentified themselves with the white doll, and at age 7, 13% of the children still misidentified. This was widely interpreted as evidence of Negro self-rejection, but such conclusions were unfounded because no control group of white children was included in the study. What proportion of white children might similarly choose the "wrong" doll as looking most like themselves? This methodological flaw was corrected in a later study (Greenwald & Oppenheim, 1968) which included a control group of white children and dolls with three differing degrees of skin pigmentation: white, light brown, and dark brown. The proportion of children who "misidentified" was equivalent for both black and white children, but the proportion of black children who "misidentified" was lower than in the Clark study. Thus, while there is evidence that white as well as black students may make "erroneous" choices in a task which requires them to choose a doll that looks most like themselves, both black and white children showed preference for the white doll. This is consistent with Clark's finding that black children showed preference for white dolls more often than for black dolls, and their choices were interpreted as evidence of self-rejection. It was assumed, probably correctly so, that black children's preferences reflected the evaluative stance of the dominant social environment. More recent investigations (e.g., Fox & Barnes, 1971; Hraba & Grant, 1970) along this same line have shown that black children now more often express preference for black dolls and perceive them as more like themselves than was true in earlier studies. It is our guess that this is a direct reflection of the racial pride movement of recent years, and of the fact that successful black models (however unrealistically critics may feel they depict black culture) are much more frequently seen than before through the medium of television. Again, the evidence relevant to the issue of racial identification and self-esteem indicates that older children from both majority and minority backgrounds are more likely to identify with their own group than are younger children. This has been demonstrated with black, American-Chinese, and white children (Fox & Barnes, 1973), and may be the result of both increasing specificity in environmental information and the increasing abilities of cognitive differentiation that come with advancing maturity.

Racial pride and change in self-esteem

The general consensus of these studies seems to be that black children have become more self-accepting than their counterparts who were studied two or three decades ago, but that they are still less self-accepting than white children (Silverstein & Krate, 1975).

Antecedents of self-esteem.   Coopersmith (1967) studied a large number of pre-adolescent boys and their parents in an attempt to identify the antecedents of self-esteem. He did this by administering a self-esteem measure to the boys, and by collecting information relating to child rearing from the parents. Since both sets of measures were administered at the same point in time, the attitudes expressed by parents cannot really be accepted as antecedents of self-esteem in the sense that the conditions under which the boys were reared could predict their self-esteem. Nevertheless, Coopersmith's findings are generally in agreement with those from an earlier longitudinal study (Sears, Maccoby, & Levin, 1957) which employed similar instruments and procedures and studied children of both sexes. The compatibility of the findings from these two investigations increases the level of confidence we can place in Coopersmith's conclusions.

Coopersmith found a number of important differences between boys with high or low self-esteem, as measured by his instrument. Boys with high self-esteem were more likely than their low-esteem counterparts to express confidence in their own opinions. Their confidence seemed likely to permit them to follow their own judgments, but they were also able to consider novel ideas. Individuals with high self-esteem were likely to show greater creativity, and more social independence than boys with lower self-esteem. It is easy to see the relationship between the apparent autonomy which Coopersmith found in boys with high self-esteem, and the greater resistance to external influence reported as a quality of high-esteem children in experimental studies (cf., Gelfand, 1972). Coopersmith also found high self-esteem boys more likely to be active in group discussions and to report less difficulty in forming friendships. They appeared to be less preoccupied with personal problems and less self-conscious than boys expressing low self-esteem. The composite picture of the boys with low self-esteem is almost the exact opposite. They are not likely to be active participants in a group, are self-conscious and preoccupied with their own problems, and the resulting limitations on their social interactions further decrease the likelihood of developing friendly and supportive relationships.

Confidence and autonomy

Peer relationships

Personal adjustment

Some differences in the characteristic behaviors of parents of high and low self-esteem boys were also revealed. Boys with high self-esteem had parents who were also high in self-esteem. These parents were also self-reliant and emotionally stable. They had relatively high expectations for their sons and provided consistent encouragement and support. Mothers of high self-esteem sons were more likely than mothers of boys with low self-esteem to establish rules and to enforce them consistently. Their preferred mode of influencing their children was by rewarding desired behavior, although they also used punishment. When used, punishment was appropriate and straightforward. They did not generally use harsh treatment or withdrawal of love as a disciplinary measure. When punishment was judged necessary, it was usually administered by the father and, interestingly enough, was usually perceived as justified by high self-esteem boys. In contrast, the disciplinary practices of parents of low self-esteem boys were characterized by harsh and disrespectful treatment by the parent. Rather than using reward to promote desired behaviors, parents of low self-esteem boys favored practices characterized by force and threat of loss of love.

Encouragement and support

Consistently enforced rules

Punishment

Parents of high self-esteem children displayed respect for the child by recognizing his rights and opinions and by soliciting his views. They stressed decision making and reasoning in seeking the child's cooperation. As you can see, there is a striking similarity between the child-influence strategies employed by parents of high self-esteem boys in this study, and the modes of control suggested as being appropriate and effective for the management of aggression, as discussed

Respect and reasoning

in chapter 9. The practices which seem to produce the best results appear to be those which establish a warm nurturant relationship, establish reasonable standards for behavior, provide reinforcement for good behavior, and stress reasoning and decision making.

Self-expectations. There is an additional point which should be underscored. In some cases, poor self-esteem may result from holding unreasonably high self-expectations and selectively attending to failure experiences in relation to those expectations, while denying or inadequately symbolizing experiences which are discrepant with negative self-evaluations. In such cases individuals may need help in setting reasonable self-expectations and in symbolizing self-administered reinforcement for meeting those reasonable standards. The fact should not be overlooked, however, that while "some competent people may undergo distress because of excessively high standards of self-reinforcement . . ." in many other cases ". . . unfavorable self-attitudes stem from behavioral deficits and are reinforced through failure experiences occasioned by the person's inability to meet realistic cultural expectations" (Bandura, 1969, p. 614). In view of the rather consistent evidence that self-esteem is enhanced by successful performance, it seems reasonable that in programs dealing with children high priority should be given to assisting them acquire whatever skills are necessary to successfully fulfill cultural expectations, or to change those expectations where possible when they are unreasonable.

SEX-TYPING

In every society children learn behaviors which are culturally defined as characteristic to or appropriate for one or the other of the sexes. Those behaviors which are culturally sanctioned and considered characteristic of one sex but which are ridiculed and considered inappropriate when performed by members of the other sex are called sex-typed behaviors. The process by which individuals come to value and acquire the behaviors considered characteristic of and appropriate for his or her own sex is *sex-typing.* Children's ideas about their own masculinity or femininity, as shaped by feedback from the actions of people in the environment, constitute an important component of their concept of self, so sex-typing is an important process in the development of personal competence. But just as important as one's knowledge of the sex role expectations of his or her

Role options and sex-role stereotypes

own society is a knowledge of and appreciation for a diversity of role options, and the ability to remain unbound by sex-role stereotypes which may artificially restrict the opportunities available to an individual. Children have only the information available from the observation of models in the environment available as the raw material for sex-role formation, and that information may be misleading, even if it is an accurate reflection of the status quo of contemporary society. One of the authors and his family were driving to the mountains on a camping trip when his oldest daughter, then eight years old, asked why it was that all the interesting jobs were only for men. Her question was apparently prompted by the ranger station just passed. When asked why she thought that was so, she elaborated by observing that all the forest rangers, airline pilots, and astronauts were men. It is rather difficult and totally unconvincing to explain that such need not be the case when every shred of objective evidence from personal observation and vicarious experience via the electronic media suggests otherwise.

Generally from birth children are designated as members of one of the sexes, and information about one's sex status is communicated in myriad ways. Ap-

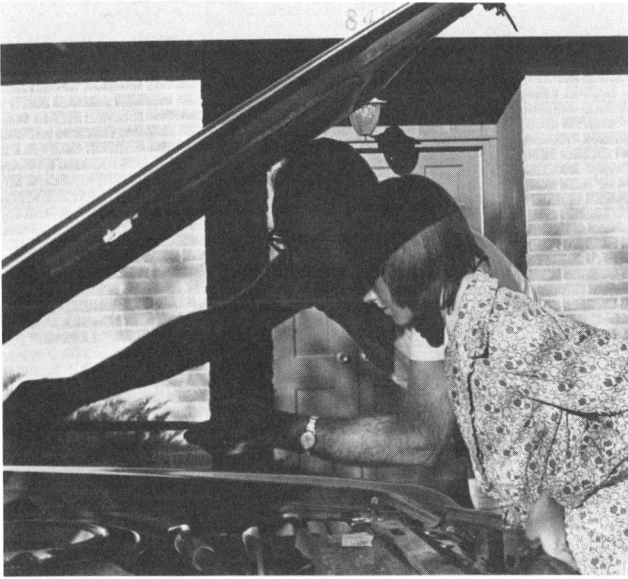

parently the effects of early sex-role assignment are very important. Money (cited in Mischel, 1970) and his associates have carried out a number of studies with hermaphrodites, and the results of these studies suggest that:

> . . . the development of normal sexual behavior requires that the individual be labeled and raised in accord with one sex before he reaches the age of 3 or 4 years. When hermaphrodites were reassigned after that age (in order to be more consistent with their internal sex characteristics) severe maladjustment seemed to result. (p.3)

Descriptive research (Kagan, 1964) on sex-typing shows that children display very definite sex-typed behavior preferences before they go to school. Boys, for example, tend to choose play objects related to sports, aggression, and mechanical things, while objects associated with home and babies are selected by girls. However, there is less crossing of sex-lines by boys than girls; that is, girls frequently select objects or activities that are generally associated with boys' activities, while boys seldom choose objects generally associated with girls' activities. There are plenty of tomboys, but few examples of the male equivalent of that behavior pattern. In fact, we do not even have a name for the male counterpart of the "tomboy," unless perhaps it is "sissy." Boys generally scorn girls' tasks, games, and future life roles, and while girls not infrequently express the desire that they were boys, such a wish to change sexes is virtually unheard of for boys.

Sex-typed behavior preferences

Dependency and Aggression

Among the major behavioral dimensions on which male and female children tend to differ are those behavior patterns associated with dependency and aggression, and these sex-typed behaviors have been studied more than any others. Aggression may be generally defined as behavior aimed at inflicting injury on others, while dependency is evidenced by behavior aimed at receiving the attention of a significant person. Mischel's (1970) major review of literature on sex-typing indicates that by about the age of three, sex differences in aggression may be

Sex differences in aggression

noted. Boys display more physical aggression, more negative attention getting, start more fights, and are more prone to resist attacks initiated by another than are girls. This pattern is apparently fairly consistent across cultures. The Whitings (cited in Mischel, 1970) reported more physical aggression among boys than girls in six cultures, but according to other ethnographic accounts, the pattern is by no means universal (Mead, 1935). The pattern of more frequent aggression among males than females appears to be consistent from childhood to adulthood, and the greater tendency for boys to adopt aggressive behaviors has been documented in both observational and experimental investigations (Mischel, 1970).

Sex differences in dependency

Sex differences in dependency do not seem to originate as early as differences in aggression. With the exception of negative attention getting, there are no major differences in the dependency behaviors of nursery-school-aged boys and girls. Throughout childhood, sex differences in dependency are less clear than for aggression, with the most striking differences occurring in the teens through adulthood, when girls tend to express more dependency than boys. The pattern of greater dependency in older girls tends to be accompanied by greater social passivity and conformity (Mischel, 1970).

Sex-Role Stereotypes

Cross-cultural differences

Just how arbitrary the assignment of particular culturally approved norms for sex-typed behavior may be is dramatically illustrated in Margaret Mead's (1935) comparisons of sex-role behavior in three societies in New Guinea. In one of these societies, the Arapesh, behaviors which we normally think of as masculine were typically engaged in by females, while men displayed behavior which we ordinarily consider feminine. The scope of "feminine" behavior patterns available to the men was of course restricted by their obvious biological limitations. The culturally shared expectations about the typical behaviors which are supposed to be characteristics of members of a given sex constitute sex-role stereotypes. Much of the research on sex-typing has involved the measurement and description of such stereotypes. In our culture, for example:

> . . . females are supposed to inhibit aggression and open display of sexual urges, to be passive with men, to be nutrient to others, to cultivate attractiveness, and to maintain an affective, socially poised, and friendly posture with others. Males are urged to be aggressive in face of attack, independent in problem solving situations, sexually aggressive, in control of regressive urges, and suppressive of strong emotions, especially anxiety. (Kagan, 1964, cited in Mischel, 1970, p. 7)

Pervasiveness of stereotypes

To a contemporary male chavinist, that characterization may sound like the good old days. Obviously that statement does not now, and most likely in 1964 did not well describe many particular males or females who might come to mind. Interestingly enough, even though individuals may reject the stereotypes associated with their sex and may behave in ways which are substantially different from the popular stereotypes, such stereotypes nevertheless are quite widely shared within a culture, and to a certain extent, across cultures (Mischel, 1970). The sex-role stereotypes of a particular culture serve in a sense as evaluative standards against which to judge one's own behavior, even though there are wide variations in the specific sex-role behaviors adopted by individuals. Just as the categories available to an individual for the description of the behavior patterns of one's self restrict and filter one's self-perceptions, so do stereotypes play a part in the organization of information concerning sex roles and have an influence on future perceptions (Mischel, 1970).

Sex-Typing Processes

It is obvious that the significant people in children's environments have an important influence on the development of sex-typed behavior. Theorists and researchers of different theoretical persuasions differ in the degree to which they invoke the concepts of *identification* or *imitation* to explain the formation of sex-typed behavior.

Identification. Much of the research on the development of sex differences in behavior has been guided by the Freudian concept of identification. Supporters of the concept of identification claim that it is a more subtle and complex process than imitation. Imitation is seen as a superficial kind of behavioral mimicry, while identification is said to involve a more pervasive and stable process of internalizing the qualities of significant agents of socialization. Identification is viewed as the principal process by which children develop behavior patterns and personality characteristics similar to those of significant people in their lives.

Since Freud's thinking about the process of identification shifted over the course of the development of his theory, the concept has been used by Freud and his followers to refer to different phenomena. Identification may refer to behavioral similarity between a child and a significant adult, or to motives or dispositional states which presumably influence a child to emulate the standards of parents or other significant people with whom he has contact, or it may refer to the process by which a child comes to emulate various agents of socialization (Bronfenbrenner, 1960).

The concept of identification has also been used to refer to a child's belief that he posseses some of the characteristics of attractive, competent, or powerful people in his environment (Kagan, 1964). For example, a six-year-old boy who identifies with his father will believe that he possesses some of his father's qualities, such as masculinity. When things happen to the father it is as though they were happening to the boy, and thus he shares in his father's victories, his sorrows, his happiness, and his defeats (Kagan, 1964). There is no clear distinction between the process of identification, as viewed in this way, and the concept of empathy discussed in the previous chapter. Mischel (1970) has pointed out that such an empathetic relationship, viewed by Kagan as an aspect of identification, could just as easily apply to the empathetic response of a father to his son. As a popular black comedian of the mid 1970s might have said, "Just who is the identificator, and who is the identificatee?"

Freud distinguished between two mechanisms of identification (Mischel, 1970). The intense dependency relation which a child develops for its mother forms the basis for anaclytic identification. For girls this dependency on the mother is supposed to form the principal basis for identification. Tangentially, it is interesting to note in this regard that while the earliest years of a child's life are presumed to be of crucial importance in the identification process, consistent differences in dependency among boys and girls are not generally identified in the early childhood years.

For boys, the principal mechanism is identification with the aggressor, which we discussed in chapter 8. This process soon supplements the boy's anaclytic identification with the mother, according to the Freudian view.

In both types of identificatory mechanisms, a strong affective relationship between parent and child is assumed, but identification with the aggressor also implies ambivalent feelings in which the boy's love for his father is mixed with hostility resulting from Oedipal urges. Castration fears create anxiety, which the boy resolves by emulating the father and repressing his aggressive wishes (Mischel, 1970).

Researchers who have studied the identification process generally assume that a broad cluster of presumably related behavioral characteristics result from the process of identification. Among the products which have been assumed to result from identification are:

> . . . sex-typing, adult role formation, self-control, self-recrimination, prosocial forms of aggression, guilt feelings, and other expressions of conscience. (Sears, Rau, & Alpert, 1965, p. 1)

As Mischel says;

> It would be elegant if one unitary identification process could be shown to account for such seemingly diverse behavioral manifestations as conscience and self-control, for the formation of enduring sex roles and sex-typing patterns, and for the acquisition by the child of appropriate adult role behavior. (1970, p. 19)

Behavioral variation within categories

Dependency

Categories of dependency

Unfortunately, empirical research has not revealed the consistency among these behaviors that would be necessary to validate the assumption that they all result from the same process, i.e., identification. Even within a single category, e.g., sex-typed behavior, and a single subcategory, e.g., dependency, behaviors are not impressively consistent. Dependency, for example is regarded by many writers as a single global trait, one whose critical relationship to traditional conceptualizations of the process of identification has already been discussed. It has been demonstrated that dependency takes a number of different forms, and individual children may display a good deal of one form of dependency but little of another. This was nicely illustrated in a study in which Sears (1963) defined five categories of dependency and objectively observed and coded instances of these behaviors in a sample of nursery school children. The five categories of dependency were: negative attention seeking, as when children gained attention by behaving aggressively or disruptively, positive attention seeking, as, for example, attempting to elicit praise, nonaggressive touching or holding, being near, as in following or standing beside the teacher, and seeking reassurance.

A total of 21 boys and 19 girls were observed for seven to ten hours each. The intercorrelations among the dependency categories are displayed in table 10-1. Only one of the correlations, that for the relationship between *touching* and *holding and being near,* were statistically significant, and then only for the girls. A number of other studies have reported congruent findings (e.g., Mann, 1956; Heathers, 1953; Gewirtz, 1956), buttressing the conclusion that dependency is not a highly consistent trait even within individuals. Since dependency is crucial to anaclytic identification, and the evidence provides little support for a unitary concept of dependency (Mischel, 1970; Sears, Rau, & Alpert, 1965), the assumption that dependency is a crucial factor in identification is left with little empirical support.

Lack of distinguishing criteria for identification and imitation. Since the concept of identification has so many varied meanings, including behavioral similarity, motives, and processes, and since there is little empirical support for the view that identification is a more subtle and significant process in the acquisition of sex-typed behavior than imitation, traditional distinctions between identification and imitation seem unwarranted. Bandura (1969) has reviewed the usage of the concept of identification and concluded that there is little agreement about the criteria differentiating identification from imitation, and that both terms generally refer to the tendency of one individual to reproduce the actions, emotional responses, or attitudes of others. It is not a one-way process of influence from socialization agent to child. Rather it seems to be a reciprocal process (Mischel, 1970), with influence flowing in both directions. Witness the middle-aged men who adopted the longer hair and clothing styles of their sons in the late 1960s.

Imitation. As imitation is conceptualized in social learning theory, it is not the simple, direct behavioral matching or mimicry which more psychoanalytically oriented psychologists contend. Like many other behaviors and conceptual rules, sex-typed behaviors may be acquired through observation of a variety of different models in the environment. Research on imitation resulting from observational learning demonstrates that behaviors can be acquired without reinforcement, although direct reinforcement or the expectation of reinforcement certainly influences the actual performance of behaviors learned through observation. In addition to learning specific behavioral forms, an observer also learns about the characteristics of the physical and social environment. From this the learner can deduce the probable consequences of performing given behaviors. When children learn through the observation of a variety of different models, and when they witness the outcomes of given behaviors, they are able to adopt various components from the behavior of different models, and vary their behaviors on the basis of their acquired expectations about behavioral consequences in different situations. Social learning research also demonstrates clearly that a child's sex-role learning is not restricted to the qualities displayed by the like-sex parent, but is also greatly influenced by other children (Mischel, 1970) and undoubtedly

Selective adoption of behaviors

Intercorrelations among Categories of Dependency　　　　Table 10-1

Dependency Categories	Girls					Boys				
	I	II	III	IV	V	I	II	III	IV	V
I. Negative Attention		.06	.10	.15	.37		−.24	.23	.04	−.03
II. Reassurance			.25	.19	.26			−.11	.14	.12
III. Positive Attention				.11	−.03				−.16	−.14
IV. Touching and Holding					.71*					.13
V. Being Near										

*Significant .01 level

(Adapted from "Dependency Motivation," *Nebraska Symposium on Motivation*, by R. R. Sears, by permission of The University of Nebraska Press, Copyright © 1963 by the University of Nebraska Press.)

also by vicarious influences provided by television, movies, reading material, and perhaps even by the lyrics of popular songs.

As we indicated in chapter 8, research on observational learning processes has identified some of the specific conditions, such as characteristics of models, that influence the likelihood that given behaviors will be adopted. It becomes clear that model characteristics such as nurturance and power to control resources do not invariably influence children to imitate the behaviors of those models, even though this is often the case. The effects of nurturance and power over resources may differ depending on the type of behavior displayed by a model, and the situation in which it is displayed. It would be nice if the influences on the adoption of sex-typed or other categories of behavior were so simple as theories postulating unitary influences propose, but wishing will not make it so. What does seem to be suggested is that generally, a model who is liked, respected, powerful, or competent is more likely to influence the developing child than one who has no such relationship to her. Moreover, the restricting effects of sex-role stereotyping should be easier to overcome when children have a chance to observe both male and female models displaying a diverse range of behaviors. It is highly likely that cultural influences institutionalized in the form of media programming and instructional materials used in schools may restrict the opportunities of children to emulate models whose behaviors represent the entire range of opportunity which will probably be available to individuals of both sexes by the time today's children become adults. This issue will be explored in chapter 12.

SUGGESTED READINGS

Bandura, A. Social-learning theory of identificatory processes. In D. A. Goslin (Ed.), *Handbook of socialization theory and research*. Chicago: Rand McNally & Co., 1969.

Bronfenbrenner, U. Freudian theories of identification and their derivatives. *Child Development*. 1960, *31*, 15-40.

Caldwell, B. M., Wright, C. M., Honig, A. S., & Tannenbaum, B. S. Infant day care and attachment. *American Journal of Orthopsychiatry*, 1970, *40* (3).

Crandall, V. C., Katkovsky, W., & Crandall, V. J. Children's belief in their own control of reinforcement in intellectual-achievement situations. *Child Development*, 1965, *36*, 91-109.

Harlow, H., & Harlow, M. H. Learning to love. *American Scientist*, 1966, *54* (3), 244-72.

Hetherington, E. M. The effects of familial variables on sex-typing, on parent-child similarity, and on imitation in children. In J. P. Hill (Ed.), *Minnesota Symposium on Child Psychology*. Minneapolis, Minn.: University of Minnesota Press, 1967. Pp. 82-107.

Maccoby, E. E., & Jacklin, C. N. *The psychology of sex differences*. Stanford, Calif.: Stanford University Press, 1975.

Mead, M. *Sex and temperament in three primitive socities*. New York: U. Morrow & Co., 1935.

Mischel, W. Sex-typing and socialization. In P. H. Mussen (Ed.), *Carmichael's Manual of Child Psychology*, Vol. 2 (3rd Ed.). New York: Wiley, 1970.

Rosen, B. C., & D'Andrade, R. The psychosocial origins of achievement motivation. *Sociometry*, 1959, *22*, 185-218.

Swanson, R., & Henderson, R. Achieving home-school continuity in the socialization of an academic motive. *Journal of Experimental Education*, (in press).

Part Five

Socialization

11

The Socialization Process

Instructional Objectives

Recognize or recall
Compare and contrast
Describe or demonstrate
Evaluate

the sociological view of the outcomes of socialization.

the definition of and the use of norms in socialization.

the definition of the terms *role* and *social structure*.

the ways in which roles are assigned.

the influence of socializing agents on role-related behavior.

task requirements for the analysis of social structure.

the behavioral view of the outcomes of socialization.

the meaning, situational specificity, and analysis of *behavior-contingency units*.

the trait view, personality-structure position, and intellectual-structure position regarding the outcomes of socialization.

the analysis of personality and the analysis of the intellect.

the use of Gordon's concepts of door openers and active listening in the analysis of personality.

the use of Piaget's clinical method of investigation in the analysis of the intellect.

the sociological, behavioral, and interactive views of the outcomes of socialization.

the meaning of the terms *cuing, modeling, reinforcing, shaping, extinguishing,* and *punishing.*

the advantages, uses, and conditions influencing cuing and modeling in socialization.

the meaning of the terms *positive* and *negative reinforcement*.

types of positive reinforcers and advantages and limitations associated with each of these types.

the meanings of the terms *primary reinforcer* and *secondary reinforcer*.

intermittent or partial reinforcement schedules including fixed-ratio, fixed-interval, variable-ratio, and variable-interval schedules of reinforcement.

the meanings of the terms *token economy* and *point system*.

the steps involved in setting up a token economy or point system.

the effects of inadvertent reinforcement on socialization.

the uses, limitations, and influences related to shaping, extinction, and punishment.

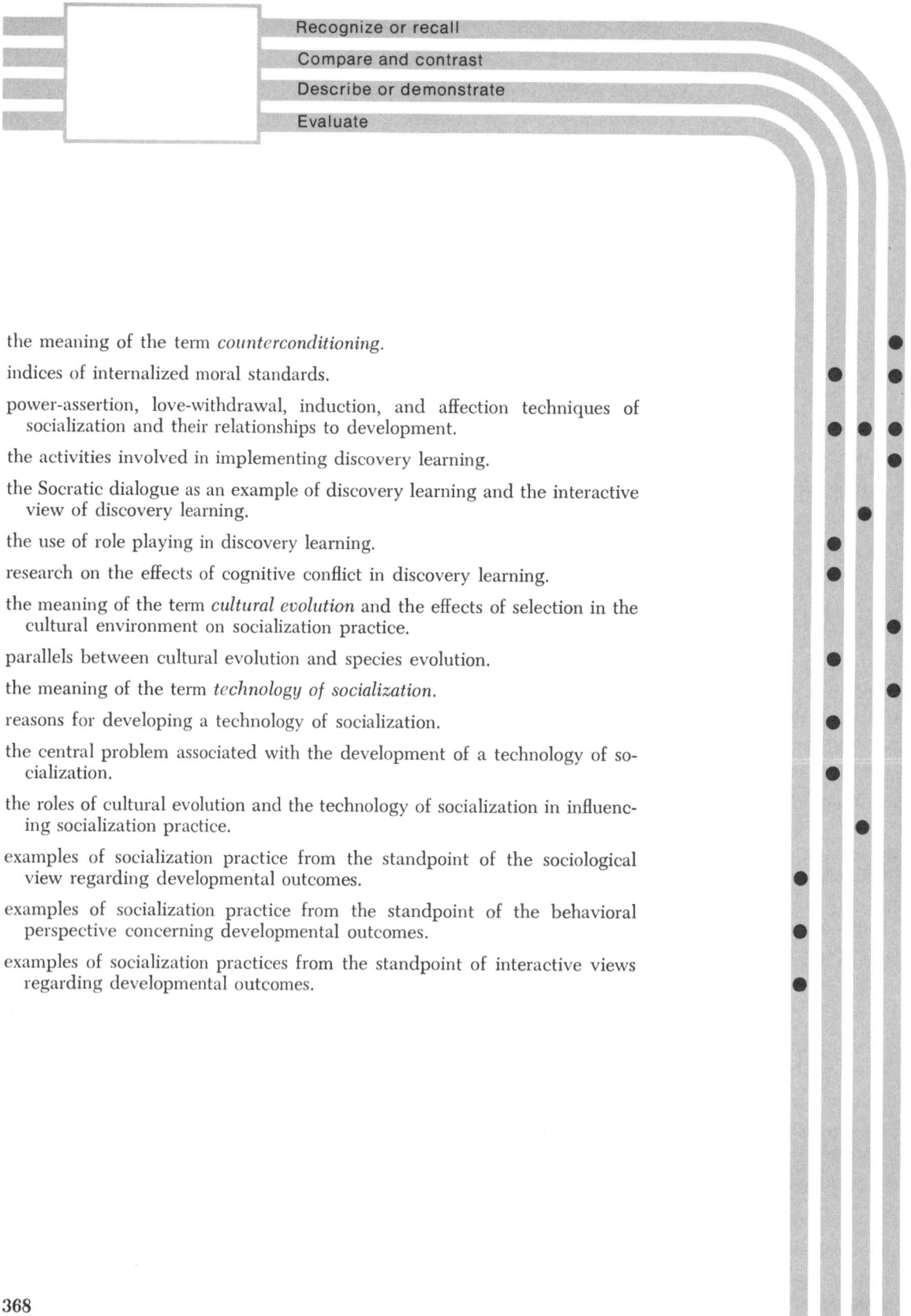

Recognize or recall

Compare and contrast

Describe or demonstrate

Evaluate

the meaning of the term *counterconditioning*.

indices of internalized moral standards.

power-assertion, love-withdrawal, induction, and affection techniques of socialization and their relationships to development.

the activities involved in implementing discovery learning.

the Socratic dialogue as an example of discovery learning and the interactive view of discovery learning.

the use of role playing in discovery learning.

research on the effects of cognitive conflict in discovery learning.

the meaning of the term *cultural evolution* and the effects of selection in the cultural environment on socialization practice.

parallels between cultural evolution and species evolution.

the meaning of the term *technology of socialization*.

reasons for developing a technology of socialization.

the central problem associated with the development of a technology of socialization.

the roles of cultural evolution and the technology of socialization in influencing socialization practice.

examples of socialization practice from the standpoint of the sociological view regarding developmental outcomes.

examples of socialization practice from the standpoint of the behavioral perspective concerning developmental outcomes.

examples of socialization practices from the standpoint of interactive views regarding developmental outcomes.

Socialization is an extremely broad topic that has been defined in a variety of ways. Stanford University psychologist Robert Hess describes socialization as ". . . the patterns of antecedent variables which shape behavior and tie it to the social system in which an individual lives" (1970, p. 457). The emphasis in Hess's definition is on the environmental conditions that affect social learning. *Definition of socialization*

Hess's definition provides a suitable conception of socialization for our purposes. Our emphasis in this chapter is on what socializing agents do to influence child development and on why they do the things they do. The pursuit of this emphasis will lead us to address a number of specific questions about socialization. For instance, what are the kinds of things that parents and teachers may accomplish through their child-rearing efforts? What practices can they use to achieve their child-rearing goals? What factors determine the techniques that socializing agents employ? Finally, what role can developmental science play in the socialization process?

As we examine the above questions, we shall discuss a number of theoretical perspectives and concepts with which you will have become familiar in previous chapters. However, we will be viewing these theories and concepts from a changed perspective. Whereas in earlier chapters we presented theories and principles as conditions and explanations of development, in the present chapter we shall view them as tools and explanations of socialization. For example, reinforcement may be regarded as a condition affecting development. However, it may also be thought of as a tool used by parents and teachers to guide development.

CHILD-TRAINING PERSPECTIVES AND THE OUTCOMES OF SOCIALIZATION

What a parent, teacher, or other socializing agent believes regarding the outcomes of socialization will probably determine the methods that he applies in guiding development. As indicated in table 11-1, there are currently three basic views regarding the outcomes of socialization: the sociological view, the behavioral view, and the interactive view. The sociological position holds that the central outcome of socialization efforts is adherence to group standards. The be-

havioral view is that socialization leads to the development of behaviors which
are under the control of specific stimulus conditions. Finally, the interactive
stance is that socialization produces stable intellectual structures and personality
characteristics which control behavior.

Table 11-1   *Perspectives Regarding Socialization Outcomes and Practices.*

Theoretical Perspective	Socialization Outcomes	Guides for Socialization Practice
The Sociological View	acquisition of behavior patterns conforming to norms and roles	the analysis of social structure
The Behavioral View	acquisition of behavior contingency units	the analysis of behavior-contingency units
The Interactive View	acquisition of intellectual structures, traits, and personality structures	the analysis of intellectual structures and personality structures

Each of the above views regarding the outcomes of socialization suggests a
different set of guiding principles for socialization practice. When socializing
agents act in accordance with the sociological view, they tend to govern their
actions in accordance with analyses of group standards. When they operate
within the behavioral perspective, they guide their socialization efforts primarily
on the basis of analyses of environmental conditions influencing specific behaviors. Finally, when they are influenced by the interactive view that socialization
produces stable intellectual structures and personality characteristics, they derive
guidance primarily from analyses of the characteristics of the child.

At one time or another, socializing agents may act in accordance with all the
above perspectives. A parent, for example, will often use behavioral principles
to produce conformity to group standards. Similarly, a teacher may explain a
child's failure to conform to group expectations as a manifestation of an undesirable personality trait, such as aggressiveness.

The Sociological View

Socialization and conformity

The sociological view regarding child rearing is that what a child learns through
child training is to conform to societal expectations. Adherence to social expectations serves the vital function of perpetuating culture. If the individuals within
a culture did not behave to a significant degree in predictable and socially appropriate ways, social institutions would soon break down. Chaos would replace
order, and the cultural knowledge base accumulated across successive generations would quickly disappear (LeVine, 1973). Under these conditions both the
survival of the culture and of the people within it would be in jeopardy.

Although conformity to societal expectations perpetuates culture, it does not
necessarily impede change within a culture. In societies in which there are relatively few standards which remain fixed over long periods, very little change
occurs. However, in the complex technological societies of Western culture, there
are many standards. Moreover, new standards derived from scientific research
and social experimentation are continually arising. As a result, change and

diversity are among the few stable features in technological societies. Ironically, conformity to societal expectations in technological cultures tends to perpetuate cultural variability (Hess, 1970).

Socialization and conformity to norms.   Some of the expectations which a group holds for its members apply to all individuals in the group. Expectations of this kind are called group norms. For example, if you belong to that group of individuals who drive automobiles in this country (and if you are not a member of some special class of persons such as police), you are expected to stop your vehicle when you come to a red light. The expectation that drivers stop at red lights constitutes a norm which, if violated, may result in societal sanctions against the violator. *Norms*

In part, socialization can be regarded as the process of transmitting norms to the young. A mother taking her young child shopping in the car might be asked: *Why are we stopping? We always stop at red lights.* She may answer: *If we don't stop we could be hit by another car, or we might get a ticket. Then we would have to pay money to the city.* Later when the child is at home playing with friends, he may say: *You just went through a red light. I'm going to give you a ticket.* Through this kind of play, societal expectations are rehearsed and communicated to other young members of the culture.

Individuals in a society generally belong to a number of groups, each of which may have unique norms. In America virtually everyone belongs to what is generally called the mass culture (Kopan, 1974). This culture is comprised of the shared norms and values communicated mainly through mass media such as television. In addition to the mass culture, individuals in American society may belong to various ethnic and social groups.

Variations in group norms associated with different groups within a culture are one of the major sources of cultural diversity and, to some degree, cultural conflict within societies. For example, one of the most familiar sources of conflict in many societies is that associated with group norms that differ across generations. The old lament the errant ways of the young, and the young, for their part, generally find it necessary to challenge the established cultural patterns and traditions of the adult world.

Socialization as the acquisition of roles.   Many group expectations apply only to a particular class of individuals within the group. In the family group, sons are expected to behave differently from daughters. Similarly, fathers are expected to behave differently from mothers. Expected behavior patterns for a specific category of individuals are called roles (Sarbin & Allen, 1968). *Definition of role*

Roles, like norms, can be transmitted to the young in a variety of ways. Parents, of course, play a particularly important part in role transmission. They interpret roles for their children by describing and explaining societal expectations (Hess, 1970). In addition, they model role behavior for their children as they perform the routine tasks in their daily lives (Maccoby, 1959).

As discussed in detail in chapter 8, role taking begins quite early in life (Hetherington & McIntyre, 1975). In the course of development, the child acquires extensive knowledge about roles, practice in enacting them, and a highly sophisticated set of role-taking capabilities (Flavell, 1973).

The total set of roles within a group is called the social structure for the group. For example, the social structure associated with a school includes roles for students, teachers, secretaries, maintenance staff, administrators, and so on. *Social structure*

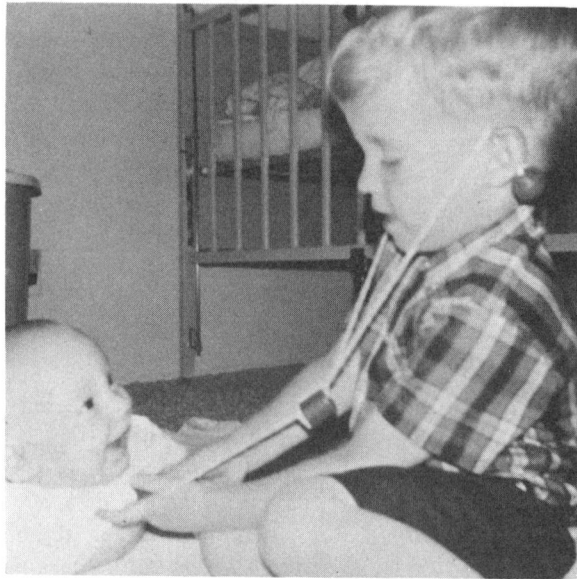

Roles in a social structure are not assigned directly to individuals. Rather they are allocated to positions which individuals may occupy within a group. Each position in a social structure will entail certain behavioral expectations. For instance, an individual may occupy the position of child, boy, student, and peer within a group. Each of these positions will require highly specialized behavioral patterns. As a student the individual may be expected to do his homework, raise his hand when he has a point to make in class, and recite when he is called upon. As a peer he may be expected to play baseball, build forts in the field behind his house, and put frogs in the teacher's desk.

Some of the positions that an individual may occupy in a group are assigned independently of his behavior. Roles associated with positions of this kind are *Ascribed roles* called ascribed roles. A child, for instance, has no choice with respect to occupying the position of child. As a consequence he cannot readily go into business, make people take his views on politics seriously, or tell adults to be careful when they're crossing the street.

Many of the positions that an individual may occupy are earned. Roles associated with positions of this kind are said to be achieved. A high-school girl *Achieved roles* might achieve the role of class president by campaigning vigorously for that office. Similarly, she might achieve the role of homecoming queen by emitting the necessary behaviors to earn that honor.

Child training and the analysis of social structure. As implied in the above discussion, according to the sociological view the principal function of parents, teachers, and other socializing agents is to instill behavior patterns in the young that conform to societal expectations. From the sociological standpoint, the way in which socializing agents establish behavior patterns is not a matter of particular concern. The issue of importance is what behavioral expectations are communicated to the young.

A child learns something about societal expectations through direct contact with his or her social environment, but he or she also learns a great deal through the interpretations of socializing agents. As Hess (1970) remarks, "The points of contact between the child and the environment are . . . mediated through parents, siblings, other adults or agents (not excluding mass media)" (p. 464).

What the child learns from the interpretations of socializing agents can markedly affect the kinds of roles he or she may later occupy. For example, there is evidence that children's educational goals are significantly related to parental aspirations. Kandel and Lesser (1970) asked mothers of high school students to indicate the highest educational level that they hoped their children would complete. They then asked close friends of the children to provide an estimate of the maximum level of education that the children would probably reach. Finally they requested the children to describe their own educational plans. Children's plans tended to correspond more closely to parental aspirations than to peer estimates.

Socializing influences on role-related behaviors

Freud, in an autobiographical remark quoted by Ernest Jones (1953), attests further to the influence which parents may have on the role-related aspirations of their children: "A man who has been the indisputable favorite of his mother keeps for life the feeling of a conqueror, that confidence of success that often induces real success" (p. 5).

Socializing agents other than parents can have a significant impact on a child's aspirations. The influence of peers is particularly important. For instance, Bandura and Kupers (1964) conducted a study in which peers modeled either high or low standards of self-reinforcement. Children observing models who displayed low standards subsequently tended to reward themselves liberally for rather mediocre task performance. On the other hand, children who had observed models displaying stronger self-reinforcement standards tended to make self-reinforcement contingent upon the achievement of highly demanding goals.

Young Sigmund Freud and his mother. (Kind permission of Mrs. E. L. Freud.)

Adults responsible for socialization interpret the social environment for the children in their charge through an informal analysis of social structure. As Robert LeVine (1969) points out:

> Every adult individual perceives the environment around him and notices to some degree the evaluative and distributive operations of the sociocultural system. From observation of individual instances of conformity and nonconformity, positive and negative evaluation, success and failure, social reward and punishment: in a process equivalent to the vicarious trial-and-error or observational learning of reinforcement theorists: he draws conclusions about which behavioral dispositions are favored and which disfavored. These inductive conclusions become part of his cognitive structure, joining the attitudes, beliefs and values already there, and becoming consistent with them to some degree. From this cognitive structure comes his definition of the situation in which he sees his children growing up and his prescriptions and proscriptions for their adaptive performance. This is his ground plan for the deliberate socialization of his children, guiding their training toward certain goals and away from others. (p. 513)

The analysis of social structure involves three basic tasks. The first is the determination of available roles within a social structure. The second is the acquisition of knowledge of required behaviors for the effective enactment of available roles, and the third is an evaluation of the desirability and appropriateness of roles.

The knowledge that socializing agents have of available roles is a factor of obvious importance in socialization. If a parent is aware of only a limited number of roles to which his or her child might aspire, the parent's ability to convey available opportunities to the child is severely curtailed. In a culturally diverse and rapidly changing society such as that which exists in America today, the problem of acquiring and maintaining awareness is formidable. For instance, a vast array of occupational choices which are available to young people today did not exist a generation ago. Job titles such as systems analyst, computer programmer, and resource teacher were nonexistent just a few decades ago. It is a difficult task for parents and teachers to keep abreast of changes in role options of relevance to children.

The knowledge that socializing agents have of the ways in which various roles are enacted can also be a significant factor in determining development (Hess, 1970). For example, if a parent is attempting to train a child to occupy a position of authority in society, he or she must have some knowledge of the kinds of skills needed to assume positions of that kind.

The evaluation of the desirability and appropriateness of roles by socializing agents may influence the motivation of a child to pursue various roles. Adult evaluation of roles may be influenced not only by the perceived prestige and rewards afforded by roles, but also by assumptions about the feasibility of role attainment. If, for example, a parent continually communicates to a child the belief that the child lacks the ability to achieve high-status roles, he or she may influence the child's assumptions regarding the attainability of such roles (Hess, 1970).

The Behavioral View

According to behavioral theory, what a child learns through socialization is a complex set of behavioral patterns controlled in the main by events in the immediate environment in which behavior occurs. Despite their insistence on environmental control, behaviorists recognize that some of the behavior patterns that are acquired through socialization may serve a self-regulatory function

(Bandura, 1969). After hearing his mother say on countless occasions, *Wipe the mud off your feet before you come in,* a child may begin to control his own foot-wiping behaviors by covert self-instructions similar to those of his mother. However, even though foot-wiping may become a self-regulated behavior, both it and the self-regulatory responses used to control it will still be subject to environmental influence. Thus, if the child in the above example were hurrying in from play to watch his favorite television program or to get a special treat from his mother, he might well forget to wipe his feet at the door.

Socialization as the acquisition of behavior-contingency units. Walter Mischel (1973) describes the behavioral outcomes of socialization as behavior-contingency units. A behavior-contingency unit is comprised of a behavior and the conditions which control the likelihood of its occurrence. For instance, a young boy suffering from awkwardness and an overabundance of adolescent pride might be prone to emitting long strings of verbal abuse toward any of his peers who criticized his athletic performance. Criticism in this example would be a cue setting the occasion for verbal abuse. Temporary cessation of criticism during and following verbal abuse might be reinforcing the behavior. The complete set of events including the cue, behavior, and reinforcement would be a behavior-contingency unit.

Definition of a behavior-contingency unit

According to the behavioral view, the behavioral patterns that occur in behavior-contingency units tend to be situationally specific (Mischel, 1968, 1973). Thus, even though the boy in the above example displayed aggression in response to criticisms of his athletic ability, he might not emit aggressive responses to jibes about his intellectual prowess. Societal recognition of the specificity of conditions controlling behavior is illustrated in the many department stores which carry signs saying: *Shoplifting is stealing.* Presumably the store owners find it necessary to remind their customers that shoplifting and stealing are equivalent acts because people do not behave as though this were the case. It is well known that there are many individuals who would never hold up a convenience market or burglarize a home who would, nevertheless, fill their pockets or purses with department store merchandise that is not theirs.

Situational specificity of behavior-contingency units

The behaviors emitted in a behavior-contingency unit are categories of behavior. However, the categories, like the situations in which they occur, tend to be rather narrow in scope (Mischel, 1968). Accordingly, it would be quite possible that the boy who lashed out at his peers with verbal invectives would never attempt to harm them physically. The actions of a junior high school girl in a violent quarrel with a classmate offer a striking illustration of the specificity of behavior-contingency units. The girl slashed her peer viciously with a razor, cutting the child's throat. However, before she inflicted this wound upon her adversary, she lifted her classmate's hair aside. The reason that she subsequently gave for this action was that she did not want to spoil her friend's hairdo.

Behavioral specificity in behavior-contingency units

Child training and the analysis of behavior-contingency units. From the behavioral perspective, the principal guiding factor for socializing agents attempting to produce planned changes in child behavior should be the analysis of behavior-contingency units. Such analysis involves a precise specification of behaviors to be changed through socialization and a description of the conditions controlling those behaviors (Bergan & Tombari, 1975).

The initial step in the analysis of behavior-contingency units is to specify the child behaviors to be changed in the process of socialization. As any parent or teacher can attest, there are countless numbers of these. A child at dinner may

Behavioral specifications

kick her brother under the table, cut her meat with a spoon, spill her milk, and wipe her greasy hands on her chair all in the span of a few seconds.

Because there are so many behaviors of concern in socialization, it is not possible to specify them all. The general strategy followed by socializing agents using behavioral principles has been to focus on a limited number of behaviors of immediate concern in the socialization process (Bergan & Caldwell, 1967). As an illustration, consider the problem faced by two young parents who had made the mistake of rewarding their child's crying behavior at bedtime by bringing the child into their bed with them. The child would goo and coo in the bed for hours making it impossible for the parents to sleep. Moreover, an occasional leaky diaper sometimes drove the parents from their soft bed to the hard, but dry bedroom floor. If the parents tried to put the child in his own bed, he would blare like a fire truck late into the night. Needless to say, it was not difficult for these blurry-eyed parents to decide what behavior ought to be the immediate focus of their child-rearing efforts.

Although the strategy of focusing on a limited number of behaviors of immediate concern is quite serviceable in many instances, it has certain drawbacks. The parent or teacher who focuses mainly on behaviors of the current moment may fail to relate his or her socialization efforts in any systematic way to the achievement of significant long-range developmental goals. Behaviorists have often been criticized for applying their powerful technology to achieve trivial and sometimes questionable socialization goals (e.g., see Winett & Winkler, 1972). Many contemporary educators doubt that any benefit is achieved by the behavior modifier who has been successful in making a young child sit in his or her seat or keep silent throughout the long course of the school day (Silberman, 1970). It is possible that one reason for the trivial outcomes of some behavioral programs is that behaviorists have sometimes failed to articulate specific concerns of the moment to long-range developmental purposes.

Of course there is nothing inherent in the behavioral position which would prevent it from being applied toward the achievement of long-range developmental objectives. Indeed in some instances behavioral principles have been used in the pursuit of significant long-range goals. For example, behavioral programs involving the design of instructional systems have often been directed toward the attainment of long-range objectives of clear significance to children's intellectual development (e.g., see Gagné, 1970; Glaser & Nitko, 1971).

Adults in American culture have a tendency to describe the behavior of other people in rather global terms (Mischel, 1973). A teacher may depict a child as immature, listless, lazy, or obstreperous. Similarly, the child's Boy Scout leader may describe him as helpful, courteous, kind, obedient, loyal, trustworthy, and so forth. While terms like these may be useful in providing a general description of a child, they do, nevertheless, fail to communicate anything very specific about the child's behavior.

In order to use behavioral principles in socialization, it is necessary for socializing agents to translate their global impressions about a child's behavior into specific terms. Thus, if a mother is trying to eliminate a child's temper tantrums, she must begin by clarifying what the child actually does when he has a tantrum. It may be that the child screams. It may be that he bangs his fists against a wall. It may be that he lies on the floor thrashing his arms and legs. Or it may be that he emits all or some combination of these behaviors. In any case, before the parent can do anything about the child's behavior, she must indicate in a rather precise way what constitutes a temper tantrum.

The key to specifying behaviors clearly is to use words that describe observable acts. For example, terms such as *aggression, anxiety,* or *hostility* convey nothing about what an individual actually does. By contrast words such as *hits, kicks, bites,* and *swears* provide a sufficiently vivid description of action to be well understood by potential observers. In behavioral socialization, it is necessary to describe behavior in observable terms even if the socializing agent has no intention of communicating the behavior to someone else. Behavioral specification clarifies socialization concerns not only for others, but also for the socializing agent himself. When a mother takes on the task of indicating exactly what a child actually does to warrant a label such as *immature* or *annoying,* her attention will be directed to specific acts that the child has emitted. When this occurs the parent may learn many things about the child that she had previously overlooked. Moreover, she will be forced to attach very specific meanings to labels which before behavioral specification were defined imprecisely.

After behaviors of concern have been described in observable terms, the socializing agent must specify the conditions under which behaviors that are targets for change occur. This is usually accomplished by noting what happens immediately before and immediately after behavior takes place. Consider the example of parents who sought the services of a pediatrician because of their strong belief that their four-year-old son was suffering from minimal brain dysfunction. They described their child as being uncontrollably hyperactive and asked if medication might be prescribed to calm the child down. The pediatrician, who was familiar with behavioral techniques, referred the family to a psychologist. Observation of the child in a clinical setting revealed that the boy was indeed usually on the go. However, under the influence of appropriate contingencies, his hyperactive behavior disappeared.

*Specifying
conditions*

The psychologist helped the parents to analyze hyperactivity in terms of behavior-contingency units. Hyperactive behavior was defined as jumping on furniture or on persons. This kind of behavior occurred in many types of situations, but it was particularly noticeable when the family had guests. For example, once a guest had been sitting in the living room holding an after-dinner drink, when the child leapt over the back of the guest's chair and grabbed the unwary visitor by the neck. Suitable apologies accompanied by offers to pay cleaning bills followed. When the psychologist asked what generally happened right before hyperactive behavior, the parents indicated that the child would often be sitting quietly in a chair or, in some instances, he would be attempting to initiate a conversation with his parents or the guests. When the parents were asked how they responded to this "good" behavior, they indicated that they generally did not respond to it at all since their attention was directed toward their guests. The consequences of hyperactive behavior were sharp rebukes from the parents. They had tried sending the child to his room but he had responded to this strategy by removing a pet rat from its cage, returning to the living room with the animal, where he proceeded to choke the little creature in front of the aghast guests. The parents finally resorted to taking turns holding the child on their laps when company came.

The analysis of hyperactivity in terms of behavior-contingency units caused these parents to view their child's actions in a new way. They saw parental inattention to "good" behavior as a potential cue eliciting hyperactivity. Parental actions following hyperactive behavior, i.e., rebuking and holding the chld, were regarded as possible reinforcers maintaining hyperactive behavior. As a result of their analysis of behavior-contingency units, the parents developed a new set of socialization strategies. They set up procedures for cuing and reinforcing non-hyperactive behavior and for ignoring hyperactivity. Fortunately, the results of their new approach were beneficial to all concerned.

Interactive Views

Several theories have been presented in previous chapters that view individual variations in development as the result of interactions between hereditary and environmental factors. With respect to socialization outcomes, interactive views generally hold that what a child acquires through socialization is a set of internal characteristics that are relatively stable over time and across situations.

Socialization as the acquisition of traits. Some interactive theorists (e.g., All-port, 1937; Cattell, 1957) take the position that socialization eventuates in the development of stable personality traits. Traits are defined by variations in behavior among individuals. For example, a group of children might be said to vary in the trait of aggressiveness insofar as some children emitted a greater number of aggressive acts than others.

Definition of trait

There are several characteristics which traits are presumed to possess. First of all, they are typically assumed to encompass broad classes of behavior. Thus, the trait of aggressiveness would include such behaviors as physical assaults, verbal abuse, and threats. Traits are also assumed to affect behavior across a wide variety of situations. According to the trait view, if a boy is aggressive at school, he will probably also be aggressive in his neighborhood and at home. Finally, traits are generally thought to be stable over long time spans. This view holds that if a boy is honest, friendly, and outgoing when he is young, he will probably maintain these characteristics as he grows older.

Characteristics of traits

From the standpoint of socialization, one of the most important assumptions about traits is that they are thought to control behavior. According to the trait view, a child hits because he is aggressive. He helps little old ladies across the street because he is kindhearted, and he cheats on examinations because he is dishonest.

The central aim of socialization from the trait theory perspective is to establish desirable traits. This task must be initiated during the early stages of development. As the child matures he or she will develop many traits. Once these have been acquired, they will be very difficult to modify. Thus, it is important that the traits that develop early in life are ones that will be of some benefit to the individual and to society.

Socialization and traits

Socialization as the acquisition of personality structures. Most of the theories of social development discussed in previous chapters take the position that what the child acquires as a result of socialization are personality structures that control his or her behavior. For example, according to Freudian theory, two personality structures, the ego and the superego, are developed as a result of socialization.

Structural theorists, like trait theorists, assume that internal characteristics acquired through socialization are stable across situations and over time. However, unlike trait theorists, they hold that internal structures interact to produce states within the individual that control behavior. For instance, according to Freudian theory, an individual may experience anxiety because of a conflict between different personality structures. The anxiety state, in turn, may produce avoidance reactions for certain situations. Freud (1959) illustrated this view of personality structures, states, and behavior in his famous paper "Analysis of a

Structures and states

Phobia in a Five-Year-Old Boy." The subject of this study was a little boy named Hans who at an early age manifested an extreme fear of horses. At one point his anxiety became so severe that he would not venture out of his house because of the likelihood that he might encounter a horse. Freud traced this phobia to a highly complex conflict between the superego and the id. According to Freud, the child's developing superego produced feelings of guilt and fear of reprisal associated with the boy's sexual longings for his mother. The source of the child's anxiety was his fear of being castrated as a punishment for his sexual desires. This fear was so painful to him that he repressed the reasons for it from consciousness. However, the fear itself remained. In an effort to control his persistent feelings of malaise, the child created a substitute source for his anxiety, namely, the fear that he would be bitten by a horse. In Freud's view, the biting horse was a kind of metaphor symbolizing the act of castration.

Socialization as the acquisition of intellectual structures. As pointed out in previous chapters, some interactive theorists hold that the central outcome of socialization is the acquisition of intellectual structures that govern the kinds of behaviors that an individual is capable of emitting. Jean Piaget and Lawrence Kohlberg are prime examples of theorists in this category. As we have shown previously in the book, Piaget and Kohlberg assume that in the course of successive stages of development intellectual structures are acquired which control the intellectual and moral functioning of the individual.

The control exerted by intellectual structures on behavior is indirect. Structures influence the manner in which an individual conceptualizes the events in his or her environment. The conceptualization in turn affects what he or she does. For example, young children may constitute a continuing threat to person and property because of the kinds of conceptualizations that they have of events in their environment. They may write on walls and furniture with crayons. They may attempt to eat stones or dirt, or they may poke a playmate in the face with a sharp stick. One potential reason for many of these kinds of acts is that young children are simply not aware of the probable consequences of their behavior. As Kohlberg suggests, in the early phases of development, children's actions are probably controlled in the main by anticipated rewards and punishments meted out in large measure by parents. Children lack the necessary intellectual structures to infer the effects of their actions on persons and things in their environment.

Intellectual structures and behavior control

As we have implied in earlier discussions of intellectual and moral development, interactive theorists assume that intellectual structures are stable over time. Primitive structures may give way to more advanced structures during the course of development. However, within any given stage of development, structures will remain stable.

Structure stability

Interactive theorists postulating the existence of intellectual structures assume some generality across task situations. However, like behaviorists, they recognize that the amount of generality across tasks is limited. For example, a child who knows full well that pouring liquid from a short, wide container into a tall, thin one does not change the amount of liquid may nonetheless fail to realize that rolling a round ball of clay into a long cylindrical shape does not change the overall amount of clay (Flavell, 1963).

Child training and the analysis of personality. Interactive personality theorists base their guidelines for socialization practice primarily on the analysis of personality. The analysis of personality typically includes the identification of in-

ternal forces that control behavior and that are presumed to emanate from
personality structures. For example, Freudians generally assume that male children
experience a strong sense of guilt associated with sexual desires directed toward
their mothers. Feelings of guilt are assumed to be incorporated in a personality
structure, the superego. The analysis of a child's superego, then, might include
identification of the specific feelings of guilt that the child experienced regarding
his amorous longings for his mother.

*Awareness and
personality
analysis*

Interactive theorists tend to hold that children and socializing agents are often
unaware of the underlying forces controlling behavior. For instance, from the
perspective of Rogerian theory it would be quite possible that a child's feelings
of inferiority regarding his academic ability could be so disturbing to him that he
would try to keep them out of his conscious thoughts. Moreover, the child could
feel that his parents would react negatively if he communicated his concerns to
them. Insofar as the child was successful in eliminating thoughts relating to inferiority from consciousness, he would deprive himself and his parents of the
opportunity to examine his feelings and thereby to come to some rational conclusion regarding courses of action that might be taken to improve his present
circumstances.

*Personality
analysis and the
examination
of motives*

In most interactive theories, the analysis of personality structures takes the form
of encouraging the individual to examine the internal forces controlling his or
her behavior. Encouragement usually involves reducing the fear associated with
the examination of underlying motivations. Each theory has its own unique procedures for reducing the anxiety associated with self-examination and for interpreting the material revealed in self-study. Thomas Gordon (1970), in his book
Parent Effectiveness Training, describes a method which we shall use to illus-

*A child may confide in a parent when the parent shows acceptance of what the child
has to say.*

trate the interactive approach to personality analysis as it applies to socialization. Gordon's methods are derived to a large extent from the work of Carl Rogers, whose *self-theory* was described in chapter 8.

Gordon suggests that the key factor in getting a child to examine his underlying feelings and motivations is to show acceptance of what the child has to say. The parent must be genuinely interested in the child's concerns. Moreover, the child must feel free to express himself without fear of parental rebuke. In connection with the latter point, Gordon comments that parents are often so involved in meting out discipline that children feel that they cannot communicate with them. As one girl put it:

> It got to the point where we just couldn't confide at all about even the littlest things . . . like school work. I'd be afraid I flunked a test, and I'd tell her I didn't do well. And she'd say, "Well, why not?" and then get mad at me. So I just started lying. I didn't like to lie but I did it, and it got so it didn't really bother me. . . . Finally it was just like two different people talking to each other—neither of us would show our real feelings . . . what we really thought. (Gordon, 1970, p. 30)

Gordon describes two major procedures which can be used to show acceptance. One of these he calls the door opener. The door opener is an invitation to say more about a topic of conversation. Suppose that a child said *I really had a bad day at school.* To invite the child to elaborate on his experiences at school, the parent might respond *Tell me what happened.* As the conversation proceeded, the parent might draw out the events of the day with other door openers such as *I see, Mm hmmm,* and *Did you really?*

Door openers

The second major technique that Gordon describes for showing acceptance is *active listening.* In active listening the parent shows acceptance by interpreting what the child says. Through interpretation the parent shows that he or she understands and can empathize with the child's feelings.

Active listening

Active listening is demonstrated when a parent repeats in his or her own words what he or she believes the child is trying to communicate. Gordon (1970) gives the following example:

CHILD: Daddy, when you were a boy what did you like in a girl? What made you really like a girl?
PARENT: Sounds like you're wondering what you need to get boys to like you, is that right?
CHILD: Yeah. For some reason they don't seem to like me and I don't know why. (p. 53)

Through the use of door openers and active listening, a parent can encourage a child to examine his or her feelings and problems. The result of such examination may be increased understanding for both parent and child of underlying motivations affecting behavior. A father may learn that his son really does not want to go to college. A girl may learn that she is afraid that she will not be accepted by her peers or that she is frightened by the prospect of preparing for a career. When feelings such as these have been expressed, both parent and child should be in a better position than they were before to plot the future course of development.

Child training and the analysis of the intellect. Interactive theorists, such as Piaget and Kohlberg, emphasize the role of the analysis of the intellect in guiding socialization practice. According to this view, the principal task of socializing agents attempting to foster intellectual and moral growth is to provide learning experiences selected to correspond to the developmental level of the child. In order to offer experiences of this kind, socializing agents must be able to analyze the child's intellect to determine his or her level of development.

The analysis of the intellect, like the analysis of personality, centers on the discovery of internal factors controlling behavior. As indicated in previous chapters, in interaction theories such as those of Piaget and Kohlberg, the internal mechanisms controlling behavior are described as intellectual structures. These structures must be inferred from observations of child behavior.

The basic strategy for conducting an analysis of the intellect is to encourage the child to enact and/or to verbalize his or her thinking processes. Piaget refers *The clinical* to this strategy as the clinical method of investigation. The clinical method is a *method* set of interviewing procedures which Piaget developed as a young man while working for Alfred Binet (Flavell, 1963). In the course of administering Binet's test items to many children, Piaget became fascinated with the reasoning that children used in arriving at their answers. In order to encourage children to display their reasoning processes, Piaget adapted the interviewing techniques used in psychiatric clinics of the day, hence the name *clinical method.*

In the clinical method, an adult attempts to uncover a child's thinking processes by asking the child questions. The questions are based on hypotheses that the adult has about how the child thinks. Hypotheses of this kind are often derived from observations of the child's behavior in various natural settings. For example, a child who said to her mother *In what world is New York?* not only raised the possibility that she did not understand the meaning of the term *world,* but also the likelihood that she might be conceiving of geographic location in a much different way from her parent. The parent using the clinical method would explore these hypotheses through systematic questioning. For instance, she might begin by asking: *What is the world?*

Hypotheses about children's thinking may be derived from psychological theory as well as from direct observation of child behavior. For example, the mother familiar with Piagetian theory might wish to determine whether or not her child displayed the egocentrism associated with preoperational thought. As indicated in chapter 5, one way in which egocentrism is manifested during the preoperational subperiod involves the child's tendency to attribute his or her own personal characteristics to things in the environment. He or she might assume, for instance, that inanimate objects have life. A mother could get at least a rough determination of the child's developmental level with respect to preoperational egocentrism by asking questions such as: *Is a stone alive? Is the lake alive? Are the clouds alive?*

Although the socializing agent using the clinical method should have hypotheses to guide his questions, he must be careful not to suggest answers to the child. In this regard Piaget (1963) comments:

> It is so hard not to talk too much when questioning a child, especially for a pedagogue! And above all, it is so hard to find the middle course between systematization due to preconceived ideas and incoherence due to the absence of any directing hypothesis! The good experimenter must, in fact, unite two often incompatible qualities; he must know how to observe, that is to say, to let the child talk freely, without ever checking or side-tracking his utterance, and at the same time he must constantly be alert for something definite, at every moment he must have some working hypothesis, some theory, true or false, which he is seeking to check. (p. 9)

Not only is it necessary to avoid suggesting answers to the child, but also it is essential not to criticize the child's intellectual judgments. In their zeal to insure the accuracy of their children's thinking, parents and teachers may discourage them from saying what they really think. If a child says that a picture is alive or that he wants to go to London for supper, his parents will often react almost reflexively with a criticism intended to correct the child's misguided judgment. Thus, a mother might say: *Pictures are never alive,* or *We cannot go to London for supper. It's much too far. We would have to travel across a large ocean.* Of course, corrective feedback of this kind may serve the useful purpose of eliminating some of the child's errors in judgment. Nevertheless, it also interferes with explorations of the child's thinking processes.

A socializing agent using the clinical method to find out how a child thinks will encourage the child to elaborate on his conceptions of things rather than dwell on the issue of his judgmental errors. The following protocol from one of Piaget's experimental investigations of young children's thinking illustrates the process of encouraging a child to elaborate on his ideas:

"Where does night come from? -*The sky.* -How is the night made in the sky? -*Because there's a watch, and in the morning it points right up and in the evening it's let down.* -Why? -*It's down because night-time is coming?* -And what does that do? -*Because it's night.* -What does the night do when the hand points down? -(The night comes) *because there's the hand pointing down.* Have you known this long? . . . -*Because at home there's a sort of lamp, then a hand; when it falls that makes it night."* (Piaget, 1963, p. 202)

By avoiding the temptation to provide an accurate explanation of the phenomenon of night, which incidentally the child in this example could not possibly have understood, the adult gained a number of useful insights regarding what the child's views on the matter actually were. From the child's remarks, it is clear that he is willing to entertain the notion that the night is caused. Moreover, it is obvious that he is willing to consider as a possible cause an event which an older child or adult would reject immediately as having no bearing whatever on the comings and goings of the night.

The child's comments in the above example suggest that his concept of causality may be quite different from that of adults. A parent or teacher could easily check out this possibility by examining the child's conception of causality in other situations. For example, it would be important to know whether or not the child could adequately comprehend various types of verbal explanations of cause and effect relationships. If the child's mother were to say *You mustn't hit your sister because that would hurt her,* would the child understand this communication in the same way that his mother intended it? Would he realize that hitting could cause painful tissue damage? Would he realize in addition that the prohibition against hitting ought to be generalized to other forms of aggression?

With a young child, the possibility of a lack of understanding of the consequences of aggression would certainly exist. A parent or teacher who was aware of this fact would probably behave differently toward a child than would one who was not cognizant of the possibility of such differences in thinking processes. A socializing agent who knew that a child had not yet developed an adequate conception of causality would probably not try to influence the child's behavior through the time-honored tactic of communicating verbal rules. Until the child were more mature, the socializing agent would not waste his or her energies with comments like: *don't take apart your toys because you'll break them.* As David Elkind (1974) points out, adults often fall into the unfortunate error of believing that children think just like adults do. When they make this error, they fail to adapt their behavior to the developmental level of the child. The purpose for analyzing the intellectual functioning of the child through procedures such as the clinical method is to gain information which will make it possible to adapt socialization efforts to developmental level.

CHILD-TRAINING PERSPECTIVES AND SOCIALIZATION PRACTICE

Definition of socialization practice

Socialization requires a set of child-training procedures which may be emitted intentionally or unintentionally and which either effect or are presumed to effect changes in child development. We shall call procedures of this kind socialization practices. Theories of socialization practice provide a framework for describing and analyzing child-training methods. In addition, they generally offer at least tentative guidelines as to how child-training techniques can be selected and implemented to produce desired developmental outcomes.

Socialization Practice from the Behavioral Perspective

From the behavioral point of view, socialization practices are behaviors emitted by socializing agents that are at least potentially related in a contingent fashion to child behaviors which are targets for change in the socialization process. For example, if a mother wanted a child to sit erectly at the dinner table, she might say: *You have a choice; sit up or leave the table.* If she were in a particularly affable mood, she might offer a bribe: *Sit up and you can have some ice cream.* In either case, a contingent relationship would be established specifying the consequences of the child's sitting behavior.

Antecedent and consequent practices

Behaviorists generally analyze socialization practices in terms of their temporal relationships to child behaviors that are the focus of change in socialization. Procedures that occur immediately before child behaviors of concern are labeled as antecedent practices. Procedures following child behavior are referred to as consequent practices.

Table 11-2 summarizes the major types of antecedent and consequent practices used in socialization. Many of these have been discussed in previous chapters as environmental conditions affecting development. We shall now examine them as tools of socialization.

Cuing. Cuing is among the most widely used antecedent practices in socialization. A cue is a signal for the occurrence of a response. For example, when you say *Please pass the butter,* you are emitting a cue [1] which hopefully will serve as a signal to some nearby listener to respond to your request. Behaviorists generally hold that cues do not directly control behavior. Rather, they derive their power to influence what an individual does because they have been paired in the past with reinforcement (Skinner, 1969). Thus, your dinner companion is likely to pass the butter to you because in the past that act has often been followed by signs of appreciation such as *Thank you.*

Socializing agents make deliberate use of cues countless times during the course of a day. *Pick up your room, get dressed, do your homework,* and *dinner is ready* are some of the many examples of cues that adults use in their daily socialization efforts.

Cues generally have the advantage of being relatively easy to produce. Moreover, their effects on behavior are often immediate. It takes virtually no effort for a teacher to say: *Open your workbooks to page 44.* Furthermore, there would very likely be an immediate response to such a request by most students.

---

1. The cue in this example would, of course, be a mand. See chapter 7 for a discussion of mands and other types of verbal cues.

Cuing can be a particularly effective socialization tool when it is used to provide feedback concerning the adequacy of performance. For example, Glynn and Thomas (1974) studied the effects of cuing on self-control of classroom behavior. They found that a chart providing feedback as to the extent to which children were working on classroom tasks produced stable increases in on-task behavior.

Despite its advantages, there are a number of conditions that may render cuing ineffective. If the child has not learned to discriminate cues being emitted by a socializing agent, obviously he or she will not respond to them. For example, a girl with a slight hearing loss may fail to respond to teacher directions because she does not perceive them accurately.

*Conditions
influencing cuing
effectiveness*

If the child does not know how to emit the behavior being cued, he or she will not respond as expected to the cue. A mother may ask a young child to pick up his room and be angered by his failure to comply with her request. She may fail to realize that the child has not developed a set of standards for evaluating when a room has been adequately picked up,

If a relationship between a cue and positive or negative consequences of behavior has not been established, cuing may not produce desired results. For example, in attempting to teach language skills to young children diagnosed as childhood schizophrenics, Ivar Lovaas (1967) found that before instruction could be effective it was necessary to teach the children to respond to adult cues. This was done by making aversive consequences contingent upon lack of response. If a child turned away or failed to answer when he was asked a question, his therapist-teacher would rebuke him angrily or perhaps slap him on the thigh to eliminate nonattending behavior.

The final condition under which cuing may be ineffective is that in which the

Behavioral Socialization Techniques   Table 11-2

Technique	Definition	Example
Cuing	signaling the occurrence of a response	*Pass the butter.*
Modeling	demonstrating a response to be acquired by a learner	*You say thank you when someone gives you a present.*
Reinforcing	administering a positive reinforcer or withdrawing a negative reinforcer following a response	*I really appreciated your picking up your room.*
Shaping	reinforcing successive approximations to a desired response	*That's much better. I liked your follow-through on that forehand.*
Extinguishing	withdrawing a positive reinforcer contingently related to a given behavior	*A teacher ignores a child's yelling.*
Punishing	adding an aversive stimulus or removing a positive stimulus to reduce behavior	*Since you hit Ted you can't go outside for recess.*

child is being reinforced for behavior incompatible with that occasioned by the cue. When a mother says *Come to dinner* and the child is in the middle of a highly reinforcing softball game, there is a good chance that she will not respond as desired.

Inadvertent effects of cues

Sometimes cues affect behavior in unanticipated ways which cause problems in socialization. For instance, punishment can serve as a cue signaling the subsequent occurrence of positive reinforcement. Ayllon and Azrin (1966) conducted a study with adult schizophrenics that demonstrated this fact. In their investigation a particular response was punished with a loud noise and then positively reinforced with tokens which could be exchanged for prized objects. In a subsequent phase of the investigation, the participants in the study were given a new task which was rewarded with nothing other than the noxious noise. The astonishing outcome was that participants emitted several thousand responses with no consequence other than punishment, which had been the cue for the tokens.

There are countless situations in socialization in which punishment may signal the occurrence of positive reinforcement. One parent may have the habit of comforting a child after the child has been punished by the other parent. Punishment by a teacher may be routinely followed by peer reinforcement. In circumstances like these, there is a strong possibility that socialization efforts will have unanticipated and undesirable outcomes.

Modeling. Modeling is the second major antecedent practice used in behavioral socialization. As we have discussed previously, modeling may have a marked effect on virtually all types of development. When a parent or teacher models physical skills, language behaviors, intellectual competencies, or social behaviors, a child may learn to imitate them through observation.

Uses of modeling

Modeling is a particularly useful tool when the goal of socialization is to introduce a new response or strengthen a low-rate response in a child's behavioral repertoire. Consider the familiar problem of getting young children to share toys rather than fight over them. Chittenden (1942) demonstrated that sharing behavior could be markedly strengthened by the use of modeling. In Chittenden's study, nursery-school children observed 15-minute plays in which dolls representing school children displayed either aggressive or cooperative reactions to frustrating situations. Models displaying aggressive behavior were punished whereas those manifesting cooperative responses were rewarded. In one situation two boys were depicted in a fight over possession of a wagon. The result was that the wagon was broken and neither boy got to play with it. In another version of the incident, the boys were shown enjoying themselves as they took turns with the wagon. As indicated in figure 11-1, children who observed the plays and who had been highly aggressive previously showed a substantial increase in cooperative behavior in the nursery-school setting as long as a month after the experiment.

Haskett and Lenfestey (1974) have demonstrated the effectiveness of modeling in increasing low-rate academic behaviors. In their study adults modeled oral-reading behavior for children in a preschool class. As a result the children engaged in substantially more reading-related activity, such as looking at books, than they did before modeling occurred.

Another use of modeling in socialization is to strengthen inhibitory responses in a child. Modeling used for this purpose has the highly beneficial outcome of enabling the child to escape from punishing and sometimes dangerous situations. When an individual observes a model being punished for a certain response, the

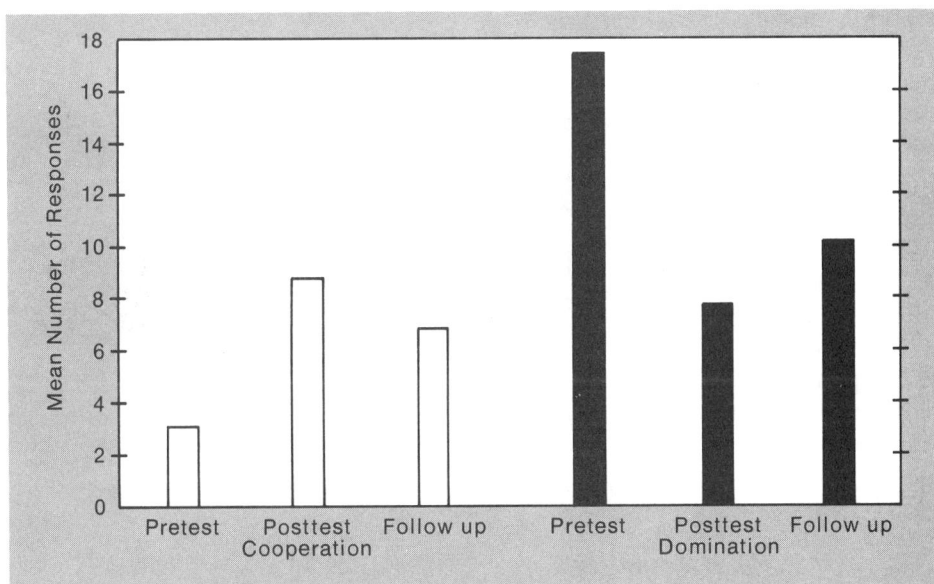

Amount of cooperative and domineering behavior exhibited by hyperaggressive children **Figure 11-1**
before and after receiving symbolic modeling treatment. (Drawn from the data of
Chittenden, 1942. In A. Bandura, Principles of behavior modification. *New York: Holt,*
Rinehart and Winston, 1969, p. 160.)

chances that the observer will subsequently imitate the response are diminished
(Bandura, 1969). Because of this fact the observer may be able to avoid potential
punishment and resulting harm. A child who has seen her playmate slip and
fall on a patch of ice on the front walk will probably have the good sense to
avoid that area. Socializing agents can assist the child to avoid punishment by
providing experiences in which a model experiences aversive consequences for
his or her actions. Chittenden's study cited in the last paragraph reveals one way
that this can be done. The dolls in Chittenden's study were punished when they
modeled aggressive behavior. The result was not only an increase in cooperation,
but also a decrease in aggression.

A third use of modeling in socialization is to produce disinhibition in behavior.
For example, Bandura and Menlove (1968) were able to reduce fear of dogs in
young children by having the children observe a film in which peer models
interacted with a dog without displaying fear. Figure 11-2 shows the behavior
of a boy who served as a model in the study as well as the reactions of a little
girl who before the experiment had been extremely afraid of dogs. As you can see,
her fear seems to have disappeared completely.

There are three major conditions which may influence the effectiveness of
modeling in socialization. One of these is the degree to which modeling stimuli
can be discriminated by the observer. For example, a high school student trying
to learn to speak a foreign language will have difficulty imitating the speech
sounds modeled by his instructor if he is unable to distinguish the subtle differences in the sound patterns of the language that he is attempting to learn.

*Conditions
influencing
modeling
effectiveness*

A second factor which may influence modeling effectiveness is the child's
ability to emit the response being modeled. For instance, Lovaas (1966) found
that a mute child who was unable to imitate the word *baby* could be taught
to imitate the separate sounds in the word. Through repeated exposure to component parts, the child eventually learned how to pronounce the word.

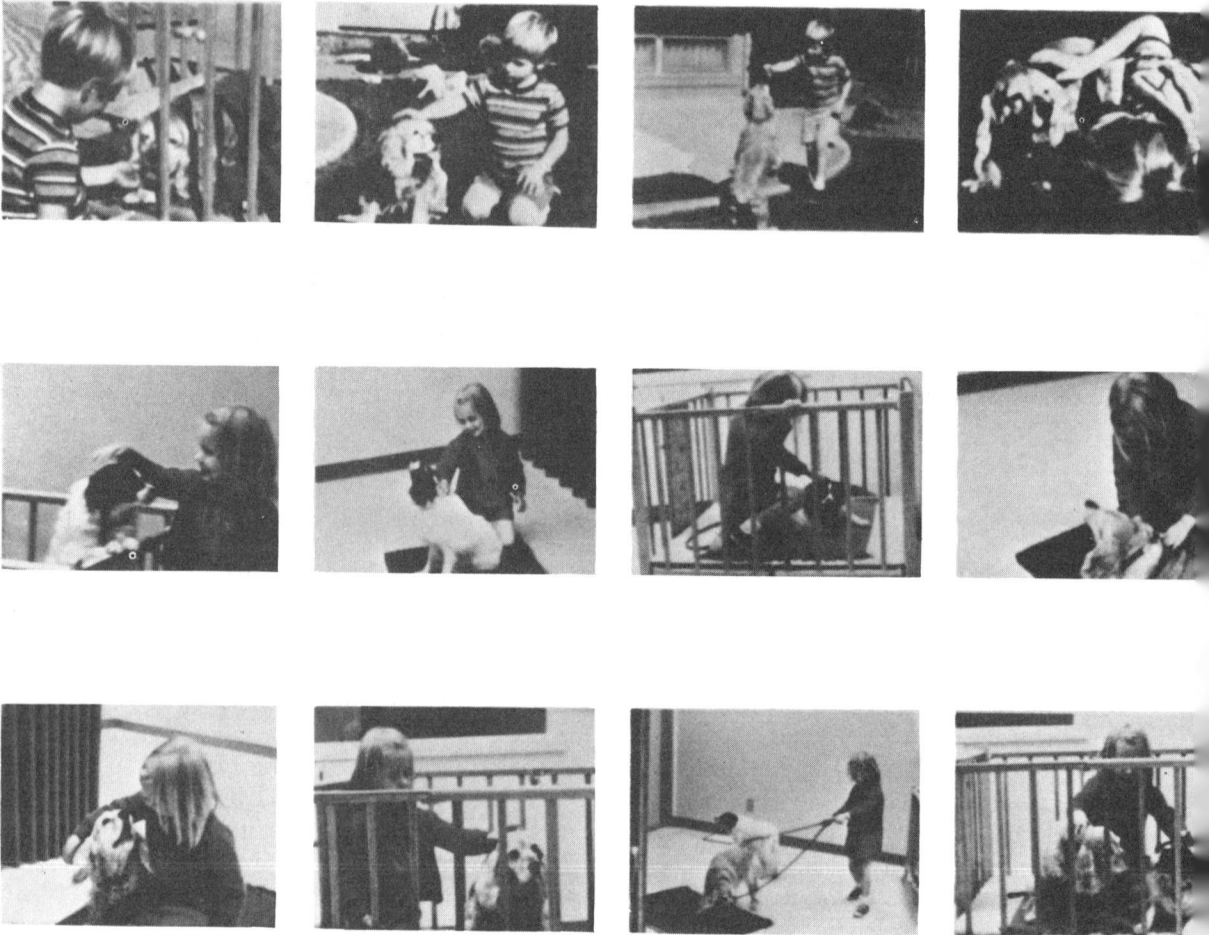

Figure 11-2   *A girl who was apprehensive about dogs engaging in fearless interactions with dogs
after exposure to the series of films in which a peer model displays progressively
threatening interactions with dogs. (From A. Bandura and F. L. Menlove, Factors
determining vicarious extinction of avoidance behavior through symbolic modeling.*
Journal of Personality and Social Psychology, 1968, 8, p. 104. *Copyrighted 1968 by
The American Psychological Association. Reprinted by permission.)*

The third major factor that may influence the effectiveness of modeling in
socialization is attention to modeling stimuli. A number of variables may affect
attention to a model. As indicated in chapter 8, these fall into two categories,
observer characteristics and model characteristics. For example, as you may
recall, prestige of the model affects attention to modeling stimuli. Personality
characteristics such as dependency in the observer also affect attention to a
model.

*Inadvertent effects
of modeling*   Modeling, like cuing, may have inadvertent effects on behavior. Children in
contemporary American society continually observe models on television displaying various undesirable behaviors, many of which are acts of violence. Available evidence suggests that such observation can adversely affect the children
(Liebert, Neale, & Davidson, 1973). This fact will be discussed in more detail in
the last chapter of the book.

Reinforcing. Reinforcement is the consequent practice that behaviorists empha-size most heavily in their writings on socialization. As you will recall, a rein-forcing event is one that increases the probability of occurrence of a response (Skinner, 1974). If teacher praise increases the probability of turning in homework assignments, then it may be regarded as a reinforcer controlling homework behavior. Similarly, if teacher reprimands for whispering to one's neighbor in-crease the probability of occurrence of that response, then reprimands may be thought of as a reinforcer for whispering.

Reinforcers may be either positive or negative. Positive reinforcement involves the addition of a consequent stimulus event to increase response probability. *Make your bed and you can go out to play. Finish your homework and you can watch television.* Remarks such as these describe contingencies involving positive reinforcement. Negative reinforcement involves the consequence of withdraw-ing a stimulus to increase response probability. An adolescent may turn off the television and do his homework or get out of bed in the morning or come to breakfast when called in anticipation of the withdrawal of the incessant carping of a nagging parent. Insofar as he does these things, his behavior can be said to have increased as a function of negative reinforcement.

Three types of positive reinforcers are typically used in socialization efforts: tangible rewards, activities, and social reinforcers. Tangible rewards are con-crete things such as food or toys which may be reinforcing to a child. Tangible rewards are particularly useful in socialization in those cases in which children have not been taught to respond to other kinds of reinforcement. For example, Vance Hall demonstrated the effectiveness of tangible rewards in increasing the IQs of economically disadvantaged preschool children (Jung, Lipe, & Wolfe, 1970). After one year in Hall's program, the average IQ of the children rose from 69 to 87. The children did not respond well to verbal praise. However, they re-sponded extremely well to rewards such as candy and snacks. In this connection Hall observed that the parents of the children rarely rewarded them verbally. From this observation he concluded that the children had never learned to respond to praise as a reinforcer.

Although tangible rewards can be useful in socialization, they sometimes have the disadvantage of being expensive and perishable. Moreover, they require storage space. One alternative to the tangible reward is the use of activities as reinforcers. Premack (1965) has demonstrated that individuals will perform an activity which is not highly valued in order to gain the opportunity to participate in an activity which is highly valued. You can determine the value of an activity simply by observing the amount of time that a child participates in it when he or she is given the opportunity to do other things. Those things that a child spends a lot of time doing can be used as reinforcers to increase the incidence of those activities that are engaged in for shorter periods. Thus, for the gregarious child, a parent might say: *Finish your reading assignment and you can go out to play.* On the other hand, with a child who favored scholarly activi-ties the contingency might be: *Go out to play with your friends for an hour and then you may read.*

Activities generally cost little or nothing. They do not have to be stored, and they are not perishable. They do, however, have the disadvantage of requiring time to administer. A parent or teacher cannot use going out to play as a rein-forcer very many times during a day. It wouldn't take many half-hour or hour play periods to use up nearly all of the time normally available for other kinds of activities.

The most extensively used reinforcement technique in socialization is social reinforcement. A social reinforcer is a social behavior which has been demonstrated to have reinforcing properties. Signs of approval and affection such as hugging, kissing, or smiling are examples. Most people tend to repeat behaviors that eventuate in approval from socializing agents.

Undoubtedly the most widely used social reinforcer is verbal praise. Verbal praise has been found to be a highly effective reinforcer. Kennedy and Willcutt (1964) summarized the findings from 33 investigations of verbal praise covering a time span of 50 years. Their review indicated that praise was a consistently effective reinforcement technique.

Praise and other social reinforcers are easy to administer, take virtually no time, cost nothing, do not have to be stored, and are not perishable. Their central disadvantage is simply that they are not effective for all individuals. Hall's experience with disadvantaged preschoolers described above provides a case in point. The children in Hall's study simply did not respond to social reinforcement.

Primary and secondary reinforcers
Some reinforcers are directly related to body-tissue needs. Reinforcers of this kind are called primary reinforcers. Food and water are examples. When a neutral stimulus (one without reinforcing properties) is paired with a primary reinforcer which is controlling a given behavior, the neutral stimulus will gradually take on reinforcing properties. Thus, verbal praise might become reinforcing to a child by being paired with various primary reinforcers such as ice cream or candy. Stimuli which acquire reinforcing properties by being paired with primary reinforcers are referred to as secondary reinforcers.

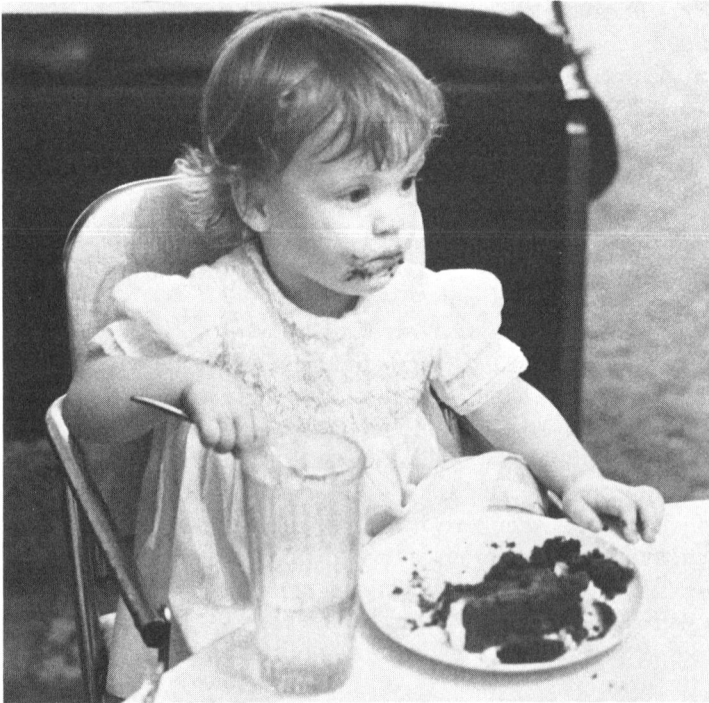

*Some behaviors have
built-in reinforcers.*

The fact that stimuli can become reinforcing by being paired with established reinforcers accounts for much of the variability in what will be reinforcing to a given individual. This variability must be taken into account if socialization efforts are to be effective. Consider the case of a child in a residential treatment center for delinquent boys. Although systematic reinforcement techniques were used with the child for a period of several months, he made little progress in changing a variety of antisocial behaviors. The principal reinforcers used in the program were telephone calls to parents and home visits. This child had been regularly beaten by his parents before entering the treatment center. Telephone calls and visits to them were not only not reinforcing, they were actually aversive. Consequences that were highly valued for many children in the program did not have reinforcing properties for this child.

In order for socializing agents to use reinforcement techniques effectively, they must find out what is reinforcing for the individuals with whom they are working. This can be done either by observing their preferences or simply by asking them to specify the kinds of things that they like.

In the course of providing positive reinforcement to increase the occurrence of a response, a socializing agent will usually deliver reinforcers on several occasions. On any given occasion the possibility exists that either intentionally or inadvertently the socializing agent will fail to deliver the reinforcer. When this occurs the child is said to be on an intermittent or partial reinforcement schedule.

There are basically two kinds of intermittent reinforcements: the interval schedule and the ratio schedule. In interval schedules, reinforcement is given after a specified time interval. For example, reinforcement might be given for the first response occurring after a two-minute time period. In ratio schedules, reinforcement takes place after a particular number of responses. For instance, a reinforcer might be given for every six responses emitted by an individual. *Intermittent reinforcement*

Interval and ratio reinforcement may occur on a fixed schedule or on a variable schedule. In the fixed schedule, the pattern of reinforcement is the same across a series of occasions. For example, in a fixed-interval schedule reinforcement might regularly occur after every five-minute time period. Similarly in a fixed-ratio schedule, reinforcement might occur regularly after every 10 responses. In the variable schedule, the pattern of reinforcement changes on each occasion, but overall conforms to a set average. For example, in a variable-interval schedule reinforcement might be given on an average of every five minutes. On one occasion reinforcement might occur after 10 minutes, and on the next occasion it might occur after one minute. However, overall the average interval would be five minutes. Similarly, in a variable-ratio schedule reinforcement might occur on the average after every 10 responses. The number of responses required to receive reinforcement would vary across occasions, but would average out to be 10.

Intermittent schedules have two characteristics that are especially important. First, they increase rate of responding. A child placed on a variable-ratio schedule while working arithmetic problems will in all likelihood work more problems than he would if he were reinforced for every response. Teachers recognize this fact when they set up competition among approximately equal contenders. Of course if the contenders are not equal, neither may be on an intermittent schedule, and competition may not produce the desired results.

A second characteristic of intermittent schedules, which is important in socialization, involves the fact that behavior acquired on an intermittent schedule is often very difficult to eliminate. This is a particularly crucial characteristic of intermittent schedules since undesirable behaviors are often inadvertently maintained by intermittent reinforcement. This point will be discussed further below.

In institutional settings such as schools, reinforcement techniques are sometimes applied in systematic programs. Such programs generally fall into two categories: token economies and point systems. In a token economy, tokens such as poker chips are used to represent reinforcers. In the point system, numerical tallies are used to signify reinforcers. *Token economies and point systems*

The first step in setting up a token economy or point system is to establish informal contracts with the children participating in the program. The contracts should specify what kinds of reinforcers are available, how long the contracts will be in effect, and what each child has to do to receive the various types of reinforcers used in the program.

The second step in establishing token or point programs is to set up procedures for recording the behaviors of the children. For example, a teacher might write down the various behaviors for which each child in her class was to receive reinforcement. She might then simply record the number of tokens or points given to each child during a specific time interval. Through this procedure, she would be able to determine how often each child emitted desired behaviors during the specified interval.

The final step in establishing a token or point program is to devise procedures for reinforcement selection and dissemination. Obviously the reinforcers chosen should be ones that are available, inexpensive, and likely to be effective. The critical point with regard to dissemination is immediacy. It may not be possible or practical to deliver tangible rewards or activities immediately after target behaviors are emitted. Nonetheless, it is typically useful to deliver the reinforcement tokens and points as soon as possible after behaviors of concern occur.

The reason for prompt delivery of reinforcement is that immediacy of reinforcement sometimes influences reinforcement effectiveness (Bandura, 1969). The ability to use symbols makes it possible for people to be influenced by reinforcers which are not immediate. A mother may tell a child that she will give him a dollar if he mows the lawn. If he thinks the price is fair, he will probably do the work even if the reinforcement is not immediately forthcoming. Nevertheless, there are circumstances in which prompt delivery of reinforcement is essential. For instance, when one is working with a behavior such as an emotional reaction which is not under verbal control, immediacy may be crucial. Similarly, when one is working with young children who have not yet developed sophisticated language skills, promptness may be of importance.

*Inadvertent
reinforcement and
behavior analysis*
Reinforcement, like other behavioral processes, may operate inadvertently to produce undesirable effects in socialization. A mother may unwittingly reward a child's whining with attention, or a teacher may bolster student mischieviousness with reprimands. The number of ways in which reinforcement can inadvertently affect behavior is almost limitless.

Analyses of behavior-contingency units in the manner described earlier in the chapter usually focus heavily on the discovery of inadvertent reinforcement effects. A central task of socializing agents conducting such analyses is to identify situations in which desired behavior is not being reinforced and/or reinforcers which are maintaining undesirable behaviors. Socialization then takes the form of altering the existing contingencies in the child's environment. The teacher who has previously reinforced reading errors by providing special help may make special help contingent upon accurate reading. The parent who has reinforced tantrum behavior by attempts to quiet and comfort a child may reserve this kind of social reinforcement for desired child responses.

Shaping.   Another consequent practice that is often used in socialization is shaping. Shaping is the reinforcement of successive approximations to a desired response. For example, if a small child displayed fear of putting his face in the water during a swimming lesson, his instructor might attempt to produce this behavior through shaping. Initially any responses which involved moving the head in the direction of the water would be reinforced. After responses of this kind had been established, reinforcement might be given for touching the water with any part of the head. Gradually the requirements for reinforcement would become more stringent until the child emitted the final behavior of putting his face in the water.

Shaping is particularly useful in situations in which the response to be acquired is one that is difficult to convey through sensory or symbolic information. The learning of physical skills provides an example. The performance of physical skills is controlled to a significant degree by internal sensory information emanating from muscles and joints (Posner & Keele, 1973). A person can learn something from watching someone hit a golf ball or a tennis ball or from being told how to perform these skills. However, no one can tell another individual how it feels to execute acts of this kind, and it's the feeling that to a significant degree controls the level of performance.

Uses of shaping

Shaping is useful in the teaching of physical skills. A watchful instructor can usually spot behavior which is moving in the direction of a desired skill. When he sees such behavior occur he may reinforce it immediately. Immediate reinforcement may alert the learner to internal stimulation associated with proper execution of the skill. Reinforcement must be immediate since sensory impressions fade from memory very quickly (Gibson, 1969).

Shaping has the disadvantage of being a much slower procedure than either modeling or cuing for initiating a response pattern. In most instances a response can be brought forth much more quickly by asking an individual to emit it or by showing him how to emit it than by reinforcing successive approximations to it.

*Limitations
of shaping*

To some extent the problem of slowness can be overcome by combining shaping with modeling and/or cuing. For example, the teaching of a physical skill might usefully incorporate verbal instructions and demonstrations as well as shaping.

Extinguishing. A third consequent practice that is often used in behavioral socialization is extinction. When the immediate goal of socialization is to reduce the rate of occurrence of a behavior, one of the easiest ways to achieve the goal is to ignore the behavior. Thus, when a father comes home from work and his wife says: *Your son is playing the stereo so loud that I can't hear myself think; what are you going to do about it,* he might appropriately respond: *Absolutely nothing.* The process of withholding a reinforcer that has previously maintained a response is called extinction. If, in the above example, parental reprimands were providing attention maintaining the behavior of turning up the volume on the stereo, then ignoring the behavior would result in a gradual reduction of that response. Of course, if loud music in itself were reinforcing to the boy, then the parents might be led to pull out the record player plug.

*Uses of
extinction*

There are a number of factors that may influence the effectiveness of attempts to extinguish a behavior. One of these is the amount of effort required to make the response being extinguished (Kimble, 1961). Responses which are highly effortful extinguish more quickly than ones which do not require a great deal of exertion. Teachers show recognition of this fact when they send restless children out for an extra long recess. Squirming, wiggling, or poking one's neighbor is hard work. When children are tired, they will tend to do these kinds of things less often than when they are not tired.

*Conditions
influencing
extinction
effectiveness*

A second factor that can influence the effectiveness of extinction is the availability of information regarding contingencies existing during extinction. For instance, Bridger and Mandel (1965) conditioned people to make an avoidance reaction to shock. Then they told some individuals that shock would no longer be administered. Extinction occurred faster for those individuals than for persons who were not told about the change in contingencies. The results of this study suggest that parents or teachers using extinction procedures could increase the rate of response reduction by telling children when reinforcement is no longer in effect. For instance, a teacher might say to a child: *You've been getting a lot of extra attention from me for cutting up in class. From now on, I'm just going to ignore that kind of behavior.*

Another factor which may influence the effectiveness of extinction is the schedule of reinforcement during acquisition of the response being extinguished (Skinner, 1938). As indicated above, a response that has been reinforced on some occasions but not others during acquisition tends to be much more difficult to extinguish than one that has been reinforced every time that it has occurred. One possible reason for this is that when a response is reinforced intermittently there is less information available regarding existing contingencies than there is when the response is continuously reinforced. A parent who has periodically reinforced tantrum behavior with attention will have a more difficult time extinguishing the behavior than would be the case if tantrums were reinforced continuously.

A fourth factor influencing extinction is the number of unreinforced repetitions of the response to be extinguished. A response on extinction generally diminishes gradually over a relatively long time span. This characteristic may make the method impractical to use under some circumstances. If a child has been physically assaulting other children, it will usually not be feasible to attempt to extinguish the behavior by withdrawing such potential reinforcers as teacher attention. A teacher cannot afford to ignore behavior that may eventuate in harm to other children.

The problems associated with the use of extinction can often be surmounted through the use of counterconditioning (Ayllon & Roberts, 1974). In counterconditioning, extinction and positive reinforcement are combined. For example, a teacher might reduce aggressive behavior by ignoring aggressive acts and at the same time positively reinforcing behavior incompatible with aggression. Thus, if she saw a child making menacing gestures toward another child she might go over to him and say: *Let me help you get started on your science project.* As the child began to work on his project, she would reinforce him by saying something like: *I like those ideas, Ted. I'm looking forward to seeing how you develop them.*

Punishing. Punishment is perhaps the most commonly used socialization practice for reducing the incidence of behavior. In technical terms, punishment is a consequent event that diminishes the probability of occurrence of a response (Azrin & Holz, 1966). The spanking that a parent says will make a child never, ever emit a given forbidden act again would be an example of punishment if indeed the parent's prediction were at least partially borne out.

Types of punishment
The consequent events in punishment may involve the addition of an aversive stimulus or the withdrawal of a positive reinforcer. Spankings, scoldings, and accidental bumps and bruises are among the many familiar aversive conditions that may reduce the incidence of behavior. Loss of free time, affection, and privileges such as using the family car illustrate the kinds of things that are often done in withdrawing positive influences on behavior.

Conditions influencing punishment effectiveness
There are a number of conditions that may influence the effectiveness of punishment. Punishment is more effective when it is administered at the onset of the act being punished than when it is given after the act has already occurred

(Aronfreed, 1968). It is best to reprimand the child with his hand in the cookie jar before he gets to the cookies rather than after he has already taken several bites. One possible reason for this is that the child who has already emitted a forbidden response receives whatever reinforcement may be attendant to producing the response. When punishment takes place before the response has had a chance to occur, positive consequences that might be associated with the punished act are eliminated. Another possible explanation for the effect of early punishment is that it may produce anxiety eventuating in avoidance reactions which suppress behavior in its early stages. According to this account the child who reaches for the cookie jar will become anxious and withdraw his hand to reduce his fear.

Long delays in the onset of punishment following behavior represent another factor that may influence the effectiveness of punishment (Azrin, 1956). When a child commits an undesirable act while playing and is punished several hours later, the effectiveness of punishment will probably be reduced substantially. This occurs frequently in socialization. A parent may not find out about a behavior which he or she feels should be punished until long after it occurs and yet go ahead with punishment. Similarly, in the case of juvenile delinquency, the punitive actions of the judicial system generally occur long after the behavior being punished has taken place.

A third factor that may influence the effectiveness of punishment is the availability of alternative responses leading to reinforcement (Herman & Azrin, 1964). If there are two responses available leading to the same reinforcement and one is punished, punishment will generally be quite effective. However, if the individual has no other way to get reinforcement than to emit the punished response, punishment may not produce desired results. If a child is able to get peer reinforcement only through disruptive activities in class, disruption may be difficult to eliminate through punishment. On the other hand, if the child commands the respect of his or her peers for socially appropriate behaviors, punishment of mischievious acts will probably reduce such behaviors.

Another major variable which may determine the effectiveness of punishment in socialization involves the reinforcement of punished responses. Behaviors which occur frequently are often maintained by positive reinforcement. The extent to which a punished response is being reinforced will influence the degree of effectiveness of punishment (Azrin & Holz, 1966). It is often possible to avoid the use of punishment altogether by discovering the reinforcers that are maintaining responses which are undesirable and removing them from the situation.

Uses of punishment

There are circumstances in socialization in which punishment can be used to advantage. Punishment generally works quickly, and there are situations in which speed may be essential. A mother's sharp rebuke to the small child who is about to venture into the street may have the immediate effect of keeping the child out of danger. Likewise, the teacher who punishes a highly aggressive child by withdrawing a privilege such as recess may quickly avert possible harm to other children.

One highly beneficial use of punishment recorded in the scientific literature on socialization involves its application in eliminating self-destructive behaviors. Self-injurious behavior sometimes occurs in severely emotionally disturbed children. A child may gouge his face with his fingernails or repeatedly bang his head against a wall. In some cases behavior of this kind becomes so severe that the child must be physically restrained almost continually for his or her own protection. Lovaas, Freitag, Gold, and Kassorla (1965) found that self-injurious acts generally followed withdrawal of reinforcement for other behaviors. Bucher and Lovaas (1968) observed that affection following self-injurious acts further increased the incidence of such acts. However, when self-injurious behavior was punished, it tended to diminish quickly. For instance, Bucher and Lovaas observed a seven-year-old boy who emitted an average of 3,000 self-injurious acts during a ninety-minute period. Through the application of a small number of shocks, this behavior was almost completely eliminated in a short time.

Limitations on the usefulness of punishment
Although punishment can produce beneficial results under certain circumstances, there are a number of factors which limit its usefulness in socialization (Bandura, 1969). One problem associated with the use of punishment is that it may suppress desirable behaviors related to the punished act. A teacher who punishes a girl with poor language skills for talking out of turn in class may discourage her from talking in school at all. Yet, presumably a major educational goal for such a child would be to help her to develop language skills.

A second difficulty associated with punishment involves avoidance reactions. Winston Churchill (1930), in his book *My Early Life,* provides a charming example of the avoidance problems associated with aversive situations:

> It was at "The Little Lodge" (the Churchill's home in Ireland) I was first menaced with Education. The approach of a sinister figure described as "the Governess" was announced. Her arrival was fixed for a certain day. In order to prepare for this day Mrs. Everest produced a book called *Reading without Tears.* It certainly did not justify its title in my case. I was made aware before the Governess arrived I must be able to read without tears. We toiled each day. My nurse pointed with a pen at the different letters. I thought it all very tiresome. Our preparations were by no means completed when the fateful hour struck and the Governess was due to arrive. I did what so many oppressed people have done in similar circumstances: I took to the woods. (p. 3)

Thousands of students continue to "take to the woods" every year just as little Winston did. However, most of them do it when they are 16 rather than three, and a goodly number do not come back.

Another major problem associated with the use of punishment in socialization is that the punishing agent may become an aversive stimulus to the child. A child may grow to hate a punitive adult to the extent that it becomes impossible for the adult to use positive social reinforcement to influence the child. Moreover, the child may exhibit avoidance behavior in the presence of the adult. The ghetto child who "tunes out" a punitive teacher is an example.

The final problem associated with punishment is that it may become reinforcing to the socializing agent. Unfortunately it is possible for parents and teachers to be conditioned to enjoy administering punishment. Jonathon Kozol (1967) describes the malevolent consequences of this state of affairs in his searing indictment of the Boston Public Schools, *Death at an Early Age:*

> I have watched a teacher giving the rattan with a look on his face which was certainly the very opposite of abhorrence, and I have heard a teacher speak of it as if it were somehow a physical accomplishment or even some kind of military feat. I am sure that teachers as a class are no more sadistic than any other people. . . . But many human beings do take pleasure in inflicting pain on others, and those who have the least to be proud of or to be happy about are often the ones who take that pleasure most. (p. 18)

Socialization Practice from the Interactive Perspective

Interactive theorists conceptualize socialization practices as broad classes of behaviors assumed to influence the development of traits and structures. In contrast to behaviorists, advocates of the interactive stance do not stress the temporal relationship between socialization practice and specific behaviors influenced through socialization. Rather, the emphasis is on broad categories of practice related to long-term developmental outcomes. For example, whereas a behaviorist might be interested in the effects of positive reinforcements on a child's proclivity to put away the toys in his or her bedroom, an interactive theorist working with the same child might be concerned about the influence of parental affection on the development of internalized moral standards.

Socialization practices identified by interactive theorists have their origins for the most part in Freudian, Kohlbergian, and Piagetian theory. Freudian theory generated interest in socialization practices related to moral development. As indicated in earlier chapters, Kohlberg and Piaget have also contributed much to current knowledge of socialization related to moral development. In addition, of course, Piaget has focused his major efforts on socialization related to intellectual development. There are five socialization practices which have been the primary targets for interactive research on the socialization process. These include: power-assertion techniques, love-withdrawal techniques, inductive techniques, affection, and discovery learning.

Power-assertion techniques. Power-assertion techniques include socialization practices involving force or threat of force to achieve compliance with the demands of socializing agents. Both physical punishment and the withdrawal of material goods are included in the power-assertion category. The mother who says *If you can't take turns, nobody will ride the bike* is using the power-assertion approach. Likewise the father who bellows *Son, you're grounded for a week— Give me the keys to the car and the credit card* has adopted a power-assertion strategy of discipline.

There is an abundance of evidence that suggests that consistent use of power-assertion techniques results in a failure on the part of children to acquire internalized standards to guide their own behaviors. Much of this evidence has been summarized by psychologist Martin Hoffman (1970). Hoffman's summary is presented in tables 11-3 and 11-4.

As these tables show, four different types of indices have been used in assessing the acquisition of internalized moral standards. These include internal orientation, guilt, resistance to temptation, and confession of responsibility for misdeeds.

Internal orientation

Indices assessing internal orientation are concerned with the extent to which the child guides his or her behavior on the basis of what he or she believes to be right or on the basis of his or her perception of societal sanctions against certain forms of behavior. The child who says that a person should not steal because of the likelihood of being caught and punished is displaying a view suggesting an external orientation to behavior control. On the other hand, the child who says that an individual should not steal because stealing is morally wrong is manifesting an internal orientation toward behavior control.

Guilt

Indices of guilt assess a child's expression of remorse associated with wrong acts. To assess guilt, children are often asked to complete a story describing someone's misdeeds. When a child indicates that the central figure in the story is sorry for his or her wrongdoings, the child has evidenced the potential for experiencing guilt.

Resistance to temptation

Resistance to temptation refers to a child's ability to refrain from forbidden acts in the absence of external sanctions against them. In many of the experimental studies which deal with this kind of internal control, children are subjected to various experimental conditions thought to affect resistance to such temptations as playing with an attractive, but forbidden toy. Then, like Adam and Eve, the children are left alone, unsupervised in the presence of the forbidden object. The child who refrains from playing with the object is described as manifesting internal moral control by resisting temptation.

Confession

Confession refers to acceptance of personal responsibility for misdeeds. When a scowling mother says *Who broke this dish* and a weak voice responds *I did*, there is evidence that a young child is willing to take some personal responsibility for his or her own conduct. On the other hand, when the response is *I don't know,* or *I think the wind blew it down,* then evidence of the assumption of personal responsibility is lacking.

Power assertion and moral development

As tables 11-3 and 11-4 show, the use of power-assertion techniques tends to be negatively related to all four of the indices of moral development described in the preceding paragraphs. From the standpoint of Freudian theory, these results are to be expected. Freudian psychology suggests that children develop internalized moral standards primarily by taking the values of their parents as their own. Parental values tend to be incorporated in verbal form (Freud, 1927).

Table 11-3   *Mother's Child-rearing Practices and Moral Development Indices*

Child Morality Index	Power Assertion	Love Withdrawal	Induction	Affection
Internal orientation	− 11 BG − 13 G − 5 B 0 13 B	− 13 G 0 13 B	+ 11 BG + 13 B 0 13 G	o + 13 G o 0 13 B
Guilt intensity	− 20 B − 13 G 0 13 B 0 20 G 0 13 BG 0 11 BG	0 13 BG	+ 13 BG + 20 B 0 20 G 0 13 BG 0 11 BG	o o o + 13 B 0 13 G
Resistance to temptation	− 20 B − 4 G 0 4 B 0 4 BG 0 11 BG	+ 4 B 0 4 G 0 11 BG 0 4 BG	+ 13 B + 4 G − 4 M 0 11 BG 0 4 B	− 4 G 0 4 B 0 11 BG 0 4 BG
Confession and acceptance of blame	− 4 M − 6 M − 13 BG 0 6 M 0 4 BG	+ 6 M + 13 G − 6 M 0 4 M 0 13 B 0 4 BG	+ 6 M + 6 M + 13 B − 4 B 0 13 G 0 4 G 0 6 M 0 4 M	+ 4 M + 6 M o + 5 B + 13 BG o − 4 B 0 4 G o 0 13 G

Key to symbols:
+, −, 0: Direction of relationship obtained.
Numeral: Approximate mean age of subjects.
B, G, M: Boys, Girls, Boys and Girls mixed.
o: Predominantly other-oriented.

From M. L. Hoffman, Moral development. In P. H. Mussen (Ed.), *Carmichael's manual of child psychology.* Vol 2 (3rd ed.). New York: Wiley, 1970. P. 291.

Parents express verbal prohibitions against various types of behavior. Subsequently children recall parental verbalizations and these become "the little voice inside the head" which in Jiminy Cricket fashion influences moral decisions.

According to Freud, the child incorporates parental verbalizations as part of a broad-scale effort to forestall loss of the parents as love objects. The child is afraid of being rejected by his or her parents because of prior misdeeds. To counteract this potential loss of love, the child attempts to recreate the parents in his or her own mind by such procedures as recalling their verbalizations.

Since power-assertion techniques are both punitive and impersonal, they are not likely to arouse much love on the part of the child. Insofar as parents do not arouse love, the child probably will not attempt to recreate them internally. Accordingly, the child is not likely to develop internalized control.

Love-withdrawal techniques. Love-withdrawal techniques are socialization practices that involve the withholding of affection or approval as a result of misdeeds. Socializing agents may manifest love withdrawal in a variety of ways. A mother may ignore her son by not looking in his direction, or she may turn her back to him or refuse to speak to him or listen to what he says. In some instances parents may express their rejection actively with comments such as: *You disgust me,* or *Get out of my sight; I don't want to be around you when you're acting this way.*

As tables 11-3 and 11-4 show, there is little evidence to suggest that love withdrawal affects the development of internalized moral standards. In well over half of the studies summarized no significant relationship was observed between love withdrawal and moral development. When viewed from the perspective of Freudian theory, this is a rather surprising finding. The Freudian view that the child incorporates parental values because of fear of loss of love suggests that love withdrawal should be an effective means of instilling internalized moral standards in the child. The rejection associated with love withdrawal ought to stimulate the child's efforts to recreate his parents internally.

Father's Child-rearing Practices and Moral Development Indices   **Table 11-4**

Child Morality Index	Power Assertion	Love Withdrawal	Induction	Affection
Internal orientation	− 13 G 0 13 B	0 13 BG	0 13 BG	o + 13 M 0 13 BG
Guilt intensity	0 20 BG 0 13 BG	0 13 BG	0 20 BG 0 13 BG	o 0 13 BG o
Resistance to temptation	− 20 B 0 4 BG		0 4 BG	+ 4 B 0 4 G
Confession and acceptance of blame	+ 4 B − 13 B 0 13 G 0 4 G	+ 13 M + 13 M 0 13 BG	0 4 BG 0 13 BG	+ 13 G o + 4 G 0 13 B 0 4 B

Key to symbols same as table 11–3.

From M. L. Hoffman, Moral development. In P. H. Mussen (Ed.), *Carmichael's manual of child psychology.* Vol 2 (3rd ed.). New York: Wiley, 1970. P. 291.

Induction techniques. Induction techniques are socialization procedures in which reasons for changing behavior are offered. *Don't pull the doggie's tail; he might bite you. Stop poking Alice with that stick; you could hurt her.* These are some examples of the many socializing efforts that fall in the inductive category.

Types of induction

In some instances inductive discipline stresses behavioral consequences involving potential harm to the child. *Put that broken glass down; you could cut yourself,* a parent might say. Or, with an older child, a father might warn: *You can't allow yourself to get such bad grades; if you continue the way you're going now, you'll never get into college.* Sometimes induction involves appeals to conform to appropriate standards for personal conduct. Verbalizations such as *Big boys don't cry,* or *Stop acting like a child, you're 16 years old* illustrate this type of induction. Finally, in some cases inductive practices may emphasize the harmful consequences of a behavior for other persons in the child's environment. For example, a parent might say: *Grandpa will be so disappointed if you're not wearing your new Easter clothes when we go there for dinner.*

Effects of other-oriented induction

Tables 11-3 and 11-4 indicate that other-oriented induction techniques tend to be related to the development of internalized moral standards. Hoffman (1970) suggests that one possible reason for this is that other-oriented procedures may arouse guilt in the child regarding misdeeds. Mark Twain's Tom Sawyer illustrates Hoffman's view in a conversation with his Aunt Polly over a practical joke:

> "Tom, I don't know what is to become of a boy that will act like that. It makes me feel so bad to think you could let me go to Sereny Harper and make such a fool of myself and never say a word."
>
> This was a new aspect of the thing. His smartness of the morning had seemed to Tom a good joke before, and very ingenious. It merely looked mean and shabby now. He hung his head and could not think of anything to say for a moment. Then he said:
>
> "Auntie, I wish I hadn't done it—but I didn't think." (Twain, 1959, p. 127)

In a recent experiment, Joseph LaVoie (1974) found age and sex differences in the extent to which other-oriented discipline resulted in internalized control. In his study children aged 7, 9, and 11 were allowed to select a toy which they regarded as attractive. They were then given a reason why they should not play with the toy. Following this, the experimenter excused herself from the experimental situation saying that she had to make a telephone call. Then the children's behavior with respect to the forbidden toy was observed through a television monitor. Nine- and eleven-year-old children who were told that they should not play with the toy because it belonged to another child resisted the temptation to use the toy to a greater extent than children of the same age who were told that the toy was a very special and unique toy and therefore should not be handled. A second finding of interest was that 9- and 11-year-olds who were told that it was wrong to want to play with the toy resisted temptation to a greater degree than children who were told that playing with the toy might have negative consequences such as toy breakage. A third finding was that the older girls were generally more resisting of temptation than boys when other-oriented induction was used.

LaVoie suggests that the effectiveness of other-oriented induction may be a function of the child's level of cognitive development regarding moral judgments. This explanation would be in accord with Piagetian and Kohlbergian views on moral development. He goes on to point out that the findings with respect to sex suggest a behavioral interpretation of the data. Girls in middle childhood may be reinforced for responding to other-oriented discipline whereas this may not be the case for boys.

Affection techniques. Affection techniques include all the various activities that socializing agents may use in delivering positive reinforcers to children. Hugs, kisses, gifts, and verbal praise are all examples of practices evidencing affection.

The concept of affection is closely related to that of positive reinforcement. Yet there are important differences. Specifically, the idea of affection does not necessarily imply a contingent relationship between positive stimulation and behavior. For example, a little girl might walk into the house after school, and her mother might say: *It's so good to have you home. Did you have a nice day?* From the behavioral perspective, a remark of this kind might have the effect of increasing the probability of the response immediately preceding it, which in this example would be walking in the door. Whether or not the remark influenced walking in the door would be of little concern to the interactive theorist. The critical question would be the effect of that kind of positive statement as well as other positive stimuli on aspects of personality development such as the development of internalized control.

Affection and reinforcement

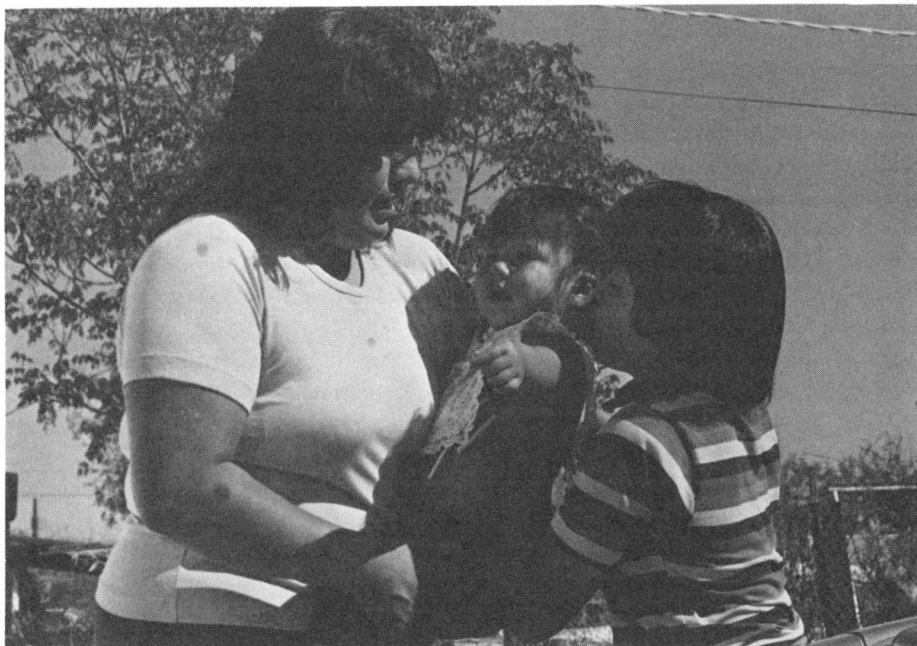

Parents influence the socialization of their children through affection.

Hoffman's summary of research presented in tables 11-3 and 11-4 suggests that the use of affection is related to the development of internalized moral standards. About half of the studies in the summary revealed a significant relationship between affection and moral development. This finding is not directly implied by Freudian theory. As indicated above, in the Freudian view internalization comes about through fear of loss of love, not through the reception of affection. Hoffman suggests as one explanation for the findings on affection the view that affection increases the child's receptivity to parental influence. According to this view, the threat of loss of love from a parent who displayed a great deal of af-

Affection and moral development

fection would be more severe and therefore more influential in determining internalization than would be the case when fear of loss of love involved a parent who displayed little affection.

Discovery-learning techniques. As indicated in previous chapters, Kohlberg and Piaget suggest that developmental progress is governed largely by the child's discovery of truths gleaned through continuing commerce with the environment. For example, a child's concepts of right and wrong are thought to be fashioned from his or her own judgments of moral behavior. Consider the following conversation between Tom Sawyer and Huck Finn:

> "Looky-here, Huck, being rich ain't going to keep me back from turning robber."
> "No! Oh, good-licks, are you in real deadwood earnest, Tom?"
> "Just as dead earnest as I'm a-sitting here. But Huck, we can't let you into the gang if you ain't respectable, you know."
> Huck's joy was quenched.
> "Can't let me in, Tom? Didn't you let me go for a pirate?"
> "Yes, but that's different. A robber is more high'toned than what a pirate is, as a general thing. In most countries they're awful high up in the nobility, dukes and such." (Twain, 1959, p. 217)

These remarks surely do not represent the kind of moral judgment likely to come from parental preachments. The implication is that Tom arrived at his views on robbers through his own powers of reasoning and observation. One wonders if many of today's children are not coming to similar conclusions.

Although many of the discoveries which children make in the course of development occur as part of their day-to-day intercourse with the environment, it is possible for socializing agents to stimulate developmental progress at least to a small degree by arranging circumstances which will facilitate discovery learning (Kohlberg, 1969; Piaget, 1973; Turiel, 1973). Such deliberate efforts to stimulate discovery comprise what we are calling discovery-learning techniques of socialization.

As indicated in chapter 2, discovery learning is generally initiated by confronting the child with a problem-solving situation. The child's task is to solve the problem by discovering a rule on the basis of examination of various concrete circumstances related to the rule. For example, as shown in figure 11-3, a child might discover the rule that the area of a parallelogram presented in the manner depicted in the illustration equals the length times the height of the figure. This rule could be discovered by examination of concrete examples revealing that a parallelogram can be converted into a rectangle having the same area as the parallelogram (Wertheimer, 1959). Providing that the child understands the rule for determining the area of a rectangle, he or she should have no difficulty in discovering the rule for determining the area of a parallelogram.

Steps in discovery learning   Discovery-learning techniques generally involve four kinds of activities. First, a problem is posed for the learner. This typically entails indicating a rule to be discovered by the learner. Second, the learner is given the opportunity to examine instances related to the rule to be discovered. The third step is used only in what is called guided discovery learning. It involves giving hints to the learner to help him or her in rule discovery. In the final step, the learner indicates the rule to be acquired. This may be done either by enacting the rule or by verbalizing it. For example, a child might demonstrate mastery of the rule for determining the area of a parallelogram by computing the areas of a number of parallelograms or by verbalizing the rule governing such computation.

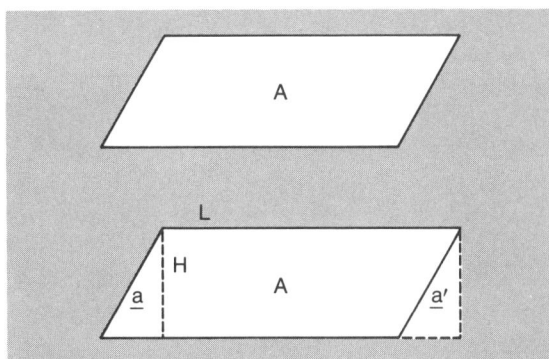

Figure 11-3

Discovering the formula for computing the area of a parallelogram. The dotted lines demonstrate that a parallelogram can be converted to a rectangle having the same area as the parallelogram by moving a to a'. After the conversion has been made, area can be computed by applying the formula for computing the area of a rectangle: L × H = A (L = length, H = height, and A = area).

Discovery learning was formally introduced into socialization in the writings of Plato. The dialogues that Plato describes between Socrates and his students provide many examples of the approach. One which is particularly interesting is between Socrates and Meno. In this dialogue Socrates leads Meno to discover the "truth" (today it would be called a theory) that knowledge is innate and that learning through discovery simply enables one to recall what was always known, but forgotten.

Socratic discovery learning

The concrete instance that Socrates uses to guide Meno in the discovery process is itself an example of discovery learning. Socrates demonstrates to Meno that a slave boy who has had no formal schooling can discover the proof of the Pythagorean theorem that in a right triangle the square of the hypotenuse is equal to the sum of the squares of the sides.

After successfully demonstrating the discovery-learning approach with the slave boy, Socrates leads Meno in inexorable fashion to the conclusion that knowledge is inborn:

Soc. And this knowledge which he now has must he not either have acquired or always possessed?

Men. Yes.

Soc. But if he always possessed this knowledge he would always have known; or if he has acquired the knowledge he could not have acquired it in this life unless he has been taught geometry; for he may be made to do the same with all geometry and every other branch of knowledge. Now, has any one ever taught him all this? You must know about him if, as you say, he was born and bred in your house.

Men. And I am certain that no one ever did teach him.

Soc. And yet he has the knowledge?

Men. The fact, Socrates, is undeniable.

Soc. But if he did not acquire the knowledge in this life, then he must have had and learned it at some other time?

Men. Clearly he must.

Soc. Which must have been the time when he was not a man?

Men. Yes.

Soc. And if there have been always true thoughts in him, both at the time he was and was not a man, which only need to be awakened into knowledge by putting questions to him, his soul must have always possessed this knowledge, for he always either was or was not a man?

Men. Obviously.

Soc. And if the truth of all things always existed in the soul, then the soul is immortal. Wherefore be of good cheer and try to recollect what you do not know, or rather what you do not remember. (Plato, trans. 1949, p. 44)

As we have indicated previously in the book, the notion of a preformed intellect, which is essentially what Plato is arguing for in this dialogue, is still ascribed to by some theorists today. Chomsky's view that certain rules which govern language production and reception are inborn is a case in point. Both Piaget and Kohlberg, as we have shown, hold that some aspects of intellectual functioning are innately determined. However, they also assume that the intellect is modified through experience.

The interactive view of discovery learning

The interactive view that the intellect is shaped in part by experience has eventuated in a significant modification in discovery-learning procedures. Discovery learning, as it is used by contemporary Piagetians and Kohlbergians, requires that problems posed in the discovery-learning process be related to the developmental level of the child. It is generally assumed that through repeated attempts at discovery a child can advance from a given level of intellectual functioning to the next higher level of functioning (Hickey, 1972; Holstein, 1970; Keasey, 1973; Flavell, 1963; Turiel 1973). For example, a child who is about ready to advance from preoperational thought to concrete operations might be assisted to achieve this higher level of functioning through discovery learning.

Kohlbergian and Piagetian efforts to promote discovery learning generally proceed as follows. First, the developmental level of the child is assessed. For instance a mother might use Piaget's clinical method to assess her daughter's role-taking ability. In implementing the clinical approach, she might begin by saying: *How do you think Carol feels when you call her names?* After developmental level has been established, a problem is posed in such a way that the child's existing manner of conceptualizing things is placed in conflict with the mode of conceptualization associated with the developmental level toward which the child is moving. For instance, suppose the child in the above example did not clearly comprehend the fact that Carol's feelings would probably be hurt by name calling. Under these conditions, the mother might tell her daughter a story in which the central character was a little girl who was a constant target for name calling. At the end of the story, the mother might attempt to create conflict by juxtaposing the feelings described for the child in the story with the daughter's previously stated views about Carol's feelings. For instance, she might say: *You said that Carol doesn't mind name calling, but Alice in our story certainly did. Would Carol be likely to feel differently about name calling than Carol?*

Recent research by Arbuthnot (1975) indicates that role playing is a highly useful tool in discovery learning. In Arbuthnot's study, college students enacted roles in one of Kohlberg's (1969) moral dilemmas. In this dilemma, which was described in an earlier chapter, a man (Heinz) whose wife is dying of cancer steals a needed drug from an unscrupulous druggist who demands more money than Heinz can obtain for the drug. Students were assigned to play either the role of Heinz or the role of the druggist. They were instructed to argue as effectively as they could that their position in the dilemma was justifiable. In those cases in which an opponent was more mature in moral judgments than the student with whom he or she was arguing, role playing produced a significant increase in developmental level of the less mature student.

The effectiveness of discovery-learning procedures

Despite successes such as that revealed in the Arbuthnot study, there has been a substantial amount of controversy regarding the effectiveness of discovery-learning procedures in stimulating development. Kohlbergians and Piagetians

Differences in socialization create different patterns of response to the environment.

generally hold that development cannot be greatly accelerated through teaching. A child who is in a transitional phase between two developmental levels may be assisted to make the transition to the higher level through the use of discovery learning (Turiel, 1973). However, the amount of change in developmental level will usually be quite small and will not involve skipping developmental stages.

Interactive theorists hold that the critical condition for facilitating transition from one developmental level to the next is the presence of cognitive conflict. Children must be placed in a situation in which they have the opportunity to observe that their current reasoning abilities lead to illogical and incongruous conclusions about things. However, even when a situation of this kind is produced, children will not recognize conflict unless they are developmentally ready to do so. For example, Langer (1969) conducted a study in which he presented children with 10 round beads (seven red and three blue). He then asked the children to place the round beads on one side of a table and the red beads on the other. The younger children in the experiment were not troubled in any way by this impossible task. They apparently did not consider the fact that in every case red beads were also round beads.

Peterson, Peterson, and Finley (1974) obtained similar results in a study of moral judgment. These investigators induced conflict by setting two characteristic beliefs of young children in opposition. One of these was the view that adult conduct is generally correct. The other was the idea that the amount of damage done by an individual rather than his or her intentions when causing damage is the key factor in determining the extent of wrongdoing. Conflict was created by telling the children a story in which an adult unintentionally caused a substantial amount of damage and a child committing a misdeed caused a small amount of damage. Second grade children in this conflict-inducing condition tended to make moral judgments characteristic of a higher developmental level than the judgments of children who had not experienced conflict induction. Specifically, they were more likely than their age-mates to judge severity of wrongdoing on the basis of the intention of the wrongdoer rather than on the basis of the amount of damage caused.

As indicated in chapter 6, behaviorists take the view that development can be accelerated when appropriate training methods are used. In support of this view, they have demonstrated on a number of occasions that developmental progress can be accelerated through the use of modeling and reinforcement techniques. For example, Bandura and McDonald (1963) were able to facilitate moral development using modeling and reinforcement procedures. More recently Zimmerman and Rosenthal (1974), among others, have demonstrated that conversation skills can be taught using modeling and reinforcement techniques.

Cognitive theorists have criticized behavioral research demonstrating the facilitation of developmental change on several grounds (Turiel, 1973). Among these is the lack of stability over time of behaviorally induced changes, the use of inappropriate measures of change, and failure to recognize that children participating in research studies may be at a transitional phase of development which renders them more susceptible to influence than they would otherwise be. Despite these criticisms, there is a substantial amount of evidence which suggests that developmental progress can be facilitated by behavioral techniques.

CULTURE, SCIENCE, AND SOCIALIZATION

A modern technological society, such as that existing in America today, places heavy social, emotional, and intellectual demands upon its citizenry. Because of family mobility and societal complexity, men and women in today's culture must have highly developed social skills which will enable them to interact effectively with many different types of people occupying a vast array of different roles. They must be prepared emotionally to face the social, political, and economic uncertainties of a rapidly changing culture. Finally, they must have the intellectual capabilities to cope with the social and technical changes attendant to the explosion of new knowledge which inevitably occurs in a technological society.

In a culture which places such extensive demands upon its people, the effectiveness of socialization practices in producing desired developmental outcomes is a matter of critical importance. When an individual fails to achieve necessary developmental competencies, his or her productivity in society will be impaired and his or her ability to derive the social and economic benefits that the society has to offer will be decreased. In light of the significant influences that socialization practices may have on development, it becomes critical to determine the factors that influence the socialization process. This is the topic that we shall consider in the remainder of the present chapter.

Socialization and the Evolution of Culture

Socialization can be viewed as the process of transmitting culture from one generation to the next. Without effective socialization practices, no culture could survive for very long. Yet it is clear that most socialization techniques are not specifically designed to produce the effects which they achieve. As B. F. Skinner (1971) points out, "Much of what a person does to promote the survival of a culture is not 'intentional' —that is, it is not done *because* it increases survival value" (p. 135).

If socialization practices are in the main not planned, how do they come to be adopted? A number of social theorists representing diverse disciplines have suggested that socialization practices are selected and maintained by the cultural environment in accordance with their effect on cultural survival. For example, anthropologist Leslie A. White (1959), developmentalist Robert LeVine (1969), and behavioral psychologist B. F. Skinner (1971) have each argued that socialization is an aspect of cultural evolution.

Evolutionary parallels between cultures and species
The idea of cultural evolution is an extension of Darwinian thought regarding the evolution of species. Skinner (1971) has indicated the parallels between cultures and species which support the concept of cultural evolution. The first among these is the fact that the characteristics of cultures, like the characteristics of species, are transmitted from generation to generation by group members. For example, some cultures place heavy stress on obedience in children whereas others emphasize initiative and independence. These emphases are communicated from generation to generation by individual members of the cultures involved. Similarly, the pouch for carrying young is transmitted from generation to generation by individual members of the marsupial species.

In Skinner's view, cultural characteristics, like species characteristics, are selected through the necessity for adapting to environmental demands. Marsupials with pouches were very likely selected over other versions of that species because the pouch enhanced the probability of survival of the young. Similarly, emphases on obedience or independence may have been incorporated into cultures because of the impact of these behavioral characteristics on survival. Work by Barry, Child, and Bacon (1959) suggests that this indeed may be the case. In a study of 107 different cultures, these investigators found that obedience tended to be stressed in cultures in which the principal basis for economic subsistence

was agriculture. In societies of this kind, conscientious adherence to behavioral routines associated with agricultural production is essential to survival. Cultures in which economic subsistence was based on hunting and fishing tended to stress initiative and independence in children. Barry, Child, and Bacon suggested that these characteristics in all likelihood contribute to the success of hunting and fishing ventures.

The concept of selection explains how practices which already exist are maintained in a culture. Some consideration must also be given to the matter of how new practices are acquired. From the perspective of cultural evolution, new practices correspond to genetic mutations. They arise by accident. Moreover, their role in enhancing cultural survival is often overlooked. For example, socializing agents in cultures stressing obedience or initiative may not be fully aware of the role which these characteristics play in enhancing survival.

Cultural evolution occurs when new practices further the survival of those who practice them. Evolution of this kind takes place continuously in contemporary society. For example, views on child rearing have changed markedly in Western societies during the last 100 years. Western culture has become much more humane in its attitudes toward children than it was previously. Regarding this point, Lloyd deMause (1975) writes:

> A child's life prior to modern times was uniformly bleak. Virtually every child-rearing tract from antiquity to the 18th century recommended the beating of children. We found no examples from this period in which a child wasn't beaten, and hundreds of instances of not only beating, but battering, beginning in infancy.
> One 19th-century German schoolmaster who kept score reported administering 911,527 strokes with a stick, 124,000 lashes with a whip, 136,715 slaps with his hand and 1,115,800 boxes on the ear. The beatings described in most historical sources began at an early age, continued regularly throughout childhood, and were severe enough to cause bruising and bloodying. (p. 85)

Fortunately, contemporary views on socialization are poles apart from the punitive practices of the past. In this respect we can say with some assurance that our culture has evolved. Contemporary socialization, with its emphasis on the humane

treatment of children undoubtedly has survival value. A culture such as ours
which requires cooperative behavior, social responsibility, and a high degree of
creativity from a broad segment of the population cannot afford the wholesale
abuse of children.

Science and the Technology of Socialization

Many theorists have argued that in modern technological culture it is neither
prudent nor practical to base socialization practices solely on the accidental innovations which may arise in the course of cultural evolution. Regarding this
point psychologist Urie Bronfenbrenner (1970) writes:

The control of
socialization

> We are . . . faced with the necessity of developing a new style of socialization,
> one that will correct the inadequacies of our contemporary pattern of living as it is
> affecting our children and provide them with the opportunities for humanizing
> experience of which they are now bereft.
> . . . it is not a question of whether or not there will be changes in the way in
> which we bring up our children, but rather what direction the changes shall take.
> Shall we continue to drift, or shall we try to determine our course? (p. 119)

One reason for socializing agents to seek greater control over the socialization
process has to do with the current rate of cultural change. Rapid cultural change
creates time demands for adaptation which probably cannot be met through selection based on accidental change in the socialization process. For example, the
rapid expansion of knowledge in contemporary society has produced demands
for a high level of intellectual competency from an extremely broad segment of
the citizenry. Society cannot wait for unplanned evolution to produce a citizenry
with high-level intellectual skills. It must find and implement procedures to
produce required skills in the young now.

Another major reason for seeking greater control over socialization involves
variations in socialization practice related to social class. An abundance of
evidence indicates that there are class-related differences in socialization that
may affect the social, emotional, and intellectual development of children (Bronfenbrenner, 1958; Hess, 1970). These differences constitute a highly significant
factor in determining the kind of job that a child will ultimately hold, the amount
of money that he will make, and his social position in the society. Class-related
differences in socialization are in all likelihood adaptations to environmental
circumstances (Hess, 1970). Planned socialization is required to give individuals
across class levels greater freedom in producing desired developmental outcomes.

Control and
technology

Many contemporary social theorists argue that what is needed to enable socializing agents to achieve increased control over developmental outcomes is a
technology of socialization (LeVine, 1969; Skinner, 1971). Such a technology
would relate socialization practices to scientific knowledge regarding socialization. In addition it would provide a delivery system which would insure the
broad-scale availability of research-based techniques of socialization.

The idea of a technology of socialization is not new. It was clearly present in
practice, if not in name, in the child-study movement which, as indicated in
chapter 2, was launched by G. Stanley Hall at the beginning of this century.
Moreover, socialization technology has continued to develop throughout the
course of the twentieth century. Much of the material in this chapter attests
to the fact that a great deal of scientific knowledge regarding socialization has
been accumulated during the last four decades.

The major problem associated with currently available socialization technology is that what is known about socialization is not known by enough people.
The vast majority of socializing agents are simply unaware of available information which could be used in guiding development. In light of this fact, the central
task associated with the future development of socialization technology must be
to establish methods of delivering knowledge to an increasingly broad segment
of the socializing agents in the culture (Havelock, 1969).

It is, of course, not possible to know precisely what form methods of delivery
will take in the years ahead. However, there is one factor regarding socialization
that seems clear. The manner in which various forms of socialization technology
evolve will be determined to a significant degree by the character of socialization institutions such as the home and the school. Policy regarding socialization
is formulated by social institutions. Moreover, the rate at which and manner in
which new knowledge is incorporated into child training is determined by the
policies and practices of socializing institutions. As we shall discuss in the next
and final chapter of the book, socializing institutions are undergoing rapid
changes which have had and will in all likelihood continue to have dramatic
effects on the socialization process.

SUGGESTED READINGS

Aronfreed, J. *Conduct and conscience*. New York: Academic Press, 1968.

Ayllon, T., & Roberts, M. D. Eliminating discipline problems by strengthening academic
performance. *Journal of Applied Behavior Analysis*, 1974, 7, 71-76.

Bandura, A., & McDonald, F. J. Influence of social reinforcement and the behavior of
models in shaping children's moral judgments. *Journal of Abnormal and Social
Psychology*, 1963, 67, 274-81.

Bandura, A., & Menlove, F. L. Factors determining vicarious extinction of avoidance
behavior through symbolic modeling. *Journal of Personality and Social Psychology*,
1968, 8, 99-108.

Freud, S. The analysis of a phobia in a five-year-old boy. *Collected Papers* (Vol. 3).
New York: Basic Books, 1959.

Gordon, T. *Parent effectiveness training*. New York: Wyden, 1970.

Kandel, D., & Lesser, G. S. Relative influences of parents and peers on the educational plans of adolescents in the United States and Denmark. In M. W. Miles &
W. W. Charters, Jr. (Eds.), *Learning in social settings*. Boston: Allyn and Bacon,
1970.

Kohlberg, L. Stage and sequence: The cognitive-developmental approach to socialization. In D. A. Goslin (Ed.), *Handbook of socialization theory and research*.
Chicago: Rand McNally, 1969.

LeVine, R. A. *Culture, behavior and personality*. Chicago: Aldine, 1973.

Peterson, C., Peterson, J., & Finley, N. Conflict and moral judgment. *Developmental
Psychology*, 1974, 10, 65-69.

Skinner, B. F. *Beyond freedom and dignity*. New York: Knopf, 1971.

12

Socialization Institutions

Instructional Objectives

Recognize or recall
Compare and contrast
Describe or demonstrate
Evaluate

nuclear and extended families.

conditions contributing to the demise of the extended family.

contemporary American and Arapesh (as described by M. Mead) child rearing.

experimental and naturalistic evidence of the influences of sensory stimulation and sensory deprivation on infant development.

evidence on the permanence or reversibility of effects of early stimulus deprivation.

the conditions hypothesized to contribute to continuity and discontinuity in development.

the components of socioeconomic status.

the major characteristics distinguishing middle and lower SES life-styles, with special reference to authority patterns and disciplinary practices.

the definitions of phenotypic and genotypic intelligence.

the relationships between IQ and SES.

the general results and conclusions of Lesser, Fifer, and Clark's study of SES, ethnicity, and mental ability.

the definition of and hypothesized cause of *cumulative deficit* in intellectual functioning.

the impact of evidence relating to the development of intellectual performance on public policy in the 1960s.

the social science rationale for "compensatory" education.

Bruner's views on the cultural specificity of cognitive growth.

psychodynamic assumptions about the influence of father absence on the development of boys.

the conditions that mediate the influence of father absence on the behavior and development of children.

observational learning processes influencing sex-role development in boys from father-absent homes.

the general results of Hetherington's study of daughters of widows and divorcées.

the relationships among family size, SES, and intelligence.

the effects of birth order on development.

differences in parental care of first- and later-born children.

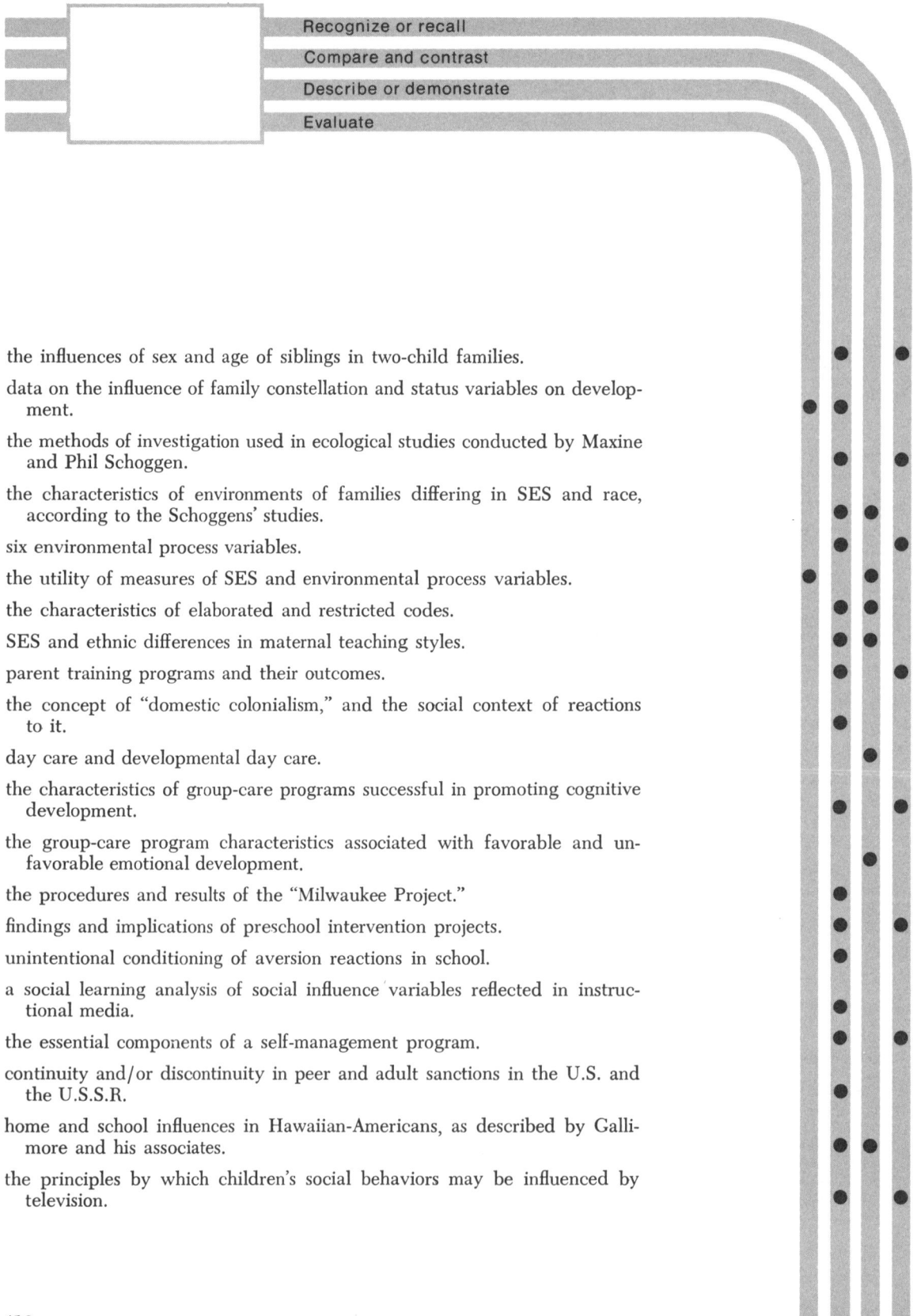

	Recognize or recall	Compare and contrast	Describe or demonstrate	Evaluate
the influences of sex and age of siblings in two-child families.	●		●	
data on the influence of family constellation and status variables on development.			●	●
the methods of investigation used in ecological studies conducted by Maxine and Phil Schoggen.	●		●	
the characteristics of environments of families differing in SES and race, according to the Schoggens' studies.		●	●	
six environmental process variables.	●		●	
the utility of measures of SES and environmental process variables.		●		●
the characteristics of elaborated and restricted codes.		●	●	
SES and ethnic differences in maternal teaching styles.		●	●	
parent training programs and their outcomes.	●		●	
the concept of "domestic colonialism," and the social context of reactions to it.			●	
day care and developmental day care.		●		
the characteristics of group-care programs successful in promoting cognitive development.	●		●	
the group-care program characteristics associated with favorable and unfavorable emotional development.		●		
the procedures and results of the "Milwaukee Project."			●	
findings and implications of preschool intervention projects.	●		●	
unintentional conditioning of aversion reactions in school.			●	
a social learning analysis of social influence variables reflected in instructional media.			●	
the essential components of a self-management program.	●		●	
continuity and/or discontinuity in peer and adult sanctions in the U.S. and the U.S.S.R.			●	
home and school influences in Hawaiian-Americans, as described by Gallimore and his associates.		●	●	
the principles by which children's social behaviors may be influenced by television.	●		●	

CHAPTER CONTENT

In contemporary society, developmental science offers more than descriptions of developmental processes and child characteristics or even intellectual advice to parents and other caregivers. It is becoming a force which influences social legislation and the design of social institutions. In the decade of the 1960s, developmental psychology and related sciences were called upon to advise in public policies which, it was hoped, would "cure" many of the ills of American society. In their enthusiasm over this newfound influence, some scientists implied a promise that their respective disciplines were not prepared to fulfill. In retrospect, the expectation that the behavioral sciences could engineer quick and effective solutions to problems of education, poverty, inequality, and violence seems both presumptuous and naïve.

Child development and public policy

Perhaps because the science of child development overpromised and could not deliver the results the public came to expect, disillusionment set in, both among the public and among the makers of public policy. But in the wake of these experiences, careful examination of the results of social experimentation suggests that some advances were made, and some important lessons were learned. With greater wisdom regarding the difficulties of implementing ideas suggested by what is known about conditions that foster development and with greater humility about the power of developmental science to influence events in the complex world of social reality, knowledge of child development may make realistic contributions to public policy and planning.

A fair amount is known about the ways in which events which are embedded in social institutions influence the development of children. It is probably fair to say that even more remains to be learned than is already known, but there does exist a vast reservoir of basic knowledge about socialization processes from descriptive and laboratory research which awaits translation into purposeful attempts to facilitate development. In this chapter we shall review some of the knowledge base relating to the influences of the family, extrafamilial child care, schools and preschools, peer groups, and the public media on children's development. We shall also identify some of the attempts that have been made to introduce change into these institutions for the purpose of optimizing conditions thought to foster development.

FAMILY INFLUENCES ON DEVELOPMENT

Nuclear family

When we mention the family, the image that comes to the minds of most Americans is that of the nuclear family: a social unit composed of a pair of parents and their own children. Members of some minority groups, Mexican-Americans, for example, are apt to think not so much of a living unit of parents and their children as a family as they are to think of an extended family. The extended family may consist of two or more generations of direct biological descent, such as grandparents, parents, and children, plus a range of cousins, uncles, aunts, and even fictive kin, such as godparents. Ordinarily there are well-defined role relationships among the members of extended families, which usually include such reciprocal expectations as mutual help or cooperative arrangements. If you need to fix your roof on the weekend, members of the extended family will probably show up to help, and a range of nurturant and caring adults are available to take care of one of your children when needed.

Extended family

Some societies have highly complex and elaborated extended family arrangements, and even in the United States the extended family has not always been restricted to various minority groups. Extended families were common in rural settings in the United States, and still are in some regions. But occupational mobility and a life-style that takes people off the land and puts them in factories and offices is not conducive to the maintenance of extended family arrangements, so in contemporary society young couples starting their families are expected to do so without the wider circle of helping relatives and friends that characterized earlier generations. These changes hold profound implications for the socialization of children, especially as more and more women assume professional roles outside the home.

Cultural Differences in Child Rearing

The Arapesh

Child rearing among the Arapesh of New Guinea provides a sharp contrast to the socialization practices most characteristic of contemporary American families. That at least was the case when Margaret Mead (1935, 1953) studied these people in the 1920s. The Arapesh are gentle, receptive people, and Mead wondered how in that homogeneous society socialization works to assure that the child becomes such an adult. How is the child trained so that it will be "placid and contented, unaggressive and non-initiatory, non-competitive and responsive, warm, docile, and trusting?" (Mead, 1953, p. 127). Only a few of the facts of Arapesh child rearing can be presented here to convey the flavor of the process.

During the infant's earliest months it is never far from someone's comforting arms. At any time the child becomes fretful it is offered the mother's breast. A child's crying is considered a tragedy and must be avoided at all costs. Contrast that attitude with the belief of many Americans of about the same era that crying strengthened the child, or that one should not give into an infant's cries of distress lest it become "spoiled" and come to dominate its adult caretakers. That attitude is not so different from the view of some contemporary operant psychologists who believe that unless the child is in pain or danger, its cries should be ignored so as to avoid strengthening "operant crying" responses. We should hasten to add that some operant psychologists of our acquaintance do not accept this point of view, but rather regard crying as the infant's principal means of communication and feel that it should not be extinguished. Authorities on emotional development during infancy feel the baby's cries should not be ignored during the first year of life (Ainsworth, 1973).

As with any people, there are times when the Arapesh mother is occupied with other things, but there are always others around to comfort the infant with the sound of their voices and the touch of human skin. Little boys and little girls *Body contact* alike are enthusiastic about babies. With their verbalizations the mothers regularly point to the good in things around, the good taro root, the good dog, good pig, and good child. Relationships of people are identified repeatedly, from the child's earliest days, and the people in the child's circle of relations are identified as sources of comfort and nurturance. *This is your other mother* (mother's *Significant adults* sister). *See your other mother. She is good. She brings you food. She smiles. She is good.* As the child grows older its close relationships extend well beyond the circle of its parents. A 4-year-old may stay for a week or so with an aunt, who may send him home to his parents via other relatives. Thus, while he sees his own parents more than he does other adults, there are many significant adults in his life, and his circle of trust extends to many "parents" other than his biological ones.

All in all, Arapesh children seem to live a happy-go-lucky life. Adults make no attempt to make sure that the child grows up rapidly. Children are free to try things out for themselves, even at tasks where the risk of some accident which could result in physical injury is high. Parental concern with "efficient" methods of child training, designed to encourage precocious development in American children, seems to be entirely lacking in Arapesh society. In fact, in most Arapesh activities there is little of the concern with accuracy and efficiency that is characteristic of so much of modern American life. For example, the Arapesh have few well-defined, standardized skills and techniques in their material technology. The knots used to tie various parts of their houses together are of varied styles and forms. Lengths are measured haphazardly, and when a mistake is made, it usually goes uncorrected. Rather, the rest of the house is adjusted to accommodate to the error. Handicrafts reflect the same characteristic lack of concern for accuracy and detail.

Viewed from Mead's (1953) account of it, Arapesh child rearing stands in marked contrast to typical practices of American caregivers, and the warm, noncompetitive, trusting adult character that seems to result is almost the antithesis of the suspicious, competitive urban American. Such a contrast gives one cause to wonder whether warmth and positive interpersonal affect must inevitably be sacrificed and precocious skill development stressed in order to prepare children for productive roles in industrial societies.

There are striking differences in the amount and kind of stimulation to which *Infant stimulation* infants are subjected in various cultures. This fact holds policy implications in a pluralistic society because many psychologists believe that children are most malleable during infancy (e.g., White, 1971), and that the foundations of intellectual development are laid down during that period (Bloom, 1964). Perhaps the most striking differences in developmental stimulation may be seen in the contrasts between the conditions of child rearing in American middle-class homes and in institutions such as foundling homes. As indicated in chapter 4, Dennis and his colleagues (Dennis, 1960; Dennis & Najarian, 1957) observed the behavior of children reared in foundling homes in Iran. The children were given reasonably good physical care, but resources were too scarce to permit adults to spend much time playing with the infants. Even during feeding children were not held. They drank from a bottle propped on a pillow as they lay on their backs. Sheets were hung from the rails of the cribs to prevent drafts, resulting in an unchanging white visual environment all around, topped off by a stark ceiling above. The children were also swaddled, according to Near Eastern custom, until they were about eight months old. Children reared under these conditions were markedly retarded in the development of intellectual performance and motor skills, such as walking. Even the sequence of creeping to crawling to walking, observed among most children reared in natural settings, did not occur. Retardation appeared to be temporary, since by 4½ to 6 years of age performance was comparable to American norms. Before the children learned to walk they moved about by scooting on their bottoms, rather than by crawling.

Stimulus deprivation and developmental retardation

The cause of retardation in motor skill development does not seem to be related to physical restraints on movement resulting from swaddling and restriction to cribs, because observation in other cultures indicates that under certain circumstances children whose physical movements are restricted during infancy show no retardation in the development of motor capabilities. For example, Hopi children who are reared on traditional cradle boards learn to walk as early as those whose movements are unrestricted (Dennis, 1940). There are, however, important differences in the sorts of stimulation available to a child reared on a Hopi cradle board on the one hand, and stimulation available to an institutionalized infant, on the other. The infant on the cradle board is almost always within sight of other people. She observes them going about their business, and experiences the sensation of moving in an upright position as her mother goes about with the child strapped to her back. When adults are engaged in work, the cradle board is likely to be propped in a semi-upright position, from which vantage point the child can see everything that is going on. The fact that infants who are restricted physically in this way nevertheless display no retardation in the development of motor capabilities has led Hunt (1961) to speculate that visual experiences may be incorporated into sensorimotor schemata and contribute to readiness for the development of motor skills.

Sensory stimulation

As we pointed out in chapter 4, there is some support for the general point of view that development may be accelerated by tactile-kinesthetic, auditory, and visual stimulation. For example, infants typically develop prehension skills through a relatively fixed sequence of perceptual-motor advances between the ages of about eight weeks and 36 weeks (White & Castle, 1964). The sequence begins at two months of age when infants display general motor activity and make a closed-fisted sweeping motion toward a presented object. Next, one-armed swipes at the object decrease and efforts with both hands, clasped at the midline, are typical. By the fourth month the one-handed approach reappears, but now the child uses an open hand rather than a closed fist, and an object can be crudely grasped. By twenty months the average infant can grasp a test object with one quick direct motion, even when the hand must be moved from outside the visual field. The child begins to grasp objects between his thumb and other fingers by about 28 weeks of age. White (1969) exposed institutionalized infants to increased visual stimulation by providing them with attractive mobiles, hanging

Stimulation and developmental acceleration

pictures around the crib and other sorts of sensory stimulation. Through increased stimulation he was able to considerably reduce the period of time it took infants to progress from the random swipe at presented objects to direct and purposeful grasping with thumb and fingers. Actually, varying degrees of stimulation were provided, and only up to a point did increased stimulation result in accelerated development. Beyond some optimal level, however, further increases in stimulation seemed to have the opposite effect of slowing down the developmental sequences involved in prehension.

The mere physical handling of infants also appears to influence development. White and Castle (1964) found that infants in a hospital setting who were rocked for an additional 20 minutes per day came to spend more time exploring their visual environment than infants who did not receive this additional stimulation. The children who were rocked were blindfolded during the rocking to make sure that changes in visual stimulation associated with rocking would not contaminate the results.

These general findings from studies which have manipulated the amount and variety of stimulation find support in descriptions of infant behavior and child-rearing practices in various cultures. As indicated in chapter 4, Geber (1958) noted that infants in Uganda, Africa, were extremely precocious in their motor *Uganda* development. For a variety of behaviors such as controlling the head, sitting, and prehension, the children observed in Uganda were two or three months ahead of average European children at the same age. This accelerated development was attributed to the fact that Ugandan infants generally receive massive stimulation from the time of their birth. They are always with their mother, often with skin-to-skin contact, they hear her conversations and are the objects of continuous warmth and affection. The parallels with the child-rearing practices of the Arapesh are striking. Geber ruled out the possibility of genetic influence because such accelerated development is not found in Ugandan children who are reared in the European style.

Quite different practices have been observed in some other cultures. Kagan *Guatemala* and Klein (1973) studied the development of Indian children in two Guatemalan villages which were isolated from urban Guatemalan life in varying degrees, by geographic, cultural, and linguistic factors. Unlike the Ugandan or Arapesh cultural settings, the infants in these villages are rarely played with or spoken to. Their playthings consist of pieces of wood or clay, ears of corn, oranges, and also their own and their mother's bodies and clothing. Compared to American infants of the same age they are very passive in their motor activity, smile very little, are relatively fearful, and most strikingly, they are exceptionally quiet. These infants spend most of the first 10 to 12 months of their lives inside a small, dark, windowless hut. In this setting the infant is rarely allowed to crawl on the dirt floor, and the sun, dust and air outside the hut are considered harmful to her.

What caught the attention of these investigators was that while they observed infants who were apathetic, listless, and silent and three-year-olds who were timid, quiet, and passive, these characteristics were not at all evident in the behavior of 11-year-olds. In striking contrast to the infants and very young children, 11-year-olds seemed to be intellectually competent, active, and gay. There was no good reason to suppose that conditions had changed sufficiently since the contemporary 11-year-olds were infants to account for the differences. These observations led Kagan and Klein to entertain reservations about common assumptions concerning the continuity of development. Accordingly, they set out to examine the development of cognitive processes widely considered to reflect the development of intellectual competencies using tests of recall, recognition memory, perceptual analysis, and perceptual and conceptual inference. These devices were designed to be as free of specific cultural content as possible.

Kagan and Klein (1973) found that Guatemalan children were about two months less advanced than American infants on a number of psychological competencies which typically emerge during the first two years of life. Like economically disadvantaged American children, the Guatemalan Indian children were also retarded, by from one to three years, in developing the problem-solving skills characteristic of Piaget's stage of concrete operations. However, by the time the children reached preadolescence, the 11-year-olds performed as well as American middle-class children on tests of recognition memory, perceptual analysis, and perceptual inference. The obvious implication of this finding, although it has been challenged and needs to be replicated before firmer conclusions may be drawn, is that the effects of early stimulus deprivation are not irreversible.

The early restrictions on activity and the lack of a range of stimulation which characterizes the environment in which the Guatemalan infant spends his earliest months changes sharply when the child is about 15 months old. At that point he leaves the dark hut, plays with other children, and is faced with cognitive challenges which Kagan and Klein suspect force cognitive accommodations resulting in intellectual growth.

A Mixtecan village

Age-related cultural expectations

People in various cultures hold quite different beliefs about the nature of childhood, and these beliefs may dictate the expectations that adults hold for children of various ages, or the nature of the experiences provided and responsibilities assigned. Descriptions of child rearing in a Mixtecan Indian village in Mexico provide a case in point. During early childhood, the children in a village studied by Romney and Romney (1966) spend most of their time playing in a courtyard with other children. They are expected to learn to dress themselves, and some rather casual toileting behaviors, but other than that few demands are placed on them. This relaxed attitude seems to result in part from the belief that prior to the age of about five or six young children lack the power to reason. They are thought to learn only by imitation.

Some abrupt changes in parental expectations and demands take place when children are five or six. The children then are expected to take a hand in simple household chores and to go to school where they must learn new patterns of interaction with the more aggressive Mexican children in the central part of town. There is also a change in the ratio of punishments to rewards because the children are now thought to be capable of understanding. They must accordingly be punished for failure to obey commands. At earlier ages they were not punished much because children in the early childhood stage are thought to have no capacity for reason. If children cannot recognize the difference between right and wrong, it would be truly unreasonable to expect them to be responsible for their behavior. The distinction is well exemplified in linguistic usage. "The Mixteco word used for infants means 'in darkness,' and implies that the infant has no awareness. When speaking Spanish, Santo Domingans use the term 'creature' in referring to infants" (Romney & Romney, 1966, p. 85).

Continuity and discontinuity in development

It seems reasonable that in situations where there are clear and pervasive changes in cultural expectations for behavioral development, and when these changes in expectations are broadly supported by changes in the experiences and tasks made available to children, one would not expect continuity in development. When there is continuity in expectations and attendant experiences, we would be more likely to find continuity in developmental trends. It seems only fair to caution, however, that the children whose dramatic changes in performance were captured in Kagan and Klein's data lived in a relatively homogeneous culture, with corresponding homogeneity in experiences. Moreover, Kagan and Klein were concerned with general cognitive competencies which may bear little relationship to the specific competencies particular cultures require for successful participation. In a pluralistic culture, in which influences in different sectors of a child's life may present conflicting or competing expectations, the issue of continuity and the reversibility of effects of earlier experience may be far more problematic.

Socioeconomic Influences

In spite of our stated beliefs in social equality and egalitarianism, the United States is a stratified society. That fact is clearly evident in everyday speech, with its reference to categories of people identified as "poor white trash," "welfare rollers," and the more glamorous "jet set." Beginning in the 1920s with the Lynds' study of Middletown (1929), and peaking during the 1940s with the Yankee City series of community studies in New England (e.g., Warner & Lunt, 1941; Warner, Meeker, & Eells, 1949), social scientists have documented the fact of social stratification and devised ways of measuring it. Socioeconomic status (SES) has been measured in a variety of ways, but the most common factors to be taken into consideration are the occupation, income, and level of formal education attained by the major wage earner in the family. In the more sophisticated systems for indexing socioeconomic status, attention is given not only to the amount of income a family has, but also how it is acquired. Even if incomes were comparable for three different families, they might be assigned different SES scores if they earned their incomes in different ways. Other things being equal, a salaried worker could be considered somewhat higher on the socioeconomic scale than a family in which the breadwinner made the same amount of income from hourly wages. On the other hand, a family at the same income level but whose income was derived from interest or dividends on investments would be higher yet. These assignments are not entirely arbitrary. In some of the more elaborate work on social class, data were gathered on the actual patterns of interaction in the community—who goes to whose house for dinner, for example—and an attempt was made to develop a scoring system that would reflect the social strata observed in the patterns of interaction and association in the community (Warner, Meeker, & Eells, 1949). Type of housing, area of residence, and the state of repair of the dwelling also entered into the derivation of SES indices in the Yankee City studies. While the procedures used in these investigations were carefully developed to reflect the social reality of the New England settings in which the research was conducted, the same system clearly may be inappropriate for use in settings which are quite different.

Other community studies (Hollingshead, 1949) demonstrated that children and youth in different segments of this stratified system do not all receive the same kind of treatment and comparable advantages from the schools and other social institutions. Doubtless, there are few topics which have so captured the interest of social scientists as the question of how membership in various social strata influences the socialization and development of children. The research arising from this interest has been summarized in a number of publications (e.g., Deutsch, 1973; Hess, 1970), and addresses a vast range of questions concerning social-class differences. Some research has attempted to characterize the

Social stratification

Components of SES

SES and educational inequality

differences in life-style and circumstances of people in different social classes. The general tone of these studies may be apprehended by viewing just a sample of the conclusions which Hess (1970) identified from this body of literature.

Powerlessness, for example, is commonly agreed to be a central problem of poor people. Characteristically, the poor have had little opportunity to influence the national policies, community programs, or educational systems that influence their lives. The range of options open to the poor are restricted because of their lack of power, generally low level of educational attainment, limited occupational mobility, and perhaps most importantly, lack of patronage or sponsorship (Pearl, 1972). The middle-class parent is more likely to know a store owner or office manager, or someone who knows someone else who can help the middle-class youth to find work experience which may, in turn, increase his future prospects for work. The poor parent is less likely to be able to provide such sponsorship.

Lack of sponsorship

The poor also tend to be vulnerable to disaster. As Hess has aptly put it, "life is lived on the edge of incipient tragedy which they are powerless to avert" (1970, p. 465). This fact came home forcefully to one of the authors and his co-workers (Henderson & Garcia, 1973) when they were conducting an applied experiment in socialization which involved a number of Mexican-American mothers and their young children, who lived in circumstances of poverty. The mothers were enthusiastic about the project they were involved in, but in spite of the high motivation expressed by the mothers, absentee rates from training sessions were invariably high, requiring make-up training in the homes. Their absences, almost without exception, were occasioned by tragedies at home. For example, the frequency with which serious illness struck the immediate or extended families was greater than we ever could have imagined. Even this rate of personal and family tragedy was dimmed by comparison during the following year when we were working in a reservation setting with native-American Papago families (Henderson & Swanson, 1974). A flu epidemic which was of minor consequence in the city caused many deaths on the reservation, especially among the very young and the very old. And when tragedy strikes, there are few resources available to the poor to ease its impact.

Vulnerability to disaster

A number of studies (Whyte, 1955; Bronfenbrenner, 1958) have suggested that interpersonal relationships in lower SES or working-class homes are likely to be structured on the basis of authority and power, rather than on the basis of democratic problem-solving processes, or through strategies that take the specific characteristics of the situation into consideration. Considering the lack of power among the poor, such an orientation toward authority might be a most realistic reflection of experience since so much of the destiny of the poor seems to be in someone else's hands. If poor people are more likely than those of middle-class status to perceive the control of reinforcement as external (as discussed in chapter 10), it seems no wonder, given the circumstances governing their lives.

SES differences in family authority patterns

In addition to those studies that have attempted to capture some of the broad differences in life circumstances and attitudes among members of differing social strata, the differences in child-rearing practices of different social classes has netted a good deal of attention. One of the most widely known of these studies was one which contrasted the child-rearing techniques of lower-class and middle-class mothers in Chicago (Davis & Havighurst, 1946). One of the major conclusions was that lower-class mothers used more permissive child-rearing techniques than middle-class mothers. Just the opposite was found in another extensive study of child rearing which was done in Boston just about a decade later (Sears, Maccoby, & Levin, 1957). Of course, these differences could reflect differences between Boston and Chicago, but there were also important events affecting the entire society, such as World War II, which intervened in the years between the actual data collection for these studies. Bronfenbrenner (1958) reviewed these and an abundance of other studies of child rearing, and he concluded that in spite of apparently contradictory conclusions, both of the studies mentioned above were probably correct. After World War II many middle-class mothers, who tend to have high access to professional advice and information offered in the media, apparently took up more breast feeding than in former years and were more likely to feed on demand rather than on the basis of a rigid schedule. They also became less likely to punish sexual and aggressive impulses in their children, a change which seems likely to have been influenced by advice based on psychoanalytic views of personality development. There may be methodological and other differences among the various studies of social class and child rearing which could account for the different conclusions (Hess, 1970), but it does appear that the apparent discrepancy is due in part to the fact that social institutions, and the typical behavior of the people in them change, and the rate of change seems to be accelerating (Deutsch, 1973).

Disciplinary patterns

From his review, Bronfenbrenner (1958) concluded that a major difference between middle-class and lower-class child-rearing procedures is in the disciplinary measures that are applied. From the many studies reviewed he drew the generalization that lower-class families used physical punishment more often than did middle-class families, and that middle-class families seemed to use psychological punishment, such as shame, guilt, or withdrawal of affection, in preference to physical coercion. These differences have been encountered in our earlier discussions of disciplinary practices employed by parents of boys with relatively high self-esteem (chapter 10) and in regard to the control of aggression (chapter 9). The effectiveness of withdrawal of affection has been widely assumed in descriptive studies of socialization, but little experimental work has been conducted to compare the differential effectiveness of punitive control and withdrawal of affection as disciplinary techniques.

IQ and SES

Large numbers of studies have examined the relationship between IQ and socioeconomic status. As indicated in chapter 5, there is a consistent relationship between SES and various measures of intelligence. There are a number of reasons for interest in the relationship between social class and IQ. Some investigators undoubtedly have considered the IQ to be an index of phenotypic intelligence and have investigated its relationship with various other measures on the assumption that it provides a good estimate of genotypic intelligence (Deutsch, 1973), but other investigators have been interested in the relationship between IQ and social-class status because the IQ has proved such a reliable measure, and because it has been assumed to provide a good prediction of other performances, such as academic achievement. A major difficulty that cuts across most studies of relationships between socioeconomic indices and measures of IQ is that socioeconomic status is heavily confounded with race and ethnicity factors. Minority racial and ethnic groups are heavily overrepresented in the lower strata of socioeconomic status. Therefore, many studies comparing the performance of minority groups against middle-class standards inadvertently bias the results against minority-group members.

SES, ethnicity, and intellectual functioning

Lesser, Fifer, and Clark (1965) conducted a most revealing study which begins to sort out some of the confusion inherent in studies of relationships among socioeconomic status, ethnic group membership, and intellectual functioning. They administered specially constructed tests of verbal ability, space conceptualization, reasoning, and numerical ability to middle- and lower-class samples of Jewish, Chinese, Puerto Rican and Negro children. Within each ethnic group, performance of middle-class children on all measures was significantly superior to their lower-class counterparts. The greatest difference between middle- and lower-class scores was found among the black children. These results come as no surprise. The most striking discovery was that within each ethnic group the *pattern* of performance of both middle- and lower-class children was the same, while these patterns differed from one ethnic group to another. These patterns are illustrated in figure 12-1. Jewish children, for example, were highest on verbal ability, while Chinese were highest on reasoning and space. The fact that within a given ethnic group patterns of performance were similar while level differed for middle- and lower-class children is illustrated for the Jewish and Negro samples in figure 12-2.

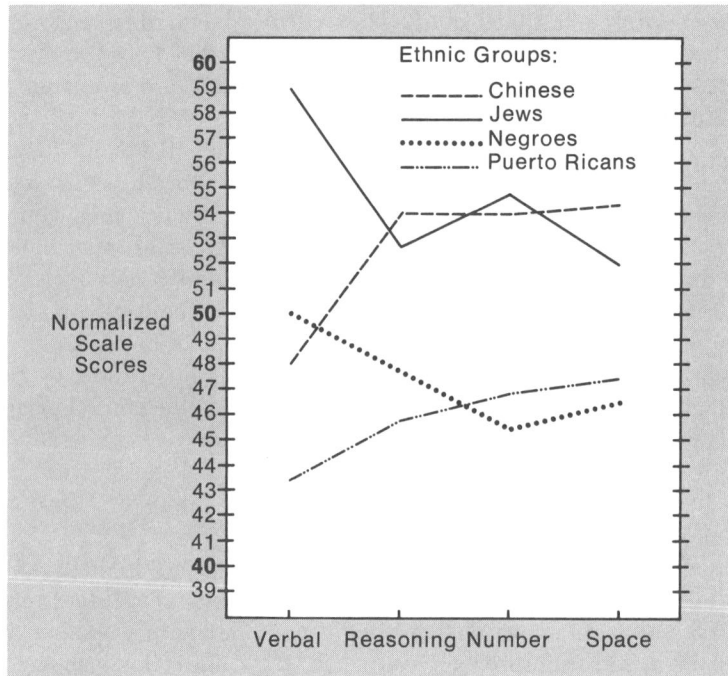

Figure 12-1   *Pattern of normalized mental-ability scores for four ethnic groups. (From G. S. Lesser, G. Fifer, and D. H. Clark. Mental abilities of children from different social-class and cultural groups. Monographs of the Society for Research in Child Development, 30, [serial no. 102], Copyright 1965, The Society for Research in Child Development. Used by permission of the publisher and Gerald S. Lesser.)*

The results of the Lesser, Fifer, and Clark study suggest that different ethnic groups may value, promote, and provide more learning opportunities for their children on some kinds of intellectual tasks than on others. Unfortunately, there are no data on the specific kinds of child-rearing practices which might account for these differences, except that verbal behavior is known to be highly valued and modeled in Jewish households. It seems extremely unlikely that factors other than environmental experiences could account for differences in patterns of such specific mental abilities.

Isolated children   Another type of evidence with implications for the socialization of competencies in children went little noticed for many years. In 1932 Sherman and Key (1932) studied "hollow children" in the Blue Ridge Mountains, and found that average IQs declined from about 84 for the age range six to eight to 70 at ages eight to ten, and finally to 53 at ages ten to twelve. Similar IQ declines were noted even

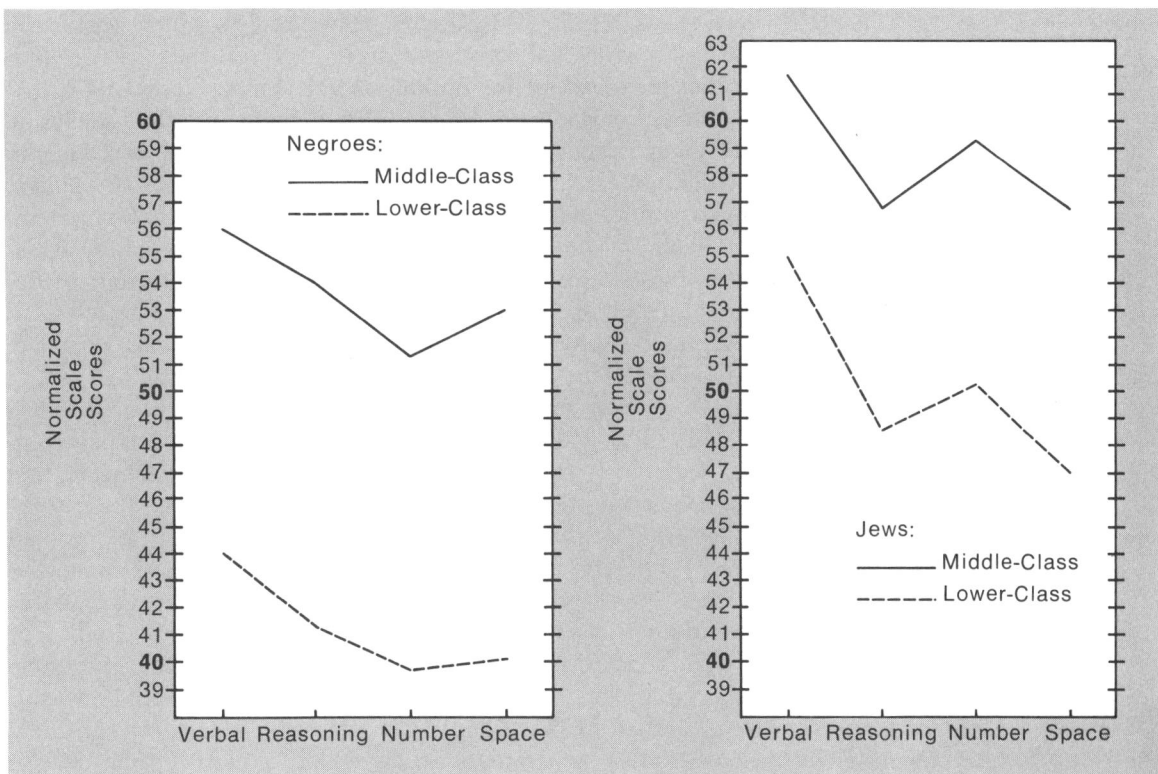

Patterns of normalized mental ability scores for middle- and lower-class Negro and Jewish children. (From G. S. Lesser, G. Fifer, and D. H. Clark. Mental abilities of children from different social-class and cultural groups. Monographs of the Society for Research in Child Development, 30 [serial no. 102], Copyright 1965, The Society for Research in Child Development. Used by permission of the publisher and Gerald S. Lesser.)

Figure 12-2

earlier in a study of gypsy barge children (Gordon, 1923). Children in both of these populations were reared in environments characterized by a very restricted range of social contacts, and what has been considered a general lack of intellectual stimulation. These reports were read with interest by some social scientists, but they gained little public visibility and certainly had no notable influence on social policy. In the 1960s observations that inner-city black children displayed a similar (but less extreme) cumulative deficit in intellectual performance, and that poor children in a small town in the South displayed "progressive retardation," (Klaus & Gray, 1968) had a greater social impact.

Cumulative deficit

Cumulative deficit simply means that a given group of children falls further and further behind the test norms as they grow older. With reference to school achievement it implies the paradox that the longer children from a given population are in school, the greater is the discrepancy between their performance and the performance of their middle-class peers, who contribute disproportionately to the norms for most standardized tests. This general pattern has been identified in a great variety of settings and among various ethnic groups who are over-represented in the low income groups of our society (e.g., see Henderson, 1966).

The reports of "cumulative deficit" in the 1960s created more interest and activity than the reports of IQ decline among isolated children in the 1920s and 1930s probably because the time was right for society to be responsive to such data. These reports came amid public sensitivity to the causes of inequality

Developmental data and social policy

and the aims of civil rights activity. They also came at a time in which most social scientists believed that intellectual development is very malleable and that it requires a stimulating environment for optimal development (Hunt, 1961). At the same time there had been wide popular dissemination of the conclusion (Bloom, 1964) that a major proportion of intellectual development is laid down in the years before a child enters school. In this receptive climate of social opinion, the 1960s saw the spawning of large numbers of federally supported programs, such as Head Start, Follow Through, and other educational endeavors designed to "compensate" for deficiencies which were presumed to result from inadequate socialization in the family.

Cultural specificity of intellectual performance   The experiences provided to children, and the cultural conditions to which they are subjected, influence the intellectual performance of children. According to Bruner (1964), cognitive growth depends upon the mastery of specific, culturally transmitted, skills and techniques used in solving the problems encountered in a particular culture. It should therefore not be surprising to find that individuals reared in an ethnic subculture in which certain of these techniques are not highly functional would lack them when faced with tasks valued in another culture. There are undoubtedly experiences which are somewhat common across various ethnic groups, but which differ by socioeconomic status because of the conditions poverty imposes on the quality of life. Studies of relationships between social class and IQ or social class and school performance provide little information on the processes by which differential levels of learning take place. Neither do they identify those areas in which strength may be developed as a result of experiences in an ethnic or social group whose unique abilities are not assessed or valued in conventional educational programs.

Family Constellation

The constellation of families may influence the development of children. In attempts to understand influences on developmental processes, a considerable amount of attention has been given to the ways in which children reared in one-parent families differ from those reared in two-parent families. The interest here has focused almost exclusively on the impact of "father absence" on child development. Other constellation factors of interest include family size, birth order of the siblings in a family, and the spacing between siblings. We will turn our attention first to fatherless families, a topic which turns out to be surprisingly controversial.

Sex-role development   *Father absence.*   If we recall the central importance of the child's identification with his father in psychodynamic theory, especially with regard to the sex-role development of boys, it is not surprising that so much attention has been given the influence of father absence on development. The assumption is that lacking a father with whom to identify may have particularly devastating effects on the development of boys, since the resolution of the Oedipal situation is supposed to be of central importance in the development of emotional maturity and appropriate sex-role identification. Empirical studies give the impression of supporting the proposition that the lack of a father figure may have serious and generalized negative influences on children. Evidence can be mustered to suggest that the absence of a father during childhood may result in delinquency, impaired intellectual functioning, and emotional disorders.

Father absence and IQ   Researchers at the Insitute for Developmental Studies (IDS) in New York City, one of the earliest organizations to become involved in the study of relationships between poverty and intellectual functioning, studied a sample of

543 black and white children who were selected from various socioeconomic levels. They found that IQ was significantly related to the presence of a father in the home, for children at both the fifth and the first grade levels. The evidence suggests that academic performance as well as IQ may be negatively affected by father absence (Blanchard & Biller, 1971; Landy, Rosenberg, & Sutton-Smith, 1969). The possibility that father absence may have progressive effects is reflected in the IDS finding that the level of association between IQ scores and father presence was higher for fifth than for first grade children. The evidence on this issue is inconsistent, however. Some investigations have found no differences in intelligence-test performance between lower-income black children reared with or without fathers (Hess et al., 1968). When data from a large number of studies of father absence and scores on tests of intellectual functioning are examined closely, what seems clear is that the influences of father absence on intellectual functioning are intricately interwoven with other community, family, and economic factors (Herzog & Sudia, 1963).

Mediating factors

The ways in which these factors are interrelated have not been well studied, but we could speculate that in the absence of a father to fill the role of breadwinner, a mother must assume additional time-consuming responsibilities associated with earning a living. Such responsibilities leave less time for a mother to spend interacting with and providing stimulation or expanded experiences for her child or children. Of course, even in the intact families, a traditional division of labor in which the male is the breadwinner and the mother a homemaker is becoming more and more rare. In many intact families the chores of housekeeping and child rearing are shared by men and women, but even in these cases, the loss of a parent means that there is less time for the remaining parent to interact with children. Furthermore, adequate—to say nothing of stimulating—day care arrangements are still a rarity in this country. Moreover, resources as well as time are generally more limited in single-parent than in two-parent families. The relationship between socioeconomic status and intellectual performance, as reflected in IQ measures and academic achievement, is well established. The implications of that fact are clear if one considers ". . . that one-parent families and black families are, on the whole, less prosperous than two-parent families and white families" (Herzog & Sudia, 1973). According to census figures summarized by Herzog and Sudia (1973), in 1967 the number of white families headed by a female, with incomes under $3,000, was three times the proportion of white families headed by males. Other figures based on comparisons of one- and two-parent families in a housing project suggest that the per capita income of two-parent families may be double that of single-parent families (Cagle & Deutscher, 1960, cited in Herzog & Sudia, 1973).

Time and resources for child care

It has been widely assumed that children from fatherless homes are more likely to become involved in juvenile delinquency than children from two-parent families. The evidence on this association, however, is mixed; where relationships have been found, there often appears to be contamination by other factors. For example, children from broken homes are more likely to be charged and committed for delinquent acts than are children from two-parent homes. Multiple offenses, or recidivism, among those children from broken homes who do engage in delinquent behavior further complicate the picture. Socioeconomic level again comes into the picture because blacks and children from lower socioeconomic levels are more likely to be charged and tried for juvenile offenses than are white and middle-class youngsters (Herzog & Sudia, 1973).

Juvenile delinquency

In view of these complicating factors, it is interesting to speculate why studies showing association between father absence and delinquency have been so widely and uncritically accepted, especially given the fact that the contaminating influences of community and economic factors have not been controlled in the majority of the investigations. The reason may lie in the fact that the finding of an association between delinquency and father absence is congruent with certain theoretical notions about development. In previous discussions we have suggested that once categories or assumptions about social events are formed, those categories may influence future perceptions, or act as a filter for subsequent information and perceptions. Social scientists may therefore be more apt to take note of those studies which are congruent with their preconceptions than to take note of the exceptions. One common point of view heavily influenced by psychodynamic theory is that the sex-role development of boys may be badly impaired by the lack of a father with whom to identify. Presumably, the boy reared in a fatherless home may develop doubts about his own masculinity. Aggressiveness is a salient characteristic of the masculine identity. Therefore, the boy who is unsure about his masculinity may "overcompensate" in order to convince his peers and himself of his manliness. This pattern is thought to be particularly prevalent where the neighborhood culture is characterized by a high degree of violence and antisocial acts. By logical extension, it should also be the case that black youth would be highly likely to become caught up in this pattern because of the high frequency of father absence and the "matriarchal" structure which is supposed to be common to black families (Miller, 1958).

From their extensive review of literature on father absence, Herzog and Sudia (1973) concluded that it is impossible to determine from the available information whether or not children from fatherless homes are more likely than others to engage in delinquent behavior, but it is their *impression* that there is a slight but statistically significant tendency for the incidence of delinquency among children from fatherless homes to be higher than among children from two-parent homes. However, the presence or absence of a father in itself is a variable of

Supervision and family climate

lesser importance than the kind of supervision given to the child, and the general tone or climate of the home. Family climate refers to things such as the compatibility of the parental partners, the happiness, fairness, and presence or absence of intrafamilial friction in a given home. Also more important than the presence or absence of a father per se are socioeconomic level and community factors. Adequate supervision, for example, may be impossible for mothers to maintain under certain economic circumstances where there is no father in the family (Herzog & Sudia, 1973).

Development of "masculinity"

The father's influence on sex-role development in boys is of interest beyond its hypothesized relationship to juvenile delinquency. Research suggests that boys who are reared by their mothers or other female figures may be less masculine than boys who are reared with their fathers. Much of the research on which these conclusions have been based came from studies of children who were separated from their fathers during World War II, and apparently even those boys who were separated at an early age from fathers who later returned continued to behave in a somewhat effeminate manner (Stolz, 1954). Another popular source of information has been from studies of the sons of Norwegian sailors who spent long periods of time away from home (Gronseth, 1957; Tiller, 1957). Paradoxically, when boys have shown a good deal of "masculine" behavior, the interpretation has been offered that this represents compensatory behavior designed to overcome anxiety over sex-role identity.

Unfortunately, the inferences which have been drawn from studies of effects of father absence on sex-role development and masculine identity often fail to take into consideration such important factors as the age at which separation took place, whether the separation was permanent or temporary, the duration of the separation, if it was temporary, and whether separation resulted from death, divorce or other causes. The departure of a father, for whatever reason, frequently occasions a reduction in income, and it often necessitates relocation of the family—events which might have psychological concomitants (Herzog & Sudia, 1973).

Differences in the effects of temporary and permanent separation are illustrated in a number of studies that suggest that the child who has been separated from his father on a temporary basis may maintain the presence of his father through fantasy. Children whose fathers had been away for from one to three years during World War II included enjoyable relations with their fathers just about as much in their doll play as did children whose fathers were present (Bach, 1946). Baker and his associates (1967) also found that children maintained their separated father's presence through fantasy. It seems likely that boys who perceive the absence of their father as a temporary state of affairs would tend to use fantasy to maintain his presence more than children faced with the objective reality of permanent separation through divorce or death.

Temporary and permanent separation

A good case can be made for a developmental lag in the development of "sex-appropriate" behaviors among boys who are reared without fathers, but the effects often appear to be temporary and cannot be detected in the majority of such children at later ages (Sears, 1951; Tiller, 1961; Baker et al., 1968). One important longitudinal investigation did reveal differences in adult adjustment between men who had been rated as high or low on masculinity during boyhood (Kagan & Moss, 1962), but the investigators did not take the differences to suggest that the sex-typed interests of adult males was "better" if it was more "masculine." The authors commented that:

> The social class of the family is clearly related to the sex-typed interests of the adult. The higher the educational level of the family, the less likely was the individual to prefer the traditional attitudes appropriate to his or her sex-role. The upper middle-class men rejected orthodox masculine traits; the upper middle-class women rejected orthodox feminine traits. (p. 171)

It is quite to be expected that a boy who is raised in a feminine household, with no male models regularly available for emulation, would take on some of the behavioral characteristics of the significant adults with whom he does have contact. Since these significant others are largely female during the early years, some of the observationally acquired behavioral characteristics of the child will undoubtedly be sex-typed behaviors associated with the female role. As the universe of direct and vicarious social contacts increase, a variety of same-sexed models will become available for emulation. The father is not the only male whose behavioral characteristics are incorporated even by boys who are reared in two-parent families. Kohlberg provides an anecdote which nicely illustrates the fact that multiple sources of social influence get incorporated into the developing child's stereotype of the male role. During a bed-time conversation a five-year-old boy said to his academician father:

Multiple sources of social influence

> Oh, Daddy, how old will I be when I *can go hunting* with you? We'll go in the woods, you with your gun, me with my bow and arrow. Daddy, wouldn't it be neat if *we could lasso* a wild horse? Do you think I could ride a horse backward if someone's leading me like you? (Kohlberg, 1966, p. 136, italics by the author, quoted in Herzog & Sudia, 1973)

The implications are too obvious to be belabored.

Up to this point the discussion of fatherless families has centered on the possible effects of father absence on male children. This emphasis parallels the emphasis in psychological studies on this topic. Since personality theory has generally placed greater emphasis on the father's influence on sex-role development of boys, the reasons for this bias are clear. There is, however, some interesting information on the effects of father absence on the development of girls. The relationship between father absence and intellectual performance seems similar for boys and girls (Landy & Rosenberg, 1969). The influence is particularly apparent with regard to mathematical ability, which is lower among both girls and boys who have been reared for the first decade of their lives without a father.

Fatherless girls do not appear to differ from others in their sex-typed behaviors, but in other forms of sex-role adjustment there appear to be some important differences between girls with fathers and girls without, and between girls who have lost their fathers through death and those whose loss came through divorce (Hetherington, 1972). Mavis Hetherington felt that since few evidences of effects of father absence on the development of girls had been identified among children through the elementary school years, it might be possible that the

effects do not become evident until puberty, when girls begin to engage in more frequent interaction with males. Her suspicions seemed to be confirmed, suggesting that patterns of effects from father absence may differ for boys and for girls.

As we indicated previously, the earlier effects of father absence on the development of sex-typed behavior in boys who have lost their fathers either disappear or are attenuated as time goes on. The case was just the opposite with the adolescent girls studied by Hetherington. There were no differences between girls with or without fathers on things such as their attitudes toward the feminine role or their feminine interests. Where they did differ was in their

ability to interact "appropriately" with males. The daughters of divorcees and widows both felt insecure around males, but this insecurity was manifested in very different ways by the two groups of fatherless girls. Observational measures were taken on the interactions of the girls with male and with female interviewers. The two groups of fatherless girls did not differ in their interactions with female interviewers, but the differences were striking when the interviewer was male. Daughters of widowed women were inhibited and rigid in

their interactions with males. They tended to sit stiffly or to lean away from the interviewer. Often they turned their back slightly toward him. They sat with their hands folded or in their laps. Legs were held together. The contrasting

behavior of the divorcees' daughters is best illustrated in the investigator's own words. When these girls were with a male interviewer they ". . . tended to assume a rather sprawling open posture, often leaning slightly forward with one or both arms hooked over the back of the chair" (p. 318). The daughters of widows displayed more postural attempts to increase the physical space between them and the interviewer than either the daughters of divorcees or the girls from intact families. They also showed less eye contact with him. Daughters of divorcees displayed more leaning toward the interviewer, more openness of legs and arms, and more eye contact than any of the other groups.

The results of the observational measures were generally congruent with various personality measures that were administered and with information derived from interviews, although the differences between daughters of widows and divorcees were most evident in the observational measures and in reports of heterosexual activity, in which the divorcees' daughters far exceeded the sexually restrained girls whose fathers had died. All the major differences between the groups of fatherless girls were greater for those girls who lost their fathers early than for those who lost them later.

The data from this study make an important contribution to our knowledge about the possible effects of father absence on the subsequent adjustment of female children. It is only possible to speculate about the causes of the differences noted, but at least some hints are provided in Hetherington's data from interviews with the girls and their mothers. Divorcees tended to be very hostile toward their ex-husbands, and these critical attitudes were reflected in the feelings of their daughters. On the other hand, the widows had positive feelings toward marriage and toward their lost husbands. They also had the emotional support of friends, in part perhaps because ordinarily one is considered beyond blame for the death of a spouse, while fault may be implied when loss is by divorce. It appears that both groups of fatherless girls lacked socially appropriate skills for interacting with males, but their efforts to make up for this took different forms. Hetherington speculates that the daughters of divorcees may see their mothers' lives as unsatisfying and feel that getting a man is essential to a happier life. On the other hand, the daughters of widows may have an aggrandized image of their father and feel that no other male could compare favorably with him.

Similarities and differences in adjustment

The exact reasons are left to the probing of imaginative investigators. What is clear from these and related data is that the effects of family constellation variables, such as father presence or absence, do not exert some kind of mechanical, causal influence on development and adjustment. These events are mediated by a complex network of relationships among such factors as the social context in which the event occurs, the age of the child at the time it takes place, and the child's cognitions about the meaning of the event. In order for appropriate behaviors to develop, there must be models of interaction from which the child can learn specific behavioral forms. In the case of Hetherington's study, the behaviors would be socially approved ways of interacting with members of the opposite sex in social situations. Beyond the availability of models, outcomes will be influenced by the social context in which the event of father-separation occurs, the age of the child at the time it takes place, whether or not alternative sources of role learning become available, and, perhaps most important, the culturally mediated cognitions which the child attaches to the event. Here, as in the case of differences between boys whose loss of a father is permanent or temporary, the meaning the child attaches to the loss seems to be critical.

Complex interactions

Family size. Of the many ways in which families differ from one another, perhaps one of the most obvious is the number of children in the family. The average number of children per family has declined fairly steadily over the past few decades, with time out for a baby boom just after the Second World War. In an agrarian society, and even among peoples such as Eskimos who still live by hunting, children may be an asset. In a technological society they are more often regarded as liabilities, or as luxuries. But even in contemporary Western society, there are great differences among families in the number of children they have.

Differences in the average number of children in a family tend to be associated with socioeconomic status and with religious beliefs. Larger families are most likely to be found among lower socioeconomic groups, and among the members of certain religious groups, such as Catholics and Mormons, which explicitly encourage large families. An obvious question is "Does family size in any way influence the development of children in the family?"

Studies of the influence of family size on child development have been largely restricted to examinations of relationships between children's intellectual performance and the number of children in their families. The findings have demonstrated with great consistency that as family size increases, scores on tests of intellectual performance decrease (Burt, 1946; Nisbet & Entwhistle, 1967; Thompson, 1949; Kellaghan & Macnamara, 1972; Belmont, Marolla, 1973; Henderson, 1966). These findings are based on studies of families in Great Britain, the Netherlands, and the United States. In one investigation (Henderson, 1966), which examined family structure variables among low-income Mexican-American families in a city in the southwestern United States, children who scored high on two separate measures of intellectual performance were found to come from smaller families than children whose scores were relatively lower. The average number of children in the families of the high scoring group was 4.37, compared to 6.02 children per family for the lower scoring group. The difference was highly significant. Interestingly, extended family structures were equally common in the high- and low-scoring groups, and there was no difference in marital stability of the mothers or in presence or absence of fathers in the home.

Consistency in findings of relationships between family size and intellectual performance is not absolute, however, for there are also apparently well-designed studies which have failed to find a systematic relationship between family size and intelligence (McCall & Johnson, 1972). The reasons for this discrepancy in findings is not known, but the bulk of the information suggests that an inverse *Family size, SES and intelligence* relationship between family size and intellectual performance does exist. Nevertheless, this conclusion may be misleading, because large families are more common among the poor than among more economically advantaged groups, and, as we have shown, the relationships between intellectual performance and socioeconomic status are firmly documented. Obviously, some large families are found among higher socioeconomic groups, and it has been suggested that the inverse relationships between intelligence and family size may not appear for these more economically advantaged groups. Whether or not this may be the case was a question addressed in a study of the relationships between family constellation variables and verbal reasoning among a predominantly Catholic population in Ireland. Among this population it was assumed that family size would be less confounded with socioeconomic status because large families were valued by both groups. Even in this population there was a significant relationship between family size and performance on a test of verbal reasoning when the influences of social status were statistically controlled.

The most reasonable explanation for the negative relationship between family size and intellectual functioning is that with more children in the family, *Contact time and intellectual socialization* parental contact and influence are reduced. Measures of intellectual performance are designed by adults and reflect the skills and abilities they deem important. Moreover, performance criteria are tied to age norms. This was more obvious when intelligence tests yielded scores for mental age. Standard scores on measures of intellectual performance are now derived in a different manner, but they are just as much related to age as were the old mental-age scores. Contact with adults, particularly with parents, provides the child with the opportunity for intellectual socialization, and the more children in the family, the less the proportional share of parental interaction for each child. Furthermore, when children have siblings, their interests and therefore their attention is likely to be absorbed in the child activities of their siblings, rather than in the adult activities and pursuits of the parents.

The influence of family size may exert its effects on development through complex interrelationships such as a child's ordinal position in a family and the spacing between siblings.

Birth order and spacing. Even within the same family, different children live in essentially different family environments. Inevitably, these environmental differences, especially those which influence the nature of children's experiences with other family members, exert some influences on development. There are many factors which can combine in different ways to influence development. The research on specific characteristics of the family constellation has not been notably consistent, but there seem to be a few clear trends in the observed effects of the factors of birth order and spacing.

Birth order refers to an individual child's position among her siblings (Clausen, 1966). Spacing refers to the time intervals between children. One might be the first child in a family of three, the third child in a family of three, or the middle child in a family of five. Parents have a tendency to treat children differently depending on their ordinal position, and if a child has siblings, his relationships with them will depend in large measure on the age differences between them, and whether younger or older siblings are of the same or a different sex.

A few examples should suffice to indicate the differences in interactions with other family members that may be associated with ordinal position. Bringing home a first child is an anxiety-provoking experience for most new parents. The situation may be somewhat eased if the parents have had the responsibility of caring for younger siblings when they themselves were children, but a young infant nevertheless is fragile and helpless, and in their inexperience, most parents are more anxious about their first-born child than about later ones. Their concerns are not confined to the infancy period. Parents tend to be less relaxed in their relations with first-born children, and they tend to interfere more with their activities (Clausen, 1966; Hilton, 1967). First-born children tend to get a lot of attention from their parents, and apparently as a result they generally learn to talk earlier than later born siblings, and perform better on tests of verbal intelligence. Their self-concept is greatly influenced by their parents' evaluations of them, while later born children seem to be considerably influenced by the opinions of their peers (Clausen, 1966). First-born male children tend to have greater achievement needs than their younger siblings, and first-born children are more likely than those in any other ordinal position to internalize their parents values (Altus, 1965). First-born children are sometimes said to be "highly socialized" in the sense that they have a great desire to please their parents, and they are therefore somewhat more subject to influence than later-born children (Becker, Lerner, & Caroll, 1966; Clausen, 1966). However desirable that characteristic may seem to parents, it could also have its disadvantages. But the fact that first-born children tend to out-perform children in other ordinal positions may in part reflect their motivation to gain approval by doing well at socially sanctioned tasks.

Parental anxiety

Patterns for other children are not as consistent as those for first-born children, but, in general, parents are less anxious about the rearing of second and subsequent children. They tend to be more relaxed and permissive and to spend less time with later children. Younger children spend a good deal of time

*Relaxation
of control*

interacting with their siblings—an alternative not available to a first or only child. The youngest child in a family receives the attention of older siblings as well as that of parents. As a result, youngest children may often appear "spoiled" (Clausen, 1966). The matter is confounded by the fact that it is a rare parent who, even if she knows better, does not sometimes encourage older children to give in to the "unreasonable" demands of their younger siblings in order to avoid the aversive noise and tears of open conflict.

Norms for differential treatment

The prevailing values in American society call upon parents to treat children as equally as they can. Most people think it unconscionable to openly treat one child with greater favor than another. But in some cultures differential treatment is the rule. Many cultures favor first-born children over later ones, or male children over females. Little is known about the psychological influences of such differential treatment when it occurs in a context where it is the cultural norm.

Two-child families

The complexities involved in trying to untangle the influences of a simple family-constellation dimension like birth order may be illustrated by considering the various combinations of influences operating when ordinal position is compared for families with *only two children.* Eight environmentally different sibling positions are possible in two-child families. A boy can have a younger brother or an older brother or a younger sister or an older sister, and a girl may have an older or a younger sister, and so on: eight possible positions when inquiry is limited to two-child families! One very thorough study of ordinal position influences dealt with those eight possible sibling arrangements (Koch, 1954). The results suggested that the effects of ordinal position differ depending on whether the child is a girl or a boy, and whether its siblings are girls or boys. Girls with brothers tended to display some behaviors usually associated with male sex-typing, such as aggressiveness and ambitiousness. For boys, having an older sister seems to result in less aggressive and assertive behavior. Spacing effects were different for boys than for girls. The most positive influences on the development of female characteristics in girls were found when the age gap was from zero to two years. Longer gaps of four to six years were favorable to males. Inversely, short gaps appeared detrimental to males while long gaps were more detrimental to females.

Rosenberg and Sutton-Smith (1969) hypothesized that the same age spacing which seemed to facilitate the development of female and male characteristics, respectively, would also be most conducive to cognitive development. They

Sex & spacing of siblings

found that for males, the *sex* of siblings did not seem to affect cognitive scores, but it appeared that for second-born males, *spacing* did have an influence. In the author's words, "Apparently, if you are a second-born male, the older your sibling, the less negative influence he or she has on cognitive scores" (p. 662). For females, smaller age spacing favored higher cognitive scores. Scores were higher for females with sisters than those without, and having an older sister near one's own age seemed to be the most favorable circumstance for cognitive development. Generally then, although the specific results were exceedingly complex, the hunch that close spacing facilitates functioning for females while larger spacings are more favorable for boys was supported.

It is not clear to what extent results such as these can be generalized to large families, in which the decrement in intellectual performance normally associated with increased family size may be of more serious magnitude. In the large Irish families studied by Kellaghan and Macnamara, ordinal position did contribute to the prediction of verbal-reasoning ability, even after the effects of socioeconomic status and family size had been statistically controlled. The time parents have to spend interacting with their children does seem to be a factor in the intellectual development, even though siblings also exert an influence on each other, and the nature of this influence depends on a number of family constellation factors which include sex, age separation, birth order, and number of siblings.

Environmental Press

The family variables we have discussed so far, those relating to socioeconomic status and family constellation, differ in the degree to which their relationships with various aspects of development have been documented with any consistency. The documentation for relationships between socioeconomic status and either intelligence or academic performance, for example, has been consistently established in numerous investigations. The findings on the effects of father absence, on the other hand, are much less consistent. However consistent the relationship between variables such as these and aspects of development may be, the practical value of the information is rather limited. If it is true, for example, that children from two-parent families manifest better intellectual development than those without fathers, why is that the case? And what can be done to facilitate the development of children in such circumstances? Surely to provide fatherless families with a male figure is not the answer. And what about the influences of family size? It hardly seems reasonable to try to persuade parents of large families to get rid of some of their children in the hope that the intellectual development of those who remain might benefit. And as desirable as it might be to raise the socioeconomic status of every family in the country to wipe out the effects of social status on development, that hardly seems an immediately attainable goal.

Social utility of information

The trouble with family constellation and status variables is that they tell us very little about the specific kinds of events and experiences that facilitate development. There are, after all, exceedingly brilliant, happy, and productive people who came from very humble origins, and the exalted American middle-class has produced its share of dullards, bores and ne'er-do-wells. What we really need to know is what kinds of experiences parents tend to arrange for those children who develop exceptionally well, and what kinds of forces seem to be lacking in the experiences of those who do poorly. With specific reference to those skills and abilities that are valued in traditional school systems and in the business community of an industrial society, it appears that facilitating experiences are more common in, but not exclusive to, middle-class environments. There is also the Lesser, Fifer, and Clark data (1965) which shows that even though levels of performance differ by social class, the patterns of ability are almost identical for different social strata within particular ethnic groups. What specifically do different ethnic groups tend to do, or not do, with their children that results in the development of differential ability patterns? Measures of relationships between socioeconomic status or family composition and some criterion variable, such as intellectual performance, can never tell us that.

Limitations of family constellation and status variables

Studies of the child-rearing practices of differing social classes are plentiful, but there has been little attention given to the ways in which contrasting child-rearing practices affect child behavior (Caldwell, 1964). Much of what we know about the socialization practices of different social groups is descriptive in nature (Zigler, 1970) and has been primarily restricted to descriptions of social-class differences in patterns of authority and power, emotional adjustment, and variables suggested by psychoanalytic theory, such as toilet training and weaning practices. Some investigations have been aimed at identifying relationships between child-rearing practices and children's cognitive or linguistic development (Bernstein, 1961, 1968, 1972; Hess & Shipman, 1965), but most studies have simply focused upon relationships between socioeconomic classification and various measures of intellectual or linguistic performance.

Not everyone shares our view; some investigators are enthusiastic about studies that probe the associations between indexes of socioeconomic status and intellectual performance or school achievement because measures of socioeconomic status are capable of predicting school performance. The predictive value of an index of socioeconomic status lies in the fact that it is a summarizing variable subsuming a variety of values, attitudes, and motivations related to academic performance (Lavin, 1965). A few of the variables summarized by socioeconomic class measures are suggested in the following quotation:

SES as a summarizing variable

> The kinds of specific life-style variables subsumed under social class include neighborhood or residence; value placed on education; proportion of income spent for food, housing, and entertainment; typical leisure-time activities; amount of reading done and nature of reading matter; and the like, as well as child-rearing practices. (Deutsch, 1973, p. 240)

Socioeconomic status is indeed a summarizing variable, and it is precisely for this reason that its usefulness is limited for those who are interested in planning programs or helping parents to facilitate the development of their children (Henderson, 1970, 1972; Henderson & Merritt, 1968; Wolf, 1964; Walberg & Marjoribanks, 1973). The life-style variables mentioned in the quotation above are assumed but never measured directly in socioeconomic indices. The greatest asset of SES indices is also their greatest liability when it comes to understanding how family environment influences development:

> Because SES measures are so gross and undifferentiated, they may well obscure more than they reveal. As a result, they provide no guidance for the design of programs to compensate for debilitating environments, nor to build upon the advantages provided by facilitating environments. (Henderson, Bergan, & Hurt, 1972)

The kind of knowledge that would be most useful would identify what happens, or fails to happen, in the home and neighborhood environments of children and how these events differ among children who differ in developmental abilities. Two related lines of investigation have set out to identify some of the specific environmental factors which may influence development. One approach is the ecological investigations of Maxine and Phil Schoggen (1971) in Nashville, Tennessee. The Schoggens have sent observers into the homes of children in different socioeconomic and racial groups. The observers wear a "steno-mask" which makes it possible to speak into a portable tape recorder without being heard by others in the room. To the extent possible, observers record everything they see: the physical environment is described, gestures and facial expressions are detailed, and the verbal exchanges of family members are recorded. Protocols are typed from the tapes and analyzed. One of the most important kinds of episodes to be identified is the "environmental-force unit," which involves interactions in which one individual attempts to influence the actions of another. It appears that the influence patterns of families of lower socioeconomic status differ from those of middle-class families. The patterns

Ecological investigations

Environmental force units

at each SES level seem to be equivalent for black and white families, while they differ by SES within each racial group. A striking feature of the SES differences is that a high proportion of environmental-force units in lower-SES families aim to get the child to stop doing something—to stop teasing a sister, for example. Environmental-force units in middle-class homes are more often directed at getting the child to understand or to learn something. Of course, both kinds of force units may occur in families at all SES levels, but the Schoggens' research suggests that the proportions may differ greatly across SES levels.

As indicated in chapter 5, a different approach, which has been pursued by a larger number of investigators, was initiated by students of Benjamin Bloom at the University of Chicago (Davé, 1963; Wolf, 1964). Recall that Bloom calculated that most of the basic intellectual development of children was already accomplished before they ever entered school. That premise implies that whatever experiential influences impinge on that development most likely take place in the home. Two of Bloom's doctoral students carefully surveyed the literature on possible home influences on intellectual performance, and on the basis of their reading of the literature they postulated a number of environ- *Environmental* mental process variables. Their general approach to the measurement of factors *process variables* in children's environments that may influence general intellectual development has been widely accepted, and although different investigators have added additional variables, or modified those which Davé and Wolf proposed, there has been remarkable consistency among studies carried out in different countries and with different cultural groups (Majoribanks, 1972; Henderson, 1966; Henderson & Merritt, 1968; Walberg & Marjoribanks, 1973).

Ratings for environmental process variables are derived from semi-structured interviews with parents. The environmental process variables used by Davé are representative of those used in other investigations. They included Achievement Press, Language Models, Academic Guidance, Activeness of the Family, Intellectuality in the Homes, and Work Habits in the Family.

Press for achievement refers to the parents' own aspirations and the aspira- *Press for* tions they hold for their children. The standards for academic achievement which *achievement* they hold and their standards of reward for educational attainment also contribute toward press for achievement. Parental interest in educational attainment is reflected in the kinds of concrete knowledge they have of the developmental or educational progress of their children, and in the plans and preparations they have made to attain the educational goals they hold for their children. The level of occupational and educational attainment of family friends and relatives who have contact with the child are also thought to contribute to press for achievement.

A child's linguistic and intellectual development is also influenced by language *Language models* models. Those characteristics of language models which constitute this environmental process variable include the quality of language used by parents themselves, the degree to which they are aware of specific language usages of their child, and their efforts to influence the child to use correct grammatical constructions. The quality of the parents' own language usage is reflected in such things as the richness and variety of their vocabulary, the fluency of their expression, and the organization of thought reflected in the flow of language. Environmental opportunities which encourage the enlargement of the child's vocabulary and sentence patterns are also incorporated in this variable.

Academic guidance is reflected in the amount and quality of guidance on *Academic* matters related to school work provided by parents. Parents of preschool *guidance* children provide such guidance when they read regularly to them and when they encourage them to learn letters or numbers. Academic guidance therefore begins well before the child begins school, and it is by no means limited to efforts to help children with their homework. The mothers and fathers of preschool children stimulate intellectual development in a multitude of ways as they go about their everyday, routine interactions. Some mothers, for example, encourage their young children to count the number of people who are going to eat dinner and to count out enough knives, forks, and spoons for all of them. Children are encouraged to identify words or letters when they see them in written material around the house or on signs along the road. Some educators argue that it is of no particular value for children to learn things like letters and numbers before they go to school, but the most important aspect of this guidance may be to show the child that school-like skills are valued by the parent. When the learning of tasks like these is reinforced by significant agents of socialization, successful performance may come to have secondary reinforcement value which may help to sustain academic efforts in the absence of heavy external reinforcement when the child is in a classroom situation.

*Activeness
of family*

The activeness of the family may directly influence the range of environmental stimulation available to the child. The child who is exposed to a greater variety of learning opportunities is more likely than the child with more limited opportunities to learn a large range of skills and information. The nature of the family's activities, both indoors and outdoors, and their amount of participation in various activities should influence the learning opportunities of the child. The way in which the family uses television and other media is also important. There are some families who make it a point to know in advance when programs which they think would be beneficial to the child will be aired, and they encourage their children to watch these programs. Program content is often evaluated, elaborated, and extended in family discussions. In other families, very little of this kind of guidance in the use of media is provided. Parents also model the informational use of television when their children see them watch news broadcasts and documentaries regularly, and when they discuss the content of these programs. The activeness of the family also includes their use of books, magazines, and other reading materials, and the degree to which they use libraries, museums, and other sources of information.

*Intellectuality
in the home*

Intellectuality in the home may contribute to intellectual development. Intellectuality, according to the criteria set by Davé (1963), may include such things as the kinds of toys and games available to the child and the kinds of hobbies engaged in by the child and other family members. It also includes the kinds of opportunities provided for the use of thought and imagination in daily life.

*Work habits
in the family*

It has also been thought that work habits in the family may influence development. Presumably, relatively disorganized households in which there is no established structure and routine in home management, and in which work responsibilities are not defined and distributed among family members, would be less conducive to intellectual progress than a home atmosphere in which this kind of routine and order exists. Work habits have also been defined to include the degree to which the family expresses a preference for educational activities over other pleasurable ways of spending their time.

There have been variations in the specific ways in which environmental process variables have been defined in various investigations, but, in general, they have tried to get at specific differences in the kinds of experiences available to children and to examine the relationship of such experiences to intellectual development, as reflected in intellectual ability tests and school achievement. The findings within various ethnic groups and in various countries have demonstrated, with remarkable consistency, that environmental process variables account for much more of the variation in intellectual performance than do measures of socioeconomic status. Rarely does socioeconomic status account for more than 25% of the variance in intellectual performance, whereas environmental process measures usually account for about 60% of the variance. At least two investigations have followed children over a period of time to see if the relationship between home environment and intellectual performance is durable. Mexican-American children whose home environments were studied when they entered first grade were located at the end of their third year in school. With the exception of "work habits in the family," all the environmental process variables previously discussed, plus additional data on the range of adult models available to interact with the child, the social-system linkages of the family with other community institutions, and the family's perception of the value of education, all provided significant predictions of reading achievement at the end of third grade (Henderson, 1972). For this population there is convincing evidence that measures of the home environment provide better predictions of future school achievement than individually administered tests of intelligence (Henderson & Rankin, 1973).

Predictive value of environmental measures

In another follow-up study, Wolf (personal communication) tested the children from his original sample four years after environmental process variables in their homes had been measured. There was little or no deterioration in the correlations between home environment and achievement over a four-year period of time. The original correlation between environmental process measures and academic-achievement scores taken concurrently was .79. Four years later the correlation was .75, indicating that a measure of home environment may be an extraordinarily good predictor of achievement over time.

The fact that environmental process variables "account for" variation in performance does not necessarily mean that these variables "cause" intellectual development. There is no way to tell from correlational evidence whether or not the variables are causally related, but the identification of specific events which are so highly related to intellectual performance and academic achievement provides an excellent starting point for research designed to examine the specific effects of such variables.

The disadvantage of using environmental-process variables as the basis either for probing the relationship between experience and intellectual development, or as guides for the development of educational programs, is that the list of specific kinds of experiences which might make contributions to development could presumably be extended almost indefinitely. Like the generation of lists of "needs" which we discussed earlier, the number of environmental process variables which could be generated is conceivably limited only by the imaginativeness of the investigator. An alternative way of conceptualizing the dimensions of environmental events which may influence development is suggested by social-learning theory. A Canadian investigator (Williams, 1974) has suggested that the relevant dimensions within a social learning framework would center around the stimuli parents provide for a variety of behaviors, the reinforcements they employ, and the encouragements and expectations they provide. In a reanalysis of the data from some of the major studies of environmental process variables, Williams has asserted that these dimensions fit the data better than the environmental process variable dimensions, and that the explanations from such a model are more parsimonious than the dimensions provided by models of influence based on environmental press theory.

Even so, research on environmental process variables has provided valuable insights into the specific kinds of activities and stimulation provided by families whose children tend to perform well on the kinds of tasks that have been traditionally valued in Western, industrialized societies. The data in these investigations are based on self-report, and among the many disadvantages of *Limitations* using self-report instruments is that respondents may not always be entirely *of self-report* truthful—there is a temptation to tell the interviewer that you do those things that you think would be most socially acceptable, whether you really do them or not. Besides, when people are asked about things they have done in the past, their memories do not serve them with complete reliability. Nevertheless, confidence in the relationships found between environmental process variables and intellectual performance is enhanced by the consistency displayed among the findings of different investigators, and for differing populations. Moreover, the results match well with the intensive studies of children from birth to six years of age who were observed by psychologist Burton White (White & Watts, 1973) and his associates in the natural environments of their own homes. These investigators contrasted the home environments of children who were assessed to be developing very well, or comparatively poorly. Their data are richer with description than the environmental investigations based on information from interviews, but their conclusions are basically in harmony with the environmental dimensions from existing studies of environmental process variables.

Parental Teaching Styles

Studies of environmental press provide information about the dimensions of home environments that differ among families, and about the relationship between those differences and cognitive development. In this way this information goes well beyond the general insights about the manner in which socioeconomic status or father absence or birth order may influence development. At an even finer grained level of analysis, the specific styles of parental interaction with children and the differing teaching styles which parents use with their children have been probed to determine how these highly focused dimensions of parental behavior may influence intellectual development.

Since language is so intricately related to intellectual development and enters to a substantial degree into almost any attempt to assess intellectual performance, much of the effort to discern the influence of parental behavior on children's cognitive development has centered on language. Recall from chapter 7, if you will, that Basil Bernstein (1961, 1968, 1972) concluded from his studies of socioeconomic class differences in England that working-class and middle-class families use different linguistic codes. He postulated that the *Elaborated* speech of middle-class people tends to be "elaborated" while working-class *and restricted* people speak a "restricted" code. Presumably, the "elaborated" code is highly *codes* flexible, making extensive use of complex word forms and sentence constructions. It is supposed to be better adapted to the expression of abstract ideas. The "restricted code" or "public language" of the working-class person, in contrast, lacks complexity, is inflexible, is heavy with well-worn idioms, and relies heavily on implicit meanings rather than providing overt differentiation. The speaker of the "elaborated" code supposedly justifies statements to her children and appeals to reason and logic. The speaker of the "restricted" code relies more on unexplained, authoritarian commands. Bernstein feels that the use of the restricted code by parents produces poor thinking in their children. As we have indicated earlier, Bernstein's point of view has invited considerable criticism by those who argue that the poor are just as capable of using elaborated and abstract language as are middle-class people, but the linguistic behaviors in question are situation specific. Labov's demonstrations of the operation of situational constraints on the language production of black ghetto youth are often presented as evidence for the opposing point of view. Nevertheless, Bernstein's idea stimulated a great deal of research on parental teaching styles.

One of the earliest efforts to test Bernstein's ideas in this country was carried out by Robert Hess and Virginia Shipman (1965, 1968) who were located at the time at the University of Chicago. As indicated in chapter 5, they examined the interaction styles of black mothers and their children from differing socio-economic status levels. They found the language codes were more restricted among the lower-class than among the middle-class mothers.

Other investigators have generally confirmed Hess and Shipman's conclusion that parental teaching styles differ by social class (e.g., see Bee et al., 1969), although one pair of investigators (Steward & Steward, 1973) compared the maternal teaching styles of Anglo-American, Mexican-American, and Chinese-American mothers, and found that teaching styles were more closely related to ethnicity than to social class.

Even though there is a high level of agreement among studies of social-class differences in teaching style, a few words of caution should be observed in interpreting these relationships. We have stressed repeatedly that correlation does not mean causation, but there is always a temptation to jump to the conclusion that a particular maternal teaching style causes a particular kind of intellectual development, because to most of us it seems logical that one should lead to the other. A more subtle problem in the interpretation of this literature may be illustrated by examining one large research project. Lower-class and middle-class mothers were observed with their children in a waiting room situation (through a one-way mirror) and in a house-building task that was supposed to present a problem-solving situation. In addition, the mothers were interviewed and the children were tested on a number of tests of cognitive and motivational behavior. Most of the lower-class mothers were black. The middle-class sample consisted primarily of university faculty and graduate students. The interview protocols were used to analyze the speech of the mothers.

Cautions

Some significant questions have been raised about the methods and conclusions of this research (Sroufe, 1970). First, it is well established that factors such as the race and ethnicity of experimenters can significantly influence the ways in which members of different ethnic and social-class groups respond, although findings on the precise ways in which responses are influenced are mixed. In the research under consideration the examiners were middle-class and white. Moreover, the testing and interviewing were conducted in a university facility, in which it is conceivable that the faculty and graduate students may have felt more natural and relaxed than the lower-class parents.

More subtle yet is the possibility that the same behaviors may have different meanings to different groups. This point is nicely illustrated in a comparison of the conclusions offered by the authors of the study and an alternative interpretation suggested as plausible within a different meaning system by Sroufex (1970). Bee and her associates (Bee et al., 1969) concluded that:

Alternative interpretation

> Middle-class mothers, regardless of the situation, used more instruction, less physical intrusion, less negative feedback, and were generally more in tune with the child's individual needs and qualities. (p. 732)

Sroufe's alternative summary of the data emphasizes the role of value judgements in interpreting the results of the experiment. The conclusions covered in points *a* through *d* in the following quotation refer to the results of the cognitive and motivational testing:

> White, middle-class parents can be seen to be much more subtly manipulative and controlling of their children, fostering great dependence and conformity through the use of powerful psychological reinforcers. Such subtle control, in ways more potent than physical control, reveals its effects in the following ways in the child's behavior: (a) rigid persistence in a meaningless, boring key-tapping task merely because of instructions to do so from an adult, (b) drawing a line more slowly than lower-class controls, again with no internal satisfaction or external reward, but merely to conform with adult wishes, (c) compulsive imitation of an adult model, and (d) an inability to dare or aspire to greatness as manifest by an only moderate level of aspiration. (They were, however, no less curious than lower-class children at this young age). (p. 143)

The point of this quotation is not to imply that there are no differences in the performance of middle-class and lower-class children, or in the teaching styles of their parents. The point is that the ways in which differences are most often described *implies* that the behaviors of lower-class people are not just different; they are interpreted as being deficient and inferior. Children from lower-class or ethnic minority backgrounds may well need to learn standard English and certain academic skills, in addition to the language and skills that are functional within their own background, because those abilities are required for access to certain benefits in the dominant society. But to imply inferiority may in the long run prove counterproductive.

Family Intervention

Whether one takes the point of view that poor children and children from racial or ethnic minorities (often they are the same children) have more than their share of difficulty with schoolwork because of deficits or differences in their intellectual repertoires, the fact remains that the schools have not been notably successful in imparting important skills and knowledge to children from these sections of the population. There is a widespread interest in our society in finding ways to optimize the conditions under which children develop their intellectual, social, and personal competencies. Given the prevailing opinion that the early years are particularly critical in establishing the foundations of development it is not surprising that many educators and psychologists have looked to the home as the most appropriate place to bring about change. Parents are, after all, the first and perhaps the most important teachers of their own children. Accordingly, many intervention programs have included parent-education components aimed at providing parents with the knowledge and skills with which to provide a more stimulating home environment for their children. Efforts have been directed almost exclusively at cognitive stimulation. In many cases, family intervention was mixed with other treatments in a way that makes it impossible to separate the effects of one program component from those of another. This discussion is therefore limited to a few examples of efforts which have focused primarily on the family, and for which some evaluative data are available. Readers who are interested in learning about a wide range of intervention programs are referred to reviews by Chilman (1973) and Horowitz and Paden (1973).

Gordon's approach   One of the most widely known parent intervention projects has been the Florida Parent Education Program devised by Ira Gordon (1968, 1969). Gordon's approach was strongly influenced by Piaget's conceptions of developmental processes. Gordon trained low-income women to visit the homes of low-income mothers and to teach these mothers concrete activities to carry out with their infants. These activities were designed to promote the cognitive and affective growth of the infant. During weekly home visits the trainer demonstrated activities with a doll, while the trainee-mother followed suit using her own baby.

Gordon studied four different groups of mothers and their infants. One group received continuous weekly instruction from the time the infant was three months old through age two. A second group also began weekly instruction at age three months, but instruction was terminated at age one year. For the third group the weekly instruction was of one year duration, beginning at age one year, while the fourth group received no home-instructional visits. The results indicate that both the group which received instruction for two years, and the group which received a year of instruction beginning at age one performed better on a scale of infant development than infants who received no instruction. Infants who received instruction from age three months to one year, but no instruction during the second year, did no better at the end of year two than did controls who received no instruction. It appears that, at least within the first two years, continuity of intervention may be more important than how early it begins.

Gordon's approach has been extended to children in kindergarten through third grade in communities which adopted it as a Follow Through model. The national Follow Through program was a federally funded program which enabled selected school districts to choose one of a variety of "innovative" educational programs in an effort to maintain whatever benefits Head Start graduates may have derived from that program. Evaluation criteria included an increase in parental competency and self-esteem as well as improvement in self-image and intellectual development among project children. Information from at least one well-implemented project suggests that the program has been responsible for improvements in the amount and quality of mother-child interactions among those who have received training, and that project children are superior to control group children in the development of pre-academic skills (Evans, 1975).

Several other programs have used some form of home visitation to teach parents ways of providing their children with cognitive stimulation. Weikart and Lambie (1960) were interested in the fact that some of the four-year-old children in their program in Ypsilanti, Michigan, seemed to benefit far more than others. Their analysis indicated that the children whose Stanford-Binet intelligence scores increased the most were those who came from the most "disadvantaged" homes. The mothers who were judged most effective were those who gave positive verbal reinforcement to their children for learning, but with large numbers of children in the home it was very difficult for mothers to deliver verbal praise, contingent on learning behavior. This observation offers some support to the supposition that one of the ways in which large families influence intellectual development is by reducing the amount of specific attention and guidance parents can provide for each child.

Weikart and Lambie

Conditions restricting influences

Certain kinds of toys are thought to have educational benefits, and toys may also serve to mediate the interaction between parent and child, and to provide the parent with distinct cues which may guide her or his efforts to provide intellectual stimulation for the child. Gordon's home visitors provided parents with help in constructing stimulating toys from cast-off articles around the house. The Far West Regional Educational Laboratory has experimented with a toy-lending library, accompanied by instructions for parents in the use of the toys.

Toys and mediation of interactions

A successful program in Nassau County, New York, provided cognitive stimulation through weekly home visits by "toy demonstrators" who each week demonstrated the use of an educational toy and left it in the home as a gift (Levenstein, 1968).

Programs such as the examples given here, which reach parents through home visitors who demonstrate cognitive stimulation activities and often provide informal emotional support as well, have in general been more effective than group education for parents (Chilman, 1973). It is difficult to attract and hold low-income parents, especially fathers, with parent-education groups, and parent education with groups at any socioeconomic level has not generally been successful in changing either the attitudes or the behavior of parents (Chilman, 1973).

Restricted focus of programs

On the other hand, programs which work with parents in their own homes, and which assist them in becoming the primary teachers of their children, show promising results (Chilman, 1973; Nedler, 1973) by producing modest but statistically significant IQ score gains. Existing programs have been criticized for being too narrowly focused on cognitive enrichment, to the neglect of children's emotional and moral development (Chilman, 1973; Maccoby, 1968). It is true that the scope of most programs has been restricted, but the emphasis on cognitive development is certainly understandable in the context of the *Zeitgeist* of the 1960s when most of these programs originated. As Evans (1975) has stated, even though ". . . little is yet known about the noncognitive effects of such parental teaching . . . there is little reason to believe these efforts would be negative" (p. 344).

Domestic colonialism

A new *Zeitgeist* emerged in the late 1960s and became prominent in the 1970s. The kinds of parent education programs which were typical of the early and mid-1960s came to be seen as a form of domestic colonialism, in which programs were devised for poor people by social scientists and policy makers who thought that they knew better than the people for whom programs were designed what was good for poor people and minority groups. After all, the reasoning went, if the poor people knew the solutions to their problems would they still be poor? The shift in emphasis which became most visible in the early 1970s really got under way in the 1960s through programs which attempted to give poor people more power and influence over the programs which affect their lives. Parent participation has been advocated in programs such as Head Start and Follow Through, which tend to be regarded by the general public as either primarily or exclusively *educational* programs. Within the social sciences, the shift in orientation has been influenced by sociologists. In one reviewer's opinion,

> Unlike psychologists, who generally seek to aid people by helping them change their individual behavior, sociologists tend to believe that the behavior and structure of society should be changed and that this is a far more viable and effective approach to a solution of the problems of a mass society. (Chilman, 1973, p. 407)

Increasingly, people who have been outside the structure of power and influence in this country are coming to feel that they should have a decisive voice in determining the kinds of programs that will be implemented for them and their children. Interestingly enough, if psychologists are responsive to this orientation they may still be able to apply their expertise to the design of programs to optimize the development of children, but within a framework that escapes the devastating effects of arguments about deficits versus differences. An example from the work of one of the authors and his colleagues may help to illustrate the point we are trying to make here.

The Papago Indians live on a vast reservation on the Arizona-Sonoran desert. Their resources are meager and their lives extremely isolated from the activity of the large urban areas to the north of them. A number of Papago Native American leaders have expressed concern over the difficulties which their children have in school, and believe that these problems could be reduced if parents were more actively involved in the education of their children. In an initial project we were approached to see if we could help to devise a way of providing parents with some concrete procedures for influencing school-related capabilities in their children. Discussions with the school superintendent indicated that Papago children ask very few questions, and that this behavior might be a reasonable one to start with in an attempt to see if parent training was feasible in a reservation setting in which family residences are scattered over a wide area, and to determine if a focused program could be effective in influencing a particular class of children's cognitive behaviors. The parent advisory group agreed that traditionally, question asking has not been promoted as a customary way of obtaining information. The ethnographic literature also indicated that traditionally Papagos depend on observation rather than question asking as a primary means of acquiring skills and information. The parents recognized that their natural environment does not promote the development of question-asking skills, but given the realities of the reservation situation they saw it as important to begin to promote this capability in their children. In dealings with the Anglo bureaucracies on the reservation, it is critical to be willing and able to ask good questions.

The training program was designed on the basis of social-learning theory, and it employed several linkages from the university-based organization that contracted to do the work in the field setting on the reservation. A Native-American student at the university was trained to train indigenous parapro-

Mothers role-play parent-child interactions in a training project.

fessional parent trainers who in turn trained mothers to model, cue, and reinforce question asking in their children. The emphasis of the training program
was teaching causal questions, those which inquire about relationships and cause
and effect connections, because such questions represent a relatively "mature"
form of questions. In small groups and through home visits, the paraprofes-
sionals demonstrated how to discriminate questions from statements, how to
identify causal questions in interactions with children, and how to reinforce
children for asking causal questions. The mothers were enthusiastic and learned
the techniques well. Between training sessions they practiced what they had
learned at home with their first grade children. The children made significant
improvements in their question-asking skills, and the changes were clearly attributable to the parent's activities with their own children. The modeling and
reinforcing procedures employed by the mothers clearly accounted for the
acquisition and performance of this particular cognitive skill.

Given the success of this limited demonstration, the parent advisory group
asked for an extension of the project in order to see if parents could have any
effect on some aspect of their children's reading behavior. Again, no one on the
outside was attempting to remediate a presumed deficiency in the children. The
initiation came from parent representatives. The children learned many things
in their home environment, but few parents read very much, even though they
wanted their children to become proficient in this skill. In asking for help with
this problem they were in effect asking that parents be helped to influence a
specific aspect of their children's behavior which would be acquired *in addition to* the behaviors traditionally fostered in the family environment on the
reservation.

Papago boys, for example, are highly motivated to learn the skills of horse-
manship. During the winter, hardly a week goes by that one cannot find an
amateur rodeo underway in some village on the reservation. Large numbers
of the boys' fathers are involved in the rodeos, or they work with horses and
cattle during the week. Boys imitate their fathers and other significant males in
their lives and approval is implicitly given to successful performance of behaviors that demonstrate the boys' developing manhood. This emphasis on aggressive masculinity is often referred to as a "macho" complex. One of the most
frequently observed imaginative play activities among Papago boys at Head
Start centers is the rough-and-tumble depiction of horse-riding and calf roping.
Few Anglo boys, with the exception of those raised on ranches, can handle
a lasso like a Papago preschooler.

On the other hand, models of reading behavior, reading materials, and parental
reinforcement for reading behavior are generally lacking in the home environments of these children. If children are to be motivated to become successful
readers, it would conceivably help to have home experiences which lead to the
development of reading activity as a secondary reinforcer.

*Promoting
home-school
continuity*
In consideration of this rationale, mothers were provided with reading materials and with other attractive materials for children. Mothers were trained to
discuss a book with the child in a positive way. Materials were selected so that
the books could be discussed on the basis of pictorial material if the mother
lacked skills necessary to deal with the printed material. Mothers were also
trained to set up a free-choice situation at regular intervals, in which the child
could select either to engage in a self-initiated reading activity, or to select from
competing, attractive play materials. The mothers were trained to attend to the
children positively and to provide explicit verbal reinforcement whenever the
reading materials were chosen. The child was simply not attended to while in-

volved with the competing activity. These procedures were effective in increasing the frequency of self-initiated reading activity when a choice of activities was presented to the children in a structured free-choice situation. The effects also generalized from the home to the classroom setting, as evidenced by a significant difference in preference for reading which favored experimental over control group children (Swanson & Henderson, in press).

This experiment used scientific knowledge about the kinds of socialization conditions that foster the development of a particular motive to bring about an outcome which the parents wanted, but which was not regularly facilitated within the framework of their traditional socialization practices. By working with a set of behaviors valued by both the parents and by the school personnel, it was possible to bring about better continuity between the goals and socialization practices of the Anglo-dominated schools and the home environments of the children. The aims were modest, however, and any comprehensive program to bring about better continuity between home and school goals will require both parents and educators to interact and to become familiar with each other's expectations and aspirations for their children. Few schools seem prepared to make the kind of commitment of time and resources required to bring about this continuity.

EXTRAFAMILIAL CHILD CARE AND EARLY INTERVENTION

More and more children spend much of their time in settings other than the family. Increasing numbers of mothers work outside the home, either out of necessity or the desire for greater stimulation and challenge than they find at home. It seems likely that this trend will increase, so an evaluation of alternative child care arrangements, and their possible effects, seems clearly in order.

Day Care

Traditionally, the most common means of providing care for children whose parents worked was to place them with a baby-sitter. In former times this was most likely to be a grandmother, an aunt, or at least a neighbor who might have ties of affection to the child and who would be responsive to the child's behaviors. With industrialization, mobility away from family roots, and residence patterns in which next-door neighbors may not know each other or even speak, such informal arrangements are clearly on the decline. They may still represent the mode among certain populations, such as Mexican-Americans in some communities where they have been able to maintain extended family relations and residential stability. In most cases, however, other arrangements are being developed to fill the void and to accommodate the increasing numbers of working mothers.

Changes in child-care arrangements

Institutionalized day care arrangements are still in short supply, when compared with the demand, but they are clearly on the increase. Home day care is one variation in which an individual may be licensed to care for several children in her own home. In addition there are day care centers which accept children from infancy through school age, and some of which provide care for school-aged children during the interval between school dismissal and their parents' return from work. Day care programs are supported in numerous ways, through community agencies funded by community fund-raising efforts, by the industries which employ the parents, or by fee payments from parents or govermental agencies. While there have always been a few privately operated day care

Home day care

centers around for parents who could pay the fees, large corporations have now entered into the act and there are strings of franchised day care centers from coast to coast.

A major problem is not only that there are few day care services available that parents can afford, but also that the services are quite variable and unco-ordinated. Various states and communities have created umbrella agencies to attempt to coordinate these services. Most of the present programs are little more than custodial; they meet most of the children's physical needs while the parents are working. Programs of comprehensive services, referred to as *Developmental day care* developmental day care, are now widely advocated to replace custodial day care. Such programs would include medical and social services, diagnostic services, a nutritional and an educational program (Feeney, 1973). The need for such services is broadly acknowledged. According to Zigler (1972), about half of American mothers are employed outside the home on a full-time basis, and this proportion seems destined to increase. The fact that there is a well-established need, however, should not lull the public nor interested professionals into wide-scale acceptance of programs which violate the conditions information from developmental research suggests are necessary to healthy development.

Effective programs First, those group-care programs in which the educational components have enhanced cognitive development seem to have been exceedingly well planned and managed, and used staff who were highly trained for the particular tasks they were assigned (e.g., see Caldwell, 1968). Very few day care programs which claim an educational component can boast such careful design and implementation of instructional activities. The majority of caregivers in either home or center day care programs have little, if any, specific training.

Consequences for emotional development In all likelihood, the lack of well-planned educational components in day care is less serious in its possible consequences for intellectual development than the possible effects that inadequate day care arrangements may have on the emotional development of children. Ainsworth (1973) has carefully re-viewed the literature on the development of attachments between infants and their mothers. Some of this information was presented in chapter 10. From her synthesis of the research literature, Ainsworth has drawn important implica-tions which should be considered in decision making at both the level of policy making and individual family choice.

Reliable and responsive mother figure First, it seems vital to the child's healthy emotional and social development that the environment provide a reliable and responsive mother figure. In any kind of institutional setting in which the attention of adult figures is spread over many children and other competing pressures. ". . . it is difficult to arrange enough individual care and continuity for an infant to be able to establish the basic infant-mother attachment that is one of the foundation stones of healthy social development" (Ainsworth, 1973, p. 77).

First year of life The first year of life is a particularly sensitive period for the formation of attachments. Under certain circumstances attachments may be formed later, but the longer the delay, the more likely are anomalies in social development to occur. This is a particularly important consideration in placing children for adoption or with foster parents. Every effort should be made to provide plenty of stimulation and physical contact, and regular caretakers, for children reared apart from their parents.

Ainsworth's (1973) third conclusion is stated with conviction. She asserts that "there *is at present no known substitute for a family environment for child-rearing*" (p. 77, author's original emphasis). A requirement of healthy develop-ment that none of our current institutions seem able to satisfy is to provide for sufficient continuity of interaction with a single or with a small number of specific individuals for attachment to occur. Countless families work out informal arrangements meeting these requirements, but it is becoming increasingly difficult.

Ainsworth (1973) also concluded from her study of the literature on separation that most infants in our society adapt well to minor separations during the day, and even to being left for a few hours with baby-sitters once in a while. But full-time child care involves more than such minor separations, and some research suggests that for children under four, group day care may have adverse affects. On the other hand, there are children whose home situations are far from optimal and who may be better off in a good day care situation than they would be at home. There is much to be learned about the effects of various arrangements for substitute care on children's social and emotional development.

Major and minor separation

As matters stand, it appears that substitute care-givers should be well trained to provide cognitive stimulation for children for whom they are responsible. Humanistic concerns also demand that care-givers be carefully selected for their capacity to be responsive to the behavioral cues of children, especially for infants. Additionally, care-givers should apparently be responsible for only a very few children in order that they may be responsive and attentive. And finally, there should be some assurance of stability of care-givers, and that the child's care is entrusted to a sufficiently small number of adults so that attachment relationships will not be spread over too many figures. This condition seems unlikely to be met in most day care center operations in which pay is generally low and staff turnover high.

Among the substitute care arrangements which we rarely think of until the occasion arises is the confinement of children to a hospital for some period of time. This constitutes a major separation—a situation clearly to be avoided if possible. Major separations may be especially serious in the age range from about six months until the child is about three years old (Ainsworth, 1973). Ainsworth suggests that if hospitalization is unavoidable during this age range, the mother should arrange to stay at the hospital with the child if it is at all possible. Otherwise, she should at least stay with the child for extended periods of time whenever it it possible.

Preschool Intervention

One of the most intensive early intervention efforts ever undertaken has been the Milwaukee Project developed by Rick Heber (Strickland, 1971; Garber & Heber, 1973) at the University of Wisconsin. This program differs from the intervention efforts discussed earlier in this chapter in that it does not aim primarily at the improvement of parenting skills in the family to achieve its aims. There is an effort to prepare mothers for employment opportunities and to improve their homemaking and parenting skills, but the major part of the intervention with children is in the hands of project staff members. The goal of the program has been to prevent mental retardation among "high risk" children through intensive intervention early in life. It has been statistically determined that children whose mothers have low IQs (below 70), who come from large families of low socioeconomic status, and whose siblings have low IQs, have a high probability of becoming mentally retarded.

The Milwaukee project

High risk children

Home visits of several hours duration begin shortly after the child's birth, and within a few months they are taken daily to a center where intervention designed to provide cognitive stimulation is continued for several hours per day through interactions with adults. By the age of two, the children are assigned to

Home visits

small instructional groups with multiple adults where they receive instructions in such things as problem solving, language and science, and where they watch "Sesame Street" and take field trips.

So far the cognitive development of the project children is so superior to their controls that some critics are skeptical about the results. Beyond the fact that predicted retardation seems to have been prevented, as reflected in differences between the intellectual performance test scores of experimental and control children, Heber and his associates report that the first group of experimental children are now in school, and not one has yet been assigned to classes for the retarded (Garber & Heber, 1973).

The Milwaukee Project is probably too costly to be instituted on any wide-scale basis, but if its results can be replicated, scientists will undoubtedly set to work to identify those components that produce the effects and to design less costly means of accomplishing the same ends (White, 1975).

The early training project

Like the Milwaukee Project, the Early Training Project designed by Gray and Klaus (1970; Klaus & Gray, 1968) and discussed in chapter 5 was based on a deficit model. Along with the successful Ypsilanti-Perry Preschool Project it was one of the first systematic attempts to design a program specifically aimed at prevention of the progressive retardation in intellectual and academic performance which had been noted among children from backgrounds of poverty. Children went to summer school in a highly organized program, and between summer sessions home visitors called upon the mothers weekly and provided activities which they could carry out with their children. Some of the children received three successive summer sessions and two years of home visitation. Another group entered the project when they were about a year older than the children in the first group and received two summer sessions and the intervening year of home visits. There was a local control group and a distal control group located in a community some distance away. Because the groups were not initially equivalent, the results of the experiment are difficult to evaluate,

Durability of effects

but it appears that both experimental groups were superior to the controls on word knowledge and reading subtests of the *Metropolitan Achievement Test* at the end of grade three; but by the end of grade four the advantage of the experimental over the control groups appeared to have disappeared (Gray & Klaus, 1970). Since this was an early effort, the experiences of this project have been of value to other researchers and educators. Two implications that might be drawn are that summer programs are insufficient to produce sustained effects, and that effective preschool programs must be followed by effective programs in the elementary grades if early gains are to have any chance of being maintained.

Need for continuity

The same conclusions could probably be applied to the outcomes of the early Head Start efforts. Head Start began as a summer program. It seems to have been viewed by many people, rather naïvely, as a sort of inoculation. Give the kids a shot of summer Head Start and they will be immune to school failure. It very soon became clear that nothing of the sort was going to happen, and Head Start became a full-year program. As we indicated earlier, evaluations of the effects of Head Start have not met the expectations of those who expected it to dramatically and permanently increase IQ scores and improve academic achievement in conventional schools for those children who attended. Nevertheless, parents and Head Start staff members seem largely convinced that Head

Subjective evalutations

Start has had positive influences on the social and emotional development of children who attend, and it seems destined to survive in spite of whatever the evaluators' statements about it suggest (White, 1975). There are no existing measures of proven value for many of the social and emotional outcomes which supporters of Head Start attribute to it, and there is a desperate need for the development of good evaluative techniques for this purpose.

SCHOOL INFLUENCES

When children start school, the range of people and conditions that influence them enlarges dramatically. They are exposed to teachers, peers, and instructional media, all of which may influence their development. In previous passages we have referred to various attempts to intervene in the lives of families and their children for the purposes of attempting to use knowledge of learning and development to facilitate development. We often overlook a fact pointed out by Horowitz and Paden, that "our system of public education has been designed to provide widespread environmental enrichment or intervention. . ." (p. 331).

Schools as Intellectual Enrichment

Traditionally the schools have been interested in intellectual development to the virtual exclusion of objectives related to social and emotional development. This fact is reflected in the methods and curricula of schools from first grade through graduate school, and it is clearly evidenced in the examples of preschool intervention programs we have mentioned. Follow Through, for example, *Follow Through* was a program devised to test the effectiveness of a broad range of different educational approaches to determine which ones were more effective in maintaining and improving on whatever advances children made in Head Start. The original question was not just "Which of several alternative programs is most effective?" but rather "What aspects of which approaches are most effective for what outcomes?" The answer to the second and more important of the two questions may never be known, for several reasons. First, there were among the alternative program approaches some which placed a high value on social and *Social and affective* affective objectives. But for the most part the developers of the various programs *objectives* were not able to specify very clearly just what social and affective outcomes they expected. Objectives tended to be phrased in abstract terms, such as "self-concept," "task persistence," or "trust," but these qualities are difficult to operationalize and measure unless the program developers can tell the program evaluators quite specifically what behaviors they would accept as evidence, for example, that a child's self-concept is developing nicely.

Second, well-developed measures of academic performance were already available when the project began, and these were ready and waiting to be used in the program. Measures used during the first year of any evaluation have a high priority for selection during the second and succeeding years because the continuous use of the same instruments provides continuity in the evaluation data. Therefore, after several years of operation, the best and most convincing data are those on academic progress of children enrolled in the various Follow Through model programs. That fact is bound to have policy implications which *Continued* may have the net effect of supporting continued emphasis on cognitively oriented *emphasis on* school programs. *cognitive goals*

Affective Learning in School

Even though they are not generally planned, there are conditions in the schools which do influence social and emotional development, even if that is not the explicit intent. For example, in the Southwest it was a general practice for many years to prohibit Mexican-American children from speaking Spanish when they attended school. By implication that practice seemed to say that Spanish was not a worthy language or that it had no place in an academic setting. Moreover, there were generally no Mexican-American teachers or administrators. Only the low status jobs in the schools were held by Mexicans. Many children were influenced to feel ashamed of their heritage, and even in recent years one of the authors has seen children whose lunches contained traditional Mexican items, such as tortillas, retreat from the rest of the children at lunch time to eat their lunch as inconspicuously as possible. Even more subtle is the fact that coming to a place where you cannot understand what people are saying, and where you cannot express yourself to others, may be a frightening experience. A Yaqui Indian boy in junior high school once related his vivid memories of attending school for the first time, not understanding directions, not knowing where to go, and not being able to ask anyone anything. One thing he wanted to ask was where the lavatory was. Unable to communicate his need he wet his pants, only to be ridiculed by the teacher

School as a conditioned aversive stimulus

and other children. School and all that it entailed became an aversive stimulus for him, evoking anxiety reactions that were not easily shed. With the rise of ethnic nationalism and the influences of humanistic concerns in education, most situations are much less blatant today, although exceptions are easily at hand.

Instructional Media

The media and curriculum materials used in schools constitute another subtle source of influence. Textbooks provide a prize example. Although there are many exceptions, most children receive the largest portion of their reading

Basal readers

instruction from basal reading textbooks. Every publisher has its own cast of characters, but most readers will remember the bland families of first grade primer fame. Their names may differ, but usually they are some minor variation on the theme of Dick, Jane, mother, father, baby Sally, Spot the dog, and Puff the kitten. Almost invariably the male child is the oldest child. They live in a comfortable suburban neighborhood. Now that may sound quite innocuous, but consider how few of the children who use these materials live in such circumstances. The families represented in the readers are always intact—father comes home regularly after work and spends weekends with the family. We are not aware of specific data on the effects of these stereotypes on the children who use readers, but there is some evidence that the content of readers may exert some rather subtle influences on the attitudes and perceptions of children.

Multi-ethnic readers

For example, until quite recently all of the children portrayed in the basal readers were good middle-class white children. With the advent of the civil rights movement and the growth of concern about racial equality, some publishers began to introduce black characters into the readers. Actually, in most cases all that was done was to give dark faces to a few of the characters. There is usually nothing else to distinguish these characters as blacks or as members of any other specific racial or ethnic minority. We certainly would not expect such a superficial alteration of the content of basal readers to have any effect, but there is at least one study (Litcher & Johnson, 1969) that suggests we are wrong, and none that we know of to suggest that we are correct in that assumption. Pretests and posttests were given to one group of children who used an ethnic reader and to another group who used the traditional reader to determine if multi-ethnic readers have any effect on children's racial attitudes. The children who participated in the study were second graders. The multi-ethnic readers used in the study portrayed blacks ". . . as having middle-class characteristics (works hard, dresses nicely, is clean) in integrated situations" (Litcher & Johnson, 1969, p. 61). The results of the study indicated that the use of the multi-ethnic readers resulted in more favorable attitudes toward blacks. The differences between experimental and control children were quite dramatic. It should be noted, however, that the study was conducted in a community in which the actual population of blacks constituted less than 0.2 percent of the population, and the children had therefore had little direct experience with blacks. Nevertheless, the results are of some interest because there are innumerable communities in the Midwest and West where the only representatives of the black population children are likely to see will be those represented in the media.

Although the content of readers is highly stereotyped, those stereotypes do often reflect real changes in our society. DeCharmes and Moeller (1962) analyzed the imagery themes reflected in the content of children's readers in use in the United States from 1800 to 1950. They found evidence of a continuous rise in achievement imagery, which reflects the Protestant ethic, from 1800 to about 1900. After that there was a steady decline in achievement imagery. The investigators expected to find an increase in affiliation imagery over the same period, reflecting what observers of the social scene have described as a transition from the Protestant ethic to a social ethic (Whyte, 1956). In Riesman's terminology, which we discussed earlier, the transition would be phrased as a change from inner-direction to other-direction (Riesman, Glazer, & Denney, 1950). The themes in the readers reflected a trend in this direction, but it was not statistically significant. The amount of moral teaching incorporated in the readers steadily declined during the period from 1800-1950.

Stereotypes and social reality

Achievement imagery

Affiliation imagery

Moral teaching

The fact that moral teaching incorporated into children's reading materials has declined is certainly understandable. In a pluralistic society how does one determine what values should be expressed in instructional materials? Since it would be all but impossible to get everyone to agree, the easiest alternative is to leave them out. But where then do developing children and youth learn about values? Values are implicitly incorporated in many sources of social influence, perhaps most notably in the mass media. Many parents, psychologists, and educators are concerned that the values presented are rather one-sided, and that children have little opportunity to explicitly identify the values that guide their actions and to evaluate them against alternative value systems. Because of such concerns, there has been a growing effort to incorporate values education into the curriculum (Kohlberg, 1970; Rest, 1974), and a movement called Values Clarification has gained momentum in schools in many areas of the country. Values clarification is basically a set of procedures designed to help young people identify the values underlying certain choices they may make, and to evaluate these values by contrasting them with alternative ones. These procedures seem to influence the verbal statements people make about their values, but research is needed to determine if such training has any influence on behavior other than verbal statements.

Values in education

A study conducted several years ago on the themes expressed in children's readers is highly significant from the perspective of social-learning theory. All general third grade readers published from 1930 up to the time of the study were subjected to content analysis. Among the most interesting generalization to emerge from the study was the fact that in the material presented in the readers, there was little encouragement of the characters depicted for intellectual activity. When acquisition of skills or knowledge was rewarded it was generally a kind of knowledge which was dependent on people in a superior

Social influence variables in readers

Intellectual activity

position—parents or teachers, for example. There was very little evidence of original thinking on the part of central characters.

On the other hand, behavior directed toward affiliation or nurturance was always rewarded in the readers. From these findings we would not expect the children who read these books to be motivated to engage in intellectual activity, to be creative, innovative, or independent of the influence of adults, if social influence factors in printed material operate in anything like the same way they work in live modeling or film-mediated modeling situations.

Sex-typing

Perhaps most blatant was the degree to which the readers assigned stereotypic sex-typed behaviors to boys and girls. Females were depicted as being affiliative, nurturant, and keeping out of harm's way. Only infrequently did female characters display qualities such as activity, achievement, or construction. Girls and women were thus stereotyped as being kind, timid and sociable, and inactive, unambitious, and certainly uncreative. Males were portrayed as the bearers of wisdom and knowledge. It is from male figures that children could expect to find knowledge.

More striking than the stereotyped treatment of sex roles was the simple fact that women and girls were simply neglected in the stories. If the stories had been about people who had somehow achieved recognition in the society, the overrepresentation of males as central characters might have been understandable. There have, after all, been institutional barriers to achievement among women, and the stories might then at least be thought to depict reality with some accuracy. The contrary fact is that the stories were not about people who had achieved any degree of greatness. They were primarily stories about very ordinary people in very ordinary, and if we read accurately between the lines of the report of the study, pretty humdrum situations.

*Incidental
learning*

There is little reason to believe that the content of children's readers has changed much in the past thirty or so years. The impression one gets from more recent descriptions of reader content (e.g., see Zimet, 1968) is that the themes identified by Child and his associates are still fairly typical, although some publishers are attempting to correct this situation. Since the function of the readers is ostensibly to teach reading skills, it is common for parents and teachers to consider the specific content as irrelevant, as long as it is not so deadly boring that children refuse to read it regardless of the contingencies. But if we can extrapolate from the social-learning influences which have been demonstrated with live models and with film media, there is every reason to think that the actions portrayed, the behaviors that are reinforced and encouraged, and the kinds of story models who depict the behavior, would influence children's attitudes and behaviors. Surely parents and teachers should be alert to this possibility, and recognize that instructional materials may inadvertently influence rigid sex-role stereotyping and foster compliant rather than aggressive or creative intellectual activity.

Self-management in School Learning

Of the many ways in which knowledge about learning and development may be used to humanize the treatment of children, none offers more exciting possibilities than the explorations that are under way in behavioral self-control. Adults and college students have been taught to use behavioral principles to manage their own behavior effectively. By deciding on specific target behaviors they want to affect, by controlling the stimulus situations and consequences which govern those behaviors, and by using effective monitoring techniques to track the progress of their efforts at self-control, large numbers of people have been helped to control

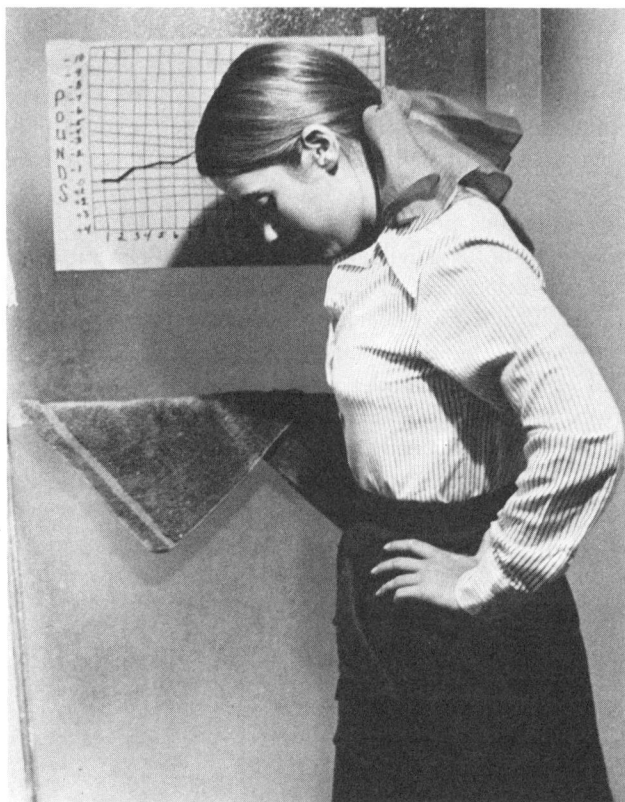

*Children and youths can
learn to apply behavioral
principles to achieve
their own goals.*

their eating habits, their smoking, their study habits, and numerous other behaviors which are subject to ordinary human frailties. (For examples, see
Mahoney & Thorsen, 1974; Thorsen & Mahoney, 1974; Watson & Tharp, 1972;
Kanfer & Philips, 1970.) More recently it has been proposed that elementary-
school children might be taught to identify specific goals they want to achieve,
to have some control over stimulus situations and reinforcement contingencies
which would facilitate behavior directed toward those goals, and to evaluate
their own progress toward those goals (Bergan & Dunn, 1976; Henderson,
1974). Rarely have all of these components been put together for an empirical
test of effects, but various parts of such a system have been employed with
success.

It has been demonstrated that students may be reasonably accurate in re-   *Self-monitoring*
cording their own progress (Knapczyk & Livingston, 1973; Glynn, Thomas, &
Shee, 1973), and that reading performance (Knapczyk & Livingston, 1973) and
on-task behavior (Glynn, Thomas, & Shee, 1973) may be facilitated when
students record their own behavior and control their own reinforcers. Klein   *Self-reinforcement*
and Schuler (1974) demonstrated that academic performance of third graders
may be enhanced through the introduction of contingent self-evaluation procedures. No powerful back-up reinforcement systems were used, as has been the
case in most studies of self-evaluation and self-reinforcement. The only reinforcement was self-administered praise, which was contingent on the children
meeting their own criteria. Test performance exceeded the level achieved when
evaluation was done by the teacher. Hopefully, detailed studies such as these
will provide the information necessary to provide children with the behavioral
techniques they need to take a larger hand in controlling their own educational
progress.

Children and Their Peers in School

One of the most significant things that happens to children when they enter school is that their social world expands dramatically. For most American children sources of social influence prior to going to school are restricted almost exclusively to parents and other significant family members and adult care-givers. In school they interact with a range of peers whose influence generally becomes more and more important as time goes on. Parents often become frustrated as children come to justify their requests for privileges on the basis of the rationale that all their friends are allowed to do it, or on the other hand, they may argue that certain responsibilities should not be expected of them because none of their friends have to do it. Some of the most obvious influences of peers are seen in the mannerisms, figures of speech, and modes of dress which children and *Peer and parental* adolescents adopt from their peers. More subtle characteristics such as educational *influence* and occupational aspirations are also influenced by peers (Haller & Butterworth, 1960; Kandel & Lesser, 1969), but discrepancies between peer and parental influences may often be more apparent than real. Young people are certainly influenced by their friends, but although there are exceptions, they also tend to choose their friends on the basis of the attitudes and values which prevail in their homes (Bandura & Walters, 1963).

The peer group is an important influence in the lives of adolescents.

Traditionally, schools have made no deliberate efforts to capitalize on the influences peers do exert on one another. Often teacher and peer influences seem to be in direct competition with one another. Other societies have approached the manner of using peer and teacher influences on children's behavior quite differently. In the Soviet Union, for example, subgroups are deliberately organized within classrooms to work toward group goals, to promote mutual assistance within the groups, and to employ peer sanctions to promote goal-oriented effort among individual group members. In this case there is high congruence in the values and standards of adults and peer groups, decreasing the likelihood of children yielding to deviant peer pressure (Bronfenbrenner, 1967).

In other cultural settings, the discrepancy between the values and patterns of social influence that are typical of the home setting and those which are incorporated into instructional arrangements in the schools may be so great as to promote serious conflict. Among Hawaiians, for example (Gallimore, Boggs, & Jordan, 1974), children depend upon and learn a great deal from their siblings. Early in their lives affiliative relationships with their peers become important. Accordingly, they are less likely to attend to adults and to go to them for help than they are to relate to and depend upon their peers. The schools, however, are arranged on an authority and influence pattern that does not differ from most schools on the mainland. The teacher is the authority, and it is the teacher to whom one should attend in order to learn, and go to for assistance. Native Hawaiian children do not seem to adapt well to such a system, and they might well learn more effectively under a more informal structure in which they could work in groups with their peers, and help one another to achieve goals of mutual benefit. Instead, "teachers may regard peer interaction in the classroom as disruptive or 'cheating'" (Gallimore, Boggs, & Jordan, 1974, p. 264).

Discontinuities in home and school influence

Peer and adult influence

The inclination of children from certain cultural groups to cooperate rather than compete could well be used to advantage in the educational programs that serve them. Remember also, if you will, that the emphasis on competition that pervades the socialization practices of many middle-class American homes, and the contingency patterns used for motivational purposes in our schools, seem to have produced children who may behave competitively to the point that it becomes maladaptive. There are many tasks in adult life that require cooperative effort directed toward group goals, and even in these situations many individuals cannot escape their impulse to compete rather than cooperate. Perhaps there is no better place to see maladaptive competition in operation than among "highly educated" university faculty. The teaching of group skills required for cooperation has been almost entirely neglected in the school, but some highly interesting research on the teaching of cooperation to preschool children has shown promising results.

Cooperation and competition

Jackie Kimbrough and her associates have developed a research and demonstration program designed to teach cooperative, community-oriented behavioral styles to black preschool children in Los Angeles. Initial results suggest that the program has been successful in teaching adaptive cooperation, as evidenced by performance on generalization tasks such as the Madsen marble-pull game which was described in chapter 9.

Leadership is another area of social competence that has been systematically neglected in schools and other institutions that deal with groups of children. Some children develop a knack for leadership "naturally." That is to say no one deliberately set out to teach them how to influence others, and we would be hard put to determine in retrospect just how they acquired their skills. However it happens, once leadership qualities are displayed, teachers, scout leaders, and other adults who work with children seem to call upon the same youngsters time and time again to take whatever leadership responsibilities are available in the settings in question. The children called upon must, of course, have

Leadership

whatever skills are specific to the situations in which leadership is to be expressed, but certainly not all children who have those skills have the additional leadership qualities that seem to be necessary.

Group process skills

In one bilingual program that emphasized small-group processes (Baker, 1971, 1974; Baker et al., 1971), children were systematically taught some of the skills which seemed to be requisites to providing leadership in small peer groups in instructional situations. For example, children were taught to lead a lesson by making sure that the directions were clear to everyone in the group, providing clarification of instructions where necessary, encouraging all group members to participate in discussions, assuring that materials necessary to complete a designated activity were available, and so on. The other children were taught to act as constructive group members. The teacher modeled the leader role, asked various children to enact the role she had depicted, while she then modeled group member behavior, and provided cues to guide the acting-leader when necessary. Leadership responsibility was shifted around among children so that all had an opportunity to learn the skills associated with group membership and with leadership. The results of the program were very encouraging and suggested that systematic instruction may indeed be effective in

Teaching vs. selecting

teaching leadership skills and assigning leadership responsibility to children who are not "natural" leaders. It seems reasonable that the role of the school should be to "teach" for leadership rather than to join other institutions in merely "selecting" for it.

MASS MEDIA

One of the most prominent features of our society is the widespread availability of communications media of all sorts. Books, magazines, and newspapers are everywhere in abundance. Movies have made something of a comeback, and with the exception of a very limited number of isolated regions, all but a few of even the most poverty-stricken homes have a television set. It is impossible to accurately estimate the exact nature and extent of the influences exerted on the development of children by the vast industries that control the media. Almost certainly the influence is great, and no aspect of the media so completely pervades our lives as does television. Because its influence is so pervasive, and because it has been subjected to more systematic research than other media of communication, our discussion will concentrate on the influence, both known and probable, of television on the lives of children.

Television as an agent of socialization

As the title of a review article on this topic aptly suggested, children's television is more than entertainment (Leifer, Gordon, & Graves, 1974). Along with parents, teachers, siblings, and peers, television has joined the ranks of significant agents of socialization in our country. At the beginning of the 1970s over 96% of American homes had at least one television set, and large numbers of homes have two or more to accommodate the viewing tastes of various members of the family. In an average home the television set is in operation for more than six hours per day, and for families with children, television set ownership has reached the saturation point of 98% to 99% (Lyle, 1972).

Children begin to watch television when they are only two or three years old. Long before they enter school they have become purposeful viewers. By that we simply mean that they have favorite programs and regular viewing times.

Extent of viewing

Obviously individual children differ greatly from one another in their viewing habits and in the amount of time they spend watching television. Nevertheless, some averages give an impression of how much of children's lives may be spent watching the tube. Most children watch television for a total of two or more hours per day (Lyle, 1972), and in one representative study it was found that boys viewed for an average of 34.56 hours per week while girls watched for an average of 32.44 hours, or *better than one-third of their waking hours* (Stein & Friedrich, 1971).

Just because children watch, does that mean that they are influenced by what they see? It seems so, although the nature and extent of the influence is tempered by other variables, such as family viewing patterns, ability to distinguish what is realistic from what poorly represents reality, and other factors which are only beginning to be probed. Much of the public and scientific concern about the possible effects of television has centered around the possible effects of televised violence on violent and aggressive behavior in children (Surgeon General's Scientific Advisory Committee on Television and Social Behavior, 1972; Friedrich & Stein, 1973; Greenberg, Erikson, & Valhos, 1972; Barker & Ball, 1969). A number of investigations conducted in laboratory settings (e.g., see Bandura, Ross, & Ross, 1963; Kuhn, Madsen, & Becker, 1967) have demonstrated that viewing filmed aggressive behavior increases the likelihood that the observer will carry out similar acts when given the opportunity. Note that we did not say viewing violence invariably leads to aggressive behavior on the part of the observer, but it *does increase the probability* that the viewer will commit similar acts. *Laboratory studies*

It is appropriate to question whether findings derived from laboratory analogues of real-life situations accurately reflect what might happen under naturalistic conditions. Friedrich and Stein (1973) did conduct research on this question under more naturalistic conditions in which children viewed various kinds of programs in a nursery school setting. This research provided confirmation for the laboratory investigations and gave us increased confidence in the contention that the influences of viewing aggressive models on children's aggressive behavior is not confined to the brief experimental interludes of the psychologists' laboratory.* *Naturalistic studies*

These findings may give some cause for alarm, because to the casual viewer it often seems that there is more violence on television than any other single category of behavior. Violence is not confined to prime time and late evening programming. It is perhaps most conspicuous of all on the Saturday morning "cartoons" which are targeted on children. But there is a brighter side. It is possible that television *has the potential* of fostering pro-social behaviors and attitudes. Research on this topic is extremely limited, partly perhaps because there are so few children's programs designed to exert a positive influence on children's social and emotional development. Stein and Friedrich (1971) reported that "Mister Rogers' Neighborhood" was essentially the only program on television at the time of their investigation that had ". . . as its prime concern the emotional and social growth of the child" (p. 276). They reported that this program's ". . . themes of cooperation, persistence in difficult tasks, tolerance of frustration and delay, and verbalization of feelings are understood by children and alter their behavior" (p. 276). *Pro-social influences*

With this kind of encouragement, there is growing interest in the possible uses of television as a source of pro-social influence on behavior and develop-

---

* The evidence pertaining to influences of televised violence on aggressive behavior in children is summarized in *The Early Window* (Liebert, Neale, & Davidson, 1973).

ment. Only in recent years have there been many programs on the commercial networks with explicitly pro-social themes, and empirical research in this area has barely begun.

While the potential for television to serve a positive function in the socialization process is real, the *actual* content of most commercial television programming seems better designed to provide misinformation and to influence the development of attitudes which few parents would knowingly inculcate into their children. Ethnic minorities, for example, tend to be underrepresented on television. When they are represented, they often are presented in roles that are the subject of ridicule, as in situation comedies, or their characterizations are completely noncontroversial and nondescript (Clark, 1969).

Just as surely as ethnic minorities are unrealistically portrayed, so too are occupational roles. The kinds of occupations depicted are unrepresentative of those which children are most likely to someday adopt, and the nature of the work-roles portrayed are highly distorted in order to emphasize dramatic aspects of the occupation. In a society in which fewer and fewer children have any opportunity for firsthand observation of people working at the various occupations of the community (Bronfenbrenner, 1970; Goslin, 1975), the distorted portrayal of occupational roles in the one medium in which the average child has any access to what goes on in the world of work seems particularly unfortunate.

The place of women in the structure of society also seems badly represented. Recently a few female characters have escaped the traditional homemaker's role on television, but it is problematic how many of today's young female viewers may find placement in future years in the dramatic occupations of detective sergeant or chief of police, or whatever fad a season's round of new television shows may bring. Obviously, children do not "believe" everything they see on television, and as they mature they ascribe less and less reality to television. But ". . . even tenth graders, for the most part, accept the reality of television portrayals" (Leifer, Gordon, & Graves, 1974). If it is unlikely that television networks will move toward more realistic portrayals of those important aspects of life which industrial society has cut from access for most children, then it would be helpful for parents to be sensitive to the distortions presented to their children and to exert some control on viewing and/or discuss the content of television programming with their children in order to correct the distorted perspective presented.

Much of the current interest in television as an agent of socialization centers on its influences or potential influences on social behavior, stereotypes, and attitudes relating to social issues. But television has high potential as a means of influencing cognitive as well as social development. "Sesame Street" and "The Electric Company," both productions of the Children's Television Workshop, have been enthusiastically received as a means of using the pervasive medium of television to teach cognitive behaviors. "Sesame Street" has indeed been highly successful in teaching certain cognitive behaviors. It has apparently been highly effective in teaching children to associate verbal labels (the names of letters, for example) with a visual symbol representing that concept. "Sesame Street" has also been highly successful in teaching such things as rote counting. But it was not effective in achieving some of its more ambitious goals with the disadvantaged four-year-old viewers who were studied in the evaluation program conducted by the Educational Testing Service (Bogatz & Ball, 1971). This failure raised a question concerning whether or not the medium of television was capable of teaching more complex conceptual behaviors to children. The re-

sults of field research under controlled conditions now suggests that television may be used with great effectiveness to teach complex cognitive tasks, such as Piagetian conservation, ordering arrays of objects along some dimension such as length (seriation), and question-asking (Henderson et al., 1973; Henderson, Swanson, & Zimmerman, 1975a; Henderson, Swanson, & Zimmerman, 1975b). The programming procedures employed in these studies differ considerably from those which characterize "Sesame Street" programming, and their effectiveness in broadcast situations remains to be demonstrated. Nevertheless, these findings raise the promise that television could be used more effectively than it now is as a means of facilitating the cognitive growth of young children.

PROSPECTS FOR THE HUMANIZATION OF DEVELOPMENTAL ENVIRONMENTS

Seemingly endless pitfalls lie in the path of all attempts at purposeful planning for social institutions designed for particular purposes. It nevertheless seems clear that two courses of events meet at this time in our social history and these events hold implications for the design of developmental environments. One course of events is characterized by an increasing concern for the humane treatment of children. This trend is evidenced in an extensive range of events which includes legislation aimed at identifying the causes of child abuse and devising ways to eliminate it. Further evidence for the trend is seen in movements for humanistic education with increased attention to social, moral, and emotional development. It includes attempts to legislate the availability of high quality developmental day care programs which include a wide range of child and family services. It is also reflected in the reorientation of programs for the poor, which once seemed designed to promote the *assimilation* of ethnic and racial minorities, but which increasingly recognize the distinctive characteristics of various groups, and strive to preserve their uniqueness. Many new programs attempt to give programmatic control to the populations to be served by the programs and strive to preserve the richness and variety of our nation's heritage by promoting cultural pluralism. These events and many others reflect a growing awareness of and appreciation for individual and group uniqueness, and thus show humanistic concern.

The second set of potential influences is found in the continuing growth of knowledge about the conditions that influence the development of children. Recent advances have moved from knowledge about the relationships between gross socioeconomic or demographic variables and development, to more specific knowledge which identifies much more specific elements of experience that are related to development. Experimental demonstrations of the effects of some of these specific variables on the acquisition of specific developmental skills and abilities suggest their potential for environmental design. This' knowledge offers the possibility of guiding the design of developmental environments which are both more effective than environments designed by chance, folk wisdom, and expediency, and which take the full range of children's developmental needs into consideration. Having learned some important lessons from the overconfident and narrowly conceptualized social-engineering efforts of the 1960s, the science of child development stands in a position to make cautious and constructive contributions to the humanization of developmental environments.

SUGGESTED READINGS

Bell, R. Q. A reinterpretation of the direction of effects in studies of socialization. *Psychological Review*, 1968, *75*, 81-95.

Blanchard, R. W., & Biller, H. B. Father availability and academic performance among third grade boys. *Developmental Psychology*, 1971, *4*, 301-5.

Brittain, C. V. Adolescent choices and parent-peer cross-pressures. *American Sociological Review*, 1963, *28*, 385-91.

Bronfenbrenner, U. *Two worlds of childhood: U.S. and U.S.S.R.* New York: Russell Sage Foundation, 1970.

Child, I. L., Potter, E. H., Levine, E. M. Children's textbook and personality development. *Psychological Monographs*, 1946, *60* (3), Whole No. 279.

Henderson, R. W., & Merritt, C. B. Environmental backgrounds of Mexican-American children with different potentials for school success. *Journal of Social Psychology*, 1968, *75*, 101-6.

Henderson, R. W., Swanson, R., & Zimmerman, B. J. Training seriation responses in young children through televised modeling of hierarchially sequenced rule components. *American Educational Research Journal*, 1975, *12*, 000.

Hilton, I. Differences in the behavior of mothers toward first- and later-born children. *Journal of Personality and Social Psychology*, 1967, *7*, 282-90.

Leifer, A. D., Gordon, N. J., & Graves, S. B. Children's television more than mere entertainment. *Harvard Educational Review*, 1974, *44* (2), 213-45.

References

Adkins, D. C., Payne, F. D., & O'Malley, J. M. Moral development. In F. N. Kerlinger & J. B. Carroll (Eds.), *Review of educational research* (Vol. I). Itasca, Ill: F. E. Peacock, 1964.

Ainsworth, M. D. S. *Infancy in uganda: Infant care and the growth of attachment.* Baltimore: Johns Hopkins Press, 1967.

Ainsworth, M. D. S. The development of infant-mother attachment. In B. M. Caldwell & Henry N. Ricciuti (Eds.), *Review of child development research.* (Vol. 3). Chicago: University of Chicago Press, 1973, 1–94.

Allison, A. C. Aspects of polymorthism in man. Cold Spring Harbor Symposium. *Quantitative Biology,* 1955, *20,* 239–255.

Allport, G. W. *Personality: A social interpretation.* New York: Holt, 1937.

Alpert, J. L. Teacher behavior across ability groups: A consideration of the mediation of pygmalion effects. *Journal of Educational Psychology,* 1974, *66,* 348–353.

Altus, W. D. Birth order and its sequelae. *Science,* 1965, *151,* 44–49.

Ames, L. B. The sequential patterning of prone progression in the human infant. *Genetic Psychology Monographs* 1937, *19,* 409–460.

Ames, L. B. The sense of self of nursery school children as manifested by their verbal behavior. *Genetic Psychology,* 1952, *81,* 193–232.

Anastasi, A. Heredity, environment and the question "How?". *Psychological Review,* 1958, *65,* 197–208.

Anderson, Scarvia, B., & Messick, S. Social competence in young children. *Developmental Psychology,* 1974, *10* (2), 282–293.

Arbuthnot, J. Modification of moral judgment through role playing. *Developmental Psychology,* 1975, *11,* 319–324.

Aronfreed, J. *Conduct and conscience.* New York: Academic Press, 1968.

Ausubel, F., Beckwith, J., & Janssen, K. Stimulus response: The politics of genetic engineering: Who decides who's defective? *Psychology Today,* 1974, *8* (1), 30–44.

Ausubel, D. P., & Sullivan, E. V. *Theory and problems of child development* (2nd ed.). New York: Grune & Stratton, 1970.

Ayllon, T., & Azrin, N. H. Punishment as a discriminative stimulus and conditioned reinforcer with humans. *Journal of the Experimental Analysis of Behavior,* 1966, *9,* 411–419.

Ayllon, T., & Roberts, M. D. Eliminating discipline problems by strengthening academic performance. *Journal of Applied Behavior Analysis,* 1974, *7,* 71–76.

Azrin, N. H. Some effects of two intermittent schedules in immediate and non-immediate punishment. *Journal of Psychology,* 1956, *42,* 3–21.

Azrin, N. H., & Holz, W. C. Punishment. In W. K. Honig (Ed.), *Operant behavior: Areas of research and applications.* New York: Appleton-Century-Crofts, 1966.

Bach, G. R. Father-fantasies and father-typing in father separated families. *Child Development,* 1946, *17,* 63–80.

Baer, D. M., & Sherman, J. A. Reinforcement control of generalized imitation in young children. *Journal of Experimental Child Psychology,* 1964, *1,* 37–49.

Baker, J. *A group process approach to bilingual instruction.* Office of Education Bilingual Branch Report (No. OEG–0–9–12011–3465). 1971.

Baker, J. Small group process in bilingual/bicultural education: Leadership education lessons. Unpublished manuscript, Behavior Associates, Tucson, Arizona, 1974.

Baker, J., Smith, T., Walters, B., & Wetzel, R. They help each other learn: A group participation leadership training manual. Dissemination Center for Bilingual/Bicultural Education, Austin, Texas, 1971.

Baker, S. L., Fagan, S. A., Fischer, E. G., Janda, E. J., & Cove, L. A. Impact of father–absence on personality factors of boys: I. An evaluation of the military family's adjustment. Paper presented at American Orlhopsychiatric Association meeting, Washington, D.C., March 1967.

Baker, S. L., Fagan, S. A., Fischer, E. G., Janda, E. J., & Cove, L. A. Impact of father absence. III. Problem of family reintegration following prolonged father absence. Paper presented at American Orthopsychiatric Association Meeting, Chicago, March 1968.

Baldwin, A. L. *Theories of child development.* New York: Wiley, 1967.

Bandura, A. Influence of models' reinforcement contingencies on the acquisition of imitative responses. *Journal of Personality and Social Psychology,* 1965, *1,* 589–595.

Bandura, A. *Principles of behavior modification.* New York: Holt, Rinehart and Winston, 1969.

Bandura, A. Behavior theory and the models of man. *American Psychologist,* 1974, *29,* 859–869.

Bandura, A., & Huston, A. C. Identification as a process of incidental learning. *Journal of Abnormal and Social Psychology,* 1961, *63,* 311–318.

Bandura, A., & Kupers, C. J. Transmissions of patterns of self-reinforcement through modeling. *Journal of Abnormal and Social Psychology,* 1964, *69,* 1–9.

Bandura, A., & McDonald, F. J. Influence of social reinforcement and the behavior of models in shaping children's moral judgments. *Journal of Abnormal and Social Psychology,* 1963, *67,* 274–281.

Bandura, A., & Menlove, F. L. Factors determining vicarious extinction of avoidance behavior through symbolic modeling. *Journal of Personality and Social Psychology,* 1968, *8,* 99–108.

Bandura, A., & Mischel, W. Modification of self-imposed delay of reward through exposure to live and symbolic models. *Journal of Personality and Social Psychology.* 1965, *2,* 698–705.

Bandura, A., Ross, D., & Ross, S. A. Transmission of aggression through imitation of aggressive models. *Journal of Abnormal and Social Psychology,* 1961, *63,* 575–582.

Bandura, A., Ross, D., & Ross, S. A. Imitation of film-mediated aggressive models. *Journal of Abnormal and Social Psychology,* 1963, *66,* 3–11.

Bandura, A., & Walters, R. H. *Social learning and personality development.* New York: Holt, Rinehart and Winston, 1963.

Baratz, J. C. Teaching reading in an urban Negro school. In J. C. Baratz & R. W. Shuy (Eds.), *Teaching black children to read.* Washington, D.C.: Center for Applied Linguistics, 1969.

Baratz, S. S., & Baratz, J. Early childhood intervention: The social science basis of institutional racism. *Harvard Educational Review.* 1970, *40,* 29–50.

Barber, T. X., Silver, M. J. Fact, fiction, and the experimenter bias effect. *Psychological Bulletin,* 1968, *70* (6, Pt. 2).

Barker, R. G., Gump, P. V., Friesen, W. V., Willems, E. T. The ecological environment: Student participation in non-class situations. In M. W. Miles & W. W. Charters, Jr. (Eds.), *Learning in social settings.* Boston: Allyn and Bacon, 1970, pp. 12–42.

Barker, R. K., & Ball, S. J. *Mass media and violence: A report to the National Commission on causes and prevention of violence.* Washington, D.C.: U.S. Government Printing Office, 1969.

Barry, H., Child, I. L., & Bacon, M. K. Relation of child training to subsistence economy. *American Anthropologist,* 1959, *61,* 51–63.

Bayley, N. The development of motor abilities during the first three years. *Monographs of the Society for Research in Child Development,* 1935 (1).

Bayley, N. Consistency and variability in the growth from birth to 18 years. *Journal of Genetic Psychology,* 1949, *45,* 1–21.

Bayley, N. *Bayley scales of infant development: Birth to two years.* New York: Psychological Corp., 1969.

Beaglehole, E. *Notes on Hopi Economic Life.* Yale University Publications in Anthropology, Vol. 17, 1937.

Becker, W. C. Consequences of different kind of parental discipline. In M. L. Hoffman & L. W. Hoffman (Eds.), *Review of Child Development Research* (Vol. 1). New York: Russell Sage, 1964.

Becker, S. W., Lerner, M. J., & Carroll, J. Conformity as a function of birth order and type of group pressure.

Journal of Personality and Social Psychology, 1966, *3,* 242–244.

Bee, H. L., Van Egeren, L. F., Pytkowiez, S., Nyman, B. A., & Lockie, M. S. Social class differences in maternal teaching strategies and speech patterns. *Developmental Psychology,* 1969, *1,* 726–734.

Beez, W. Influence of biased psychological reports on teacher behavior and pupil performance. *Proceedings of the 76th Annual Convention of the American Psychological Association,* 1968, *3,* 605–606. (Summary)

Bell, R. Q. A reinterpretation of the directions of effects and studies of socialization. *Psychological Review,* 1968, *75,* 81–95.

Belmont, L., & Marolla, F. A. Birth order, family size and intelligence. *Science,* 1973, *182,* 1096–1101.

Benedict, R. Continuities and discontinuities in cultural conditioning. *Psychiatry,* 1938, *1,* 161–167.

Bergan, J. R. Effects of verbal pretraining on letter identification under variations in response number. *Proceedings of the 80th Annual Convention of the American Psychological Association,* 1972, Vol. 1. 7 (Part 1), 479–480.

Bergan, J. R., & Caldwell, T. Operant techniques in school psychology. *Psychology in the Schools,* 1967, *4,* 136–141.

Bergan, J. R., & Dunn, J. R. *Psychology and education: A science for instruction.* New York: Wiley, 1976.

Bergan, J. R., & Tombari, M. L. Verbal interactions in consultation. *Journal of School Psychology,* 1975, *13,* 209–226.

Bergan, J. R., Zimmerman, B. J., & Ferg, M. Effects of variations in content and stimulus grouping on visual sequential memory. *Journal of Educational Psychology,* 1971, *62,* 400–404.

Berkowitz, L. *The development of motives and values in the child.* New York: Basic Books, 1964.

Berkowitz, L. Control of aggression. In B. M. Caldwell & H. N. Ricciuti (Eds.), *Review of child development research* (Vol. 3). Chicago: The University of Chicago Press, 1973, 95–140.

Berkowitz, L., & LePage, A. Weapons as aggression-eliciting stimuli. *Journal of Personality and Social Psychology,* 1967, *7,* 202–207.

Bernstein, B. Social class and linguistic development: A theory of social learning. In A. H. Halsey, J. Floud, & C. A. Anderson (Eds.), *Education, economy, and society.* Glencoe, Ill.: Free Press, 1961, 288–314.

Bernstein, B. *Language, primary socialization and education.* London: Routledge and Kegan Paul, 1968.

Bernstein, B. A socio-linguistic approach to socialization with some references to educability. In J. J. Gumperz & D. Hymes (Eds.), *Directions in sociolinguistics.* New York: Holt, Rinehart and Winston, 1972.

Bever, T. G. The cognitive basis for linguistic structures. In J. R. Hayes (Ed.), *Cognition and the development of language.* New York: Wiley, 1970.

Bever, T. G. The integrated study of language behavior. In J. Morton (Ed.), *Biological and social factors in psycholinguistics.* London: Logos Press, 1971.

Bexton, W. H., Heron, W., & Scott, T. H. Effects of decreased variation in the sensory environment. *Canadian Journal of Psychology,* 1954, *8,* 70–76.

Bijou, S. W. Ages, stages, and the naturalization of human development. *American Psychologist,* 1968, *23,* 419–426.

Bijou, S. W., & Baer, D. M. *Child development I: A systematic and empirical theory.* New York: Appleton-Century-Crofts, 1961.

Bissell, J. S. *The cognitive effects of pre-school programs for disadvantaged children.* Washington, D.C.: National Institute of Child Health and Human Development, 1970.

Blanchard, R. W., & Biller, H. B. Father availability and academic performance among third grade boys. *Developmental Psychology,* 1971, *4,* 301–305.

Block, J., Block, J. H., & Harrington, D. M. Some misgivings about the Matching Familiar Figures Test as a measure of reflection-impulsivity. *Developmental Psychology,* 1974, *10,* 611–632.

Block, J., Block, J. H., & Harrington, D. M. Comment on the Kagan-Messer reply. *Developmental Psychology,* 1975, *11* (2) 249–252.

Bloom, B. S. *Stability and change in human characteristics.* New York: Wiley, 1964.

Bogatz, G. A., & Ball, S. *The second year of Sesame Street: A continuing evaluation.* Princeton, N.J.: Educational Testing Service, 1971.

Bogue, D. J. *Principles of demography.* New York: Wiley, 1969.

Bowlby, J. *Attachment.* New York: Basic Books, 1969.

Borke, H. Interpersonal perception of young children. *Developmental Psychology,* 1971, *5,* 263–269.

Borke, H. Chandler and Greenspan's Ergatz egocentrism: A rejoinder. *Developmental Psychology,* 1972, *7,* 107–109.

Bourne, L. E., Jr., & Dominowski, R. L. Thinking. *Annual Review of Psychology.* 1972, *23,* 105–130.

Bower, G. H., Trabasso, T. R. A concept identification. In R. C. Atkinson (Ed.), *Studies in mathematical psychology.* Stanford: Stanford University Press, 1964.

Bower, T. G. R. The development of object-permanence: Some studies of existence constancy. *Perception and Psychophysics,* 1967, *2,* 411–418.

Bower, T. G. R. The object in the world of the infant. *Scientific American,* 1971, *225,* 30–47.

Bower, T. G. R., Broughton, J. M., & Moore, M. K. The coordination of visual and tactual input in infants. *Perception and Psychophysics,* 1970, *8,* 51–53.

Bower, T. G. R., & Paterson, J. G. Stages in the development of the object concept. *Cognition,* 1972, *1,* 47–55.

Bowers, K. S. Situationism in psychology: An analysis and a critique. *Psychological Review,* 1973, *80,* 307–336.

Bowman, M. J. Learning and earning in the post-school years. In F. N. Kerlinger & J. B. Carroll (Eds.), *Review of research in education* (Vol. 2). Itasca, Ill.: Peacock, 1974.

Boyd, W. C. *Genetics and the races of man.* Boston: D. C. Heath and Company, 1950.

Bridger, W. H., & Mandel, I. J. Abolition of the PRE by instructions in GSR conditioning. *Journal of Experimental Psychology,* 1965, *69,* 476–482.

Bronfenbrenner, U. Socialization and social class through time and space. In E. E. Maccoby, T. M. Newcomb, & E. L. Hartley (Eds.), *Reading in social psychology.* New York: Holt, Rinehart, & Winston, 1958.

Bronfenbrenner, U. Freudian theories of identification and their derivatives. *Child Development,* 1960, *31,* 15–40.

Bronfenbrenner, U. Response to pressure from peers versus adults among Soviet and American school children. *International Journal of Psychology,* 1967, *2,* 199–207.

Bronfenbrenner, U. *Two worlds of childhood: U.S. and U.S.S.R.* New York: Russell Sage Foundation, 1970.

Bronson, G. W. Infants' reactions to unfamiliar persons and mood objects. *Monographs of the Society for Research in Child Development,* 1972, *37,* (3), (Serial No. 148).

Brown, P., & Elliott, R. Control of aggression in a nursery school class. *Journal of Experimental Child Psychology,* 1965, *2,* 103–107.

Brown, R. *A first language: The early stages.* Cambridge: Harvard University Press, 1973.

Brown, R., & Fraser, C. The acquisition of syntax. In C. N. Cofer & B. Musgrave (Eds.), *Verbal behavior and learning: Problems and processes.* New York: McGraw-Hill, 1963.

Brown, R. E. Organ weight in malnutrition with special reference to brain weight. *Developmental Medicine and Child Neurology,* 1966, *8,* 512–522.

Bruner, J. S. *The process of education.* New York: Vintage, 1960.

Bruner, J. S. The course of cognitive growth. *American Psychologist,* 1964, *19,* 1–15.

Bruner, J. S. The growth and structure of skill. In K. Connolly (Ed.), *Mechanisms of motor skill development.* New York: Academic Press, 1970.

Bruner, J. S., Goodnow, J. J., & Austin, G. A. *A study of thinking.* New York: Wiley, 1956.

Bryan, J. H. Children's reaction to helpers: Their money isn't where their mouths are. In J. Macaulay & L. Berkowitz (Eds.), *Altruism and helping behavior.* New York: Academic Press, 1970, pp. 61–73.

Bryan, J. H., & London, P. Altruistic behavior by children. *Psychological Bulletin,* 1970, *73,* 200–211.

Bucher, B., & Lovass, O. I. Use of aversive stimulation in behavior modification. In M. R. Jones (Ed.), *Miami Symposium on the prediction of behavior, 1967: Aversive stimulation.* Coral Gables, Fla.: University of Miami Press, 1968.

Burke, B. S., Harding, V. V., & Stuart, H. C. Nutrition studies during pregnancy: 4. Relation of protein content of mother's diet during pregnancy to birth length, birth weight, and condition of infant at birth. *Journal of Pediatrics,* 1943, *23,* 506.

Burt, C. *Intelligence and fertility.* London: Eugenics Society, 1946.

Burt, C. The inheritance of mental ability. *American Psychologist,* 1958, *13,* 1–15.

Burton, R. V. Generality of honesty reconsidered. *Psychological Review,* 1963, *70,* 481–500.

Butts, R. F. *A cultural history of western education: Its social and intellectual foundations* (2nd Ed.). New York: McGraw-Hill, 1955.

Cagle, L. T., & Deutscher, I. Social mobility and low-income fatherless families. Paper presented at Society for the Study of Social Problems, Montreal, Quebec, September 1964.

Caldwell, B. M. The effects of infant care. In M. L. Hoffman & L. W. Hoffman (Eds.), *Review of child development research* (Vol. I). New York: Russell Sage Foundation, 1964.

Caldwell, B. M. The fourth dimension in early childhood education. In R. D. Hess & R. M. Bear (Eds.), *Early education: Current theory, research and action.* Chicago: Aldine, 1968, 71–81.

Caldwell, B. M., & Ricciuti, H. N. *Review of child development research* (Vol. 3). Chicago: University of Chicago Press, 1973.

Calhoun, J. B. Population density and social pathology. *Scientific American,* 1962, *206,* 139–148.

Casler, L. The effects of extra tactile stimulation on a group of institutionalized infants. *Genetic Psychology Monographs,* 1965, *71,* 137–175.

Cattell, R. B. *Personality and motivation: Structure and measurement.* Yonkers-on-Hudson: World Book, 1957.

Cazden, C. B. The neglected situation in child language research and education. In F. Williams (Ed.), *Language and poverty: Perspectives on a theme.* Chicago: Markham, 1970.

Cazden, C. B. The acquisition of noun and verb inflections. In C. A. Ferguson & D. I. Slobin (Eds.), *Studies of child language development.* New York: Holt, Rinehart and Winston, 1973.

Central Advisory Council for Education (England). *Children and their primary schools. Vol. 1: Report.* London: Her Majesty's Stationery Office, 1967.

Chandler, M. H., & Greenspan, S. Ersatz egocentrism: A reply to H. Borke. *Developmental Psychology,* 1972, *7,* 104–106.

Child, I. L. *Humanistic psychology and the research tradition: Their several virtues.* New York: Wiley, 1973.

Child, I. L., Potter, E. H., & Levine, E. M. Children's textbooks and personality development. *Psychological Monographs,* 1946, *60* (3, Whole No. 279).

Chilman, C. Programs for disadvantaged parents. In B. M. Caldwell & H. N. Ricciuti (Eds.), *Review of child development research* (Vol. 3). Chicago: University of Chicago Press, 1973.

Chittenden, G. E. An experimental study in measuring and modifying assertive behavior in young children. *Monographs of the Society for Research in Child Development,* 1942, 7 (1, Serial No. 31).

Chomsky, N. A review of *Verbal Behavior* by B. F. Skinner. *Language,* 1959, *35,* 26–58.

Chomsky, N. *Language and mind: Enlarged edition.* New York: Harcourt Brace Jovanovich, 1968.

Churchill, W. S. *My early life: A roving commission.* New York: Scribner's, 1930.

Citizen's Board of Inquiry into Hunger and Malnutrition in the United States. *Hunger, U.S.A.* Boston: Beacon Press, 1968.

Claiborne, W. L. Expectancy effects in the classroom: A failure to replicate. *Journal of Educational Psychology,* 1969, *60,* 377–383.

Clark, E. E. Television and social control: Some observations on the portrayal of ethnic minorities. *Television Quarterly,* 1969, *8,* 18–22.

Clark, K. B. Learning obstacles among children. In A. L. Roaden (Ed.), *Problems of school children in depressed urban centers.* Columbus, Ohio: The Ohio State University, 1969.

Clark, K. B., & Clark, M. P. Racial identification and preference in Negro children. In T. M. Newcomb, & E. J. Hartley (Eds.), *Readings in social psychology.* New York: Holt, 1947, 164–178.

Clausen, J. A. Family structure, socialization and personality. In L. W. Hoffman & M. L. Hoffman (Eds.), *Review of child development research* (Vol. 2). New York: Russell Sage Foundation, 1966, 1–54.

Coghill, G. E. *Anatomy and the problem of behavior.* Cambridge: Cambridge University Press, 1929.

Cole, M., & Bruner, J. Cultural differences and inferences about psychological processes. *American Psychologist,* 1971, *26,* 867–876.

Coleman, J. S. Equal schools or equal students? *The Public Interest,* 1966, *4*(Summer), 73–74.

Coleman, J. S., Campbell, E. Q., Hobson, C. J., McPartland, J., Mood, A. M., Weinfeld, F. D., & York, R. L. *Equality of educational opportunity.* Washington, D.C.: U.S. Department of Health, Education and Welfare, U.S. Government Printing Office, 1966.

Coopersmith, S. *The antecedents of self-esteem.* San Francisco: Freeman, 1967.

Coppersmith, S., & Feldman, R. Fostering a positive self-concept and high self-esteem in the classroom. In R. H. Coop & K. White (Eds.), *Psychological concepts in the classroom.* New York: Harper & Row, 1974, 192–225.

Crandall, V. C., Katkovsky, W., & Crandall, V. J. Children's beliefs in their own control of reinforcement in intellectual-academic achievement situations. *Child Development,* 1965, *36,* 91–109.

Darwin, C. *Origin of the species.* London: Murray, 1859.

Davé, R. H. The identification and measurement of environmental process variables that are related to educational achievement. Unpublished doctoral dissertation, University of Chicago, 1963.

Davis, A., & Havighurst, R. J. Social class and color differences in child rearing. *American Sociological Review,* 1946, *11,* 698–710.

de Charms, R., & Moeller, G. H. Values expressed in

American children's readers, 1800–1950. *Journal of Abnormal and Social Psychology*, 1962, *64* (2), 136–142.

Deese, J., & Hulse, S. H. *The psychology of learning.* New York: McGraw-Hill, 1967.

deMause, L. Our forebears made childhood a nightmare. *Psychology Today*, 1975, *8* (11), 85–87.

Dennis, W. The effect of cradling practices upong the onset of walking in Hopi children. *Journal of Genetic Psychology*, 1940, *56*, 77–86.

Dennis, W. Spalding's experiment on the flight of birds repeated with another species. *Journal of Comparative Psychology*, 1941, *31*, 117–120.

Dennis, W. Causes of retardation among institutional children: Iran. *Journal of Genetic Psychology*, 1960, *96*, 47–59.

Dennis, W., & Najarian, P. Infant development under environmental handicap. *Psychological Monographs*, 1957, *71*, No. 7.

Dennis, W., & Sayegh, Y. The effect of supplementary experiences upon the behavioral development of infants in institutions. *Child Development*, 1965, *36*, 81–90.

Deutsch, C. P. Social class and child development. In Bettye M. Caldwell & Henry N. Ricciuti (Eds.), *Review of child development research* (Vol. 3). Chicago: University of Chicago Press, 1973.

Deutsch, M. Cooperation & trust: Some theoretical notes. In M. R. Jones (Ed.), *Nebraska Symposium on Motivation*. Lincoln, Nebraska: University of Nebraska Press, 1962, 275–320.

DeVos, G. A. Achievement and innovation in culture and personality. In E. Norbeck, D. Price-Williams, & W. M. McCord (Eds.), *Personality: An interdisciplinary approach*. New York: Holt, Rinehart & Winston, 1968.

Doland, D. J., & Adelberg, K. The learning of shaming behavior. *Child Development*, 1967, *38*, 695–700.

Dollard, J., Doob, L. W., Miller, N. E., Mowrer, O. H., & Sears, R. R. *Frustration and aggression*. New Haven: Yale University Press, 1939.

Dollard, J., & Miller, N. E. *Personality and psychotherapy: An analysis in terms of learning, thinking, and culture*. New York: McGraw-Hill, 1950.

Dornbusch, S. M., Hastorf, A. H., Richardson, S. A., Muzzy, R. E., & Vreeland, R. S. The perceiver and the perceived: Their relative influence on the categories of interpersonal cognition. *Journal of Personality and Social Psychology*, 1965, *1*, 434–440.

DuBois, C. The dominant value profile of American culture. *American Anthropologist*, 1955, *57*, 1232–1239.

Dubos, R. *So human an animal*. New York: Charles Scribner's Sons, 1968.

Duncker, K. Experimental modification of children's food preferences through social suggestion. *Journal of Abnormal Psychology*, 1938, *33*, 489–507.

Dunn, L. C. *Heredity and evolution in human populations*. Cambridge, Mass.: Harvard University Press, 1959.

Durkheim, E. *Moral education*. New York: Free Press, 1961.

Elkind, D. *Children and adolescents: Interpretive essays on Jean Piaget* (2nd ed.). New York: Oxford University Press, 1974.

Elkind, D., & Duckworth, E. The educational implications of Piaget's work. In C. E. Silberman (Ed.), *The open classroom reader*. New York: Vintage, 1973.

Epstein, R. Aggression toward outgroups as a function of authoritarianism and imitation of aggressive models. *Journal of Personality and Social Psychology*, 1966, *3*, 574–579.

Epstein, R., & Komorita, S. S. Self-esteem, success-failure, and locus of control in Negro children. *Developmental Psychology*, 1971, *4*, (1), 2–8.

Erikson, E. H. *Childhood and society*. New York: Norton, 1950, 1963.

Erlenmeyer-Kimling, L., & Jarvik, L. F. Genetics and intelligence: A review. *Science*, 1963, *142*, 1477–1478.

Ervin-Tripp, S. M. Children's sociolinguistic competence and dialect diversity. In Ira J. Gordon (Ed.), *Early childhood education: The seventy-fifth yearbook of the National Society for the Study of Education*. Chicago: University of Chicago Press, 1972.

Ervin-Tripp, S. M. *Language acquisition and communicative choice*. Stanford, Calif.: Stanford University Press, 1973.

Evans, E. D. *Contemporary influences in early childhood education* (2nd Ed.). New York: Holt, Rinehart & Winston, 1975.

Evans-Pritchard, E. E. *Social anthropology*. Glencoe, Ill.: The Free Press, 1951.

Eysenck, H. J. Symposium: The development of moral values in children. VII—The contribution of learning theory. *British Journal of Educational Psychology*, 1960, *30*, 11–21.

Faust, M. S. Developmental maturity as a determinant in prestige of adolescent girls. *Child Development*, 1960, *31*, 173–184.

Feeney, S. Child care debate: Key question. *Compact*, 1973, July–August, 25–26.

Ferster, C. S., & Skinner, B. F. *Schedules of reinforcement*. New York: Appleton-Century-Crofts, 1957.

Feshback, S. The catharsis hypothesis and some consequences of interaction with aggressive and neutral play objects. *Journal of Personality*, 1956, *24*, 449–462.

Festinger, L. *A theory of cognitive dissonance*. Stanford, Calif.: Stanford University Press, 1957.

Fischer, W. F. Sharing in preschool children as a function of amount and type of reinforcement. *Genetic Psychology Monographs*, 1963, *68*, 215–245.

Flanagan, J. C. Individualizing education. *Education*, 1970, *90*, 191–206.

Flavell, J. H. *The developmental psychology of Jean Piaget*. New York: Van Nostrand, 1963.

Flavell, J. H. The development of inferences about others. In T. Mischel (Ed.), *Understanding other persons*. London: Blackwell, 1973.

Fleming, A. *Nine months: A practical guide for the expectant mother.* New York: Barnes and Nobel Books, 1972.

Fodor, J. A., & Bever, T. The psychological reality of linguistic segments. *Journal of Verbal Learning and Verbal Behavior,* 1965, *4,* 414–420.

Fox, D. J. and Barnes, V. B. Racial preference and identification of Black, American Chinese, and White children. *Genetic Psychology Monographs,* 1973, *88,* 229–286.

Fraser, A. *Heredity, genes and chromosomes.* New York: McGraw-Hill, 1966.

Freud, S. *The ego and the id.* London: Hogarth Press, 1927.

Freud, S. *The basic writings of....* (A. A. Brill, Ed. and trans.). New York: Random House, 1938.

Freud, S. *Collected papers* (Vol. 3). New York: Basic Books, 1959.

Freud, S. *The ego and the id.* New York: Norton, 1960.

Freud, S. *The complete introductory lectures on psychoanalysis.* (J. Strachey, Ed. and trans.). New York: Norton, 1966.

Friedrich, L. K., & Stein, A. H. Aggressive and prosocial television programs and the natural behavior of preschool children. *Monographs of the Society for Research in Child Development,* 1973, *38* (Serial No. 151).

Fry, C. L. A developmental examination of performance in a tacit coordination game situation. *Journal of Personality and Social Psychology,* 1967, *5,* 277–281.

Gage, N. L. I.Q. heritability, race differences, and educational research. *Phi Delta Kappan,* 1972, *53,* 308–312.

Gagné, R. M. Contributions of learning to human development. *Psychological Review,* 1968, *75,* 177–191.

Gagné, R. M. *The conditions of learning* (2nd ed.). New York: Holt, Rinehart and Winston, 1970.

Gahagan, D. M., & Gahagan, G. A. Talk reform: Explorations in language for infant-school children. *Primary socialization, language and education* (Vol. 3). Sociological Research Unit Monograph Series, B. Bernstein, Director. London: Routledge and Kegan Paul, 1970.

Gallimore, R., Boggs, J., & Jordan, C. *Culture, behavior and education: A study of Hawaiian-Americans.* Beverly Hills, Calif.: Sage Publications, 1974.

Gallimore, R., & Howard, A. (Eds.), Studies in a Hawaiian community: Namamaka o Nanokuli. *Pacific Anthropological Records.* No. 1. Honolulu: B. P. Bishop Museum. 1968.

Galton, F. *Hereditary genius: An inquiry into its laws and consequences.* New York: Macmillan, 1869.

Garber, H., & Heber, R. The Milwaukee Project: Early intervention as a technique to prevent mental retardation. National Leadership Institute Teacher Education/ Early childhood. The University of Connecticut Technical Papers. Storrs, Conn.: University of Connecticut, 1973.

Garcia, A. B., & Zimmerman, B. J. The effect of examiner ethnicity and language on the performance of bilingual Mexican-American first graders. *Journal of Social Psychology,* 1972, *87,* 3–11.

Gardner, J. W. *Excellence: Can we be equal and excellent too?* New York: Harper and Row, 1961.

Garrett, M., Bever, T., & Fodor, J. A. The active use of grammar in speech perception. *Perception & Psychophysics* 1966, *1,* 30–32.

Geber, M. The psychomotor development of African children in the first year and the influence of maternal behavior. *Journal of Social Psychology,* 1958, *47,* 185–195.

Gelfand, D. M. The influence of self-esteem on rate of verbal conditioning and social matching behavior. *Journal of Abnormal and Social Psychology,* 1962, *65,* 259–265.

Gesell, A. *The mental growth of the preschool child.* New York: Macmillan, 1925.

Gesell, A. *Infancy and human growth.* New York: Macmillan, 1928.

Gesell, A. *The first five years of life.* New York: Harper, 1940.

Gesell, A., & Ilg., F. L. *Infant and child in the culture of today.* New York: Harper and Row, 1943.

Gesell, A., & Thompson, H. Learning and growth in identical infant twins: An experimental study by the method of co-twin control. *Genetic Psychology Monographs,* 1929, *6,* 1–124.

Gewirtz, J. L. A factor analysis of some attention-seeking behaviors of young children. *Child Development,* 1956, *27,* 17–36.

Ghesquiere, J. L. Interdependence analysis of physical performance and growth in boys. *Annales Paediatriae Fenniae,* 4: Suppl. 11, 1958.

Gibson, E. J. *Principles of perceptual learning and development.* New York: Appleton-Century-Crofts, 1969.

Glaser, R., & Nitko, A. J. Measurement in learning and instruction. In R. L. Thorndike (Ed.), *Educational measurement* (2nd ed.). Washington, D.C.: American Council on Education, 1971.

Gleason, J. B. Code switching in children's language. In T. E. Moore (Ed.), *Cognitive development and the acquisition of language.* New York: Academic Press, 1973, 159–167.

Glynn, E. L., & Thomas, J. D. Effect of cueing on self-control of classroom behavior. *Journal of Applied Behavior Analysis,* 1974, *7,* 299–306.

Glynn, E. L., Thomas, J. D., & Shee, S. M. Behavioral self-control of on task-behavior in an elementary classroom. *Journal of Applied Behavior Analysis,* 1973, *6* (1), 105–113.

Goddard, H. H. *Human efficiency and levels of intelligence.* Princeton, N.J.: Princeton University Press, 1920.

Good, T. L. Which pupils do teachers call on? *Elementary School Journal,* 1970, *70,* 190–198.

Goodenough, F. L., & Maurer, K. M. *The mental growth of children from two to fourteen years: A study of the* predictive value of the Minnesota Preschool Scales. Minneapolis: University of Minnesota Press, 1942.

Gordon, E. W. The child: His cognitive, personal, social, and physical development—a false trichotomy? In S. B. Anderson & J. Dopplet (Chm.), Untangling the tangled web of education. (ETS rm 69–6). Princeton, N.J.: Educational Testing Service, 1969.

Gordon, I. J. A parent education project for culturally disadvantaged. Preliminary report to the Children's Bureau. Gainesville: University of Florida, 1968.

Gordon, I. J. Early child stimulation through parent education. Final report to the U.S. Children's Bureau. Gainesville: College of Education, University of Florida, 1969.

Gordon, T. Parent effectiveness training. New York: Wyden, 1970.

Goslin, D. Improving the community as a socialization system. Paper presented at the annual meeting of the American Educational Research Association, Chicago, March 1975.

Graffar, M., & Corbiar, J. Contribuiton à l'étude de l'influence socio-économique sur la croissance et le développement de lénfant. Courrier, 1966, 16, 1–25.

Gratch, G. A study of the relative dominance of vision and touch in six-month-old infants. Child Development, 1972, 43, 615–623.

Gray, S. W. Children from three to ten: The early training project. Early Education Papers and Reports (Vol. 5, No. 3). Nashville, Tenn.: George Peabody College for Teachers, Demonstration and Research Center for Early Education, 1971.

Gray, S. W., & Klaus, R. S. The early training project: A seventh year report. Child Development, 1970, 41, 909–924.

Greenberg, B. S., Erikson, P. M., & Valhos, M. Children's television behavior as perceived by mother and child. In Television and social behavior (Vol. 4), Washington, D.C.: U.S. Government Printing Office, 1972.

Greenberg, M., Pelliteri, O., & Barton, J. Frequency of defects in infants whose mothers had rubella during pregnancy. Journal of the American Medical Association, 1957, 165, 675–678.

Greenwald, H. J., & Oppenheim, D. B. Reported magnitude of self-misidentification among Negro children—Artifact? Journal of Personality and Social Psychology, 1968, 8, 49–52.

Gronseth, E. The impact of father absence in sailor families upon the personality structure and social adjustment of adult sailor sons. Part I. In N. Anderson (Ed.), Studies of the family. Gottengen: Vandenhoeck & Ruprechh, 1957, 2, 97–114.

Guilford, J. P. The nature of human intelligence. New York: McGraw-Hill, 1967.

Guthrie, E. R. Relationships of teaching method, socioeconomic status, and intelligence in concept formation. Journal of Educational Psychology, 1971, 62, 345–351.

Halford, G. S., & Fullerton, T. J. A discrimination task which induces conservation of number. Child Development, 1970, 41, 205–213.

Hall, E. T. The hidden dimension. Garden City, N.Y.: Anchor Books, Doubleday & Co. Inc., 1966.

Hall, C. S., & Lindzey, G. Theories of personality (2nd Ed.). New York: Wiley, 1970.

Haller, A. O., & Butterworth, C. E. Peer influence on levels of occupation and educational aspiration. Social Forces, 1960, 38, 289–295.

Halverson, H. M. An experimental study of prehension in infants by means of systematic cinema records. Genetic Psychology Monographs, 1931, 10, 110–286.

Handlon, B. J., & Gross, P. The development of sharing behavior. Journal of Abnormal and Social Psychology, 1959, 59, 425–428.

Harasym, C. R., Boersma, F. J., & McGuire, T. O. Semantic differential analysis of relational terms used in conservation. Child Development, 1971, 42, 767–779.

Hardin, G. Biology: Its human implications (2nd Ed.). San Francisco: W. H. Freeman, & Co., 1953.

Harlow, H., & Harlow, M. H. Learning to love. American Scientist, 1966, 54 (3), 244–272.

Harlow, H., & Zimmermen, R. R. Affectional responses in the infant monkey. Science, 1959, 130 (3373), 421–432.

Harris, J. A., Jackson, C. M., Paterson, D. G., & Scammon, R. F. The measurement of man. Minneapolis: University of Minnesota Press, 1930.

Harris, P. L. Examination and search in infants. British Journal of Psychology, 1971, 62, 469–73.

Harris, P. L. Development of search and object permanence during infancy. Psychological Bulletin, 1975, 82, 332–344.

Hartshorne, H., & May, M. A. Studies in the nature of character. Studies in Deceit (Vol. 1). New York: MacMillan, 1928.

Hartup, W. W. Peer interaction and social organization. In P. H. Mussen (Ed.), Carmichael's Manual of Child Psychology (Vol. 2). New York: Wiley, 1970, 361–456.

Haskett, G. J., & Lenfestey, W. Reading-related behavior in an open classroom: Effects of novelty and modelling on preschoolers. Journal of Applied Behavior Analysis, 1974, 7, 233–241.

Havelock, R. G. Planning for innovation through dissemination and utilization of knowledge. Ann Arbor: The University of Michigan Institute for Social Research, 1969.

Hawkins, P. R. Social class, the nominal group and reference. Language and Speech, 1969, 12, 125–35.

Heathers, G. Emotional Dependence and Independence in a physical threat situation. Child Development, 1953, 24, 169–179.

Henderson, R. W. Environmental stimulation and intellectual development of Mexican-American children. Final Report for U.S.O.E. Cooperative Research Project (No. 6–8068–2–12–1), 1966.

Henderson, R. W. Research and consultation in the natural environment. Psychology in the Schools, 1970, 7, 335–341.

Henderson, R. W. Environmental predictors of academic performance of disadvantaged Mexican-American children. *Journal of Consulting and Clinical Psychology,* 1972, 38, 297.

Henderson, R. W. Defining goals in open education. In B. Spodek & H. Walberg (Eds.), *Studies in open education,* New York: Agathon Press, 1974.

Henderson, R. W., Bergan, J. R., & Hurt, M. Development and validation of the Henderson Environmental Learning Process Scale. *Journal of Social Psychology,* 1972, 88, 185–196.

Henderson, R. W., & Garcia, A. The effects of a parent training program on the question-asking behavior of Mexican-American children. *American Educational Research Journal,* 1973, 10, 193–201.

Henderson, R. W., & Merritt, C. B. Environmental backgrounds of Mexican-American children with different potentials for school success. *Journal of Social Psychology,* 1968, 75, 101–106.

Henderson, R. W., & Rankin, R. J. WPPSI Reliability and validity with disadvantaged Mexican-American children. *Journal of School Psychology,* 1973, 11, 16–20.

Henderson, R. W., & Swanson, R. The application of social learning principles in a field setting: An applied experiment. *Exceptional Children,* 1974, September, 53–55.

Henderson, R. W., Swanson, R., & Zimmerman, B. Inquiry response induction in preschool children through televised modeling. *Developmental Psychology,* 1975a.

Henderson, R. W., Swanson, R., & Zimmerman, B. Training seriation responses in young children through televised modeling of hierarchially sequenced rule components. *American Educational Research Journal,* 1975b.

Henderson, R. W., Zimmerman, B. J., Swanson, R., & Bergan, J. R. Televised cognitive skill instruction for Papago Native American Children. Technical Report on Grant No. OCD–CB–479 from the Office Child Development, H.E.W. Tucson: Arizona Center for Educational Research and Development, University of Arizona, July, 1974.

Herman, R. L., & Azrin, N. H. Punishment by noise in an alternative response situation. *Journal of the Experimental Analysis of Behavior,* 1964, 7, 185–188.

Herson, P. H. Biasing effects of diagnostic labels and sex of pupil on teachers' views of pupils' mental health. *Journal of Educational Psychology,* 1974, 66, 117–122.

Herzog, E., & Sudia, C. E. Children in fatherless families. In B. M. Caldwell & H. N. Riciutti (Eds.), *Review of child development research* (Vol. 3). Chicago: University of Chicago Press, 1973.

Hess, R. D. Social class and ethnic influences upon socialization. In P. H. Mussen (Ed.), *Carmichael's manual of child psychology* (Vol. 2). New York: Wiley, 1970.

Hess, R. D., & Shipman, V. C. Early experiences and the socialization of cognitive modes in children. In M. W. Miles & W. W. Charters, Jr., *Learning in social settings.* Boston: Allyn and Bacon, 1970.

Hess, R. D., Shipman, V., Brophy, J., & Bear, R. Cognitive environments of urban preschool Negro children. Report to the Children's Bureau, Social Security Administration, H.E.W., 1968.

Hetherington, E. M. Effects of father absence on personality development in adolescent daughters. *Developmental Psychology,* 1972, 7 (3), 313–326.

Hetherington, E. M., & McIntyre, C. W. Developmental psychology. *Annual Review of Psychology,* 1975, 26, 97–136.

Hickey, J. E. The effects of guided moral discussion upon youthful offenders' level of moral judgment. (Doctoral dissertation, Boston University, 1972). *Dissertation Abstracts International,* 1972, 33, 1551A. (University Microfilms No. 72–25, 438)

Hicks, D. J. Imitation and retention of film-mediated aggressive peer and adult models. *Journal of Personality and Social Psychology,* 1965, 2, 97–100.

Hiernaux, J. Heredity and environment: Their influence on human morphology. A comparison of two independent lines of study. *American Journal of Physical Anthropology,* 1963, 27, 575–589.

Hiernaux, J. Weight/height relationship during growth in Africans and Europeans. *Human Biology,* 1964, 36, 273–293.

Hilton, I. Differences in the behavior of mothers toward first- and later-born children. *Journal of Personality and Social Psychology,* 1967, 7, 282–290.

Hoffman, M. L. Moral development. In P. H. Mussen (Ed.), *Carmichael's manual of child psychology* (Vol. 2). (3rd ed.). New York: Wiley, 1970.

Hofstaetter, P. R. The changing composition of "intelligence": A study in T-technique. *Journal of Genetic Psychology,* 1954, 85, 159–164.

Hollingshead, A. B. *Elmtown's youth.* New York: Wiley, 1949.

Holstein, C. The relation of children's moral judgment to that of their parents and to communication patterns in the family. (Doctoral dissertation, University of California, Berkeley, 1969). *Dissertation Abstracts International,* 1970, 31, 1888A–1889A. (University Microfilms No. 70–17, 579)

Honnigman, J. J. *Culture and personality.* New York: Harper, 1954.

Honzik, M. P., Macfarlane, J. W., & Allen, L. The stability of mental test performance between two and 18 years. *Journal of Experimental Education,* 1948, 4, 309–324.

Horowitz, F. D., & Paden, L. Y. The effectiveness of environmental intervention programs. In B. M. Caldwell, & H. N. Riciutti (Eds.), *Review of child development research* (Vol. 3). Chicago: University of Chicago Press, 1973, 331–402.

Houston, S. A sociolinguistic consideration of the black English of children in Northern Florida. *Language,* 1969, 45, 599–607.

Hraba, J., & Grant, G. Black is beautiful: An examination of racial preference and identity. *Journal of Personality and Social Psychology,* 16, 398–402.

Hulse, F. S. *The human species*. New York: Random House, 1963.

Hunt, E. B. *Concept learning*. New York: Wiley, 1962.

Hunt, J. McV. *Intelligence and experience*. New York: Ronald Press, 1961.

Inhelder, B., & Piaget, J. *The growth of logical thinking from childhood to adolescence*. New York: Basic Books, 1958.

James, W. Talks to teachers on psychology and to students on some of life's ideals. In S. A. Rippa (Ed.), *Educational ideas in America: A documentary history*. New York: McKay, 1969.

Jencks, C., Smith, M., Acland, H., Bane, M. J., Cohen, D., Gintis, H., Heyns, B., & Michelson, S. *Inequality: A reassessment of the effect of family and schooling in America*. New York: Basic Books, 1972.

Jenkins, J. J., & Paterson, D. G. *Studies in individual differences*. New York: Appleton-Century-Crofts, 1961.

Jensen, A. R. How much can we boost IQ and scholastic achievement? *Harvard Educational Review*, Reprint Series No. 2, 1969, 1–124.

Jensen, A. R. The heritability of intelligence. *Engineering and Science*, 1970, 33 (6), 1–4.

Jensen, A. R. The phylogeny and ontogeny of intelligence. *Perspectives in Biology and Medicine*, 1971, 15, 37–43.

Jensen, A. R. The ethical issues. *The Humanist*, 1972, 32, 5–6.

Johnson, O. G., & Bommarito, J. W. *Tests and measurements in child development: A handbook*. San Francisco: Jossey-Bass, 1971.

Johnson-Laird, P. N. Experimental psycholinguistics. *Annual Review of Psychology*, 1974, 25, 135–160.

Johnston, M. K., Kelley, C. S., Harris, F. R., & Wolf, M. M. An application of reinforcement principles to development of motor skills of a young child. *Child Development*, 1966, 37, 379–387.

Jones, C. A. Some relationships between creative writing and creative drawing of sixth-grade children. Unpublished doctoral dissertation, The Pennsylvania State University, 1960.

Jones, E. *The life and work of Sigmund Freud* (Vol. 1). New York: Basic Books, 1953.

Jones, H. E. The California adolescent growth study. *Journal of Educational Research*, 1938, 31, 561–567.

Jones, J. E. The environment and mental development. In L. Carmichael (Ed.), *Manual of Child Psychology*. New York: Wiley, 1954.

Jones, M. C. A study of socialization patterns at the high school level. *Journal of Genetic Psychology*, 1958, 92, 87–111.

Jones, M. C., & Bayley, N. Physical maturing among boys as related to behavior. *Journal of Educational Psychology*, 1950, 41, 129–148.

Jung, S. M., Lipe, D., & Wolfe, P. S. Study of the use of incentive in education and the feasibility of field experiments in school systems. Contract number OEC–0–70–5025. Washington, D.C.: U.S. Department of Health, Education and Welfare, Office of Education, 1970.

Kagan, J. Acquisition and significance of sex-typing and sex-role identity. In M. Hoffman & L. Hoffman (Eds.), *Review of child development research* (Vol. 1). New York: Russell Sage, 1964, 137–167.

Kagan, J. Individual differences in the resolution of response uncertainty. *Journal of Personality and Social Psychology*, 1965a, 2, 154–160.

Kagan, J. Reflection impulsivity and reading ability in primary grade children. *Child Development*, 1965b, 36, 609–628.

Kagan, J., & Klein, R. E. Cross-cultural perspectives on early development. *American Psychologist*, 1973, 28, 947–961.

Kagan, J., & Messer, S. B. A reply to "Some misgivings about the matching familiar figures test as a measure of reflection-impulsivity." *Developmental Psychology*, 1975, 11 (2), 244–248.

Kagan, J., & Moss, H. A. *Birth to maturity*. New York: Wiley, 1964.

Kagan, S., & Madsen, M. C. Cooperation and competition of Mexican, Mexican-American, and Anglo-American children of two ages under four instructional sets. *Developmental Psychology*, 1971, 5 (1), 32–39.

Kagan, S., & Madsen, M. C. Rivalry in Anglo-American and Mexican children of two ages. *Journal of Personality and Social Psychology*, 1972, 24 (2), 214–220.

Kandel, D. B., & Lesser, G. S. Parental and peer influences on educational plans of adolescents. *American Sociological Review*, 1969, 34, 213–223.

Kandel, D., & Lesser, G. S. Relative influences of parents and peers on the educational plans of adolescents in the United States and Denmark. In M. W. Miles & W. W. Charters, Jr., *Learning in social settings*. Boston: Allyn and Bacon, 1970.

Kanfer, F. H., & Philips, J. S. *Learning foundations of behavior therapy*. New York: Wiley, 1970.

Kantor, J. R. *Interbehavioral Psychology* (2nd ed.). Bloomington, Ind.: Principia Press, 1959.

Kaplan, B. J. Malnutrition and mental deficiency. *Psychological Bulletin*, 1972, 78, 321–334.

Karlins, M., & Andrews, L. M. *Biofeedback: Turning on the power of your mind*. New York: Warner, 1972.

Keasey, C. B. Experimentally induced change in moral opinions and reasoning. *Journal of Personality and Social Psychology*, 1973, 26, 30–38.

Keesing, F. M. *Cultural anthropology: The science of custom*. New York: Holt, Rinehart & Winston, 1965.

Keliher, A. V. *Life and growth*. New York: Appleton-Century, 1938.

Kellaghan, T., Macnamara, J. Family correlates of verbal reasoning ability. *Developmental Psychology*, 1972, 7, 49–53.

Kendler, T. S., Kendler, H. H., & Wells, D. Reversal and nonreversal shifts in nursery school children. *Journal of Comparative and Physiological Psychology*, 1960, 53, 83–88.

Kennedy, W. A. Van de Riet, V. & White, J. C. A normative sample of intelligence and achievement of Negro elementary school children in the Southeastern United States. *Monographs of Social Research in Child Development,* 1963, 28 (6).

Kennedy, W. A., & Willcutt, H. C. Praise and blame as incentives. *Psychological Bulletin,* 1964, 62, 323–332.

Kessen, W. *The child.* New York: John Wiley & Sons, Inc., 1965.

Kessen, W., Haith, M. M., & Salapatek, P. H. Infancy. In P. H. Mussen (Ed.), *Carmichael's manual of child psychology* (Vol. 2). (3rd ed.). New York: Wiley, 1970.

Kester, S. W. The communication of teacher expectations and their effects on the achievement and attitudes of secondary school pupils. Unpublished doctoral dissertation, University of Oklahoma, 1969.

Kimble, G. A. *Hilgard and Marquis' conditioning and learning* (2nd ed.). New York: Appleton-Century-Crofts, 1961.

Kimbrough, J. *The Children's Collective Program Proposal.* Submitted to the Office of Child Development, Department of Health, Education and Welfare, 1974.

Kimbrough, J., & Bikson, K. *Cooperative community orientation project.* Final report submitted to the Office of Child Development, Department of Health, Education and Welfare, 1972.

Kirk, S. A. *Early education of the mentally retarded.* Urbana, Ill.: University of Illinois Press, 1958.

Klaus, R. A., & Gray, S. W. The early training project for disadvantaged children: a report after five years. *Monographs of the Society for Research in Child Development,* 1968, 33 (4, Serial No. 120).

Klein, R. D., & Schuler, C. F. *Increasing academic performance through the contingent use of self-evaluation.* Paper presented at the annual meeting of the American Educational Research Association, Chicago, April 1, 1974.

Klineberg, O. *Negro intelligence and selective migration.* New York: Columbia University Press, 1935.

Kluckhohn, C. *Culture and behavior.* New York: Free Press of Glencoe, 1962.

Kluckhohn, C., & Leighton, D. *The Navaho.* Cambridge: Havard University Press, 1958.

Kobayashi, S., & Saito, M. An experimental study of leadership function in young children's groups. *Japanese Journal of Educational Psychology,* 1958, 5, 195–199.

Koch, H. L. The relation of primary mental abilities in five- and six-year-olds to sex of child and characteristics of his sibling. *Child Development,* 1954, 25, 209–223.

Koch, H. L. Some personality correlates of sex, sibling position and sex of sibling among five- and six-year-old children. *Genetic Psychology Monographs,* 1955, 52, 3–51.

Kohlberg, L. The development of children's orientations toward a moral order: 1. Sequence in the development of moral thought. *Vita Humana,* 1963, 6, 11–33.

Kohlberg, L. Development of moral character and moral ideology. In M. L. Hoffman & L. W. Hoffman (Eds.), *Review of child development research* (Vol. 1). New York: Russell Sage Foundation, 1964.

Kohlberg, L. A cognitive-developmental analysis of children's sex-role concepts and attitudes. In E. E. Maccoby (Ed.), *The development of sex differences.* Palo Alto, Calif.: Stanford University Press, 1966, 82–173.

Kohlberg, L. Stage and sequence: The cognitive-developmental approach to socialization. In D. A. Goslin (Ed.), *Handbook of socialization theory and research.* Chicago: Rand McNally, 1969.

Kohlberg, L. The developmental approach to moral education. In C. Beck, B. Crittendon & E. Sullivan (Eds.), *Moral education: Interdisciplinary approaches.* Toronto: University of Toronto Press, 1970.

Kohlberg, L., & Mayer, R. Development as the aim of education. *Harvard Educational Review,* 1972, 42, 449–496.

Kohlberg, L., & Turiel, E. Moral development and moral education. In G. S. Lesser (Ed.), *Psychology and educational practice.* Glenview, Ill.: Scott Foresman, 1971, 410–465.

Konapczyk, D. R., & Livingston, G. Self-recording and student teacher supervision: Variables within a token economy structure. *Journal of Applied Behavior Analysis,* 1973, 6 (3), 481–486.

Kopan, A. T. Melting pot: Myth or reality? In E. G. Epps (Ed.), *Cultural pluralism.* Berkeley, Calif.: McCutchan, 1974.

Kopp, C. B., Sigman, M., & Parmelee, A. H. Longitudinal study of sensorimotor development. *Developmental Psychology,* 1974, 10, 687–695.

Kozol, J. *Death at an early age.* New York: Houghton Mifflin, 1967.

Krasner, L., & Ullmann, L. P. (Eds.), *Research in behavior modification: New developments and implications.* New York: Holt, Rinehart and Winston, 1965.

Kroeber, A. L., & Kluckhohn, C. *Culture: A critical review of concepts and definitions.* New York: Vintage Books, 1952.

Kubany, E. S. The effects of incentives on the test performance of Hawaiians and Caucasians. Unpublished doctoral dissertation, University of Hawaii, 1971.

Kuhn, D. Z., Madsen, C. H., Jr., & Becker, W. C. Effects of exposure to aggressive model and "frustration" on children's aggressive behavior. *Child Development,* 1967, 38, 739–345.

Labov, W. *The social stratification of English in New York City.* Washington, D.C.: Center for Applied Linguistics, 1966.

Labov, W., & Cohen, P. *Systematic relations of standard and nonstandard rules in the grammars of Negro speakers.* Ithaca, N.Y.: Cornell University, Project Literacy Reports, No. 8, 1967.

Landauer, T. K., & Whiting, J. N. M. Infantile stimulation and adult stature of human males. *American Anthropologist,* 1963, 66, 1007–1028.

Landy, F., Rosenberg, B. G., & Sutton-Smith, B. The

effect of limited father-absence on cognitive development. *Child Development*, 1969, *40*, 941–944.

Langer, J. Disequilibrium as a source of development. In P. Mussen, J. Langer, & M. Covington (Eds.), *Trends and issues in developmental psychology*. New York: Holt, Rinehart, and Winston, 1969.

LaPointe, K., & O'Donnell, J. P. Number conservation in children below age six: Its relationship to age, perceptual dimensions, and language comprehension. *Developmental Psychology*, 1974, *10*, 422–428.

Laughlin, P. R., Moss, I. L., & Miller, S. M. Information processing in children as a function of adult model, stimulus display, school grade, and sex. *Journal of Educational Psychology*, 1969, *60*, 188–193.

Lavin, D. S. *The prediction of academic performance*. New York: Russell Sage, 1965.

LaVois, J. C. Type of punishment as a determinant of resistance to deviation. *Developmental Psychology*, 1974, *10*, 181–185.

Lee, E. S. Negro intelligence and selective migration: A Philadelphia test of the Klineberg hypotheses. *American Sociological Review*, 1951, *16*, 227–233.

Leifer, A. D., Gordon, N. J., & Graves, S. B. Children's television more than mere entertainment. *Harvard Educational Review*, 1974 (May) *44* (2), 213–245.

Lesser, G. S., Fifer, G., & Clark, D. H. Mental abilities of children in different social class and cultural groups. *Monographs of the Society for Research in Child Development*, 1965, *30*, (Serial No. 102).

Lester, B. M., Kotelshuck, M., Spelke, E., Sellers, M. J., & Klein, R. E. Separation protest in Guatemalan infants: Cross-cultural and cognitive findings. *Developmental Psychology*, 1974, *10* (1), 79–85.

Levenstein, P. *Aiding cognitive growth in disadvantaged pre-schoolers: Mother-child programs*. Family Service Association of Nassau County, Mineola; N.Y. Progress report to the U.S. Children's Bureau, 1968.

Levine, M. Cue neutralization: The effects of random reinforcements upon discrimination learning. *Journal of Experimental Psychology*, 1962, *63*, 438–443.

LeVine, R. A. Culture, personality, and socialization: An evolutionary view. In D. A. Goslin (Ed.), *Handbook of socialization theory and research*. Chicago: Rand McNally, 1969.

LeVine, R. A. *Culture, behavior and personality*. Chicago: Aldine, 1973.

Lewis, O. *Life in a Mexican village: Tepoztlan restudied*. Urbana, Ill.: University of Illinois Press, 1961.

Licher, J. H., & Johnson, D. W. Changes in attitudes toward Negroes of White elementary school students after use of multi-ethnic readers. *Journal of Educational Psychology*, 1969, *60*, 148–152.

Liebert, R. M., Neale, J. M., & Davidson, E. S. *The early window: Effects of TV on children and youth*. New York: Pergamon Press, 1973.

Linton, R. *The study of man*. New York: Appleton-Century-Crofts, Inc. 1936.

Linton, R. The scope and aims of anthropology. In R. Linton (Ed.), *The science of man in the world crisis*. New York: Columbia University Press, 1945.

Lorenz, K. Z. *King Solomon's ring*. New York: Thomas Y. Crowell, 1952.

Lovaas, O. I. A program for the establishment of speech in psychotic children. In J. K. Wing (Ed.), *Early childhood autism*. New York: Pergamon Press, 1966.

Lovaas, O. I. A behavior therapy approach to the treatment of childhood schizophrenia. In J. P. Hill (Ed.), *Minnesota symposia on child psychology* (Vol. 1). Minneapolis: University of Minnesota Press, 1967.

Lovaas, O. I., Freitag, G., Gold, V. J., & Kassorla, I. C. Experimental studies of childhood schizophrenia: Analysis of self-destructive behavior. *Journal of Experimental Child Psychology*, 1965, *2*, 67–84.

Lowie, R. H. *The history of ethnological theory*. New York: Holt, Rinehart and Winston, 1937.

Lyle, J. Television and daily life: Patterns of use (overview). In *Television and Social Behavior* (Vol. 4). Washington, D.C.: U.S. Government Printing office, 1972.

Lynd, R. S., & Lynd, H. M. *Middletown: A study in contemporary American culture*. New York: Harcourt Brace, 1929.

McCall, J. N., & Johnson, O. G. The independence of intelligence from family size and birth order. *Journal of Genetic Psychology*, 1972, *121*, 207–213.

McCarthy, D. Language development in children. In L. Carmichael (Ed.), *Manual of child psychology* (2nd ed.). New York: Wiley, 1954.

McClearn, G. E. Genetic influences on behavior and development. In P. H. Mussen (Ed.), *Carmichael's Manual of Child Psychology* (2rd Ed.). (Vol. 1). New York: John Wiley & Sons, Inc., 1970, 39–76.

McClelland, D. C. *The achieving society*. Princeton, N.J.: Van Nostrand, 1961.

McIntyre, C. W., Vaughn, B. E., Flavell, J. H., Early developmental changes in the ability to infer the visual precepts of others. *Proceedings of the 81st Annual Convention of the American Psychological Association*, 1973, *8*, 99–100.

Maccoby, E. E. Role-taking in childhood and its consequences for social learning. *Child Development*, 1959, *30*, 239–252.

Maccoby, E. E. The development of moral values and behavior in childhood. In J. A. Clausen (Ed.), *Socialization and society*. Boston: Little, Brown, 1968, 227–269.

Maccoby, E. E., & Wilson, W. C. Identification and observational learning from films. *Journal of Abnormal and Social Psychology*, 1957, *55*, 78–87.

Maccoby, E., & Zelmer, M. *Experiments in primary education: Aspects of Project Follow-Through*. New York: Harcourt Brace Jovanovich, 1970.

Madsen, M. C. Cooperative and competitive motivation of children in three Mexican-American Sub-cultures. *Psychological Reports*, 1967, *20*, 1307–1320.

Madsen, M. C. Developmental and cross-cultural differences in the cooperative and competitive behavior of young children. *Journal of Cross Cultural Psychology,* 1971, *2* (4), 365–371.

Madsen, M. C., & Ariella, S. Cooperative and competitive behavior of urban Afro-American, Anglo-American, Mexican-American, and Mexican village children. *Developmental Psychology,* 1970, *3* (1), 16–20.

Mahoney, M. J., & Thoresen, C. E. *Self-control: Power to the person.* Monterey, Calif.: Brooks/Cole, 1974.

Malinowski, B. *Sex and repression in savage society.* New York: Harcourt Brace, 1927.

Mallick, S. K., & McCandless, B. R. A study of catharsis of aggression. *Journal of Personality and Social Psychology,* 1966, *4,* 591–596.

Mann, R. D. A review of the relationship between personality and performance in small groups. *Psychological Bulletin,* 1959, *56,* 241–270.

Marjoribanks, K. Ethnic and environmental influences on mental abilities. *The American Journal of Sociology,* 1972, *78,* 323–337.

Masland, R. L., Sarason, S. B., & Gladwin, T. *Mental subnormality: Biological, psychological, and cultural factors.* New York: Basic Books, 1958.

Maslow, A. H. A Theory of human motivation. *Psychological Review,* 1943, *50,* 370–396.

Maslow, A. H. *Toward a psychology of being.* New York: Van Nostrand, 1968.

Mead, G. H. In C. W. Morris (Ed.), *Mind, self and society from the standpoint of a social behaviorist.* Chicago: University of Chicago Press, 1934.

Mead, M. *Sex and temperament in three primitive societies.* New York: William Morrow and Co., 1935.

Mead, M. Social change and cultural surrogates. *Journal of Educational Sociology,* 1940, *14,* (2), 92–109.

Mead, M. Early influences that mould Arapesh Personality. In M. Mead & N. Calas (Eds.), *Primitive heritage: An anthropological anthology.* New York: Random House, 1953.

Meadows, D. H., Meadows, D. L., Randers, J., & Behrens, W. W., III. *The limits to growth.* New York: Potomac Associates, 1972.

Meichenbaum, D. Enhancing creativity by modifying what subjects say to themselves. *American Educational Research Journal,* 1975, *12,* 129–146.

Menninger, W. C. Recreation and mental health. *Recreation,* 1948, *42,* 340–346.

Mercer, J. R. *Labeling the mentally retarded.* Berkeley: University of California Press, 1973.

Merton, R. K. *Social theory and social structure.* Glencoe, Ill.: The Free Press, 1957.

Midlarsky, E., & Bryan, J. H. Training charity in children. *Journal of Personality and Social Psychology,* 1967, *5,* 400–415.

Milgram, S., & Hollander, P. Murder they heard. *Nation,* 1964, *198,* 602–604.

Miller, G. A., & Isard, S. Free recall of self-embedded English sentences. *Information & Control,* 1964, *7,* 292–303.

Miller, N. E. & Dollard, J. *Social learning and Imitation.* New Haven: Yale University Press, 1941.

Mischel, W. *Personality and assessment.* New York: Wiley, 1968.

Mischel, W. Sex-typing and socialization. In P. H. Mussen (Ed.), *Carmichael's Manual of Child Psychology* (Vol. 2). (3rd Ed.). New York: Wiley, 1970.

Mischel, W. *Introduction to Personality.* New York: Holt, Rinehart and Winston, 1971.

Mischel, W. Toward a cognitive social learning reconceptualization of personality. *Psychological Review,* 1973, *80,* 252–283.

Mischel, W. Processes in delay of gratification. In Leonard Berkowitz (Ed.), *Advances in experimental social psychology.* New York: Academic Press, 1974.

Mischel, W., & Ebbesen, E. B. Attention in delay of gratification. *Journal of Personality and Social Psychology,* 1970, *16,* 329–337.

Montagu, M. F. A. Constitutional and prenatal factors in infant and child health. In M. J. E. Senn (Ed.), *Symposium on the healthy personality.* New York: Josiah Macy, Jr. Foundation, 1950, 148–175.

Montagu, M. F. A. *Prenatal influences.* Springfield, Ill.: Charles C. Thomas, 1962.

Moore, B. S., Underwood, B., & Rosenhan, D. L. Affect and altruism. *Developmental Psychology,* 1973, *8,* 99–104.

Moos, R. H. Situational analysis of a therapeutic community milieu. *Journal of Abnormal Psychology,* 1968, *73,* 49–61.

Morgan, G. A., & Ricciuti, H. N. Infants' responses to strangers during the first year. In B. H. Foss (Ed.), *Determinants of infant behavior IV.* London: Methuen, 1965; New York: Wiley, 253–272.

Mosteller, F., & Moynihan, D. P. (Eds.). *On equality of educational opportunity.* New York: Random House, 1972.

Mullener, Nachanael, & Laird, J. D. Some developmental changes in the organization of self-evaluations. *Developmental Psychology,* 1971, *5* (2), 233–236.

Murray, H. A., et al. *Explorations in personality.* New York: Oxford, 1938.

Mussen, P. H. Some antecedents and consequences of masculine sex-typing in adolescent boys. *Psychological Monographs,* 1961, *75,* (2, Whole no. 506).

Mussen, P. H., Conger, J. J., & Kagan, J. *Child development and personality* (4th ed.). New York: Harper and Row, 1974.

Mussen, P. H., & Jones, M. C. Self conceptions, motivations, and interpersonal attitudes of late and early maturing boys. *Child Development,* 1957, *28,* 243–256.

Nedler, S. Parent education and training: Literature review. Austin, Texas: Southwest Educational Development Laboratory, 1973.

Nelson, K. E. Organization of visual-tracking responses in human infants. *Journal of Experimental Child Psychology,* 1968, *6,* 194–201.

Nisbitt, J. D., & Entwhistle, N. J. Intelligence and family size, 1949–1965. *British Journal of Educational Psychology*, 1967, *37*, 188–193.

Nuthall, G., & Snook, I. Contemporary models of teaching. In R. M. W. Travers (Ed.), *Second handbook of research on teaching*. Chicago: Rand McNally, 1973.

Oakland, T. Assessing minority group children: Challenges for school psychologists. *Journal of School Psychology*, 1973, *11*, 294–303.

O'Connell, E. J., Dusek, J. B., & Wheeler, R. J. A follow-up study of teacher expectancy effects. *Journal of Educational Psychology*, 1974, *66*, 325–328.

Olson, W. C. *Child development* (2nd ed.). Boston: Heath, 1959.

Opler, M. E. Themes as dynamic forces in culture. *American Journal of Sociology*, 1945, *51*, 198–206.

Opler, M. K. Cultural induction of stress. In M. H. Appley & R. Trumbull (Eds.), *Psychological Stress*. New York: Appleton-Century-Crofts, 1967, 209–241.

Osborn, J. Teaching a teaching language to disadvantaged children. In M. A. Brottman (Ed.), Language remediation for the disadvantaged preschool child. *Monographs of the Society for Research in Child Development*, 1968, *33*, 36–48.

O'Sullivan, M., & Guilford, J. P. *Cartoon predictions*. Orange, Calif.: Sheridan Psychological Services, Inc., 1965.

Painter, G. A tutorial language program for disadvantaged infants. In C. S. Lavatelli (Ed.), *Language training in early childhood education*. Urbana, Ill.: University of Illinois Press, ERIC Clearinghouse on Early Childhood Education, 1971.

Palmer, C. E. Height and weight of children of the depression poor. *Public Health Reports*, 1935, *59*, 33.

Paradise, E. B., & Curico, F. Relationship of cognitive and affective behaviors to fear of strangers in male infants. *Developmental Psychology*, 1974, *10* (4), 476–483.

Parke, R. D., & Walters, R. H. Some factors influencing the efficiency of punishment training for inducing response inhibition. *Monographs of the Society for Research and Child Development*, 1967, *32* (1, Serial No. 109).

Parten, M., & Newhall, S. Social behavior of preschool children. In R. S. Barker, J. S. Rounin, & H. F. Wright (Eds.), *Child behavior and development*. New York: McGraw-Hill, 1943, 509–525.

Pasamanick, R., & Knobloch, H. Retrospective studies on the epidemiology of reproductive causality: Old and new. *Merrill-Palmer Quarterly*, 1966, *12* (1), 7–26.

Patterson, G. R. Responsiveness to social stimuli. In L. Krasner & L. P. Ullman (Eds.), *Research in behavior modification*. New York: Holt, Rinehart and Winston, 1965.

Payne, D. E., & Mussen, P. H. Parent-child relations and father identification among adolescent boys. *Journal of Abnormal Psychology*, 1956, *71*, 124–135.

Paz, O. The labyrinth of solitude: Life and thought in Mexico. (L. Kemp, trans.) New York: Grove Press, 1961.

Pearl, A. *The atrocity of education*. St. Louis, Mo.: New Critics Press, 1972.

Pestalozzi, J. H. Leonard and Gertrude. In S. A. Rippa (Ed.), *Educational ideas in America: A documentary history*. New York: McKay, 1969.

Peterson, C., Peterson, J., & Finley, N. Conflict and moral judgment. *Development Psychology*, 1974, *10*, 65–69.

Piaget, J. *The moral judgment of the child*. New York: Harcourt, Brace, 1932.

Piaget, J. *The psychology of intelligence*. New York: Harcourt, Brace, 1960.

Piaget, J. *Play, dreams, and imitation in childhood*. New York: Norton, 1951.

Piaget, J. *The origins of intelligence in children*. New York: International Universities Press, 1952.

Piaget, J. *The construction of reality in the child*. New York: Basic Books, 1954.

Piaget, J. *The child's conception of the world*. Paterson, N.J.: Littlefield, Adams, 1963.

Piaget, J. *Science of education and the psychology of the child* (D. Cottman, trans.). New York: Orion Press, 1970.

Piaget, J. *To understand is to invent: The future of education*. New York: Grossman, 1973.

Piaget, J., & Inhelder, B. *Le développement des quantités chez l'enfant*. Neuchâtel: Delachaux et Niestlé, 1941.

Piaget, J., & Inhelder, B. *Memory and intelligence*. New York: Basic Books, 1973.

Plato. *Plato's meno* (B. Jowett, trans.). New York: Liberal Arts Press, 1949.

Posner, M., & Keele, S. W. Skill learning. In R. M. W. Travers (Ed.), *Second handbook of research on teaching*. Chicago: Rand McNally, 1973.

Prader, A., Tanner, J. M., & von Harnack, G. A. Catch-up growth following illness or starvation. *Journal of Pediatrics*, 1963, *62*, 646–659.

Premack, D. Reinforcement theory. In D. Levine (Ed.), *Nebraska Symposium on Motivation, 1965*. Lincoln: University of Nebraska Press, 1965.

Provence, S., & Lipton, R. C. *Infants in institutions*. New York: International Universities Press, 1962.

Pufall, P. B., & Shaw, R. E. Precocious thoughts on number: The long and the short of it. *Developmental Psychology*, 1972, *7*, 62–69.

Purpel, D. E., & Belanger, M. *Curriculum and the cultural revolution*. Berkeley, Calif.: McCutchan, 1972.

Radcliffe-Browne, A. R. *A natural science of society*. Glencoe, Ill.: The Free Press, 1957.

Rau, L. Conscience and identification. In R. R. Sears, L. Rau, & R. Alpert (Eds.), *Identification and child-rearing*. Stanford, Calif.: Stanford University Press, 1965.

Redel, F., & Wineman, D. *The aggressive child*. Glencoe, Ill.: Free Press, 1957.

Redfield, R., Linton, R., & Herskovits, M. J. A memorandum on acculturation. *American Anthropologist*, 1936, *38*, 149–152.

Reed, S. C. *Counseling in medical genetics*. New York: W. B. Saunders Co., 1955.

Reese, H. W., & Lipsitt, L. P. *Experimental child psychology*. New York: Academic Press, 1970.

Reese, H. W., & Overton, W. F. Models of development and theories of development. In L. R. Goulet & P. B. Baltes (Eds.), *Life-span developmental psychology*. New York: Academic Press, 1970, 115–145.

Reisman, D. *Individualism reconsidered*. Glencoe, Ill.: Free Press, 1954.

Rest, J. R. The hierarchical nature of moral judgment: A study of patterns of comprehension and preference of moral stages. *Journal of Personality*, 1973, *41*, 86–109.

Rest, J. R. Developmental psychology as a guide to value education: A review of Kohlbergian programs. *Review of Educational Research*, 1974, *44* (2), 241–259.

Restle, F. The selection of strategies in cue learning. *Psychological Review*, 1962, *69*, 329–343.

Reynolds, E. L. Degree of kinship and pattern of ossification. *American Journal of Physiological Anthropology*, N. S., 1943, *1*, 405–416.

Rheingold, H. L., Gewirtz, J. L., & Ross, H. W. Social conditioning of vocalizations in the infant. *Journal of Comparative and Physiological Psychology*, 1959, *52*, 68–73.

Rich, J. M. *Humanistic foundations of education*. Worthington, Ohio: Charles A. Jones Publishing Co., 1971.

Ridberg, E. H., Parke, R. D., & Hetherington, E. M. Modification of impulsive and reflective cognitive styles through observation of film-mediated models. *Developmental Psychology*, 1971, 5 (3), 369–377.

Riegel, Klaus F. Influence of economic and political ideologies on the development of developmental psychology. *Psychological Bulletin*, 1972, *78*, 129–141.

Riesman, D., Glazer, N., & Denny, R. *The lonely crowd*. New Haven: Yale University Press, 1950.

Rippa, S. A. *Educational ideas in America: A documentary history*. New York: McKay, 1969.

Roberts, E. An evaluation of standardized tests as tools for the measurement of language development. Unpublished paper. Cambridge, Mass.: Language Research Foundation, 1971.

Rogers, C. R. A theory of therapy, personality and interpersonal relationships, as developed in the client centered framework. In S. Koch (Ed.), *Psychology: A study of a science* (Vol. 3). New York: McGraw-Hill, 1959, 184–256.

Rogers, C. R. Interpersonal relationships: U.S.A. 2000. In D. E. Purpel and M. Belanger (Eds,), *Curriculum and the cultural revolution*. Berkeley, Calif.: McCutchan, 1972, 411–424.

Romney, K., & Romney, R. *The Mixtecans of Juxlahuaca, Mexico*. (Six Cultures Series, Vol. 4). New York: Wiley, 1966.

Rosen, B. C., & D'Andrade, R. The psychological origins of achievement motivation. *Sociometry*, 1959, *22*, 185–218.

Rosenberg, B. G., & Sutton-Smith, B. Sibling age spacing effects on cognition. *Developmental Psychology*, 1969, *1*, 661–668.

Rosenthal, A. M. *Thirty-eight witnesses*. New York: McGraw-Hill, 1964.

Rosenthal, R., & Jacobson, L. *Pygmalion in the classroom*. New York: Holt, Rinehart and Winston, 1968.

Rosenthal, T. L., Zimmerman, B. J., & Durning, K. Observationally-induced changes in children's interrogative classes. *Journal of Personality and Social Psychology*, 1970, *16*, 681–688.

Rotter, J. B. Generalized expectancies for internal versus external control of reinforcement. *Psychological Monographs*, 1966, *80* (Whole No. 609).

Rush, B. A plan for the establishment of public schools and the diffusion of knowledge in Pennsylvania; to which are added thoughts upon the mode of education proper in a republic. Address to the legislature and citizens of the state. In S. A. Rippa (Ed.), *Educational ideas in America: A documentary history*. New York: McKay, 1969.

Sarbin, T. R., & Allen, V. L. Role theory. In G. Lindzey (Ed.), *The handbook of social psychology* (Vol. 1). Reading, Mass.: Addison-Wesley, 1968.

Savin, H. B., & Perchonock, E. Grammatical structure and the immediate recall of English sentences. *Journal of Verbal Learning and Verbal Behavior*, 1965, *4*, 348–353.

Scammon, R. E. The measurement of the body in childhood. In J. A. Harris, C. M. Jackson, D. G. Paterson, & R. E. Scammon. *The measurement of man*. Minneapolis: University of Minnesota Press, 1930.

Scheinfeld, A. *Your heredity and environment*. Philadelphia: J. B. Lippincott Co., 1965.

Schoggen, J., & Schoggen, P. *Environmental force units in the home lives of three-year-old children in three population subgroups*. Demonstration and Research Center for Early Education Papers and Reports, George Peabody College for Teachers, Nashville, Tennessee, 1971, *5* (2), 1–116.

Sears, P. S. Child-rearing factors related to playing at sex-typed roles. *American Psychologist*, 1953, *8*, 431 (Abstract).

Sears, P. S. Doll play aggression in normal young children: Influence of sex, age, sibling status, father absence. *Psychological Monographs*, 1956, *65* (6, Whole no. 323).

Sears, R. R. Dependency motivation. In M. R. Jones (Ed.), *Nebraska Symposium on Motivation*. Lincoln, Nebraska: University of Nebraska Press, 1963, 25–64.

Sears, R. R., Maccoby, E., & Levin, H. *Patterns of child rearing*. Evanston, Ill.: Row Peterson, 1957.

Sears, R. R., Rau, L., & Alpert, R. *Identification and child rearing*. Stanford, Calif.: Stanford University Press, 1965.

Shapira, A., & Madsen, M. C. Cooperation and competitive behavior of Kibbutz and urban children in Israel. *Child Development*, 1969, *4*, 609–617.

Shatz, M., & Gelman, R. The development of communication skills: Modifications in the speech of young children as a function of listening. *Monographs of the*

Society for Research in Child Development, 1973, *38* (5, Serial No. 152).

Shaw, G. B. *Four plays by.* . . . New York: Modern Library, Random House, 1953.

Sherif, M., & Sherif, C. W. *Reference groups.* New York: Harper and Row, 1964.

Sherman, M. The differentiation of emotional responses in infants. I. Judgements of emotional responses from motion picture views and from actual observations. *Journal of Comparative Psychology,* 1927, *7,* 265–284.

Sherman, M. The differentiation of emotional responses in infants. II. The ability of observers to judge the emotional characteristics of the crying of infants and the voice of an adult. *Journal of Comparative Psychology,* 1927b, *7,* 335–351.

Sherman, M., & Key, C. B. The intelligence of isolated mountain children. *Child Development,* 1932, *3,* 279–290.

Shirley, M. M. A motor sequence favors the maturation theory. *Psychological Bulletin* 1931, *28,* 204–205.

Shirley, M. M. *The first two years: Vol. II. Intellectual development.* Minneapolis: University of Minnesota Press, 1933.

Siegel, L. S., & Goldstein, A. G. Conservation of number in young children: Recency versus relational response strategies. *Developmental Psychology,* 1969, *1,* 128–130.

Siegler, R. S., Liebert, D. E., & Liebert, R. M. Inhelder and Piaget's pendulum problem: Teaching preadolescents to act as scientists. *Developmental Psychology,* 1973, *9,* 97–101.

Silberman, C. E. *Crisis in the classroom.* New York: Random House, 1970.

Silverstein, B., & Krate, R. *Children of the dark ghetto.* New York: Praeger, 1975.

Skinner, B. F. *The behavior of organisms: An experimental analysis.* New York: Appleton-Century-Crofts, 1938.

Skinner, B. F. *Walden two.* New York: Macmillan, 1948.

Skinner, B. F. *Science and human behavior.* New York: Macmillan, 1953.

Skinner, B. F. The science of learning and the art of teaching. *Harvard Educational Review,* 1954, *24,* 86–97.

Skinner, B. F. *Verbal behavior.* New York: Appleton-Century-Crofts, 1957.

Skinner, B. F. Pigeons in a pelican. *American Psychologist,* 1960, *15,* 28–37.

Skinner, B. F. *Contingencies of reinforcement A theoretical analysis.* New York: Meredith Corp., 1969.

Skinner, B. F. *Beyond freedom and dignity.* New York: Knopf, 1971.

Skinner, B. F. The free and happy student. *Phi Delta Kappan,* 1973, *55,* 13–16.

Skinner, B. F. *About behaviorism.* New York: Knopf, 1974.

Sloggett, B. B., Gallimoe, R., & Kubany, E. A comparative analysis of fantasy need achievement among high and low achieving male Hawaiian-Americans. *Journal of Cross-Cultural Psychology, 1,* 53–61.

Spalding, D. A. Instinct: With original observations on young animals. Reprinted *British Journal of Animal Behavior,* 1954, *2,* 2–11.

Spearman, C. General intelligence objectively determined and measured. *The American Journal of Psychology,* 1904, *15,* 201–292.

Spearman, C. *The abilities of man: Their nature and measurement.* New York: Macmillan, 1927.

Spelke, E., Zelazo, P., Kagan, J., & Kotelchuck, M. Father interaction and separation protest. *Developmental Psychology,* 1973, *9* (1), 83–90.

Spiro, M. E. *Children of the kibbutz.* Cambridge, Mass.: Harvard University Press, 1965.

Spitz, R. A. Hospitalism: An inquiry into the genesis of psychiatric conditions in early childhood. A follow-up report. *Psychoanalytic Study of the Child,* 1945, *1,* 53–74.

Spitz, R. A. Hospitalism: A followup report. *The Psychoanalytic Study of the Child,* 1946, *2,* 113–117.

Spitz, R. A. *The first year of life.* New York: International Universities Press, 1965.

Spitz, R. A., & Wolf, K. M. Anaclitic depression. *The Psychoanalytic Study of the Child,* 1947, *2,* 313–342.

Sroufe, L. A. A methodological and philosophical critique of intervention-oriented research. *Developmental Psychology,* 1970, *2,* 140–145.

Staats, A. W., & Staats, C. K. *Complex human behavior.* New York: Holt, Rinehart and Winston, 1963.

Stayton, D. J., Ainsworth, M. D. S., & Main, M. B. Development of separation behavior in the first year of life: Protest, following, and greeting. *Developmental Psychology,* 1973, *9* (2), 213–225.

Stein, A. H., & Friedrich, L. K. Television content and young children's behavior. In *Television and Social Behavior* (Vol. 2). Washington, D.C.: U.S. Government Printing Office, 1971.

Stephens, M. W., & Delys, P. A locus of control measure for preschool children. *Developmental Psychology,* 1973, *9* (1), 55–65.

Stern, C. *Principles of human genetics.* San Francisco: Freeman, 1949, 1960.

Steward, M. S., & Steward, D. S. The observation of Anglo-, Mexican-, and Chinese-American mothers teaching their young sons. *Child Development,* 1973, *44,* 329–337.

Stoch, M. B., & Smythe, P. M. The effect of undernutrition during infancy on subsequent brain growth and intellectual development. *South African Medical Journal,* 1967, *41,* 1027.

Stogdill, R. M. *Handbook of leadership: A survey of theory and research.* New York: Free Press, 1974.

Stolz, L. M., et al. *Father relationships of war-born children.* Stanford, Calif.: Stanford University Press, 1954.

Strickland, S. P. Can slum children learn? *American Education.* U.S. Department of Health, Education and Welfare, Office of Education, July 1971, pp. 3–7.

Sunley, R. Early nineteenth-century American literature of child rearing. In M. Mead & M. Wolfenstein (Eds.), *Childhood in contemporary cultures.* Chicago: University of Chicago Press, 1955.

Surgeon General's Scientific Advisory Committee on Television and Social Behavior. *Television and growing up: The impact of televised violence.* Washington, D.C.: U.S. Government Printing Office, 1972.

Swanson, R., & Henderson, R. W. Achieving home-school continuity in the socialization of an academic motive. *Journal of Experimental Education* (in press).

Swift, J. W. Effects of early group experience: The nursery school and day nursery. In M. C. Hoffman & L. W. Hoffman (Eds.), *Review of child development research.* New York: Russell Sage Foundation, 1964, 249–288.

Tanner, J. M. *Growth at adolescence* (2nd ed.). Oxford: Basil Blackwell, 1962.

Tanner, J. M. Physical growth. In P. H. Mussen (Ed.), *Carmichael's manual of child psychology* (Vol. 1). (3rd ed.). New York: Wiley, 1970.

Thompson, H. Physical growth. In L. Carmichael (Ed.), *Manual of child psychology* (2nd ed.). New York: Wiley, 1954.

Thompson, W. R., & Grusec, J. E. Studies of early experience. In P. H. Mussen (Ed.), *Carmichael's manual of child psychology* (Vol. 1). (3rd ed.). New York: Wiley, 1970.

Thomson, A. M. Maternal stature and reproductive efficiency. *Eugenics Review,* 1959, *51,* 157–162.

Thomson, G. H. Intelligence and family size. In Scottish Council for Research in Education, *The trend of Scottish intelligence.* London: University of London Press, 1949.

Thoresen, C. E. *Behavior humanism.* Palo Alto, Calif.: Stanford Center for Research and Development in Teaching, 1972.

Thoresen, C. E., & Mahoney, M. J. *Behavioral self-control.* New York: Holt, Rinehart and Winston, 1974.

Thorndike, R. L. Review of R. Rosenthal and L. Jacobson, *Pygmalion in the Classroom. American Educational Research Journal,* 1968, *5,* 708–711.

Thorndike, R. L. But you have to know how to tell time. *American Educational Research Journal,* 1969, *6,* 692.

Thurstone, L. L. Psychological implications of factor analysis. *American Psychologist,* 1948, *3,* 402–408.

Tiller, P. O. Father absence and personality development of children in sailor families. A preliminary research report, II. In N. Anderson (Ed.), *Studies of the Family* (Vol. 2). Gottingen: Vandenhoeck & Ruprecht, 1957, 115–137.

Toffler, A. *Future shock.* New York: Bantam Books, 1970.

Torrance, E. P. *Guiding creative talent.* Englewood Cliffs, N.J.: Prentice-Hall, 1962.

Torrance, E. P. *Rewarding creative behavior.* Englewood Cliffs, N.J.: Prentice-Hall, 1965.

Tuddenham, R. D. Soldier intelligence in World Wars I and II. *American Psychologist,* 1948, *3,* 54–56.

Tuddenham, R. D. The nature and measurement of intelligence. In L. Postman (Ed.), *Psychology in the making.* New York: Knopf, 1962.

Turiel, E. Stage transition in moral development. In R. M. W. Travers (Ed.), *Second handbook on research in teaching.* Chicago: Rand McNally, 1973, 732–758.

Twain, M. *The adventures of Tom Sawyer.* New York: New American Library, 1959.

Tylor, E. B. The origins of culture, Part I of *Primitive culture.* New York: Harper Torchbooks, 1958.

Ugurel-Semin, R. Moral behavior and moral judgement of children. *Journal of Abnormal and Social Psychology,* 1952, *47,* 463–474.

Vernon, P. Ability factors and environmental influences. *American Psychologist,* 1965, *20,* 723–733.

Walberg, H. J., & Marjoribanks, K. Differential mental abilities and home environment: A canonical analysis. *Developmental Psychology,* 1973, *9,* 363–368.

Walker, D. K. *Socioemotional measures for preschool and kindergarten children.* San Francisco: Jossey-Bass, 1973.

Walker, J. Aspects of fetal environment. In H. Wolff (Ed.), *Mechanisms of congenital malformation.* New York: Association for the Aid of Crippled Children, 1955.

Walters, R. H., & Brown, M. Studies of reinforcement of aggression. III. Transfer of responses to an interpersonal situation. *Child Development,* 1963, *34,* 563–571.

Warner, W. L., & Lunt, P. S. *The social life of a modern community.* New Haven, Conn.: Yale University Press, 1941.

Warner, W. L., Meeker, M., & Eells, K. *Social class in America: A manual of procedure for the measurement of social status.* New York: Harper and Row, 1949.

Warren, N. Malnutrition and mental development. *Psychological Bulletin,* 1973, *80,* 324–328.

Watson, D. L., & Tharp, R. G. *Self-directed behavior: Self-modification for personal adjustment.* Monterey, Calif.: Brooks/Cole, 1972.

Watson, J. B. Psychology as the behaviorist views it. *Psychological Review,* 1913, *20,* 158–177.

Watson, J. B. *Psychology from the standpoint of a behaviorist.* Philadelphia: Lippincott, 1919.

Watson, J. B. *Behaviorism.* New York: Norton, 1930.

Watson, J. B. Psychology as the behaviorist views it. In S. A. Rippa (Ed.), *Educational ideas in America: A documentary history.* New York: McKay, 1969.

Watson, J. B., & Rayner, R. Conditioned emotional reactions. *Journal of Experimental Psychology,* 1920, *3,* 1–14.

Wattenberg, W. W., & Glifford, C. Relation of self-concepts to beginning achievement in reading. *Child Development,* 1964, *35,* 461–467.

Weatherley, D. Self-perceived rate of physical maturation and personality in late adolescence. *Child Development,* 1964, *35,* 1197–1210.

Weikart, D. P., & Lambie, D. Z. Preschool intervention through a home teaching program. In J. Hellmuth

(Ed.), *The Disadvantaged child*. Seattle, Wash.: Special Child Publications, 1968, 2, 437–500.

Weisberg, P. Social and nonsocial conditioning of infant vocalizations. *Child Development*, 1963, 34, 377–388.

Wertheimer, M. *Productive thinking*. New York: Harper & Row, 1959.

Westinghouse Learning Corporation-Ohio University. *The impact of Head Start*. Springfield, Va.: Clearing House for Federal Scientific and Technical Information, U.S. Department of Commerce, 1969.

Wheeler, L. R. The intelligence of east Tennessee mountain children. *Journal of Educational Psychology*, 1932, 23, 351–370.

Wheeler, L. R. A comparative study of the intelligence of east Tennessee mountain children. *Journal of Educational Psychology*, 1942, 33, 321–334.

White, B. L. The initial coordination of sensory-motor schemes in human infants—Piaget's ideas and the role of experience. In D. Elkind & J. H. Flavell (Eds.), *Studies in cognitive development: Essays in honour of Jean Piaget*. Toronto: Oxford University Press, 1969, 237–256.

White, B. L. *Human infants*. Englewood Cliffs, N.J.: Prentice-Hall, 1971.

White, B. L., & Castle, P. W. Visual exploratory behavior following postnatal handling of human infants. *Perceptual and Motor Skills*, 1964, 18, 497–502.

White, B. L., & Held, R. Plasticity of sensory-motor development. In J. F. Rosenblith & W. Allinsmith (Eds.), *Readings in child development and educational psychology* (2nd ed.). Boston: Allyn and Bacon, 1966.

White, B. L., & Watts, F. C. (with I. C. Barnett, B. T. Kabon, F. R. Marmor, & B. B. Shapira). *Experience and Environment* (Vol. 1). Englewood Cliffs, N.J.: Prentice-Hall, 1973.

White, G. M. *The elicitation and durability of altruistic behavior in children*. (Research Bulletin No. 67–27) Princeton, N.J.: Educational Testing Service, 1967.

White, L. A. *The evolution of culture: The development of civilization to the fall of Rome*. New York: McGraw-Hill, 1959.

White, R. Motivation reconsidered: The concept of competence. *Psychological Review*, 1959, 66, 297–333.

White, S. *Speculations on the future fate of early childhood education*. Paper presented at the annual meetings of the American Educational Research Association, Washington, D.C., April 1975.

Whiting, J. W. M. *Becoming a Kwoma*. New Haven: Yale University Press, 1941.

Whyte, W. *Street corner society: The social structure of an Italian slum* (2nd ed.). Chicago: University of Chicago Press, 1955.

Whyte, W. *The organization man*. Garden City: Doubleday, 1956.

Wiley, D. E., & Harnischfeger, A. Explosion of a myth: Quantity of schooling and exposure to instruction, major educational vehicles. *Educational Researcher*, 1974, 3 (4), 7–12.

Williams, R. L. Stimulus/response: Scientific racism and

IQ—The silent mugging of the black community. *Psychology Today*, 1974, 7 (12), 32–100.

Williams, T. *Competence dimensions of family environments*. Paper presented at the annual meetings of the American Educational Research Association, Chicago, Illinois, April 1974.

Wilson, R. S. Twins: Mental development in the preschool years. *Developmental Psychology*, 1974, 10, 580–588.

Winett, R. A., & Winkler, R. C. Current behavior modification in the classroom: Be still, be quiet, be docile. *Journal of Applied Behavior Analysis*, 1972, 5, 499–504.

Winick, M., Rosso, P., & Waterlow, J. Cellular growth of cerebrum, cerebellum, and brain stem in normal and marasmic children. *Experimental Neurology*, 1970, 26, 393–400.

Winterbottom, M. The relation of need for achievement in learning experiences in independence and mastery. In J. Atkinson (Ed.), *Motives in Fantasy, Action, and Society*. Princeton: Van Nostrand, 1958, 453–478.

Wissler, C. The correlation of mental and physical tests. *Psychological Review*, Monograph Supplement, 1901, 3 (16).

Witty, P. A., Kinsella, P., & Coomer, A. A summary of yearly studies of televiewing—1949–1963. *Elementary English*, October 1963, 590–597.

Wolf, R. M. The identification and measurement of environmental process variables related to intelligence. Unpublished doctoral dissertation, University of Chicago, 1964.

Wolfe, R. M. The identification and measurement of environmental process variables related to intelligence. Unpublished doctoral dissertation, University of Chicago, 1964.

Wolfenstein, M. Fun morality: An analysis of recent American child-training literature. In M. Mead & M. Wolfenstein (Eds.), *Childhood in contemporary cultures*. Chicago: University of Chicago Press, 1955.

Wolfle, D. L., & Wolfle, H. M. The development of cooperative behavior in monkeys and young children. *Journal of Genetic Psychology*, 1939, 55, 137–175.

Yarrow, L. J. Separation from parents during early childhood. In M. L. Hoffman & L. W. Hoffman (Eds.), *Review of child development research* (Vol. 1). New York: Russell Sage Foundation, 1964, 89–136.

Yarrow, M. R., Scott, P. M., & Waxler, C. Z. Learning concern for others. *Developmental Psychology*, 1973, 8, 240–260.

Zelazo, N. A., Zelazo, P. R., & Kolb, S. Walking in the newborn. *Science*, 1972, 176, 314–315.

Zigler, E. Social class and the socialization process. *Review of Educational Research*, 1970, 40, 87–110.

Zigler, E. Child care in the seventies. *Inequality in education*, 1972, 13, 17–28.

Zigler, E. Project Head Start: Success or Failure? Unpublished manuscript, 1972. Quoted in S. Anderson & S. Messick, Social competency in young children. *Developmental Psychology*, 1974, 10, 282–293.

Zigler, E. F., & Child, I. L. *Socialization and personality development*. Reading, Mass.: Addison-Wesley, 1973.

Zimet, S. G. American elementary reading textbooks: A sociological review. *Teachers College Record*, 1969, *70*, 331–340.

Zimmerman, B. J., & Bergan, J. R. Intellectual operations in teacher question-asking behavior. *Merrill-Palmer Quarterly*, 1971, *17*, 19–26.

Zimmerman, B. J., & Dialessi, F. Modeling influences on children's creative behavior. *Journal of Educational Psychology*, 1973, *65*, 127–134.

Zimmerman, B. J., & Rosenthal, T. L. Conserving and retaining equalities and inequalities through observation and correction. *Developmental Psychology*, 1974, *10*, 260–268.

Glossary

Abstract thinking	A form of rule-governed behavior distinguished from other varieties in that it involves the use of complex rules expressing relationships among concepts representing possible rather than actual conditions.
Accommodation	A Piagetian concept indicating adaptive changes occurring in the manner in which an individual interacts with the environment.
Acculturation	The process of change that results from individuals from different cultures being in prolonged contact with each other. The process may result in changes in the cultural patterns of one or both groups, but each culture maintains much of its own original character.
Achieved role	A role associated with an earned social position.
Achievement motivation	Motivation based on the desire to achieve internal standards of excellence in academic or entrepreneurial undertakings.
Affect	Emotion or subjective feeling state.
Affiliation motivation	Motivation based on the desire to "fit in" and be accepted by a reference group.
Alleles	Alternative forms of a gene.
Altruism	Behavior directed to the well-being of other people. Generosity and sharing are examples of altruistic behavior.
Amaurotic family idiocy	A genetically transmitted metabolic disorder that leads to mental impairment.
Behavior-contingency unit	A behavior and the accompanying conditions which control the likelihood of its occurrence.
Behavioral construction	The active process by which an individual organizes and transforms acquired information and capabilities, and constructs his/her own reality.
Behaviorism	The general body of psychological theory which holds that the proper focus of psychological science is the description, prediction, and control of behavior.
Bilingualism	In a strict sense, the capability to speak two languages. However, for educational purposes the term *bilingual* is sometimes applied to children from minority groups who speak little or no English. Moreover it is occasionally used in connection with the classification of children for bilingual educational programs—to refer to children from ethnic minorities who speak only English.
Birth trauma	Shocks experienced by an infant during delivery, including anoxia and physical injuries that may attend the birth process.
Black English	A nonstandard dialect spoken by blacks living for the most part in urban ghettos.
Blastocyte	The stage of development beginning when cells of the zygote begin to differentiate and ending with implantation in the uterine wall. At this point the organism is designated as an embryo.
Cephalocaudal development (principle of)	The principle that morphological and behavioral development proceed from the head downward.
Chaining	The learning of a set of responses in sequence as in learning to tie shoes.

Chromotids	The "daughter" chromosomes that are formed when chromosomes split along their length, or reduplicate, during the process of mitosis.
Chromosomes	Microscopic, rod-shaped bodies which are the physical vehicles of hereditary material.
Amniotic fluid	The fluid which fills the amniotic sac, insulating the embryo and protecting it from shock.
Anaclitic identification	In psychoanalytic theory, identification based on the child's anxiety over loss of love of the mother or other first love object.
Anal stage	In psychoanalytic theory, a developmental stage in which pleasurable sensations are centered in the anal region.
Anoxia	Shortage of oxygen.
Anxiety	A state of painful emotional tension, characterized by fearfulness and apprehension.
Ascribed role	A role associated with a social position which is assigned independently from behavior. The role associated with being a child is an example.
Assimilation	A Piagetian concept referring to the acquisition of new information represented by an existing intellectual structure. In anthropological theory, the process by which the members of one cultural group become completely integrated and absorbed into a dominant group.
Attachment	A tie of affection that one person forms with reference to another specific individual. Such attachments tend to bind the people who form them together over time.
Autoclitic	A verbal operant involving verbal behavior based upon or dependent upon other verbal behavior. Expressions that qualify meaning illustrate the autoclitic; for example, in the sentence *I want no bread* the word *no* alters the meaning of the utterance and thereby serves an autoclitic function.
Classical conditioning	Process by which a conditioned stimulus is paired in time with an unconditioned stimulus and thereby acquires the capability to elicit a response previously under the control of the unconditioned stimulus.
Clinical method	The method of investigation used by Piaget in his developmental studies. The clinical method is comprised of a set of interviewing procedures to encourage a child to enact or to verbalize his/her thinking processes.
Cognition	The processes of knowing and thinking.
Cognitive dissonance	A state in which new information is discrepant from the established beliefs or cognitive structures of the individual. According to cognitive dissonance theory, the individual attempts to reduce the discrepancy by reinterpreting the facts.
Cognitive distraction	Processes involving thinking of things other than temptation objects as a strategy to facilitate delay-of-reward choices.
Cognitive style	*See* conceptual tempo.
Cognitive transformations	A term used by Walter Mischel to designate the process of thinking of designated qualities of reward objects.
Compensatory education	A term referring to a broad range of educational programs, usually designed for poor and minority group children, to "fill in intellectual deficiencies" which program planners assume exist because of "inadequate" intellectual socialization in the ethnic subculture.
Competence motivation	The innate need of the organism to interact with the environment in a manner that develops competence. A concept proposed by Robert White.
Competition	Activity in which individual goals can be attained only at the expense of others involved in the activity. As individuals act to increase their chances of attaining their goals, chances for others to reach their goals are reduced.
Concept	A rule for classifying things, for example other rules or objects.

Conceptual tempo	A term referring to the degree to which children respond slowly and reflectively or with quick impulse under conditions of uncertainty. Also referred to as cognitive style.
Concrete-concept learning	Rule learning involving acquisition of the ability to classify concrete objects.
Concrete operations	The second major developmental period designated by Piaget. During this period the child learns to represent concrete experiences with symbols and to classify concrete objects in terms of their relationships to other objects.
Conditioned stimulus	A stimulus which, as a result of being paired with an unconditioned stimulus, acquires the capability to elicit a response.
Conditioning	The process whereby a previously neutral stimulus gains control over behavior.
Conservation	A Piagetian term referring to intellectual actions displaying recognition that a whole must remain unchanged despite variations in the arrangement of its parts.
Conservative focusing	A strategy in which hypotheses in a rule-discovery task are tested by varying one element in the task at a time while holding all other elements constant.
Contents (of intelligence)	A term used by both Guilford and Piaget. For Guilford it means the types of material upon which intellectual operations are performed. For Piaget it denotes the specific behavioral capabilities of an individual which are manifestations of the operation of intellectual structures.
Convergent thinking	Problem-solving behavior which leads to one correct problem solution.
Cooperation	Group effort in which goals and activities are so arranged that as each individual acts to increase his/her chances of attaining an objective, chances are simultaneously increased for the group to achieve its goals.
Correlation	A statistical technique which measures the relationship between two variables by quantifying the extent to which they vary in the same way.
Counter culture	A term applied to collective patterns of behavior that are in opposition to prevailing patterns of behavior in the larger culture.
Critical periods	Points in the developmental sequence of an organism during which a particular type of stimulation is essential to the development of specific characteristics or capabilities. Lacking appropriate experience during the critical period, the aspect of development associated with that period may not occur.
Cross-sectional method	A method of research in which individuals differing in age are studied during the same time period.
Crossing over	A process by which recombinations of maternal and paternal genetic material occur during meiosis.
Cue	A. A signal to emit a response. B. The act of emitting a signal for the occurrence of a response.
Cultural evolution	The process by which cultural practices that promote cultural survival are acquired and maintained.
Cultural goals	Purposes that are considered appropriate aims of action for members of a particular culture.
Cultural pluralism	The condition in which varied subcultures exist side by side within a single society. The term is also sometimes used to designate the ability of some individuals to move freely from one subculture to another, displaying the skills and behaving within the norms of either culture.
Cultural relativity	The view that no form of behavior is inherently good or bad, moral or immoral. Behavior can be judged only in terms of its relationship to the behavioral patterns extant in the society in which it occurs.

Cultural theme	An overriding postulate that subsumes a number of related societal goals and which may direct or stimulate action.
Cultural values	Preferences among alternatives, hierarchically organized and widely shared among the carriers of a particular culture.
Culture	The patterns of behavior, including those embodied in artifacts and social institutions such as religion and law, which are transmitted through symbolic communication and overt modeling or demonstration.
Cumulative deficit	A phenomenon in which a given population of children falls progressively further behind standardized test norms as they progress through school.
Cumulative learning	Learning involving cumulative effects in which simple forms of learning facilitate subsequent complex forms of learning.
Deep structure	A linguistic structure which relates syntax to meaning.
Delay of gratification	Voluntary postponement of immediate gratification for the sake of obtaining more distant goals or rewards that are expected to be more substantial.
Denial	An ego defense mechanism in which an individual simply refuses to perceive unacceptable impulses or thoughts that evoke anxiety. Generally employed by children because this mechanism is incompatible with cognitive maturity.
Deoxyribonucleic acid (DNA)	The amino acid which comprises the genes and contains the genetic code that is carried by ribonucleic acid (RNA), providing the instructions that determine how the organism will develop.
Dependency	Two types of dependency may be distinguished. Both may be considered forms of attachment. *Instrumental dependency* refers to seeking help and attention. Seeking the affection, approval and physical proximity to others is designated *emotional dependency*.
Dependent variable	A variable subject to influence by an experimental treatment.
Descriptive method	A method of research involving the specification of individual characteristics and relationships among characteristics in different individuals.
Development	Changes in structure, behavioral capability, and process occurring over time.
Developmental norm	A standard against which to judge level of development with respect to a particular developmental process. Developmental norms specify average, below average, and above average functioning at successive age levels.
Developmental process	Structural and/or behavioral changes which occur within an individual over time.
Developmental stages	Qualitatively distinct levels of development.
Dialect	Speech patterns based on language rules characteristic of a particular cultural subgroup.
Discovery learning	An instructional method in which the learner is expected to discover a rule as a result of examining specific instances of the rule to be discovered.
Discrepant events	Events that are incongruent with established intellectual structures of an individual, and which therefore cannot be readily assimilated into existing schemata.
Discrimination	The act of distinguishing among stimuli.
Discriminative stimulus	A stimulus which serves as a signal for a particular response.
Disequilibrium	A Piagetian concept indicating a condition in which intellectual structures used to represent reality are not in harmony with information extracted from the environment.
Disinhibition	The release or reduction of self-restraints or behavioral suppression.

Displacement	An ego defense mechanism in which an emotion is transferred from one object to another, or symbolic meaning is transferred from one object or event to a less threatening object or event.
Divergent thinking	The generation of a variety of different information products (e.g., ideas) about a given subject. Divergent production may be assessed both in terms of overall quantity of production and in terms of the number of qualitatively different products generated.
Dizygotic twins	Twins resulting from two separate fertilized eggs. Popularly referred to as fraternal twins.
Dominant trait	A characteristic which is observable in both homozygous and heterozygous conditions. In the heterozygous condition the dominant allele masks the effects of the recessive allele.
Down's syndrome	A disorder resulting from an abnormal chromosome condition. Characteristics include mental deficiency, physical features such as a flat, sunken nose bridge, a fold of skin giving the eyes a slanted appearance, and susceptibility to infections and disease.
Drive	A physiological or psychological state that impels action.
Ectoderm	The outer layer of cells in the blastocyte. This layer develops into specific tissues and organs including the outer layer of skin, hair, nails, and the nervous system as differentiation proceeds.
Effectance motivation	A concept proposed by Robert White, referring to an innate desire to interact effectively with the environment; to have an effect on it. Thus playful exploration of the environment facilitates the development of competence.
Ego	A theoretical construct in Freudian theory. The ego is described as a mental structure responsible for rational thought.
Egocentrism	A term used by Piaget to denote a child's failure to distinguish between his or her own construction of things and the objective reality of the phenomena which he or she experiences.
Ego defense mechanism	One of a variety of "unrealistic" means developed by the organism to avoid painful anxiety when more realistic methods fail.
Ego strength	The characteristic of acting on the basis of internalized standards. The ability to exercise self-control.
Eight-month anxiety	A characteristic response pattern appearing in about the eighth month of life, wherein the sight of a stranger in close proximity elicits a fear response. Also referred to as fear of strangers.
Elaborated code	A term suggested by Basil Bernstein to characterize the language of the middle class. Characteristics of the elaborated code include a tendency to use abstract terms, a tendency to display concern in speech for the intentions and motivations of others, and an emphasis on personal consequences rather than social status as a basis for guiding behavior.
Electra complex	In psychoanalytic theory, the excessive emotional attraction of a daughter to her father, and hostility toward the mother.
Embryo	The term designating an early period of prenatal development. In humans, from the time the blastocyte is implanted in the uterine wall to the eighth week of development.
Emotion	Strong generalized feelings of psychological excitement, with accompanying physiological reactions.
Empathy	The capacity to find pleasure in the pleasure expressed by another person; or to experience pain, sorrow, or any other affective state in response to the plight of another. To experience empathy requires that an individual be able to perceive things from the perspective of another person.
Enactive mode of thinking	Physical acts used to represent objects or events in the environment.

Encounter groups	Groups of individuals brought together for the purpose of bringing people into "meaningful" contact with one another.
Enculturation	The process by which the skills and behaviors characteristic of a culture are transmitted to an individual.
Environmental process variables	Variables consisting of collections of environmental characteristics hypothesized to influence the intellectual development of children reared in those environments.
Epilepsy	A term encompassing a number of disorders involving convulsive seizures and loss of consciousness.
Equilibration	A Piagetian term referring to the process by which an individual achieves a state of equilibrium.
Equilibrium	A Piagetian term referring to a condition in which intellectual structures used to represent environmental conditions are in harmony with information extracted from the environment.
Erogenous zones	Parts of the body that give rise to sexual feelings when stimulated.
Erythroblastosis fetalis	A condition arising from Rh incompatibility of a fetus and its mother. If Rh substances from an Rh positive fetus get through the placenta into the Rh negative bloodstream of the mother, the mother's blood may manufacture antibodies which get back into the blood of the fetus, causing red blood cells of the fetus to clump. The condition is more likely to occur with later than first born children. Without medical attention the fetus may die in utero or shortly after birth, or suffer brain damage.
Ethnic group	Any group of people distinguished from other groups by their customs, which may include language.
Eugenics	The science of controlling genetic makeup for the purpose of improving genetic endowment.
Expectancies	Individual predictions, based on past experience, concerning the contingencies likely to attend given behaviors in specific situations.
Experimental method	A method of research in which an effort is made to determine the effects of variations in one or more independent variables on one or more dependent variables.
Extended family	A social unit composed of two or more generations of direct biological descent, such as parents, grandparents, and children, plus a range of cousins, uncles, aunts, and fictive kin.
External control	*See* locus of control.
Extinction	A process in which the probability of occurrence of a response is reduced by withholding the reinforcer previously maintaining the response.
Fetus	The designation for the developing human organism in the mother's womb, from the beginning of the third month until birth.
Fixation	The arrestment of emotional development on a level earlier than that expected for the chronological age of the individual. Fixation involves preoccupation with the satisfaction of instincts characteristic of an earlier stage of psychosexual development.
Fixed interval schedule	A reinforcement schedule in which reinforcement takes place following the first response to occur after a fixed time period.
Fixed-ratio schedule	A reinforcement schedule in which each reinforcement occurs after a fixed number of responses.
Formal operations	The third major developmental period designated by Piaget. During this period, the individual acquires abstract thinking capability making it possible to represent symbolically the full range of hypothetical realities that might exist with respect to a given situation.

Frustration- aggression hypothesis	The assumption that frustration occurs when social realities present barriers to the expression of instinctual energies. The reservoir of accumulated aggressive urges must be released through catharsis which takes many forms, including direct aggression, displacement, sublimation, and fantasy.
Gene	The basic unit of hereditary transmission. Composed of deoxyribonucleic acid, genes are arranged as segments along the chromosome. Each gene occupies a specific position (locus) on a specific chromosome.
Genital stage	The period of development in which the individual moves from preoccupation with self-love, to the capability of loving others for altruistic reasons. Roughly corresponds to the period of pubescence and adolescence.
Genotype	The specific genetic endowment of an individual.
Germ cells	The sex cells, referred to as male and female gametes, or sperm for the male and ovum for the female germ cells.
Gestalt	A form or configuration. In psychology, associated with the view that the response of an organism cannot be analyzed in isolation from other elements of experience. The behavioral configuration of an individual or cultural group is more than the sum of its parts.
Grammar	A system of rules which specifies the sound-meaning relationships for a language.
Growth	This term is sometimes used only to refer to the enlargement of body organs. However, in the present text, growth is a synonym for development.
Hemophilia	A sex-linked genetic disorder in which the blood-coagulating process fails to work properly because of a defective gene on the X chromosome.
Hermaphrodite	A sexual abnormality in which an individual has sex organs characteristic of both sexes.
Heterozygous	The state in which an individual carries alleles for contrasting characteristics on the two members of a homologous pair of chromosomes.
Higher order conditioning	The process by which a neutral stimulus becomes conditioned to a previously conditioned stimulus.
Homeostasis	The tendency of organisms to maintain their physiological functioning within a range of fixed limits.
Homologous chromosomes	Chromosomes that normally form pairs during the process of meiosis, each of which becomes incorporated into a separate daughter cell during the reduction-division process.
Homologs	The members of a pair of homologous chromosomes.
Homozygous	The state in which an individual carries two alleles for the identical characteristic on a pair of homologous chromosomes.
Humanism	A system of thought or philosophical position that emphasizes those qualities that are unique to the human organism, particularly the active role humans take in directing their own behavior and creating their own reality.
Hydrocephaly	A genetically determined disorder in which the skull fills with abnormal amounts of cerebrospinal fluid. If untreated, this condition results in enlargement of the skull and mental deficiency.
Id	A theoretical construct within Freudian theory. The id is described as a mental structure controlling instinctual behavior.
Identification	The process or product of internalizing the qualities of significant agents of socialization.
Imagistic mode of thinking	Perceptual behavior used to represent objects in the environment in cases in which such objects are not physically present to the senses.
Imitation	The display of behavior corresponding to the category of behavior emitted by a model.
Imprinting	A process by which certain animals become fixated on an object (usually

their mother) with respect to a specific function, such as following. Imprinting must occur within a critical period of development if it is to occur at all.

Impulsiveness	A response style in which children react quickly, with little reflection, to test situations presenting conditions of uncertainty.
Independent assortment	The principle discovered by Gregor Mendel that certain genetically determined characteristics are transmitted independently of each other. Also referred to as Mendel's second law, or the principle of recombination.
Independent variable	A potential influence variable which is altered in an experiment without affecting other variables that might affect experimental outcomes.
Induction techniques	Discipline techniques in which reasons are given for compliance to the demands of the socializing agent.
Information products	A term used in Guilford's structure of intellect model to describe types of information (e.g., classes or relations) upon which intellectual operations are performed.
Inhibition	A psychological process that restrains or suppresses a behavior.
Intellectual operations	A term used in Guilford's structure of intellect model to describe mental activities or processes such as memory and cognition.
Intellectual structure	A systematic arrangement of elements within the mental apparatus limiting the kinds of intellectual capabilities which an individual can display behaviorally.
Intelligence	Intellectual capability. There is wide variation in the definitions which various theorists give to intelligence. It may be described as complex rule-governed behavior, as the construction of reality based on interactions with the environment, or as performance on an intelligence test. There is rather widespread agreement that intelligence in its highest form is creative problem-solving ability.
Internal control	*See* locus of control.
Intraverbal operant	A verbal operant made up of verbal behavior under the control of verbal stimuli. Verbal chains such as *horse and buggy* are examples of intraverbal operants.
IQ	Intelligence quotient. The term IQ originally referred to the ratio of mental age (computed from a test score) to chronological age. Today the term refers to performance on an intelligence test which is described by specifying an individual's relative standing in a norm group established for the test.
Irradiation	Exposure to radiation.
Klinefelter syndrome	A condition in which male testes are not fully formed and are incapable of producing sperm. Deficiencies in the production of male hormones hinder the normal development of male secondary sex characteristics. The condition is most common in males with an extra X chromosome (XXY).
Language Acquisition Device (LAD)	A theoretical construct advanced by Noam Chomsky referring to an innate mechanism comprised of those language rules which apply to all languages.
Latency period	The period following the phallic stage, during which, according to psychoanalytic theory, overt sexual activity in all forms is reduced.
Leadership	The capability of an individual to influence the norm setting and activities of others in a group.
Learning	The process of acquiring new responses, capabilities, or associations as a result of experience.
Learning history	All of an individual's past experiences in which learning has occurred.
Life space	The psychological reality of an individual. All of the facts, as perceived by an individual, that may influence that person's behavior.

Linguistic markers	Features of speech which are interpreted as signs of a speaker's social and cultural affiliations. The omission of the *r* sound in the speech of New Yorkers is an example.
Locus of control	A term designating individual differences in expectations regarding control of events that influence their lives. Individuals who usually think they control their own contingencies are said to manifest "internal control." Those who believe they have little influence over their own destiny are said to display belief in external control.
Longitudinal method	A method of research in which the same individuals are studied at different age levels.
Love-withdrawal techniques	Socialization practices involving the withholding of affection or approval as a result of misdeeds.
Mand	A verbal operant in which the verbal behavior of the speaker is generally reinforced by a characteristic consequence. For example, the utterance *Pass the butter* is a mand.
Match	A term used by J. McV. Hunt to designate the degree of "fit" between a new experience and the intellectual structures already developed by an individual on the basis of related experiences.
Maturation	Developmental change controlled by genetic factors.
Meiosis	The process of reduction division by which the sex cells divide.
Mesoderm	The middle layer of cells of the blastocyte. This layer develops into such organs as muscle tissue, circulatory and excretory systems.
Microcephaly	A genetic disorder in which the brain and skull cease to grow at an early age, resulting in severe mental retardation.
Mimicry	The exact duplication of a model's behavior.
Mitosis	The process of cell division by which body cells divide and replicate themselves.
Model	A. An individual who emits behavior to be imitated by another person. B. The act of emitting behavior to be imitated by another person. C. The act of imitating behavior.
Modeling	The act of emitting behavior to be imitated by an observer. Also the act of imitating the behavior of a model.
Mongolism	A once popular but now disfavored term for Down's syndrome. Based on the somewhat mongoloid appearance of individuals displaying symptoms of Down's syndrome.
Monozygotic twins	Twins originating in a single egg fertilized by a single sperm. Early in its development the fertilized egg (zygote) splits and develops into two organisms. Popularly referred to as identical twins.
Morpheme	The smallest sound unit to which a meaning is attached in a language.
Motivation	A general term employed for the processes involved in the operation of needs, drives, and incentives.
Motor skills	Sequences of muscular movements which conform to predetermined standards of acceptable performance.
Multiple discrimination	Distinguishing among individual stimuli in a set which generally includes several stimuli.
Mutation	An "altered copy" of genetic material, resulting in a sudden variation in inherited characteristics.
Nature	Innate influences on development.
Recessive traits	A characteristic observed in the phenotype only when the allele controlling it exists in the homozygous condition. In the heterozygous condition the

effects of the allele controlling it are marked by the effects of the dominant allele.

Need	A physiological or psychological condition that impels and directs behavior. Sometimes used synonymously with drive.
Negative reinforcement	A behavioral consequence involving the withdrawal of an aversive stimulus to increase response probability.
Neutral stimulus	A stimulus without reinforcing properties.
Nonstandard dialect	A dialect based on rules which vary from the standard form (i.e., the form defined by the culture as being correct) of a language.
Norm-referenced assessment	Measurement which establishes an individual's level of performance by describing the individual's relative standing in an appropriate norm group.
Nuclear family	A social unit composed of a pair of parents and their biological offspring.
Nurturance	A term referring to the rewardingness characteristics of a caretaker's relationship to a child.
Nurture	Environmental influences on development.
Objective morality	According to Piagetian theory, the characteristic tendencies of young children to judge actions on the basis of the objective consequences of an act rather than on the basis of the actor's probable motives.
Objectivity	A construct used by Piaget to denote a child's ability to distinguish between his or her own construction of things and the external reality of his or her experiences.
Observational learning	Sometimes used synonymously with social learning or modeling, this term refers to learning by watching the behaviors of other people in the environment.
Oedipus complex	In psychodynamic theory, the tendency of a male child to be attracted to his mother and hostile toward the parent of the opposite sex.
Ontogenetic traits	Characteristics which are possessed by some members of a species, but not by others.
Operant conditioning	The process whereby a reinforcing consequence acquires control over the probability of occurrence of the behavior that precedes it.
Oral stage	The stage of development in which the infant is totally dependent upon its caretakers, and personality development is strongly influenced by the ways in which pleasure-seeking impulses centered in the mouth are satisfied.
Organismic theory	A point of view attempting to take the entire biological organism into consideration. With Gestalt theory this point of view shares the assumption that no component of the organism or its behavior can be understood if abstracted from the whole.
Ovum	An egg, or female germ cell.
Phallic stage	A psychosexual stage of development in which instincts associated with the genital organs play a predominant role.
Phenemenological theory	A point of view that asserts that it is not the reality of events, but rather the individual's perception of events that influences behavior.
Phenotype	Observable characteristics of an individual.
Phenylalanine	An amino acid involved in the disorder phenylketonuria. Individuals having two recessive genes for phenylketonuria cannot metabolize phenylalanine properly, resulting in the accumulation of phenylpyruvic acid in the body, which damages the nervous system of the infant.
Phenylketonuria	A genetically determined condition which leads to mental deficiency because of damage to the developing nervous system of an infant. It is inherited through a simple recessive gene which leads to a breakdown in the production of the enzyme required for proper metabolism of the amino acid phenylalanine.

Phobic reaction	A reaction characterized by "irrational" fears.
Phoneme	The smallest categories of sound in a language which the speakers of the language are generally able to distinguish.
Phonetics	That aspect of grammar comprised of rules which specify the types of sounds used in a language.
Phylogenetic traits	Characteristics shared by all members of a species.
Physical growth	The enlargement of various body structures during the course of development.
Placenta	A vascular organ within the uterus that serves as the structure through which the fetus receives nourishment from and eliminates waste into the circulatory system of the mother.
Point system	A systematic reinforcement program in which numerical tallies are used to signify reinforcers.
Power-assertion techniques	Socialization practices involving force or threat of force to achieve compliance with the demands of socializing agents.
Prehension	Seizing or grasping.
Preoperational subperiod	A subperiod of the period of concrete operations characterized by the acquisition of the ability to represent concrete experiences through the use of symbols.
Prepotency	Exceeding others in power, as in Maslow's motivational hierarchy in which needs lower in the hierarchy are prepotent over, or exceed in power, those at higher levels.
Primacy effect	The circumstance in which an event experienced early has a greater influence on behaviors or perceptions than events experienced later.
Primary drive	Drives based on innate physiological requirements, such as the need for nourishment, water and oxygen.
Primary reinforcer	A reinforcer directly related to body-tissue needs.
Problem solving	Rule-governed behavior requiring rule discovery.
Projection	An ego defense mechanism by which one's unacceptable impulses are attributed to someone else.
Projective test	Any one of a variety of tests consisting of ambiguous stimuli. An individual's responses to or interpretation of these stimuli are assumed to reveal information about his/her internal personality state.
Proximodistal development (principle of)	The principle that morphological and behavioral development proceed from the trunk to the extremeties.
Psychodynamic	A term referring to the Freudian point of view that individual social and emotional functioning involves the dynamic interactions of internal structures that constitute personality.
Psychogenic needs	Needs which are not directly tied to physiological drives, but operate across diverse cultures.
Psychological ecology	The study of complex relationships between individuals and their environments. Ecological research approaches are derived from the work of Kurt Lewin and take a wholistic approach to the study of environmental influences, and avoid dealing with "arbitrary" categories of behavior or environmental stimuli.
Psychometrics	The techniques of assessment used to measure level of performance related to psychological processes.
Psychosexual stages	Stages of development in which different pleasure-sensation motives dominate the behavior and adjustment of the individual.

Psychosocial stages	Stages of development which, in Erikson's theory, present unique social crises for individuals of different ages. The crises associated with each age must be resolved successfully if optimal psychological development is to occur.
Puberty	That period of physical development marked by the rapid enlargement of organs related to reproduction.
Punishment	The application of a consequent condition that decreases the probability of occurrence of a response.
Rationalization	An ego defense mechanism in which anxiety is reduced by thinking of socially acceptable justifications for behaviors that are otherwise unacceptable to the ego.
Reaction formation	An ego defense mechanism in which unacceptable impulses are excluded from consciousness by adopting behavior or attributes antithetical to the anxiety-provoking desires.
Readiness	The degree to which the level of development of the individual matches the learning experiences provided for him/her.
Reflectiveness	A response style in which children react slowly and with forethought to test situations presenting conditions of uncertainty.
Regression	An ego defense mechanism in which an individual attempts to deal with anxiety by reverting to a form of behavior that was formerly acceptable, but which has become age-inappropriate.
Reinforcer	Something which increases the probability of occurrence of a behavior.
Repression	An ego defense mechanism in which an anxiety-provoking cognition is blocked or removed from consciousness.
Response latency	The period of delay between the presentation of a stimulus and a subject's response.
Restricted code	A term suggested by Basil Bernstein to characterize the language of lower-class speakers. Characteristics of the restricted code include a tendency to use concrete rather than abstract terms, failure to be concerned with the motives and intentions of others, and an emphasis on social status as a standard for guiding behavior.
Rh factor	An agglutinating factor present in the blood of some individuals. Individuals who have the factor are Rh positive; those who do not are Rh negative.
Role	Expected behavior patterns for a particular category of individuals.
Role taking	The adoption and performance of behaviors considered socially appropriate for a given situation, or for a specific status, such as age, sex, father, daughter.
Rubella	German measles.
Rule	A set of specifications which describe relationships among phenomena.
Rule-governed behavior	Behavior which conforms to a rule.
Rule learning	A. Learning to state a rule or to emit behaviors which conform to a rule. B. One of Robert Gagné's eight types of learning. As used by Gagné, the term *rule learning* refers to learning which involves the specification of relationships among concepts.
Rules of formation	Linguistic rules which generate the deep structure of a sentence.
Rules of transformation	Linguistic rules which convert the deep structure of a sentence into a surface structure.

Secondary drive	Originally neutral events that acquire the capacity to impel behavior because they are regularly paired with the satisfaction of primary drives.
Secondary reinforcer	A stimulus which has acquired reinforcing properties through conditioning.
Secular trend	The general increase in developmental levels which has been occurring across generations for the last 100 years.
Self-actualization	A motivation state that may activate behavior only when lower-order needs, such as physical, social, and achievement needs, have been reasonably well satisfied. This level of need influences one to be open, nondefensive, loving, creative, autonomous, spontaneous, and to act for the good of society.
Self-concept	The beliefs, feelings, attitudes, and personal qualities a person views as salient qualities of him/herself.
Self-esteem	The judgments one characteristically makes about his/her self-concept.
Semantics	That aspect of grammar concerned with the meanings conveyed through language.
Sensorimotor period	The first major period of development designated by Piaget. During this period the child learns to represent concrete experiences through physical acts.
Separation protest	A form of emotional reaction generally displayed toward the end of the first year of a child's life. The reaction is evidenced by crying or attempts to follow when the mother or other principal caretaker leaves the room.
Sex-linked inheritance	A condition of genetic inheritance in which certain genetically determined characteristics are inherited along with one's sex, because the genes controlling these characteristics are located on the sex chromosomes.
Sex-role stereotypes	Culturally shared expectations about the typical behaviors that are supposed to be characteristic of members of a given sex.
Sex typing	The process by which individuals come to value and acquire the behaviors and attitudes considered characteristic of and appropriate for his or her own sex.
Shaping	The reinforcement of successive approximations to a desired response.
Sickle cell anemia	A genetic disorder characterized by the formation of defective red blood cells. The condition is lethal only in the homozygous condition, and occurs in a disproportionately high proportion of people of African ancestry.
Signal learning	Learning resulting from classical conditioning.
Social class	Social level in a society defined primarily in terms of economic status.
Social competence	Capabilities involved in managing one's own behavior and affect, and in managing interpersonal relationships in a manner that benefits oneself and society.
Social-learning theory	A cognitive behavioral theory which asserts that development is shaped largely by observational learning occurring in social situations.
Sociolinguistic rules	Rules which specify linguistic alterations associated with variations in social factors.
Social norms	The modes of behavior and standards of conduct that prevail at a given period of time in a particular society.
Socialization	The patterns of antecedent variables which shape behavior and tie it to the social system in which an individual lives.
Socializing agent	An individual responsible for the socialization of another person or group.
Social organization	The institutions and roles through which the behavior of individuals toward one another is organized.
Social structure	The total set of roles within a group.

Society	The aggregation of individuals who live together in an organized population.
Socioeconomic status (SES)	An index of status or position within the vertical social and economic structure of the social organization. Components of SES include factors such as occupation, income, and level of formal education.
Specific grammar	Grammatical rules which are unique to a given language.
State	Conditions (e.g., anxiety) within an individual that may control behavior.
Stimulus generalization	The capability of different stimuli to elicit or signal a particular response.
Stimulus-response learning	Learning through the presentation of a cue which signals a response that is subsequently reinforced.
Strategy (of rule discovery)	Hypothesis testing during rule discovery which evidences an orderly sequence.
Subjective morality	According to Piagetian theory, the mode of moral judgment in which the intents of a transgressor are taken into consideration in assessing the gravity of his/her action.
Sublimation	An ego defense mechanism by which an individual transforms unacceptable instinctive impulses into some socially acceptable form, such as athletics. The unacceptable instincts which are sublimated are frequently sexual urges.
Successive scanning	A strategy in which hypotheses in a rule discovery task are tested one at a time by examining variations in one element of the task at a time. In the scanning strategy no provision is made for holding constant elements other than the one currently being considered.
Superego	A theoretical construct in Freudian theory. The superego is described as a mental structure formed from the incorporation of representations of parents' behaviors, attitudes, and values into the mental apparatus. The superego exerts a guiding influence on behavior.
Surface structure	A linguistic structure which relates syntax to the language sounds involved in producing a verbalization.
Symbolic models	Behavioral cues or instructions presented via symbolic materials, such as books, which transmit information about the form and consequences of certain behaviors.
Syntactics	That portion of grammar comprised of rules which determine the arrangement of words into phrases, clauses, and sentences.
Tact	A verbal operant signaled by an object or property in the environment. The act of naming objects illustrates the tact.
Tay-Sachs disease	A form of amaurotic family idiocy, resulting when the recessive genes for the trait occurs in the homozygous condition. The condition may produce mental deficiency, blindness, and death at an early age.
Temperament	Constitutional qualities of an individual that may have a generalized influence on behavior.
Test reliability	Test consistency. Reliability may be established by assessing the extent to which the various items within a test measure the same thing, by measuring consistency across parallel forms of the test, or by assessing stability in test performance across different occasions.
Test validity	The extent to which a test actually measures what it purports to measure. Validity is generally established by correlating the test with other measures with which the test ought to correlate if it is an effective measure of the processes which it purports to assess.
Thalidomide	A tranquilizing drug used in the 1950s and 1960s that resulted in severe abnormalities in infants whose mothers were administered the drug during pregnancy.

Themes	*See* cultural themes.
Token economy	A systematic reinforcement program in which counters such as poker chips are used to represent reinforcers.
Toxemia	A disorder that may strike expectant mothers during pregnancy. Symptoms include dysfunctions of the kidneys and circulatory system. May have damaging effects on both the mother and the developing fetus.
Trait	Internal characteristics that control classes of behavior which vary among individuals, and which are assumed to be relatively stable over time and across situations.
Transfer of learning	The effect of prior learning on subsequent learning. Transfer may be positive or negative. In the case of positive transfer, prior learning has a facilitative effect on subsequent learning. In the case of negative transfer, prior learning impairs subsequent learning.
Transformational grammar	Noam Chomsky's grammar, which assumes that the deep structure of a sentence may be converted into a surface structure through the use of rules of transformation.
Trophoblast	Those tissues of the blastocyte that, together with the membrane of the mother's uterine wall, develop into the tissues that nourish and protect the embryo.
Turner syndrome	A chromosomal disorder resulting in the incomplete development of female sex characteristics.
Unconditioned response	A response elicited by an unconditioned stimulus prior to conditioning.
Unconditioned stimulus	A stimulus which, prior to conditioning, has the power to elicit a response.
Universal grammar	The phonetic, semantic, and syntactic rules which relate sound to meaning in all languages.
Values	*See* cultural values
Variable-interval schedule	A reinforcement schedule in which reinforcement takes place after the first response following a variable time interval.
Variable-ratio schedule	A reinforcement schedule in which reinforcement occurs after a variable number of responses.
Verbal association	Chaining in which the various links in the chain are verbal behaviors.
Verbal mode of thinking	Thinking in the form of covert verbal behavior.
Vicarious conditioning	Conditioning in which an observer's behavior is changed by witnessing stimuli, reactions, and consequences in the behavioral sequence of a model. The observer acquires the reactions and response patterns observed in the model display.
Zeitgeist	The spirit of the age. The prevailing trend of thought and feeling in a period of history.
Zygote	A fertilized ovum.

Index